# Knowledge Reuse and Agile Processes:
## Catalysts for Innovation

Amit Mitra
*TCS, Global Consulting Practice, USA*

Amar Gupta
*University of Arizona, USA*

Information Science REFERENCE

**INFORMATION SCIENCE REFERENCE**
Hershey · New York

Acquisitions Editor: Kristin Klinger
Development Editor: Kristin Roth
Senior Managing Editor: Jennifer Neidig
Managing Editor: Sara Reed
Copy Editor: April Schmidt
Typesetter: Cindy Consonery
Cover Design: Lisa Tosheff
Printed at: Yurchak Printing Inc.

Published in the United States of America by
Information Science Reference (an imprint of IGI Global)
701 E. Chocolate Avenue, Suite 200
Hershey PA 17033
Tel: 717-533-8845
Fax: 717-533-8661
E-mail: cust@igi-global.com
Web site: http://www.igi-global.com

and in the United Kingdom by
Information Science Reference (an imprint of IGI Global)
3 Henrietta Street
Covent Garden
London WC2E 8LU
Tel: 44 20 7240 0856
Fax: 44 20 7379 0609
Web site: http://www.eurospanonline.com



Mitra, Amit, 1949-

Knowledge reuse and agile processes : catalysts for innovation / Amit Mitra & Amar Gupta.

p. cm.

Summary: "This book addresses flexibility of both business and information systems through component technology at the nexus of three seemingly unrelated disciplines: service-oriented architecture, knowledge management, and business process management. It provides practitioners and academics with timely, compelling research on agile, adaptive processes and information systems, and will enhance the collection of every reference library"--Provided by publisher.

Includes bibliographical references and index.

ISBN-13: 978-1-59904-921-2 (hardcover)

ISBN-13: 978-1-59904-023-3 (ebook)

1. Knowledge management. 2. Management information systems. 3. Business logistics--Data processing--Management. 4. Computer network architectures. 5. Information theory. I. Gupta, Amar. II. Title.

HD30.2.M58 2008

658.4'038--dc22

2007024489

British Cataloguing in Publication Data
A Cataloguing in Publication record for this book is available from the British Library.

# Dedication

*I dedicate this book to my late mother, Sevati Mitra, for her unflagging encouragement. She would have been a proud and delighted mother had she lived to see the book in print. I also dedicate this book to my wife Snigdha and my children, Tanya and Trishna, for their understanding and support as I spent long hours of time that were rightfully theirs to create this book.*

**Amit Mitra**

*I dedicate this book to my parents-in-law, Mr. Ram Roop Gupta and Mrs. Pushpa Guta, on their 50th wedding anniversary. They have been a tremendous source of encouragement and inspiration for me. I owe a lot to them!*

**Amar Gupta**

# Table of Contents

# Detailed Table of Contents

# Foreword

New technologies, like new ideas, take time to become established. When they are first presented, they are met with a mix of enthusiasm and skepticism. Once tried, if success is not immediate—and it hardly ever is—those who opposed the innovation are quick to point out that they said the innovation would never work. Later, after the idea and the culture have had time to get to know one another and the new idea or technology is understood better, it often begins to flourish.

The idea of describing business processes as knowledge networks and sets of rules began in the 1980s with what were then called expert or knowledge systems. The first expert systems used rules to capture the knowledge of business experts and then made that knowledge available to other experts by putting the rules into a software system that, given information about a specific problem, could make an expert-level recommendation. As the early expert systems got larger, it was determined that rules alone were too clumsy. Hence, by the mid-1980s, most of the more sophisticated expert system-building tools incorporated objects (they were called Frames in those days).

In essence, the objects in a sophisticated expert system-building tool formed a network that described the vocabulary of problem, and rules were added to reason about the facts as they were accumulated by the system. When one used these more sophisticated expert system-building tools, one began by accumulating knowledge from experts. Thus, if one wanted to build an expert system to assist with home loans, one would begin by working out the vocabulary of loans. One would probably identify vocabulary objects like Home, Payment, Credit, Interest, Calendar, and so forth. Payments would probably have attributes like down payment and monthly payment, while Credit might have attributes like income, credit history, and so forth. In other words, one would construct a cognitive model of all of the concepts or words that a loan officer typically used—questions, in effect, that the loan officer would ask. Then, one would begin to add rules that could reason with the information one had about a specific case. For example:

*If the individual's credit history was superior, and her salary was $130,000 a year, and she could make a down payment of $50,000, what type of loan would she qualify for?*

The objects and rules formed an abstract model of the concepts and rules an expert could use to organize knowledge about a particular subject and to reason about it to reach conclusions.

By the end of the 1980s, most companies had given up on expert systems. They concluded that expert systems could be built but that the knowledge in the systems degraded too rapidly. One could capture human expertise in an expert system, but the system quickly became obsolete. Real human experts are constantly learning, reading journals, talking with colleagues about their latest experience, and attending conferences. They are constantly updating the knowledge structures and rules they use to analyze and solve problems. Thus, the problem with expert systems was not in the construction but in the maintenance.

It was easier to keep the expert, because the system that would replace him required that you keep him anyway, to maintain the expert system.

This might have been the end of the idea that rules could be useful, but, in fact, it was only the beginning. Individuals who had learned about rules while building expert systems quickly realized that they could build systems to capture and automate more mundane human decisions—those based on well-defined corporate policies. Policies and associated business rules were easier to capture and changed less frequently. Thus, the interest in expert systems in the 1980s mutated into an interest in Business Rules in the 1990s and that application of rule technology is now flourishing. Many financial companies have large business rule groups that are responsible for defining and managing the business rules used throughout their organizations.

At the same time that the business rules movement was showing how business rules could be used in practical situations, others were exploring patterns, business processes, and automated software tools that support business process modeling. Today, business rules and business processes are being integrated in new and creative ways.

Amit Mitra and Amar Gupta propose to apply what I think of as a mixture of the expert systems approach to business process modeling and to the now popular business rules approach. In essence, they would build object models that described the vocabulary and business rules of an area of business—say Financial Management. If one then sought to create a business process in the area of Financial Management, one would, in essence, create process objects that would inherit information from the more generic Financial Management model. Mitra and Gupta refer to their high-level constructs as reusable patterns of business knowledge. They have written three books explaining this approach. This is the third.

In the first, *Agile Systems,* they proposed a Universal Pattern that includes objects like Event, Fund, Energy, Physical Object, Person or Organization, Place, and Information. They work out the basic attributes of these objects and define some of the rules or constraints that apply to them. Then they start to create submodels for more specialized business activities. They consider, for example, a shipment and transportation cluster, a document and information cluster, a task-resource cluster, a meeting and agreement cluster, and a buying and selling cluster.

Mitra and Gupta went on to propose that companies consider creating a knowledge machine. In essence, it would be a huge expert system that had all the knowledge of all the terms used by businesses and all the critical constraints or business rules. Anyone with a specific process problem would define the process, determine what elements of the process inherited what vocabulary, and instantly get an analysis of all the considerations and rules that might apply.

To provide a foundation for the knowledge machine, Mitra and Gupta have explored all the technical problems one faces in creating this type of inheritance hierarchy. This kind of system cannot rely on the simple inheritance one finds in simpler object-oriented languages. It requires that one object can inherit from multiple parents and that some objects can inherit some features but not others from a given parent. These are programming problems that bedeviled the expert systems designers in the mid-1980s, and they still create technical and conceptual problems today. I mention this only to suggest that the first book is not light reading. It not only offers a survey of the high-level vocabulary and concepts of business but a survey of some very complex programming concepts as well.

The second book, *Creating Agile Business Systems with Reusable Knowledge*, discusses the underlying ideas that form the foundation of the earlier book. This book probes the truly fundamental concepts involved, including the nature of reality and business, the nature of objects and attributes, and the meaning of domains.

This book, the third in the series, describes how the underlying concepts described in the first book can be transformed into the business patterns described in the first book. Admittedly, the books were not published in what would seem to be the logical sequence, but now that all three are available, they can be read in whatever order the reader prefers. I found it easier to begin with the first book, which shows how everything fits together to create a business system and then to work back into the underlying theory once I understood why I would need it. Most, I suspect, will want to do that. Others may prefer to start with the first and then go to this volume that provides more on knowledge patterns and the automation of the business system.

No matter where you begin, the journey will be challenging. It will also be rewarding if you really want to understand the potential for systematic, rule-based business systems analysis. These are ideas whose time is about to come, and this book and the other two in the series will give you the technical foundation and the vision to be ready when that time comes.

*Paul Harmon is executive editor and founder of BPTrends. Harmon is a noted consultant, author, and analyst concerned with applying new technologies to real-world business problems. He is the author of* Business Process Change: A Manager's Guide to Improving, Redesigning, and Automating Processes *(2003). He has previously co-authored* Developing E-business Systems and Architectures *(2001),* Understanding UML *(1998), and* Intelligent Software Systems Development *(1993).*

# Preface

This book is part of a series of three complementary books (Figure P.1). The series addresses the pivotal issue of providing automated support for attaining business process resilience and information systems agility with little or no recurring manual intervention.

The first two books, *Agile Systems with Reusable Patterns of Business Knowledge: A Component Based Approach* and *Creating Agile Business Systems with Reusable Knowledge*, were published by Artech House Press, Norwood, MA in October 2005 and Cambridge University Press, Cambridge, UK, in January 2007, respectively. The series as a whole addresses the basic organization of knowledge and how an integrated knowledge repository can be created from its shared components. This book, which is the final book of the series, addresses business rules and processes.

In terms of content, *Creating Agile Business Systems with Reusable Knowledge* developed the semantics of Pattern and the concepts of Measurability, Distinction, Rules, Value, and Constraint, which are the basis of all knowledge. This book summarizes that foundation in Chapter IV and then builds upon it in subsequent chapters to provide additional depth. It addresses to a greater extent the components from which business rules and business processes are assembled and demonstrates how these components can automate reasoning and even some kinds of innovation. Each book is self-contained and may be read independently of the others.

*Figure P.1. Reusing business knowledge: The three books*

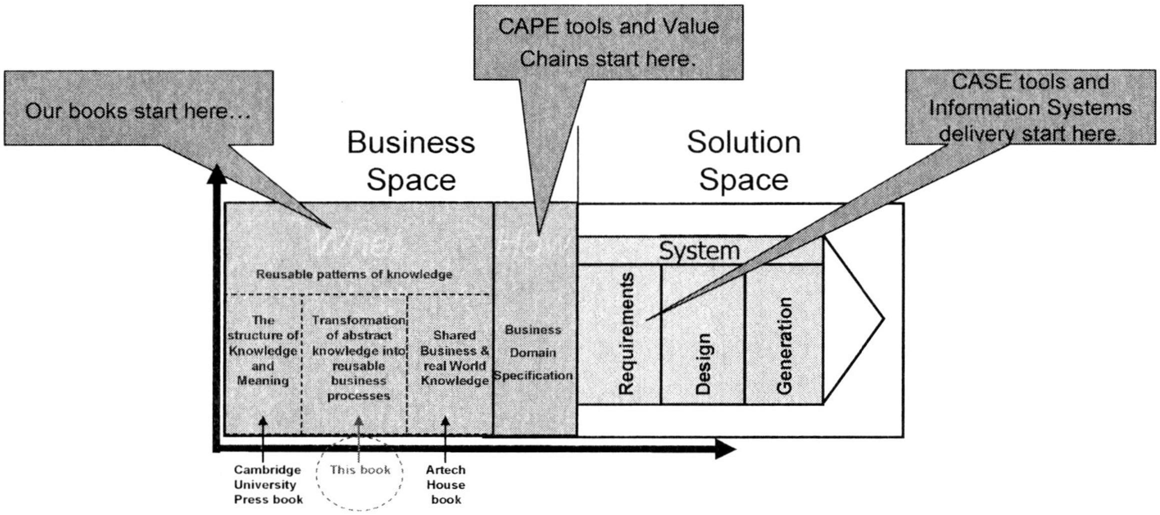

The patterns that will be described in the following chapters facilitate the design of resilient services, business processes, and information systems. These patterns will also facilitate development of tools that can automate the design of "self aware" business services and adaptive information systems. The Semantic Web is a vision of the future, in which the World Wide Web operates on the plane of meanings. It envisions a future in which automation processes and integrates a World Wide Web of information based on the meanings of individual items of data. The patterns of information in this series of books describe meanings. These patterns do not need the Web to exist. However, they can be the cornerstone of the Semantic Web.

The purpose of the semantics of knowledge we develop in this book is to normalize business rules and knowledge in order to reduce chaotic interactions and unintended side effects under the pressure of continual and rapid changes in scope, objectives, perspectives, and functionality. This book focuses on the concepts and models that integrate ontology, measurability, business rules, and business processes. The intent of this book is to anchor this integration in a cogent, overarching, nonstochastic model of knowledge and to demonstrate how such a model will result in agile and adaptable processes and information systems. Human, perceptual, and organizational issues, governance, and change management were addressed in the first book (Mitra & Gupta, 2005). This latest book discusses the risks associated with information quality and discusses processes for managing risks associated with violation of constraints.

The long-term success of business is increasingly dependent on its underlying resilience and agility. Most analysis, methodologies, and traditional business process engineering practices place emphasis on operational efficiency and net profits at the expense of innovation and agility. However, innovation, agility, and coordination of information in support of value, from customers' perspectives, are paramount in the global knowledge economy. In such an environment, research and processes that transcend departmental, corporate, and even national boundaries drive global excellence; innovation is not only supreme but is also made routine. This series of three books is tailored to support such an environment. The series demonstrates how new learning may be absorbed by flexible processes and information systems, which can be aligned automatically in lock step.

The series supports the stated intent of the Object Management Group (OMG) to drive towards semantic integration of business rules, ontology, processes, and services in support of service orientation and self-aware business processes. The OMG has published its SBVR standard for business rules and is close to completing the BPDM model for business processes, which it eventually intends to integrate with SBVR. *The Metamodel of Knowledge*, in this series of books, supports OMG's strategy by integrating the semantics that define business rules, business processes, reasoning, and shared knowledge.

Read on to see how this can be done and discover the inhuman patterns of machine reasoning that will surprise you at the nexus of knowledge, process, and information.

# Acknowledgment

We would like to say a very special thank you to Kristin Roth of IGI Global for her patience and guidance through the publishing process. We also thank Dane Sorenson, David Branson Smith, Katie James, Jessica Duran, Ruchika Agarwal, Julie Ovadia, and Trishna Mitra for their hard work, suggestions, and assistance in proofing and preparing the manuscript. We acknowledge, with sincere thanks, the valuable feedback provided by the reviewers. One of the authors (Amar Gupta) would like to thank his colleagues at the University of Arizona and at the Massachusetts Institute of Technology (MIT) for their support and encouragement.

# Chapter I
# Introduction to This Book

## AGILITY AND THE PROBLEM OF CHANGE

Change is difficult, complex, and risky because it has unintended side effects. Effects of change ricochet through systems via interactions between its parts. The larger the number of components, the more convoluted the system and the greater the chance of unintended side effects of change: more interactions imply a greater risk of multiple, complex impacts of change. Each impact has many consequences, which in turn will have many more until there is a cascading avalanche of changes, interactions, and impacts, which are difficult to manage, foresee, and qualify. This is the problem of change.

The problem of change has persisted through 50 years of automation. Its solution has resisted every technology devised by man. In the beginning, our systems were small, simple, and of limited scope. However, automation opened up new opportunities to improve and integrate processes by coordinating ever larger numbers of elements in previously unanticipated ways. This meant coordination of information across continually broadening horizons, which led to processes that were more dependent on automated systems; further, these processes and systems were more complex, had even more interactions, and were therefore even riskier to change. Paradoxically, it also led to the information economy, which thrives on change and innovation. We have created new technologies and methodologies at a prodigious rate to solve the burgeoning problem of change as our systems have evolved, matured, and integrated over the last 50 years. However, a solution to the problem of change has eluded us because every new approach has been the catalyst for the next level of complexity, which has then required a better, more sophisticated approach to managing change and innovation (Figure 1.1).

Change impacts diverse business processes and cascades through multiple layers of the legacy information systems in a rapidly growing avalanche such that the initiator of the change is faced with the Hobson's choice—either to make the change with huge overheads of cost, time, and risk, or to abandon the potential innovation because of the associated cost, time, and risk factors. The Y2K problem was a classic example. It cost the world around $600 billion (Yuen & Mitchell, n.d.) and exhausted a considerable part of the world's professional resources, just to convert a two-digit representation of the calendar year to four digits[1], which enabled automation to deal with the new millennium.

As systems and processes became more integrated and tightly coupled, it became imperative to isolate and manage the effects of change. The strategy was to encapsulate densely clustered

*Figure 1.1. The evolution of information technology*

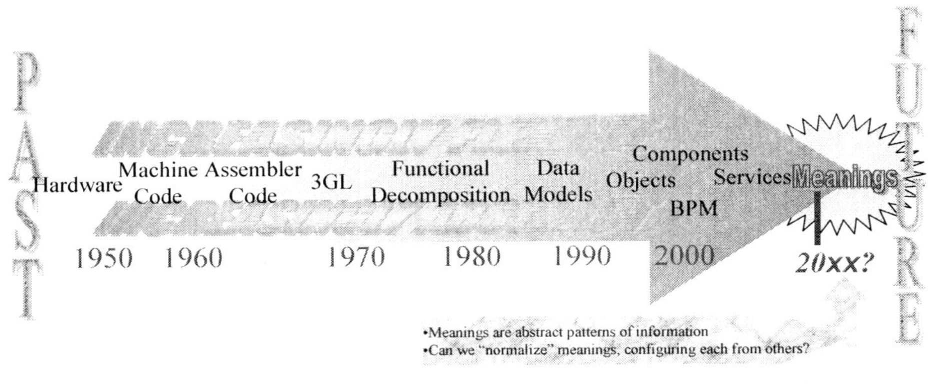


interactions into components, which were coupled loosely with other similar components to produce requisite behaviors and outcomes. These components became the parts of more integrated, more modular systems across larger scopes, which were more maintainable because the impact of change was better managed within modules. This approach required abstraction of information. Each step of the journey in Figure 1.1 not only made business more agile and scalable but also led to higher levels of abstraction. The levels before it did not disappear; rather they hid themselves behind more malleable constructs that became the primary interface between man and machine or machine and machine. This helped the system to become more agile.

As business processes became more tightly coupled with automation, the lack of agility in information systems became a serious bottleneck to product and process innovation. Several frameworks have attempted to solve this problem. Most have failed, or at best, have had very limited arguable success: Structured Programming, Reusable Code Libraries, Relational Databases, Expert Systems, Object Technology, CASE[2] tools, code generators, and CAPE[3] tools, to name a few. They failed because they did not adequately address the ripple effects of change—how business rules and knowledge may be represented so that we may change a rule once and send corresponding changes rippling across all the relevant business processes. To do this, we need ontology, a schema of interrelated meanings, which are derived from each other. Ontology is a study of the meanings of things. It was a philosophical concept that became concrete and computable and, in so doing, took computation into the plane of meanings (see Appendix IV). It is the next advancement in the evolution of automation (see Figure 1.1).

Currently, business rules are replicated in dissimilar formats in multiple, intermingled ways in multiple information systems and business processes. They must all be coordinated when any rule is changed. It makes change and innovation complex, perilous, and problematic to implement. This has been the most critical problem related to change.[4] Purely technical approaches have failed miserably. Despite some claims to the contrary, the problem was not resolved in the 1950s when computer professionals replaced the intertwined programming code of machine language with assembly languages, or in the 1960s when the next generation of these professionals replaced the cumbersome code of assembly languages with that of third generation languages like COBOL and FORTRAN. During the 1970s and 1980s, it was not solved either, when the expert systems, relational databases, and CASE tools were deployed. In addition, in the 1990s, object technology was considered to be a panacea until tangled object inheritance became so much of a problem that many advocated making multiple inheritances illegal in tools of the day. Finally, in very recent years, as one hurtled towards business process management (BPM) and service oriented architecture (SOA) with their plug-and-play business services, the problem had not been solved either. This has happened because new and better automation triggered more tangling of these business rules.

Therefore, the authors asked entirely different questions when initiating the research leading to this book:

- What is the natural structure of information that is used to represent business knowledge and services in a fully normalized and reusable form across diverse global business environments?
- What information is needed to model the stimulus response behavior of business processes and host organizations?
- If so many approaches have failed, why would a new one work?

The framework described in this book addresses these three issues by untangling business rules with an ontology derived from the inherent structure of information. By untangling business rules, even in complex legacy models and systems, one gains the unique capability to represent specific elements of business knowledge once, and only once, in a knowledge repository. Using this repository, the specific elements of knowledge can be designed to naturally manifest themselves, in appropriate forms, to suit the idiosyncrasies of different business contexts. Changes made at appropriate places will ripple through and impact relevant places within the concerned business systems with minimal or no human intervention. Not surprisingly, business professionals have long perceived that business information gained in one context may be used in another situation. However, in order to attain this objective in automation, one must specify the knowledge with greater precision in the appropriate framework. This book addresses the quest to define a fundamentally reusable structure of knowledge in a language that can be understood by most business professionals and also by machines.

These patterns of knowledge flow from theory and are validated by practice across a spectrum of different industries. Indeed, they had their genesis, not in abstract theory, but in the practical need to build the semantics of agile business for large diversified corporations, such as AIG and Verizon, in programs which one of the authors (Mitra) spearheaded.

This series of three books provides a connection between the world of systems engineering and the world of business process engineering. It is a generalized framework that applies with equal ease to diverse industry and business applications, ranging from transportation to defense and agriculture to medicine. Figure 1.2 describes the overall scheme of the framework.

The scheme in Figure 1.2 can assist in identifying reusable business services and predicting principal requirements, predicated on common patterns of knowledge, even before users articulate them. This can dramatically reduce the time needed to develop and to market new products and services. Moreover, the strategy can be a crucial asset in our intensely competitive business world, which increasingly depends on putting new ideas on the table in ever-shortening periods of time.

Industry consortiums such as the OMG and W3C are developing standards for business rules and business processes (like SBVR for business rules and BPDM for business processes from OMG and RDF for metadata from W3C). The W3C also has a recommendation called OWL (see Appendix IV) for a limited part of the ontology layer at the apex of the pyramid in Figure 1.2. However, these models are not integrated yet and are therefore limited in their ability to

*Figure 1.2. The business knowledge engineering framework*

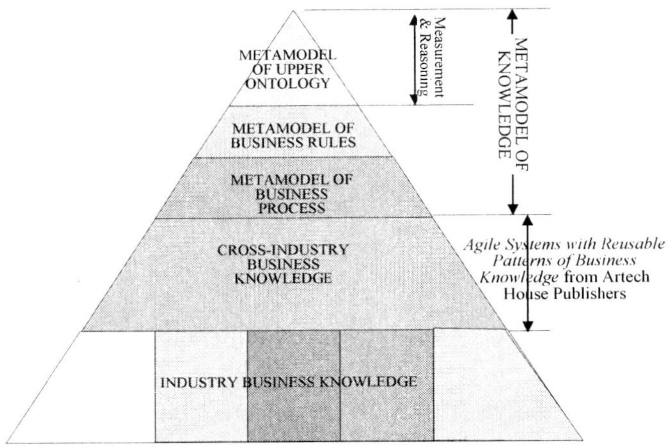


represent integrated knowledge and reasoning that flow through all aspects of business. This book shows how this can be done and presents a cogent integrated model of knowledge.

Corporations such as IBM are developing the industry models at the base of the pyramid in Figure 1.2. Some examples are the IAA model for insurance, IBM's health care models, Telecordia's TMN architecture for telecommunications, the Supply Chain Council's SCOR model for manufacturing, and others. In terms of the theme in Figure 1.2, these industry models are integrated neither horizontally nor vertically. This limits their ability to orchestrate and reuse knowledge across the diversity of business partners that form modern extended enterprises. These are the very enterprises that are enabled by the World Wide Web and the global knowledge economy and have the potential to make quantum leaps in the value they bring to end users of products and services. To bring true integration, agility, and coordination to the information enabled extended enterprises of the 21st century, the cross-industry layer of knowledge is critical. It allows a firm to innovate and reinvent its product markets, coordinates across business partners, and enables the business-on-demand concepts, enabled by the Web, which corporations like IBM have envisioned for the future.

Making business systems entirely maintenance free is the ultimate vision. Systems based on software will automatically adapt to chaos and change. These systems will be assisted by automated intelligent agents that will hopefully, someday, maintain software and adapt to change even as it occurs. They might even anticipate change, and perhaps thrive on it, like the businesses of the 21st century, which they will support.

## SCOPE OF THIS BOOK

This book and the other two books in the series focus on normalization, encapsulation, and reuse of business knowledge across a broad spectrum of industries and dissimilar business functions.[5] This book identifies the information that describes normalized knowledge. It does not describe the sequence of tasks that are required to capture this information (how the information is captured may vary widely). Thus, it is not a cookbook of sequenced activities to build components of normalized knowledge; rather it provides the foundation for cookbooks of that kind and a basis for evaluating how complete existing cookbooks are in terms of the information they must collect to model business knowledge.

Although business knowledge and technology are considered independent entities, the knowledge that is embedded within processes must be supported by an array of technologies, both manual and automated in nature, in order to derive full benefits. Frequently, large organizations and extended enterprises that are in close partnership in a supply chain have difficulty in coordinating their processes. This leads to waste, inefficiency, lack of coordination, and loss of agility. Different divisions and units of these enterprises have different and sometimes confusing business rules. On closer analysis, it becomes apparent that these apparently different rules, manifested in different procedures, implemented in different systems, which might run on different technology platforms, are merely different expressions and implementations of the same generic rules. The dissimilar implementations are driven by different local legacies, characterized by their own geographical, technological, whimsical, political, and environmental parameters.

It is possible to extract the shared business knowledge and intent from these diverse implementations. This shared knowledge focuses on the intent and semantics of the business. It is platform and procedure independent. It provides the basis for a shared "federated" business model. The federated model can coordinate the shared semantics of the business, which includes processes, rules, and information in the "federation" of businesses. If the federation wishes to reuse this shared knowledge, it must store it in an electronic repository. Although the federated model itself is technology independent, in the repository, it will be an array of information expressed explicitly on physical media in physical formats. It is thus an electronic artifact. We have named these artifacts Business Knowledge Artifacts, often abbreviated to Knowledge Artifacts, in this book.

Traditional software and hardware components differ from these Knowledge Artifacts. These Knowledge Artifacts are the components from which business knowledge and its semantics may be configured. New learning leads to adaptation by changing configurations of Knowledge Artifacts. This book identifies these Knowledge Artifacts and shows their relationship to software components. It also shows how automating these configurations can automate reasoning and the creation of the right processes for a business. As such, these Knowledge Artifacts encapsulate business intelligence as meanings and reasoning that can be stored as reusable components within an electronic knowledge repository.

## THE 24-HOUR KNOWLEDGE FACTORY AND THE SEMANTIC WEB

The purpose of the 24-Hour Knowledge Factory is to drastically reduce the time needed to develop information systems, and to facilitate effective knowledge-based processes. It is like a relay race that envisions a globally distributed work environment, in which global teams work on projects around the clock. Each team member works a normal workday in his or her time zone, and at close of business passes the baton to another member in a different time zone, who then continues the same task[6]. One of the authors (Gupta) has done extensive research on the concept and has successfully tested the efficacy of this approach in large industrial and academic environments.

Knowledge artifacts will facilitate the operation of such a factory because they are the components from which business knowledge and its semantics are configured, coordinated, and used to automate the creation of information systems and services. New learning and other changes lead to adaptation by changing configurations of knowledge artifacts, and thereby changing the behavior of automated systems and services. This kind of automation is needed to support the stringent demands that the 24 Hour Knowledge Factory imposes on the business, for rapid response and flawless coordination, across a spatially and temporally distributed network of workers and work centers. Ideally, such a knowledge factory would be built on the Semantic Web (see Appendix IV).

## SERVICE ORIENTED ARCHITECTURE

Were it not for the Web, this model of knowledge would remain an interesting academic exercise with very limited practical application. The World Wide Web has enabled e-commerce and the information economy by facilitating the exchange of information within and between corporations. This has led to the concept of service oriented architecture. In SOA, reusable services are published on the Web or an Enterprise Service Bus. Other services may then invoke and reuse these services via predetermined contracts for exchanging information. Not only may these loosely coupled services be assembled into business processes as needed, but processes themselves may too be constructed on demand (see the note on the State Machine). These processes can also provide for "business fail-overs" across a supply chain of collaborating enterprises, in which the user of a service has a choice of similar services from several competing partners to choose from. This is IBM's concept of on-demand business in an extended enterprise, limited only by the reach of the Web. There is a great deal of work being done on realizing this vision by standardizing messaging between services with Web services and their extensions. Web services are enabling communication and setting the stage for the next quantum leap in interoperability of diverse businesses in supply and demand chains—the standardization and expression of reusable business knowledge and services at the semantic level. This is a critical need.

At present, there is no way of identifying what business semantics are reusable in what scopes, and therefore there is no scientific method of identifying reusable services. Thus, the definition of business services in SOA has to be an art based on intuition and experience. The definition of reusable business services is the fundamental business value obtained by investing in SOA. Thus, current engineering methodologies do not address the very reason for the existence of SOA, leaving this as a soft art form, fraught with risk. The knowledge artifacts described in this series fill this gap. They are standardized, reusable patterns of business services. Web services have enabled their use, and these patterns can be the basis for standards that facilitate identification and definition of business services in service oriented architectures.

## OTHER APPROACHES

Business agility has been traditionally addressed from a management and organizational perspective. The focus has been on management of people, training, communication, organization, governance, soft skills, and change. This series takes a different approach. It focuses on engineering the semantics of reusable services, processes, and knowledge.

Chapter III discusses some of the business modeling techniques commonly used today and why they fail when we cross a critical threshold of scope and complexity. Our businesses today are not only complex and their boundaries often cross not only departments and geographies, but also entire enterprises that collaborate across the globe. A senior manager of a Fortune 100 firm recently asked one of us if we needed functional decomposition to model his business. The answer is that there are better techniques, although, for pragmatic reasons we would permit the use of functional decomposition, and accept the engineering risks this would involve. The reason was that process engineers and business modelers understand the technique, are comfortable with it, and in a large organization, the risk of sudden change would exceed the engineering risks involved (Mitra & Gupta, 2005 discuss the governance and enabling of change). However, as history has repeatedly demonstrated, the risk of chaotic behavior and unintended side effects is high when we apply this technique to complex business processes and information systems. We manage the risk by being pragmatic: taking more time, increasing our resource commitments, and reducing our expectations, scope, and complexity, trading them off against business benefits. This often has a high cost that is not recognized: the cost of opportunities lost.

We must substitute functional decomposition with something else when we engineer across large scopes because we need a method of adding detail incrementally so that we can divide and conquer complex problems in incremental steps. In theory, we can do this with a properly designed ontology. This book shows how we can create executable processes even when detail is missing. Thus, we can refine our model in steps, adding detail and tracking moving targets as scopes, objectives, and priorities shift in a changing business environment.

However, in practice, ontological design is a very difficult problem and involves a great deal of abstraction. In addition, this is not always the best method of communicating with the business and even professional modelers might find it difficult. This series of books presents an approach that creates a "packaged ontology" of knowledge to simplify and accelerate the process.

The Web Ontology Language (OWL) from W3C takes a similar approach. This is why there is a separate section dedicated to OWL in Appendix IV. The model in this series subsumes and extends OWL. It starts with the engineering premise that knowledge is based on the ability to recognize patterns and that a pattern increases predictability because its information content is less than the collective information content of its constituents. The properties of knowledge thus emerge from the semantics of pattern. These properties include OWL constructs. They also provide the foundation for integrating measurability, inference, rules, and processes into an overarching model of knowledge.

## SUPPLEMENTARY MATERIALS AND ORGANIZATION OF THIS BOOK

*To elaborate further on various themes, this book makes frequent references to supplementary chapters and notes on the Web. The Web site also includes more elaborate examples of practical application of the concepts in this book than we could include in print. Readers of this book may access this material at:*

***http://www.igi-global.com/mitrabook***

*All references to "our Web site" in this book refer to the above URL. You will need a user ID and password to access the material on the Web site. The user id is "Mitra" and the password is "Gupta". Remember that the user ID and password are case sensitive.*

The boxes in this book and the notes in Appendix II amplify technical details for the sophisticated reader.

Appendix III suggests articles and books for further reading. The process of expressing knowledge in reusable, componentized form draws upon many areas of business experience as along with active research. Appendix III categorizes and organizes these areas and provides brief notes and descriptions for most publications. URLs have been provided, where possible, to enable rapid online access to information. The Internet, however, is constantly updating and changing, and therefore the authors cannot guarantee that certain sites will exist on an indefinite basis. Readers may, however, try to access old Web sites with the "Wayback Machine" available at http://www.archive.org/index.php.

A serial number has been assigned to each item in Appendix III. When we have suggested additional reading on a discussion or argument in this book, we have bracketed its serial number [like this]. The companion books in the series, Creating Agile Business Systems with Reusable Knowledge from Cambridge University Press and Agile Systems with Reusable Patterns of Business Knowledge: A Component Based Approach from Artech House publishers, are the 337th and 338th items in Appendix III. They are referenced in the remainder of this book as (Mitra & Gupta, 2006) and (Mitra & Gupta, 2005), respectively.

## REFERENCES

Mitra, A., & Gupta, A. (2005). *Agile systems with reusable patterns of business knowledge*. Artech House.

Mitra, A., & Gupta, A. (2006). *Creating agile business systems with reusable knowledge*. Cambridge University Press.

## ENDNOTES

1 The Y2K problem at the end of the 20th century addressed converting 2 digit representations of the year into 4 digit representations. For example, 1/1/2001 instead of 1/1/01. Computer calculations involving dates beyond 1999 had a very high risk of error if the year was not expressed in terms of 4 digits.

2 CASE is an acronym for Computer Aided Software Engineering.

3 CAPE is an acronym for Computer Aided Process Engineering.

4 Human and organizational comfort levels with change are also major impediments, and arguably the less quantifiable, but larger risk. However, solving the engineering problems related to quality and coordination of changing rules are the prerequisites that create the need to address the human and organizational dimensions of change. The companion book from Artech House by the same authors addresses both dimensions of change.

5 See Appendix II on Normalization.

6 For more information on the 24 Hour Knowledge Factory, see [343] and [344] in Appendix III.

# Chapter II
# Introduction to Structure of Knowledge


## ABSTRACT

*This chapter introduces the concept of the metamodel of knowledge. The chapter:*

- *Defines knowledge and introduces the concept of the atomic rule as the building block of knowledge*
- *Describes the need for coordinating business knowledge, the difficulty of doing so, and how normalization of knowledge can facilitate its coordination and lead to the development of agile software*
- *Introduces the concepts that show how knowledge can be normalized and assembled from components*
- *Introduces the concept of a business process and services as derivatives of business knowledge*
- *Introduces the concept of modeling of behavior*
- *Introduces the problem of multiple clashing perspectives of reality from which knowledge is assembled*


*Figure 2.1. Knowledge is the meaning of business practices, rules, goals, guidelines, and their respective roles in the integrated whole*

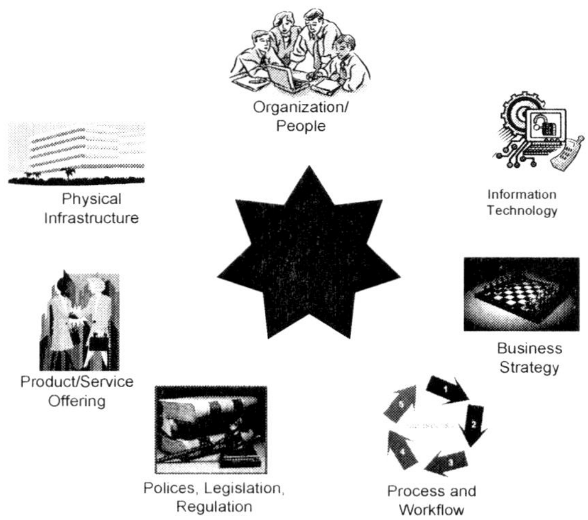

## INTRODUCTION TO KNOWLEDGE

Knowledge involves understanding, the understanding of meanings. Business knowledge involves understanding of goals and guidelines, opportunities and operations, threats and constraints, strengths and weaknesses, policies and practices, reasons and rationales, as well as their interrelationships. Knowledge is also a pattern of information that includes breach and recovery: what must be adhered to, what can be overlooked, and under what circumstances. In today's fast paced global environment, one must possess intimate knowledge of the rapidly evolving global marketplace and its impact on the current and planned set of products and services.

Knowledge represents a coordinated set of information: rules of business, imposed by man or nature, either explicitly stated or implied. Knowledge must address both what one should do and what one should not, as well as how to do it and how not to do it. In some business schools today, students are taught both implementation and counter-implementation strategies; the latter focuses on the use of knowledge to avoid getting into painful situations.[1]

Knowledge consists of assertions, described by rules, caveats, constraints, issues, and guidelines. Knowledge possesses structure. Engineers have long fabricated complex structures from simple parts. Relatively small components are first assembled into simple subassemblies, which in turn serve as the building blocks for larger, more complex, assemblies. This process is continued until the final machine or equipment is produced. Knowledge is similar: it is aggregated from isolated facts, but unlike a machine, its components are harder to perceive because they are abstract patterns of information; we understand information but cannot see, hear, taste, touch, or smell it. However, we *can* understand it by abstracting the inputs of our five senses.

Meaning and understanding are abstract, but they are similar to the physical world in yet another way. We learned from fundamental chemistry that we can divide and subdivide substances until we reach the stage of molecules without losing information on what the substance is. However, if we divide the molecule, we change the identity of the substance and lose information on its behavior and properties. Similarly, to identify the components of knowledge, we must distinguish between assertions whose division will involve no loss of information, and assertions whose division will sacrifice meaning: if an assertion is decomposed into smaller parts and the "lost" information cannot be recovered by reassembling the pieces into a "subassembly of knowledge," then the decomposition has gone too far. The fundamental rules that cannot be decomposed further without irrecoverable loss of information are called *indivisible rules, atomic rules,* or *irreducible facts.*[2]

Ambiguity, uncertainty, or a different meaning imply loss of information. Consider the following assertion:

*Frank is a man who has a daughter named Sarah*

This fact consists of two simpler facts which, when considered together, unambiguously mean *Frank is a man who has a daughter named Sarah*:

1. Frank is a man
2. Frank has a daughter named Sarah

Because the meaning, "*Frank is a man who has a daughter named Sarah,*" may be reconstituted from simpler, shorter facts, it is not an atomic rule (also known as an irreducible fact). However, if we tried to break the second of the two assertions above into smaller assertions, we would lose information.

Now consider the assertions:

2.1. Frank has a daughter
2.2. A daughter is named Sarah

The last statement asserts that somebody's daughter, not necessarily Frank's, is named Sarah. Thus, taken together, the statements above assert that Frank has a daughter, but Sarah may or may not be Frank's daughter. We have lost information because of the uncertainty we created by attempting to break *Frank has a daughter named Sarah* into smaller components. Therefore, *Frank has a daughter named Sarah* is an irreducible fact, which if decomposed, will result in loss of knowledge.

Irreducible facts embody pivotal information and constitute the root of coordinated requirements. These irreducible facts are woven together to create normalized knowledge. Normalized knowledge can then be utilized to coordinate complex activities in transnational corporations and intercompany supply chains. In the legacy systems of today, the process of making a single change opens up a Pandora's box primarily because irreducible facts are scattered across systems. By finding better ways for representing irreducible facts, one can potentially mitigate the problem of uncontrolled chain reactions caused by change.

Consider a situation, derived from a real company, in which a customer orders new voice mail services from a telephone company (called "Flashy" Telecom). The service is added to the customer's record and the company subsequently starts billing the customer. In order to activate the service, the telephone company needs to reprogram some telephone switches. At this particular company, the software instructing the switch cannot recognize voice mail services, although the billing system can. This causes the customer to be unhappy at the billing commencing prior to the start of the service, and the phone company is spending time and effort to manually activate the change and to correct the bill.

That voice mail is a feature of telephone service is an irreducible fact because this assertion cannot be broken down into simpler assertions without losing information. The billing system properly recognized this fact (that voice mail is a service offering); however, the service provisioning system was unable to do so. The root of the problem was that knowledge was not normalized.

To show that the problem is not necessarily confined to the telecommunications industry, let us consider reuse of knowledge by taking a different example, from a different industry. "Hasty" Delivery Services used two different systems: one for scheduling deliveries to geographic locations over roadways and the other for scheduling the delivery of packages to trucks through conveyor belts, picking, packing, and staging systems. In both systems, multiple routes could be used to deliver their shipments, and in each system, such routes may be filled to capacity. These facts are atomic rules about routing masquerading as different requirements in different systems. Indeed, the same rule may be used in a project management system to model the flow of tasks, resources, and work products. If this knowledge is implemented in computer code and stored in an electronic repository as a knowledge artifact, it may be reused by diverse systems. It could therefore be considered to be a reusable service from which business processes may be composed.

However, if Hasty and Flashy are like most firms, it would be difficult for them to use the software and design artifacts of one system to incorporate appropriate changes in another. Most of today's technology processes and best practices are not geared to do this. This is why each change involves more time and more money than it should. Systems designers may argue, with some justification, that their systems meet the stated requirements. However, these systems are often not designed to meet evolving needs of either the customer or the market.

The authors have encountered several similar situations in their consulting experience, where systems failed because firms were large and their operations had evolved in a way that made it difficult to effectively coordinate knowledge across the diverse functions of the enterprise. In a number of instances, systems have failed because knowledge was reflected in systems differently from the manner as it was in the real world. In order to become agile, our artifacts must reflect real world knowledge as it is in the real world, and thus encapsulate our understanding of how reality governs meaning, reasoning, and information.

## MODELING THE REAL WORLD

A model *represents* information about reality in a limited scope and context, in a repeatable, consistent, and accurate manner. The reliability and accuracy of the model within its scope are governed by the range of error, or inconsistency, that one is willing to tolerate—tolerances defined in terms of deviations from unbiased (accurate) and repeatedly consistent (reliable) predictions of target behaviors.

## METAWORLD OF INFORMATION

To normalize and reflect real world knowledge in our systems, one needs to understand and model such knowledge as a set of more fundamental attributes.

*Box 2.1. Model for making tea*

This model demonstrates:

1. How limited a model is compared to reality
2. How easily knowledge becomes denormalized in artifacts which must then be coordinated

The process of making tea can be depicted as a model that involves information about a sequence of events. The arrows show succession from event to event. The event at the end of an arrowhead cannot occur until the event at the beginning of that arrow has occurred. We cannot remove the tea packet unless we have boiled the water and inserted the tea packet.

Events like starting the stove, acquiring the pan to heat the water, and drinking the tea are beyond the scope of this model. The behavior of the water, such as boiling over heat, mixing with the tea flavor and sugar, its color, and its fragrance are also out of scope.

The content in the model could have been expressed in a different syntax. For example, instead of a set of labeled boxes connected with arrows, the information could have been presented as a set of English sentences. The model or its meaning would not have changed, but rather it would have changed the syntax, or technique, for expressing information. The information and its meaning would be the same in both versions.

Although the meaning and content of the model are the same in the two syntaxes, there are now two artifacts, or deliverables, with identical information, or meaning. To be consistent, the two must be synchronized. This is an example of how easily the information and meaning of a single real world phenomenon can become replicated in our records. If one changes, then the other must also change. By repeating information in two different artifacts, we have denormalized real world knowledge about making tea and made the process of incorporating change more complex. We did not even try. It just happened!

*Figure A. Model for making tea*

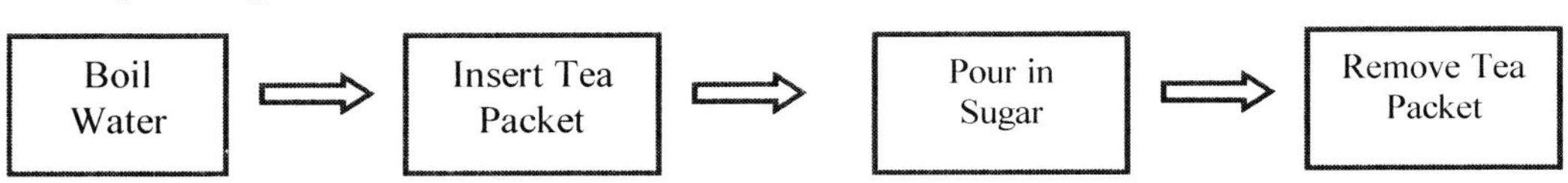

## Objects, Relationships, Processes, and Events

In the real world, every object conveys information. The information content of physical objects is conveyed to us via one or more of our five senses. That is how we know the object exists and perceive it as such. Our perception of the object is our mental model of the information it conveys. Objects are also impacted and influenced by each other. For instance, a piece of glass can be hit by a hammer and it will break. This too is information. In Box 2.1, the water, the tea packet, the hot stove, and the tea maker interact with each other in order to produce a cup of tea. Objects acting in concert with each other create the real world. Thus, the essence of the real world is a pattern of information.

Objects are associated with one another. While some associations involve the passage of time (such as making tea), other associations, such as locations of physical objects, are relationships that do not involve time. These relationships and associations are natural storehouses for particular behaviors of real world objects acting in unison. These relationships too are objects in their own right.

One could interrupt and stop "Make Tea" before the cup of tea is fully prepared. Here are other examples of how objects can be natural repositories of behavior: A person may be born, and later, the *same* person may be transformed into an *employee* through an employment relationship with an organization or a *spouse* by marrying another person. In *addition* to behaviors common to *Persons* in general, such as breathing and growing older, *Employees* and *Spouses* exhibit special properties. For example, spouses may get divorced and employees may be promoted. As such, these objects are concepts, abstracted from reality, based on shared behavior and information content. This is also an example of how meanings are created by extending shared meanings by adding behavior, constraints, and other kinds of additional information.

These were also examples that showed how *Processes are artifacts for expressing information about relationships that involve the passage of time*, that is, those that involve *before and after effects*. The "Make Tea" object, shown in Figure 2.2, is characterized by the information carried by the "Make Tea" relationship. The only item that distinguishes the process from a mere association is the fact that the resources for making tea, which

*Figure 2.2. Processes represent a special kind of relationship and possess information on "before and after" effects related to objects.*

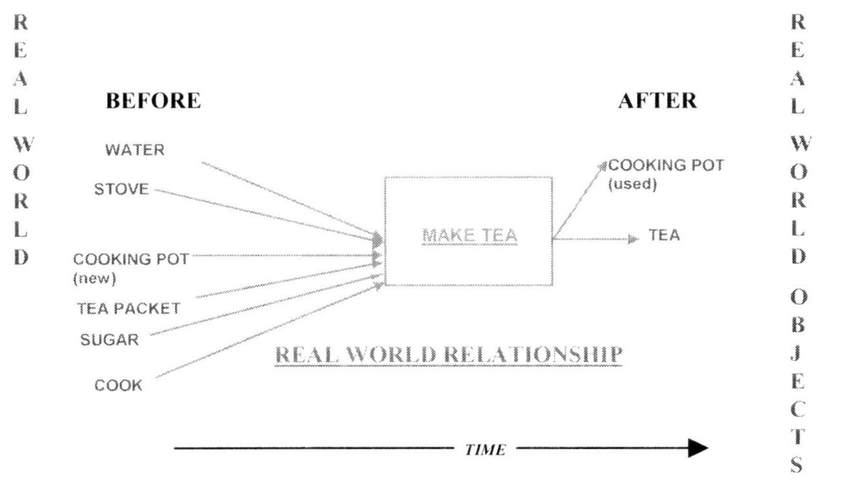

are objects, such as the water and tea bags, had to precede tea, the work product of the process. Thus, the process is not only an association, but also an association that describes a causative temporal sequence and passage of time.

*Make Tea* relates eight objects in the model: Water, Stove, Cooking Pot (new and used), Cook, Tea Packet, Sugar, and the Tea; it also *sequences* them. The object "Make Tea" specifies that the objects to the left in Figure 2.2, namely the Water, the Stove, a New Cooking Pan, the Tea Packet, the Sugar, and the Cook must exist before those objects on the right happen. *Make Tea* is a process because it facilitates the transfer of information through a sequence based on the passage of time. *Thus, a process, besides being an object in its own right, is a special kind of association because it contains a sequence of information.* This is also how the meaning of causality is born: the resources and the process that create the product are its causes.

Objects respond to events,[3] with their response being a certain kind of behavior.[4] Glass is hit by a hammer and broken; the hammer strike is an event. The process of making tea may have been initiated by the chef asking the cook to do so. The chef's request would then have been the trigger. Triggers are events too. Events are occurrences in time such as the occurrence of a condition (e.g., the value of an order exceeding a threshold that calls for special scrutiny), a trigger such as the beginning or end of another process, or the occurrence of a time of day (e.g., close of business), the passage of a certain duration of time (e.g., a three day waiting period before a contract becomes binding on both parties), or some other occurrence in *time*.

An event could also be an occurrence in time that transforms nothing. This distinguishes *Event* from *Process*. Unlike a full-blown process, an event is not a causal relationship and does not need to result in products or link resources to products. An event only conveys information about the passage of time. Events, when joined with relationships between objects, create causality and process by infusing temporal information about before and after into the relationship. Causality is information about which objects in the relationship (causes) precede which successor objects in a cause and effect relationship. Similarly in a process, resources come before products. As such, a process can be considered a special kind of causal relationship—one that uses resources to create products or services. This is how the meanings of *Causality* and *Process* are created from *Event* and *Relationship*.

A process always makes a change or seeks information.[5] Business process engineers often use the term *cycle time* to describe the time interval from the beginning of a process to its end. A process, like the event it is derived from, can even be instantaneous or may continue indefinitely. The deep space probe *Pioneer* will travel into deeper interstellar space for an indefinite period of time, whereas the cook may trigger the baking process for a batch of cookies instantaneously by pressing a button. The trigger for bake cookie is an event with negligible duration, whereas the journey of the Pioneer is a process with no known end. Processes that do not end, or have no known end, are called *Sagas*. Thus, a process is a relationship, and also an event, which may be of finite, negligible, or endless duration.

Events are important because they also act as triggers for actions, processes, and behaviors. The cook may turn the stove off and interrupt the *Make Tea* process in Box 2.1. Turning the stove off would then be the event that leads to the suspension of the *Make Tea* process. Processes are special kinds of objects with special kinds of behavior. Turning the stove off is an event that triggers specific behavior of the *Make Tea* object. The start of a process is an event that is implicit in every process, but as we have seen, the end of the process is implied for many, not all, processes.

*Figure 2.3. How is information naturally manifested in the real world?*

*Reproduced by permission from Mitra, A., & Gupta, A., Agile Systems with Reusable Patterns of Business Knowledge, Norwood, MA: Artech House, Inc., 2005. ©*

## Perception and Information Naturally Speaking: Meaning, Measurability, and Format

In order to normalize knowledge, we must separate meaning from its expression, as described in Box 2.1. This may be done by augmenting our metamodel to represent entities of pure information that exist beyond physical objects and relationships. This section will introduce three of these objects: *Domain*, *Unit of Measure (UOM)*, and *Format*.

Just as matter and energy exist in the real world, so too does information; the only difference between these items are the rules governing each. In terms of tangibility, matter is the easiest to grasp both physically and mentally. The debate over energy being equally real is old. It took over a thousand years for our ancestors to settle this debate,[6] and it took humankind even longer to observe that energy and matter could neither be created nor destroyed. Information is no less real than matter or energy, but it is even more abstract and its laws harder to grasp than those for matter and energy. Although information cannot be touched or felt, it is *manifested* through the behavior of real objects and physical energy and therefore must be understood.

Unlike the situation with matter and energy, a *meaning* is not located at a particular place in space and time; only its *expression* is.[7] All physical objects or energy manifested at a particular place at a point in time convey information, and in the example of Box 2.1, we saw how they may convey the same information: the same meaning occurred in two different artifacts that had no spatial or temporal relationship with each other. They only shared meaning, that is, information *content*.[8] This was their only relationship. Although *meaning* in its true sense (and hence the *information* it conveys) does not occupy space and is immutable in time, it is ironic that one can only know the meaning from information *expressed and observed* in the physical world framed by space, time, and real world objects.

A single meaning may be characterized by multiple expressions.[9] The same piece of information may be stored (and disseminated) in multiple forms and places: on the printed envelope sent to a customer and on a company's Web site; in the French and English versions of a new computer owner's manual; and in the Chinese president's speech and its English translation distributed at the meeting of the United Nations General assembly.[10] Indeed, an item composed of matter or energy will always convey information, even if it is only information about itself. Accordingly, matter and energy may be considered to hold a constrained form of information: information constrained to a single physical location at a moment in time or a pattern in information space shaped by a constraint. It is here that the fundamental difference between Information vs. Matter and Energy is displayed. Unlike a specific material object or a packet of energy that is bound to only a single location at a single point in time,[11] identical information can exist at many different places at several different times.

Our observation of information is mediated by matter and/or energy; we can only *observe* the *behavior* of reality as it is *manifested in the behavior of objects* located in space and time. Whereas specific physical objects are *local*; that is, their existence corresponds to a particular place at any given moment in time, information carried by *meaning* is *nonlocal*; that is, it is completely independent of space and time. The need to understand the underlying natural structures that connect information to its physical expression(s) is inherent in the effort to normalize business rules.

Information mediation and expression within the real world is achieved by two metaobjects. One is intangible; it emerges from the concept of measurability and deals with the amount of information[12] that is inherent in the *meaning* being conveyed. The other is tangible; it deals with the format—or physical form—of expression. The format is easier to recognize, and many tools and techniques provide the ability to do so explicitly. It is much harder to recognize the *domain of measurability* (called *domain* in this book).[13] If we are careless and club domain with format,[14] like some of the older modeling tools did, this information will return to plague us through inflexible software and replicated business rules.

## Measurability and Information Content

Through the behavior, or properties, of objects we observe, the information content of reality manifests itself to us. People have anniversaries; they gain or lose weight, prefer some fruit more than others, have genetic traits that determine eye color and other physical attributes, and so forth. Let us consider two completely different objects, say, a bottle of juice, and you, a person. The amount of juice in the bottle can be measured, just as it is possible to weigh yourself. The volume of juice in the jug as well as your weight can both be quantified with numbers that express their individual (and inherently different) magnitudes.

You are able to realize that these two values—the volume of juice in the jug and your weight—are quite dissimilar qualities of inherently dissimilar objects (a person's weight and the volume of juice). Despite this difference, both values are drawn from a *domain of information* that contains some common behavior. This common behavior—that each value can be quantitatively measured—is inherent in the information being conveyed by the measurement of these values, but not in the objects themselves. Date is another example of a shared quality of these disparate objects that can be applied to each of them. We can measure the date of three separate events: when the bottle was made, when the juice was produced, and when the person was born. The kind of information that *domains* naturally normalize can be understood by comparing the *amount* of information *intrinsically* conveyed by each of these qualities of people and the bottles of juice, as we will see next.

## Nominal Domains

Let us start with domains that only distinguish one kind of object from another, for example, living objects from nonliving objects. We know that the living/nonliving classification conveys that living things are different from nonliving things. However, the classification has no information on how living and nonliving objects can be arranged in any natural sequence; nor does the classification include any quantitative information regarding the differences between living and nonliving things.

If this information is *stored* on a physical medium, "living things" could be arbitrarily represented with a numeric code 1, and "nonliving things" with 2. If we claimed that living things precede nonliving things because the number 1 precedes 2,[15] we would come to the conclusion that this assertion is nonsensical because the domain conveys no natural sequencing information for this classification scheme (meaningless assertions are considered to be "null," a special value that we will examine further on in this book[16]).

This fact will always assert itself regardless of how the information is coded or *physically* expressed: it is also without meaning to subtract 1 from 2 in an attempt to quantify the difference between living and nonliving things, just as it is meaningless to divide 1 by 2 to find the ratio by which the meaning of "living" exceeds or is a fraction of the meaning of "nonliving." *That information is just not carried in the domain.* It is immaterial how the information is physically expressed.

The term *nominally scaled domains* (*nominal* domains, in short) denotes domains that contain just enough information needed to classify objects based on their properties or relationships.

## Ordinal Domains

Next, consider a person's preference for fruit. Jane is a woman who likes blueberries more than grapes and apples and, above all, loathes oranges. She really has no preference between grapes and apples.

*Box 2.2. Formats, objects, and domains*

Domains convey meaning and information content. For example, the age domain conveys information on the time lapse between the moment of creation and a later point in time. Objects frame the context of the meaning that is conveyed by domains. The intersection (relationship) between the age domain and a person conveys that the age of a person is the meaning we wish to convey. Thus, the combination of Objects and Domains conveys *meaning*. Formats on the other hand, specify the manner in which information is *physically presented* or transmitted to a person, a system, or an instrument.[17] For instance, the age might be displayed in decimal numbers on a screen for a human observer, or sent in binary format as electromagnetic pulses to a computer.

Consider, another example, in which we convey nominal meanings about living vs. nonliving objects: we could use a numeric code of "1" for "living" and "2" for "nonliving," or "L" for "Living" and "N" for "Nonliving"; or we could use icons or pictures to convey the information. These symbols would all be different physical representations of the same meaning; they cannot change the meaning assigned to them. They are all examples of format. The meaning is a fact—that living objects breathe, whereas nonliving objects do not. Thus, this domain normalizes the common meaning and behavior of living and nonliving things. A living object can place this behavior into context, thereby giving it a context-specific *meaning*. For example, how a plant breathes may be very different from how a man breathes.

The domain conveys the fact that the property "living," related to a class of objects, maps to the life/nonlife domain, subject to the condition that only a living *or* nonliving classification is permitted for an instance of this object. The fact that an object must be either living or not is an *irreducible fact*.

At times, more than one property of an object can map to the same domain. Each property represents an irreducible fact related to the real world. The length, the breadth, and the height of a building all map to the length domain. The domain normalizes the facts that these three properties of building are characterized by the same units of measure, with identical conversion factors. Accordingly, this information does not need to be repeated for each property. The same reasoning holds when different properties of various kinds of objects are mapped to the same domain, such as a person's height and the length of a bridge both mapping to the length domain. The length domain provides a common basis for units of measure and also for conversion rules between various units of length. (Also, see the note in Appendix II on gender.)

Jane can easily rank the four fruits in order of preference: blueberries, followed by apples and grapes as equal, and finally oranges at the end. However, if someone asks Jane to quantify the *amount* of her liking for each fruit by assigning a number to each, a problem arises. She would not know how to respond to the demand. She would know that she should give blueberries the highest score, followed by an equal score for grapes and apples, and a lower score for oranges, but would not know what these scores should be because the information does not exist.

The domain on which Jane classifies her *preference* for fruit contains sequencing (ranking) information but no information about *quantitative magnitude*. If the person asking Jane insists that she enumerate her preference of fruit, some numerical values may be assigned, but regardless of how these preferences are recorded—whether with numbers, letters, colors, or graphic icons—these numbers will convey no information beyond Jane's ranking of fruit preferences.[18] *Domains like this, that have no quantitative information, but do convey enough information to arrange objects in some sequence or order, are called ordinal domains.*[19]

Because Jane is able to rank different fruits in order of her preference, she can *automatically* arrange fruits into separate groups (e.g., grapes and apples would be grouped together, and both oranges and blueberries would constitute their own separate groups—the criterion is her fruit *preference*). However, *if she simply groups, rather than ranks, the fruit in order of her preference, information is withheld regarding her preferences.* Thus, we come to the conclusion that *ordinal domains intrinsically carry more information than nominal domains.*[20] Ordinal domains carry sequencing information and classification information, the latter by implication.

Now let us suppose that Jane's questioner has become frustrated by her inability to quantify her preferences and demands that she assign some order of numbers to her preferences—say, for the sake of argument, the rank Jane assigned to each fruit is 1 to blueberries, 2 to apples and grapes, and 3 to oranges. We know that it would be entirely wrong to conclude on this basis that Jane likes blueberries 3 times as much as she likes oranges. Nor can it be concluded that the *gap*, or difference, in Jane's preference between blueberries and apples is equal to the gap between her preferences for apples and oranges. The domain simply does not *have* this information.

## Difference Scaled Domains

Let us consider birthdays. Say another individual, Jim, was born on January 1, 1965 whereas Jane was born on January 1, 1975. It is meaningless to divide the date on which Jim was born by the date on which Jane was born. The ratio has no meaning. On the other hand, one *can* say Jim is 10 years older than Jane. In other words, one *could* meaningfully subtract one date from the other to obtain their quantitative difference. Domains of this type are called difference scaled domains. They contain adequate information to include all operations such as comparison and ranking that apply to ordinal domains and also the information that permits meaningful subtraction of values in the domain, but they carry no information in terms of ratios. Note that it is also meaningless to mutually add or multiply dates. Addition and multiplication are meaningless in difference scaled domains. Note also that the date (time) domain is distinct from the age (elapsed time or time difference) domain, in which ratios, addition, and multiplication *are* meaningful operations.

## Ratio Scaled Domains

Ratios are meaningful in ratio scaled domains because, in addition to the information in difference scaled domains like the time domain, they carry information about a natural nil magnitude. Suppose it is now January 1, 2000, and Jane has a daughter named Jenny who was born on January

1, 1995. We can meaningfully say that Jane is five times older than her daughter because Jane is 25 years old, whereas her daughter is 5 years old. This is because the age (i.e., elapsed time) domain has a natural nil value. All operations that apply to nominal, ordinal, and difference scaled domains, along with addition, division, and multiplication, and indeed all arithmetic, are also valid in the case of ratio scaled domains.

## Physical Expression of Domains

Domains convey the concepts of measurability and existence. They are a key constituent of knowledge.[21] There are four fundamental domains that we will consider in this book; two of them convey qualitative information and the other two convey quantitative information, as follows:

- **Qualitative domains:**
  - Nominal domains convey no information on sequencing, distances, or ratios. They convey only distinctions, distinguishing one object from another or a class from another (a class is also an object).
  - Ordinal domains not only convey distinctions between objects but also information on arranging its members in a sequence (a value is also an object, hence the concept of magnitude may be deemed to start here). However, ordinal domains posses no information regarding the magnitudes of gaps or ratios between objects (values).
- **Quantitative domains:**
  - Difference scaled domains not only express all the information that qualitative domains convey, but also convey magnitudes of difference; they allow for measurement of the magnitude of point-to-point differences in a sequence. However, they cannot convey any information about ratios between objects because the domain does not contain a value in it that one can call nil or zero.
  - Ratio scaled domains perform three functions: assist in the classification and arrangement of objects in a natural sequence, able to measure the magnitude of differences in properties of objects, and take the ratios of these different properties. Ratio scaled domains always contain a natural zero.

In order to give information a physical expression, it must be physically formatted and recorded on some sort of medium. A single piece of information must be recorded on at least one medium and may be recorded in many different formats. For example, different types of equines may be coded as a number (say, 1 for Horse and 2 for Zebra), or as a letter (say, H for Horse and Z for Zebra) or as a picture of a brown equine for Horse and a striped equine for Zebra. This information could also be spoken aloud or written as a hexadecimal code on floppy disk that only computers can read. This physical representation of information is its *Format*. A Format is an item of information, which may be attached to a meaning but is a distinct component of information that should be distinguished from the abstract meaning it is attached to.

A symbol is sufficient to physically represent the information conveyed by nominal and ordinal domains. Of course, ordinal domains also carry sequencing information, and it would make sense to map ordinal values to a naturally sequenced set of symbols like digits or letters. (If there is no limit to the number of values in an ordinal domain, obviously the set of 26 letters in the alphabet will not suffice, but numeric digits would, provided that we understand that quantitative differences between numbers are meaningless.)

Unlike qualitative domains, quantitative domains need both symbols and units of measure to physically express the information they carry. This is because they are *dense domains*; that is, given a pair of values, regardless of how close they are to each other, it is always possible to find a value in between them. A discrete set of symbols cannot therefore convey all the information in a quantitative domain. However, numbers have this characteristic of being dense. Therefore, it is possible to map values in a dense domain to an arbitrary set of numbers without losing information. These numbers may then be represented by physical symbols such as decimal digits, roman numerals, or binary or octal numbers. There may be many different mappings between values and numbers. For example, age may be expressed in months, years, or days; a person's age will be the same regardless of the number used. To show that different numbers may express the same meaning, we need a Unit of Measure (UOM). The UOM is the name of the specific map used to express that meaning. Age in years, days, months, and hours are all different UOMs for the elapsed time domain.

Both the number and UOM must be physically represented by a symbol to physically format the information in a quantitative domain. Indeed, a UOM may be represented by several different symbols. The UOM "Dollars," for the money domain, may be represented by the symbol "$" or the text "USD." In general, a dense domain needs a pair of symbols to fully represent the information in it: a symbol for the UOM and a symbol for the number mapped to a value. We will call this pair the *full format* of the domain.

Domains, UOMs, and Formats are all objects that structure meaning. For this reason, we call them Metaobjects in Figure 2.4. They are some of the components from which the very concept of knowledge is assembled. The Metamodel of Knowledge is a model of the meaning of knowl-

*Figure 2.4. (Partial) metamodel of domain*

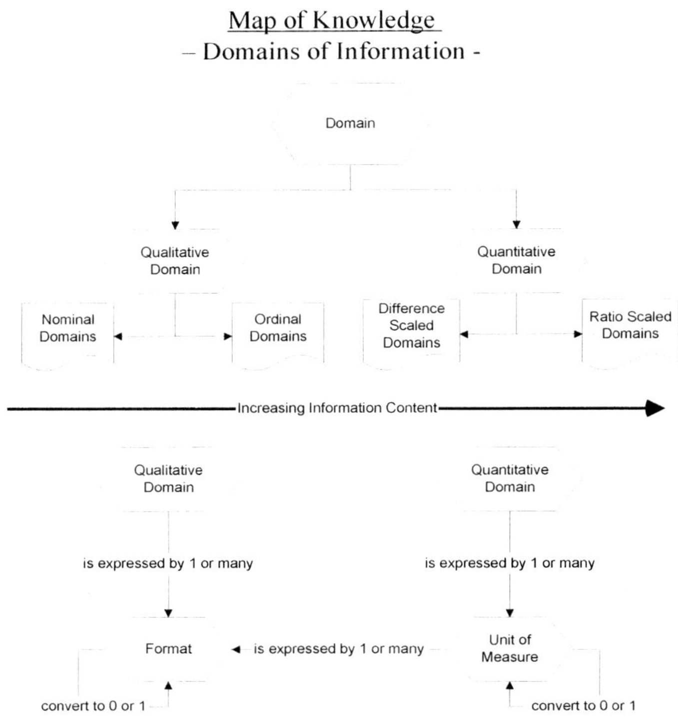

edge built from abstract components. We will describe more of these components later in this book. Our model will describe the mutual interaction between these components that creates the patterns of information we call "knowledge." These interactions are semantic relationships between objects. These patterns may be considered to be equivalent to the engineering blueprints that describe physical structures. Figure 2.4 is an example of the technique we will use.

Metaobjects in Figure 2.4 are represented by rectangles, and their relationships are arrows. We caution readers who are used to input and output diagrams commonly used in information systems and process engineering that Figure 2.4 is different. The arrows in Figure 2.4 do not represent the *flow* of information from one place to another. However, they do show how objects *interact*. Figure 2.4 is a semantic model. To understand the rules, you must read along the arrows and form a sentence.

Starting with "Quantitative Domain," for example, the sentence reads "(A) Quantitative Domain *is expressed by 1 or many* Unit(s) of Measure." The lower limit (1) on the occurrence of Unit of Measure highlights the fact that each quantitative domain must possess at least one unit of measure. This is because the unit of measure is not optional. A quantitative value cannot be expressed unless a unit of measure can characterize it. The arrow that starts from, and loops back to, Unit of Measure reads "Unit of Measure *converts to none or at most 1* Unit of Measure." Conversion rules, such as those for currency conversion or distance conversion, reside in the Metamodel of Knowledge. This relationship provides another example of a metaobject (since relationships are objects too) and demonstrates how a metaobject can facilitate the storage of the full set of conversion rules in a single place.

The conversion rule is restricted to conversion from one UOM to only one other UOM; this constraint is necessary to avoid redundancy and to normalize information. A single conversion rule enables navigation from one UOM to any other arbitrary UOM by following a daisy chain of conversion rules. If you needed to convert yards to inches, and you had only the conversion factor to feet, you could convert yards to feet by multiplying by 3 and then to inches by multiplying by 12. The upper bound of one on the conversion relationship in the metamodel also implies that if you add a new UOM to a domain, you have to add only a single conversion rule to convert to any of the other UOMs, and that such information will suffice to enable conversion to every UOM defined for that domain.

## METAOBJECTS, SUBTYPES, AND INHERITANCE

Metaobjects help to normalize real world behavior by normalizing the irreducible facts we discussed earlier.[22] The metaobjects that we have discussed so far are object (a pattern, the fundamental metaobject described Chapter IV)[23]; property; relationship; process; event; domain; unit of measure; and format. The kind of atomic rules normalized by each type of metaobject are summarized in Figure 2.5. Although they are simple in of themselves, they are extremely important because they serve as the building blocks of knowledge.

The ontology in Figure 2.5 organizes objects in a hierarchy of meaning. Lower level objects in the ontology are derived from objects at higher levels by adding information. Figure 2.5 tells us that the meaning of *Process* is configured by combining the meanings of *Relationship*, an interaction between objects, with the meaning of *Event*, the flow of time.[24] This kind of relationship is special. It is called a subtyping relationship and forms the basis of the ontology. Subtyping relationships convey information from higher levels to lower levels of an ontology. The lower level object becomes a special kind of higher-level object. Figure 2.5 shows that *Ratio Scaled Domain* is a special kind of *Domain* because of the chain of subtyping relationships

*Box 2.3. Transformation between multiple units of measure*

In any Difference Scaled domain or Ratio Scaled domain, a value can be transformed from one Unit of Measure to another by simply multiplying the particular value by a specific conversion factor. If one or more UOMs with corresponding conversion factors exist in a particular domain and a new UOM is introduced, only one new conversion ratio needs to be added in order to transform a value to enable us to revise measurements expressed in the new UOM to all the other UOMs. More specifically, individual ratios will not be needed for making conversions from the new UOM to all of the old UOMs. Indeed, knowledge would be denormalized if every conversion ratio was individually specialized. This is because a single conversion ratio between the new and any one of the older UOMs can deduce each ratio.

The following exemplifies the real world facts. By basing it on the weight domain, the example remains simple. However, the same arguments will always apply to UOMs, no matter whether it is the ratio-scaled domain or the difference-scaled domain.

Assume that governments of different nations decide that they want to conduct a survey to find the average weight of persons in their respective countries. Just after the project was started, however, they realize their scales of measurement are all different. This means that to succeed, all participating governments will have to compromise on a single unit of measure. The basic conversion rules between pounds, grams, and kilograms include, (see Figure A).

To convert kilograms to pounds using the table, find "*kilograms*" beneath the "From" column on the extreme left, and then follow the "Kilogram" row until you find the "Pounds" column. The cell specifies "x 2.2"; this means that to convert kilograms to pounds, simply multiply by 2.2 (therefore, 5 kilograms = 5 x 2.2 = 11 pounds). Along the same lines, the rule to convert kilograms to grams is "multiply by 1,000." Since it is common knowledge that division is the inverse of multiplication, the table actually contains three atomic rules.

Only these three rules are necessary to convert between any units of measure represented in the table. The table does not hold any explicit rule for converting pounds to kilograms, but by knowing that division and multiplication are inverses of each other, we can derive the rule to convert pounds to kilograms; this is: divide by 2.2 in order to convert pounds to kilograms. Moreover, we can derive the rule to convert grams to kilograms using the table's information, even though no definitive rule is stated for it. Grams to kilograms can be converted by dividing by 1,000. It would have been redundant to include the conversion ratio for explicitly converting grams to kilogram in the table; further, knowledge would then be denormalized. (Note: all diagonal cells of the table are all blank.)

Note that there would be no need to convert if all nations had standardized the same units. In such a world, conversion rules would not be needed at all. However, in some nations, surveyors were uncomfortable with UOMs because they were unfamiliar with grams, pounds, or kilograms. If the governments opt to add ounces to the list of UOMs for weight, the conversion rule table will have change as follows, (see Figure B).

Note how only one conversion rule must be added to the table: "*multiply by 0.035 to convert from grams to ounces.*" This single new rule will ensure that ounces can be converted to any of the other units presented in the table. Thus, even though there is no definitive rule in the table to convert ounces from kilograms, there is an implied rule, which may be inferred (derived): we could multiply kilograms by 1,000 to convert to grams and then multiply the result by 0.035 to further convert to ounces. Thus, inference flows from the normalization of the information content of business rules.

*Figure A. Conversion table*

| FROM | TO | | |
|---|---|---|---|
| | *Kilograms* | *Pounds* | *Grams* |
| *Kilograms* | | x 2.2 | x 1,000 |
| *Pounds* | | | |
| *Grams* | | | |

*Box 2.3. continued*

*Figure B. Conversion table*

| FROM | TO | | | |
|---|---|---|---|---|
| | *Kilograms* | *Pounds* | *Grams* | *Ounces* |
| *Kilograms* | | x 2.2 | x 1,000 | |
| *Pounds* | | | | |
| *Grams* | | | | x 0.035 |
| *Ounces* | | | | |

*Note that none of these metarelationships represent processes because they do not involve time; in the real world, there is no data flow or conversion process. Everything is just Knowledge. Later we will see how these ideas can be mapped to computer-based implementation and continue to stay normalized.*

*Figure 2.5. Basic metaobject inventory: Kinds of rules each metaobject normalizes*

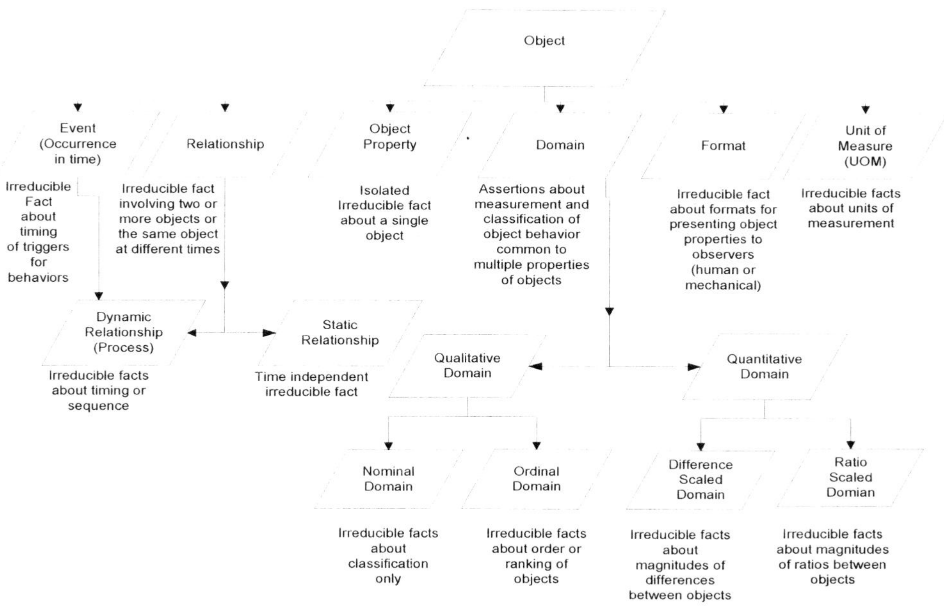

that lead from *Domain* to *Ratio Scaled Domain* via *Quantitative Domain*.

We now introduce two new metaobjects: the subtyping relationship and its corollary, the Subtype. They serve as containers for encapsulating and normalizing knowledge and as conduits for sharing this knowledge with other objects. Shared behavior is normalized in the supertype object and automatically shared with subtypes by implication through the subtyping relationship. For example, aging, birthdays, gender, credit rating, names, ring size, social security numbers, and telephone numbers are common to all persons. People can be customers, employees, or both. The object class "Person" will normalize information common to people, such as social security number and birthday, without regard to the person being an employee, customer, or both. Subtypes will add specific information that gives the object special, more specific meanings, which are distinct and more restrictive than the meanings of their supertypes. For instance, *Customer* and *Employee* are subtypes of *Person*. *Employee* adds the employment relationship with another person or organization, while *Customer* has the same effect for the purchasing relationship. This is the information that *Employee* and *Customer* normalize and add to the information conveyed by *Person*. They create new meanings by extending the meaning of Person. This example demonstrates why subtypes, the subtyping relationship, and inheritance are all needed to normalize information, and are therefore critical to the discussion in this book.[25]

Note also that the subtyping hierarchy between qualitative and quantitative domains, specifically from nominal, ordinal, difference to ratio scaled domains, has been ignored in Figure 2.5. They are subtypes because, as we have seen, each adds information and hence behavior as we descend down the hierarchy from nominal domain to ratio scaled domain through ordinal and difference scaled domains. The information we lose when we ignore a subtyping hierarchy is information we might have reused. For example, the irreducible fact that ratio scaled values may be arranged in order of magnitude was inherited from ordinal domains. If we ignore this hierarchy in our electronic knowledge repository, we will need to replicate the comparison operators of the ordinal domain in ratio scaled domains. With the hierarchy, they will be automatically inherited. Indeed, integrating the concept of ontology into the repository of knowledge gives it the power of reason. As we will see later, this will enable automated support for innovation.[26] Box 2.4 shows different kinds of information that subtypes may add to their parent objects.

The next section shows, with an example, how knowledge may be configured from components and how inheritance can automate the process of reuse of knowledge.

## THE REPOSITORY OF MEANING

The atomic rule is not only the most basic building block of knowledge; it is also the ultimate repository of information. It is a rule that cannot be broken into smaller, simpler parts without losing some of its meaning. The metaobjects of Figure 2.5 are the natural repositories of knowledge. They provide the basis of real world meaning. The intent of this section is to create an intuitive understanding of the principles involved with a simple example. *Creating Agile Business Systems with Reusable Knowledge* provides more coverage of this topic.

Just as molecules react with molecules in chemical reactions to produce molecules of new substances with different properties from the original reagents, atomic rules may be built from other atomic rules. As we continually polish our business positions with product and process innovation, some atomic rules are reused. These rules are perfect examples of those that can act as reusable components of knowledge. In order to build specialized domains of knowledge, entire

*Box 2.4. Subtyping criteria*

By changing their state, object instances can react to events. A change of state has the power to either make the instance a member or take it out of the subclass. For instance, a company will hire a person to make him or her an employee. Employee is a subtype of Person (see the discussion above). Likewise, an employee who is fired is no longer an instance of the Employee, a subclass of Person. This is an example of how individual objects, in response to certain events, leap in and out of subclasses. Basically, their roles change. Morphism is the ability to have shape and form. When something appears in numerous different forms, it is referred to as polymorphism. For that reason, subtypes may be called polymorphisms of their supertypes. Thus, in the example about living things in Box 2.2, "Breathing" assumed different forms in different life forms. Each form of breathing was a polymorphism of the generic feature called "breathing." This notion is the foundation for many key concepts presented in this book. (Appendix II discusses polymorphism under the theory of categories.)

A guard condition is a rule that determines whether a certain object will be affected by an event. For example, one cannot modify the terms of a sealed agreement. Consequently, the agreement is a guard condition because of the sealed state. Guard conditions present another opportunity for constraining and thereby subtyping objects (all constraints are features of objects as we will discuss later in this book; constraints convey information, and increased information content is the basis for subtyping). Agreements could have been divided into two categories: those that are sealed and those under negotiation. The modification effect would only be a property (behavior) of Open Agreements (in the generic agreement, the existence or not of the modification effect is "unknown"). A separate guard condition on the parent object to verify its state would not be compulsory, if the Agreement object were designed in this manner. Indeed, if the request to renegotiate an agreement occurs, and its state is not known, this framework would imply that the software automatically query the state before updating the agreement. Note how the framework implicitly defines some of the key services that are required by the concept of "Agreement" ([338] in Appendix III has more information on reusable business services).

*Figure A. Effects of events on subtypes*

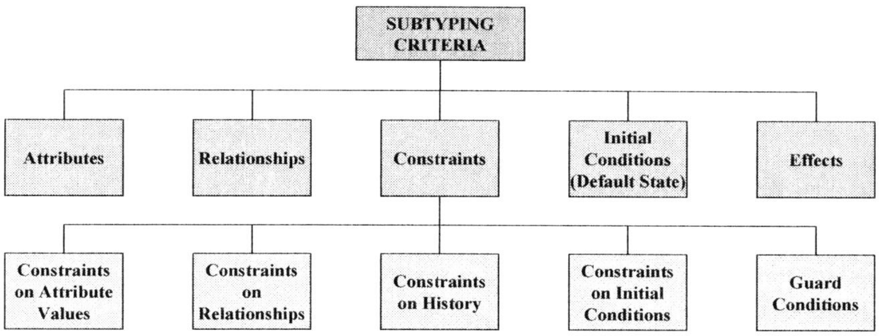


structures and configurations may be reused. This is similar to manufacturers creating reusable subassemblies to build machines from ordinary parts. The end product may incorporate many versions and modifications of these reusable subassemblies. The structure of metaobjects sparks reusability. The following example will show how the spark of innovation starts within metaobjects when these objects are normalized repositories of atomic rules.

Consider the example in Box 2.1. Each process in Box 2.1 is an object. They are strung in a chain that shows which process must lead which others. These links are relationships, and, as was stated previously, these relationships are also objects in their own right. These relationships transfer irreducible facts about mutual dependencies among the processes that they connect. This chain of processes forms a *structure* assembled from

*Figure 2.6. A rule, Organization Ships Product, assembled from Objects*

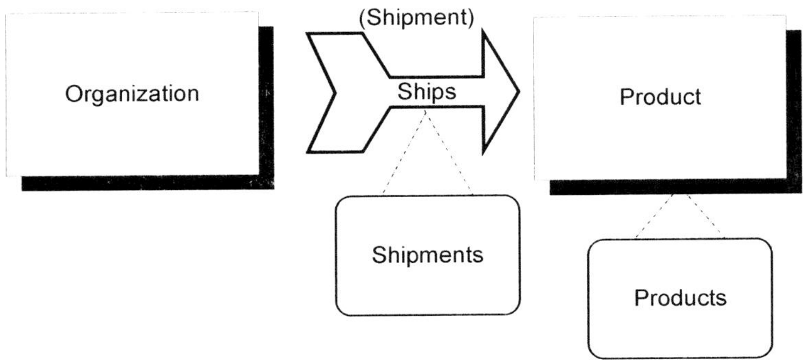


atomic rules. It is a very simple arrangement of atomic rules.

Look at Figure 2.6 to understand how atomic rules can be created from other atomic rules, and to comprehend how subassemblies of rules may be reused: Figure 2.6 is an example of a simple atomic rule which is common to many businesses: that of *Organization Ships Product*.

The shipment between organization and product is a relationship; it is also an object in its own right (like all relationships). Figure 2.6 shows a diagram of the *Organization Ships Product* rule.[27] Read it just as you would the diagram of Figure 2.4; only remember that the arrows (that is, relationships) are objects in their own right as well.

Figure 2.6 illustrates two atomic rules:

1. Many shipments may be made by an organization, and
2. Each separate shipment can have multiple products.

This is an example of a simple configuration of knowledge. There are two atomic rules, and they are not mutually linked in any structure. Each rule stands on its own.

Watch how the rules are reconfigured in the following scenario:

*Assume that a flat rate per shipment had been negotiated, but this contract has expired. In the new contract, shipping cost will depend on the total volume of the shipment. The scope of the shipping model must be enhanced to include the total volume.*

*Assume also that the firm has, at its disposal, components of knowledge as a part of an inventory of knowledge artifacts that have already been built and stored by its process-reengineering department. The relevant knowledge in the repository must first be found.*

*We locate the volume domain in the repository. This is a ratio scaled domain. We understand (from Figure 2.4 and Box 2.3) that it must be associated with some particular UOM. The conversion rules between units of measure are shown in Figure 2.4. We also know that volume must be a positive number. It is a constraint (and an atomic rule) associated with the domain (constraints are also objects, and may be features of objects[28]). As such, there exists a natural structure of irreducible facts that is correlated with this volume domain. Let us assume that the artifact in the repository reflects this. This natural structure may then be considered to be a subassembly of knowledge stored in the repository. This is the second structure from the left in Figure 2.7.*

When we assemble Shipment with volume, Shipment Volume, a new meaning derived from

*Figure 2.7. Adding components to assemble configurations of rules*

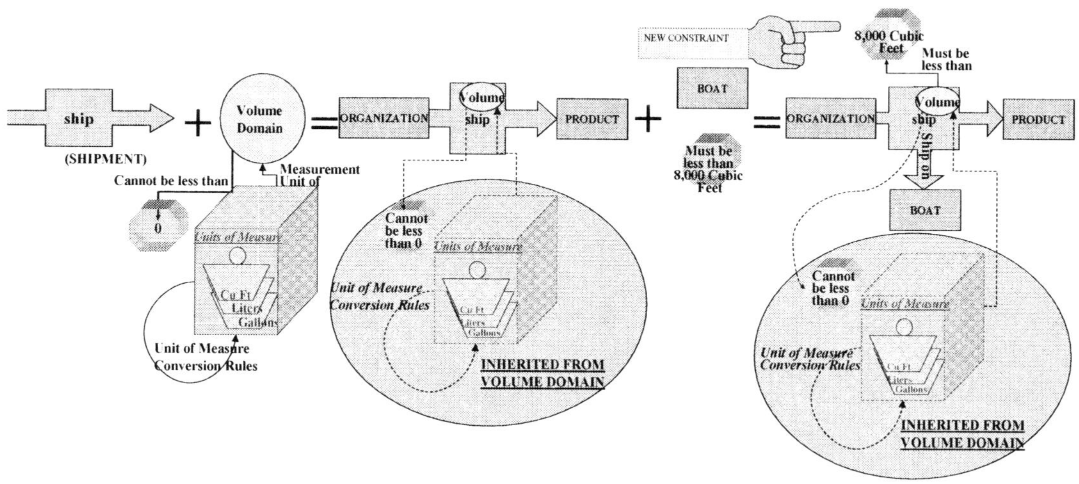


*Reproduced by permission from Mitra, A., & Gupta, A. , Agile Systems with Reusable Patterns of Business Knowledge, Norwood, MA: Artech House, Inc., 2005. ©*

Volume and Shipment, inherits the information associated with the volume domain, including units of measure of volume, rules for converting between units of measure and the fact that the shipment volume cannot be negative. These are irreducible facts that flow into the subassembly of knowledge automatically and are examples of how knowledge can be reused.

If the unit volume of the *product* were needed as well, the volume domain would be reused again. The same structures and rules would be inherited, and we would then assemble the object with the volume domain. These constraints, UOMs, and conversion rules, would not have to be separately redefined for shipment volume and product volume separately. If a conversion rule had been changed or a new unit of measure added to the volume domain, the availability to both the shipment volume and product volume would occur *automatically* due to the fact that knowledge in the volume domain is normalized.

Let us see how the reuse of irreducible facts can assist in building other irreducible facts. Assume that a new contract with the shipping company stipulates that all products be shipped as cargo (by boat). The atomic rule will then read: *Organization Ships Product by boat.*

First, this rule must be tested to ensure its validity as an atomic rule. It is an atomic rule if we lose information when we break the rule into the following parts:

1. Organization ships product
2. Organization ships by boat

The two assertions taken together do not necessarily mean that the *product* will be shipped by boat. For example, the organization could ship products by air and other items by boat without violating either rule. Therefore, information has been lost by dividing *Organization Ships Product by boat* into the two separate assertions above. Therefore, *Organization Ships Product by boat* is an atomic rule. We obtained this atomic rule by changing *Shipment* from a two-way relationship involving *Organization* and *Product,* into a three-way relationship between *Organization, Product,* and *Boat.* We have created one atomic rule from another by adding information to it to make a general rule more specific. It shows how generic rules may be made specific by adding information.[29] The assembly of this structure of information from knowledge artifacts is shown in Figure 2.7.

Now we have another requirement: we find that boats cannot carry more than 8,000 cubic feet, i.e., the total volume of each shipment by boat must be no more than 8,000 cubic feet. This too is an irreducible fact. This does not act as a generic constraint attached to the volume domain; rather it is specific to shipments made by boat. Therefore, the constraint is attached to *Shipment Volume*, a property of *Shipment*, instead of the generic volume domain (see Figure 2.5). Accordingly, this constraint will not be automatically inherited by volumes of all items (e.g., Product Volume).

The effect of attaching this constraint of 8,000 cubic feet to *Shipment Volume* implies that two separate constraints now apply to the property of *Shipment:*

1. Inherited automatically from the Volume domain that no volume may be negative.
2. Specific to Shipment volume, that no shipment may exceed 8,000 cubic feet.

The combined effect of both of these constraints is to restrict Shipment volume from zero to 8,000 cubic feet. The structure on the far right of Figure 2.7 shows how these rules have been organized to reflect knowledge about product shipments.

If the process to ship by air as well as boat was reengineered, we would use the structure *Organization Ships Product* in Figure 2.7 again but *Airplane* would substitute *Boat* in the structure on the far righthand side of Figure 2.7. This is another example of how subassemblies of knowledge can be reused.

On an airplane, the volume limitations might be different. All units of measure and conversion rules will again be automatically inherited from the volume domain, and in our example, this can enable interoperability between U.S. and European operations.

The patterns in this book and its companions provide the most generic and widely reused irreducible facts, along with templates for analyzing and identifying more specific irreducible facts. The Semantic Web of the future would be the ultimate repository of these components of knowledge (see Appendix IV).

## THE PROBLEM OF PERSPECTIVE

We understand the world around us by experiencing its behavior and then forming *concepts* by differentiating and classifying objects (relationships between concepts are also objects) based on behaviors that are mutually shared and contrasting those that are not. These concepts are generalizations that have filtered out information we consider irrelevant to our estimation of how our world behaves. Our perspective is a subjective model of reality, valid within the scope of our perception or problem space. Differences in scope, experience, and individuals' thinking lead to different models, in which generalizations of what is shared and what is unique may be different. The graphic in Box 2.5 may be perceived very differently, depending on which color we think of as representing empty space. This is the problem of perspective.

The example in Box 2.5 also demonstrates that communication can be difficult between individuals when their concepts do not match, and consequently, their models of reality are different. This happens because objects and relationships are sets of properties that are based on classification of common behavior, and classes are based on individual judgments, experience, and perceptions. This is a fundamental problem on which many modeling projects have foundered.[30]

As scopes shift, new behavior is recognized, old constraints end, and the *same individual* may change the way he or she classifies common

*Box 2.5. Perspective is an object*

*Figure A. The problem of Perspective*

What do you see in the picture above? Is it a chalice or two people conversing in private? How you perceive the picture is dependent upon on how you classify the black and white spaces—which color is solid and which color is empty? This picture is a perfect demonstration of the fact that Perspective is a point of view and a model. A Perspective is the composite of interconnected objects that anchor knowledge. Thus, the structure that we label knowledge or, more explicitly, our perspective of knowledge, is a blend of classes, constraints, aggregations, domains, state spaces, and all the other metaobjects mentioned in this book. It is an aggregate object with a structure. We have called it "composition" in this book. Each individual person's outlook is an instance of a model. If, in response to a new insight of information, the model changes, the model has changed its state and created a novel perspective.[31]

The changes are often small—a new relationship, an additional effect, a new attribute, or an additional subtype. Yet, sometimes the change can be fundamental and may cause classification schemes to change, possibly both in the relationship and the object.

Concepts and things that have propertier are referred to as object instances. While some properties are shared with one set of things, other properties are shared with different sets. When looking from different perspectives, it may seem that the same object belongs to different object classes. A change in perspectives has the power to eliminate entire relationships and to replace them with others.

Consider the transformation that will occur when classification schemes change. Object classes are classification schemes generated from similar properties of object instances—all properties of instances in a class do not match in all cases. While matching properties are shared, others are not. Shared properties are controlled with the concept of superclass (supertype) and unshared properties are controlled with the concept of subclass (subtype). A subclass will only survive within a superclass. If a superclass disappears, the subclasses will cease to exist too. Further, if entire objects start disappearing, then all their relationships, constraints, and subclasses will be taken down as well. This will, in turn destroy the relationships and constraints of those subclasses, as well.

A domino effect may collapse the whole model if these classification schemes (i.e., taxonomies/ontologies) change. Entire subclasses and myriads of relationships will be annihilated. Partitions, constraints, and all other structures that relate objects and subclasses into a cogent configuration of knowledge will be destroyed. New structures will have to replace the old ones. The appearance of the new and the disappearance of the old will impact yet other structures, which will lead to other changes. Accordingly, change will start at the top and percolate down through the structure of knowledge until it settles into a fresh arrangement. This will be referred to as a paradigm shift—a radically different model of the universe or a perspective that has completely changed its state. For example, the change from Newton's to Einstein's perspective of the physical world was an example of a paradigm shift.

This is why the Universal Perspective is necessary, along with its universal object classes and specific relationships that identify ideas about reality and business that are well known. The secret of universal objects[32] that anchor the knowledge of all possible perspectives is not hidden within some covert and abstract detail; rather, it is explicitly specified within the sweeping generalizations that can withstand the persistence of continual change and the vast diversity of creative thought and innovation. The makeup of the Universal Perspective includes structures and objects that are masked as objects in different perspectives. These disguised objects are actually different compositions, states, and roles of universal objects. Therefore,

*continued on following page*

*Box 2.5. continued*

understanding the Universal Perspective and universal objects help to pinpoint the fundamental nature of universal reality and the unity of all perspectives. All perspectives are states of the Universal Perspective, which paradoxically, is changeless because it underpins change. The Universal Perspective is the integrated model described in this book and the two companion books of this series.[33]

behavior, that is, his or her perspective changes. Did you just experience that in Box 2.5? Under the pressure of change, object classes can become chimerical, and object models can become chimeras that descend rapidly into chaos, as waves of change overtake each other in rapid succession. The broader and more complex the reality we try to model, the greater the risk of this happening. Almost all data, process, and object modelers have experienced it, and many managers consider building large scope, enterprise level models to be risk prone for this very reason. This is also a critical bottleneck in designing resilient business processes and agile information systems, which will support adaptation, innovation, and change, all of which are required by corporations to thrive in the turbulence of the global information economy. This highlights the need for a Standard Universal Perspective; it will allow us to rapidly leverage and automate shared understanding, so that we may focus on adding those special components to this common understanding that will differentiate our products, systems, services, and processes to enable us to gain the competitive edge.

## Does a Universal Perspective Exist?

We know we communicate and can understand each other. The Universal Perspective models these widely shared ideas. This series captures the semantics of this shared reality, which is rooted in the natural ontology of information described in Chapter 4.[34]

Our perspectives can converge rapidly when we model simple situations because of these shared ideas. This convergence does not need a formal model in simple situations, but it becomes harder when our models are broader in scope and more complex in detail. The value of a formal semantic model of shared concepts increases as models span complex corporations and cross corporate boundaries into the world of intercompany alliances and supply chains. Such a model becomes almost indispensable when we consider concepts of "Business on Demand." In today's world, organizations require extreme agility and innovative business models: such agility can be facilitated with patterns of service based on a Standard Universal Perspective. They can do this because the Universal Perspective resolves individual perspectives and facilitates automated communication through shared understanding even as it allows the free play of diversity in support of creativity, individuality, and innovation.

The Standard Universal Perspective, like the foundation of a building, is a component that binds both standard and custom parts of individual understanding to make the whole work. The standard parts are the universal object classes and patterns highlighted in this book and its two companion books. These objects normalize shared ideas. Custom components will inherit these concepts and will add to the special behavior, constraints, and creative ideas that today's innovative companies need. The universal pattern of shared ideas in our "foundation" will therefore integrate special behavior automatically with the standard concepts needed to communicate with systems and stakeholders within and beyond the enterprise. These standard concepts may be considered "stock themes," which are the patterns and objects described in this series (Mitra & Gupta, 2006).[35]

The intent of this introductory chapter was to present a "feel" for the Metamodel of Knowledge and its capabilities. The next chapter will describe the layered architecture of knowledge and how it may be leveraged to mitigate the problem of chaos under the pressure of rapid, successive waves of change.

## REFERENCES

Mitra, A., & Gupta, A. (2006). *Creating Agile Business Systems with Reusable Knowledge.* Cambridge University Press.

Siegrist, K. (1997-2001). *Sets and Events in Virtual Laboratories in Probability and Statistics.* Retrieved September 27, 2007, from http://www.ds.unifi.it/VL/VL_EN/prob/prob2.html & http://www.ds.unifi.it/VL/VL_EN/ index.html

## ENDNOTES

1 Many approaches to knowledge engineering discuss asserting what should go with what. Few discuss what must *not* happen. We will discuss both: patterns of inclusion and patterns of exclusion when we discuss patterns—the source of all knowledge and meaning.

2 These rules are called *atomic rules* or *irreducible facts* as they cannot be decomposed further without loss of information. Atomic rules: Ross, R. G. (1997). *The Business Rule Book: Classifying, Defining and Modeling Rules.* Database Research Group Inc. ([294] in Appendix III) Irreducible Facts: Nijssen, G. M., & Halpin, T.A. (1989). *Conceptual Schema and Relational Database Design: A Fact Oriented Approach.* Prentice Hall ([297] in Appendix III). [252] in Appendix III (Krifka, M. (WS 2000-2001). A Paper on Semantics. HU Berlin, Germany) provides an advanced discussion on coordination of rules.

3 How events are related to object behavior is described in [166] Appendix III (Siegrist, 1997-2001).

4 Objects may sometimes exhibit spontaneous behavior. This type of spontaneous behavior is not triggered by any obvious external event. For example, stock prices may move at random each second. Spontaneous changes are also events.

5 Information Technology professionals call processes that are reused "services." Service Oriented Architecture is an information architecture in which business processes are configured from these reusable services that are loosely coupled (see the note on the State Machine in Appendix II). The central problem in SOA is the identification of reusable services. The patterns of information described in the three books of this series address that problem. [338] in Appendix III identifies the reusable elements that may be composed into business services. SOA also assumes a service level agreement (SLA) for each service. The SLA is a "contract" a service presents to other services that seek to use it. The SLA describes, among other items like availability and timing, the information it expects, its format and accuracy, and the information it will produce, its format, and accuracy. This book separates meanings from how they are rendered and focuses on the assembly of these meanings from components. Thus, it addresses the central problem of service identification and assembly from more granular services, but not the all components of the SLA, such as formats and the precision of data.

6 Appendix II describes how the concepts of matter and energy were developed.

7 Appendix II describes Shannon's Information Theory, which measures the *quantum* of information. Meanings *structure* information. The two concepts complement each other.

8 Physical phenomena may share information that just *is*, as opposed to obtaining information that is transmitted spatially and temporally by messages. The Aspect Experiments in Appendix II, under the note on messages between objects, validate this concept.

9 In our metamodel, *meaning*, *expression*, and the *quantum of information* are separate objects.

10 Refer to Appendix II on how information relates to physical objects.

11 Appendix II on the locale of matter and energy has more information: pure information is a concept, meaning, or knowledge. Unlike matter and energy, pure information is not restricted to be in one and only one place at a time. Adding this constraint expresses information in the form of matter or energy. For instance, information on this printed page is represented by material particles of printing ink, information riding on a beam of light, or radio waves is expressed in radiant energy, and information in an individual's mind is expressed by the material processes in that individual's brain.

12 Appendix II, under Shannon's Information Theory, discusses the measure of information.

13 Several mathematical and engineering texts, including [308], [232], [233], [234], and [235] (all found in Appendix III) describe sets, domains, and functions.

14 Many CASE tools and professional publications join *domain* with format and call the composition "domain." In this book, we will distinguish between the two.

15 This is called "coercive polymorphism." It is described in Appendix II, under Polymorphism, in the Mathematical Theory of Categories.

16 Null values, which denote the lack of meaning, are different from nil values, which denote the absence of magnitude, and both are different from "unknown." [337] in Appendix III examines these differences in more detail.

17 Termed *actor* in the parlance of Object technology or *observer* in the language of physics. For more information about actors, please refer to books on UML and the resources listed in Appendix III. Universal Modeling Language has become the de-facto standard. The Object Management Group is a strong proponent of UML concepts. See http://www.omg.org.

18 Appendix II, under the Theory of Categories, has more information on coercive polymorphism.

19 [211] in Appendix III describes the mathematical theory that supports the ordinal domain described in this book (Davies, 2000).

20 Appendix II, under Shannon's Information Theory, describes the mathematical measure of information.

21 [337] in Appendix II discusses domains in detail.

22 Metaobjects provide normalized containers for shared *irreducible facts*, discussed in detail in [297] of Appendix III, which are also Ross' *atomic rules* discussed in detail in [294] of Appendix III.

23 The semantics of Pattern are the foundation of the Metamodel of Knowledge. They are described in detail in [337] in Appendix III.

24 As discussed earlier in the chapter, process is a before-and-after interaction. Resources are used to create the products of a process.

The resources come before and the products after.

25 A relationship mutually connects several objects. The subtyping relationship is a special kind of relationship and a subtype may have multiple parents, a fact inherited from *Relationship*. See *Process* in Figure 2.5 for an example of this concept.

26 [337] in Appendix III shows how domains emerge from the semantics of Pattern and describes the integration of Ontology into the Metamodel of Knowledge. Both this book and [337] describes how this will support innovation, but each deals with different aspects of innovation and absorption of new learning.

27 In order to keep the diagrams simple, cardinality and other constraints familiar to advanced business modelers have been deliberately omitted. The intent of this chapter is not to be technically comprehensive, but rather to convey the essential concepts. Please refer to [337] in Appendix III for more information.

28 Constraints on values are discussed in detail in [337] of Appendix III. The generic concept of a constraint and how features of objects spring from this concept are described further on in this book.

29 The Universal Perspective and the Metamodel of Knowledge have the most frequently used, generalized rules, a starting point for reusable components.

30 Some analysts have proposed that we do not try to classify objects intuitively. Instead, they recommend that we mathematically analyze similarities between objects in terms of their properties in order to group them into object classes and subtypes [283]. While this approach may be useful, it will not guarantee stable object classes. If the scope of the process changes in a way that some properties under consideration change, so might the classification scheme. Inclusion or exclusion of behavior may change affinities between object instances, which in turn can change the taxonomy of objects and relationships. We did not address the root problem; we only automated it. Facet modeling is another approach in which *aspects* of an object might be reused. This concept is described in Appendix II, under Multiperspective Modeling. For more information, see [15], [53], [13], [21], and [23] in Appendix III.

31 This book and [337] focus on the components from which all perspectives of knowledge are configured, whereas [338] focuses on the components and patterns from which all perspectives of *business* knowledge are created.

32 Note that relationships are objects too.

33 [338] in Appendix III describes the Universal Perspective for business applications.

34 Item [338] of Appendix III captures shared patterns of business knowledge and the shared ontology of business concepts, which, in turn, are derived from the shared semantics of the Metamodel of Knowledge described in this book and [337]. Thus, together the three books capture the semantics of shared reality, which is rooted in the natural ontology of information.

35 The themes in items [337] and [338] in Appendix III describe how context sensitive meanings and names are all parts of the Metamodel of Knowledge, as is changing of perspective in step with new learning. The stock themes of collaboration, conflict, and processes that may resolve or intensify them or even turn one into the other emerge from these themes. Item [338] in Appendix III describes these Topoi (stock themes) in detail. They too are components of knowledge.

# Chapter III
# The Architecture of Knowledge


## ABSTRACT

*This chapter introduces the layered structure of knowledge and describes why chaos rides wings of change and adaptation. It tells us how traditional analytical approaches, like functional decomposition, can lead to chaos when the size and complexity of business processes and information systems exceed a critical threshold.*


## THE END OF COMMON SENSE: HIDDEN CHAOS IN THE HEART OF COMPLEXITY

Why has change been so hard on information systems? What methods worked in a smaller, simpler age and why have they started failing? Why does the impact of change ricochet through our systems explosively and chaotically, and above all, why is it so hard to manage?

We must have these answers to understand root causes. Only then can we fashion solutions that will fit the age of knowledge with its unceasing, pitiless, and ravenous appetite for rapid change driven by the race of survival in a shifting landscape of high stake, chimerical, and short-lived opportunities. Therefore, let us digress briefly to understand lessons learned and the reasons why older methods are failing.

Systems analysis and design methodologies had their conceptual beginning in two basic techniques for building abstract models. Both approaches had their genesis in the behavior of physical and engineering, not business, systems.[1] Many of our problems with managing change and reusing knowledge stem from the intrinsic limitations we inherited from these two techniques. They cannot scale up to satisfy our current needs for far more complex and vastly larger *business* systems. Most analysis and design techniques in use today were derived from one of two fundamental techniques, and, unaware, we still carry their hidden legacy of limitations. The two fundamental techniques are:

1. Black box process decomposition technique
2. Node branch technique

Variations of these two themes were later extended to modeling business systems. These early models of physical and engineering systems involved fewer objects and relatively simple behaviors compared to modern, industrial-strength business systems.

To understand why neither method can scale up to satisfy the demands of 21st century business, we must understand the two approaches and their limitations. Only then can we chart a new course away from the pitfalls of the old.

## Black Box Process Decomposition: Why it Failed

The black box approach[2] was a simple stimulus-response model consisting of inputs, outputs, and a set of rules, called a *transform* or *transfer function,*[3] relating outputs to inputs. Inputs and outputs were called variables.

Implicit in the model was the assumption that values of output variables would respond to changes in values of input variables (possibly with a time delay) as described by rules within a box linking inputs to outputs. The box was called a *black* box because it was opaque or dark: the mechanisms inside the box, those that created or manifested their external behavior in the rules, were unknown and irrelevant to the model. Only the rules themselves were of interest. Figure 3.1 illustrates the concept.

There are four inputs and three output variables in Figure 3.1. Variables 1-7 are each represented by labels v1 through v7. V1 through v4 are input variables, represented by arrows pointing into the black box, whereas v5 through v7 are output variables, represented by arrows emerging from, and pointing away from, the black box.

The graph on the left shows how values of input variables change over time, whereas the graph on the right shows how values of output variables change over time in response to changes in values of input variables.

*Figure 3.1. The black box perspective of behavior*

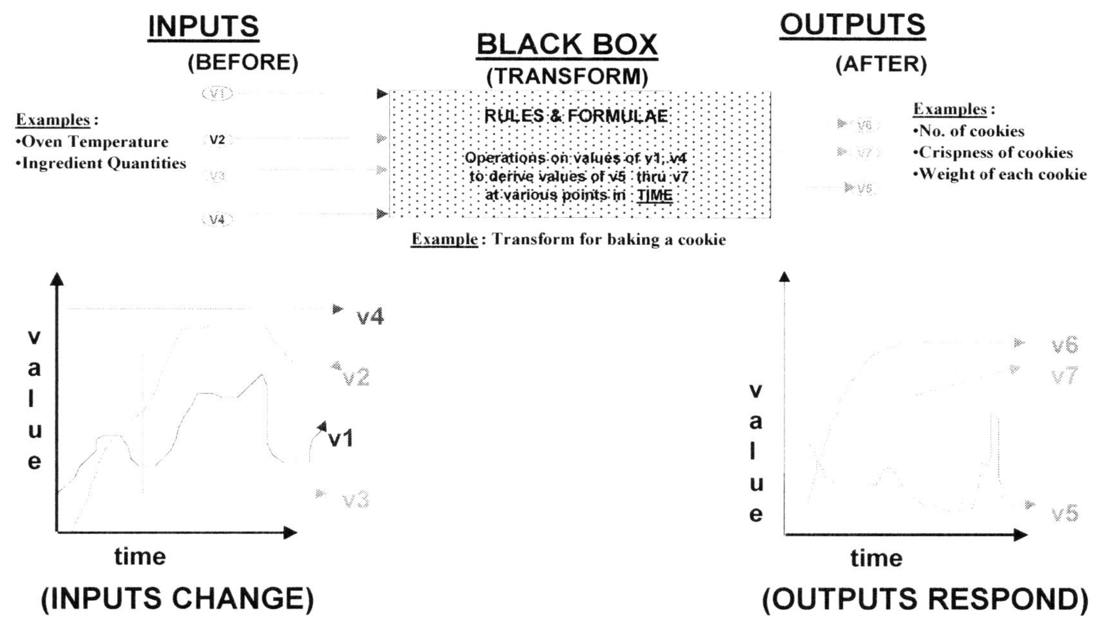


*Reproduced by permission from Mitra, A., & Gupta, A., Creating Agile Business Systems with Reusable Knowledge, New York, NY: Cambridge University Press, 2006.©*

The black box does not explicitly recognize that it is the behavior of real world objects we are interested in. Rather, the technique focuses on an amorphous mass of information. It only classifies information into inputs, or causes, and outputs, or effects and an amorphous set of causal rules, which do not have to be, and are usually not, irreducible facts. In any case, these rules are usually unknown when we create the black box. The black box is an amorphous, intuitive, and ungoverned classification scheme for yet-to-be-discovered business rules intended to impose order on complex real world problems, where large numbers of objects are in constant flux—behaving, interacting, and changing in complex ways. The black box cannot scale up because it is too simplistic.

The black box approach worked when systems were simple; their scope was small, and rules were few. Then every variable and every response could be determined up front, before designing the automated information system. In the real world, causes not only have effects, but these effects, in turn, may be causes of yet other effects, some of which might loop back through complex causal chains to impact the original causes themselves. When variables are many, and the rules complex, small differences in rules, timing of responses, and values of variables can lead to unpredictable, unmanageable, and chaotic effects that cascade through the system.[4] It becomes hard to foresee every exception and every contingency. Quality assurance, development, deployment, and modification of information systems can become a daunting task: resource intensive, time consuming, and fraught with risk. This happens because the black box technique recognizes neither the natural structure of knowledge, nor the inherently reusable components of knowledge, which are the irreducible facts that facilitate flexible, scalable, and adaptive business behavior.

There is another more serious problem. It is the problem of business requirements. In large business systems, rarely are all rules known and available readily. Rather, a general sense of what the system must do is stated, and analysts must then fill in the rules through a time consuming process of discovery. Neither is there any assurance that the discovery is complete and accurate at the end, nor is there any guarantee that rules they *have* discovered will stay the same when the system is ready for deployment.

To manage complexity and scale, analysts try to classify rules and isolate the impact of change within the black box (*even before they really know what these rules are!*) into hierarchies (*with little help from any objective classification scheme*) of component black boxes (*little wonder that these are rarely reusable components!*). It is a tribute

*Figure 3.2. Process decomposition*

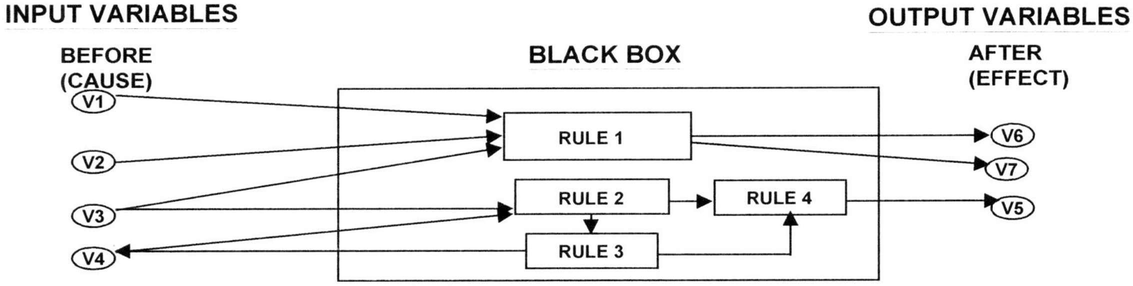


*Reproduced by permission from Mitra, A., & Gupta, A., Creating Agile Business Systems with Reusable Knowledge, New York, NY: Cambridge University Press, 2006.©*

to the skills and perceptive power of the analysis community that these black boxes were useful at all and that this technique, *process decomposition*, was considered the solution to the problems of complexity and size for decades.

Process decomposition is a rule-centered approach, but it does not recognize the special character of atomic rules. It tries to arrive at detailed rules by trying to classify the-not-quite-known-yet-rule in the black box into component rules, that is, create black boxes within black boxes, as illustrated in Figure 3.2.[5] Process decomposition met with only limited success when systems were small and simple. It was doomed to fail when scale, complexity, and scope of systems expanded in support of integrated, cross-functional, business knowledge.

Process decomposition was doomed because there are almost unlimited ways in which black boxes may be divided. There is little guidance or clarity about what divisions will yield reusable black boxes that contain reusable components of knowledge. If rules change, a few schemes for dividing the black box may isolate the change or reduce the number and complexity of its impact, but most schemes will not. Finding the right process decomposition is a question of luck that, at best, depends on the subjective judgments of seasoned analysts.

For example, when analyzing the business of a firm, analysts may subdivide the firm into a "human resources process," a "production process," a marketing process," and so on. The Human Resources Process may be further subdivided into a Payroll Process, an Appraisals Process, a Training Process, a Promotions Process, a Recruitment and Terminations Process, and so on. Until the bitter end, no one really knew what inputs, outputs, and rules these transformations represented.

Subdividing a black box is a skilled art more than an objective science. It works in a limited way, in a limited context, but mostly not. Indeed, by its very nature, process decomposition creates hierarchies that make it harder to identify reusable business components. The hierarchical scheme in the preceding example will try to allocate a subprocess to one of several mutually exclusive hierarchies, say the Human Resources Hierarchy *or* the Production Hierarchy *or* the Marketing Hierarchy. Common behavior such as ageing a transaction or changing an address (be it the address of an employee or customer, for example, to include both international and domestic addresses) will be fragmented and replicated across hierarchies. When common rules change or the scope of the model grows to include a new envelope of behavior, it will have many impacts. These will be complex, often chaotic, and hard to manage.

For these reasons, systems were usually brittle and difficult to change. It became harder and harder to manage the cascading and chaotic domino effect of change as business systems became more sophisticated. Requirements grew more complex, the need to take an integrated view of business operations became more urgent, and the amount of information as well as the numbers of objects involved kept increasing. Business systems rapidly outstripped the envelope of size and complexity that this technique could handle.

The root causes were:

- Too much detail was needed up front: Business systems have many variables and complex rules, too few of which are known up front.
- Requirements flow from business knowledge and this technique was not synchronized with the natural structure of knowledge. (The natural structure of knowledge was introduced in Chapter II. Its architecture will be analyzed in this chapter and those that follow.)
- Consequently, there were no precise criteria for classifying information or finding a firm foundation of common rules to build on.
- Therefore, reusable components of knowledge were hard to recognize and even harder to come by.

- The domino effect of change was difficult to manage because rules were fragmented and replicated randomly, with little control.

## The Node-Branch Method and Why it Failed

This technique grew out of the need to model behavior when large numbers of variables and many mutual interactions were involved. It took a more holistic perspective than the black box method.

Variables were considered to be components of a causal *network*, rather than data strung together in a linear cause-and-effect *chain*. Each variable was a node in this causal network. (See the example in Figure 3.3, and Object and Data Modelers, and note the resemblance with Entity Relationship Diagrams.[6]) The arrows between nodes showed what changes would impact which variables. In Figure 3.3, the two arrows from $v_1$ and $v_2$ converging on $v_6$ indicate that a change in either $v_1$ or $v_2$ (or both) would cause a change in the value of $v_6$. The *state of the system*[7] was considered, by definition, to be the set of values of all variables in the model at any given instant.

In some ways, this holistic view was better suited for building semirealistic models of systems with large numbers of variables. Causal loops in which values of variables would respond to mutual changes in a continuing cycle of change were easier to model.[8] The loop between $v_4$ and $v_5$ in Figure 3.3 is an example of one such causal loop.[9] (The black box approach handled this with a *feedback mechanism*, where the output variables were linked to input variables through another, feedback black box. The black box labeled "Rule 3" in Figure 3.2 is an example of this.)

Sometimes, in real life, a value of a variable will depend on its past values. The growth of the principal in a money market account depends on the quantum of investment, which changes each

*Figure 3.3. Node-branch representation*

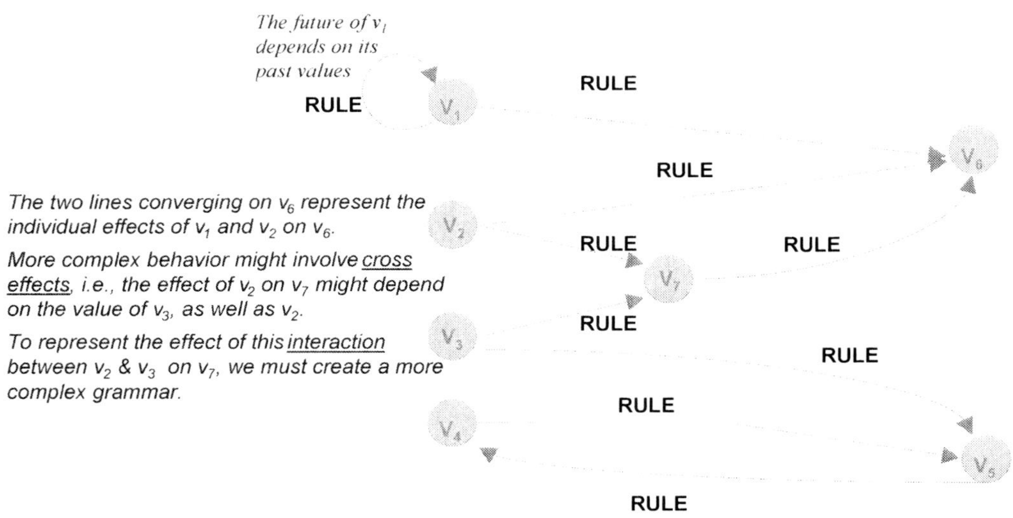


*Reproduced by permission from Mitra, A., & Gupta, A., Creating Agile Business Systems with Reusable Knowledge, New York, NY: Cambridge University Press, 2006.©*

time interest earned is credited to the account and added to the principal amount. This kind of rule would be shown with an arrow looping back on a single node as with $v_1$ in Figure 3.3. (The black box approach handled this by considering the past value to be an input variable and the future value to be the output variable. As such, the output of the black box would become the input of the feedback black box. The output of the feedback black box then looped back as the input of the original black box.)

However, we run into many of the same problems we had with the black box method when we try to scale up. Too much detail is needed up front:

- If all variables are not modeled up front when rules are complex and variables many, the chaotic behavior described for black box models will prevail, and the state of the system predicted by the model may be very different from the reality it is trying to represent.
- Only in the simplest business systems are all variables known upfront. As such, this cannot be a tool for modeling modern industrial strength complex systems of the 21st century that span entire enterprises and supply chains consisting of many corporations. Too much detail is needed up front, and there is no prescription for starting with broad categories of information and gradually adding detail in successive steps. Neither is the need for atomic rules, nor is the natural structure of knowledge explicitly recognized. This is why this technique cannot scale up.
- There is also another problem: Although it is easy to show the existence of mutual influences between variables in the causal network and to represent rules with arrows when the effect of each variable can be isolated from others in the causal net, real life rules may be more complex and not easily represented by arrows between *pairs* of variables. Complex behavior can involve cross effects, i.e., the effect of $v_2$ on $v_7$ might depend not only on the value of $v_2$, but also the value of $v_3$ and other variables in the causal net. This cannot be easily shown in a diagram of the kind in Figure 3.3.

For example, the purchase price of an air ticket ($v_7$) may depend on both the number of tickets purchased together ($v_2$), as well as how much in advance the flight reservations were made ($v_3$). If tickets are bought the day before flying, there may be no discount on price regardless of how many tickets were bought; if reservations for 100 tickets were made up to 30 days in advance, the price might be discounted 75%, whereas 50 tickets bought up to 15 days in advance might be discounted only 40%.

To represent the effect of this interaction between $v_2$ and $v_3$ on $v_7$, we must create a more complex grammar.[10] This is often done by augmenting the simple node branch syntax with special kinds of nodes and arrows that describe formulae and mathematical operators (such as addition, subtraction, multiplication, division, time delays, and sequences). Atomic rules *can* be expressed in this syntax, but the technique does not explicitly seek atomic rules, or try to arrive at detail from broader categories of information, as we did in the example under The Repository of Meaning heading in Chapter II. Unless all rules are included up front (an impossible task for any large business application development project) the model can be woefully inadequate.

There is no emphasis on categorizing rules or variables with an eye on reuse. The same rule may be repeated in many places of the causal net. The rule used to calculate the age of a customer order might be the same as the rule used to calculate the age of a purchase order, the age of an employee, and the age of a manufactured batch of items,[11] but the node branch method will repeat the rule each time it is needed. It cannot normalize and reuse knowledge. As such, it cannot manage the explosive and chaotic impact of change on large and complex business systems.

The Node Branch technique could not scale up for the same reasons the Black Box technique could not. The root causes were:

1. Too much detail was needed up front: Business systems have many variables and complex rules, too few of which are known up front.
2. Requirements flow from business knowledge and this technique was not synchronized with the natural structure of knowledge.
3. There were no precise criteria for classifying information or finding a firm foundation of common rules to build on.
4. Reusable components of knowledge were hard to recognize and even harder to come by.
5. The domino effect of change was difficult to manage because rules were fragmented and replicated randomly, with little or no control.

## Service Oriented Architecture (SOA)

Service Oriented Architecture was described in Chapter I. It is a variation of the Black Box theme, in which reusable services are black boxes that call (use) each other. The calling service provides the inputs to the service it calls, and the called service responds by returning its outputs to the service that called it. Neither service needs information about how the other service produces its outputs or transmits its inputs. These services are also "stateless," in that the called service retains no information about prior calls or results. Retention of that information is the responsibility of the calling service. For this reason, services are said to be "loosely coupled" (as opposed to "tightly coupled"). For instance, a billing service may call a currency conversion service to invoice overseas customers in foreign currency. The currency conversion service will not preserve information on the history of inputs received from, or outputs provided to, the billing service. If this is needed, the billing service will retain the information. Moreover, each service presents a common "contract" to services that call it. This "contract" describes the inputs the service requires, their formats and precision, and the outputs it will provide, their formats and precision. Thus, SOA overcomes the problem of vaguely defined, ambiguous functions endemic in the typical functional decomposition described earlier.

The emphasis in service-oriented architecture is on communication, making services "visible" on the network, service discovery and orchestration (sequencing of services in a business process). Although the intent of SOA is to identify reusable services and configure them into business processes, SOA does not actually address how these reusable services will be identified.

The concept of normalization lies at the heart of reuse. Reusable services can be identified only if we can normalize knowledge, so that the same behavior and information is not replicated in an uncontrolled manner in multiple services. Only then will the impact of change be isolated, and not ricochet chaotically through the components of systems. SOA does have constructs that support normalization. For instance, a service called "Assemble" may assemble items from their parts. The service can be designed so that it accepts the kind of item it must assemble as an input parameter, and if the parameter passed to it is "boat," it will execute the steps required to assemble a boat from boat parts, whereas if the parameter is "car," it will assemble a car from car parts. This behavior is called polymorphism, and the example shows how the meaning of "Assemble" may be generalized to support service agility. Although SOA provides mechanisms to support agility, the state of the SOA art does not provide a clear method of identifying what these services are and or how they may be generalized. The patterns in this book and its companions fill this gap. The patterns and objects in this book and its companions normalize knowledge, and may be used to identify reusable services as well as data.[12]

Moreover, although SOA advocates focusing on business services, it does not have a formal set of criteria that clearly distinguishes a business semantic from data transfer or interfacing services. A single business rule, as we will see further on in this chapter, may be implemented in several ways. Therefore, if we cannot clearly and consistently distinguish the business semantic from its implementation, knowledge will not always be normalized, and chaos will not be reliably controlled. In this series, we delineate how business rules may be distinguished from rules of automation.

## The Structure of Knowledge and First Principles of Reuse

The heart of our problem with both the black box and the node branch techniques was our inability to create cogent and stable classes of reusable behavior. Both methods failed to scale because:

- In the absence of consistent classes of known behavior, both needed too much detail up front.
- Large complex systems need to understand the "big picture" and take a top-down approach where detail is filled in successive steps. This requires a stable method of categorizing information and generalizing business rules. Neither technique had robust criteria for classifying variables and rules to facilitate this. Both focused on detail at the expense of "the big picture." (Process decomposition attempted to look at "the big picture," but it was subjective, imprecise, and by its very nature, not suited to discovery of common behavior.)
- Reusability requires generalizing and categorizing rules into reusable groups. Neither technique focused on reusability or common behavior of real world objects. Consequently, the domino effect of chaotic change was difficult to isolate and control.

To circumvent these pitfalls, we must find a method of grouping rules that:

1. Recognizes atomic rules are the basic building blocks of knowledge. Atomic rules are precise and will help us avoid chaos even as they address complexity. Reusability will flow from reuse of atomic rules.
2. Recognizes that knowledge is a configuration of atomic rules. Precision of meaning will flow from the structure of configurations. Reusability will flow from reuse of common configurations (see the example in The Repository of Meaning section in Chapter II).
3. Recognizes reusable behavior so that we can recognize reusable rules and configurations. Object classes identify common behavior. We will recognize reusable behavior by:
    - First, classifying rules to reflect the natural relationship between business meaning and its implementation. This is the natural architecture of knowledge described in the next section. It helps us isolate variables relevant to business rules, and thus reduce the number of variables we must address to build the business model.
    - Then, applying the theory of sets[13] to fine-tune our classification scheme. We will focus on meaning to identify and classify the basis of common real-world *business* behavior. Thus, we will normalize the semantics of business rules and business processes.

      We do this by describing an ontology of meanings and their interrelationships based on the natural structure of information (described in Chapter IV) that becomes progressively more complex, because meanings at the lower levels of the ontology inherit information and behavior from higher levels, while progressively adding information in terms of new behaviors, relationships and constraints (the ontology in this book and its companion, *Creating Agile Business Systems with Reusable Knowledge,* from Cambridge University Press, describe the ontology from which concepts such as *Pattern, Rule, Perspective, Process, Constraint, Behavior,* and *Knowledge* are created

- Finally, identifying the most frequently reused and normalized business rules at the heart of business knowledge. This business ontology is described in a companion book, *Agile Systems with Reusable Patterns of Business Knowledge: A Component Based Approach,* from Artech House publishers, but is derived by adding information and applying the principles described by the ontology of knowledge in this book. The companion book also contains a practical model for implementing the technology in a business organization.
- To minimize the chaotic effects of change in large scale complex systems, we apply the *Principle of Parsimony,* described in Chapter IV and also Appendix II of this book. The Principle of Parsimony admonishes us to apply only the bare minimum of information to unambiguously describe a given business rule.

  Thus, as we discover new information on the behavior of a complex, large-scale business system iterative steps, we start with the generalized semantic patterns in this series, and use them as-is (with perhaps only cosmetic name changes and synonyms to fit the business domain). We add information only when we must add new constraints, data, relationships, and behavior not represented in the generalized models within this series. We do this by adding new, deeper, information rich layers to the ontology in this series of three books.

  For example, if we wish to assert that the terms of sale in a master agreement may be selectively overridden by riders in individual sale agreements, we inherit this rule from the generalized "agreement" pattern, and do not assert this in the more specific "sales agreement" pattern at a lower level of the ontology of business meanings. The "sale agreement" pattern would add more specific information, such as sale price. (Both these patterns are described in *Agile Systems with Reusable Patterns of Business Knowledge: A Component Based Approach* from Artech House publishers, which drives the ontology of knowledge down to business levels.)
- *Liskov's Principle,* described in Chapter V, is another tool we use to foster agility. Liskov's principle asserts that objects, concepts, and rules that add information to those derived by the Principle of Parsimony can replace each other in business rules and processes and preserve the business semantic. In other words, these will be mutually mutable objects in business rules and mutable resources in business processes, and may replace one another, depending on their availability (see the examples in chapters V and VII).

Together, these principles will address the problem of scale and complexity. In concert, they will solve the problem of classifying rules and understanding the big picture before filling

*Figure 3.4. The architecture of knowledge*

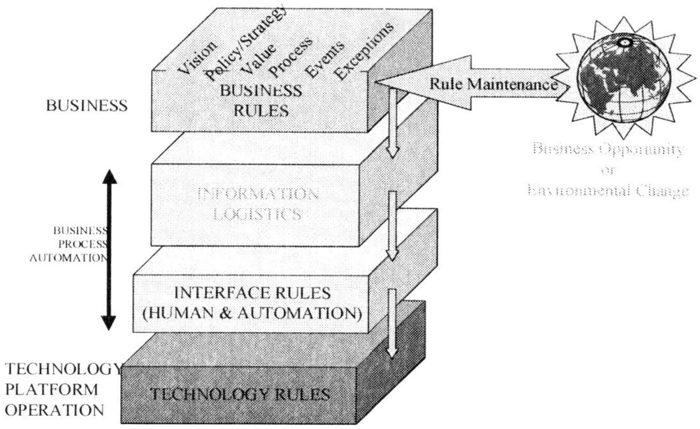


*Reproduced by permission from Mitra, A., & Gupta, A., Creating Agile Business Systems with Reusable Knowledge, New York: Cambridge University Press, 2006.©*

in detail. They will provide robust and stable criteria for grouping rules and variables, the key to common behavior and shared components. The first principle of reuse is the Architecture of Knowledge, described in the next section.

## THE ARCHITECTURE OF KNOWLEDGE

The bedrock of knowledge in a business system is requirements: Information Systems are built only to satisfy business requirements.[14] Business requirements can be automated in many ways and supported by a wide choice of technological resources. Each choice imposes its own requirements that flow from the capabilities of chosen technologies and processes. Requirements are not only the key, but also the foundation of information systems, *and they can be reused.*

Although requirements are the most critical component of any information system, to this day, almost half a century after business process automation first appeared, "Requirement" has remained a nebulous concept in the industry. There is no common understanding, let alone agreement, on what requirements really mean. Poorly formulated and ill-managed requirements are at the heart of the vast majority of problems information systems projects currently face. Our first task is to understand the meaning and structure of requirements. Only then will we know how we can reuse them.

Requirements flow from knowledge. Knowledge is formal, informal, common sense, and intuitive wisdom encapsulated in configurations of atomic rules.[15] Knowledge of information systems involves configurations of (atomic) rules of business as well as technology. Nature has provided a simple and elegant structure to integrate business and technology knowledge. This structure *naturally* facilitates business process innovation, knowledge reuse, and design of flexible and scalable business operations supported by technology.

The structure is not only the conceptual underpinning of reusable information systems components, but also the first principle of the metamodel of business knowledge. Let us call this natural structure of knowledge the *Architecture of Knowledge*. To understand the metamodel, we must first understand the Architecture of Knowledge.

The basic premises of the Architecture of Knowledge are simple:

- Knowledge is a configuration of atomic rules.
- Atomic rules of business are different from atomic rules of technology.
- Rules of business are related to rules of information technology through Business Process Automation.
- Each atomic rule must be implemented in information systems by one or *more* information flows. Each information flow must be supported by one or *more* interfaces. Each interface must be supported by one or *more* information technology platforms (see Box 3.1).[16]
- An information system is a *configuration* of atomic rules of business, information flow, interfaces, and technology platforms.

Rules of business, technology, and process automation, *naturally normalized in the real world*, must be reflected in systems as they are in the real world.[17]

The architecture of knowledge requires that we:

- Recognize atomic rules to configure reusable components of knowledge.
- Separate atomic business rules from atomic rules of technology.

There are few practitioners who would debate the need to separate business rules from rules of technology. The problem is that there are few guidelines and even less agreement on the *criteria* for distinguishing business rules from rules of technology. Many practitioners try to separate business rules from rules of technology intuitively because the distinction is often clear. However, the distinction is not *always* clear. It is this lack of consistent clarity and separation criteria that has resulted in a great deal of confusion in the industry about where to draw the line between business rules and technology (or "systems") rules.

This problem is compounded in complex supply chains and large firms, particularly the larger global corporations and organizations built through acquisitions and mergers. These firms (and supply chains) operate in complex and diverse environments, and different parts of these organizations often have different legacies and standards of technology.

These legacies have either been bequeathed by the different histories of individual organizational units or have resulted from their efforts to tailor their technology to match local environments, skills, and infrastructure. In such firms, similar business rules often have to be implemented in different technological environments. To reuse and coordinate business knowledge in these environments, it becomes even more important to distinguish business rules from rules of technology.

Unless we draw the line between business rules and rules of technology correctly, we will not realize the benefits of nimble or scalable processes supported by nimble and scalable systems. On the other hand, if we *do* distinguish rules of business rooted in reality from those rooted in technology, we can reuse and coordinate business rules across complex corporations and supply chains, which will help make our businesses nimble and more cost-effective. With this thought in mind, let us first understand what business and technology rules are, and why it is sometimes difficult to separate the two.

Rules of business are expressions of pure business meaning. They assert business intentions, strategy, and procedure that flow from constraints, risks, opportunities, threats, strengths, and weaknesses of the real world, that is, the physical, competitive, regulatory, personal, and cultural environment in which businesses must flourish. A policy that asserts that all prices must be negotiated in U.S. dollars is clearly a business rule.

Rules of automation are those that are the basis for systems performance-, reliability-, security-, or technology-imposed constraints. They are usually easy to identify. A policy that asserts that *all new development will be on UNIX platforms* is clearly a technology rule. Similarly the assertion: "*If a SQL query accesses over 1/3 of the rows of a DB2 table, a tablespace scan will be faster than an index scan*" is definitely a technology rule, not a business rule.

The confusion between business and technology rules stems from the fact that some atomic rules are rules of technology *and* business. They link the business and technology when business leverages technology. Workflow then depends on capabilities and features of automation. For example, this happens when a librarian uses a laser pen to scan information about a book being returned by a customer, from the bar code on the book. Should this be a technology or business rule? Is the requirement for 24x7 customer information systems availability (the system must be available 24 hours a day, 7 days a week) a business or technology rule? The answer is that these are neither pure rules of business, nor pure rules of technology; rather, they are rules of Business Process Automation.[18]

The ever-tightening embrace between business and technology means that business and automation will increasingly and inextricably become enmeshed with business process and business opportunity. That is why the line between business and technology has blurred, and *will continue to blur even more*. Indeed, not only will business innovation spring from reengineering pure rules of business to position firms at a competitive advantage, but Business Process Automation will increasingly be a vibrant area of opportunity in our age of technological innovation. This is why normalizing not only business behavior, but also the transforms that link business behavior to business process automation are critical to the reuse of knowledge.

Driven by market diversity and environmental constraints, businesses must support different scales of operations in different technology environments in various geographical footprints. Different kinds of business process automation are appropriate in support of different technologies and scales of operation. The key question is where do we draw the line between the world of business and the world of technology in order to normalize knowledge, reuse it, and make our business operation both flexible and scalable? The answer is that there is not one, but actually four lines we must draw: A business rules layer for "pure" business rules, Business Process Automation layers consisting of Information (Data) Flow and information storage rules, collectively called Information Logistics,[20] Interface rules layers, and finally the Technology rules layer for "pure" technology rules that optimize or constrain platform performance. That is shown in Figure 3.4. We can reuse rules in each layer to build configurations of knowledge. The four layers of Figure 3.4 are examined in the following paragraphs.

## The Business Rules Layer

The Business rules layer in Figure 3.4 contains rules rooted in the world of business meaning or physical reality. These are generic rules independent of any technology or mechanism used to implement them, *or involve mechanisms that do not directly capture, process, or present information.*

Business rules do not care about the logistics of information storage, transportation, and transformation. These rules are usually assertions about the firm's position, opportunities, threats, and resources; products, services, and markets; strengths, weaknesses, and goals; regulations,

*Box 3.1. The architecture of knowledge reuse can help make information systems flexible and scalable.*

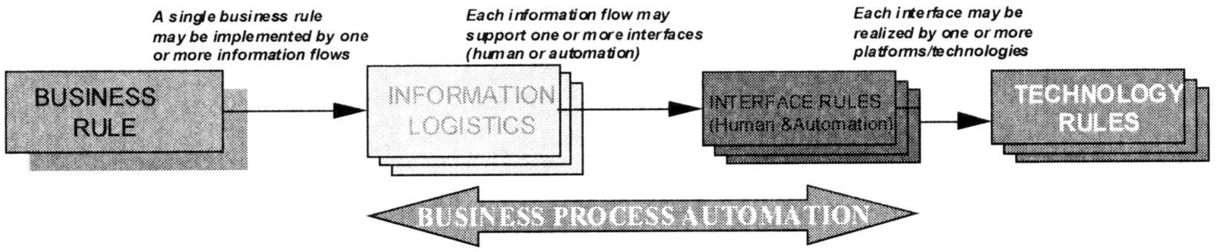


Figure A. Business process automation

*Reproduced by permission from Mitra, A., & Gupta, A. , Creating Agile Business Systems with Reusable Knowledge, New York, NY: Cambridge University Press, 2006.©*

In the natural world, a single rule of business may be implemented in different ways with different kinds of automation. This gives business an enormous amount of flexibility and opportunity for innovation, and the opportunity to reuse knowledge resident in every layer of Figure 3.4. To understand how this can happen, let us start with a pure rule of business, for example, "take order." Each business rule can be implemented in different ways. Let us look at the two different data flows that can implement the single business rule "take order."

Let us start by considering two diametrically opposite business environments:

A small new market where customers are new and few. In this market, orders are usually taken during sales calls to customers' offices. Both order values and volumes are small. Consequently, orders are keyed into salespersons' laptop computers during sales calls and consolidated in a desktop PC at the branch office at close of business every day. No customer validation is required against a customer master file (as most customers are new, and customer information must be recorded during order entry). Orders are consolidated once a week and e-mailed to the head office.

A well-established market, where high value, high volume, repeat orders are the rule, and customers are many. The firm is well known and has a good reputation. Most customers like to place orders on the telephone. Orders are keyed into PCs located in a call center. It is a client-server system. Orders are validated against customers' S&P rating on a master file, and checked against availability of items on the inventory file. Inventory is reserved for the customer on the inventory master file; if items are not available off the shelf, the salesperson at the call center gives the customer a date when the order can be filled and asks if the customer would like to place a back order. Only then is the order stored on the order master file and an order confirmation notice is mailed to the customer. All orders that were declined are placed in a Declined Orders file. Management reviews reports are generated from this file once a month to determine opportunity cost of, and reasons for, lost orders.

Two very different data flows to cater to two very different scales of business in two very different kinds of markets, but both reuse the same root business rule "take order." This is how business can scale up or down and be innovative in different environments without needing to change the core rule of business meaning.

Now let us see how each data flow might be supported by several interface rules and how that can be the basis for innovation.

The firm decides to supplement its call centers with a Web-based ordering system. The firm can reuse the data flow already deployed for its client-server system. Data entry, however, is pushed out to customers, and new screens added to make it easy for customers to confirm back orders. Now there are two kinds of interfaces, a Web interface and a call center interface, to support the same data flow. The single business rule, "take order," may be supported by an even larger multiplicity of configurations, consisting of data flow and presentation options, which makes room for an enormous amount of flexibility, innovation, and scalability.

Next, let us consider only the client-server call center system, and how many technology platforms can support it. The number of possible choices of data flow-interface-technology configurations that the firm can deploy can be much more than the choices available if only data flow-interface configurations are considered. This increases the flexibility and scalability of "take order" even more. In the U.S., the inventory files may be physically on an IBM mainframe under

*continued on following page*

*Box 3.1. continued*

MVS as a part of a legacy ERP systems based on DB2, whereas in India, inventory files may be smaller and the firm may have ready access to Microsoft skills and support. Consequently, management may use an IBM PC server that runs Windows NT and Microsoft access for database management in that country. In Europe, on the other hand, the scale of operation may be larger than in India, and local management may have a special deal that gives them a large discount on purchases of SQL server Database Management Software. Therefore, they may prefer to use SQL server databases to optimize platform performance at minimal cost.

In the above manner, the implementation of the single business rule becomes even more scalable, and the opportunity for innovation increases further when the technology rules layer[19] is considered with the two Business Process Automation layers and the Business Rules layer.

ethics, and public opinion; strategy, tactics, and business practices.

The following atomic rules are examples of "pure, abstract" business rules that *do not* involve implementation mechanisms:

- "New employees must be oriented."
- "New employees must be oriented within one month of joining the firm."
- "New employees will be allowed two working days to get oriented."
- "A physical object must be located in a single geographical place at any given moment in time."
- "All products will be considered untested when they are first acquired" (a rule about an initial condition of a business object.)
- "Each product will be considered saleable only after it has been tested."
- "Send shipment."
- "Take customer order."
- "The surface area of a sphere." (This is a real world concept; the actual procedure for calculating the area, that is, the algorithm that describes the sequence of mathematical operations that cubes the radius of the sphere and multiplies the result with the appropriate number to yield a measure of the surface area, is a transform that links the meaning to the information logistics layer.)

The following examples are atomic business rules that *do* involve implementation mechanisms *but do not directly involve information technology*:

- "Send shipment on a boat." The boat, a mechanism for implementing "Send Shipment," does not directly involve information. *Shipment* is a real world business concept and *Boat*, a real world object; hence, "Send shipment on a boat" is a *business rule,* not a business process automation rule.[21]
- "Bake Cookie in Oven." The oven, a mechanism for implementing the real world abstract process "Bake Cookie," does not directly involve information. *Cookie*, *Oven*, and "Bake Cookie" are all real world objects, hence "Bake Cookie in Oven" is a business rule.

The following are examples of rules that are *not* business rules:

- "YYY Database management systems will assign a default zero value to all numeric fields." This is a rule about an initial condition, but not a business rule because it is a rule imposed by a *technology platform* (the database management system) and not the *real world of business.*
- "Accumulate telephone call records in the message file" is not a business rule because

it involves *information movement* from the telephone switch to a file.

- "Key customer order into the order entry screen" is a *business process automation*, not *business*, rule because it is an assertion about the *information capturing mechanism* for implementing a business rule. Let us take this example to understand how business rules are different from rules in other layers.

"Take customer order" is a pure business rule. It does not assert any mechanism for taking the order, whereas "key customer order into the order entry screen" is a Business Process Automation rule because it mixes the mechanism for taking orders with the pure rule that a business must take customer orders. The architecture in Figure 3.4 mandates that this mixed rule must be reduced to a pure atomic business assertion and an atomic assertion about the data entry interface. We will then be at liberty to standardize and reuse (or not) the rules of business divorced from the rules of Business Process Automation and technology.

Are all atomic rules that include the implementation mechanisms disqualified from the Business Rule layer? The answer is no. Only atomic rules that involve automation do not belong to the Business Rule layer. To understand this answer, we must first understand that there are many mechanisms, technologies, and tools, including manual methods that might implement a "pure" technology independent rule of business like "Take Order" or "Send Shipment," and not all will directly involve information. "Send Shipment" might be implemented with a Boat (making Boat the implementation mechanism), and the atomic implementation rule would read "Send Shipment by Boat." This is a business rule. The truck has nothing to do with information capture, presentation, or processing. On the other hand,

*Figure 3.5. Business process automation is only one of several mechanisms that implement abstract business rules in the physical world.*

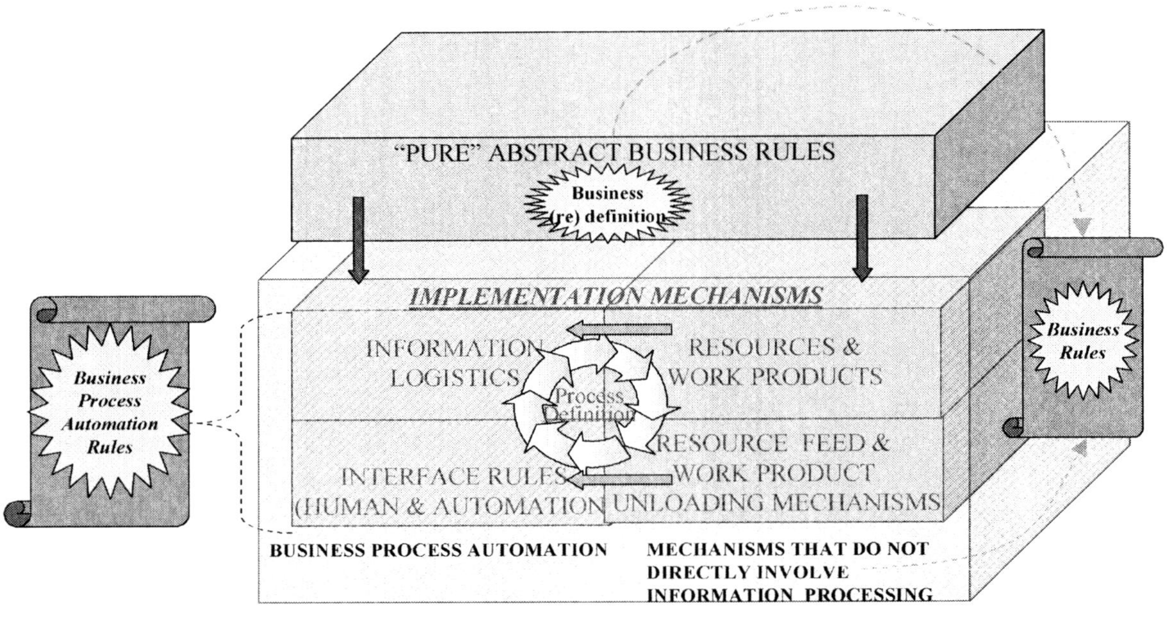


*Reproduced by permission from Mitra, A., & Gupta, A., Creating Agile Business Systems with Reusable Knowledge, New York, NY: Cambridge University Press, 2006.©*

the primary purpose of other kinds of implementation mechanisms, such as bar code scanners, keyboards, screens, voice synthesizers, sensors, robots, and biometric devices, is to capture, present, or process information. Business implementations that involve rules about these mechanisms are rules of business process automation.[22] These examples demonstrate that *automation is only one of several kinds of mechanisms that might be used to implement "pure" technology independent of business rules.*

The *natural* fact is that there is usually a wide choice of implementation methods for abstract business concepts.[23] Some might involve automation whereas others might involve other kinds of tools and technologies. This behavior of the real world gives us room to innovate, be flexible, and be able to design business processes that scale appropriately. However, not all mechanisms are components of *knowledge*. Our objective is to understand how to build reusable components of *business knowledge*, not physical piece parts. Our goal is to make our *information systems* robust under the continual and intense pressure of change. It is for this reason we focus on business process automation and separate atomic rules that link business to information technology from those that link abstract business concepts to other kinds of implementation technologies.

Rules that link business concepts to implementation mechanisms *belong to the Business Process Automation layers only if these mechanisms capture, present, or process information*. Otherwise, they belong to the business rules layer because they involve real world objects like boats and ovens. Therefore, "Send Shipment by Boat" belongs to the business rules layer, whereas "Key Customer Order into the Order Entry Screen" belongs to the Business Process Automation layers.

Rules of Business Process Automation involve information flow, storage, exchange, and calculation procedures. They may be different in different parts of the complex and diverse empire that characterize most large organizations and supply chains. The Business Process Automation layers recognize these variations for what they really are: different means for implementing the same business concepts (i.e., rules) with different kinds of information technology in different environments.

In the natural world, a single rule of business may be implemented in different ways with different kinds of automation. This provides business with an enormous amount of flexibility and opportunity for process innovation by leveraging automation. It is also an opportunity for reusing business rules. Box 3.1 shows how scalable and flexible systems can flow from business rule reuse framed by the knowledge architecture shown in Figure 3.4.[24]

## Business Process Automation Layers

Business process automation links pure business meaning and intent to its physical implementation in information systems. Atomic rules in these layers must involve *both* business meaning and *features of information technology platforms.*

Confusion about which atomic rules belong here and which belong to the Technology rules layer often stems from confusion over which features of technology *directly* impact business functionality and which do not. Is a limitation on the size of e-mail attachments that users may send via an email service a Business Process Automation rule or a technology rule? In order to determine this, it is important to remember that it is the applications program that links the real world to the technology platform. Consequently, any rules that link business meaning to technology concepts (objects) *visible either to users or to applications programmers* must be considered to be rules of Business Process Automation. A *Functional Feature* of an information system is a special kind of business process automation rule: *it is a rule of business process automation that is visible to both users and application*

*Box 3.2. How rules shift between business process automation and technology layers*

**An example of how a functional feature became a technology rule in step with advancing automation**

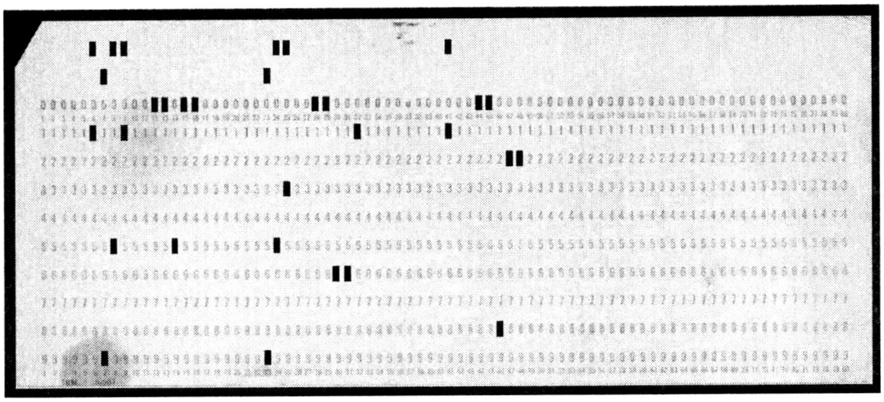

Figure A. Punch Card

In the 1960s, business information was keyed into punch cards. Each card was divided into 80 columns along its length, and each column held one character (the pattern of holes punched into rows under a column was a code that represented the character keyed into the column). As such, each card could accommodate only 80 characters. After all business transactions were keyed in, the deck of cards was loaded into the hopper of a card reader that would read the information into memory. Cards were read in the sequence they were arranged in the deck. The application program usually assumed that each item of information (called a field) in a transaction would reside between specific columns of the card.

When information in a business transaction exceeded 80 characters, it had to be continued on multiple cards. The user was responsible for keying in a code (usually at the beginning of the card) to tell the program what information to expect on the card. Depending on the code, the program would determine what fields to expect in which card columns. It was the responsibility of the user to arrange cards in the right sequence. Cards for each transaction were grouped together and arranged in the right sequence in the deck before the deck was loaded into the card reader. Mistakes could lead to incorrect results and other errors.

The current use of terminals and screens to enter data has taken that responsibility away from users. It is the platform that now determines, based on the screen, which inputs belong to which transactions, and where the transaction ends and the sequence in which inputs will be accepted. This is one example of how advancing technology has turned a functional feature of business process automation into a technology rule to the user's advantage.

**An example of how a non-functional rule of business process automation became a technology rule**

In the early 1960s, applications programmers had to worry about blocking and deblocking data records stored on files to access or store individual records of business information. These rules were relationships between business information, their organization inside software programs, and the physical storage media. Since these rules were relationships between business information and items inside the technology platform and they were about information access, they belonged to the Interface Rules layer of Figure 3.4.

Modern file management software has hidden the need for grouping data records into blocks of data on the physical storage medium. Physical organization of business data into contiguous blocks of information still happens, but now it is done automatically. It is now a relationship between the database (or file) management software, the operating system, and the physical storage device, all of which are internal to the technology platform. These rules have become rules of technology that reside in the Technology Rules layer of Figure 3.4. This is how rules about blocking and deblocking data records in computers have moved from the Interface Rules layer to the Technology Rules layer.

*programmers*. The constraint on the size of the e-mail attachment is visible to both users and programmers who created the e-mail application. Therefore, it is a functional feature and a business process automation rule. (Box 3.2 provides more examples.)

Functional Features are important because they provide the interface that the business user sees. It is the *business* end of business process automation so deeply wedded to technology that it is dependent on capabilities and features of the technology platform for its very existence. For example, you cannot have a graphic with links to Web pages without a browser and a GUI display device.

This criterion (visibility to users or to applications programmers) for business process automation does have one disadvantage: some technology platforms are more automated than others are. Different choices of technology may make some features visible and hide others from applications programmers or users. This may mean that the *same* rule can change the layer it belongs to, depending on choice of technology. Our contention is that this shifting of rules between layers is a *natural*, albeit inconvenient, consequence of technological progress.

Progress implies that information technology platforms (hardware, software, operating systems, networks, etc.) will continue to become more automated and that constraints of technology will be progressively handled internally by platforms and hidden from users and applications programmers. This is one reason why rules of business process automation are (and should be) different for different technology implementations. It is these differences that provide businesses the opportunity to steal a march on competition by leveraging information technology to make business processes and workflow innovative, automatic, flexible, scalable, and economical.

In the midst of this arcane discussion of technology's shifting goal posts, it is important to keep the objective in mind: Whatever scheme we use must lend itself to the ability to configure components that will facilitate innovation, flexibility, and scalability under the pressure of change. We get the space to do this from the multiplicity of choices that flow from the one-to-many relationships in Box 3.1. Later in the book, we will examine how objects and relationships in the metamodel of business knowledge *naturally* support this capability.

To obtain this flexibility, we must understand that there are two distinct kinds of atomic rules that belong to two different layers of Business Process Automation. These are discussed in the following subsections.

## Information Logistics Layer

Information Logistics are the rules of (business) information flow and availability. They are the *platform independent* logistics of information sourcing and distribution visible to application developers or users. These rules will include data flow, such as rules about the source and destination of business data, data distribution in terms of (intermediate and final) destinations of data, storage in terms of physical files and logical data stores, as well as queuing and (business) information staging. Information Logistics include rules about where and for how long business information will be available in which staging areas. This layer has all rules and requirements that involve movement or storage of *business* information in terms of location, *but not format, accuracy, presentation, or timing.*

Irreducible facts that involve the following kinds of information belong to this layer:

- Source of information: Files, records, and data elements.
- Destination of information: Files, records, and data elements.
- Records and data elements transported, stored, or staged.
- Retention periods, storage media, volumes, growth, and security of information stored or staged.

- Initial condition of any or all of these items. (Initial conditions apply to objects in all layers of Figure 3.4.)
- *Relationships* between any of the following: data flows, data stores, initial conditions of these items, retention periods, storage media, volumes, growth, and security of information stored or staged.

The following illustrative rules all belong to the information logistics layer:

- "Store orders in order file," and "Store unmatched customers' telephone usage in exception file" are rules about *where to store* information.
- "Match customer on order entry screen with customer in customer file" and "Obtain customer credit rating from S&P" are rules about data flow/*sourcing*.
- "Store customer telephone call records file on disk" and "Store customer telephone call records that are between 4 and 10 years old in tape files" are rules about storage media that belongs to this layer.
- "Preserve customer telephone call for 10 years" is a rule about availability of data that belongs to this layer.
- "YYY Database management systems will assign a default zero value to all numeric fields" is a rule about an *initial condition* of *stored business information* that maps to quantitative domains[25] *imposed by choice of a technology platform* (the database management system), not the real world. It relates real world business information to the technology platform. Hence, it is a rule of Business Process Automation. It belongs to the information logistics layer because it is a rule about the initial condition of business data.
- "An employee's security clearance in the personnel file must match that in the departmental security clearance file" is a *relationship* between data stores.

Rules in this layer involve *business* information flow visible to users or applications programmers. There may be other kinds of information flows related to the internal working of technology platforms. These *do not* belong here. Rather, they belong to the *technology* layer. The following illustrative rules involve information flow, but do not belong to this layer:

- "If memory overflows, dump its contents to disk." Both computer memory and disk are parts of the technology platform. The rule does not refer to any business information. Rather, it deals with the flow of information related to technology objects internal to the platform that executes software. Therefore, it is not a rule of Business Process Automation.
- "Store the last three orders in the screen buffer area." Although orders are business information, the Screen Buffer Area is internal to the technology platform. If movement to and from, and storage of information in, buffer areas is transparent to application programmers, this rule will belong to the technology layer. (If this is *not* transparent to application programmers, it will belong to the Business Process Automation layer, *but not be a functional feature* of data flow because, presumably, programmers would hide this technical complexity from users.)[26]
- Assume a nationally distributed radar network is tracking air traffic. An "airplane" business object in the system reflects each airplane in the air. The information system is physically distributed across nodes of a computing network that runs the application on computers located at each major airport and dynamically optimizes resource use by moving processes and data between nodes. The rule "move the business object that represents an airplane in the information system to the node that is nearest to the physical airplane at any given time" is an instance of this kind of optimization. The rule involves

flow of business information between nodes. Nodes are information technology objects. So why have we said that this is not a rule of Business Process Automation?

- Although "airplane" in the system carries business information, moving "airplane" between computers in the network will not be a rule of business process automation if we assume that the movement and storage of information between these nodes is the responsibility of the network communications software, transparent to business applications programmers and users. Instead, it will be a *technology rule* because the rule involves movement of information between nodes that are internal to the technology platform, and information movement or storage between these nodes is transparent to applications programmers and users.

## Interface Rules Layer

Interface Rules are rules of information exchange between information systems and people, other information systems or instruments, such as sensors, effectors, or robots. These rules usually involve workflow.

When information flows between an information system and people, instruments, other information systems or files that store and stage information, it must pass through an interface. This interface may be thought of as a conceptual contract that determines how entities exchanging information will present information to each other. Since we are dealing only with *business* information flows, *this layer will exclude interfaces that involve exchange of purely technical information internal to technology platforms, or exchange of any information between concepts or parts that are internal to the functioning of the technology platform.*

Interface rules are rules for presenting information, such as sequencing, access and security, formats and format conversions, accuracy requirements, availability and timing of the *interface*, timing of batch runs or mass updates, and data transformation (such as truncation and rounding). Irreducible facts that involve the following kinds of information belong to this layer:

- Interface schedule, batch timing, schedule for refreshing information business being presented at the interface (update cycles), exception and other events, availability of the interface and time-outs.
- Responsibility/approvals for the interface and its operation.
- Interfacing file layout, Interfacing Record layout, Interfacing data element, corresponding formats and units of measure (if any), and encryption.
- Access permission or denial rules; there could be several kinds of permission—permission to know an item exists, permission to see its contents, and permission to update its contents.
- Presentation of information to a human or automated actor, such as Accuracy, Format (including size limitations), Units of measure, Sort sequences, screens, and reports.
- Terminal devices/special equipment specifications.
- File audit and control specifications, such as record balancing or check digit processing.
- File or information transfer methods.
- Relationships between any of these.

The following rules are all examples of interface rules:

- "Key orders into order entry screen" and "Scan item with wand" are interface rules because they describe *mechanisms* for capturing business information.
- "Display service location on a map" and "Show stock prices in fractional format" are interface rules because they are rules about business data *presentation and formatting* at the system's human interfaces.

- "Highlight all data entry errors in red" and "The twenty fifth line of the screen will be reserved for error messages" are interface rules because they are rules about human *interface standards* (screens and data presentation formats).
- "Report revenues to the nearest $1000" is an interface rule because it is a rule about the *accuracy* with which business information must be presented to an actor (human or not).
- "Allow only subscribers access to stock prices" is an interface rule because data *access* rules are rules about an actor's (human or not) interface to business information stored in the system.
- "Update customers' S&P credit ratings at Close of Business every day" is an interface rule because it is a rule about *timing of an interface* to an S&P business data source.
- "Present order data in customer number sequence" is an interface rule because it is a rule about *presenting business information* to a human or automated actor.[27]
- "Present the Welcome Screen at the Start of Business every day" and "Generate report at Close of Business" are interface rules because they are rules about the *timing of human interfaces*.
- "The system must be continuously available 24 hours a day, 7 days a week" is also an interface rule because it is a rule about the *timing of the interface* from an actor's perspective.
- Assume that a depository markets a software product for buying and selling financial instruments it holds in trust. Customers who install the software must be activated to allow them to access information on financial instruments held by the depository. In this system "Activate New Customer" is an interface rule of Business Process Automation because it is a rule about enabling, that is, *setting the condition of a human interface* to make it available to customers.
- "Scan barcode" is an interface rule because it is a rule about the *format* for presenting business information to the application.
- Convert barcode to EBCDIC characters is an interface rule because it is a rule about *format* conversion of business information.
- "Commit information when the user hits the enter button" and "Commit the record on confirmation that the transmission is complete" are interface rules because they involve *business information transfer methods*.
- "Alphanumeric fields in XXX database management systems cannot be larger than 1024 characters" is not only a rule about the (storage) format of business information, but also a rule imposed by choice of a technology platform: the database management system in this case. It links business information to a specific implementation technology. The rule is also *visible to users and application programmers*; therefore, it is a rule of Business Process Automation that belongs to the Interface Rules layer.
- SMS is a data transfer technology for cellular telephones and wireless hand held devices. The rule "SMS messages cannot exceed 160 characters" is a (business process automation) interface rule because it is *visible to both users and applications programmers* of devices that support SMS.
- "Send batched transactions in compressed format" is an interface rule because it is a rule about the format in which *business information* must be presented to another system and is *visible to application programmers*.

If the platform that executed each system had a feature that automatically and *transparently* (to applications programmers and users) compressed and decompressed information being sent, then this rule would have been internal to the platform and would have belonged to the Technology Rules layer.

On the other hand, if applications programmers wrote programs to make this compression and decompression automatic and *transparent to users*, then this would remain a rule of Business Process Automation in the interface layer, but will not be a *functional feature* of the system.

Yet, another variation might be that application programs automatically compress and decompress the data and flash the information to a screen to make users aware of the activity. Although no action is required from users, they *are* involved with the interface—even if it means they are passively involved. Because users are aware, *this rule will be a functional feature* as well as a rule of the business process automation interface under these conditions.[28]

Some kinds of interfaces are excluded from *Business Process Automation* layers because they are interfaces between concepts and components that are strictly internal to technology platforms. These rules *usually* (but not *always*, as we will see further on) involve:

- Communications software
- Modem requirements
- Transmission rates
- File blocking factors and other technology dependent rules transparent to application programmers and users
- Line characteristics and protocols
- Communications protocols

Examples of interface rules that are *not* Business Process Automation rules are:

- "Disallow access to memory addresses 1 to 5000." Memory addresses are internal to the working of the technology platform.
- GSM is a standard for sending data in wireless telephony. "Accept information in GSM format" is an interface rule because it is a rule about the format in which data must be presented to the wireless device that belongs to the technology layer. It belongs to the technology layer because it relates to a *communication protocol* internal to the design of the technology platform: the wireless device.

CDMA and GSM are two different standards for wireless telephony. "Convert the signal from CDMA to GSM format" is a rule about format conversion that belongs to the technology layer because it is internal to the technology platform.

## Technology Rules and Constraints Layer

These are rules that only involve performance optimization and constraints of technology platforms. They too are requirements, but requirements imposed by choice of technology. In many ways, they have parallels in the universe of business that we have covered in the other layers. The universe of technology, like the universe of business, has objects, relationships, data movement, and interfaces. However, unlike the business universe, these items involve concepts and parts that are internal to the working of the technology platform. Some earlier examples are consolidated and repeated here for the reader's convenience:

- "If memory overflows, dump its contents to disk" is rule of information movement that belongs to the technology layer because it refers to technology, not business concepts, that are internal to the functioning of the platform for executing software.
- "Disallow access to memory addresses 1 to 5000" is a technology rule because it is an information movement (access) rule about concepts internal to the technology platform for executing application software.
- "Model ZZZ computers will physically execute only one thread at a time" is a technology rule because it is a rule about processes that are internal to the working of the technology platform.

- "The platform must have at least 256 MB of RAM to run the trading system" and "The trading system must be run on Windows 98 operating system" are technology rules because they are relationships between objects that are internal to the working of the technology platform: RAM is computer hardware, and both Windows 98 and Trading System are computer software.

On the other hand, even though the following rules involve modems, communications lines, and software, they are not pure technology rules resident in the bottom most layer of Figure 3.4. Instead, they are rules of business process automation because at least one business object is involved in each rule:

- To download stock prices in real time, you must have a DSL modem. *Stock price* is business information. This rule describes an interface mechanism required to access Stock Price, hence it is an interface rule.
- To watch the concert in real time, you must install streaming media software and a T1 communications line. *Concert* is business information. This rule describes an interface mechanism required to access Concert, hence it is an interface rule.

## How Businesses Can Use the Architecture of Knowledge

What kinds of opportunity for innovation and improvement does each layer present and what kinds of changes will each layer normalize?

The business layer helps us assemble components of knowledge into business concepts, such as products, services, markets, regulations, and business practices. It caters to change and innovation in the universe of business *meaning*. It supports businesspersons striving to adapt, excel, and innovate in order to position their firms, products, and services at an advantage by "thinking out of the box." It caters to changing fundamental rules of business (see Figure 3.5).

For example, a telephone services provider may integrate cable TV and entertainment media into its business. These changes in the Business Rules layer will impact business functions and systems functionality (which can have a domino effect on the layers below it), whereas changes to process automation layers alone will impact only availability, timeliness, accuracy, reliability, and presentation of information. Changes in business process automation, in turn, can impose new requirements for performance, reliability, and accuracy on technology platforms, which will impact the technology layer.

Business Process Automation is usually changed to leverage information technology or to focus on those processes that create most value while eliminating those of little value.[29] It can make business processes more reliable, accurate, or less resource intensive. It can impact business process activity cost, cycle times, workflow, resource requirements, and process ownership. Changes in this layer seldom impact the fundamental business of the firm. For example, the firm could deploy its ordering process on the Web, but not make any fundamental change in the nature of its products, services, or markets.

The technology layer is changed primarily to improve computer performance in terms of speed, cost, reliability, availability or alignment, and support for Business Process Automation.

## An Example: Separating Business Rules from Implementation Technology

Let us analyze an example from the telephone industry in some detail to understand this concept. This example is about procedures that are intimately connected with the kind of automation used to record telephone customers' use of telephone services for billing purposes. Telephone customers' call data are first downloaded from the telephone switch to magnetic tape at the telephone exchange. Once a day, these tapes are shipped to the data center and copied to disk files. These data are then validated and used to update the "Message" Customer Records Information System (MCRIS) file. The MCRIS file is input to the customer billing system.

## Business Layer

At the business layer, we would only have an assertion that *Subscriber* may use *Telephone Service* to call another *Subscriber*. *Phone Call* a three-way relationship between *two Subscribers* and *Telephone Service* that would be a repository of real world information such as call start time, end time, call duration, and geographical locations.

## Example of Policies That Reside in the Business Layer

Not only products and services, but also business policy springs from this layer. For example, the following policies reside in this layer:

1. The firm will penetrate untapped markets.
2. The firm will develop wholesale business.
3. The firm will obtain the necessary market freedoms to effectively compete.
4. The firm will purchase or lease competitors' fixed assets.
5. The firm will create unbranded and cobranded wholesale products.
6. The firm will creatively match products to market segments.
7. The firm will provide seamless telephone voice conversation service to all telephone subscribers in any geography; such a policy may have domino effects on information logistics, interface, and technology layers such as requiring data movement between, interfaces to, and interconnectivity with other telephone company networks.

## Example of a Change in the Business Layer

The original business rule reads, "*Subscriber* may use *Telephone Service* to call **another** *Subscriber*." If the telephone company introduces a new product, such as a party line or telephone conferencing facilities, it will have to add a calling relationship to read "*Subscriber* may use *Telephone Service* to conference with one or more *Subscribers*." The change would make *Phone Call* a relationship between two or *more* Subscribers and Telephone Service, instead of a relationship between only two subscribers and Telephone Service.

## Business Process Automation Layers

Rules related to transporting and presenting the information would belong to the *Business Process Automation* layers, not the pure business layer. Figure 3.4 shows how Business Process Automation consists of two layers. The Information Logistics layer is the repository for rules related to the logistics of *moving and storing information* in files, and the Interface layer is concerned with how this information is *presented* to human operators or other automation as follows:

## Business Process Automation: Information Logistics Layer

Moving data from the switch to magnetic tape is a pure technology rule because it involves only objects internal to the technology platform (the switch, the tape drive, and tape), but where does transporting the tape to the data center fit in? Is it a business rule, since it involves real world objects such as transportation vehicles, or does it belong to the Information Logistics layer of Figure 3.4 because it involves moving information?

Transporting the tape to the data center with a courier service involves the source and destination of information about calls made from subscribers' telephones. It is this *business information* that is being moved. Transportation of these tapes also involves information on how and where this *business information* is staged (for example, the loading dock and transport vehicle). These rules fulfill all the criteria needed to call them Information Logistics rules; hence, that is what they are.

## Example of a Policy That Resides in the Information Logistics Layer

Apart from operational detail, strategic and policy rules could reside in each layer of Figure 3.4. A policy that asserts that *MCRIS will be the central data resource to support and authenticate all commercial call information* is an Information Logistics rule that belongs to this layer. It is an Information Logistics rule because it is a rule about information storage. It is worth noting that this information storage policy can be changed without having to change the business rule it supports: "*Subscriber may use Telephone Service to call another Subscriber.*"

## Example of a Change in the Information Logistics Layer

A key premise of the natural architecture of knowledge was that a single business rule might be implemented by several kinds of process automation. For example, the information framed by the single business rule—*Subscriber* may use *Telephone Service* to call one other *Subscriber*—may be recorded in different ways, with different mechanisms. It could be done either by recording, manually shipping and copying from magnetic tape, as described earlier, or by sending the call information directly over the network to programs that will validate, summarize, and store it in MCRIS.

If the network is used, the rules of data staging and transportation interfaces will change, whereas other rules such as the source of data and the final destination in MCRIS files are data flow components that will not change and may be reused.

Both methods may co-exist. Some switches may be polled over a network and call data downloaded at predetermined intervals over the network to MCRIS files, whereas other switches might record information on magnetic tapes, which may be sent by courier to data centers for consolidation on the MCRIS file. Both are mechanisms for capturing information about telephone calls that are instances of the single business rule, "*Subscriber may use Telephone Service to call another Subscriber.*" This business rule remains unchanged, and is a common component in the knowledge configurations that represents each of these two systems.

## Business Process Automation: Interface Layer

If we ship tapes manually by courier and no automation is involved, why do we call it an interface rule? Transporting the tape to the data center via a courier service is a file transfer rule, albeit an unusual one, because the file transfer method involves manual transportation instead of an electronic file transfer. Rules that involve file transfer methods are interface rules. This is why this manual method of shipping telephone call information must also be an interface rule.

This rule also satisfies other criteria that interface rules must transfer schedule, responsibility, and approval for the operation of the interface (someone in the firm must have responsibility and ownership of the transfer process) and provide audit and controls (assuming validation procedures are built in to ensure accurate, reliable, and timely transportation).

This manual file transfer method *is* a relationship between business data and the mechanism for moving it; hence, it *is* Business Process Automation. Like any other file transfer method, certain protocols must support this movement of information.

Electronic file transfer protocols are confined to components of technology inside the information technology platform and belong to the Technology Rules layer of Figure 3.4. Unlike electronic transfers, this manual file transfer method must be supported by protocols that involve real world mechanisms, unrelated to information technology, such as couriers, trucks, and lock boxes, and is visible to staff. Therefore, these protocols, which, if automated, would have involved only the technology layer, will now involve business process automation because they are manual procedures: the manual file transfer protocol will be a business system in its own right, supported by automation of its own.

For example, the manual operation of passing the tape to the courier, getting an acknowledgement or receipt from him, tracking the movement, the way-bill, the receipt, and validation of the tape at its destination are part of the file transfer protocol and may be supported by automated tracking systems and procedures.

If the firm switched to sending all call records from switches to the MCRIS file over the network, these business process automation components could be deleted from the knowledge base without risking explosive and chaotic impact on the billing system *because knowledge of the interface was normalized* and isolated in this tracking system.

The interface rules layer will also contain other, more commonly expected kinds of components, such as formatting rules, screens, and terminal devices. Assume that human customer service operators require access to subscribers' call information on a screen; then the screen layouts and standards, as well as presentation components, would belong to the interface layer.

To summarize, for *each* set of rules related to the logistics of transporting and storing data in specific files (either the system of manual transport of magnetic tapes *or* the system for supporting electronic data shipment over the network), there may be several kinds of interfaces. For example, there could be one set of standards for a Graphical User Interface (GUI), for those who have access to networked PCs and another for those stuck with legacy IBM3270 line terminals without graphics capabilities. These will be separate irreducible facts, divorced from rules of where and when data are stored or transported.

## Example of a Policy That Resides in the Interface Layer

Not all interface rules will be operational rules. Some may be statements of policy or strategy as well. For example, a policy might state that all GUI screens will follow Microsoft's Inductive User Interface standards (Microsoft Inductive User Interface Guidelines, n.d.).[30]

## Example of a Change in the Interface Layer

Interface rules may not always be related to human interfaces. Sometimes they will involve interfacing with automation. For example, let us assume that other telephone firms lease the network to provide telephone services independently to customers. The firm that owns the network is obliged to provide telephone call information to firms that have leased their network. The timing and format for presenting usage data to the lessee's systems may change independently of what file the data is sourced from. Indeed, even if there is a single source of data, different timings, update frequencies, and formats may be needed to satisfy lessees with different needs.

## Technology Rules Layer

Like the other layers in Figure 3.4, the Technology Rules layer may involve both operational and strategic (atomic) rules. For example, the architect for billing systems may decree that call volumes are so heavy that the firm will optimize performance of its computer systems by storing call records on flat files rather than any relational database management software; then, this is a policy that will reside in the Technology Rules layer.

The firm might decide that it wishes to reduce its technology risk by standardizing on a single reputed vendor for all their hardware and systems software. This will be a strategy rule that will reside in the technology layer. Changing these rules might impact software code as well as interfaces between software and hardware components internal to the platform, all of which reside in the bottom layer of Figure 3.4, but business process automation (data flow and interface rules) will not be impacted.[31]

Of course, at more operational levels, the Technology layer may also have rules about data transfer, records, fields, formats, and transformations between technology objects internal to the platform or network, such as "Bit value 0, of bit zero of an IP address means it is an Internet class A address" (a rule about a field in an IP address used internally by Internet software).[32]

## An Example of Process Improvement by Leveraging New Technology

Automated instruments or other automated information systems may also set formatting and file requirements. To illustrate this, let us consider the operation of a warehouse. Inventories of items stored in a warehouse are validated periodically by physically counting them. When inventories are physically counted, employees tally inventory items by keying the physical inventory into portable palm top devices equipped with a keyboard. The data are downloaded from the palm top devices and consolidated in an inventory file.

The firm decides to make the process faster and more efficient by replacing the palm top devices with bar code reading wands. The wands scan a bar code to tally items. These counts are then down loaded to the same inventory file as before. Wands may present data to the inventory system in one format and palm top recorders in another. These rules involve format and hence belong to the interface layer.

Thus, the logistics of storing and transporting data stay the same, but formatting requirements might depend on the technological environment. If new kinds of devices become available, or should the firm change its standards (for example, its bar coding standards), only the interface components will change.[33] Components related to pure business rules and the logistics of data movement would remain the same and may be configured with the new interface and technology components to improve the business process.

Below the business process automation layer lie the rules of pure technology—those required to optimize performance, stability, and reliability of chosen platforms.

## Configuring Rules to Build Components

We examined examples of how knowledge can be assembled from knowledge artifacts under The Repository of Meaning in Chapter II. The rules we assembled there were not executable software or even the technical specifications for executable software. Instead, they were business requirements from which designs and technical specifications would flow.

An example of reusable components of business information appears in the uppermost layer of Figure 3.6.[34] These reusable components are *business* requirements for applications software (and specifications for business processes as well). Reusable *business specifications* (i.e., requirements), not executable components, flow from the metamodel at this level.

To turn these business specifications into executable software, we must round out this metamodel of business knowledge with imple-

*Figure 3.6. The architecture of reusable knowledge components*

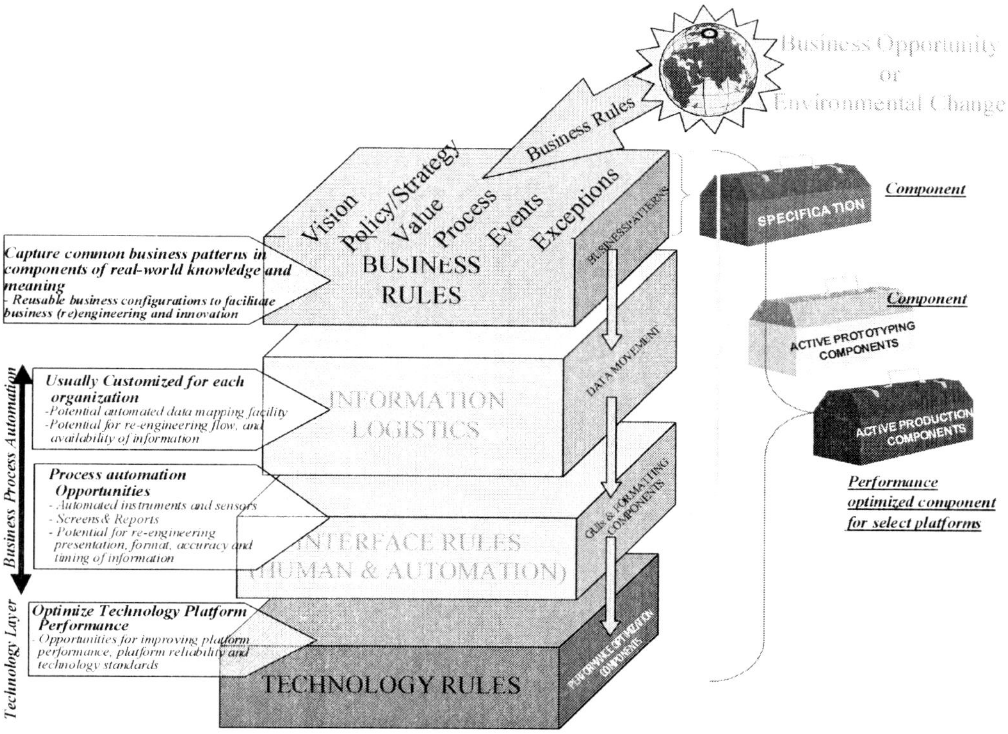


*Reproduced by permission from Mitra, A., & Gupta, A. , Creating Agile Business Systems with Reusable Knowledge, New York, NY: Cambridge University Press, 2006.©*

mentation components. These active executable components will then consist of business semantics of the kind we had assembled into subassemblies of pure business process knowledge in The Repository of Meaning section in Chapter II, assembled with information logistics and interface components. Such structures will be reusable subassemblies of executable code and hence reusable components in their own right. These executable components may then be assembled into proof-of-concept prototype systems, even if they are not performance optimized. When executable components *are* performance optimized for specific platforms, they may be assembled into production systems (see Figure 3.6).

## Scope of the Metamodel of Core *Business* Knowledge

(Note that each of the layers in Figure 3.7 may have a vision component supported by policies, strategies, tactics, operations, events, exceptions, and standards. Each of these must ideally be aligned with the corresponding component in the layer immediately above it, so that the firm's information systems can be in harmony with the business that it serves.)

The objective is to normalize real-world business behavior; the purpose is to facilitate business agility with Knowledge Artifacts. This business focus will provide the maximal return. Therefore, this book focuses on the core—the metamodel

*Figure 3.7. The scope of the metamodel of knowledge in this book is confined to pure business rules.*

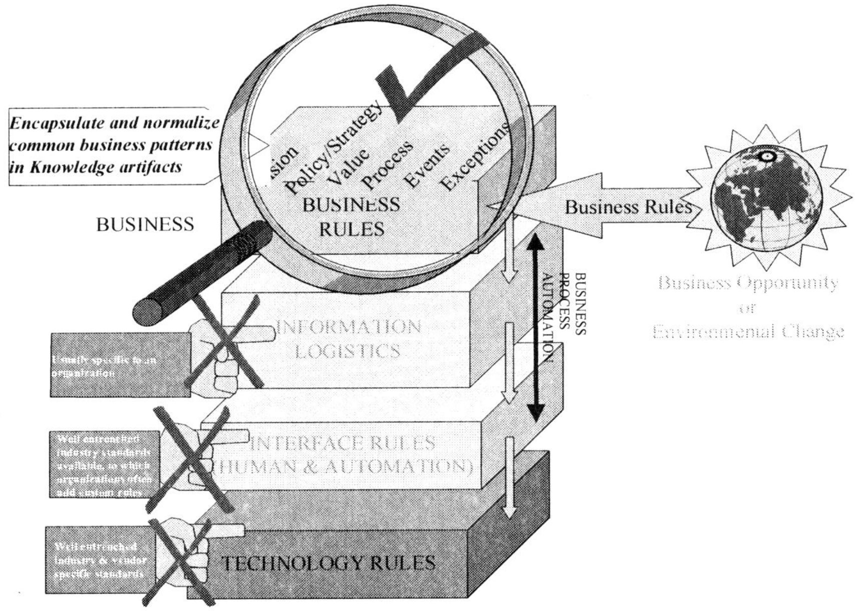


*Reproduced by permission from Mitra, A., & Gupta, A. , Creating Agile Business Systems with Reusable Knowledge, New York, NY: Cambridge University Press, 2006.©*

of pure business rules and meanings—not the logistics of data flow or the complexities of performance optimization. The framework of Figure 3.4 provides a tool for filtering irreducible facts so that we can focus on pure business behavior independently of mechanisms that implement or reflect these requirements in information systems that are prone to change in step with technology. This will facilitate business knowledge reuse and coordination, make our automation flexible, our businesses more agile and innovative, and above all, help reduce time to market new products, services, and systems.

There are several GUIs and other interface and information exchange components and standards readily available in the marketplace, as are those that focus on platform technology and performance. The metamodel of *business behavior* does not care about how it is implemented in information systems. It is reusable and flexible. It can be manifested in many different and innovative ways. Indeed, once we understand the metamodel of business knowledge, it is relatively simple to incorporate the other three layers of Figure 3.4 to build an integrated metamodel of systems knowledge.

The rest of this book describes the metaobjects that normalize atomic *business* rules found in the uppermost (Business Rules) layer of the architecture of knowledge. In this book, we will learn the behavior of metaobjects that flow *naturally* from the layer of pure business rules and understand transforms that turn these rules of business into rules of information exchange and transportation.

## ENDNOTES

1 Techniques of systems analysis and design were borrowed from cybernetics and the theory of finite state automation, which

was the origin of both the "Black Box" and "Node Branch" method. See Appendix II on State Machines. [325] also describes the concept. The figure on page 84 of [325] in Appendix III captures it succinctly.

2 See the chapter on black boxes in [325] in Appendix III and Appendix II on State Machines.

3 The Transfer function may depend on the state of the black box. See Appendix II on State Machines.

4 The chaotic behavior of complex systems is a specialized topic. See [323] in Appendix III.

5 Interactions between the subprocesses inside a black box are through inputs and outputs of subprocesses inside the black box, which are invisible at its interface. Figure 3.2 shows these "hidden" variables with arrows confined entirely inside the perimeter of the original black box. The need to introduce these additional variables increased the complexity of the model and made it even more difficult to obtain reuse and manage the domino effects of change.

6 Entity relationship diagrams are based on the node branch technique: entities are groups of variables, and relationships are their time agnostic associations.

7 See the State Machine in Appendix II.

8 The *Logical Unit of Work* is a fundamental concept in analysis of business systems. It assumes the system is in stable condition (equilibrium) and is returned to equilibrium after each change caused by business activity. For example, a business' customer list will be stable until the activity of acquiring a new customer occurs. After it is completed, the result will be a new, stable customer list. Equilibrium is fundamental to the concept of Logical Unit of Work, but causal loops in the real world do not guarantee equilibrium. Logical Unit of Work assumes that change occurs in discrete steps, which result in equilibrium at the end of each step. If we take a limited view of the causal network, this could happen. If we consider only one of the two arrows in the loop between $v_4$ and $v_5$ of Figure 3.2, we may assume a temporary equilibrium in the hiatus between successive changes. The Logical Unit of Work is valid only under conditions of discrete, not continuous, change.

9 For example, $v_4$ might represent the number of products and v5 the number of customers. A larger product portfolio might increase market penetration, which might be reason to increase product diversity even more to satisfy this larger customer base. This could then be the reason for acquiring even more customers. The cycle would keep repeating until market saturation.

10 The *Arms Race Model* on page 281 of [326] and section 1.4.9, Determining Events and Variables in [327] of Appendix III describes how the simple node branch representation may be enhanced to model complex interactions.

11 The note on polymorphism under the Mathematical Theory of Categories, in Appendix II, explains how categorization can support rule reuse with mathematical precision.

12 The patterns in [338] in Appendix III focus on business services, which are polymorphisms of components and models described in this book. The components and patterns in this book and [337] in Appendix III may be used to describe the generic services that describe knowledge and inference.

13 The theory of sets is fundamental to classification.

14 Lest we give the wrong impression, we will point out that Information Systems projects are not always undertaken to add or alter business functionality. Sometimes they are undertaken to implement purely technical changes. Case in point, the recent Year 2000 projects, which collectively vost the world

more than $600 billion. Many of us have come across projects where the sole purpose was to update technology or to conform to technical standards and platforms. However, there should always be cogent business justification even for projects like these, and their software is always wrapped around business rules. Even pure technology projects cannot ignore business rules. For Information Systems projects, they are neither respite from reality nor from business rules.

15 Atomic Rules were described in Chapter II.

16 This multiplicity of choice in how each business rule can be implemented is the basis for building scalable and flexible information systems with reusable components.

17 Rules may be reflected in systems as they are in the real world if they are stored in an electronic repository where they are conceptually normalized, although they may be physically replicated purely to optimize computer performance. If these rules *are* replicated, they must be replicated in a closely controlled and well-managed way in order to manage the impact of change and avoid the problem of explosive and chaotic change.

18 This particular requirement is not a pure business rule because it is not an assertion about any new business functionality required of the system. A pure business rule exists regardless of the availability of systems. Its existence does not depend on whether the information system can record its operation or not. These "pure" business rules are the kinds of rules that reside in the business rule layer of Figure 3.4.

19 In the Technology Rules layer, we find many parallels with the business layers, including the existence of objects, initial conditions, relationships, processes, information movement, information stores, and interfaces, except that these involve platform specific technology objects rather than business objects. Although the metamodel in this book focuses on the business rules layer, and analysis of links between business process automation and technology platforms is not in the scope of this metamodel, the metamodel of technology will have many parallels with the metamodel of business, and indeed, will be an extension of the core model developed in this book.

20 Ed Peters of Index Technology developed the science of Information Logistics.

21 Section 5 of Chapter II describes how a similar atomic rule, *Organization ships Product by Boat*, may be assembled from reusable components.

22 Automation in this context means actors that produce, capture, or process information.

23 Process improvement programs focus on *execution* of business concepts through redefinition of business processes, not redefinition of the business itself. See Figure 3.5.

24 The metamodel of business knowledge, developed in this book, helps to normalize business rules. Normalized business rules will be the reusable business components of Figure 3.6. The Universal Perspective has the rules reused most frequently by businesses.

25 Domains will be discussed in Chapter IV.

26 Just as there are rules that link "pure" business rules to Business Process Automation, there are rules that link Business Process Automation to technology platforms. This is one example of this kind of rule. However, the focus of this book is the Business Rules layer in the architecture of knowledge, and rules related to technology platforms are beyond the scope of this book. [296] in Appendix III discusses technology platform issues related to building reusable components in more detail.

27 A person, system, or instrument that accesses or processes (i.e., acts on) information is called an *actor*.

28 Some readers might ask how we might classify this rule if it had mentioned what the source and destination(s) of the compressed data were. The architecture of knowledge in Figure 3.4 mandates that had the rule included either the source or the destination of data, it would have had to be broken into a source-destination, or data flow rule, and an interface, or formatting rule.

29 Business Process Automation only refers to process innovation and change that leverages *information* technology. Other kinds of technological innovations that have little to do with information technology, but a lot to do with how business rules are physically realized in the real world, may also be leveraged for similar reasons and have similar effects. A glue maker may add a new specialty chemical to her formula to reduce the time it takes to cook the mix of raw materials to glue, or a shipper who has traditionally used trucking to ship goods might add air shipment to his repertoire. These implementations of "pure" business rules ("make glue" and "ship items," respectively) have little to do with automation, but they can, and do, impact workflow, cycle times, activity cost, resource requirements, process ownership, and other items just as Business Process Automation does.

30 The Microsoft inductive user interface is an example of policies that reside in the interface layer. Further reading on this topic is available at [154] in Appendix III.

31 Some readers might argue that standardizing on a single vendor may impact terminal devices and that, in turn, might impact business process automation (at the interface layer). However, it is not the *manufacturer*, but the *functionality* of the terminal device *visible to business information* that is in question in this layer. Only if the new manufacturer's equipment does not support all interface requirements of the terminal, such as graphics, keyboard characteristics, multimedia, or biometric capabilities, will business process automation be impacted. If this happens, we must understand that it is not the business process automation that has moved; rather it is a new technology constraint that must be incorporated at the interface between technology and interface layers. The firm must then make an informed trade-off between the requirement of business process automation and the technology constraint. The purpose of the knowledge artifact is served: to minimize the uncontrolled and chaotic impact of change. This will have been achieved by representing the system as a configuration of normalized atomic rules organized into the layers shown in Figure 3.4 so that each layer can be considered in terms of its interaction with the other layers in the architecture of knowledge.

32 Internet Protocols are described in Chapter 49 of [334] in Appendix III. This book is an excellent introduction to networking, data transfer, and telecommunications technology. Policy changes in the technology layer will impact technology rules such as those that involve communications software, line characteristics, and so forth. These are objects internal to the technology platform and are not considered business objects.

33 Technology rules such as those that involve communications software and line characteristics may also be impacted, but they only involve objects internal to the technology platform, which is not the focus of this book.

34 It was also an example of how this business information may be assembled from reusable business knowledge components

into full-blown business requirements for an application system. These assembled requirements, too, are structures of business logic that live in the Business Rules layer of Figure 3.6.

# Chapter IV
# The Pattern at the Root of It All

*The world came out of a single spark, the creator is in the creation and the creation is in the creator*
- Kabir Das, a 15th-century poet-philosopher from India


## ABSTRACT

*This chapter describes the concept of a Pattern, and describes why patterns are the basis of knowledge. It establishes the semantics of Pattern, and describes the concept of "information space," an abstract arena in which patterns of information create meanings. It shows how the concept of measurability is the basis of all meaning and how meanings are structured by patterns in information space. It also distinguishes a meaning from its physical representation and establishes the identity between objects and patterns. It shows how joining and constraining meanings creates new patterns of information, which lead to new meanings and hence the ability to configure meanings from other meanings. This is the basis on which components of knowledge are derived in this book and also in its companions in the series.*


The concept of Pattern and Information Space is where our journey begins. Meanings are abstract patterns of information. We conceive of these patterns of information as patterns in an abstract place called Information Space. We cannot physically see, hear, touch, or sense information space or the abstract meanings that swirl and twist though Information Space. This makes it difficult for most of us to visualize these patterns and to understand how they are assembled from other patterns, which may also be meanings and are always components of meanings.

*Pattern* is the fundamental object from which all meanings are born. The metamodel of Pattern is also the metamodel of *Object*[1]. In this chapter, we summarize the key characteristics of Pattern.

A pattern is a pattern of objects. A pattern cannot be a pattern unless the arrangement of its constituent objects follows some kind of law. In order to be considered a pattern, the information conveyed by the law cannot exceed the information conveyed by the ensemble of objects that constitute the pattern in the absence of the law (that is, the law must not make things more unpredictable; see Appendix II on Shannon's information theory). A pattern exists in state space. State Space is also a pattern of information. Fundamental to the concept of a pattern are the criteria that its constituents must satisfy to be considered parts of the pattern. These criteria compose the law that defines the identity and shape of the pattern. Since it is a pattern in state space, its constituents are located in state space. For this reason, we consider that its Law of Location defines a pattern.

The following example will illustrate this concept. Cars have properties such as weight and color. Its weight and color contain information about the car; hence, the pattern of information that defines the car includes the dimensions of weight and color. The physical location of a car at a particular time is also information about the car, and hence an aspect of its state. Its physical location is therefore also a property of the car. Physical space and time may also be facets of the state space of cars. State space extends and subsumes the concept of physical space by extending physical space into additional dimensions to account for the all the information conveyed by an object. This leads to the concept of information space.

Concepts and meanings need not have a physical presence. They could be abstractions. For instance, the concept of enumeration is an abstraction. Information content of objects like these, which are actually meanings, may not involve physical space, time, or properties like color and texture related to our senses. These objects exist in information space as pure concepts, which are abstract patterns of information. As stated earlier, information space can extend into physical space to accommodate physical objects with physical and temporal locations. Hence, the concept of information space subsumes and extends the physical concepts of space, time, and physical properties of objects.

Information space contains all the information conveyed by an object, which could be a physical object or an abstract concept. Indeed, it may be argued that objects that convey exactly the same information in every way are mutually indistinguishable and are therefore identical to each other because they possess exactly the same footprint in information space. The concept of object class conveys information that is common to all object instances in the class. Reusable information flows from the concept of Class. On the other hand, the instance identifier of an object is a symbol for all the unshared information in information space that makes an individual object different from the other individuals in its class, and thereby lends the object instance its very identity. To create a pattern, we must have a measure of similarity, which will serve as the basis for the arrangement of objects in the pattern: i.e., concepts of similarity and contrast are at the heart of every pattern.

## MEASURE OF SIMILARITY: THE PROXIMITY METRIC

Similarity and contrast between the constituents of a pattern are the basis for including or excluding an item from the pattern. The proximity of items in state space is a measure of their mutual similarity. The closer they are, the greater their similarity. For this reason, we call a measure of similarity between a pair of objects a *Proximity Metric*. The Proximity Metric is an integral part of the Law of Location and is derived from it. Other things being the same, two blue cars will be considered closer in information space than a blue and red car. Similarly, other things being the same, if two cars are physically close to each other, their states are considered to be closer, and in that aspect, they are considered more similar than a pair of cars separated by a larger physical distance. Any measure may be considered to be a proximity metric, provided it satisfies the following common-sense criteria:

- The proximity between a pair of dissimilar objects cannot be nil or less;
- The proximity of an object to itself must be nil;
- The proximity between a pair of objects must be the same in both directions; and
- The proximity of a pair of objects cannot exceed the summation of proximities of objects over any trajectory that connects the pair.

Physical distance satisfies all of the criteria above and is therefore an example of a proximity metric, or a measure of closeness and similarity between objects. See Appendix II, on generalizing measures of distance, for a more complete discussion of the proximity metric.[2]

## THE ONTOLOGY OF INFORMATION SPACE

A pattern conveys information. The quantum of information in a message is "the degree of surprise" in its contents; the more unexpected an item of information is, the more information it is considered to convey (see Appendix II on the measure of information). Therefore, it is somewhat paradoxical that the concept of "everything" conveys no information. The broader and more general a concept, the less is its information content and the larger its scope. When a concept is broad enough to cover everything, so that it distinguishes nothing, it conveys nothing.

*Figure 4.1A: The ontology of pattern*

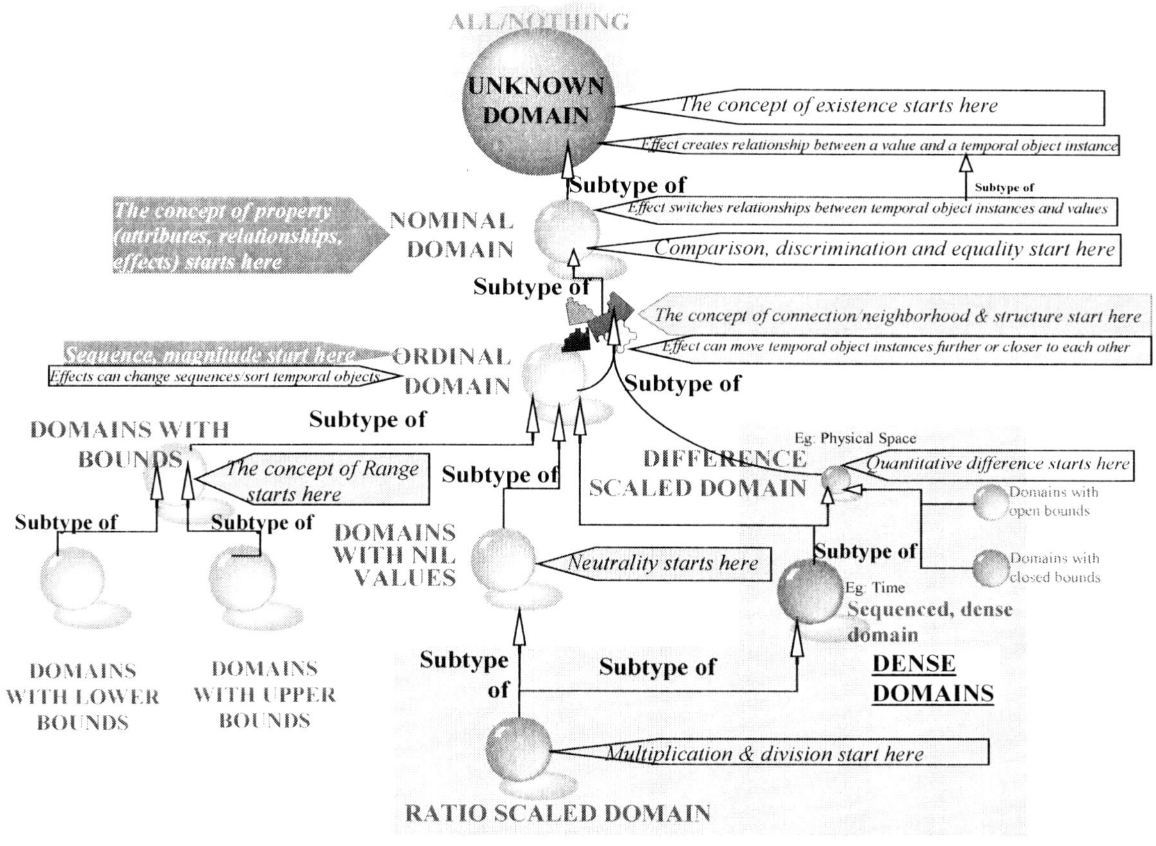


*Reproduced by permission from Mitra, A., & Gupta, A., Creating Agile Business Systems with Reusable Knowledge, New York, NY: Cambridge University Press, 2006.©*

To this kind of information space, add only the fact that distinctions exist. Classification schemes may now exist in this space so that we can make distinctions between instances of objects, such as one vehicle being distinct from another, and with a little more information between classes of objects being distinct, like the class of cars being distinct from the class of horses. Patterns of distinction can exist in this space, but they will convey little information on the quantum of distinction between objects in it. The Nominal domain of Chapter II emerges in this manner.

The information space may consist of collections of domains like these, as well the other domains that we describe in this chapter. Each domain could be considered to be a dimension of information space. This concept is explained using Candu Compoot's Story.

## Candu Compoot's Story: The Tale of Higher Dimensional Arrays

*Candu Compoot's Story describes four and higher dimensional arrays in a parable with a business example. It shows how arrays need not always be patterns of concrete symbols but could also be patterns of meanings. It demonstrates how lower dimensional slices of higher dimensional arrays may also be formatted as arrays:*

Count Albeans, the Chief of the accounting firm of Creative Accounting Inc. is concerned about the firm's ability to attract creative, bright young employees. Count Albeans asks his old school friend, Canut Compoot, now a corporate image consultant, to find the kind of image his firm should project to attract bright and creative young employees.

Canut Compoot conducts a survey of young accounting professionals to determine the kind of reputation they prefer in prospective employers. In the survey, Canut classifies respondents in terms of their creativity and intelligence on an ordinal five-point scale. The lowest position on the scale is "terrible," followed by "poor." "Average" is in the middle, "Good" follows "Average," and "Superb" is highest. He also measures respondents' willingness to be employed by firms on an ordinal five-point scale. The lowest position on the scale is "never work for the firm," the highest on the scale is "love to work for the firm," and the middle is anchored at "perhaps work for the firm." Every respondent is asked to rate his or her willingness to work for five firms on this scale, and his or her willingness to work for each is recorded. The firms are presented to respondents not by name but in terms of their reputation. The reputation consists of six parameters: pay, ethics, conventionality, financial stability, growth, and concern for work-life balance. Each parameter is rated on a three-point scale. The lowest position on the scale is "poor," the highest position is "good," and the middle is "average." Canut must now find what images make creative and bright respondents like a prospective employer in terms of these parameters.

Candu Compoot, Canut's brother, suggests Canut build a multidimensional array and analyze the pattern. Respondents' creativity rating, their intelligence rating, their willingness to work for the firm, as well as the firms' six image parameters will each be a dimension of this array. In all, the array will have nine dimensions:

- Respondents creativity ( "*Terrible,*" "*Poor,*" "*Average,*" "*Good,*" "*Superb*")
- Respondents intelligence ("*Terrible,*" "*Poor,*" "*Average,*" "*Good,*" "*Superb*")
- Attractiveness of firm as employer ("*Never,*" "*Perhaps,*" "*Love to*" work for firm)
- Firm's reputation as paymaster ("*Poor,*" "*Average,*" "*Good*")
- Firm's reputation in terms of ethical behavior ("*Poor,*" "*Average,*" "*Good*")
- Firm's reputation in terms of conventional or unconventional culture ("*Poor,*" "*Average,*" "*Good*")
- Firm's reputation for financial stability ("*Poor,*" "*Average,*" "*Good*")

- Firm's growth prospects (*"Poor," "Average," "Good"*)
- Firm's reputation in terms of concern for work-life balance (*"Poor," "Average,"* "Good")

Each cell of the array would map to a position on each of the nine dimensions above. Thus, there would be a cell for superbly creative respondents of average intelligence who would love to work for a conventional firm of average ethics, good financial stability, average growth and good concern for employees' work-life balance, but poor pay. Similarly there would be another cell for individuals with good creativity and superb intelligence who would never work for a firm of questionable ethics and financial stability, which is unconcerned about employees' work-life balance and has a reputation for being unconventional, even if the firm offers good pay and has good growth prospects.

The cells of the array, suggests Candu, should contain the percentages of respondents that match the parameters of each cell. Then, Candu tells him, Canut can compare the incidence of respondents of each kind with the kind of image that bright and creative respondents prefer.

Canut has trouble visualizing a nine dimensional array, but Candu asks him not to worry. He says Canut can always print two-dimensional slices, one at a time to look for patterns. For example, says Candu, if he looks at the data for only those who were rated Superb on creativity and intelligence, and would love to join an unconventional employer that pays well, has good ethics, is financially stable, then Canut can compare employers' reputations, among this group only, in terms of their growth prospects vs. concern for work-life balance in the following two-dimensional table. The table, explained Candu, will be a two-dimensional slice of this nine dimensional array because values the other seven dimensions have been fixed. This is equivalent to slicing through them.

Canut does this and meticulously fills in percentages of respondents in each cell. He finds responses of only 39% of candidates fit this profile, and they are distributed into the various cells of the two-dimensional table as follows:

| | **Concern for Work-Life Balance** | | |
|---|---|---|---|
| **Growth Prospect** | **Poor** | **Average** | **Good** |
| **Poor** | 0% | 1% | 5% |
| **Average** | 1% | 2% | 10% |
| **Good** | 2% | 3% | 15% |

*A two dimensional slice of Candu's nine dimensional array*

"There you are!" exclaims Candu, "Look at the pattern in the table! It clearly tells you that the employer's concern for work-life balance is very important. True, the firm's growth prospects are important too, but only if the employer is concerned about employees' work-life balance. The two parameters *interact* with each other very significantly."

Canut is quite pleased and calls Count Albeans to schedule a meeting in which he will present his recommendations. Count Albeans invites Dr. Candy Beanstalk, his Vice President of Public Relations, Mr. Candid Beanstalk, his Vice President of Human Resources, and Mesher Creatively, his Vice President of Marketing, to the meeting.

When the results are presented, everyone but Mesher seems satisfied. "I have a concern," says Mesher. "Sometimes prospective clients put a premium on creative accounting. If we only consider potential employees who insist on the highest ethical standards, we may crimp our growth prospects. Instead, we must look at preferences of bright, creative young people who would be willing to work for employers of average ethics."

Count Albeans looks concerned at this. After a thoughtful pause, he chimes in: "Yes, Mr. Creatively, you are right. We may miss the big picture if we consider only two patterns at a time." He turns to Candu and asks, "Is there some way we can look at more dimensions simultaneously?"

"No problem," says Candu. "I have brought this latest laptop computer with a three-dimensional display from Gizmos Unlimited, our corner electronics store. It has the latest display technology. It has a very special screen that projects three-dimensional holographic images into the air above it. Let us look at a three dimensional slice of our nine dimensional array. As we did in the two dimensional slice in the table above, we will consider preferences of respondents of superb intelligence and creativity, who would love to work for an unconventional employer that pays well and is financially stable, but now, with this three-dimensional display, we will also look for patterns of ethics, in conjunction with the parameters we already have in this table."

He types furiously into his new laptop and a three dimensional projection springs into the air above it:

"Excellent, my friend!" exclaims a beaming Count Albeans as he turns from the pattern in the air to Candu. "I knew you and Canut were just the team for this job!"

However, Dr. Beanstalk is still not satisfied. "It might be even better if we can search for patterns in all nine dimensions together," he says.

Candu is rarely at a loss. This is one of those rare occasions. "Dr. Beanstalk, how on earth would you do that?" asks Candu. "We exist in only three dimensions, how could we ever display nine, even with the best technology that mankind can ever create, today or in future?"

"I apologize," says Dr. Beanstalk. I did not mean to be critical. You have really done a superb job. All I was thinking was that we could perhaps use pattern recognition software to look for patterns in nine dimensions. That way we will not have to actually display the nine-dimensional array."

*Figure 4.1B. Candu Compoot's three-dimensional array*

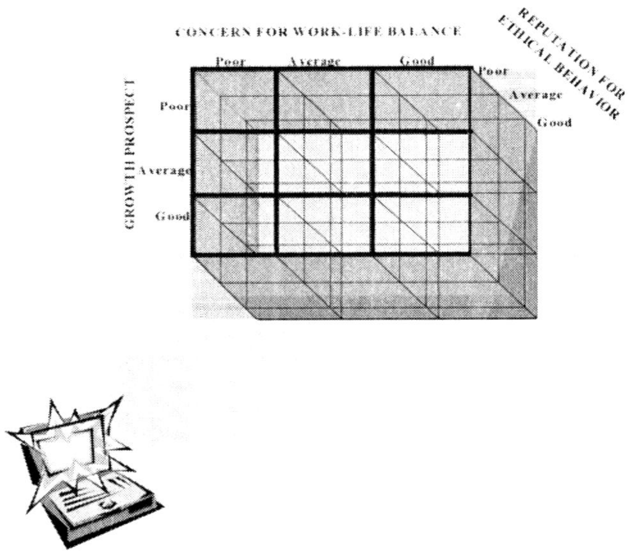


*Reproduced by permission from Mitra, A., & Gupta, A., Creating Agile Business Systems with Reusable Knowledge, New York, NY: Cambridge University Press, 2006.©*

Candid suddenly looked very interested. "I have just bought a package to do just that!" he exclaims. I intend to use it to look for patterns in our employees' demographic information, and this might be an excellent opportunity to put it to good use."

And that is just what they did. Of course, because they bypassed the human element to find these patterns, they did not have to *format* the information in arrays that people could see. After all, Dr. Beanstalk explained, "The arrays we could see were merely *symbols* that *represented* abstract information. They were symbols that made it easier for humans to *see* patterns in discrete, multidimensional state spaces. Arrays are formats when they are *symbols imbued with meaning.* If they remain concepts, like Candu's nine-dimensional array, which we cannot sense with any of our senses, they are still arrays, but they are *not formats*. They are arrays of meaning. We can still analyze patterns in these arrays, even if we cannot physically *see* their contents arranged in nine dimensions."

The *Array* in Figure I.2 in Appendix I subsumes both roles of arrays. It can be a symbol or an array of meaning. Arrays that are formats are visual symbols like the table above, or Candu's three-dimensional projections in physical space. These symbols are subtypes with two parents—*Pattern in Physical Space* and *Array*—both of which are present in Figure I.2 in Appendix I. The latter figure incorporates the framework to support both arrays of abstract meaning as well as formatting arrays that are symbols we can see.

To simplify our discussion, we will begin our argument by considering only a single dimensional, nominally scaled information space. The proximity metric in a space like this may only assert whether a pair of objects is distinct or not. The concept of the Unknown Domain and the Unknown Value also emerge from this proximity metric: those items do differ, but the quantum of difference is unknown. The Unknown Domain emerges from the Domain of Nothing, and the nominally scaled domain emerges from the Unknown Domain.

Add a little more information to information space so that it is possible to rank similarities between objects in it. In such a space, we can assert that an object is closer to one object than to another and that the mutual distance between the two neighbors is larger, smaller, or equal to the distance of the first object from either neighbor. However, we have no information about the actual magnitudes of the distances involved. The concept of Neighborhood implies that there is an association between objects and that some objects may be closer than others. The concept of sequence, or order, also emerges from the ability to rank objects relative to other objects. As such, association leads to the concept of neighborhood and ranking. The Ordinal Domain of Chapter II emerges in this manner.

For example, we could say that the rank of a sergeant in the military is located between the ranks of a private and the major and that military ranks may be arranged in ascending order. However, we have no quantitative information on the magnitude of a sergeant compared to the magnitudes of a private or major. On the other hand, we may know that a sergeant is two ranks above a private and that a major is three ranks above the sergeant. We have quantitative information on *differences* between ranks, even though we have no quantitative information on the magnitudes of individual ranks. However, the pattern has room for only discrete differences. Unlike physical space, continuously varying quantitative difference may not be available in this space.

Consider a space with a Neighborhood again. Take any pair of points in this space. We could insert an object into the gap between a pair of neighboring objects so that the inserted object is closer to the objects at the two ends of the gap than they are to each other. We could then repeat this procedure, inserting another object into the gap between the inserted object and one of the ends of the original gap, and continue repeating the procedure ad-infinitum, until we have a space in which it is always possible to find an object between two others, regardless of how small the gap between them is. Spaces like these are called *dense* spaces. A dense space is a continuum. Like ordinal space, it has enough information to quantitatively measure the proximity between a pair of points; however, unlike ordinal space, differences in proximity are not discrete. They form a continuum. The information in a discrete ordinal space of infinite extent, and a dense continuum, are structured differently but their degrees of freedom and information carrying capacity may be similar. This is how the difference scaled domain emerges from ordinal domains and the concept of neighborhood.

Physical space is an example of a dense, difference scaled space. We cannot quantify magnitudes of points in physical space, but we can quantify distances between them and also the ratios of these distances. We can also conceive of a nil distance between collocated objects. This leads to ratio scaled space. Ratio scaled space has the highest information carrying capacity of all the spaces that we have discussed, which includes the nil value. Nil denotes absence of magnitude, which is different from "Don't Know," "Any," or "Null." (Null is the absence of meaning.)

For example, the state space for the intensity of light is ratio scaled. The absence of light, nil light intensity, is manifested as total darkness and is a special point of nil magnitude in intensity space. Contrast this with a point in physical space, where each point is similar to every other, serving only to locate its neighbors, but conveying no information on any intrinsic magnitude relative to other points. As such, ratios between light intensity are meaningful whereas ratios between points in physical space are not.

Ordinal space may also have a nil value. Consider an individual's preference for fruit. She might like blueberries the most, followed by apples and grapes; she may be indifferent to bananas and dislike oranges. This domain carries more information than a domain that merely asserts an order of preference because it conveys not only the order of preference but also information on the absence of preference, that is, a nil magnitude for preference (in our example, indifference to bananas). Difference scaled spaces and ordinal spaces with nil values are both obtained from ordinal spaces and can be considered different polymorphisms of ordinal space. Dense ordinal spaces are a difference scaled polymorphism with two parents: ordinal space and difference scaled space. See the endnote on the flow of time.

Ratio scaled space joins the two concepts and is a polymorphism (subtype) with two parents. Its parent spaces are difference scaled space and the space with nil values (see Figure 4.1A).

The information carrying capacity of information space depends on these properties of its dimensions as well as the number of dimensions involved. We will call the number of dimensions of a space its dimensionality. All of these properties are polymorphisms of degrees of freedom. Naturally, the information content of a pattern in information space cannot exceed that of the space that holds it.

A pattern in space may be multidimensional but cannot exceed the dimensionality of the space that holds it. The larger the number of dimensions of the pattern and the greater information content of each dimension of the space that holds the pattern, the greater the information content of the pattern. When we consider patterns of multiple dimensions that consist of differently scaled dimensions, properties of the same patterns may appear to be different depending on the direction of our perspective in information space. Moreover, it is always possible to represent the complete information content of one pattern in another, provided the information carrying capacity of the pattern representing the other equals or exceeds the information carrying capacity of the pattern it is representing (Mitra & Gupta, 2006). Indeed, in an ontological sense, two patterns of equal information carrying capacities may be considered different expressions of their common parent(s).

We usually think of space as though it were physical space, in which we can locate a point with a set of numbers that measures distances, angles, or both (see Figure 4.2). The preceding discussion showed that information space can be very different, lacking any information on magnitude, direction, and sometimes even neighborhood. Moreover, there are a few disadvantages in using numbers to represent values. Every domain contains three values that are absent from the domain of numbers, namely "All," "Unknown," and "meaningless." (We will call meaninglessness "Null," as opposed to "Nil"; the Nil conveys absence of magnitude, whereas Null conveys the absence of meaning, which includes things that are impossible. These values are inherited from the "All" and "Unknown" domains at the top of the hierarchy in Figure 4.1.) Not all domains have the Nil value represented by zero in the domain of numbers. For instance, ratios are meaningless for difference scaled quantities because the nil value is unknown. For the same reason, adding two points in physical space is meaningless: physical space is difference scaled, which means that there is no nil value capable of being mapped to the number zero and that no number can represent "unknown." Some of these issues are resolved in ratio scaled space. For instance, we can meaningfully add intensities of light, which are points in the ratio scaled intensity space because ratio scaled space does have a nil value that we can map to the number zero. However, it remains impossible to represent the concept of an unknown intensity with a number.

The operation of creating subspaces by removing dimensions is ambiguous. For instance, we could create a two-dimensional plane from the three-dimensional space in Figure 4.2 by constraining height to a fixed value or by eliminating the dimension of height by asserting we do not know it or do not care about it. This amounts to assigning "Unknown" or "Any" values to heights. A constraint increases information, the Unknown value reduces information, and "Any" reduces it even more. In general, the two-dimensional spaces derived by each of these operations will have different meanings and be very different from each other in terms of their properties and information content.

*Figure 4.2. Cartesian and polar coordinates in physical space*

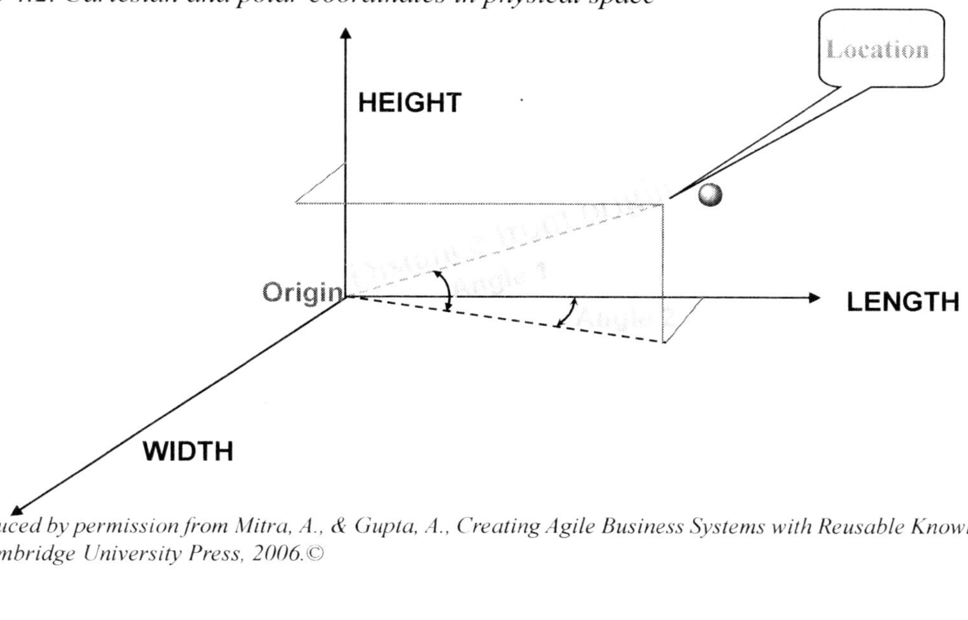


*Reproduced by permission from Mitra, A., & Gupta, A., Creating Agile Business Systems with Reusable Knowledge, New York, NY: Cambridge University Press, 2006.©*

A constrained pattern may be derived from a less constrained pattern. The constrained pattern will then be a polymorphism of its less constrained parent, inheriting its parent's behaviors and adding its own. A constrained plane is a polymorphism of a volume, whereas the relationship is reversed for a volume derived by making unknown values of an axis known. These concepts are important when we carve patterns in information space (Mitra & Gupta, 2006).

## PROPERTIES OF PATTERNS IN INFORMATION SPACE

The most fundamental and abstract property of a pattern is the concept of freedom, as measured by its degrees of freedom. The other properties of a pattern depend on the kind of information space that holds it. Each of these properties is a polymorphism of the generic concept of constraint, which restricts the freedom of the pattern to give it a structure and shape and thereby a special identity and meaning. This is why every property of a pattern is a polymorphism of the topos, or theme of freedom, obtained by adding information to distinguish one kind of freedom from another.

Consider an example to illustrate the concept. The concept of a triangle has more freedom than the concept of an upright triangle because the meaning of Triangle will not change if we rotate it in space, whereas the upright triangle will cease being an upright triangle if we reorient it. Note that "Upright Triangle" conveys more information than "Triangle" because "Upright" adds information on orientation. Note that the meaning of Triangle also contains the meaning of Upright Triangle. Therefore, unlike our physical concept of constraints curbing or physically truncating physical patterns, adding a constraint to a pattern

*Figure 4.3. Universal properties of pattern*

| Parameter/ Feature | Directional? | Subtypes | Valid in (Space) |
|---|---|---|---|
| Association | Y | Patterns of Associations | All |
| | | Sequencing Patterns | Ordinal |
| Dimensionality | N | Dimensionality of state space | All |
| | | Dimensionality of pattern | Ordinal & subtypes |
| Cohesion/ Separation | Y | Patterns of distinction | All |
| | | Ranking patterns | Nominal & Subtypes |
| | | Patterns of separation in terms of quantitative *differences* (eg: differences in military rank) | Ordinal & Subtypes |
| | | Patterns of separation in terms of ratios of separation (eg: Physical distance) | Difference scaled & Subtypes |
| Location | Y | Absolute location | Spaces with "Nil" value (Ratio scaled and Ordinal with Nil value) |
| | | Differences in absolute location | Ordinal with Nil value |
| | | Ratios of absolute location | Ratio scaled space |
| Inclusion vs. Exclusion | Y | Patterns of inclusion | Nominal & Subtypes |
| | | Patterns of exclusion | Nominal & Subtypes |
| Extent | Y | Infinite | Nominal & Subtypes |
| | | Finite | Nominal & Subtypes |
| Delimitation | Y | Unbounded (Undelimited) | Nominal & Subtypes |
| | | Bounded (Delimited) | Ordinal & Subtypes |
| | | Open | Difference Scaled & Subtypes |
| | | Closed | Difference Scaled & Subtypes |

May be infinite
Cardinality (No. of participating Objects)
Degrees of freedom (information carrying capacity)
Order of a pattern (pattern of patterns, pattern of pattern of patterns, pattern of pattern of pattern of patterns etc.)
Partition
Subtype of

of information actually extends the meaning of the pattern in information space by making distinctions and including these new meanings in the scope of the pattern it constrained to create the new meaning.

The *essence of a pattern* is the minimum information required to define the identity of the pattern. If all we need is a triangle, the essence of the pattern will be "triangle," not "upright triangle." The concept of "essential" emerges from the concept of the essential pattern (Mitra & Gupta, 2006). (See Appendix II on the Principle of Parsimony. It asserts that we provide just enough information and no more information than necessary to describe a concept unambiguously.)

We could also create a new meaning, "Not an upright triangle," by adding a constraint that excludes all upright triangles. Then we will have a pair of mutually exclusive items, thereby creating a partition. Polymorphisms in an exclusion partition are mutually exclusive; that is, an object instance may only belong to one subclass in the exclusion partition at any given moment. We could also have inclusion partitions, in which an object instance must belong to every subclass in the inclusion set if it is a member of any one of them (Mitra & Gupta, 2006). Unless we otherwise qualify it, the word *partition* always implies exclusion partition in this book.

Every constraint shapes a pattern of information by adding more information to other patterns in information space, which may be meanings, making them more specific and narrower in scope. Constraints always bear information and thereby derive new meanings from old. Conversely, relaxing or removing a constraint changes the shape of the meaning in information space by generalizing the meaning, reducing the information payload of the pattern, and broadening its scope. This is how new learning and innovation are absorbed.

Each kind of space in the ontology of Figure 4.1 inherits the capability of conveying all the information its parent does, and adds more, creating room for richer and more specific meanings. Naturally, the information carrying capacity of a pattern in information space cannot exceed the information carrying capacity of the space that holds it.

Based on these principles, we can infer several universal properties of patterns from their information content. Many of these properties will depend on the direction from which we experience the pattern in information space. Figure 4.3 summarizes the discussion below and asserts which properties of patterns can be directional in information space; for example, the cylinder in Figure 4.4 is a pattern that is delimited in some directions but not in others. In Figure 4.3, items in a "Partition" are mutually exclusive.[3] For the purposes of this book, it will suffice to understand that the universal properties of patterns, which flow from the concept of its essence and its degrees of freedom, are:

1. **Association:** Conveys information and is the basis for the concept of pattern; all patterns are patterns of association. The fact of association only establishes which objects are mutually involved in a pattern. The concept of neighborhood starts with association. The association may have no information on sequence, direction, or the nature of the association.
2. **Inclusion/exclusion:** A pattern may be a pattern of inclusion or a pattern of exclusion. A pattern of inclusion asserts which objects are associated with which, whereas a pattern of exclusion asserts what is not associated, that is, excluded or dissociated.

   The certainty that an association does *not* exist conveys as much information as the certainty that the association exists. Both are polymorphisms of the topos (the theme) of association, which merely asserts that the existence of an association, or a bar against it, is a certainty. Contrast this with the absence of information, when we do not know if either constraint applies.

3. **Cardinality:** Cardinality is the number of objects that compose the pattern. Dense domains are a subtype of domains of infinite cardinality. Patterns like serial numbers, for example, may not be dense but may go on endlessly and be constituted of infinite numbers of members.
4. **Sequence:** The law that defines the pattern may or may not consider sequences. Sequence is a polymorphism of the concept of association and neighborhood. Association merely asserts that two objects are connected in some way (or not), whereas sequencing rules reduce the degrees of freedom of the pattern by specifying the order in which objects must be arranged in the pattern. A pattern that asserts that a blue bead must follow two adjacent red beads on a necklace is a polymorphism of a pattern that merely asserts that blue and red beads must comprise the necklace.
   Naturally, there can be no sequence for objects that are located at the same point. As such, patterns of collocation cannot be sequenced. Sequence is meaningful only when there is enough information to make distinctions between points in information space to enable one to distinguish a beginning from an end.
5. **Extent:** The concept of extent flows from the concepts of cardinality and order. The extent of a pattern might be infinite or finite. For instance, a straight line of infinite length, "Serial Number" and "Ancestor," are all patterns of infinite extent, whereas "Parent" and the shapes in Figure 4.3 are patterns of finite extent. Constraints may reduce the extent of a pattern. Patterns of finite extent are polymorphisms of patterns of infinite extent. In this way, "Enumeration" is a finite polymorphism of Cardinality, and the concept of Scope is a polymorphism of Extent (Mitra & Gupta, 2006).
6. **Delimitation:** Patterns of finite extent may be delimited by boundaries or not. For instance, in Figure 4.4, the pattern on the left occupies a finite two-dimensional space marked by a clear boundary whereas a similar pattern to its right also sits on a finite two-dimensional surface but is undelimited by boundaries that mark its edge because it has no edge.
   Delimiters of patterns are also patterns. For instance, a circle at its rim delimits a disk; a word is delimited by a space on both sides, a sentence by a space at the beginning and a period at the end, and the concept of "Grand Parent" by the concept of "Generation."
   On the other hand, a circle is a finite pattern, but has no boundaries. Similarly, the concept of a cycle of 24 hours is finite but is a boundless pattern. Naturally, patterns of infinite extent

*Figure 4.4. Delimiters and boundaries*

*Reproduced by permission from Mitra, A., & Gupta, A., Creating Agile Business Systems with Reusable Knowledge, New York, NY: Cambridge University Press, 2006.©*

are unbounded and can have no delimiters. The concept of time is a one-dimensional pattern with no boundaries at either end. We could think of the pattern as an infinitely long line. When we add the concept of a 12-month cycle to the concept of time, it becomes a polymorphism, which we might visualize as resembling a helix wrapped around the cylinder in Figure 4.3 with its boundaries removed so that the cylinder stretches from an infinite past to an infinite future. Each complete turn of the helix will advance one year along the time line. The 12-month cycle is finite but unbounded, whereas the dimension of time stretches to infinity on both ends. If we add the information that the year begins on January 1, then a new polymorphism emerges, which modifies the helical visualization of the pattern in information space. The helix now has a delimiter: a "cut," or edge, on the rounded surface that marks the beginning and the end of the cycle of months.

Not all patterns in information space can be visualized as easily. As we have discussed, information space may not look like any space we know; however, patterns in information space will share these qualities of extent and, for pattern of finite extent, the quality that marks the presence or absence of delimiters.

7. **Open and closed patterns:** A delimiter is a boundary that marks the edge of a pattern. It may be specified as an inclusion constraint that includes the delimiter or an exclusion constraint that excludes the delimiter. The two forms are equivalent when we consider discrete, finite patterns. However, a distinct polymorphism of delimitation emerges when a pattern is finite and dense. A pattern may extend up to its boundary if the boundary is included or could get arbitrarily close, even infinitesimally close but cannot touch its boundary if the boundary is excluded. A disk that extends to its rim is a subtly different pattern from a disk that stays inside the circle that encloses it without being able to ever actually touch the enclosing circle. A boundary that is included in the pattern it delimits is called a closed bound, whereas a boundary excluded from the pattern is called an open bound. In general, dense patterns are richer in information than patterns that are not dense, which is how these additional polymorphisms of delimiters are obtained.

   The concept of open bound gives rise to the concept of "Many" in *non-dense* patterns of infinite extent. "Many" is a polymorphism of cardinality, in which a delimiter at infinity is excluded from the pattern. For instance, we may have an infinite series of whole numbers. To this pattern, we may add a constraint that infinite numbers are excluded. The series can include arbitrarily large numbers but not infinitely large numbers. This is how the meaning of "Many" emerges.

   Indeed, we could also hold the information in the non-dense pattern of infinite extent in a dense pattern of finite extent and map the boundary to a finite value. "Many" would then translate to a finite open bound that limits the extent of the pattern. This equivalence may not be intuitive, but information space does not always resemble the space we live in, and its laws are different. This leads to meanings that are "open." For instance, the meaning of "squeeze" is delimited by the concept of no pressure. It is an open bound. Squeezing can involve very little pressure, but the complete absence of pressure is excluded from the meaning of squeeze, whereas negative pressure may become "stretch."

8. **Cohesion/Separation:** This parameter measures the mutual proximity of the constituents of a pattern. The more cohesive a pattern, the less the mutual separation of its constituents, compared to their distance from objects that

do not constitute the pattern. In information space, it describes how "loose" or cogent a meaning might be.

The cohesiveness of a pattern is based on its proximity metric. As we have discussed before, nominal patterns may only assert whether there is a difference between a pair of constituents or not. In a space with a little more information, but one that is not quite ordinal yet, we could also add the concept of neighborhood and have patterns asserting that some objects are closer than others but not by how much. Ordinal space can quantify differences but not ratios. Similarly, dense spaces can quantify differences and ratios of differences. In ratio scaled space, proximity to the natural nil value may also be used as a measure of cohesion. As such, the measure of cohesion could not only use all of the measures of a nominal, ordinal, and difference scaled space but also involve ratios of magnitudes of points in that space.

9. **Density:** Density is a polymorphism of cohesion that we discussed while considering information space. A dense pattern may only exist in a dense space. A dense pattern carries more information than one that is not dense, and a dense domain has an infinite cardinality.
10. **Dimensionality:** The dimensionality of a pattern may not exceed the dimensionality of the space that holds it. A three-dimensional space may contain zero-, one-, two-, and three-dimensional patterns. One and two-dimensional patterns in a three-dimensional space may be straight lines and flat planes respectively or could twist and warp in three dimensions (just as the one-dimensional line might warp into two or three dimensions). The information content of a pattern will depend on its dimensionality as well as on the minimum dimensionality of the space required to hold the pattern. Generally, the greater the dimensionality of a pattern and the higher the dimensionality of the space that holds it, the larger the information content of the pattern.
11. **Equivalence of patterns:** A pattern may represent another without loss of information if its information carrying capacity equals or exceeds the information content of the essential pattern it is representing. This is why nominal and ordinal patterns of finite extent only require symbols to represent them, whereas dense patterns need symbols and units of measure, which in turn must be physically represented by other symbols. A symbol is a discrete pattern in physical space, which we can sense. When it represents information, we call it a format. Symbols are discrete, countable patterns. On the other hand, dense patterns have infinite cardinality. Therefore, symbols by themselves do not have enough information carrying capacity to convey all the information in a dense pattern. However, there are infinitely many numbers. Therefore, numbers may represent dense domains without losing large amounts of information. (We will still lose "Unknown," "Any," and "Null.") Numbers can be formatted as symbols. Each map from value to number is a unit of measure, which can be represented by a symbol. For example, weight is a dense pattern; the textual words *pounds* and *lbs* are symbols for the measure of weight called pound.

In this book and its companions, the term *full format* refers to the format of the number and the format of the unit of measure considered as a set. Full formats are required to physically represent dense patterns such as difference and ratio scaled values in information space. There are an infinite number of possible units of measure and uncountable numbers of formats for each (Mitra & Gupta, 2006). Non-dense patterns of infinite extent also have infinite cardinality. Finite sets of symbols cannot completely convey all the

information in them. However, dense patterns of finite extent can represent the information in them. The kind of pattern required would depend on the cohesion of the infinite pattern it is representing. Patterns of infinite extent may be represented by dense patterns of finite extent without loss of information (see the additional reading on set theory and cardinality of classes suggested in Appendix III for a more complete coverage of these issues).

Each of the parameters of the pattern that we have described is a polymorphism of its degrees of freedom, and each contributes to the overall degrees of freedom of the pattern. Many of these polymorphisms are directional in state space (see Figure 4.3) and can interact in complex ways. For instance, in a mirror image, both separation and sequence must be preserved, except in the direction of reflection, when separation is preserved but not sequence (sequence is inverted, turning left into right).

Similarly, when size and orientation are not essential parts of the pattern but only shape is; the angular separation is preserved but not absolute positions or linear separation. Both angular and linear distances satisfy the criteria for being a proximity metric and each is a polymorphism of that concept.

12. **Order of a pattern:** Patterns may be constituted of patterns, which in turn may constitute patterns and so on. The order of a pattern is defined as the number of levels of patterns involved in defining a pattern. Accordingly, a pattern of patterns is a second order pattern. A pattern of patterns of patterns is a third order pattern, and so on. The concepts of a governing process and the order of governance are derived from this concept.

The figures in Appendix I capture the semantics of Pattern.

## DOMAINS OF MEANINGS VS. FORMAT

The preceding sections showed how the generic concept of measurability is derived from patterns and normalized in the concept of *Domain*. The ontology of domains follows the ontology of Pattern, which recognizes both qualitative and quantitative measurement. The concept of a property of an object is derived from its measurable behavior and thus from its relationship with *Domain*. Meanings are derived from the bald domains in Figure 4.1, described in previous sections, by adding information to them until they acquire business and physical meanings as described in Box 4.2. Boxes 4.5 and 4.6 describe how relationships between domains can create new meanings. This is one way that automation can assemble new meanings from its legacy of learning, adapting, and change in response to new knowledge.[4] Domains are stateless classes of values. Temporal objects like buildings, organizations, and persons cannot exist unless they exist for a finite span of time. They are stateful objects, and their properties are derived from domains. Every feature of a temporal object draws its value from a domain of meaning. At any given moment, the feature can have only a single value, which includes "Unknown," "Any," a range, or a region of state space. The collection of values of all features of a temporal object at a given moment in time is its state at that time. A temporal object like a car would qualify and limit the meaning of a value like "weight" drawn from the Weight Domain and constrain its meaning to "Weight of Car." Events may then change these values. Boxes 4.5 and 4.6 describe domains and their interactions.

Abstract concepts must be physically represented in an information system with symbols that we can sense. Symbols are objects that we can see, hear, touch, smell, or taste. A symbol must

be a physical pattern we can see (like a shape or text), a pattern of sound (for example, a spoken word or a chime), a haptic (touch) pattern we can feel with our sense of touch, or a pattern of odor or taste. When symbols represent information, they are said to format it. Box 4.1 describes how symbols may format information.

Note that our five senses are the basis of five formatting domains, based on sight (for example, figures, pictures, and written words), sound (for example, a spoken message or a tone), touch, odor, and taste (not widely prevalent representations in information systems yet), each of which normalizes different kinds of behavior. For instance, the visual domain normalizes the sensation of color as well as behavior like rotation of symbols in physical space, the auditory domain normalizes sensations such as the pitch and loudness of sound, and the haptic domain normalizes sensations such as heat and roughness.[5]

*Box 4.1. Metamodels of format, format conversion, encryption, and formatting constraint*

**Formatting Rules:** The metamodel of Format merely maps a value to a symbol. Figure 2.4 illustrates this. Figure A shows the detail behind "*expressed by*" of Figure 2.4. Note that the Object Set in the "*expressed by*" relationship enables multiple (optional) context dependent expressions of a value.

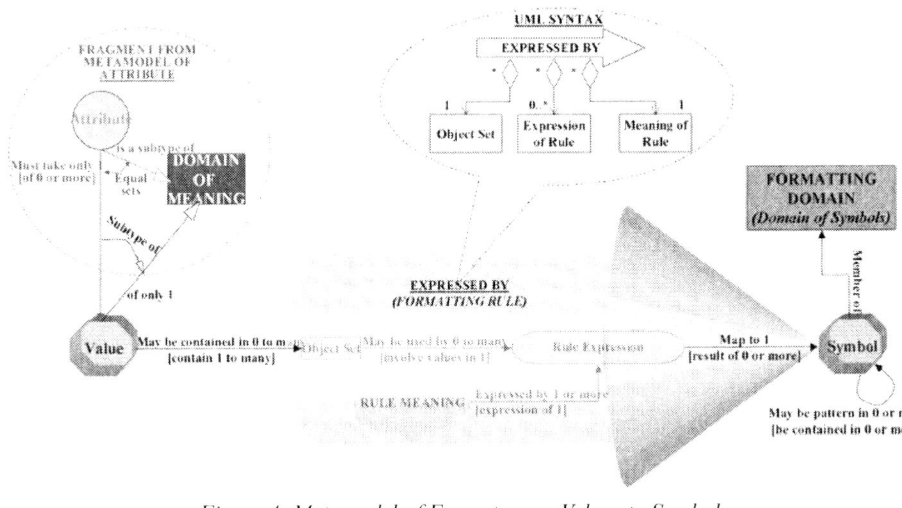


*Figure A. Metamodel of Format maps Values to Symbols*

*Reproduced by permission from Mitra, A., & Gupta, A., Creating Agile Business Systems with Reusable Knowledge, New York, NY: Cambridge University Press, 2006.©*

Note that symbols may consist of arrangements of other symbols. A string of characters is a one-dimensional sequence of symbols. Similarly, written sentences are sequences of written words, which in turn are sequences of alphabets. Symbols may be patterns of other symbols, which in turn may be symbols that consist of yet other symbols that are themselves patterns of symbols and so on. These symbols within symbols may thus be patterns that can be reused across more than one set of symbols. Patterns need not always be one-dimensional strings of characters. They could be multidimensional visual, auditory, and other patterns in any of the five fundamental formatting domains, or their combinations, based on our five senses.[6] The recursive relationship on Symbol in Figure A represents this fact.

Consider the role of *Object Set*. The *Object Set* of Figure A is one role of *Set of Object States* shown in Appendix I, Figure I.2. *Set of Object States* had two partitions we had discussed. One partition of this space contained the pattern—the symbol in Figure A, while another contained objects that influenced the pattern. The *Object Set* in Figure A is the set of objects that influence the pattern. The foundation of format is the object being formatted. Therefore, that is the single

*continued on following page*

*Box 4.1. continued*

most critical object that influences the symbol it is mapped to. The particular object must always be a member of *Object Set* in Figure A. This is mandated by the inverse relationship between *Object Set* and *Value*. *Object Set* in Figure A must always have one member—the value being formatted.

Consider the formatting behavior of the Object Set in Figure A. It gives us the capability of representing values in different formats depending on the context of the value. The object set has the context, and the rule expression has the context sensitive map. The rule expression could map different values to different formats depending on states of objects in *Object Set*. For example, the size of a drawing may be automatically scaled up or down, depending on the size of the frame it will be displayed in; the color of text may be black, if the background is light, or white, if the background is dark and so on. Figure A of Box 4.1 is the metamodel of format. The Object Set in Figure A of Box 4.1 not only maps values to symbols but contains the context of the map as well. The map is polymorphic, and its parameters are members of *Object Set*.

Consider how the recursive relationship on Symbol in Figure A normalizes the information content of *Format*. Suppose all values of an attribute (such as the temperature of an oven) in a certain range are displayed in red and are accompanied by an audible signal. The audible signal is merely a different expression of the value, as are the colored visual symbols of value. Each is a different format of the same *Attribute Value*. Together, the formats constitute a pattern synchronized in time. Equally, with its constituent symbols, this composite pattern is a format too. The composite pattern normalizes rules of synchronization between its constituents. Each constituent inherits different normalized behavior from a fundamental formatting domain. This is how the recursive relationship on *Symbol* in Figure A normalizes the behavior of *format* and how the normalized behavior flows from format to the expression of an attribute.

We have seen how the state of the symbol that represents it may be contingent on the state of the object it represents. We have also seen how the state of the symbol could also be contingent on states of other objects in *Object Set*. These states may even involve "don't know" and null values. As such, formats may depend on whether certain objects or states exist and whether they are known or not. If the originator of an e-mail attachment is unknown, the mail header might be highlighted in red. Similarly, an operation that adds to the height of a shape is meaningless in two dimensions. Two-dimensional shapes have only length and breadth, and hence their heights are "null." The symbol that represents the operation on a screen may be grayed out (a format) or excluded (the state of the excluded item is "null"). The members of *Object Set* establish the context of *Format*, the symbol.

Often a formatting rule will apply only to values of a specific attribute. For example, a formatting rule might assert that heights of mountains greater than 9999 must be expressed in exponential format. This formatting rule applies only to a specific attribute of a specific object class—the *height* (an attribute) of a *mountain* (an object class). Formatting rules can also apply to values of all attributes that map to a domain. These generic formatting rules will be directly linked to domains, and all attributes that map to the domain will inherit the rule. The link between Value and Attribute in Figure A of Box 4.1 represents rules that apply to values of specific attributes, whereas the direct link between value and domain is for rules that are generic to all attributes that draw on that domain. (See the discussion of Figure C in Box 5.1 to understand why the relationship between *Attribute* and *Value* is a subtype of the relationship between *Value* and *Domain*). An example of a generic formatting rule is a rule that maps all values with an absolute magnitude greater than 9999 to an exponential format. It is a rule attached to the *Quantitative Domain* of Figure 2.4. All quantitative domains such as height, weight, and money are subtypes of the *Quantitative Domain* of Figure 2.4 and will inherit the particular rule.

Formats are the bridge between meaning and its presentation in tangible symbols to man or machine. This bridge was not built by nature, but is arbitrarily determined by the hands of men and women who design business processes and information systems. That is why we must make it context dependent by making the expression of a value depend on *Object Set* in Figure A of this box.

Meanings may be context sensitive. Polymorphism supports this concept. A set of objects may be parameters that influence the form a relationship or object assumes. Figure A shows that representation may also be influenced thus. *Object Set* is a pattern that establishes the context of the format. The object set has all the attributes and emergent properties that we had discussed under patterns, earlier in this chapter. *Object Set* could be a true set, in which items are not repeated, or a list. *Format* may depend on states of members of *Object Set* and on emergent properties of *Object Set*, the *pattern*.

For example, the number of repetitions of a specific object is an emergent property of *Object Set*, the pattern (see *Object Occurrence Value* in the metamodel of *Pattern*). We could color symbols that represent duplicated objects red.

*continued on following page*

*Box 4.1. continued*

The color of a symbol is an indicator of its state. This is an example of how the state of *format* can depend on an emergent property of *Object Set*, the pattern.

Indeed, there is no bar on making the format contingent on any emergent property of *Pattern*, like extent, dimensionality, and the other attributes we discussed under *Pattern*, or the states of any of its constituents. Remember, relationships are objects too and may be among the pattern's constituents. Relationships represent interactions between objects, and there is no bar on making formats contingent on complex interactions if need be. Indeed, constraints imposed by technology are constraints imposed by physical devices[7] used to support requisite formats. This is an integral part of business process automation. *Figure A is a bridge and a transform that links business meanings with symbols and information systems.* It is a bridge between Business Rules and Interface Rules layers of the Architecture of Knowledge in Figure 3.4. (Later in this book, we will articulate other transforms that take us from one layer of Figure 3.4 to another.)

**Format Conversion Rules:** Formatting Rules map Values to Symbols, and Format Conversion Rules map one set of symbols (or patterns of symbols) to other sets of symbols (or patterns of symbols). The metamodel of format conversion is very similar to Figure A. The sole difference is that *Value,* on the left side of the diagram, is replaced by *Symbol*, and the *Object Set* must contain the Symbol, not the Value being mapped to a symbol. Naturally, in Figure B, the fragment from the metamodel of Attribute in the top lefthand corner of Figure A will be replaced by the structure relating *Symbol* and *Formatting Domain* on the right side of the figure. Figure B follows from Figure A.

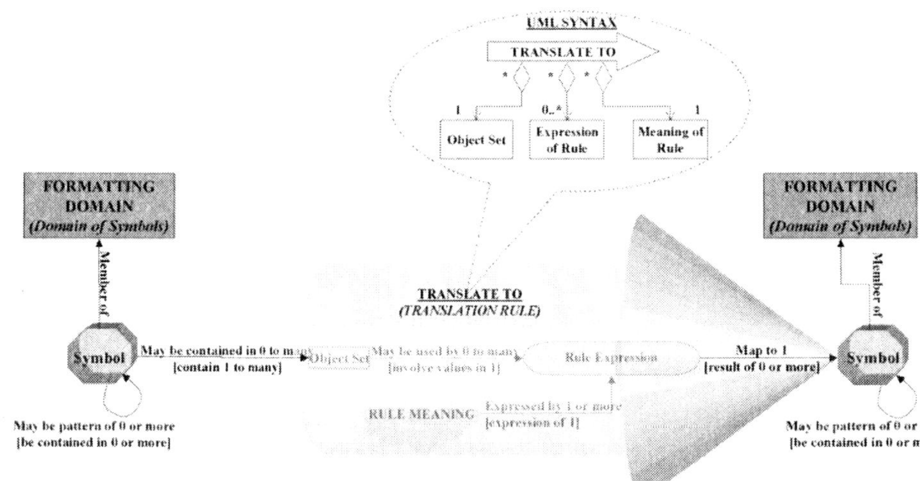


*Figure B. Metamodel of Format Conversion maps Symbols to Symbols*

*Reproduced by permission from Mitra, A., & Gupta, A., Creating Agile Business Systems with Reusable Knowledge, New York, NY: Cambridge University Press, 2006.©*

Figure B is another polymorphism of *Represent*, in which both the object that is represented, and the object that represents it, are symbols. The object set in Figure B of this box provides the capability to represent translation rules that depend on combinations of *objects*. This structure supports context sensitive translation.

Just as it was mandatory for the object set in Figure B to contain the value it was formatting, it is mandatory for the object set in Figure B to contain the symbol that it is converting. Symbols, as discussed under patterns, are perceptible patterns. At least one object in the object set of Figure B, if not more, must be a pattern.

Patterns are arrangements of objects. We have discussed how a pattern involves existence, sequence, extent, delimitation, position, proximity, and all the other attributes described by its metamodel (shown in Appendix I, Figures I.2 and I.3). All of these attributes describe the state of a pattern and may influence the translation of one symbol (or pattern) to another. The metamodel in Figure B supports this kind of behavior.

Symbols are not abstract like the meanings they represent. They must exist in physical space and time. In addition to space and time dimensions, symbols inherit dimensions from their formatting domains, such as color and size from visual

*continued on following page*

*Box 4.1. continued*

domains, or cadence, pitch, loudness, and timbre from audible domains, and yet others from olfactory, tactile, and taste domains. Symbols are patterns in one, two, three, or higher dimensional state spaces,[8] and so are formats. The metamodel of *Format Conversion* is simple, but it supports complexity; it also supports simplicity. When an object set consists of a single symbol, the translation rule becomes a simple symbol substitution rule. For example, a tone may also be mapped to a waveform on an oscilloscope. This is a translation from the audio domain to a two-dimensional visual domain; it is also a substitution of a symbol in one kind of formatting domain with that in another.

Format conversion is constrained by physical devices used to support requisite formats (which is an integral part of business process automation), as well as by whims of users and systems designers. Therefore, they may be arbitrary and complex[9] or intuitive and simple. *Object Set*, the pattern in Figure B, can support simple, complex, and even arbitrary format conversion rules because it is a pattern, and patterns may be simple, complex, and even arbitrary (see nominally scaled proximity metrics and "patterns by decree" under Proximity Metric). The business process to populate *Object Set* with the right members, such as actors (systems or individuals), devices, and business processes that frame the context of format conversion and the conversion, will take them into account.

Thus, the object set in Figures A and B could account for complex context sensitive rules. For example, it might mandate inclusion or exclusion of specific states and regions in state space for formatting symbols; it could account for interactions between values or interactions between states of the symbol. Interactions between objects are represented by their relationships with other objects. Relationships are objects too and may belong to object sets. Object sets support the far greater complexity that patterns demand for context sensitive formatting and context sensitive format conversion. *Format* and *format conversion*, after all, are patterns of rules.

As with formatting rules, format conversion rules can be either generic or specific. A given conversion may apply to all symbols, only to specific numbers, only to specific domains, specific values, specific objects, specific attributes of objects, or combinations of these. It all depends on their membership in *Object Set*.

A domain can be inferred from a value and an object from an attribute; hence *either* a value *or* a domain, and *either* an object *or* its states may participate in such combinations. When it is the domain that matters, then all values in that domain will be formatted in the same way (or will influence the format conversion in an identical fashion). When specific values (or ranges) matter, only specific values or ranges will be formatted the same (or will influence the format conversion). When conversion is contingent on only the existence (or not) of object instance(s), the format will depend only on the membership of the object in *Object Set*; but when the state of the object also matters, the value set must contain relevant states (or regions of state space) and only those states in the *Object Set* will be converted (or influence format conversion). Note that the object set in Figure B must contain at least one object—the symbol being translated.

Format conversion is a relationship between two symbols. Thus, *Format conversion* is recursive on *symbol*.

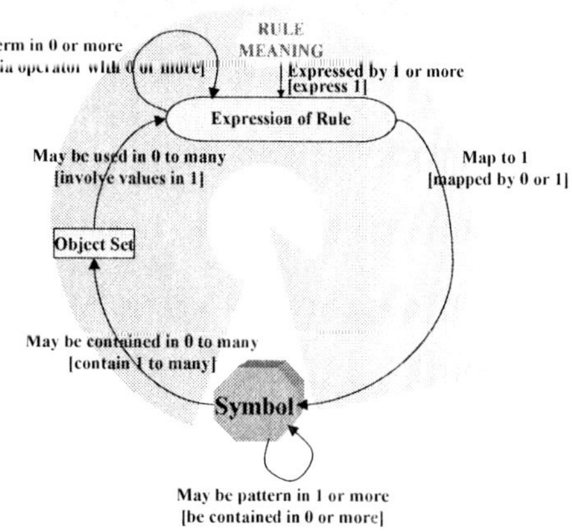


*Figure C. Format conversion is a recursive aggregate relationship.*

*Reproduced by permission from Mitra, A., & Gupta, A., Creating Agile Business Systems with Reusable Knowledge, New York, NY: Cambridge University Press, 2006.©*

*continued on following page*

*Box 4.1. continued*

**Format Conversion and Encryption:** Symbols are patterns, and patterns are lists or sets in state space. Format conversion rule expressions like those in Figure C may involve not only states of patterns but also impute values to patterns. Imputed values stem from the fact that we can arbitrarily associate a value or rank with a symbol (or pattern of symbols). Imputing a rank or magnitude to a symbol is a map from Symbol to Value; it is similar to the relationship in Figure A, except that it is in the reverse direction. To arrive at this reverse relationship, we could switch *Value* with *Symbol* and *Value Set* with *Symbol Set* in Figure A. It is another polymorphism of the generic *Represent* relationship.[10]

Indeed, imputed values constitute a pattern of arbitrary, unsequenced association between a value and a symbol (see *Patterns* in State Space). Let us return to Candu Compoot's story. Instead of rating reputation for ethical behavior in terms of *Poor, Average*, and *Good*, Candu Compoot may have assigned an arbitrary value of 10 points to the first cell of the three-dimensional array in Figure A, 20 points to the next cell, 30 points to the third cell, and so on, increasing the imputed value of each cell by 10 points until he reached the last (81st) cell, and imputed a value of 810 to it. Of course, had he treated these as ratio scaled scores and done any statistical tests that ignored the true ordinal nature of his measurements, he might have arrived at erroneous conclusions, but there is no bar against merely imputing a value to a symbol. He would merely be creating a pattern.[11] Imputed values are useful in encrypting or decoding information. Imputing a value, or pattern, to a symbol or another value is merely another role of the *Represent* relationship and is similar to format conversion.

As stated early in this chapter, formatting symbols have attributes they inherit from the formatting domains. Format conversion may therefore involve not only symbol conversion but conversion of symbol states as well. It boils down to mapping symbols being converted to specific states of symbols they are converted to.

Indeed, each formatting symbol may be distinguished from every other symbol based on both the meaning and value of its attributes. The brightness of a visual symbol may be mapped to the loudness of an audible signal; its color might convert to pitch, the shade to timbre, and its size to cadence. These are maps between *meanings* in each formatting domain. On the other hand, it is not just brightness, the meaning that is mapped to loudness, another meaning. A specific *magnitude* of brightness is also mapped to a specific *magnitude* of loudness. This is a map between *values* of attributes. States are patterns of unsequenced association between attribute values. Format conversion converts not just bare symbols but their states and patterns as well.

These maps are relationships. The relationship between attributes is the *class* of the relationship object, and those between instances of attribute values are *instances* of the *class*. These maps can normalize and represent the extent of our knowledge as well as the extent of our ignorance about format conversion. The state of the class level map between the attribute being represented, as well as the attribute representing it, may be "*do not know*." If this happens, the instance level maps to become "*do not know*." The class level map could also be "*null*"; that is, we know that it does not exist because it is barred, and therefore we know that the instance level maps also cannot be.[12] The state of the class level map may also be constrained by a value constraint to "*Null or Unknown*."[13] When this happens, we do not know if the instance level maps can even *exist*. The same constraints, similarly applied to instance level maps, indicate the extent of our knowledge about conversion between specific states.

This discussion tells us why, when we configure knowledge from knowledge artifacts in an electronic repository, the configuration management software must automatically check for consistency between instance level and class level rules. The software must issue an exception if rules will become inconsistent so that one can make the right amendments to keep knowledge normalized as one adapts software to changing business rules or to align software with new information in new scopes.

**Accuracy of Formats and Encrypted Information:** Symbols carry meaning. Only then are they formats. This meaning is information. If they lose information when one format is converted to another, they will lose some (or all) of their meaning. Remember how meaning was lost in the examples in Chapter II when we divided irreducible facts. In order to preserve the information content of the symbol being converted, the governing rule is: the *degrees of freedom of the essential pattern being converted must not exceed the degrees of freedom of the symbol it is converted to.* Otherwise, meaning will be lost. We will call this the golden rule of encryption. The discussion on information carrying capacity of symbols on page 181 of [337] of Appendix III makes it clear why this must be so. Meaning will be preserved if information is not lost in the conversion of symbols to symbols or meanings to symbols.

An object is a collection of attributes that lend meaning to its state. Attributes have values that instantiate the state. As we have seen in the example above, when one object represents another, we must not only map attributes of the object

*continued on following page*

*Box 4.1. continued*

being represented to those of the object representing it, but also map *values* of attributes of the object being represented to *values* of attributes of the object representing it. Two laws apply to *represent* the relationship between objects—one for mapping the meaning of state and the other for mapping instances of state. This is true for formatting rules, format conversion rules, and rules that impute values to symbols. All these relationships are subtypes of the generic representation relationship. The laws for mapping states of objects to states of the objects that represent them are inherited by each subtype of *represent*.

The generic *Represent* relationship (the relationship class) articulates the fact that an object may represent one or *more* objects and, in turn, be represented by one or *more* objects. There is no injunction against mapping a single state of the object being represented to many states of the object that represents it, *nor is a single state of an object representing another object barred from representing several states of the object(s) it is representing* (see the example in the footnote).[14] This is true for both kinds of maps—the one that maps meanings of attributes, as well as the one that maps instances of states. Ill-considered representations of both kinds can be problematic. When many states represent one state, we might denormalize information and create the very problem we are trying to solve in this book. When one state represents many, we may lose information.

We will lose information when an object with fewer degrees of freedom represents an object with greater degrees of freedom because the object with less information carrying capacity (fewer degrees of freedom) will simply not support the requisite number of states needed to represent all the information that the object it is representing may carry. For example, if we map ratio scaled states to an object with a nominally scaled state space, we will lose information. Nominally scaled states are discrete and cannot represent the continuum of states that a ratio scaled attribute can. As such, some ratio scaled states will be lost.

Objects are patterns, and if the object being represented does not fully use its information carrying capacity to store the essential pattern in it (see The Essence of a Pattern in Chapter IV), we might preserve the meaning of the essential pattern even if we represent it with another pattern with fewer degrees of freedom. We can do this if the degrees of freedom of the essential pattern do not exceed that of the symbol that represents it. For example, in Candu Compoot's story, Candu Compoot could have imputed a score of 1 to a "poor" rating, 2 to "average," and 3 to "good" (see Figure 4.1B). However, the essential pattern in the ratio scaled state space of these scores would remain an ordinally scaled pattern, and it could be mapped back to an ordinally scaled state space without losing its meaning.

Fortunately, there is a simple solution. However, simplicity comes at a price. We will need to sacrifice the set of *all* possible ways one object may represent another and focus on only those conversions that map a single attribute of the object being represented to a single attribute of the object representing it. We will also map a single state of the object being represented to a single state of the object representing it (and thereby sidestep the problem of denormalization).

The metamodel of Proximity Metric in Appendix I can help to identify a subset of objects that can carry *all* information in the objects it is representing and denormalizes none of it. The following rules are based on the information content of the different kinds of patterns we discussed in this chapter:

1. ***Each attribute of the object being represented will map to exactly one attribute of the object that represents it.***
2. ***A single value may not be represented by several values.***
3. ***Multiple discrete values may not be mapped to a single discrete value that subsumes the discrete values mapped into it.***
4. ***Attributes that have a continuum of values may not be mapped to attributes with discrete values.***
5. Ratio scaled attributes must be mapped to ratio scaled attributes only.
6. Difference scaled attributes may be mapped to difference or ratio scaled attributes.
7. Ordinally scaled attributes may be mapped to ratio, difference, or ordinally scaled attributes.
8. Nominally scaled attributes may be mapped to ratio, difference, ordinally, or nominally scaled attributes.

*Rules 1 and 2 ensure that normalized information stays normalized. Rules 3-8 prevent information loss.* We will call the collection of the eight rules above *Rules of Simple Representation*. Rules 5-8 are tabulated as follows. Checked cells in

*continued on following page*

*Box 4.1. continued*

the table indicate that corresponding representations will preserve information. Unchecked cells show which representations may lose information.

| REPRESENTING ATTRIBUTE | REPRESENTED ATTRIBUTE Nominal | Ordinal | Difference Scaled | Ratio Scaled |
|---|---|---|---|---|
| Nominal | ✓ | | | |
| Ordinal | ✓ | ✓ | | |
| Difference Scaled | ✓ | ✓ | ✓ | |
| Ratio Scaled | ✓ | ✓ | ✓ | ✓ |

*Rules 5-8 of Simple Representation*

The internal structure of the symbol, on the right side of Figure B, is a hierarchy like the hierarchy of domains (because information carrying capacity is progressively added as we go down the hierarchy).

*Rules of Simple Representation* always ensure that an object representing another object does not violate the golden rule of encryption. Symbols are objects, and the *Rules of Simple Representation* will apply to formatting symbols. The *Rules of Simple Representation* will ensure that we can convert formats and impute values without losing information. As such, we can encrypt information in a way that will not distort meaning and convert formats without losing information in the conversion. Once the meaning is lost, it cannot be reacquired by merely decoding encrypted information or by converting one symbol to another. Lost information is simply not present in the symbol or object, and one cannot wring blood from stone!

Of course, there may be more complex maps that also preserve meaning, but we have sacrificed them. The *Rules of Simple Representation* listed above will not exhaustively give us *all* possible symbols that have enough degrees of freedom to represent the meaning in an object, but they *will give us only those that do,* and that is often good enough.

However, as we have seen, *Simple Representation* can sometimes exclude some very useful patterns and formats such as arrays that categorize states of objects into categories represented by cells of the array. (Note how Rules 3, 4, and 6 would have excluded the array in Figure 4.6.) Arrays can help us to classify and to recognize complex multidimensional patterns (like object instances, their states, and their histories). When we map object instances into cells of an array, we must abandon the *Rules of Simple Representation.* Each cell of the array may categorize several states of the object that map to it. In contrast, as we will soon see, *Simple Representation* is also not good enough when encryption requirements mandate violation of *Simple Representation* in order to deliberately obfuscate meaning. Here is an example of a complex object that has enough information carrying capacity to represent another but obfuscates meaning and is excluded by the rules of simple representation:

In Candu Compoot's story, we could map a single ordinal attribute, *Concern for Ethical Behavior*, to two ordinal attributes, one nominal attribute and two objects. One object would have two attributes. One attribute would be ordinally scaled and be restricted to only two values: *poor* and *average.* The second attribute would be a nominal *yes*/no attribute that would represent the value *good.* Furthermore, we could add a mutual exclusivity constraint between the value *yes*, of the *yes/no* attribute, and values of the other attribute (via relationships between partitions).

The other object would contain the order of each attribute in the first object. Accordingly, this object will rank *Good* above *Average.*

The ordinally scaled attribute of the first object has ensured that *Poor* and *Average* are mutually exclusive and *Average* is ranked above *Poor.* The constraint between partitions has ensured that *Good, Average*, and *Poor* are mutually exclusive. The second object has established that *Good* is better than *Average* (which has already been established as better than *Poor*). The information on ranks of values has been preserved by this pattern and all three values, *Good, Average*, and *Poor*, would also continue to be mutually exclusive in the resulting pattern.

The original attribute has not lost any information in the translation, but the composite pattern, the object it is translated to, is indeed a complex pattern. It is also clumsy. Regardless of how complex and clumsy it might be, it is a pattern that does not violate the terms of *represent*, the relationship, or the golden rule of encryption. Hence, the model is "correct," if clumsy. It can express *all* the information in the pattern it represents accurately and completely, even if it does not do so simply and elegantly. The Rules of Simple Representation will exclude this configuration of objects.

*continued on following page*

*Box 4.1. continued*

The eight Rules of Simple Representation are often good enough, but they may not be good enough for complex encryption needs. Sometimes, when the need for security is paramount, the requirement might be to deliberately obfuscate meaning, and rules of encryption may be deliberately made commensurately obtuse. Encrypted information may even be deliberately denormalized, and the same information may be represented in different formats in different places and times. Encrypted information may be deliberately fragmented and distributed among multiple objects, some of which are called "keys" to others. The results may be deliberately made complex and clumsy because the purpose of this kind of encryption is not elegance and simplicity. Rather it is obfuscation.

Patterns lose degrees of freedom, and their capacity for representing and conveying meaning as constraints are slapped onto them. No translation, however much it might obfuscate meanings being translated, may violate the golden rule of encryption and still preserve all its original meaning. Appropriately, unrestricted formats must be chosen to represent objects commensurate with their richness of meaning, *the information content*, of the object the format is representing. For example, the full meaning conveyed by a single image of a rich and complex painting by a master artist can never be described by an epiphany of words, whatever its volume, elegance, or scale.

Figure D shows what kind of maps may go between what kinds of states when one object represents another. It articulates the detail behind the *Represent* relationship and demonstrates the polymorphic nature of *represent*.

The broken lined arrow is a value constraint between the information carrying capacities of the object being represented and the object representing it. If we remove the value constraint (or weaken it—say, by limiting the difference between information carrying capacities), representation may still be possible but with less and less precision once the information carrying capacity of the object that is representing the other object falls below that of the object it is representing. If we go on reducing the information carrying capacity of the object that is representing the other object, it will eventually become a mere token for the existence of the object it represents, like the diagramming symbols in this book are only tokens for the meanings you have been studying in it.[15]

In following figure, when the object on the right is a symbol, Figure D will become the metamodel of format—the additional detail behind Figure A. When both objects, that being represented and that representing it, are symbols, Figure D will become the metamodel of format conversion—the additional detail behind Figure B. When only the object on the left is a symbol, Figure D will become the metamodel for imputing values (or objects, as we have been doing in our diagrams) to a symbol. Thus, Figure D captures the polymorphic nature of *represent*.

Different components of knowledge may be "snapped" into place and the behavior of the represent relationship will change commensurately to serve different ends. In the description of Figure D that follows, we will emphasize its role in format conversion, but keep in mind that the same description will apply to its other roles as well, including that as the metamodel for encryption of both symbol and meaning.

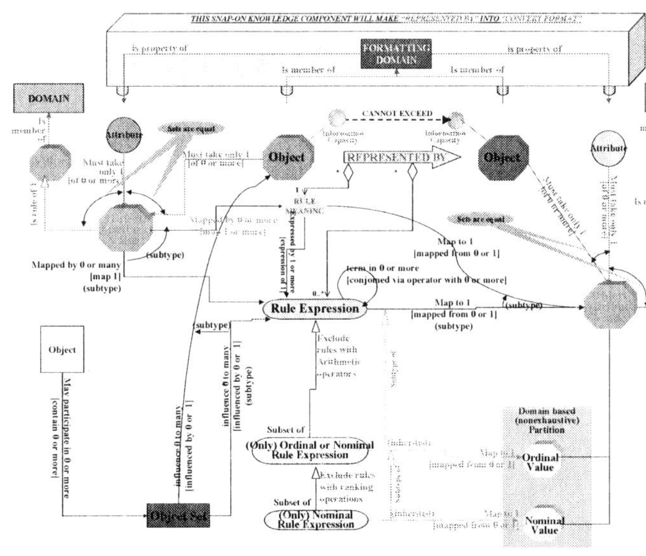


*Figure D. Metamodel of representation*

*Reproduced by permission from Mitra, A., & Gupta, A., Creating Agile Business Systems with Reusable Knowledge, New*

*continued on following page*

*Box 4.1. continued*

*York, NY: Cambridge University Press, 2006.©*

Start at the top left hand corner of Figure D. Attributes may be nominally, ordinally, difference, or ratio scaled. We understood how symbols inherit attributes from formatting domains early on in this chapter. Formatting attributes are attributes of the formatting symbol.[16] The object labeled *Object Attribute Value* in Figure D is the value of an attribute (at a given moment in time) of a specific object. If the object is a symbol, the attribute value is a property of its formatting domain. The attribute is the meaning of the property, and the value is an instance of the property. For example, if the object is a tone, the attribute may be the pitch of the tone. A tone is an audio symbol and pitch is its attribute.

The three relationships shown separately between *Object Attribute Value* and *Object*, *Attribute*, and *Value* are intrinsically a part of a single atomic rule, a three way relationship represented by *Object Attribute Value*. The three relationships are inseparable. The equality constraint between the three represents their inseparability. (We will understand that *Object Attribute Value* is a kind of relationship between an *attribute*, an *object*, and a *value* in a domain of meaning.)

A characteristic of the object being translated may map to one or more characteristics of the object it is translated to. For instance, the loudness of a tone may map to the brightness of an image, and pitch might map to color. This mapping may be mediated by a rule expression. The rule expression is not a meaning; it is a formula or procedure, the expression of a meaning. The meaning may be expressed in several equivalent ways (see the examples in Box 5.1).

Figure D makes this clear. Each map has a meaning. It is this meaning that makes it unique. Different maps with the same meaning may employ different rule expressions to mediate between objects, but these maps will always be equivalent; the results will be identical.

Consider the relationship between the object being represented and the meaning of the rule that represents it. Naturally, an object may or may not be represented by another object, and if it is, several may represent it (although this will denormalize its meaning). Each such map between source and target attribute values will have a different meaning in terms of the *identity of the meaning* of the *Represented by* relationship between these attribute values. The relationship between the object being represented and *Rule Meaning* in Figure D articulates this in terms of its cardinality ratio.

Indeed, close inspection of Figure D, from the *Object Attribute Value* on the righthand side of Figure D to that on the lefthand side of the figure, across *Rule Meaning*, shows that the map is between source and target *Object Attribute Values*. Each is a conjunction of an object, an attribute, and a value, and it is possible for a given attribute value of one object to map to several states of another object or even several states of *several* other objects—inelegant and complex?—Difficult, but possible?—Yes, certainly. Note that the *Rules of Simple Representation* would not permit this. As an exercise for interested readers, what alterations would you have to make to the model in Figure D to support only Simple Representation? Can these relationships and cardinality ratios be considered "snap-on" components and another polymorph of *represent*?

When considering arrays, the represent relationship in Figure D also implies that a cell of an array may map to cells of other arrays of different dimensions. For example, we could "unfold" the array in Figure 4.6 and map every cell in it to a cell of a one-dimensional array or a position on a line. The opposite is also supported by the metamodel in Figure D. Cells of an array with more dimensions could represent cells of an array with fewer dimensions.

The inverse of the relationship between *Object Attribute Value* and *Rule Meaning* is less intuitive. It asserts that each *Rule Meaning* may represent more than one *Object Attribute Value*. To see the truth of that assertion, consider the three dimensional array of Figure 4.6. Each time slice was a region in the object's state space and represented a continuum—an infinitude—of moments in time. It was an example of how several attribute values may be represented by a single attribute value, the *identity* of the time slice. Figure D also articulates the possibility of attribute values of different objects mapping to a single attribute value of a third object. This value subsumes (serves as a common category) for all attribute values that map to it. *Rules of Simple Representation* would not permit this either (an exercise for readers: what changes to Figure D would prevent this?).

The relationship between *Rule Meaning* and *Object Attribute Value*, in conjunction with that between *Rule Meaning* and *Rule Expression*, *implies* the relationship between *Object Attribute Value* and *Rule Expression*. This implied relationship does not stand on its own. It is a *subtype* of the relationship between *Object Attribute Value* and *Rule Meaning*—one that only adds information about the specific formula or algorithm (of perhaps several) that *implements* the *Rule Meaning.*[17]

Should we have included *exclude* in Figure D? Can the *absence* of a symbol imply the *presence* of a meaning—or can the absence of one object imply the presence of another? Yes, it certainly can. If a partition with two subtypes is exhaustive and instances of one subtype are missing, it implies that instances of the other exist. However, we can articulate the

*continued on following page*

*Box 4.1. continued*

same rule more intuitively, with greater simplicity and elegance, if we articulate exhaustivity and mutual exclusion at the object class level, just as we have done with partitions. It is therefore okay to exclude *exclude* from the relationship in Figure D. We have other means for inferring the presence of a value from the absence of another.

The Object Set in the left bottom corner of Figure D adds a different dimension to the polymorphism of *represent*. The rule meaning (and by implication the rule expression) may depend on the objects in *Object Set*, as well as their interactions and states. Indeed, the object set may contain object states, interactions (relationships) between states, regions of state space, interactions between regions, and even between specific states and specific regions of state space. In *Object Set*, specific states and regions of state space may be represented by subtypes of objects classes that satisfy those criteria and their interactions by relationships between these subtypes. We have discussed some examples of this kind of polymorphic behavior earlier in this box and demonstrated how *Object Set* normalizes complex rules of representation.

Figure D describes the structure of the Represent relationship. There can be several subtypes of the rule expression in Figure D, and each will give rise to a different kind of representation, a polymorphism. The Object Set in Figure D shows that representation may be context sensitive because other objects in the environment may influence the representation.

It is worth noting that maps between attributes and states that instantiate the metamodel in Figure D may be between like domains as well as between unlike domains. For example, a tone may be mapped to an identical but louder tone. This kind of format translation is the reusable component that supports the common act of adjusting the volume of an audio signal—something we do so often that we rarely even think about it. It is a translation between like formatting domains—audio domain to audio domain.

*When it maps meanings to symbols, turning them into formats or converting one format to another, Figure D becomes a context sensitive bridge—a polymorphic transform—that takes us from the world of business meaning to the universe of supporting information systems. It is then a bridge from the Business Rules layer to the Interface Rules layer in the architecture of Knowledge* (Figure 3.4).

**Formatting Constraints:** Formats may be constrained in four basic ways:

- States of symbols may be constrained: This amounts to attaching a value constraint to Attribute Value or, when the constraint is generic to all attributes in that domain, by attaching the Value Constraint directly to the domain. When several values are constrained, the constraint on *State* is merely a collection of *Attribute Value Constraints* attached to various attributes of the format. Second order constraints may involve attaching value constraints to bounds and other parameters of Value Constraint, as well as to members of Object Set in Figure D.
- By constraining symbols that may express value(s): This constraint would go to the heart of Format—its instance identifier. Symbols may be barred or made mandatory by attaching inclusion or exclusion constraints that limit the kinds of instance identifiers that are permitted for qualified formats. This is merely a special case, a subtype, of the constraint on the state of a symbol. The type of symbol is also an indicator of state.
- By constraining formatting domains that may express value(s): This constraint would go to the heart of *Formatting Domain*—its type. Domains may be barred or made mandatory by attaching inclusion or exclusion constraints that limit the kinds of states that are permitted for qualified formats. Naturally, if the Domain itself is barred, so are all symbols that map to it.
- By constraining one or more emergent properties of *Format*, the pattern: This can limit multiplicity of occurrence, size, dimensionality, delimitation, various statistical properties like variability, similarity, direction, and others we have discussed under the architecture of patterns.

Where values have been imputed to symbols, formatting constraints may even be defined by attaching inclusion and exclusion constraints to imputed values. These constraints may determine permitted, mandatory, and impermissible symbols (for example, in a cipher).

### Attaching Value Constraints to Format

Basic Formatting Constraints 1 and 2 are constraints on constituents of symbols or objects that influence them (i.e., members of *Object Set* of Figure D). Value Constraints may be attached to states of the object being formatted, as well

*continued on following page*

*Box 4.1. continued*

as to the symbol formatting it. We have seen several examples earlier in this box and Basic Formatting Constraints 1 and 2 need no further elaboration. Basic Formatting Constraint 3 describes constraints attached to formatting domains and inherited by all objects that have attributes that map to the constrained domain.

All symbols exist in physical space-time. Nature constrains physical space-time to a maximum of three spatial dimensions and one time dimension. The dimensionality of a pattern is an emergent property (see the architecture of Pattern in this chapter and its metamodel in Appendix I, Figures I.2 and I.3). *Pattern in Physical Space-Time* is a subtype of *Pattern* and symbols are patterns in physical space and time. The dimensionality of such patterns is limited to a maximum of four—three for space and one for time. This constraint is dictated by the metamodel of *Pattern* in Appendix I, Figure I.2.

Physical space and time are examples of a natural constraint on an emergent property of *all* formatting domains. As was discussed under patterns, physical space is a pattern of unsequenced association. It consists of the length domain, repeated one, two, or three times. Thus, physical space is a *list* of length domains. The multiplicity of Occurrence (Occurrence Value) of the Length domain in this list is limited to three (see Appendix I, Figure I.2) because nature has decreed that physical space cannot exceed three spatial dimensions. Similarly, physical space-time, within which all symbols (and hence formats) are expressed, is a pattern of unsequenced association of four domains. It too is a list, in which the length domain is constrained to three occurrences and the time domain to one occurrence. These are examples of how constraints may be attached to emergent properties of patterns in the metamodel of knowledge.

Some constraints exist in only specific perspective(s) and others in the Universal Perspective (Mitra & Gupta, 2005). In a repository of Knowledge Artifacts, perspectives may be subtypes of similar perspectives that do not have these constraints. Remember the principle of subtyping by *adding* information. Each constraint is an item of information. Indeed, every component is an item of information. Adding a component to a perspective makes it a subtype of the perspective it was added to. Thus, perspectives themselves can be reusable models. The Universal Perspective is at the top of this hierarchy and contains only universal constraints.

The value constraint attached to the Length domain and the dimensional limitation on physical space and space-time are examples of constraints that reside in the Universal Perspective. Other perspectives inherit the rule from the Universal Perspective. That all symbols must have one to three spatial dimensions and at most one temporal dimension is a constraint on *Formatting Domain*. It is dictated by the metamodel of Pattern and resides in the Universal Perspective. Therefore, it is inherited by every format, every perceptible symbol, in every perspective.

Appendix I, Figures I.2 and I.3 describe the emergent properties of patterns. Let us examine what constraints on each emergent property of *format*, the pattern imply. Constraints on dimensions, direction, extent, and information carrying capacities of formats are experienced most frequently.

**Constraints on Dimensionality of a Symbol's State Space:**

Dimensionality of state space is the number of attributes in our model that describe the state of the object. An object is a pattern and so is a symbol. Value constraints on the dimensionality of a pattern limit the number of attributes we may consider in determining the state of the object or symbol. We have discussed dimensionality of state space at length and have just discussed, with examples, how dimensionality of physical space is naturally constrained and how dimensionality of state space may be constrained by technology. We have also seen where to attach these constraints to normalize this knowledge.

**Constraints on Dimensionality of a Symbol:**

Naturally, the dimensionality of a pattern may not exceed that of the space that holds it. The metamodel of pattern in Appendix I, Figures I.2 and I.3 also make this clear. This atomic rule is the most fundamental value constraint on the dimensionality patterns in general and, specifically, on the dimensionality of formatting symbols in physical space. It is also true in state space. We have just discussed how constraints on dimensionality are imposed by business process automation. Have you ever wished for the kind of display device Candu Compoot showed Count Albeans in Candu Compoot's story? Not only may value constraints limit the dimensionality of symbols, but they may also bar the existence of the time

*continued on following page*

*Box 4.1. continued*

dimension in a format. A constraint that bars the time dimension in a visual (graphic) format makes a still picture—a snapshot at a moment in time of the object being represented. Similarly, barring the time dimension in other formatting domains bars change and movement over time.[18]

Now let us consider a nonspatial, nontemporal dimension of state space for a visual symbol. Constraining the range of colors to black and white will create a black and white image. Unlike the constraint that froze the flow of time by barring an entire dimension, this is a constraint on *values*, not on the *existence* of color, a dimension of state space. If there is no color, there is no vision. Some formatting domains cannot exist without certain sensory attributes because it is those attributes that define them. The existence of these attributes is the basis for distinguishing them as special subtypes of the general formatting domain. We cannot constrain the existence of these dimensions (i.e., constrain their values to equal "null") without losing the domain and driving all states of symbols in it to "null."

Process automation may force constraints like these on states of formats and even formatting of domains. Consider an example that drives home the point so obviously that it might be considered even ridiculously obvious by some—a voice synthesizer cannot support color and therefore cannot support visual formatting domains. The constraint may be obvious to people but must be made explicit to automation by explicitly stating it in the metamodel. Only then will automated intelligent agents[19] be able to link meaning to format in business process designs they generate in different technology environments.

New attributes literally add new dimensions to our presentation of symbols. For example, in the visual formatting dimension, color is an attribute and a dimension added to the three spatial and one temporal dimension. We have discussed color but not all its attributes like brightness and shade. Both the hue and brightness of a color convey information through our sense of sight and hence are attributes of visual domains.

Indeed, color is a subjective sensation, as are attributes of all formatting domains. Some of these sensations form the basis of the domain and cannot be constrained without losing the meaning of the domain itself and hence all symbols in it, while others can be constrained and will only constrain our perceptions of those symbols. Constrained symbols will lose some variety and may become less "rich" in terms of their perceived properties but will continue to be perceived.

Color has three dimensions.[20]

- Hue – the kind of color it is (e.g., red, yellow, blue, green, etc.).
- Brightness – how luminous or light the color is.
- Purity – The shade or strength of the color in proportion to its brightness, also called its saturation, "richness," or "colorfulness" (see Appendix II on dimensions of color).

Subjective sensations cannot, strictly speaking, be "measured," but they can be described. It is the *meaning* of these descriptions that are the basis for states of symbols—meanings such as hue, its purity, and brightness that are dimensions of state space.

Indeed, the subjective sensation of color is even impacted by other colors near it. The same color looks different against different backgrounds.[21] When we discuss color or, for that matter, *any property of a perceptible symbol*, it is not the physical measurement that we mean (like the wavelength of light or the amplitude of a sound wave) but rather a description of the subjective sensation.

The dimensionality of a symbol in state space is defined by how much values of these descriptive attributes can change independently of others. For example, brightness is a dimension in state space for visual symbols. Even if value constraints limit the brightness of an image to a narrow band, the image will still extend a little in the brightness dimension, but if a value constraint freezes brightness to a single value, then the symbol will not extend at all in that dimension of state space. In such a case, the *symbol* (not its state space) would lose that dimension. The symbol would continue to exist in a seven dimensional space that has three spatial, three visual, and one temporal dimension, but the symbol itself would lose one visual dimension, brightness, because its brightness cannot change (remember how cross sections of arrays lost dimensions—see the discussion on arrays under Patterns in this chapter).

Similarly, if brightness and hue were related so that the brightness of the image was exactly determined by its hue, the symbol would lose a dimension. Its shape would be a subspace that tilts or curves with respect to both the hue and brightness axis (like a tilted, curved, or twisted two-dimensional surface in three-dimensional space; the exact shape will

*continued on following page*

*Box 4.1. continued*

depend on the exact relationship between hue and brightness). This concept of dimensionality in state space applies not only to visual symbols, but also to any formatting domain and indeed any object. The number of attributes determines the dimensionality of its state space. The dimensionality of a symbol is determined by constraints on its states and those of its constituents. Each value constraint, that defines the value of an attribute exactly, reduces the dimensionality of the symbol (or the lawful state space of an object) by one dimension.

**Constraints on Directions:**

A dimension in state space is a direction. A direction in state space can also involve several dimensions. Directions in state space are described by a coordinate system.[22] Relative locations of a *set* of attribute values, compared with another *set* of attribute values, establish the twin concepts of direction and proximity in state space. A direction in state space represents possible sets of interactions between sets of attribute values. Constraints on these interactions can constrain the extent of state space in these directions.

The discussion on patterns emphasizes that the direction of a pattern has meaning only in the context of its directional attributes. Patterns may be constrained differently in different directions in state space and symbols and formats may too. Moreover, the meaning of the constraint will depend on the attribute in question. Therefore, constraints on directions are best discussed separately under each directional attribute as follows:

**Constraints on Extent:**

Extent describes the size and shape of a *region* of state space (see Appendix I, Figure I.2). Constraints on Extent limit the shape and size of the region. This translates to limiting the scope and size of the format. The extent of the pattern *being mapped* determines the *scope* of the object being represented by the format, the extent of *the pattern it is mapped to*, and the *size* of the symbol that represents it. One can visualize this in physical space and time; therefore, clarity will be best served by considering the meaning of extent in physical space first.

Consider an object, any object in physical space that is represented by another. Say, a home that the owner wishes to sell. The owner can post an image of the home on a Web page to advertise the home. The home will be represented by its image, a format, on a Web page. The picture may include only the building, or its extent may be increased to cover the yard or even the immediate neighborhood. This is the extent of the object being mapped. It can be different in different directions. For example, the roof may be cut off, but the picture might include the playground next to the home. These are different ways in which the extent of the scene being mapped to the image may be curtailed in different directions. This kind of limitation on the scope of the format is a set of value constraints attached to the extent, in different directions, of the object being formatted.

In addition to the scope of the format, the format too has an extent that may be different from the object it formats. In the example above, the image extends in different directions on the screen. Its size in any given direction represents the extent of the image in that direction. This is quite different from its scope. The scope of the image is the extent of the object it is formatting. The size of the image (possibly framed differently in different directions) is the extent of the *image*, a format, not its scope. The image of the home may even be projected onto a screen in different sizes. The extent of the image, a format, is different in each projection. The size of the image, the space it occupies, may be limited by different value constraints in different directions, just as its scope was. This kind of limitation on the size of the format is a set of value constraints attached to the extent, in different directions, of the format—the symbol a formatted object is mapped to.

- In terms of components and structures of knowledge, Value Constraints are components, and the size is a set of value constraints on the extent of the format. Contrast these value constraints with those that determined the scope of the format: the constraints we have just discussed are attached to the extent of the *format*, the symbol, not the extent of the object being formatted. The value constraints that determined the scope of the format were attached to the extent of the *object being formatted*, not the symbol formatting it.
- Accordingly, where a Value Constraint is attached, it determines the behavior of *Format*. The same Value Constraint

*continued on following page*

*Box 4.1. continued*

attached to a different component results in different behavior and different atomic rules.

- This is another example of how components of knowledge are meanings that engage each other like gears in a machine to produce new meanings. These meanings are subassemblies of knowledge, which, in turn, are also components of knowledge that can engage other components. The metamodel of knowledge contains components that will help normalize other knowledge.

We could reduce or enlarge the extent of symbols in space. The extent of the format will change, but not the amount of information it conveys. Thus, reduction or enlargement of an image is an operation on the spatial extent of a format. The formatting domain normalizes it.

Changing the spatial extent of a symbol is not restricted to visual domains. It is generic to all formatting domains because formatting symbols must occupy space and exist in time. The extent of an audible tone, an audible symbol, may be limited in space without necessarily limiting its loudness in the space it is confined to; for example, with soundproof barriers or electronic sound cancellation devices.

Consider how the extent of a format may be limited in time. The scope of a moving picture in a documentary film is limited by both the space and the time span it covers. Speeding up or showing a film in fast or slow motion (without editing it) preserves the extent of the scene that was filmed in both space and time but changes the extent of its format, the moving image, in time. The movie becomes longer or shorter (but does not lose any information). As such, in physical space and time, the extent of the format translates to size, whereas the extent of the object represented by the format translates to scope, and value constraints may limit either item.

Based on this understanding, consider nonphysical directions in state space. Let us start by considering the extent of a written word. The word occupies space on the page it is printed on. It is a two-dimensional pattern in physical space and we have seen how its extent in physical space may be constrained by value constraints. Physical space is only a part (subspace) of its state space. In state space, the word has more dimensions. One of these is a nominal dimension. This dimension contains the set of letters that make words. Each letter is a point in this nominally scaled dimension. Constraining this set by excluding some letters (points) on this nominally scaled axis of state space would curtail the spellings and existence of words. Exclusion constraints are one kind of value constraint. Hence, the "size" of words in terms of the diversity of letters in their spelling would be curbed by value constraints in this "direction" of state space.

This kind of constraint must be considered when formatting words in Chinese. The character set the language may potentially use is enormous, and in the days when mechanical typewriters were used, typewriters would come with a partial character set, that customers could replace as needed with additional characters. The customers' choices of "typewriter technology" constrained the choice, that is, extent of words in this alphabet dimension of state space.

A word is a sequence of letters. It is not merely the occurrence of the letter in the word but also the position of a letter in it that spells the word. The spelling of the word is the pattern that defines it. Hence, in addition to its spatial dimensions and permitted character set, the word has another dimension—the location of a letter in terms of its serial number in the word.

Truncation:

Let us assume a mapping rule like that in Figure B is translating a word—mapping it back to the same state space. An upper bound on this serial number dimension, applied to words being mapped, will curb its extent along this dimension and truncate it. Applied to the format it is being mapped to, it might make it impossible to map long words that exceed this upper bound (unless the mapping rule maps several positions of letters in the word being converted to fewer positions in the word it is converted to and loses information. The mapping rule could also use more symbols. The additional symbols could be codes for letters in positions that had to be truncated. Thus, a translation rule could increase the extent of one dimension when another is curbed in order to preserve information carrying capacity of formats.)

Remember that the extent of a pattern is along a direction, and directions may be straight and simple or complex and convoluted. There is no rule in the metamodel of pattern that bars us from considering the extent of a pattern along *any* trajectory in state space, unless we explicitly formulate rules that ban paths or positions in state space. Remember how even circular trajectories were considered in Figure 4.4.[23] However, a detailed discussion of the topology of state space is beyond the scope of this book.[24]

*continued on following page*

*Box 4.1. continued*

**Delimited Extent and Constraints on Delimiters:**

We have seen how one pattern may delimit another. If one symbol delimits another, they may not overlap because the delimiting symbol delimits the extent of the symbol it delimits (in one or more directions in state space). Symbols that do not delimit the other could overlap; that is, they could occupy overlapping regions of state space and even have common constituents in state space (see the overlapping trapezoids in Figure 5.9). On the other hand, the letters on these words you are reading cannot overlap. Each letter is not only a pattern and a symbol but also a delimiter for others of its kind. Constraints on delimiters may limit their identity or states. Invisible paragraph marks in Microsoft Word documents delimit paragraphs; their identity and their state are both determined by value constraints. The identity is determined by a value constraint that forces it to be a paragraph mark (Basic Formatting Constraint 2, discussed previously), while the state is determined by value constraints on attributes that hide it or make it visible (Basic Formatting Constraint 3, discussed previously).

Delimiters of the object being formatted (or represented) determine the scope of the format or representation (i.e., the mapped extent of the object), and delimiters in the format determine the extent of the format. For instance, the frame of the scanning surface on a copying machine delimits the area that will be scanned, whereas the edges of the paper in the paper tray delimit the extent of the copy.

**Constraints on Information Carrying Capacity (Degrees of Freedom):**

Consider the image of the home in the example above. Increasing or decreasing its extent in physical space conserved the information in it. Curbs on the extent of the object being represented (the home and its environment) limited the information content of the object being mapped, but once the scope was set, it did not matter if we reduced or increased the size of the image. The detail in the image was not lost. It might have become too small to see in a reduced image, but if our vision had been acute enough, we could have picked it out. It would still be present in the picture. On the other hand, magnifying the picture would not add any missing detail to it. Overall, the information content of the format did not depend on the extent (it *did*, however, depend on the scope, i.e., extent of the object being mapped) of the format.

However, had the image been made of pixels on a screen or a half tone print that consisted of closely packed printed dots like the pixels on a screen, its information carrying capacity would be limited by the size and density of pixels (or dots). A blurred or grainy picture carries less detail, and hence less information than a sharp picture. Value constraints on the information carrying capacity of the format (or its degrees of freedom, i.e., permitted states) would constrain its fidelity. Indeed, unlike a conventional photograph, when holographic film is sliced (truncated), the hologram does not lose extent; it loses fidelity instead. It blurs and loses resolution. The extent of the image stays the same. Information carrying capacity only depends on number of permissible states of an object. It is distinct and different from *extent* and the other emergent properties of patterns but depend on *extent* and the other emergent properties to the extent that curbs on them limit the *number* (or cardinality—see the footnote[25]) of lawful states of the symbol (or object).

The same arguments will hold for the fidelity of a format in any formatting domain. We experience this firsthand when converting music from one electronic format to another. Indeed, fidelity may even change with position or direction. Have you ever compared the fidelity of music that you hear at the side of a speaker with that in front of it?

The fidelity of the format[26] may be better in some directions of state space than in others. Our vision is most acute directly in front of our eyes, whereas we can barely make out detail at the periphery of our vision (the "corner" of our eyes). There is even a blind spot in our field of vision. The information carrying capacity at the blind spot is zero; we cannot perceive objects in our blind spot. In general, patterns may be divided into constituent patterns based on regions in state space (regions may also be subspaces), and each constituent may possess a different information carrying capacity. If its constituents do not interact (mutually constrain each other), the information carrying capacity of the pattern will be the sum of the capacities of its constituents. (Readers interested in more information may see Appendix II on the measure of information.)

*continued on following page*

*Box 4.1. continued*

**Constraints on Location and Proximity:**

A pattern's Law of Location is a constraint on location; it is also fundamental to the existence of a pattern. Any value constraint on the coordinates of a symbol in state space (or physical space and time) is a constraint on location. Confining a footnote to the bottom of this page is a constraint on its location. Constraints on location may be in terms of displacement of objects from the origin of a coordinate system or in terms of their proximity to other constituents of *Pattern*. A format is a pattern (Appendix I, Figures I.2 and I.3).

Constraints on proximity metrics also constrain location—location relative to other constituents or symbols. Proximity in state space is a measure of similarity. Value constraints on proximity metrics limit the similarity or diversity of a pattern's constituents; they make the pattern more or less homogenous (or heterogeneous). For example, a constraint on the pitch of syllables in a spoken word ensures that the word is expressed in a male voice. The syllables are constrained to be similar in pitch. Constraints on proximity metrics may also affect how close or far a pattern's constituents may be in physical space and time, and formats are exactly this kind of perceptible pattern. A proximity constraint may limit the space between characters of a one-dimensional string of characters or the distance between dots in a two-dimensional half tone print or even that between pixels on a screen. Such a constraint determines both the homogeneity (and heterogeneity) of the constituents of a symbol, as well as, in physical space-time, how tightly (or loosely) a pattern is clustered.

Limiting the extent of state space also limits the proximity of a pattern's constituents. However, constraints on proximity metrics contribute additional information because they limit proximities of a pattern's constituents not only in the context of extent but also in ways that extent cannot: The extent of a pattern determines its scope in state space whereas constraints on proximity limit how much of its extent are actually occupied by a pattern's constituents and how much is "white space" or empty.

For example, the "tightness" of clusters of constituents in a pattern may be enhanced by imposing an upper bound on proximity metrics between *constituents* within a cluster. Clusters may also be made more distinct by imposing a lower bound on the mutual proximity between *clusters* (not constituents of clusters) in the pattern. Consider a screen that shows the status of workstations on the shop floor of a factory. A design standard might mandate that the hue of all exceptions be displayed in red, all normal statuses be green, and the status of workstations under maintenance be yellow. Further, the standard might articulate permitted ranges of brightness and saturation of each color. The standard is based on clusters in state space (as we have seen earlier in this box, color contributes three dimensions to state space). The standard does this by articulating constraints on proximity of permitted colors to standard colors in each cluster.

**Constraints on Aggregation Statistics:**

Emergent statistical properties are properties of patterns that emerge from higher degree or higher order relationships between properties (see Figure B of Box 5.1) or between a pattern's constituents and the pattern itself. You could consider the messages in a voice mailbox a pattern and individual messages its constituents. The total length of a set of messages in a voice mailbox is the sum of lengths of individual messages. The total length of messages is a property of the pattern that emerges from individual lengths of the constituents of the pattern.

Technology might dictate a limit on the total length of messages stored in the voice mailbox. The messages are perceptible symbols. This makes a voice mailbox a part of business process automation. The rule of information staging belongs to the Information Logistics layer of Figure 3.4. This rule is a value constraint attached to an emergent property of a pattern—the aggregation of voice mail messages. These messages are in audio formats. We will elaborate on emergent properties of aggregate objects later in the book.

**Constraints on Object Occurrence Value:**

We have discussed this with examples in our discussion of object sets in Figure A of this box. Therefore, occurrence constraints need no further elaboration. Indeed, it is worth noting that an exclusion constraint is also a constraint on occurrence, a subtype in which the Object Occurrence Value is constrained to zero.

*continued on following page*

*Box 4.1. continued*

**Inclusion and Exclusion Constraints:**

Convention, technology, the need for security and whims of individuals designing business tasks may be some of the reasons for inclusion and exclusion constraints on *format*. We have discussed inclusion and exclusion constraints briefly in Chapter IV and in our discussion of polymorphism and business process automation in this box.[27]

**Constraints on Association and Sequence:**

Consider the diversity of conventions in different languages that express the same ideas. There are bewilderingly different ways of associating and sequencing letters, words, sentences, verbs, subjects, and objects in languages across the globe, many of which have been incubated in the cradles of diverse and different civilizations. Letters and words of Indo-European languages are arranged left to right. Arabic is a right to left sequence. Chinese goes from top to bottom. These are one-dimensional sequences of symbols in two-dimensional physical space—the plane of the paper.[28]

Sequences in nonphysical directions of state space also differ—directions like those that dictate the sequence of components of a sentence (see the ordinal dimension described under constraints on extent). Expressions in English have a subject, usually a noun or pronoun, followed by a verb, the format for an action, followed by the predicate, another noun or pronoun; this is similar to the infix notation described in Appendix II under the Theory of Categories. Indeed, the metamodel in this book follows this convention. Hindi, the language of Northern India, on the other hand, positions the verb at the end of a sentence. These language conventions are constraints on sequences of symbols that express ideas. Translating one language to another requires not only translation of symbols, but also one sequence of symbols to another. Even conventions on arrangements of alphabets differ between languages. Arabic and the European languages arrange their alphabets in a one-dimensional sequence, whereas many languages of India arrange their alphabet in a two-dimensional sequence on a matrix.

Rules may force symmetry or lack of it in formatting symbols and patterns. Like exclusion and inclusion constraints, constraints on association flow from convention, technology, the need for security and encryption, or even whims of individuals designing business tasks. Sequence and symmetry go hand in hand. Sequence signifies asymmetry, when the order of association, not the mere fact of association, matters. Lack of sequence is symmetry, when mere association, not sequences, matters. We have discussed this aspect under Patterns in this chapter; see the discussion on how symbols that do not distinguish their identity based on mirror images are laterally unsequenced patterns. Sequences give us information by distinguishing between different states of association involving the same objects. Sequenced patterns, be they meanings or formats, have more information carrying capacity than unsequenced patterns.

**Constraints on Order:**

Constraints on order of formats are rare, but given the architecture of Pattern, they are possible. We will not elaborate further on this. It will suffice that readers understand that the metamodel of knowledge has room for these constraints although they are not used often.

**Closing Remarks on Formatting Constraints:**

Usually, it is Business Process Automation and limitations of technology that are at the root of formatting constraints. All physical devices have engineering limitations that limit the scale and precision with which they can express meanings. These translate into constraints on extent and fidelity of the format. Technology may also impose constraints on states of formats. A black and white display device might exclude all colors but black and white. Color, as we have seen, is a state of *Visual Symbol*. A ticker tape may force all information to be displayed in a one-dimensional string of characters such as numbers and words. Value constraints attached to key states of the visual domain can reduce a format to a ticker tape. A device like a speaker will exclude the entire visual formatting domain. In this case, the physical device would be the

*continued on following page*

*Box 4.1. continued*

reason for an exclusion constraint that goes to the very heart of the formatting domain—the domain identifier itself.

Constraints on formats may also flow from convention. Under Patterns, we discussed how convention bars mixing of Roman and Arabic numerals in a number. These are exclusion constraints that go to the heart of the symbol—its identifier. Languages also constrain formats in terms of sequences of symbols in state space and, of course, the symbols themselves, a nominally scaled dimension of state space.

Conspicuous by their absence in this discussion on formatting constraints, have been issues related to rounding of numbers. The rules for rounding numbers are not normalized by *Format*. Rather they are normalized by measures. Mea-

*Box 4.2. Domain analysis and primary physical domains*

Engineers call the fundamental physical domains fundamental dimensions, and the study of domains that emerge from relationships between them, Dimensional Analysis.

Dimensional Analysis is based on the premise that a few fundamental physical concepts such as space, time, mass, and temperature lie at the heart of all physics. Quantified measures of the huge diversity of apparently unconnected physical phenomena can be reduced to combinations of the few fundamental physical measures (of the fundamental concepts) at the heart of all observable phenomena.

These fundamental quantities, or dimensions, are the foundation and fabric of all other physical quantities and their measures. Velocity is distance moved per unit time, and the unit of velocity is units of length combined with units of time (via the division operator). Mathematically, the unit of velocity, in terms of length and time is $LT^{-1}$ (the negative power implies division) where L is the unit of length, and T is the unit of time.[30] We call these quantities domains, instead of dimensions, in this book.

The choice of which physical quantities are termed fundamental is largely a measure of preference; the mathematical basis for this assertion is provided by the Buckingham Pi theorem.[31] We could have considered velocity a fundamental domain; had we done so, we would have had to either drop time or distance from the class of fundamental domains. This is because time may be expressed in terms of velocity and length (mathematically, $T=LV^{-1}$, where V is the unit of velocity), and length may be expressed in terms of time and velocity ($L=VT$). As such, if we promoted a secondary domain like velocity into the class of fundamental domains, we would have to exchange it with a fundamental domain that it was related to (either length or time). The domain we exchanged would have to be demoted to a secondary domain and the number of fundamental domains would stay the same. The freedom to pick fundamental domains is ours, but not the freedom to keep them. We can pick, only if we are willing to sacrifice related fundamental domains.[32]

The fact that the fundamental domains are limited to a fixed number is related to information content. Whenever a physical phenomenon is observed, it conveys information. The information content of the observed phenomenon (velocity or movement in the example above) reuses the information conveyed by one or more fundamental domains and adds to it. The added information, a meaning, is the glue that glues together fundamental domains of information, pure meanings. This glue is a relationship. The relationship may be a joint constraint—even a magnitude constraint.

The resultant is greater than its parts; this is a new atomic rule. The new rule cannot be inferred by considering each part separately; if we did that, we would ignore the meaning of their relationship. As such, a relationship engages the irreducible facts in fundamental domains to produce a new irreducible fact—the new phenomenon or physical law. Information about constituent units is normalized in the fundamental domain, and added information, the "glue," is normalized by the relationship. When the relationship is a magnitude constraint, it is called a physical "law."

Fundamental domains are sometimes termed *primary* or *base* domains and the derived domains are called *secondary* or *derived* domains. This system, whereby base domains are glued together to produce secondary domains, is called a *coherent system of measurement*[33].

In 1954, at the *Tenth General Conference on Weights and Measures*, it was agreed that length, mass, time duration, temperature, and either electric charge or electric current would be considered primary domains. (Electric current is the flow rate of electric charge, and hence the two are related, and only one of them can serve as a member of the exclusive club of primary domains.)

*continued on following page*

*Box 4.2. continued*

Physicists accept that there are four fundamental forces that shape all physical phenomena, namely, electromagnetism (represented by electric charge), gravitation (represented by mass), the strong force, and the weak force (not represented in the list of primary domains).[34] Given today's state-of-the-art in the engineering of hard products, of the four fundamental forces, engineering systems need only consider mass and electromagnetism. That is why the strong and weak forces are not represented in the list of primary physical domains. In some unimaginably far off future, we will have to include them in the list as well. Measures of all other physical phenomena such as magnetic fields, energy, and color can, in theory, be assembled from combinations of measures of primary domains.

The physical world frames information systems and business processes. Therefore, information systems and business processes must align with the physical world. For this reason, the primary domains that frame the physical world of engineering must form the basis of primary domains of components of knowledge about it. Although the list of physical primary domains published in 1954 must *frame* the world of information systems, it does not have to be *identical* with the list of primary domains that best normalize knowledge.

The list of 1954 was tailored to support physics and "hard" engineering based on the principles of physics. Among the primary domains published in 1954, temperature is related to the rate at which the energy of a physical system changes with respect to entropy (see *Thermodynamics*, Macropedia, Volume 28, page 616 of The New Encyclopedia Britannica, 15th Edition, 1988).

Entropy is a measure of orderliness, or information content of the system (see Entropy and Information Theory in Appendix II, Shannon's Information Theory). Engineering of business processes from business knowledge components is not physics, nor is knowledge a "hard" product. When we engineer knowledge, the concept of temperature is less useful as a primary domain. Knowledge is a configuration of meaning, and it is more convenient to configure meaning if we consider information primary, not temperature. We do this by substituting temperature with information in our list of primary domains. Temperature then becomes a secondary measure, derived by combining the measure of energy (units of energy are derived from mass, length, and time domains[35]) with the measure of information. Information lets us build hierarchies based on information content and adds meaning by inheritance. We can even create new meanings by associating one meaning with another. This is why information, not temperature, was in our list of primary physical domains. (The Buckingham Pi Theorem[36] justifies substitutions of this type.)

Similarly, the date and the time-lapse domains are related (see the endnote on how the flow of time is an emergent property of information). The time-lapse domain is the class of all possible differences between pairs of values in the date domain. We may substitute the time-lapse domain with the date domain in the list of primary domains, and demote time lapse to a secondary, or derived, domain. In physics, and in the engineering systems that rely on physics, it is time lapse between events that is important, not the actual date or time of occurrence. Business rules, on the other hand, may depend on both. This is why we have replaced the time-lapse domain of 1954 with the date domain in our list of primary domains.

Physicists consider the enumeration domain "dimensionless" information. The conference of 1954 did not include it the list of primary domains. However, it is obvious that enumeration normalizes knowledge about the population of an object class (or aggregate objects in general), and classes are key to configuring normalized knowledge. Therefore, the enumeration domain is also key to normalizing knowledge and has been added to the list of primary domains. (Strictly speaking, it is a subtype of the Information domain.) Meanings flow from these primary domains to every physical domain that we know today and will fashion tomorrow. We cannot leave enumeration out.

Completeness, Accuracy, Validity, and Reliability have also been recognized as subtypes of information that add specific business meanings. We cannot leave them out either.

Accuracy is the lack of bias in measurement, and reliability is the quality of consistency. A weighing scale may consistently show two pounds more than the true weight of the item it is weighing. Then the scale is reliable but inaccurate (i.e., that is, it is reliably inaccurate). In a deterministic system, reliability is either total or nil. In a stochastic system, reliability is the chance of being consistent. Completeness is extent: whether the information covers the full or partial extent of a pattern. Validity is a measure of correlation when we represent one pattern with another. For instance, it is not valid to measure length with a weighing scale, but valid to do so with a measuring tape. In a deterministic system, validity is either total or nil. In a stochastic system, validity is a measure of correlation between a pair of objects. Overall, in a deterministic system, a relationship either exists or it does not. In a stochastic system, the strength of a relationship may

*continued on following page*

*Box 4.2. continued*

be measured by the chance of it existing, which is also a measure of validity of the relationship (Mitra & Gupta, 2006).

Based on the above, we have adapted the list of primary physical domains published in 1954 to better fit the engineering of knowledge as follows: "Temperature" has been substituted with "Information," "Time Duration" with "Date," and "Enumeration" has been added. Completeness, Accuracy, Validity, and Reliability have been recognized as subtypes of Information. The original list was developed primarily in support of the hard engineering sciences. This book and its companions have adapted it to support the engineering of business knowledge.[37] To this list, we must add "Preference," an ordinally scaled domain, and its dense polymorphism, "Fund," which is the same as money. All meanings are built

*Box 4.3. The principle of subtyping by adding information*

The principle of subtyping by adding information asserts that a subtype object class has more information than its supertype class(es). Subtypes share the information in their common supertype(s) and add information of their own. Creating subtypes by adding data attributes is just one instance of this principle. Business meanings and features such as relationships and constraints also add information. Thus, a Parent is a subtype of Ancestor, Apple is a subtype of Fruit, and an Insurance Policy is a subtype of Agreement. A subtype has fewer degrees of freedom than its supertype.

The subtypes in the examples above are intuitively obvious. Other subtypes are less obvious. For instance, it may not be immediately clear that the domain of sums is a subtype of the domain of summands. The cardinality of both domains is infinite, but the domain of sums also carries information on which summations of summands result in which values.[38]

Given this fact, some readers might ask why the enumeration of fruit is not a subtype of the enumeration of apples and oranges, instead of the other way around. They may reason (falsely) that the sum of numbers of apples and oranges adds up to the numbers of fruit. Thus, if the domain of sums is a subtype of the domain of summands, the count of fruit should be a subtype of the count of apples or oranges. The truth is the other way round: The count of fruit is the supertype of the count of apples and oranges because we are counting *fruit*. Just as the enumeration of *fruit* added business meaning, information, to the bald enumeration domain and thus made enumeration of fruit a subtype of the enumeration domain, *apple* and *orange* added mutually exclusive business meanings to *fruit*. This added information made the count of apples, as well as the count of oranges, subtypes of their common parent, the count of fruit. Counts of apples and oranges are not bald counts. We know what we are counting. They have emerged from a relationship between an object *apple* (or *orange*), and the domain of enumeration. Although counts of apples and oranges add to the count of fruit, they contain more information than the count of fruit. Each is a count of a specific kind of fruit; each is a subtype of the general count of fruit.

Fruit has the freedom to be an apple or orange, but an apple or orange must be what it is. Thus, the count of fruit has more freedom, that is, contains less information than the count of either apples or oranges. Therefore, the count of fruit is the common parent of both the count of apples and the count of oranges. When mathematical operations and business meaning conflict about which object is a subtype and which a supertype based on the principle of subtyping by adding information, business meaning always wins. Follow this simple rule when in doubt and you will not go wrong.

In abstract terms, think of the object as a pattern of information. Parts of the pattern may be shared with other patterns. This is shared information. However the pattern extends beyond the portion that is identical to other patterns. These extensions add information and give the pattern its unique identity. Thus, the pattern may be conceived as a shared part (the supertype), plus extensions (the added information). The composite of the two are the subtype.

A pattern with fewer degrees of freedom has a greater burden of information than a similar pattern with more freedom. For example, a straight line is a pattern of two points: its ends and a rule about how they are connected. The line may be of any length. The pattern will not lose its identity. The rules that make the pattern a pattern also give it the freedom to retain its identity.

If we restricted the length of the line, we would add information. The pattern would lose some of its freedom. The restricted pattern will be a subtype of the unrestricted pattern. This is the principle of subtyping by adding information. The pattern with more information is always a subtype of the pattern with common information when information is shared by two or more patterns. Box 5.3 describes how this applies to values. The following discussion shows how it applies to constraints:

*continued on following page*

*Box 4.3 continued*

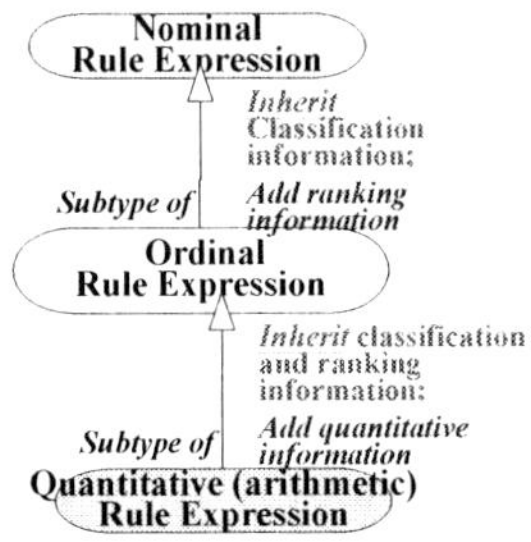


*Figure A. Subtyping hierarchy*

The subtyping hierarchy in Figure A is based on information content. A nominal (Boolean) rule expression only conveys classification information; an ordinal rule expression contains information on relative ranks—which result is larger than which, but not by how much, whereas a quantitative rule expression with arithmetic operations conveys information on relative and absolute magnitudes. Naturally, if you can rank a result, you can also classify it on that basis, but not vice versa. Similarly, if you know *how much* one result exceeds another, you can rank and classify it, but not necessarily the other way around. Thus, a nominal rule expression conveys less information than an ordinal rule expression, which in turn conveys less information than a quantitative rule expression with arithmetic operations. (*Note that occurrence relationships between objects, the "normal" relationships we have discussed thus far, are also instances of nominal rule expressions.*)

The nominal rule expression normalizes classification information, to which the ordinal rule expression adds ranking information (which it normalizes, even as it inherits classification information from its nominal parent). A quantitative rule expression normalizes and adds information on quantified magnitudes, not just their relative ranks. It inherits ranking and classification information from its ordinal parent. Based on the principle of adding information, the class of quantitative rule expressions is a subtype of the class of ordinal rule expressions, which in turn is a subtype of the class of the class of nominal rule expressions.

*Box 4.4. "Soft" information: Information content, risk and reliability, and how the scalability of domains mutates*

We intuitively refer to "soft" information. This concept has a place in the model of knowledge. To understand the "softness" of information, consider the overlap of accuracy, reliability, and enumeration, all of which are subtypes of the domain of information. Enumeration is the total number of values in a domain (domains may be infinitely large[39]). Accuracy measures proximity between two values, and reliability is how consistently we are accurate (other measures of reliability include statistical confidence levels, which measure the probability of being near enough to a target value with requisite accuracy). Accuracy, reliability, and enumeration contribute to the overall information content of the measurement. To understand this interrelationship, let us consider an individual's color preference domain as an example.

Consider a person with only a limited ability to discriminate between colors. She can only differentiate between colors she likes, colors she is neutral to, and colors she hates. The domain has three values: "like," "neutral," and "hate." She cannot distinguish between colors she only likes a little from those she likes a lot. If she is forced to state her preference in this form, her assertions will be meaningless, and meaningless degrees of preference will be spuriously introduced into her color preference domain. They will be values that do not actually exist. Unless she becomes more selective about her color preferences, the quantum of information in the domain will remain the same. The accuracy with which she can distinguish between colors will not change because she can only distinguish neutrality from hating and neutrality from liking for a color.

*continued on following page*

*Box 4.4 continued.*

This person's color preference domain is ordinal, so we intuitively know that the difference between liking and hating a color is greater than the distance between neutral and either like or hate. If she is forced to distinguish between colors she likes only a little and those she likes a lot when she simply cannot, her responses will be random. In other words, her responses will be *unreliable*, and the domain will be soft and uncertain. The overall information content determines overall "softness" and therefore the kind of scalability the domain has (see Appendix II on Shannon's Law). For this reason, if we try to impute more scalability to a domain than its information content justifies—that is, impute ordinal, difference, or ration scaled behavior to a nominal domain without increasing its intrinsic information content—values in it become less and less reliable. We characterize this situation by saying the value has become progressively "softer."

Conversely, if the size—the number of values—in a reliable domain is reduced, we will lose information in a different way. In such a domain, we can reliably distinguish between the values that are left, but we know that we can be even more accurate and maintain the same level of reliability and discrimination if there were more values in it. We call the domain "grainy" because we could fill gaps between values and continue to make reliable measurements.

As such, if the individual we discussed above became a colors aficionado who can realize very subtle distinctions in her preferences between subtle shades of color, we could increase the number of preferences (values of preference) in her color preference domain without compromising her ability to reliably distinguish between her preferences for subtly different shades of color.

As her preference for color becomes more astute, the number of values in her color preference domain will increase, and the proximity between reliable values of preference for colors will keep decreasing. Eventually we would find that she can discriminate between infinitely close values in a continuum of color. Then her color preference domain would have gathered enough information to become effectively "dense" (when an infinite number of values exist between any two values that are chosen to be arbitrarily close to each other) and of infinite cardinality. In other words, the domain has gained enough enumeration, accuracy, and reliability to become a difference scaled domain. In fact, because the individual can discriminate between like, hate, and *neutral*, this domain has a natural zero, so it has actually become a ratio scaled domain (like the money domain). This is how the information content of a domain changes its very nature and scalability.

In real life, there is no absolute certainty. A person, regardless of her talent in the area, would never be able to make infinitely subtle distinctions between her preferences. As colors and preferences get closer together, the ability to consistently distinguish between them becomes less certain. The smaller the difference, the less the chance of being consistent in our ability to distinguish between shades of color and our preference for them. In other words, the domain would get softer and softer.

The model of knowledge in this series is deterministic. The only certainty recognized would be in a digitized world of black and white. Choices in this world would be either always consistent or always inconsistent. To resolve this uncertain reality with an idealized universe of absolute certainty, it has to be determined how much uncertainty and inconsistency we will accept before we decide that a fact is absolutely certain or unknown. In our example, we would have to assert that the concerned individual absolutely can or cannot meaningfully tell the difference between color preferences that are too close. The chance of being able to distinguish between these values is not considered. When they are so close that we say that the values are indistinguishable, we also imply that the values are virtually identical. Our deterministic model *then declares that they are identical*. This also is how enumeration, accuracy, and reliability all add to the information content and cardinality of a domain.

Validity is another attribute of information. In the example we discussed, Validity lets us know for certain that we are focusing on the person's color preference, not some other quality like the rotundity of colored objects shown to her or their luster or odor that she might be confusing with preference for color. This may occur as a matter of chance; however, in our idealized model based on certainty, this either happens or does not. In other words, these properties are completely correlated or they are not (in statistical terms, the correlation coefficient is 1 or 0; there is no uncertainty involved). Validity measures the certainty of relationships, that is, with what measure of certainty a measurement of one property can substitute for another. For example, is it valid to measure the length of a column of mercury in a thermometer to deduce the temperature of an object? Is it valid to measure the weight of an object to determine its mass?

The real world is uncertain. We try to measure its uncertainty and risk by factoring chance into our models. Models that consider chance and probability are called stochastic models. Those that ignore chance are called deterministic models.

*continued on following page*

*Box 4.4. continued*

Our model of knowledge is deterministic, and we compensate for it by recognizing risk, exception, and measurability in this book.

Since the real world is shaded with uncertainty, its information content is manifested by the validity, enumeration, accuracy, and reliability of the domains that flow through the concepts (objects) that constitute our understanding of reality. The information content of each domain determines the "softness" and scalability of the domain. The information content the domain is manifested by these features of information and may be traded between them, provided its total information content is preserved. If we are willing to accept less reliability, the number of values can be increased (and gaps between them decreased, that is, increased potential accuracy requirements for measurements within the domain). As we saw in our thought experiment on color preference, if we are willing to sacrifice accuracy, we can increase reliability by making the domain more granular. Granularity implies lack of information in terms of gaps between the values in a domain. These gaps measure the meaningfulness of proximity with a level of reliability, in the pattern that underpins our understanding of our universe. It is a world where black and white exist together in shades of gray; a world in which domains may be as hard or soft as the information they convey. It is a world without absolute certainty or absolute meaning.

*Box 4.5. Partial order, fuzzy meaning, and the scaling of derived domains*

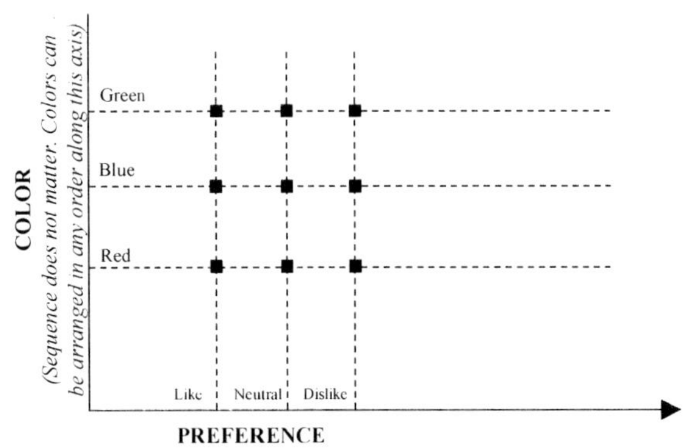


*Figure A. The color preference domain and pattern of association*

*Reproduced by permission from Mitra, A., & Gupta, A., Creating Agile Business Systems with Reusable Knowledge, New York, NY: Cambridge University Press, 2006.©*

Complex domains are made of tuples that mix meanings.[40] These domains describe state spaces.[41] For instance, Figure A is the state space created by tuple from two domains—*Color* and *Preference*. Values of color preference are points in this state space. These values are a two dimensional pattern in a discrete two-dimensional space. The collection of values, the pattern, is the color preference domain. Domains have no states because they are the immutable and changeless meanings: classes of values that create states via their relationships with objects like "Jane," which *do* exist in time and can therefore change.

If we exclude purely nominal state spaces, we are left with state spaces that have sequencing information on at least one, if not more, axis. Such a state space is called a Partial Order in mathematics.[42] Take a pair of points in Figure A, any pair. If you can find a path from one point to another such that the value increases along one or more coordinates and does not simultaneously decrease for another (or others) as you traverse the path (i.e., the path is always "upwards"), then the pair is partially ordered— "Partially" because, even if they do not decrease, other coordinates might not increase. A state space is a partial order if every pair of distinct points in it follows this dictum. Obviously, Figure A is a partial order. Given

continued on following page

*Box 4.5 continued*

any pair of distinct points in it, you can always travel in a direction of increasing preference.

When we consider partially ordered domains, we find that sequencing information is not a simple yes/no issue. Different domains may have different amounts of sequencing information. The larger the proportion of sequenced axes and the larger the sequenced domains that were joined,[43] the larger is the quantum of sequencing information in the resultant domain.

Given this definition of partial order, it follows that ordinal difference and ratio scaled domains are also partially ordered. Further, every ordinal domain and its subtypes are totally ordered (see *Total Order* under Ordered Sets and Sequences in Appendix II). As such, Total and Partial orders are not mutually exclusive. Total Order is more restrictive, and hence, based on the principle of subtyping by adding information, a total order is a subtype of partial order (strange but true, live from the logic of mathematics!).

When quantitative domains are associated with ordinal domains via a Cartesian product into a partial order, the information content of the relationship is somewhere in between that of the domains that gave it birth. We can be conservative and deem it to be an ordinal domain, but there is a cost in terms of information lost.

The information content of a relationship between domains is derived from the information content of the domains it binds together. Therefore a relationship between domains creates a new domain of at least the scaling of the most information sparse member of the participating domains (Rule 10a of domains).[44] This is an idealization of complex and uncertain reality. When the information content of the relationship (partial order) is closer to that of the quantitative domain, we are justified in ignoring Rule 10a. The circumstances that justify this will usually be clearly recognizable. They will emerge from relationships with the information domain (or its subtypes), and the new domain will be subtypes, not Cartesian products of the other domain(s) involved. For example, Economic Value emerges from the junction of preference, an ordinal domain, and information, a ratio scaled domain.[45] As our information on people's preferences increased in step with the trading population, we increased the granularity with which we could discriminate between preferences, and new values started filling the gaps between the discrete preferences. Gaps between values shrank until we reached a point where we felt that we were dealing with a continuum of values.

Economic value is really quantified preference information. Economic Value conveys "softer," more uncertain information than the engineering information conveyed by physical domains such as mass or length. We have described why this is so. Indeed, until money was discovered, primitive economies based on bartering goods and services had no unit of measure they could associate with economic value. However, when preference information of large numbers of people was involved in larger communities, the information content inherent in preferences of individuals added up, and the overall preference of the aggregate object, a population, became almost ratio scaled, and monetary exchange evolved. With monetary exchange in place, the near quantitative statistical nature of aggregate preference became evident and firmly established as the domain of money.

As we considered preferences of large numbers of individuals, the meaning of preference and the meaning of information in the composite, preference information domain, "melted" into a single continuum of values. As more individuals were considered, the information conveyed by each person's preferences added up,[46] and the relationship between preference and information got denser and denser until it could be considered a ratio scaled continuum. Hence, we are justified in considering Economic Value a primary domain that is a subtype of Preference, an ordinal domain.

Information rich domains of this type can be considered primary domains. They are domains like economic value, which have emerged by adding up many instances—large numbers—of similar, information and poor, "fuzzy" meanings to the extent that they have demonstrably become almost quantitatively scaled. These kinds of domains are found more often in the softer social sciences such as psychology, sociology, and biology. Barring economic value, few are used universally.

Domains like Economic Value, which were created by adding information to primary domains with less information until they changed into a new kind of domain are subtypes of the domains they grew from, albeit special subtypes that came into being based on inheriting the subtyping relationships in Appendix I, Figure I.4.

*continued on following page*

## *Box 4.6. Domains, relationships, and the Cartesian product*

A relationship between two or more object instances creates a pattern. When a relationship is a sequenced pattern, it is a Cartesian product between object classes.[47] Tuples[48] capture the fact that object instances listed in the tuple are "joined" in a sequence. The Cartesian product is the class of tuples. It joins the object classes that participate in the relationship. Cartesian products are antisymmetrical; that is, the direction of association matters, unless the object is referencing itself (for example, "help" in is an antisymmetrical relationship: "person helps person" is asymmetrical unless it is self help). As such, an association, (a, b), of two values "a" and "b," is considered different from the association (b, a) of the same values in asymmetrical relationships. Many relationships such as "child of" are also asymmetrical. However, some like "wedded to" are symmetrical. The direction of association does not matter. The Cartesian product and asymmetrical relationships are subtypes of relationships that are directionless associations like "wedded to."

Although a relationship is an association, it is not *only* an association. It is an association pregnant with meaning. An association is only a mathematical concept. By itself, it possesses no more meaning than a bald association. However, relationships convey richer meanings, which they normalize. The Cartesian product is the mathematical artifice that normalizes new meanings, meanings that emerge by associating one meaning with another or even several meanings with each other. Temperature Preference is a Cartesian product of the Temperature domain with the Preference domain. It has a unique meaning, but the meaning is obtained by combining the meaning of *Temperature* with the meaning of *Preference*. These meanings were combined in a tuple to create a new meaning, "temperature preference." The tuple in this case is a list of two values, a value of temperature and a value of preference. It is also a list laden with meaning, obtained by associating a temperature with a preference for that temperature. It possesses a unique meaning different from its constituents, temperature, and preference.

A relationship like this cares about its direction, and a tuple cares about sequence and so does the Cartesian product. If a set A is a set of members a1 and a2, and set B a set of members b1 and b2, then the tuple (a1, a2) is different from the tuple (a2, a1). In the same way, (a1, b1) will be different from (b1, a1), and A x B from B x A. If A and B had been objects, A x B would have been a relationship from A to B, whereas B x A would have been a relationship in the opposite direction, from B to A. Take the page you are reading in this book. The Book and Page are objects. The book contains this page. A relationship from Book to Page *contains* and connects the two objects *Book* and *Page*. It may be true that *Book* Contains *Page*, but the inverse cannot be true; obviously, this book cannot be contained in this page! As such, direction can distinguish one meaning from another, just as it can distinguish one relationship from another. Further, sequence distinguishes one tuple from another with the same elements, just as it distinguishes one Cartesian product of sets from another with the same sets.

"Contained in" was the inverse of "contain" in the example above. Not all relationships in the reverse direction may be inverses. We will return to the nature of relationships later in this book. For now, it will suffice to understand that relationships between objects can be Cartesian products laden with meaning and to remember that relationships are also object classes in their own right.

Consider a person's car color preference. It is a four-way relationship between Person and Car, two "normal" objects that may respond to events by changing their state and two domains, color and preference, that are immutable and changeless fields of meaning. The relationship is a Cartesian product that may be expressed as Person x Car x Color x Preference.

Cartesian products are associative operations on sets. Therefore, Person x Car x Color x Preference = Person x Car x (Color x Preference) = (Person x Car) x (Color x Preference). The three expressions—the four-way relationship between *Person*, *Car*, *Color*, and *Preference*; the three-way relationship between object classes *Car* and *Person* and the *Color Preference* domain; and the two-way relationship between the *Person-Car relationship* and the *Color Preference* domain—all mean the same. They are merely different expressions of the same rule meaning. It is also worth noting that, although the Cartesian product might be associative, it is not commutative (see the discussion on operators in Appendix II, under the Theory of Categories).

Domains are objects too. Cartesian product of attributes created the state space of an object class. The Cartesian product of domains is a relationship between domains that also creates a state space (a space that is a domain), a class of values, and a meaning that is changeless, eternal, and immutable.

Figure A of Box 4.5 was a state space created by the Cartesian product of two domains—*Color* and *Preference*. This is why values of color preference are points in this state space. These values are a two-dimensional pattern in a discrete two-dimensional space. The collection of values, the pattern, is the color preference domain. Domains have no states

*continued on following page*

*Box 4.6. continued*

because they are the immutable and changeless meanings: classes of values that create states via their relationships with temporal objects, like a person, which *do* exist in time and can therefore change.

**Magnitude constraint vs. Cartesian product:** Contrast the pattern created by the Cartesian product with that created by an arithmetic operation—a relationship that is a magnitude constraint between domains. Figure A of Box 4.5 was a two-dimensional pattern in two-dimensional space created by a Cartesian product. If we take the Cartesian product of the length domain with itself (once), we will get a flat two-dimensional space. We will still need two coordinates—a tuple—to describe a value (position) in this space. The price per piece domain, as we have discussed earlier, is obtained by dividing values in the money domain by values in the enumeration domain. We can describe elements of this domain in terms of a single value, not a tuple with multiple members; technically, you could also consider it to be a tuple with a single member, but that is overkill. However, the domain does contain more information than merely its value. It is a pattern. Figure A is a graph of a hypothetical price plotted against the money and enumeration axes. It is evident from Figure A that the price per piece is a two dimensional pattern, curved in three-dimensional space, like the sail of a yacht bellied out by a good breeze.

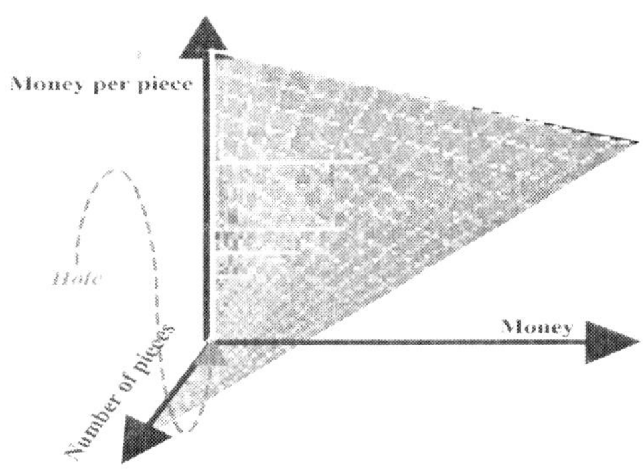


*Figure A. The money per piece pattern of association*

*Reproduced by permission from Mitra, A., & Gupta, A., Creating Agile Business Systems with Reusable Knowledge, New York, NY: Cambridge University Press, 2006.©*

Both tuples and magnitude constraints are patterns of association. Although magnitude constraints create domains that are patterns of single values, not tuples, they also create patterns of greater complexity than tuples that may twist, tilt, bend, fold, and break in more dimensions than the flat Cartesian spaces that hold mere tuples (see the discussion on patterns[49]): This is hardly surprising, given the fact that an arithmetic operation conveys more information than mere association. It tells us that the domains in question are not only associated but also associated in special ways specified by the magnitude constraint. The extra information is in the magnitude constraint.

**Null vs. nil values:** Note how the nil values in the money and enumeration domains of Figure A not only fix the nil value in the money-per-piece domain but also the null value in it. Given the number of pieces, the lower the quantum of money, the less the quantum of money per piece. Money per piece naturally falls to nil when money is nil, provided that the number of pieces is not nil. The number of pieces has the opposite effect. It is the denominator, and the less it is, the larger the value of money per piece. As it approaches zero (there may be a continuum of fractional values between a single piece and "nil" pieces), money per piece increases rapidly. Money per piece approaches infinite magnitudes as the number of pieces approaches nil, *provided the corresponding value of money is not nil.* If there are no pieces and no money, the notion of money per piece is meaningless. Note the null value in the pattern—a gap along the money per piece axis where both the number of pieces and money are nil. When both are nil, money per piece has no meaning. It is not that it has no magnitude, rather it has no meaning; it is a value that does not exist in the money per piece domain. It *cannot* when neither money nor pieces are involved. It is *null*, not nil.

This gap, a null value in the fabric of the domain when both divisor and dividend are nil, is common to all quotients. It is a property of the domain of quotients, inherited by each subtype.

*continued on following page*

*Box 4.6 continued.*

> Domains too are objects, even if they represent immutable, changeless meanings—objects that never change state but objects that lend meaning to states. "Normal" objects that change states may be related to domains or to each other. Similarly, domains may participate in relationships with other domains. Relationships between domains and objects may not be immutable. These relationships are "normal" objects that, driven by events, may switch from one value in a domain to another. On the other hand, domains are changeless and so are relationships between domains. Therefore, these relationships, be they mere association or magnitude constraints, will be changeless, immutable domains as well. This is the key distinction between domains and temporal objects. This is also how domains anchor the metamodel of knowledge on the bedrock of immutable meanings.

## THE OBJECT AND THE STATE MACHINE

A temporal object is a person, place, event, thing, or concept that exists in time. Just as domains become more meaningful in step with their information content, abstract objects also become more choate and meaningful as we add temporal and other information to them.[50] These objects and patterns become reusable business meanings by capturing our shared understanding of business and can therefore be components of knowledge from which agile business processes and business systems may be assembled.

This section summarizes how objects and their temporal states can encapsulate, normalize, and propagate knowledge through information space and, as new information flows into information space, how these objects become components that can be reconfigured in step with new learning. To exist in the real world, an object like a place, person, event, or thing must exist for some span of time, even if that time span is infinitesimally short. To distinguish these objects that exist in time from Domains, which are the immutable timeless meanings, we call them Temporal Objects. Temporal objects may be physical objects like people and buildings or concepts like organizations or budgets. All objects have properties. Properties of domains will never change because domains lie beyond the flow of time. On the other hand, properties of temporal objects can change with time. People, buildings, and organizations age, people grow taller, buildings can change hands, organizations can change their members and their charters, and budgets can lapse, increase, or decrease. We have understood how properties of temporal objects flow from their relationships with domains. The state of a temporal object at a point in time is the combination of values of its properties at the time. It describes the object at that point in time. A person being single, 5 years old, and 3 feet tall is a state of that person, which can change over time, so that 20 years later, his or her state might be married, 25 years old, and 6 feet tall.

Domains are classes of values. When a temporal object switches a relationship from one value to another in a domain, it changes its state. Objects change state in response to events. The event might be a discrete event like a wedding or an event like the continuous passage of time. The scope of our model of knowledge is limited to discrete events. However, our model does not ignore continuous changes. It merely considers them to be a series of discrete changes. The passage of time may be sliced into discrete units like years, months, or days. Continuous changes of state, like the growth of a child, would be similarly sliced into a set of discrete observations at discrete times (see Figure 4.5).

A class of objects is a group of objects with common properties. Individual objects in a class are its instances. In Figure 4.5, the state of each

*Figure 4.5. The state of an object changes in response to discrete events*

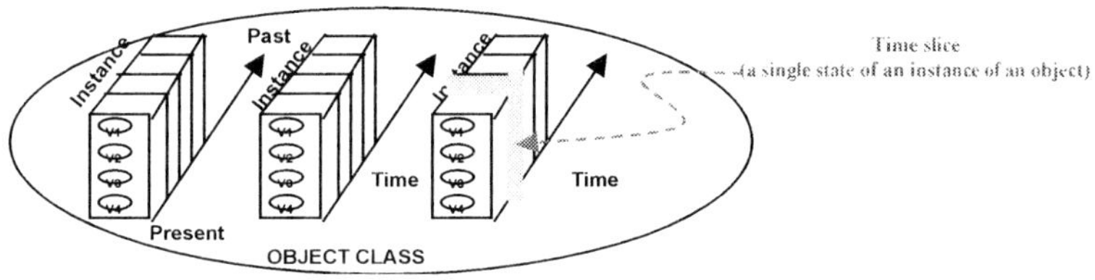


*Reproduced by permission from Mitra, A., & Gupta, A., Creating Agile Business Systems with Reusable Knowledge, New York, NY: Cambridge University Press, 2006.©*

instance is determined by four properties labeled $v_1$ through $v_4$. The relationship between the class and a domain determine what class of properties the class has. The class of persons may have properties like height via a relationship with the length domain. Individual instances of that relationship between an instance of the object class and an individual value in a domain determine the value of that property for that instance of the object. The object class in Figure 4.5 might be the class of persons and the property labeled $v_1$ could be the age of a person. An individual person may be 25 years old (a value), whereas the class of persons will have the property of Age derived from its relationship with the time-lapse domain.

Each instance in Figure 4.5 is also divided into time slices. Each time slice represents the state of the object at the time. In a discrete model such as ours, we assume that the object remains in that state for a finite time period before another event changes it. A property of an object could also be its relationship with another object instance. If the object class in Figure 4.5 were the class of male persons, a marital relationship between this object class and the class of female persons would establish the institution of marriage. At the instance level, a marital relationship between an instance of a man and a woman would establish their marital state. A wedding event would tie the two instances together with the relationship, whereas a divorce event would snap the tie, changing the state of the two object instances again. Clearly, relationships like these between instances of objects are nominally scaled. The existence of the effect of an event is also a property of an object. An agreement under negotiation may be redrafted on request from any of the parties to the agreement, whereas a sealed agreement will not be. The effect of the request (an event) is deleted by the event that seals the agreement. This too is a change of state.

From Figure 4.5, it is clear that we must have some way of identifying each instance of an object so that we can track its history. The instance identifier represents the identity of the object and conveys the information that the object is distinct from every other object. It also conveys that even though an object changes state, all the states over its history belong to the same object instance. Every instance of an object will have a unique identifier, which will never change between state transitions over its full life, even after its deáth or deletion. *This identifier cannot have the same value for any other object instance* because it is the *identity* of the object (instance) it represents, standing for all the information that makes its identity unique and different from every other object instance in the universe for all time. This identity will distinguish the object (instance) from every other object (instance) as it moves through state space, giving it a unique trajectory that is its individual history through time. It also records the irreducible fact that this specific instance of an object exists in the world.[51]

We also need a time slice identifier to acknowledge the existence of a time slice of an instance of an object (the design of the instance identifier and time slice identifier are physical design issues). Moreover, every state change will naturally be associated with:

1. The time of change;
2. Who made the change (the operator as well as process owner); and
3. The facility (automated or manual system) that was used to make the change (immediate reason, not root cause—the causal chain can always be traced to root causes and sources of change if all these audit attributes are maintained).

We will call these items, which are often required by auditors but are also the keys to the history of the object instance, the "audit attributes" of the object. Audit attributes reside in the Business Process Automation layer of the Architecture of Knowledge in Chapter III.

A temporal object class may be considered a three-dimensional pattern like that in Figure 4.6. Two-dimensional slices of this object might be perceived as history tables or relational database tables that represent the current state of the object class, but these are all implementation issues in the technology layers of the Architecture of Knowledge. In the business layer, an object is a meaning and a pattern of information, not a table of data, and this pattern has a history and trajectory through state space.

An object class is a container of object instances. Think of it as a bag of candy. The bag has an identity different from its contents. In the same way, the object class has an identity distinct from the object instances it classifies. An object class is also an object instance. A bag could be empty, and so could an object class be devoid of instances. We could conceive of an organization without members or a class of persons born with green hair that is empty because no one is born with green hair. Moreover, object classes could also be classes of object classes. Tithe class of persons includes the classes of men and women. The class of persons would normalize the common properties of all persons, whereas the class of men would normalize the properties shared by

*Figure 4.6. Perspectives of an object*

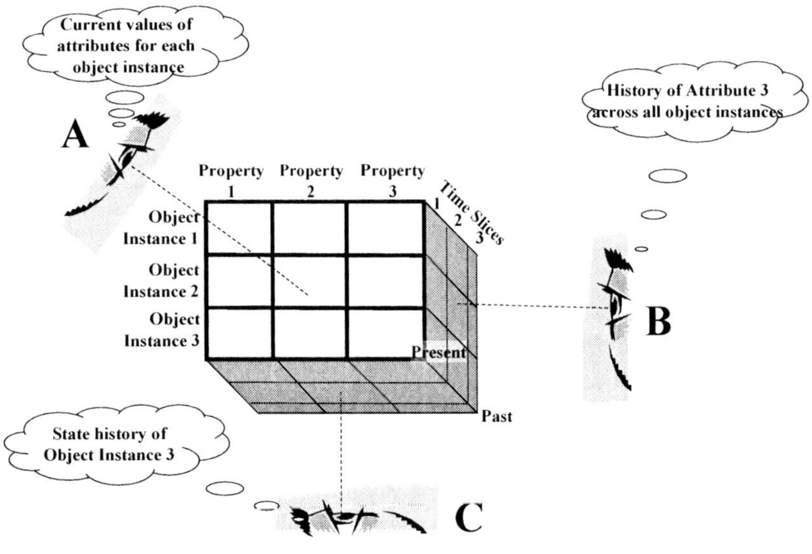


*Reproduced by permission from Mitra, A., & Gupta, A., Creating Agile Business Systems with Reusable Knowledge, New York, NY: Cambridge University Press, 2006.©*

all men, and the class of women would normalize the properties shared by all women. As such, the class of men would inherit the shared properties of all persons, but not the properties exclusive to women, and the class of women would also inherit the shared properties of persons, but not the special properties of men. If the scope of our model shifted so that we needed to add new information, like the color of a person's hair, we could add the same to the class of persons, and both the class of men and the class of women would automatically inherit this property. On the other hand, if we had to add information on the color of a man's beard, we would add this attribute only to the class of men and it would not affect women. In this way, knowledge and the impact of change are driven to the right places via the subtyping relationship.

Some experts distinguish a subtype from a polymorphism. We make no distinction between polymorphism and subtyping in this book; they are both obtained by adding information to a parent object, which creates a new meaning. We consider subtypes and polymorphisms to be synonyms. Some experts also distinguish a subtype from a role, considering that a subtype (for example, gender) will not change, whereas a role is a state obtained via a relationship like marriage, which can be changed by events. We make no such distinction. As scopes shift and new learning recognizes new events, things previously considered immutable become mutable. Even gender can change in some animals (see Appendix II on the Question of Gender). The principle of parsimony in Appendix II admonishes us against adding constraints unless they are absolutely necessary to a meaning, an interaction, or a process. We must specify the bare minimum of information in order to be resilient and agile in information space. This will lead to resilient business processes and agile information systems as the subsequent chapters of this book will show.

A meaning is abstract. It is a pattern of information. Every object conveys information. Constraining information creates new meanings, as we have understood in this chapter. Meanings can contain other meanings. The meaning of "Man" is contained in the meaning of "Person." Every object may be a place for another object. Information may be a place for information because it includes the information it contains. Not all places may be physical places. A physical place and a physical object are special polymorphisms of patterns of information, as we will discuss next.

Temporal objects convey information about their presence in time. Physical objects convey information about their presence in space and time with the caveat that a physical object may only occupy one physical place at a time. Constraints add information and reduce the degrees of freedom of a pattern. Just as physical domains morphed out of abstract domains in step with their information content, business meanings and physical objects emerge from abstract information. Figure 4.7 shows this hierarchy.

Money is obtained from the ordinally scaled preference domain as it becomes dense by including preferences of large numbers of individuals. When we add temporal behavior to this domain so that the quantum of funds may increase or decrease in response to events, it becomes Fund, which is temporal information that maps to the ratio scaled money domain.

Information can only be perceived when it is represented by physical symbols in a document. The information is physically formatted thus. Permitted formats will depend on the medium of information. Medium is therefore a class of documents based on formativeness. Individual documents are actually instances of the medium they belong to.[52] The integration of Ontology into the model of knowledge not only brings the power of reason into the model of knowledge but also enables the creation of resilient business processes from reusable knowledge. The ontology also provides ready templates for accelerating the design of business processes and information systems, as well as avenues for enabling quantum leaps in

*Figure 4.7. Temporal object ontology*

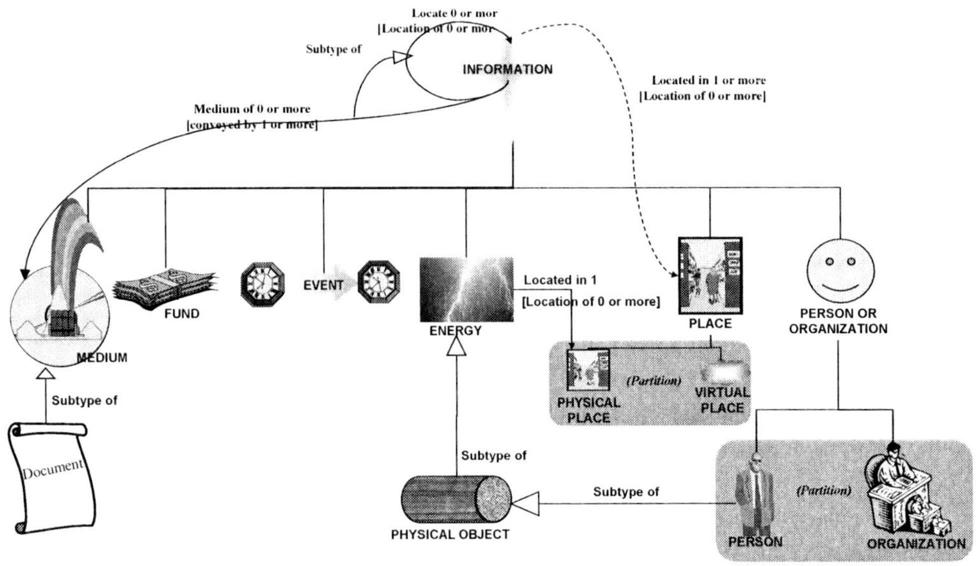


*Reproduced by permission from Mitra, A., & Gupta, A., Agile Systems with Reusable Patterns of Business Knowledge, Norwood, MA: Artech House, Inc., 2005. ©*

*Box 4.7. States, attributes, state variables, and type indicators: Much ado about nothing*

The state of an object instance is the collection of values of its attributes at an instant in time.

The State (condition) of an object instance may not only change over time (as effects of events affect the object) but also vary from object to object. These differences in state between objects, or between different states of the same object at different times, are described by values of its attributes *and the object's relationships with other objects or itself.* The existence or non-existence of a relationship is a nominally scaled item of information like many state indicators are, and indeed, there is little difference between the two.

For instance, some properties of glass panes, such as whether a pane is broken or not, might not only vary from pane to pane but also change over time in response to events such as hammer strikes, whereas other properties, such as the color and thickness of the pane might only vary from pane to pane. It is not that some attributes cannot or do not change in real life, but only those events and effects that might change them are beyond the scope of the model.

Sometimes data modelers try to draw artificial distinctions between ratio or difference scaled attributes (like the thickness of the glass pane) and nominally or ordinally scaled *state* or *type indicators.* A State indicator is a nominally or ordinally scaled attribute that captures the fact that the behavior of an object can change suddenly in response to an event or condition.[53]

A glass pane may be whole or broken; an agreement may be sealed or under negotiation. The metamodel of knowledge distinguishes facts that do not involve the flow of time, that is, things that just *are*, from facts that involve the flow of time, or things that *become. Existence* of attributes, states, types, relations, and constraints do not involve time. *Changing* values of these do. That is why, mathematically speaking, there is no distinction between attributes, participation in relationships, types, constraints, and state indicators. These distinctions do not add any meaning to the metamodel, nor do they make the metamodel any clearer. Indeed, these distinctions will only serve to complicate the metamodel. In this book, we will consider them all to be attributes that contain information about the state of the object at a point in time. Collectively, they are called features of the object.

Some analysts distinguish *roles* from state indicators. They assert that roles result from relationships, and state indicators do not. A person (an object) may assume the *role* of an employee by participating in an employment relationship.

*continued on following page*

## *Box 4.7. continued*

Roles *are* state indicators, and there is little benefit in making a distinction between role and state.[54]

Data (and object) modelers sometimes justify making distinctions between *State Indicators* and *Type Indicators* based on their assertion that states change in response to events, whereas some attributes called type indicators do not. Some practitioners might argue that since the location of a bridge or an individual's gender will never change, we must distinguish these attributes from State Variables that *do* change. For the same reasons as before, nothing will be gained by making this distinction mathematically or practically; it will only add complexity to the metamodel with no commensurate return.

Indeed, most so-called "constant" values are constant only within a limited scope. Systems change primarily because new objects and behaviors must be brought in scope as businesses they support flex and innovate for competitive advantage. The so-called "impossible-to-change, steadfastly constant" attributes may suddenly start changing in the new scope.

Most seasoned information modelers have come across several examples of this phenomenon in their professional lives. However, we will illustrate the point with two rather extreme but little known interesting real life examples:

The first is about moving bridges: Even the London Bridge moved from London to Lake Havasu City in the U.S.A.—who said bridges could not move?

The story of changing gender is even more interesting. Who said gender could not change? With so many species of plants and animals that routinely change gender, scientists have had to invent a new word, *gonochorostic*, for species that do *not* change their gender through their life span. If "individual" means an individual of any species, not just human, we would have to allow for changes in gender.

The majority of reef fish change their gender at some point in their life. Similarly, for a desert shrub called *Zuckia Brandegei*, half the plants open with male flowers and the other half open with female flowers; a few weeks later, they switch. Male and female flowers shrivel up, and new flowers of the opposite sex bloom. Because of this adaptation, these wind-pollinated shrubs are able to improve the odds that the species will flourish because the odds of mating with others of their species are increased.

## *Box 4.8. Exclusion partitions, variation inheritance, and polymorphism*

Partitions have a profound effect on inheritance—what is inherited and what is not. Sometimes the difference between Exclusion and Inclusion Partitions is subtle. It depends on how the object being partitioned into subtypes has been defined and the partitioning criteria being used. Consider the class of all people. Let us call it *Person*. Let us assume it has attributes such as *Name, Age, Gender, Height,* and *Weight*. We also understand that some persons are parents and others are not. Those who are parents have a *"parent of"* relationship with another person. This relationship does not exist for those who are not parents. This is the criterion for distinguishing parents from nonparents, and *Parenthood* is a feature of *Person*.

*Person* is the union of the class of *Parents* and the class of *Nonparents*, which makes both *Parent* and *Nonparent* subsets of *Person*. *NonParent*, the subclass, is defined by *excluding* all those who have the "parent of" relationship with another person. *Nonparent* will inherit all attributes of *Person*, except parenthood. Figure A shows how this happens; the *"parent of"* relationship is not inherited by its *Nonparent* subtype. (Technically, the value of parenthood is "unknown" in "Person," whereas it is constrained to equal "null" in nonparent.)

Inheritance with exceptions is called *Variation Inheritance*.[55] Variation Inheritance flows from exclusion partitions and supertypes that are anchored in the *union* of properties of (at least a few) subtypes (objects like these are called *parametric classes*[56]). Extension Inheritance, on the other hand, flows from supertypes anchored in the intersection of common properties of subtypes.

Restrictions on state spaces of subtypes may also lead to variation inheritance. Subtypes inherit properties, including constraints from their supertypes. We may add more constraints to a subtype. When constraints are added to subtypes, they must necessarily be stricter than or at least as strict as those it has inherited. After all, a subtype cannot violate the lawful state space the subtype has inherited from its supertype.

The subtype may not be free to roam the *entire* state space (or facets) it has inherited from its supertype. Its own constraints may restrict it to even smaller regions *inside* the inherited state space. When subtyping criteria restrict the lawful

*continued on following page*

*Box 4.8 continued*

state spaces of subtypes to regions or facets inside the supertype's lawful state space, some inherited features (effects, relationships, constraints, etc.) may become redundant[57] or incorrect (i.e., the feature would allow the subtype to violate its restricted state space). Such features must then be excluded. Hence, Variation Inheritance may flow from constraints. For example, restricting one subtype (*Nonparent*) to the set of persons who have no (0) children was cause for variation inheritance in Figure A.

### Polymorphism

Variation Inheritance, also called *Restricted Relationship Inheritance*, and *polymorphism*, is an important concept in the reuse of knowledge. It flows from the structure of relationships. Subtypes inherit relationships from supertypes along with other features. Relationships normalize facts about interactions between objects. When relationships between objects are inherited, restriction and variation inheritance can interact in special ways. Subtypes may inherit relationships unconditionally, or they may inherit relationships with caveats. The most common caveat is that the relationship inherited by a given subclass will only be between it and other specific subclass(es). Thus, if two or more superclasses are related, a subclass of one object may not always be related to all subclasses of the other object(s). In such cases, the relevant relationships do not violate constraints imposed on supertypes. This is *Inclusion Polymorphism*: "*Inclusion*" because the supertype generalizes and includes the behavior of subtype(s), and "*polymorphism*" because the relationship appears in different forms for each subtype.[58]

For example, engineering firms in general manufacture engineering products. However, if we take automobile parts manufacturers, a subtype of engineering firms, they manufacture only automobile parts, a subset of engineering products. The manufacturing relationship is inherited, but it relates automobile parts manufacturers to a subset of engineering products, not all engineering products. As such, if we said that the subtype, Automobile Parts Manufacturer, inherited the manufacturing relationship from its supertype, we would not be telling the whole truth. The manufacturing relationship is inherited but in restricted form. It only relates Automobile Parts Manufacturers to a subset of engineering products (automobile parts), not all engineering products. The inherited relationship is actually a subtype of the manufacturing relationship between corresponding supertypes. Only the subtype, not the entire relationship, was inherited. Hence, *manufacture* is a polymorphic relationship, and this is an example of *Inclusion Polymorphism*. The kind of firm is a parameter that determines the subtype of *manufacture*, the relationship that is inherited.

In Figure A, if the *Parent* subtype had been only female parent, that is, *Mother* instead of *Parent*, only those instances of "*parent of*," that belong to its subtype, "*mother of*," would have been inherited. This is another example of *Inclusion Polymorphism*.

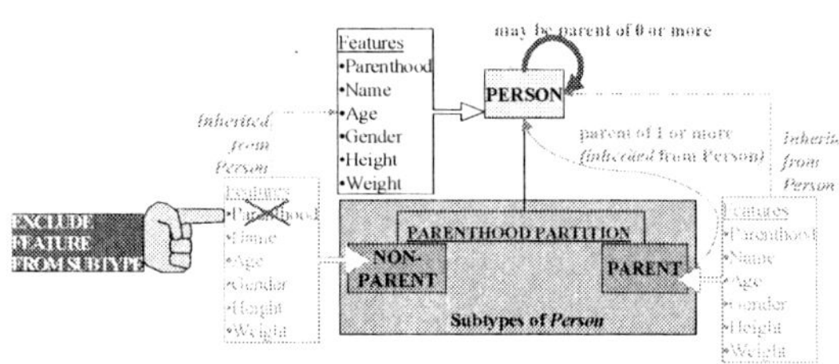


*Figure A. Partitioning criterion:* Exclusion *of parenthood relationship ("parent of" is inherited by one subtype but not the other)*

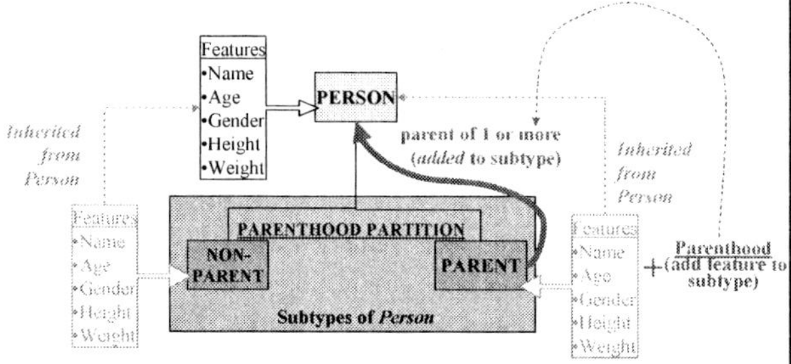


*Figure B. Partitioning criterion:* Addition *of parenthood relationship (all features inherited by all subtypes)*

### Avoiding Variation Inheritance

If we had defined *Person* sans the parenthood attribute, we could have created a Nonparent subtype of *Person* without an exclusion partition. We would have added *Parenthood* only to the *Parent* subclass. Then inheritance would flow from

*continued on following page*

*Box 4.8 continued*

*extending*, instead of *excluding*, inherited properties of the subclass, and Extension Inheritance (see Box 7.3) instead of Variation Inheritance would be at work. Figure B shows this.

The kind of inheritance that is appropriate depends on both the design of the supertype and the design of the partition, whether the partition is an inclusion or exclusion partition. If supertypes contained only behavior common to all possible subtypes, we would never need variation inheritance (with the exception of polymorphism). However, when the scope of business expands under the imperative to change, we might find that behavior that we had assumed was common to an entire object class was actually common only to subtypes in the limited scope of the old business (see Appendix II on Lungfish). Legacies like these drive variation inheritance.

As the pace of change accelerates in a world driven by new knowledge and global competition, this can happen frequently, laying layers of variation inheritance upon older layers of variation inheritance, until we end with complex, poorly understood, tangled inheritance. This greatly increases the risk of chaos under the pressure of continual change and is an imperative driving global business in the new millennium.

To minimize the risk of chaos, it is best to refactor, that is, reconfigure components of knowledge, to reduce the incidence of variation inheritance.[59] *The principle of subtyping by adding information* asserts that subtypes may be created from their parents only by adding information. It brings a common perspective to inheritance subtyping and polymorphism.[60]

Extension and Variation Inheritance are not mutually exclusive. *Unaffecting Inheritance* is a form of Variation Inheritance in which we *only* take away properties from subtype(s), as we did in the example in Figure A. There is also no bar against taking away some properties while adding others. This form of inheritance is called *Functional Variation Inheritance*. Functional Variation Inheritance boils down to subtypes over-ruling properties of supertypes. With Functional Variation Inheritance, objects can become fluid shadows of reality that shift, blur, and change fundamentally between perspectives and changes in requirements (see Chapter II, The Problem of Perspective).

To anchor objects firmly in stable perspectives and to reduce the complexity of reconfiguring processes and systems under the twin imperatives of speed and change, analysts should strive to support change by *adding* new behavior as much as possible and by *judiciously* taking obsolete behavior away (perhaps only when old behavior is incompatible or in conflict with new behavior). When we do both simultaneously, objects and perspectives can become shifting chimeras of reality.

the kinds of automated design tools we can use to support these.

The following chapters of this book highlight how automation may help to turn business knowledge into resilient business processes that nurture agility and innovation.

## ENDNOTES

1 The behavior of information space and the semantics of Pattern are discussed in detail in the companion book from Cambridge University Press. The discussion in [337] (in Appendix III) integrates the metamodel of Ontology into our model of knowledge, lending the Metamodel of Knowledge the power to reason.

2 [337] in Appendix III discusses the semantics of patterns, measurement, and the proximity metric in more detail.

3 [337] and [338] in Appendix III describe Partitions and their topoi in more detail.

4 [337] and [338] in Appendix III describe some of these aspects in greater detail.

5 [337] in Appendix III discusses formatting domains, their behavior, and how symbols in formatting domains may be organized into languages.

6 [337] in Appendix III discusses the five fundamental domains in more detail, under Patterns of Sequenced vs. Unsequenced Association.

7 Technological constraints may flow from the actual hardware of physical devices or the

systems software in the "*Technology Rules Layer*" of Figure 3.4.

8 Written scripts are visual symbols in one-dimensional sequences. Diagrams and graphics may be patterns in two or three dimensions. Patterns of movement involve time, another dimension. Animated three-dimensional graphics involves four-dimensional symbols that may consist of four-dimensional patterns. Higher dimensional arrays of symbols may also exist. Business and financial analysts often look for these patterns.

9 The science of genetics has several real world examples of complex format conversion rules. Translation of genetic information from DNA, through messenger RNA, to their expression in proteins is an example of complex real world translation rules that are the key to the field of bioinformatics. The genetic information in the DNA is expressed as proteins. The symbols that code for proteins in a strand of DNA are nucleotide molecules. An extron is a stretch of nucleotide molecules that codes for a single protein. An *extron* is a symbol in its own right. Other stretches of DNA, called introns, do not code for proteins. Instead, they contain sequences that change the expression of extrons. Depending on the symbol sequences and patterns in introns, the same extron may express different proteins. This is an example of a complex but natural real world format conversion rule. Both introns and extrons are symbols that will be members of the object set in Figures B and C of Box 4.1.

10 Represent is described in Box 36 on our Web site.

11 Imputing a value to a symbol is a form of ad-hoc polymorphism described under Kinds of Polymorphism under Mathematical Theory of Categories in Appendix II.

12 Figure 31 on our Web site has an example of unsequenced association that drives a "cannot exist" constraint from classes to instances: an attribute value is a pattern of unsequenced association between a single attribute and a single value. The two are glued to each other by a connective like the "⊠" operator in the note in Appendix II on gluing objects together.

13 Constraining a map between attribute values to be "Null or *Do Not Know*" requires that a simple inclusion constraint on values of states of the instance identifier be attached to it. The value set will have two values—"null" and "*do not know*."

14 For example, in the array of Figure 4.6, several time *values* were mapped to a single time *slice*. The time slice was an ordinal state indicator for the object instance, and the time value was a difference scaled state indicator of object instance. As such, a state of the symbol (a slice of the 3-dimensional array) representing the object actually represents several states of that object.

15 Eventually when the object doing the representation has no degrees of freedom left, it cannot be a format because it cannot represent a meaning. Constants are objects like this. They do not even have the freedom *not* to exist. They must exist and can have only one value; they have no choices, not now, not ever.

16 See under fundamental formatting domains, and also patterns, for examples of formatting attributes.

17 The metamodel of translation in Figure D is very similar to the *Rule Constrain* relationship in Figure 48 of [337] in Appendix III. The only difference is that, unlike a constraint, the rule expression does not *exclude* a value.

18 To tell the truth, all formatting symbols must have a finite or unlimited extent in

time; otherwise, they cannot exist, let alone be perceived. However, this may not be relevant to our *model*. It might suffice to bar time sensitive changes in a format and say that we have barred the time dimension *in the context of our model*. The last italicized part of the sentence is implied and often left unsaid.

19 Automated agents are discussed in Box 36 on our Web site.

20 See Appendix II on Dimensions of Color. For professionals interested in color as a part of visual formats, [324] in Appendix III deals with color, its properties, measurement, and standards in detail.

21 The phenomenon of the same color looking different against different backgrounds is called Simultaneous Color Contrast or Color Induction.

22 A direction expressed in a coordinate system is a rule expression. It is only one of several ways of describing the *meaning* of the direction. Different coordinate systems may describe the same direction on their own terms.

23 A pattern is independent of the coordinate system used to describe it. To understand this, imagine we are creatures that live in the pattern and our dimensionality is restricted to the dimensionality of the pattern. Moreover, as creatures pasted to the pattern, with no possibility of leaving it or looking at it from the "outside," we are unaware of the greater space that holds the pattern. Then the path we might follow in the space that holds the pattern will not be evident to us, but the pattern will be. Tensors are mathematical tools that let us describe laws that are independent of coordinate systems. See [256], [257], [260], and [262] in Appendix III.

24 State space is a mathematical *Topos*. See section 6.1 of [178], Chapter 11 of [314], as well as [262], [263], and [264] in Appendix III.

25 Number and cardinality (of states) are synonyms when the number of states is finite. When a continuum of states is involved, like those in ratio or difference scaled state spaces, the number of states becomes infinite. Mathematically, the set of ratio and difference scaled sets is said to have a *dense* partial order (see Box 4.5 or [208] in Appendix III). Cardinalities, or the relative sizes of these infinite numbers, must then be considered. This involves the mathematical theory of transfinite numbers and is beyond the scope of this book. Interested readers may refer to Ordinal [212], Cardinal Number [206], Continuum Hypothesis [204], Countable [202], and Countably Infinite [203] in Appendix III.

26 The fidelity of a format depends on its information carrying capacity. It deteriorates proportionately with the information carrying capacity of the object representing an essential pattern, if the information conveyed by the essential pattern exceeds that of the object that represents it.

27 Inclusion and exclusion constraints are discussed in detail in [337] in Appendix III. Also see the section on patterns in that book.

28 When it serves as the medium for expressing ideas in words, the plane of the paper has been divided into a set of one-dimensional arrays called a line. Each cell in a line has an imputed value—a sequence number. The direction that dictates the sequence of components of a sentence in state space (see the section on constraints on the extent of representation in this box) has been mapped to matching sequence numbers. The number of characters on a line is limited by a value constraint (which creates a page margin), which itself is subject to the line

delimiter, two opposite edges of the page. Lines truncate the sequence of components in sentences. The remainder is mapped to the next line and so on.

Lines are patterns that have imputed sequence numbers based on their position on the second dimension of the plane of the paper. The sequences of symbols, abstract attributes in the state space of the format, have been mapped to the two dimensional physical space of format. This map depends on convention, and different languages may have different conventions.

29 [337] in Appendix III describes the components of the Metamodel of Knowledge that normalize rounding and truncation of numbers. Each behavior is normalized at a different place in the metamodel.

30 Dimensional analysis and the fundamental physical dimensions are discussed in [271] and [272] in Appendix III.

31 The physical world and its laws flow from its information content. As we have seen, the information content of a pattern is ultimately framed by its degrees of freedom. The fundamental domains are only one of an infinite number of possible bases for framing the physical laws. We could change our perspective of what we consider fundamental by *substituting* a dimension we consider fundamental by another that we call derived, provided we do not impute more or less information content to the overall pattern. This means that we cannot add or remove fundamental domains at will: we may introduce new fundamental domains only if we turn some other fundamental domains into derived domains. Buckingham's Pi Theorem proves this mathematically and describes the kinds of changes that are permitted. [271, [272], [287], [288], and [289] in Appendix III provide additional reading on Buckingham's Pi Theorem and fundamental domains.

32 Buckingham's Pi Theorem articulates that a rule meaning may be expressed in many different ways, possibly even with different variables, but if we take a variable out of the expression, we must compensate for the information lost by including another variable that puts the information back. See [271], [287], [288], and [289] in Appendix III.

33 Fundamental (primary) domains, secondary (derived) domains, and the system of coherent measurement are described under *Measurement Theory*, Macropedia, Volume 23, page 795 of [336] in Appendix III.

34 See *Fundamental Interactions*, Micropedia, Volume 5, page 51 of [336] in Appendix III.

35 The measure of energy in terms of physical domains is $ML^2T^{-2}$, where M is the measure of mass, L is the measure of physical separation, and T is a measure of elapsed time. Albert Einstein's special theory of relativity showed that the measure of energy is even simpler—that it is identical to the measure of mass. However, this is more relevant to physicists than business modelers. Business models lose little if they consider each measure to be a domain in its own right and ignore the derivation of secondary domains from primary domains unless there is a business rule involved.

36 Buckingham's Pi Theorem articulates the fact that meanings of values are independent of the units that express them. See [271], [287], [288], and [289] in Appendix III.

37 Should we have added the strong and weak forces to our list as well? Perhaps to incorporate future technology future. However, this is not needed at this stage as the practical application of the metamodel is related to business knowledge, and business is the focus of this book.

38 [337] in Appendix III discusses domains in detail.

39 The size of (number of values in) a domain is measured by its cardinality. The cardinality of a domain may be finite or infinite. The discussion on cardinality of domains in [337] (in Appendix III) describes how even infinite numbers may be compared and how some infinite domains may be smaller or larger than others. These concepts are based on Cantor's mathematics. Cantor was a 19th century mathematician who created the theory of transfinite numbers. Several publications on number theory, metric spaces, and set theory, listed in Appendix III, provide opportunities for further reading on this topic. [172], [202], [203], [204], [206], [208], [212], [216], [219], [220], [221], [222], [230], and [231] in Appendix III deserve special mention.

40 Tuples: see Box 19 on our Web site.

41 Box 4.6 describes how relationships between domains create new domains.

42 Mathematics of Partial Order is covered in [217] of Appendix III.

43 The size of a domain is measured by its cardinality; the calculation gets complicated when one considers domains with an infinite number of values. See [202], [203], and [212] in Appendix III.

44 Rule 10a in the chapter on domains in [337] asserts that a relationship between domains creates a new domain of at least the scaling of the most information sparse member of the participating domains. The derivation of this rule is discussed in detail with examples in that book.

45 [337] in Appendix III describes how Economic Value emerges from the junction of preference, an ordinal domain, and information, a ratio scaled domain.

46 Readers interested in the mathematics of how individual preferences add up to yield domains richer in information, domains that are more than the sum of their parts, may refer to the discussion on concordance on page 229 of [311] (in Appendix III).

47 Asymmetrical and antisymmetrical relationships are Cartesian products: See Cartesian Product on our Web site in Box 19. The association between objects is a mathematical category and an object in its own right. It is the *Product Category* of [173] (in Appendix III).

48 Tuples are described in Box 19 on our Web site.

49 These patterns of curved spaces are mathematical manifolds. See [268] and [257] of Appendix III.

50 [338] in Appendix III describes how business meanings flow from the abstract objects.

51 A null value of the instance identifier implies a non-existent object instance; an "Unknown" value implies that the object instance may or may not exist. When an information system has no record of an object instance, it could have either meaning; most current methodologies do not resolve this ambiguity.

52 [338] in Appendix III expands on the discussion of Figure 4.7 and describes the patterns of business knowledge from which knowledge reuse, resilience, and agility flow. These patterns may be utilized as templates that may be used to integrate and coordinate information, to create data, object, and process models.

53 Further reading on state indicators is provided in [166] of Appendix III (Siegrist, Sets and Events in Virtual Laboratories in Probability and Statistics, 1997-2001).

54 Box 10 on our Web site amplifies on features and states of objects.

55 Appendix II and [328] of Appendix III have more information on variation and other kinds of inheritance.

56 Object classes that are collections (sets) of objects with (some) unshared properties

are called parameterized classes in UML (Unified Modeling Language, a widely used object modeling syntax. See Box 22 on our Web site). The parameter of a parameterized class is the criterion for choosing objects from the set. Parametric classes are shown like this in UML: parameters OBJECT. Parameters are sometimes called "arguments." Interested readers may refer to [50] and [329] of Appendix III for more information.

57 Meyer ([328] of Appendix III) calls this restriction inheritance. However, it is also a kind of variation inheritance.

58 Morphism is the quality of having a form or shape. Polymorphism is the quality of appearing in several apparently different forms. In mathematics, *morphisms* are maps, relationships, or rules between categories that associate objects in one category with those in other(s). When only subtypes of a relationship are inherited, it could be said that the supertype is inherited with special variations or restrictions and hence presents itself in different forms. Therefore, the relationship is *polymorphic* and this phenomenon is *polymorphism*. See Polymorphism in Appendix II under the theory of categories.

59 Appendix II, on refactoring, has more information on reconfiguring components of knowledge. [337] of Appendix III also describes refactoring in more detail, with examples in Chapter II under Default States, Subtypes, and Variation Inheritance.

60 *The principle of subtyping by adding information* is described in Box 4.3.

# Chapter V
# Relationships

## ABSTRACT

*The focus of this chapter is on how interactions between objects create new meanings. It develops a model of business rules, and shows how mutability supports innovation. It introduces the rules that support inference and innovation by manipulating the patterns of information that constitute different meanings.*

This chapter focuses on the interactions among objects. These interactions convey information and are relationships between objects. Thus, relationships between objects are also information bearing, meaningful objects. In this way, new meanings are created by objects that relate to each other. Without relationships, meanings cannot engage, patterns cannot exist, and knowledge cannot be.

Knowledge is a configuration of facts about interactions that make the world around us what it is. An interaction may be nominally scaled, ordinally scaled, difference scaled, or ratio scaled. The rule expressions in Box 4.1 were relationships. The relationship between the two signatures and the payability of the check, in which both the CFO and the CEO's signature are required to make the check payable in the case study in Module 5 on our Web site, is an example of a nominally scaled relationship between attributes. In contrast, the relationship between money per piece, number of pieces, and money in Box 4.6 is an example of a ratio scaled relationship. Relationships between object classes are nominally scaled because they merely articulate an association that asserts the mere existence, not magnitude, of a meaning.

A relationship normalizes rules about object interactions. For example, *Person* is an object class. *House* is an object class. A person may live in a house. "*Live in*" is the interaction between *Person* and *House*. "*Live in*" is a relationship and also an object. The "*live in*" relationship between *Person* and *House* will normalize information about the interaction about *Person* and *House*—information like when an individual lived in which house, why they moved, and when.[1]

## A CASE STUDY

***Authorizing a Check: Reusing and Modifying Process Knowledge*** at our Web site shows how process design may be automated with reusable components of normalized knowledge. It also demonstrates how the properties of relationships we have normalized in the different metaobjects interact to produce different business behaviors.

The case study uses a set of processes for authorizing checks. The processes are engineered differently from the same reusable components in support of different business environments. Figure 7.24 represents this process. Figure 7.24A starts with an example in which the CFO and the CEO of a company must both sign a check in order to authorize it. The case study on the Web site describes how Figure 7.24A represents this. It then describes how the processes in Figure 7.24B are polymorphisms of the pattern in Figure 7.24A and how business processes in Figure 7.24B automatically flex as rules are changed.

## INVERSE OF A RELATIONSHIP

A relationship is a map between objects. At the class level, it maps between object classes; at the instance level, it maps between object instances. The map is a meaning that springs from the gulf between objects. The objects it connects frame the meaning of the map. For example, *Person* and *House* frame the context of "*lives in*" in the assertion that a "Person lives in House." "*Lives in*," the relationship, bridges the gulf between the two objects, *Person* and *House*, to create a new meaning that depends on both *Person* and *House* for its context and thus its very existence (see Figure 5.6).

Every relationship implies another—its inverse (see Box 5.1). Inverses are special relationships that reverse the sense of the relationship that implies it *and* complements its meaning. An inverse maps back in the reverse direction, from the instance level target to its instance level source.[2] In the example above, "*live in*" is a relationship between *Person* and *House*. It is also a rule that maps the set of persons to the set of houses (see Box 5.1). An instance of "*live in*" is a rule that maps an individual in the set of persons, to a particular house, in the set of houses. That a person may live in a house also implies that a house may be *lived in by* a person. As such, "*lived in by*" is the inverse of "*live in*." If an instance of "*live in*" maps a particular individual to a particular house, an instance of "*lived in by*," its inverse relationship, maps that house back to the same individual. Every metamodel discussed so far has paired every relationship with its inverse.

*Box 5.1. Relationships between attributes, meanings, and expressions*

Box 5.1 elaborates on the behavior and the structure of relationships between attributes and the possibility of time dependent, nonstationary relationships and constraints. It discusses multiway, conjoined interactions, recursive interactions, rules, and the difference between a meaning and its expressions. It discusses, with examples, the mathematical relationship between a meaning and its possible multiplicity of expressions.

Relationships normalize atomic rules about *interactions* between objects. Attributes and features of objects are (meta)objects too, and relationships between them are repositories of knowledge about *interactions between attributes and features*.

Relationships in examples thus far have all been about *occurrences* of object instances. We could think of them as relationships between the instance identifiers of objects that participate in the relationship. Relationships between attributes are much richer and more varied. They not only carry information about existence (occurrence), but also about *value*—nominal, ordinal, and quantitative.

*continued on following page*

*Box 5.1 continued*

*Figure A. A relationship between attributes is a mapping rule.*
*Reproduced by permission from Mitra, A., & Gupta, A., Creating Agile Business Systems with Reusable Knowledge, New York, NY: Cambridge University Press, 2006.©*

Figure A illustrates how values of one attribute may map to another.[3] If attribute A in Figure A has a certain value (let us call it value A1), the mapping rule maps it to the value of a value of attribute C (let us call it value C1).[4] When C is nominally scaled, this rule could be an exclusion or inclusion relationship of the kind in Box 29 on our Web site.[5] When C is an ordinal or quantitative attribute, this relationship could be a much richer repository of far more complex and varied rules. Relationships that map to ordinal values can carry not only information on existence but also information about ranking and ranges of values.[6] Relationships that map to quantitative attributes can carry even more information. In addition to existence and ranking, they may involve mathematical formulae that that use the full range of mathematical operators such as addition, subtraction, multiplication, division, and other more complex mathematical functions.[7]

Indeed, these relationships may not only be between attributes but also between specific *values* of attributes. For example, consider a relationship between two nominal attributes of object class *Person, Gender* (male or female), and *Type of Parent* (father or mother). We know that all fathers must be male. A relationship between a specific value, *Father,* of *Type of Parent,* and another specific value, *Male,* of *Gender* establishes this. The rule is an exhaustive inclusion set between a value (*Father*), of attribute *Parent Type,* and a value (*Male*), of attribute *Gender.*

On the other hand, consider the mapping between *Car Color*, a nominal attribute of an object class called *Car,* and *Color Preference,* an ordinal attribute of object class *Person.* Assume the categories of color preference are "Likes a lot," "Likes," "Neutral," and "Dislikes." The map from *Car Color* to *Color Preference* is not merely a rule about including or excluding a specific car color but a rule about mapping car colors into one of the *ranked* categories of color preferences.

Next consider a quantitative relationship that maps to a quantitative attribute. The *Population* of an object class is the number of instances of an object class at any point in time. The population of the class is an attribute of the object *class*, not object instance. It is also a ratio scaled attribute. The existence of an instance of the class is an attribute of the *instance*, asserted by the instance identifier, a nominal attribute. The relationship between the instance identifier and the *Population* is not merely an existence or ranking rule. It involves adding 1, an arithmetic operation, for every instance identifier.

The set of values mapped from the source attribute is called the *Domain of the rule* (or *relationship*). Similarly, the set of values that the relationship maps to (of the target attribute) is called the *Codomain of the rule* (or *relationship*). Like the value set of an inclusion or exclusion set, domains and codomains of relationships between attributes need not be *proper subsets* (Proper Subset: see Box 19 on our Web site) of corresponding attribute domains.

*A relationship's codomain determines its potential.* When a relationship involves only two attributes (like in Figure A), nominal codomains will support inclusion and exclusion sets only. Ordinal codomains will support inclusion and exclusion sets by themselves or in conjunction with ranking rules. Quantitative codomains will also support inclusion and exclusion sets in conjunction with the full range of mathematical formulae. Also, based on the principle of subtyping by adding information, it is evident that ordinal relationships will be polymorphisms of nominal relationships, and quantitative relationships will be polymorphisms of ordinal relationships

Just as two attributes may be related via rules, so too may three or more attributes. For example, we know that the number of male and female persons must always add up to the population of object class *Person* (the three related attributes, *Number of Males, Number of Females,* and *Population* are all attributes of the object class *Person,* not of instances of *Person*). These are rules that map *combinations* of values of attributes to a third attribute. Figure B illustrates this. Rules like this are contained in the multiway relationship or *interactions* between attributes. These are called *Joint Constraints* in the metamodel of knowledge. Like rules that involve two attributes, the *operations* that a rule in a *Joint Constraint*

*continued on following page*

*Box 5.1 continued*

may contain (existence, ranking, and mathematical operations) will depend on the codomain of the rule—that is, whether attribute C in Figure B is nominal, ordinal, or quantitative.

Consistent with the ontology of relationships we just discussed, nominal codomains will support rules with Boolean operators (*and, or, not*) attached to inclusion and exclusion constraints only. Ordinal codomains will support Boolean operators and ranking rules attached to inclusion and exclusion constraints, whereas Quantitative codomains will also support inclusion and exclusion constraints in conjunction with the full range of mathematical operations (see Box 4.3).

***Inverse of a relationship:*** The inverse of a relationship is a relationship that maps the image of the value in the codomain back to the original value in the domain. In this book, inverses have been shown [like this] in square brackets near names of relationships.

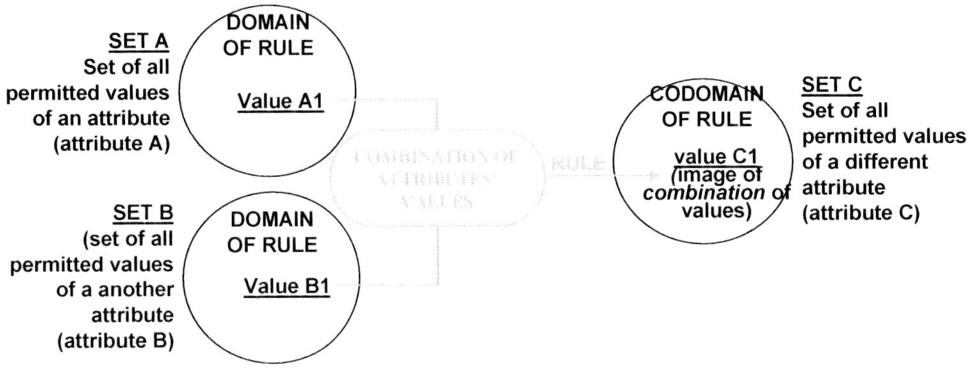


*Figure B. Multiway relationships between attributes are joint constraints that involve three or more interacting attributes.*

Reproduced by permission from Mitra, A., & Gupta, A., *Creating Agile Business Systems with Reusable Knowledge,* New York, NY: Cambridge University Press, 2006.©

***The Degree of a Relationship Between Attributes:*** The ***degree*** of a relationship between attributes is the *number of values* it involves. If a rule involves values of the two different attributes, and one of another, it will be a third degree constraint; for instance, amount = price x quantity. If the relationship had involved, not values of two different attributes, but values of an attribute in two different time slices, and a third attribute, it would still have been a third degree constraint.

***"Rule Constrain" Is an Aggregate Object with a Structure:*** The discussion above makes it clear that "rule constrain" is not only a relationship but also an aggregate object. It consists of a *Rule* and an *inclusion/exclusion relationship.*[8]

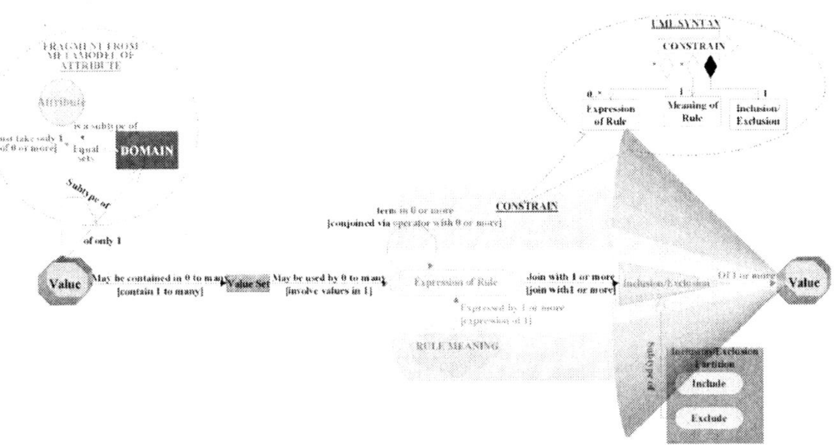


*Figure C. A "Rule Constrain" relationship is an aggregate object with a structure.*

*Reproduced by permission from Mitra, A., & Gupta, A., Creating Agile Business Systems with Reusable Knowledge, New York, NY: Cambridge University Press, 2006.©*

*continued on following page*

*Box 5.1 continued*

Figure C is the metamodel of "*Rule Constrain*." It illustrates how the "*rule constrain*" relationship is not only a relationship but also an aggregate object with an internal structure. In the figure, "*Rule Constrain*" is the large round, three-dimensional arrow between values. Components of constrain are shown inside it. That the rule may be a joint constraint is shown by the fact that the value set connected to the Rule Expression might contain several values (presumably of different attributes, or the same attribute, at different times that participate in a rule expression.

If the value set contains only the value of one attribute, the rule (expression) will be an interaction, or constraint between only *two* attributes—the attribute (value) that constrains[9] and the attribute (value) that is constrained. Whether the value set contains one or several values, each value is an "input" to the rule expression, or more appropriately, the argument of the rule expression in Figure C. Of course, a value may not participate in any constraint, joint or otherwise, hence the zero lower bound on the relationship between *Value* and *Value Set* in Figure C.

A value in a value set may be that of an attribute, illustrated by the link between *value* and *attribute* in Figure C, or it might not: values may sometimes be "constants" in mathematical formulae, drawn directly from the domain. For example, yards must be multiplied by three to convert to feet. This factor, three, is a constant drawn from the domain of numbers. Like a value set, it is a subset of a domain, except that it is a subset with a single, fixed member (a constant is a pattern with no degrees of freedom). This is why *value* is not only related to domain in conjunction with *attribute* (in Figure C) but also independently and directly linked to domain. This relationship shows that domains are classes of values.

The relationship between *attribute* and *value* is a subtype of this direct link. Whenever an attribute takes a value, the value is a value from the attribute's domain, and hence it implies this direct relationship between *attribute* and *value*. However, the reverse is not true; the relationship between *value* and *attribute* may be instantiated independently when constraints (including constants) are involved (the value of the attribute (or feature) will then be constrained to a value/feature set). Thus, the relationship between *attribute* and *value* is a subset (subtype) of the relationship between *value* and *domain*. In order to normalize knowledge, it is important to recognize this rule between the two relationships in Figure C. If we do not recognize that the relationship (of *value*) with *attribute* implies the relationship to *domain* (but not necessarily vice versa), we will replicate, not normalize, knowledge.[10]

The metamodel illustrates that a single "*rule constrain*" relationship may be applied to several values, and of course, it must constrain at least one value; otherwise it is not a constraint. Like the value set in Figure 42, the value set in Figure C may not necessarily be used to constrain values. It is only a set of values, a component that can have many and varied uses. It stands by itself, independent of other objects in the metamodel of knowledge (except domains: it is a piece of a domain, a subset of values in the domain). This is why the relationship from *Value Set* to *Rule Expression* is optional in Figure C.

***Rules, Rule Meanings, Terms, and Recursions***[11]: Most of us are familiar with the fact that mathematical formulae may consist of several terms bound together with mathematical operators. These terms are rule expressions themselves. For example, consider a business that only sells identical widgets at identical prices and offers no credit. Then:

1. *Total revenue = price per piece* x *number of pieces sold*, and
2. *Revenue per time period = Total Revenue ÷ time period over which sales transactions have occurred*

Total Revenue is a result in the first equation. It is a term in the second. Thus, the rule expression in the first equation is a term in the rule expression of the second equation. The example demonstrates that rule expressions may consist of terms that are rule expressions themselves; that is, rule expressions can be aggregate objects with linear structures (a structure in which objects are strung together in a sequence like a daisy chain or beads on a necklace rather than nodes on a lattice or network).[12] The relationship looping back on rule expression in Figure C represents this irreducible fact.

Most of us understand that the *same rule* may be *expressed* in *different terms*. For example, we could express Rule 2 above in different terms:

*Revenue per time period = (price per piece x number of pieces sold) ÷ time period over which sales transactions have occurred*

*continued on following page*

*Box 5.1 continued*

Similarly, consider that the edge of a square is a straight line that consists of two segments: one segment of length "*a*" and the other of length "*b*." The total length of the straight line will be $a + b$, and the area of a square may be expressed in two ways, both of which have the same *meaning*:

1. $Area = (a + b)^2$
2. $Area = a^2 + b^2 + 2 \times a \times b$

The meaning of the rule in both cases is exactly the same, and both expressions will always map a value in the domain of the rule to identical values in its codomain. Only the terms in which the rules are expressed, that is, their *calculation procedures*, will be different.[13] Thus, a single rule may have many expressions.[14]

Consider what it means in Figure C when "*rule constrain*," the aggregate object, consists of only one rule meaning but possibly several corresponding rule expressions. It implies that all "*rule constrain*" relationships with the same *Rule Meaning* are equivalent; they are the same constraint, at the *business rule* level, but not necessarily at the levels beneath it in Figure 3.4. All "*rule constrain*" relationships with the same *Rule Meaning* mean the same thing, and therefore point to a single object in the business rule layer of Figure 3.4. This object, a single rule *meaning*, may map to several objects, each different, but equivalent rule *expression* in the lower (business process automation) layers of Figure 3.4. This happens because different, but equivalent, rule expressions are merely different formulae or calculation procedures for the same constraint. Thus these objects in the business process automation layer are subtypes of "*rule constrain*."[15] *This is one kind of link, or transform, that takes us from business rule to process automation.* We will find more as we forge ahead into the metamodel of knowledge.

In this book, the term *Abstract Rule* means a *Value Constraint* (object) in which the *Rule Meaning* exists, but its *Terms* (Rule Expression(s)) are unknown. For example, in the real world, we may not know the formula for calculating the volume of a complex shape, but nevertheless, we know that it *does* have a rule for calculating volume, which could possibly be expressed in different ways, with different terms that we do not know. Hence, the meaning of the calculation can be independent of its expression. In Figure D, *Rule Meaning* is the sense, or *meaning*, of the rule expression.

Unfortunately, there is no general algorithm or procedure that can show the equivalence of two or more rule expressions[16]; that is, it has been mathematically and irrefutably proven that, given two or more different rule expressions, there is no single automated procedure we can apply to say for sure that they either have, or do not have, the same meaning. However, as we have seen in the examples above, this does not mean that a common meaning does not *exist*. We will call this meaning the *Rule Meaning*.

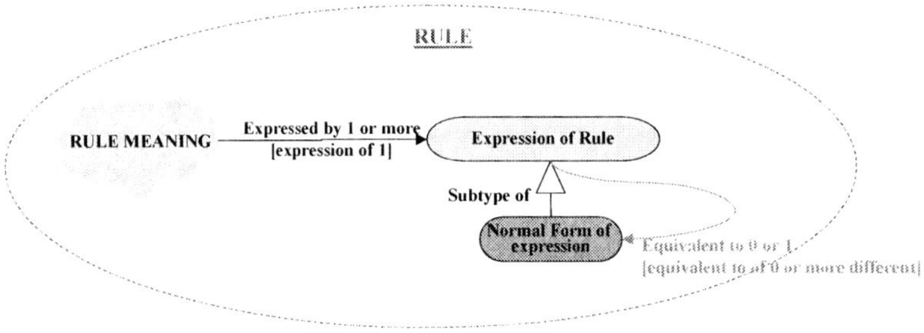


*Figure D. A rule has a unique meaning but many expressions.*
*Reproduced by permission from Mitra, A., & Gupta, A., Creating Agile Business Systems with Reusable Knowledge, New York, NY: Cambridge University Press, 2006.©*

*Rule Meaning* can be normalized by certain kinds of mathematical algorithms. These algorithms, applied to any rule expression result in an expression called a "*Normal Form*."[17] These algorithms will reduce all rule expressions with the same meaning to the same normal form. Thus, the normal form of the expression can anchor meaning. The problem is that these algorithms are not always applicable to all rule expressions (see Appendix II on the Church-Rosser theorem).

*continued on following page*

*Box 5.1 continued.*

Figure D is the backbone of the metamodel of Rule. It is a model of key natural laws about real world rules—that they can have several equivalent expressions, of which only *one* is a normal form. Figure D also states that a rule expression may not have a normal form (the relationship from Rule Expression to Normal form states that there may be zero, that is, no, normal forms equivalent to a given expression, but if there is, it must be unique (1) for all equivalent expressions).[18]

The real world does not care whether we can or cannot extract Rule Meanings from their expressions; they exist regardless. Fortunately, we *can* find the meaning and equivalence of most rules of *business* from their expressions, and vice versa. In other words, we can usually deduce its workable expression(s) given the meaning of the rule. Further, we can often (but not always) also intuitively deduce the meaning of a rule expression without arcane mathematical algorithms and theorems. However, these powerful tools are available if we need them and are required if we wish to have automation do it for us. Intelligent agents, armed with such tools, can test rule expressions for common meanings and ensure that state spaces and attribute constraints stay consistent under the pressure of changing requirements. Indeed, this fact that different but equivalent rule expressions all lead to the same end result, or meaning, is a basis for process reengineering and work flow rationalization when applied to relationships that involve the flow of time (process reengineering is discussed later in this book).

*Recursion* is the definition of a rule expression using the rule expression itself. This might sound like circular logic, or begging the argument, but it is not because we are not defining the *meaning* of the expression in terms of itself—only the procedure or sequence of calculation (terms) is being defined this way.

Consider the factorial of a positive integer "N." It is the product of a sequence of numbers starting with 1 and ending with "N." For example, Factorial(2) is 1 x 2 = 2, Factorial(3) is 1 x 2 x 3 = 6, Factorial(4) is 1 x 2 x 3 x 4 = 24, and so on. We can state this rule by asserting that for all positive integers:

Factorial (N) = N x Factorial (N-1), and Factorial (0) = 1

Here, we have used a term, factorial, to define itself in the rule expression above. This is an example of how there is no bar against rule expressions being expressed in terms of themselves. These kinds of expressions are called *recursive* sequences of terms—terms that are the same rule expression but applied to different, but related, values in reverse sequence from that implied by the "joined to" relationship in Figure C. [19] This recursive rule for computing a factorial of a number traverses the relationship that loops back to *Rule Expression*, in Figure C, backwards to Factorial(1). The argument of each term is one less than the argument of the term ahead of it; that is, the argument of each term, except the last (Factorial(1)) is constrained by the term *ahead* of it.

The meaning of this recursive calculation procedure or rule expression for computing "factorial" is identical to that of a procedure in which we move forward along the same looping relationship in Figure C. Going forward along that relationship, we would start by multiplying 1 by 2, and then the result by 3, and so on until "N." Mathematically, this procedure is described by the expression on the righthand side of the following equation:

$$\text{Factorial (N)} = \prod_{i=1}^{i=N} (i)$$

(The expression to the right of the equality (=) sign means mean that a series of numbers, *i*, starting from 1, increasing in steps of 1 to a number N, are mutually multiplied together.)

The two different expressions on the righthand side of the two procedures for calculating factorial (N) will always yield the same end result and express identical meanings. They are expressions of the same *rule meaning*[20] and an example of how a single rule may have several expressions. Figure D illustrates this natural law that flows from the metamodel of knowledge.

Rule Expression is also an object that links the meaning of the rule, in the *business layer*, to a procedure for expressing or calculating it, in the *interface rules layer* of Figure 3.4 (in the Technology Rules layer, we might have an algorithm that computes the rule expression to optimize performance and to get requisite accuracy and speed depending on technology constraints internal to the computing platform[21]). Indeed, mathematicians have conclusively proven that any iterative

*continued on following page*

*Box 5.1. continued*

computational procedure that can be implemented on a computer to express a rule can be expressed recursively and vice versa[22] (as the metamodel in Figure C shows, the relationship on Rule Expression may be traversed in either direction).

A *recursive relationship* is similar to, but not the same as, the recursion of terms in a rule expression. Unlike recursive rule expressions, a recursive relationship describes a rule or constraint that is not a mere *expression* of meaning but is a container of normalized *meaning*. Consider the recursive relationship on Value Set in Figure 42b. It shows that any given value set may merge with another, which in turn may merge with yet another and so on, following the same rules of merger. Similarly consider the bill of materials for a machine. The machine may consist of subassemblies, which in turn might consist of other subassemblies and so on until we get to individual parts that go into the machine. We will come across several recursive relationships like these in this book and in nature.

***UML Syntax:*** Figure C also illustrates the UML syntax for aggregation (UML, an acronym for Unified Modeling Language, is a standard syntax for modeling the behavior automated information systems). The diamond shapes on the relationship between "*rule constrain*" and its components assert "*rule constrain*" is an aggregate of these components; that is, it *contains* each component connected to the aggregate with a diamond. The "1" near the inclusion/exclusion component further asserts that "*rule constrain*" has one inclusion/exclusion component—no more and no less. Similarly the 0..* near the rule expression describes the lower and upper bounds of the number of rule expressions that may exist in a single "*rule constrain*." The "*" means that there is no upper bound (after all, a single rule meaning may be expressed in several ways). The "0" means that a rule expression is optional. This might seem strange at first glance. If the rule expression is missing or "null," the constraint will not be a rule constraint. Instead, it will reduce to the simpler constraints that needed only inclusion and exclusion sets to express themselves.[23]

Remember also there may be meanings we cannot express with rule expressions because we do not know the formula. In this case, the rule expression will take the "unknown" value. The rule expression being unknown is a different state of knowledge than knowing for certain that it does not exist.

Every "*constrain*" *must* have a rule meaning. The "1" adjacent to rule meaning in Figure C says it all. It not only asserts that rule meanings are mandatory for rule constraints but also that each rule constraint (obviously!) must have only one and no more.

The "*" at other end of the relationship asserts that the same rule meaning may be used elsewhere as well. For example, cubes have six identical square faces. Thus, the rule for computing the area of a square may be used to not only compute the area of a square, but may also be a component of the rule for computing the volume of a cube. In this way, not only may an *expression* be reused, but so too may the *meaning* of a rule.

The dark, solid diamond also has a meaning in UML. It asserts that "*constrain*" cannot exist unless it contains the exclusion/inclusion relationship (it also asserts that the same instance of this include/exclude component may not be used by any other object aggregation, including other "*constrain*" relationships, while it is a component of this "*constrain*." This atomic rule need not bother us because instances of *include (exclude)* are all alike. We can always use another instance of *include* or *exclude* in another aggregation if we need it).

***Stationary vs. Nonstationary Relationships Between Attributes:*** Like other relationships, relationships between attributes may change over time, that is, rules (mathematical formulae and constraints) may change over time. For example, exchange rates between currencies are in constant flux. Thus, the factor by which prices in U.S. dollars must be multiplied to convert it to prices in British pounds (and vice versa) changes continually. Constraints that do not change over time are called *stationary* constraints, whereas those that do evolve over time, like exchange rates, are called *nonstationary* constraints. Nonstationary constraints in the metamodel make room for atomic rules that are time sensitive. Indeed, the rule may require overhauling or replacing an entire formula, depending on the flow of events in time. We will discuss nonstationary constraints and the flow of time in the chapter on processes later in this book. For the moment, it will suffice to recognize that constraints can be either stationary or nonstationary.

***Equations***: Equations are a kind of constraint between attributes. Consider how equations emerge from exhaustive[24] inclusion sets:

1. If the value set in an inclusion set is exhaustive and has only a single value in it, it is tantamount to forcing an attribute to always equal that value.

*continued on following page*

*Box 5.1. continued*

2. Values in a value set may belong to attributes (perhaps in different time slices) or even the attribute being constrained at a different point in time.
3. Constraints between values (of attributes) may involve arithmetic, Boolean, and ranking operations.

These three facts, together, are manifested in the metamodel of knowledge as equations between variables of a system: An exhaustive inclusion set that contains only one attribute value (in its value set) is an equation. When the value set of the joint constraint has several (attribute) values, the equation is multivariate; that is, it involves several variables.

When only two object instances are involved, we can always infer the instance of an inverse from the class of inverses. A person may be the *mother of* another person. *Mother of*, the class, is a relationship that loops back on the same object class, *Person*. It maps one instance of *Person* to another. A person must have only one natural mother. Therefore, given a person, we can always find the inverse to "*mother of*" that person. We do not have to implicitly link each instance of "*mother of*" to each instance of its inverse to identify it as such. A class level linkage will suffice (Figure 5.1a and b).

Contrast this with the "*live in*" relationship between people and houses. Several individuals may live in the same house. Therefore, given a house, we cannot infer the inverse of "*live in*" by merely specifying at the class level that "lived in by" is the inverse of "live in." We must necessarily associate each instance level relationship with its inverse (Figure 5.1c).

When a class of relationships is constrained by a rule that bars several instances of the relationship from mapping distinct source objects (instances) to the same "target" object (instance), the inverse of the relationship may be inferred from its target

*Figure 5.1. Bijective, injective, and surjective relationships*

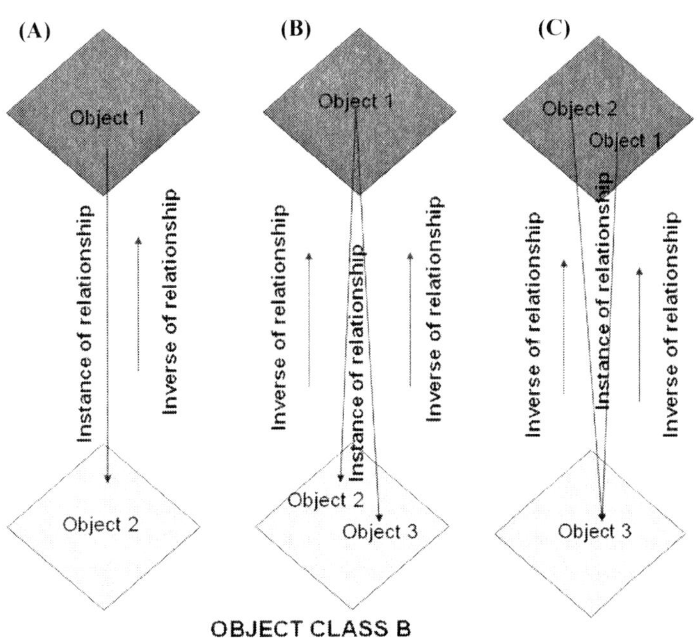

object (instance) alone. Relationships of this type are called *injective relationships*.[25] Both Figure 5.1a and b show injective relationships, but one of them is special. The *bijective relationship* in Figure 5.1a, also known as a "one-to-one relationship," is a special kind of injective relationship. In bijective relationships, only one object instance in the domain of the relationship may be related to a single object instance in its codomain (see Box 5.1). Figure 5.1a shows this. Figure 5.1b, on the other hand, shows an injective relationship in which a single object instance in the domain of the relationship may be related to several object instances in its codomain. Injective relationships of this type are also called "one-to-many" relationships.

A *surjective relationship* is a relationship of the type "*live in*," in which its target (object instance) may map back to several source object instances. When this happens, each inverse must be explicitly linked to each relationship to avoid any ambiguity about which inverse traces the relationship back to which object (Figure 5.1c).

When more than two objects are involved in a relationship (for example, in Figure 5.3), the concept of inverse is similar. Given an object instance, the inverse traces the relationship back to object instances at the other "end(s)" of the relationship. The relationship may be a joint constraint, even a value constraint, and sometimes we may have no information on the inverse. If this happens, the inverse (i.e., its instance identifier) is presumed to be "unknown."[26]

## RECURSION AND REFLEXIVITY

Consider the "mother of" relationship again. It relates objects in the same object class through *Person*. Relationships of this type are called recursive relationships. Some recursive relationships, called reflexive relationships, may even relate object instances to themselves. For example, an individual may be his own counsel in a court of law. The recursive relationship, "*counsel of*" in the rule "*Person* may be ***counsel of*** *Person*," is reflexive, whereas "*mother of*" in "*Person* may be ***mother of*** *Person*" is irreflexive because a person cannot be her own mother. Irreflexive relationships *must* relate different object instances. Reflexive relationships may weave different *or the same object instances* into a pattern of association. Figure 5.2 illustrates the difference between reflexivity and irreflexivity. The latter two are mutually exclusive subtypes of recursive relationships.

Sometimes recursive relationships are also called *homogenous facts* or *Unary Relationships* because they are rules about a single homogenous object class, as opposed to relationships that bridge different (heterogeneous) object classes.[27]

*Figure 5.2. Recursion, reflexivity, and irreflexivity*

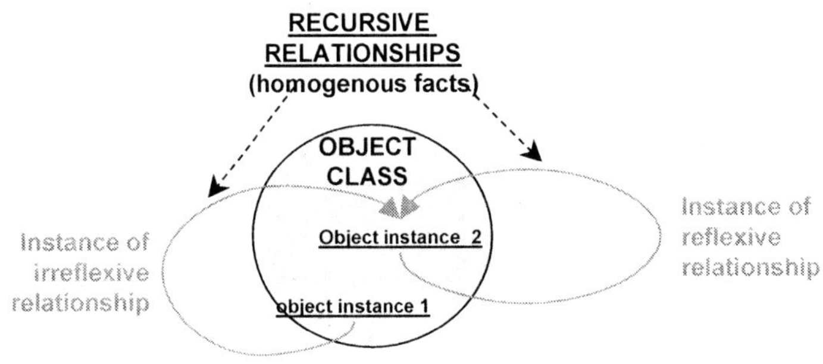

## IDEMPOTENCY

An idempotent relationship is a special kind of recursive relationship. Unlike a reflexive relationship that may, or may not, loop back to the same object instance, an idempotent relationship *must always* loop back to the same object instance. Idempotency is a stronger condition than reflexivity, and in a way, an idempotent relationship is the antithesis of an irreflexive relationship, which is *never* allowed to connect an object instance to itself. For instance, "self help" is idempotent with respect to a person. The idempotent relationship is the seed from which exchanges and returns, at the heart of business, blossom. Idempotency lends its meaning to business, and business blooms from it.

## SYMMETRICAL, ASYMMETRICAL, AND ANTISYMMETRICAL RELATIONSHIPS

Relationships weave objects into patterns. Consider the atomic rule *Person may be relative of Person.* The sequence of individuals in this pattern is irrelevant. The sequence conveys no information. Only the meaning of "*relative of*," a relationship between two individuals, and the identities of the two individuals it connects matter. The relationship and its inverse are identical. Relationships like this are called symmetrical relationships. The direction of a symmetrical relationship does not matter; only the connection does. Relationships are patterns of association. In Chapter IV, we saw that the sequence of objects in a pattern may or may not be relevant, and it is the same with relationships.

Let us add a little information to the "*relative of*" relationship above. A parent is a kind of relative. Based on the principle of subtyping by adding information (Chapter IV, Box 4.3), "*Parent of*" is a subtype of "*Relative of.*" Consider the atomic rule "*Person* may *be parent of Person*". The direction of this relationship certainly matters. We have not only added sequencing information to the pattern, but also know that a child cannot ever be a parent of his own parent. The relationship not only tells us that persons may be parents of persons but also tells us that children cannot be parents of their own parents. Obvious, but someone has to tell the computer that! "Parent of" and its inverse, "Child of," may never under any circumstances for any instance of *Person* be the same. Such relationships are called asymmetrical relationships. The inverse of an *asymmetrical relationship* can never be the same as the original—the relationship it is the inverse of.

Asymmetrical relationships, as we have just seen, crystallize from symmetrical relationships as we add information to them. They are subtypes of information-starved, symmetrical parents. Symmetrical and asymmetrical relationships may also be nonhomogenous facts bridging different kinds of objects. For instance, if a *Person* is *associated with* a *Car*, the reverse is also true—the car is also associated with the same person. "*Associated with*" is a symmetrical relationship between different object classes. On the other hand, if we are more specific about the association, it becomes asymmetrical. We know that persons may drive cars, sell cars, and fix cars, but cars cannot return the favor—cars cannot drive, sell, or fix people.

Therefore, the inverses of these relationships cannot be identical to the original. They are all asymmetrical relationships between different object classes—*Person* and *Car.*[28]

The symmetry or asymmetry of relationships is a broad concept. It applies not only to nominal patterns of the kind we have just discussed but also to any pattern, even arithmetic operations between ratio-scaled values in domains. This property is inherited from the *Join* relationship on the unknown domain in Appendix I; it springs from the universal properties of patterns. For example, arithmetic addition and multiplication are symmetrical relationships between ratio scaled values, whereas subtraction and division are not (see *Commutative Operators* in Appendix II under the theory of categories).

Obviously, symmetry and asymmetry are mutually exclusive properties of relationships; however, when we consider the symmetry or asymmetry of reflexive relationships, there is a new complication—we must consider a new class of relationships—one that emerges from the trijunction of reflexivity, symmetry, and asymmetry. Consider arithmetic subtraction of values in a quantitative domain. It is asymmetric unless the values being subtracted are the same. If the two values are the same, the sequence of subtraction will not matter; the result will be nil in either case. Such relations that are symmetric only when they loop back to the same object instance, but asymmetric otherwise, are called *antisymmetric relationships.*[29]

There are several examples of antisymmetric relationships in this book. For instance, the *convert to* relationship in Box 4.1 is an antisymmetrical relationship.

## THE ORDER AND DEGREE OF RELATIONSHIPS

Relationships are bridges between objects. Just as relationships between domains created new domains, relationships between objects create new objects—the relationship itself. Just as domains of association (see Box 4.6) were Cartesian products, so are relationships between objects Cartesian products (or a generalization of Cartesian products—see Box 5.2). Take the atomic rule we started with: *Person* may live in *House*. The association between object classes *Person* and *House* is their Cartesian product.[30] However, the relationship "*live in*" is more than a mere ordered association between individuals and houses. It is an ordered association to which a meaning has been added—the meaning of "*live in*." This makes the association special. It is distinct and different from other possible associations between the class of persons and the class of houses, such as "owns," "sells," or "decorates." Indeed, each association has its own distinct meaning that gives the association its unique identity and character. Relationships spring from Cartesian products between object classes, but they are more than mere Cartesian products—relationships are subtypes of the generic association established by a Cartesian product, with subtypes that have crystallized with clear and specific meanings.

The "live in" relationship was meaning added to the Cartesian product of two object classes—Person and House. Compare this with the atomic rule: *Product* is sold to *Customer* through *Retailer*. It is the Cartesian product of three object classes—*Product, Customer,* and *Retailer.*

Relationships are generalizations of Cartesian products of object classes (see Box 5.2) and are characterized by two properties: the number of object classes involved and the number of object instances involved.

The *constituents* of a relationship are the different objects it relates. The *order* of a relationship is the *number* of *distinct object classes* it involves, and the *degree* of a relationship is the *number* of *distinct object instances* a single instance of the relationship involves. For instance, all recursive relationships are first order relationships, but reflexive relationships are first order, first-degree relationships. On the other hand, the "*live in*" relationship between *Person* and *House* was a second order, second degree relationship—second order because it is an association between two object classes, *Person* and *House*, and second degree because an instance of "*live in*" is associated a single instance of *Person* and a single instance of *House.* Similarly, the relationship in Figure 5.3 is a third order relationship; it involves three distinct object classes—*Product*, *Customer*, and *Retailer.*

Sometimes, first order relationships are called *unary* or *monadic relationships*; second order relationships *binary* or *dyadic relationships*; third

*Figure 5.3. A three-way relationship—Product is sold to Customer who buys through Retailer*

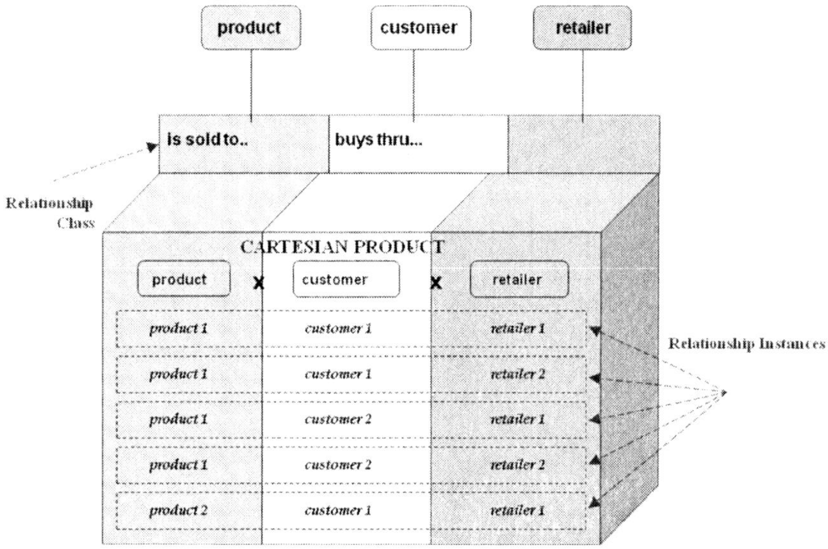


*Reproduced by permission from Mitra, A., & Gupta, A., Agile Systems with Reusable Patterns of Business Knowledge, Norwood, MA: Artech House, Inc., 2005. ©*

*Box 5.2. Cartesian products make and normalize atomic rules*

Consider the rule *Product* is sold to *Customer* through *Retailer* in Figure 5.3. Is it really an atomic rule? What information will we lose if we split it into the following distinct and unconnected facts?

1. Product is sold to Customer; and
2. Customer buys through Retailer

Assume this book you are reading is an instance of a product, and you are the customer who has purchased it. That this book has been sold to you is an instance of the first fact. It does not say who sold it. An instance of the second fact asserts that you buy from a specific retailer. However, it is not clear what you buy or have bought from the retailer. You may have bought many different items from the same retailer. It may or may not have been this book you bought from this retailer. This is the information that we have lost by breaking the three-way relationship of Figure 5.3 into two distinct facts. This example illustrates that all Cartesian products of object classes establish atomic rules. We cannot split an association established by a Cartesian product without losing information.

A Cartesian product, like the relationship in Figure 5.3, normalizes rules about the association it creates. For instance, the product class may normalize the list price of a product, but the actual price you paid for the product you bought from a particular retailer may be different from its list price. The sale price is an attribute of the sale. It belongs to the relationship in Figure 5.3, a Cartesian product. Similarly, effects like sale cancellation, sale confirmation, and others will also belong to the relationship and will be normalized by it.

Note also that a Cartesian product cares about the sequence of object classes it associates. (The Cartesian product is a noncommutative operation—see Appendix II on the theory of categories for information on commutativity.) We have seen that sequence does not matter to symmetrical relationships. Therefore, *strictly speaking, the Cartesian product is the basis of only antisymmetric and asymmetric relationships.* A more general association is the generic basis for generic relationships, and the Cartesian product is only a subtype of such generic association.

order relationships *ternary* or *triadic relationships;* and fourth order relationships *quaternary* or *tetradic relationships*. Relationships of an arbitrary order "n" are also referred to as *n-ary* or *n-adic relationships*. Often, relationships of orders greater than two are also called *higher order relationships*.[31]

## THE CARDINALITY RATIO OF RELATIONSHIPS

Relationships are patterns of association. *Order* describes the number of classes woven into the pattern, and *degree* connotes the number of distinct object instances. As we will see later in this chapter, we can constrain either one (or both) in different ways to elicit different kinds of real world behavior. However, there is also another property of relationships—the property of *cardinality ratio*. Like order and degree, cardinality ratio involves constraints on occurrence. The Cardinality Ratio specifies how many object instances in the codomain of the relationship may relate to a single object instance in its domain (codomain and domain of a relationship: see Box 5.1).

## THE CARDINALITY RATIOS OF BIJECTIVE AND SURJECTIVE RELATIONSHIPS

Consider the relationships in Figure 5.1 again. Figure 5.1a was a one-to-one relationship. As the name implied, a single instance of Object Class A in Figure 5.1a may relate to no more than one instance of Object Class B. In Figure 5.1a, the number of object instances in the codomain of the relationship was constrained to a maximum of one for each object instance in the domain of the relationship. The cardinality ratio of the relationship was therefore one. (Object Class A is the domain of the relationship, and Object Class B is the codomain of the relationship.) If we relaxed this upper bound on how many objects in object class B that a single instance of object class A may link to, we will end up with Figure 5.1b. The upper bound may be two, three, four, or any positive integer, even "many." "Many" articulates the fact that there may be no upper bound.[32] For instance, "*lived in by*," the relationship discussed under inverses, had no upper bound on its cardinality ratio.

(In addition to the one-to-one, one-to-many and many-to-one relationships of Figure 5.1, there are also "many-to-many" relationships. We will discuss these later under compositions of relationships.)

The cardinality ratio of a relationship may also be constrained by lower bounds. If the lower bound is nil, the relationship becomes optional. Consider the relationship "*live in*" between *Person* and *Home*. At first, homeless persons may be out of scope in our model, so the relationship would be mandatory, and the cardinality ratio would have a lower bound of 1. If we expanded the scope of our model to include homeless people, the relationship "*live in*" between *Person* and *House* would have become optional; the lower bound on its cardinality ratio would be nil because homeless people do not live in houses. On the other hand, consider an agreement between two or more parties. *Agreement* is an object class, as are the parties to the agreement. The rule between them asserts, "*Agreement* must bind *two* or more *Parties*." The cardinality ratio of this relationship is also constrained by a lower bound, but the lower bound is two, not nil, in this case.

Contrast limitations on cardinality ratios with those on the population of relationships. An optional relationship stipulates that not every instance of the object in the domain of the relationship need be related to object instances in the codomain of the relationship. The lower bound on the cardinality ratio of the relationship is nil. One could, without violating this constraint, make it mandatory at the class level by constraining the population of the relationship class to be one or greater. With both constraints in place, even if *every* instance of the relationship's domain is not related to instances of the relationship's codomain, *at least one will be*. The relationship will be optional at the instance level, but mandatory at the class level.

## CARDINALITY AND OTHER PROPERTIES OF HIGHER ORDER, HIGHER DEGREE RELATIONSHIPS

The cardinality ratios of unary and binary relationships have been discussed so far; the ratios of higher order and higher degree relationships are more complex. Several different kinds of cardinality ratios have to be considered, and each may have its own constraints and ranges. Consider the relationship in Figure 5.3 again. The cardinality of *Customer* may be constrained as it is in any second order relationship—the number of times a single customer appears in the set of tuples could have upper limits, lower limits, or both. The cardinality of *Retailer* may also be constrained in the same way, independently of limits on *Customer*. However, the cardinality of all possible pairs of values may also be constrained (for instance, the number of times the same customer-retailer *pairs* can occur in a triplet may be confined to a range[33]).

When it comes to the 3-tuple in a third order relationship, one enjoys little choice. The triplet in a third order relationship must be unique. A class, unlike a list, does not distinguish between identical members. However, in a fourth or higher order relationship, identical triplets embedded in a 4-tuple could repeat, and rules may restrict repetition. This pattern of repetition of parts of a tuple generalizes the concept of cardinality ratio for higher order relationships. Given cardinalities of combinations, one can always derive their ratios. In higher order relationships, the cardinalities of *combinations* are as important as cardinality ratios between individual objects bound by the relationship.

### The Cardinality of Combinations

The population of each member of the power set of *Product*, *Customer*, and *Retailer* may be constrained independently (the concept of Power Set is discussed in Box 19 on our Web site). *Product*, *Customer*, and *Retailer* are object classes. Figure 5.4 shows possible combinations that may have different populations. Each double-headed arrow in the figure represents a combination—a member of the power set of *Product*, *Customer*, and *Retailer*.

*Figure 5.4. The cardinality of multiway relationships*

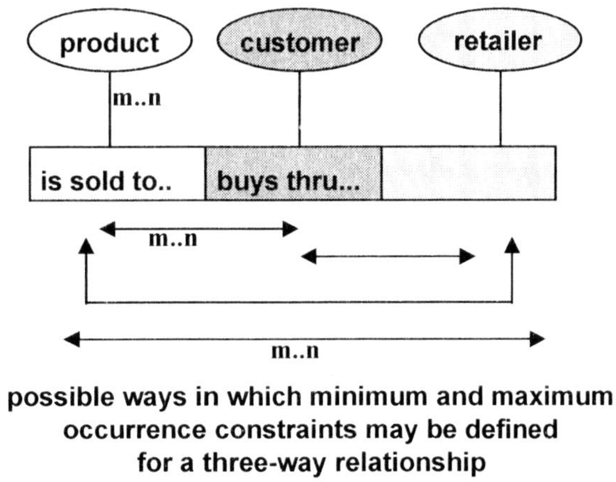

The topmost double-headed arrow, just under "*sold to...buys thru*" in Figure 5.4 represents product-customer combinations. The double-headed arrow, just under and to the right, represents Customer-Retailer combinations. The double-headed arrow under those, folded at two corners to point upwards, represents Product-Retailer pairs, and the lowest double-headed arrow represents Product-Customer-Retailer triplets.[34]

From Figure 5.3, one can see that the pairs in Figure 5.4 are actually embedded in the triplet and are an integral part of the triplet; further, the occurrences of each pair in the triplet may be individually constrained.[35]

Each double-headed arrow and each link between the relationship and the objects it relates may have maximum and minimum cardinalities (optionally) imposed on it. In NIAM,[36] upper and lower bounds are shown by the "m...n" notation in Figure 5.4. The numbers "m" and "n" represent upper and lower bounds on cardinality.

If the m...n label on the connection between *Product* and the relationship in Figure 5.4 had been 3..50, it would imply that the number of products in that relationship must always lie between 3 and 50, both inclusive; between *Product* and *Customer* (the double-headed arrow that spans *sold to* and *buys thru* in Figure 5.4), the label would restrict the occurrence of *distinct* Product-Customer pairs (in the tuples of Figure 5.3) to a number between 3 and 50; between *Customer* and *Retailer*, it would limit the occurrence of *distinct* Customer-Retailer pairs in the triple to a number between 3 and 50; between *Product* and *Retailer* (the double headed arrow with ends folded upwards in Figure 5.4), it would do the same to Product-Retailer pairs; attached to the lowermost arrow of Figure 5.4, the label would limit the number of instances of the third order relationship in Figure 5.4, the Product-Customer-Retailer combinations, to a number between 3 and 50.

Of course, if the populations of *Product, Customer*, and *Retailer* are finite, there will only be a finite set of possible *Product-Customer-Retailer* combinations. The m...n label may restrict the cardinality of the set even more but obviously cannot increase it. If, in the course of events, numbers of products, customers, and retailers falls below a point where the number of Product-Customer-Retailer combinations is less than the requisite minimum (the "m" in the "m...n" label), the relationship will cease to exist.[37]

A "distinct" Product-Customer combination means that an instance of *Product* is paired with an instance of *Customer*. Another Product-Customer combination will be distinct from this one only if a different instance of *Product*, or *Customer*, or both *Product* and *Customer* are paired. If a Product-Customer pair has exactly the same instance of Product paired with the same instance of Customer, it will not be considered a distinct combination. Rather, the pairs will be mutually indistinguishable and will be considered one – the same instance of a combination.

The combinations of *Product, Customer,* and *Retailer* in each triple of Figure 5.3 (and Figure 5.4) must be unique. Otherwise, the triple would not be an instance of an object class. It would be a member of a list instead. Each unique triple represents an instance of a *relationship* between the three objects bound into the relationship. It is the instance identifier of the relationship.[38]

Although combinations within a tuple may repeat, each tuple that represents a relationship must be a unique combination. The cardinality of a *combination* within the relationship is the number of times that the *distinct* combination occurs (in the relationship class—the set of all tuples of that kind). The population of the relationship class itself is the number of distinct tuples that represent the relationship. The combination that constitutes each instance of this tuple must be unique.[39]

(Of course, when lower and upper bounds on cardinality coincide, it implies that the cardinality exactly equal this bound. If this is the case, we will replace the "m...n" label by a single number in the diagrams that follow.)

Note that limiting the cardinality of *Product* (or *Customer* or *Retailer*) in the relationship is distinct and different from limiting the population of *Product* (or *Customer* or *Retailer*), the object class. The cardinality of *Product* in the relationship (the number of times distinct products occur in the tuple) can obviously never exceed the cardinality of *Product*, the class, but may be less (or equal). However, subject to this condition, the cardinality of *Product* in the relationship may be constrained independently of the cardinality of the class of products. The same rules will apply to the other participants of the relationship as well. The limitation obviously also applies to combinations embedded in the relationship.

In general, any higher order relationship may not only impose separate constraints on individual cardinalities of the objects it relates but may also constrain cardinalities of combinations of these objects. As the order of a relationship increases, the number of possible combinations increases explosively.

## Atomic Rules, Combinations, and Cardinality Ratios

An instance of a relationship is a unique tuple of object instances. It is also an object class in its own right. The combination in the tuple cannot repeat (if it did, the tuple would not be a relationship—an object class—it would be a list instead[40]). Several different measures of sizes for relationships exist:

1. The number of different object instances tied together (the degree of a relationship). We will discuss this later.
2. The number of different object classes tied into a relationship (the order of the relationship).
3. The number of times a *distinct* combination (combinations of the kind in Figure 5.4) occurs in a relationship class. We will call this the cardinality of the *combination*.
4. The population of a relationship class—the number of complete tuples that are instances of the relationship (like the entire 3-tuple of the third degree relationship in Figure 5.3). This is the cardinality of the relationship.

We have seen that joining tuples together (combinations like those in Figure 5.4) leads to another, higher- degree tuple. As a part of a relationship, these constituent tuples do not have to be unique combinations. For instance, in Figure 5.3, the same customer may buy the same product from several retailers. When Product-Customer combinations in the tuple are identical, the fact that each triple has different retailers makes each triple unique. The same Product-Customer combination may occur several times in the Product-Customer tuple because it is a part of another larger tuple—the Product-Customer-Retailer triple.

However, if any constituent tuple is forced to be unique, and no individual component in it has overlapping cardinality constraints with components outside the unique tuple, the particular tuple may be broken off as an *independent* relationship. Such tuples, in turn, may consist of other combinations that are unique. Those may be broken off too, subject to the same rules. We could continue doing this until we have tuples that cannot be broken. Each tuple will then be an irreducible fact about the objects it associates—an independent relationship.

When tuples within tuples are unique, but their components have cardinality constraints in concert with components outside the unique tuple, unique tuples may still be broken off as separate, *dependent* relationships. The existence of these relationships will be contingent on others. Figure 5.5 provides examples.[41]

The tuple is unique in every relationship and anchors the concept of *cardinality ratio*. In Figure 5.3, the cardinality ratio of the relationship with respect to *Customer* is the number of 3-tuples that relate to (i.e., contain) a given instance of *Customer*. This is the number of relationships a single customer may have. Similarly, combinations inside the 3-tuple that contain the *Customer* object class will also have cardinality ratios relative to *Customer*. The cardinality ratio of the Product-Customer combination relative to *Customer*, in the Product-Customer-Retailer triple, will be the number of Product-Customer combinations *per (instance of) customer*. Cardinality ratios of the other objects bound by the relationship will also be similar.

Indeed, even combinations that constitute the tuple may have cardinality ratios relative to other combinations in the tuple, or even the whole tuple. The cardinality ratio of the relationship with respect to the Product-Customer pair of Figure 5.4 is the number of triples, per *distinct* Product-Customer *combination*.

## Null Combinations

When the cardinality of a combination is constrained to be nil, such combination is barred from existing; the combination is null. When the cardinality of an entire tuple is constrained to zero, the relationship is null—it cannot exist. This is different from saying there is no relationship between them. Saying no relationship exists is equivalent to saying that there is none we know of, but it is possible that an unknown relationship may exist. Barring a relationship is a stronger constraint. We are saying that we will not permit the relationship; therefore, one is completely certain that it will not exist.[42]

Indeed, we can strengthen the conditions even further. All relationships between a given set of objects are subtypes of the generic association between them. A generic association asserts that its constituents are mutually related in some unspecified way. If we assert that no relationship may exist between two or more objects by barring the generic association between them, all associations between them will be barred. Barring the supertype automatically bars its subtypes. The objects in the set then cannot be directly connected. One cannot go from one object in the set to any other member of the aggregate without passing through other objects outside the set. Objects in the set cannot be aware of each other without "observing" the behavior of outside intermediaries. For instance, you become aware of a magnetic field only because you can see iron being attracted or a magnetized needle being deflected; you and the field cannot interact directly with each other.

## Other Properties of Combinations

Each combination is a pattern. When the sequence of members of a combination does not matter, the *combination* is symmetric. When members of a combination are identical, it is the *combination* that is reflexive. When sequences, not just identities, of instances distinguish one combination from another, it is the *combination* that is antisymmetric (identical combinations cannot be sequenced; they are collocated in information space). Just as combinations in a relationship have cardinalities, *combinations* as well as entire relationships have degrees. Degrees can be constrained by value constraints, just as combinations were, sometimes with surprising results as we will see next.

## Degrees of Combination

The length of a tuple like that in Figure 5.3 is determined by its degree—the number of object instances that participate in instances of the tuple. For example, in Figure 5.3, if the object class on the extreme right had also been *Customer*, the relationship would have been a second order third degree relationship—second order because it would have involved only two object classes, *Product* and *Customer*, and third degree because each tuple would still involve three object instances, a product and two customers. The tuple would remain a triplet, like the triplets in Figure 5.3, but two members of the triplet would now be customers instead of one.

Just as we constrained the cardinality of combinations of object classes in higher order relationships, we can constrain the number of occurrences of object instances in higher degree relationships. These constraints translate to limitations on lengths of tuples.[43]

Products and services, like telephone service or insurance coverage, may be assembled to order from a list of standard features. You can pick and choose the features you want, and together, they comprise the product or service you have bought. There may be regulatory and technical constraints on what features may be offered with which others. These constraints are first order relationships; they loop back from one feature in the class of features to others in the same class and involve only a single object class but several object instances—instances in groups of features that must (or must not) be sold together. These constraints are first order, higher degree relationships.

The imposition of limits on the degree of a relationship will constrain the size of the tuple that makes an instance of this relationship. When features are combined into service offerings, too many features in an offering may bewilder and confuse customers. We might consider it prudent to limit the number of features packaged into service offerings for customers and might formulate a guideline that not more than five features (such as voice mail and call waiting) may be packaged together in a service offering to customers. *This is a constraint, an upper bound, on the degree of the relationship* that glues features together to create a product; the degree has an upper bound of five in this case.

Constraints on combinations of instances, that is, the degree of a relationship, are similar to constraints on cardinality of higher order relationships. They follow the same pattern—patterns like those in Figure 5.4. If the constraints on the combinations in Figure 5.4 had not limited the *number of occurrences* of tuples but constrained *sizes* of an individual tuples instead, they would have constrained the degree of the *combination*. Take the combination shown by the lower-most double-headed arrow in Figure 5.4. It involves three relationship classes—one each for Person, Customer, and Retailer. A lower limit of one on the degree of the combination will force instance(s) of *at least one* of those relationships to exist at any given moment in time.

An upper limit of two would force *at most two* of the three to exist at all times—*at least* one will be dropped. Which one(s) is/are dropped will depend on responses to events, but the rule will ensure that one of the three is always dropped. Indeed, if there is no lower limit (i.e., the lower limit is nil, inherited from the enumeration domain), all of them might be dropped and the relationship itself might be obliterated by an event.

If the upper and lower bounds are the same, say two, one of the three relationships will always be dropped; which two exist might change from time to time in response to events.

Contrast this kind of constraint with constraints on cardinality. Assume that the object classes on the right of Figure 5.3 were both *Customer* instead of one being *Retailer*. Consisting still of three tuples, the relationship would now involve only two object classes—*Product* and *Customer*. *Customer* will be repeated in the tuple, taking the place of *Retailer*. The relationship will then be a second order, third degree relationship. Possible constraints on cardinalities will still follow the pattern in Figure 5.4, the only difference being that the two of the three instances that make the three tuple will belong to the same class—*Customer*. This kind of constraint is very different from the "at least" and "at most" value constraints attached to the *degree* of the combination. Constraints on cardinality and degree are different kinds of value constraints. One constrains repetition of tuples, and the other constrains the length of the tuple—the number of components it may have. Together they orchestrate the behavior of the relationship.

Generically, cardinality is a count of occurrences. So are degree and order. Each is a subtype of a generic kind of cardinality, and each is a special kind of cardinality—one describes the length of a tuple, and the other counts the *kinds* of objects that participate in a relationship. The cardinality of a *relationship* (or object class), on the other hand, counts the number of tuples (or instances of an object) in the class.

In the discussion on market segments and Borel Objects later in this chapter, we will see that constraints like these can be very important to business and flow naturally from the metamodel of knowledge as we slice and dice facts to better understand the world around us. Like any other attribute value constraint, there may be several constraints simultaneously attached to ordinalities (order), cardinalities, and the degrees of relationships. If these constraints clash, we will obtain the null set.[44] If they are consistent, we may merge them.[45]

## MUTUAL INCLUSION AND EXCLUSION OF RELATIONSHIPS

Consider what would happen to the relationship in Figure 5.3 if we forced the degree of the customer–retailer combination to always be one. This would imply that we cannot combine a customer with a retailer in a tuple. It also means that given a product, either a product-customer relationship or a product-retailer relationship may exist, but not both simultaneously. The two relationships will be mutually exclusive. Forcing the degree of any combination to equal one ensures that the relationships in the combination are mutually exclusive, and at least one of the mutually exclusive relationships must exist at all times. If we permitted a lower bound of zero, the mutually exclusive set of relationships would become optional.

Figure 5.5a is an example of a mutually exclusive pair of relationships. It asserts that a specific insurance coverage will insure either a person or an owned item (asset), but not both simultaneously. (Of course, the policy may include several different kinds of coverage, and therefore both may be covered by the complete policy, even if individual coverage covers one or the other.) This is an exclusion partition: if one object exists, the other cannot. The object in question here is a relationship. As we will see further on in this chapter, constraints on the degree and/or cardinality of a relationship can articulate mutual exclusion and more complex rules of business.

Contrast Figure 5.5a with Figure 5.5b. Figure 5.5b shows two mutually inclusive relationships. If any one of the pair exists, the other must too. A person may or may not own a car, but if she does, she must also own insurance for it. Assume that a hypothetical (fortunately!) draconian law ensures that the car insurance stands automatically cancelled the moment the car is discarded or sold, *and vice versa*—if the car's insurance is cancelled, its ownership automatically and immediately stands annulled. The existence of one relationship compels the existence of the other. Both relationships must exist simultaneously or not at all. This kind of business rule arises from cardinality constraints, not from constraints on degree. If the cardinality of the combination has a lower bound of zero, the relationship is optional. If the combination has an upper bound of "many," several may exist, but each combination implies another relationship.

Figure 5.5b is also an example of how we could lose information if we are careless with modeling atomic rules. The information lost in the representation on the left is that ownership of a car requires ownership of insurance for the *same* car. The tuple on the right captures this fact.

Of course, the degree of this relationship is exactly two, which ensures that the cardinality of *Person owns Car* will always equal the cardinality of *Person owns Car Insurance*. The constraints on the cardinality and the degree of the combination, together, ensure this. Interactions between cardinalities and degrees of combinations, together, determine the overall behavior of relationships. Remember also that strict equality implies two constraints, an upper bound and a lower bound that coincide.

Consider how mutual inclusion of mandatory relationships is different from having a pair of independent mandatory relationships. Take a group insurance policy for homes. Assume it insures several individuals against damage to their homes. Each individual is insured against damage to his individual property. Moreover, it is mandatory for at least one individual to subscribe to it; otherwise, it is null and void.

We have two mutually inclusive relationships, one from *Insurance Policy* to *Insured Individual*, and the other from *Insurance Policy* to *Insured Property*. Both are mandatory—the policy must insure *someone* and *something*. Each agreement may insure several individuals and several properties. Therefore, the upper bound on the cardinality ratio of each relationship is "many." However, by themselves, these relationships and their cardinality ratios do not convey all the information they must. Without mutual inclusion, we will not know *which properties are insured for whom*. We have no information on the *Insured Individual- Insured Property* tuple. It is a ternary relationship, an atomic rule—not two binary relationships. We lose information when we try to divide the ternary into two binaries—information on who has insured what on *that* policy. Figure 5.5b shows how sets of mutually inclusive binary relationships are actually higher order relationships.

Figure 5.5b is an equality constraint between object classes; that is, the classes are mutually inclusive. Equality constraints are only one manifestation of constraints on cardinality of relationships. Recognizing cardinality and its multiplicity in interactions between multiple objects is a broader concept than mutual inclusion. It can support a much richer repertoire of business rules than mere mutual inclusion constraints can. Constraints on cardinality subsume mutual inclusion.

In Figure 5.5c, one relationship implies another, but not vice versa—the two are not *mutually* inclusive, but inclusion *is* involved—we know that *Person Owns Wheel* includes and subsumes *Person Owns Car*. This is because a person may own wheels independently of cars. Owning a car is only one of many possible ways of owning wheels. The wheels are owned when cars are owned only because they are parts of cars. Therefore, owning a car implies owning wheels, but owning wheels does *not* imply owning a car. Therefore, *Person Owns Car* is a subset of *Person Owns Wheel*.[46]

Because the set of persons that own cars is a subset of the set of persons who own wheels, the car owner role is subsumed by a broader wheel owner role. Therefore, the cardinality (population) of car owners may, at most, equal the cardinality of wheel owners, but may not exceed it. (The cardinality of wheel owners will equal the cardinality of car owners when all wheel owners are also car owners.) Only when we force the cardinality of car owners to equal that of wheel owners (such as by attaching value constraints like those in Figure 5.5b) do we force mutual inclusion between the two relationships.

Figure 5.5c is a subsetting constraint between relationships: if the subtype exists, the supertype must also exist, but not necessarily vice versa. We will elaborate on subtyping relationships later in this book.

## THE CARDINALITY OF SUBTYPES

The subtyping relationship provides the conduit for propagating common knowledge. It is the cornerstone on which reuse of knowledge rests. Subtypes are more constrained than their parents and convey more information (see Chapter IV). Therefore, when relationships are subtyped, the cardinality constraints on the subtype may be different than those of the parent, in that the subtype may have stricter cardinality constraints than the parent relationship, but may never have looser cardinality constraints (the cardinality constraints of the subtype may also be identical to its parent because the subtype may add information to its parent in other ways, but the cardinality of the subtype can *never* violate the cardinality constraints of its parent under any circumstances). For instance, a person may have several ancestors. The upper bound on the number of ancestors each person has is "many," a number that is defined as a positive, finite number. "Person is *descendant of two or more* Person" captures this fact. *Descendant of* is the relationship we are interested in here. *Child of* is a subtype of *descendant of.* The corresponding assertion is "Person is *child of exactly 2* Person." Note that the cardinality constraint of *child of* is different from the cardinality constraint of *descendant of,* but it does not violate it. This will be true for constraints on order and degree as well. Indeed, a subtype may never violate the lawful state space of its parent but could exist within it. This is true for all objects including relationships. Note how the cardinality constraint in Figure 5.5c flows from the very nature of subtyping.

There are also subtypes of the subtyping relationship itself in which cardinality constraints may be even stricter. For instance, when an attribute of an object takes a value from a domain, it is a very special kind of subtyping relationship. In it, the cardinality of the subtype (the attribute) was exactly one; unlike most collections that may have several members, this subtype can only have one value at a time (a value is an instance of the domain).[47]

*Figure 5.5. Mutually inclusive and exclusive relationships*

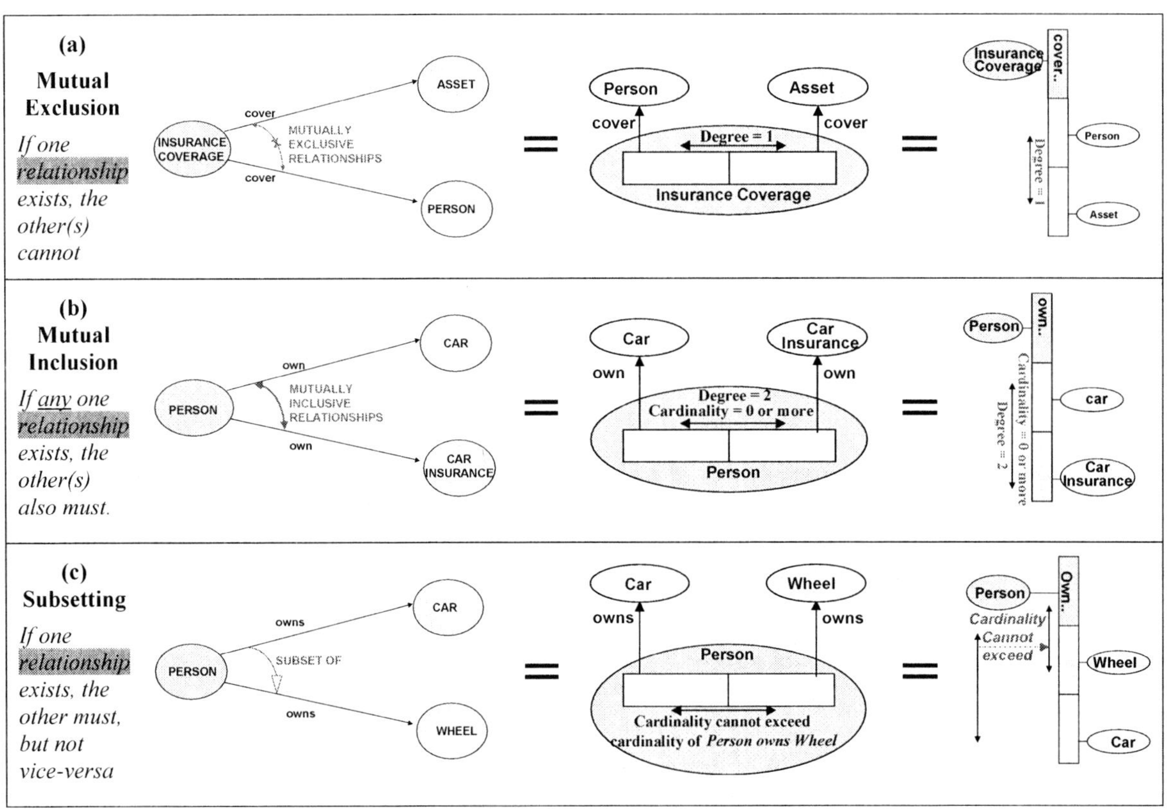

If the lower limit on the cardinality of the subtype had been nil, the attribute would have become an optional attribute. The object the attribute belonged to could then be either the supertype or the subtype; we would not know which. As such, constraints on cardinality shape the behavior of relationships—even subtyping relationships.

The class of subtyping relationships in which the cardinality of the subtype is limited to one occurs frequently in the world of business when we choose one member, an instance, out of a set of several possibilities. It is worth recognizing this as a special kind of relationship—indeed it is a special subtype of the subtyping relationship itself.

## INSTANCE LEVEL CONSTRAINTS ON CARDINALITY

So far, we have discussed class level constraints on cardinality ratios. Instance level cardinality constraints too are often found in business. Some constraints may even change between instances of relationships. Think of the "*lived in by*" relationship between *House* and *Person*. Some houses have more room than others. Each instance of house may have a different capacity for people—individual constraints on how many persons may live in it. At the class level, we had only asserted that "*lived in by*" was a one-to-many relationship. We could impose an upper bound on the cardinality of "*lived in by*," but that constraint would then apply to all houses uniformly; it will not account for individual capacities of houses. For this, we must cut the cardinality of each instance of "*lived in by*" to fit the house it belongs to.

The cardinality ratios of subtypes of relationships may stay within the range specified for its parent, and the cardinality ratio of an instance of a relationship cannot violate the cardinality ratio of the class.[48] As such, we may constrain the cardinality ratio of an instance of a relationship more than the class does, but we cannot constrain it less. It must stay within its class level limitations. For example, if the class of cottages can house five persons at most, an individual cottage may have a capacity to house fewer than five persons, but never more than five.

Cardinality maps to the enumeration domain, and cardinality ratios map to the domain of *Enumeration Quotients*. Attached to both the enumeration domain and the domain of enumeration quotients is a value constraint that imposes a lower bound of nil. This common sense constraint is inherited by all cardinalities. Lower bounds attached to the cardinality or the cardinality ratio of a specific relationship may be larger (and this will not violate this constraint inherited from the enumeration domain or the domain of enumeration quotients), but it cannot be negative. This is another example of how domains normalize knowledge and anticipate specifications (validation in this case)—specifications that might be obvious, but would otherwise need to be painstakingly documented in excruciating detail for programmers who would then manually replicate the code in equally excruciating detail to painstakingly validate every enumerated item. Instead, systems assembled from Knowledge Artifacts naturally normalize the information and automate this validation, deploying it automatically to every enumerated item—even new relationships that are born when the response to change is scope creep.

## COMPOSITIONS OF RELATIONSHIPS

Relationships begin and terminate in objects. Objects are nodes connected by a web of relationships. As much as relationships connect objects, objects connect relationships. Objects are the glue that bind relationships together end-to-end. Consider the following irreducible facts:

1. *Person* lives in *House; and*
2. *House* located in *Town.*

Together, the two rules not only imply that people live in towns, but that they do so because they live in houses and houses are located in towns. It does this by "gluing" *lives in* to *located in*. Both are relationships between object classes (*Person* and *House*, and *House* and *Town*, respectively). An object class, *House*, glues one end of "*lives in*" to the other end of "*located in*." Figure 5.6a shows this.

*House* mediates between the two relationships, and together, "*live in*," *House*, and "*located in*" mediate between *Person* and *Town*. The composite, consisting of "*live in*," *House*, and "*located in*," objects strung together on a daisy chain, is a bridge between *Person* and *House*. The composite may also be considered a relationship between the two object classes it connects. Figure 5.6b articulates this concept in a graphical manner. Conversely, daisy chains of objects are often hidden inside relationships.[49]

Indeed, given a web of objects and relationships, every possible path mediated by relationships and objects between a pair of objects, or even back to the same object[50] is a relationship. Adding detail to a model often involves opening windows into relationships to make objects and relationships in the composition explicit.[51] Later, we will see how these windows can serve as the gateway to innovation and process improvement.

A composition of objects and relationships that touches objects outside the composition is a subtype of a relationship that connects those objects together. Take Figure 2.6. It reads *Organization Ships Product*. The Shipment object and the *ships* relationship are identical. Whether we see it as an object or as a relationship is a matter of perspective—usually a matter of scope and the level of detail we need to represent.[52]

A relationship may be a token that summarizes a model—a web or daisy chain, rich and complex, or sparse and simple—of objects and relationships that are ports that "outside objects" can "plug" into—objects the token relates. These aggregates model the behavior of the token in layers of detail. The token is a relationship. The detail may merely be hidden from view or be yet unknown.

## Mutability of Compositions

Consider what would happen to the composition in Figure 5.6b if we replaced *House* with *Trailer Park*. The meaning of the composition would not change. Indeed, if we replaced *House* with a supertype called *Living Space*, or any subtype of *Living Space*, the meaning of the composition would stay the same. If we did not have a window into the components in the composition, we

*Figure 5.6. Relationships may be compositions of objects.*

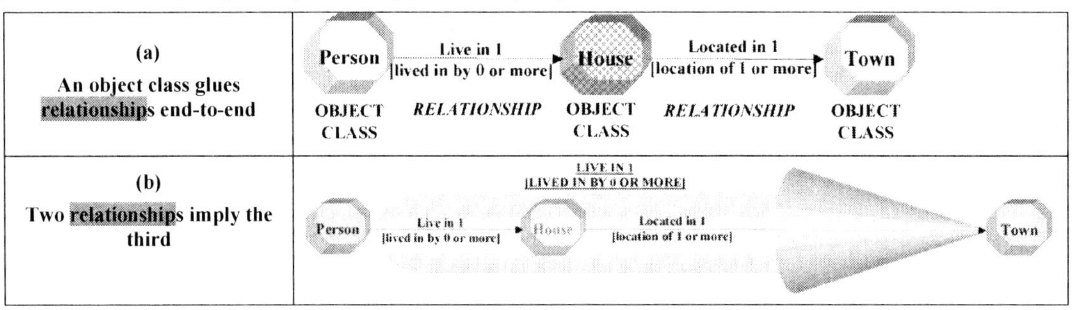


*Reproduced by permission from Mitra, A., & Gupta, A., Agile Systems with Reusable Patterns of Business Knowledge, Norwood, MA: Artech House, Inc., 2005. ©*

would not know which subtype of *Living Space* instantiates a particular instance of *Person lives in Town*. In general, each subtype of *Living Space* in the composition of objects in Figure 5.6b is mutable—maybe replaced—by another subtype of *Living Space* without affecting the meaning of the composition.

Mutability may not only mean replacement of parts; it could also imply obliteration of parts. For example, a house may consist of walls. We may remodel a house and remove inner walls. The essential meaning of the house will remain even if some inner walls are gone. These walls are mutable in the composition called a house. Compositions are patterns, and it is the essential pattern that they bring into focus.

## Perspectives of Mutability

In the first example, where we replaced *House* with *Living Space*, each composition with a different variant of *Living Space* could merely be considered as a different rule expression of the same meaning. Alternatively, we could consider each composition (e.g., *Person lives in Trailer Park located in Town* vs. *Person lives in House located in Town*) to be subtypes of *Person lives in Town*.

Based on the above, we have three equal perspectives, and a fourth that is slightly different:

1. *House* and *Trailer Park* are mutually mutable (replaceable) objects in the composition of Figure 5.6 (as are all subtypes of *Living Space*).
2. *Person lives in Trailer Park located in Town* and *Person lives in House located in Town* are different and independent expressions of the same meaning—*Person lives in Town*.
3. *Person lives in Trailer Park located in Town* and *Person lives in House located in Town* are subtypes of the composition in Figure 5.6 because they share two relationships (*live in* and *located in*) connected to two shared objects (*Person* and *Town*), and differ on account of one object (*House* vs. *Trailer Park*).
4. *Person lives in Trailer Park located in Town* and *Person lives in House located in Town* are subtypes of the composition in Figure 5.6, not because they share two relationships (*live in* and *located in*) connected to two shared objects (*Person* and *Town*) and differ on account of one object (*House* vs. *Trailer Park*), but because both *House* and *Trailer Park* are subtypes of *Living Space*.

Perspective 4 will be the obvious choice if the *Person lives in Trailer Park located in Town* conveys common information, but not exactly the same information, as *Person lives in House located in Town*. If the information conveyed by both compositions had been exactly the same (this would have happened only if *House*, *Living Space*, and *Trailer Park* had all conveyed exactly the same meaning within the scope of the model), the four perspectives would have been equivalent; they would have all conveyed the same information. However, common sense tells us that this is not so. Perspective 4 is different—subtly different because Trailer Park and House have each added different nuances (information) to the meaning of Living Space.

Even if there are no known differences in the properties of *House* and *Trailer Park* within the limited scope of the model, Perspective 4 implicitly "knows" that *Living Space*, *House*, and *Trailer Park* are not exactly the same; *Living Space* contains the shared meaning of *House* and *Trailer Park*. Moreover Perspective 4 implicitly presumes that unknown differences exist in the information conveyed by *House* vs. that conveyed by *Trailer Park*. It (implicitly) adds an *unknown number of unknown features (attributes and relationships) and unknown effects* to *House* and *Trailer Park*. Remember that the unknown value is also information. As such, Perspective 4 is richer in information than the other perspectives in the list and is not exactly the same pattern of meaning as the others.

Perspective 4 is preferable under the unrelenting pressure of change and scope creep. It conforms to the principle of subtyping by adding information and can integrate differences in behavior between subtypes easily. Many seasoned analysts prefer this approach. Subtypes may result from new learning or a larger scope and from recognizing variations in behavior that compel us to generalize objects in order to capture and to normalize their common behavior in supertypes, even as we attribute differences in behavior to subtypes. Perspective 4 can adapt more easily to change because it is different from the other two perspectives—subtly different. It adds information, adds unknown values, and adds unknown properties.

(The patterns in the Universal Perspective will use similar principles to tame the shifting chimera of Perspective and to anchor the concepts firmly in shared understanding.)

## Mutable Perspectives

A composition is a pattern of objects. When is a pattern a pattern? How much freedom does a pattern have to change its internal structure before it becomes a different pattern? Chapter IV provides the answers under Measures of Similarity. It depends on the law that makes the pattern a pattern and the proximity metric it involves. It boils down to rule meaning.

A house is a pattern of walls, roof, ceiling, floor, and other objects; it is a composition of these items. When does a house stop being a house? Can we add items such as furniture, a fireplace, and chimney? If we did, we would almost certainly consider the enlarged entity to still be a house. What if we removed its walls, but left the fireplace and furniture? Would it remain the same house, or even a house? What if we replaced the outer walls? Would we consider it the same or different house? It all depends on the law that makes a pattern a pattern and the freedom we allow before we consider it a different pattern. The key is the meaning of the pattern and the degrees of freedom buried within that meaning.

We might even leave parts of the house out and still consider it to be a different state of the same house. Of course, parts left out remove information, and parts added supplement information. Based on the principle of subtyping by adding information, a composition with information added is a subtype of the composition to which it adds information.

Remember that each combination of the kind in Figure 5.4 is a pattern, so the laws of mutability may not just make individual objects in a composition mutable with other objects, but mutability may also be articulated in terms of combinations of objects—compositions within compositions may be mutable with compositions or single objects (as the "live in" relationship between Person and Town in Figure 5.6b is a metaphor for the composition in it), as much as individual objects in a composition may be mutable with other individual objects or with compositions. After all, compositions are objects too.

Mutable objects in a composition may not all convey the same quantum of information, but they must all convey the same *essential pattern*[53] of information. If they do not, they will be mutable to the extent that they may be removed from the composition, without loss of meaning even if they are not replaced by another object.[54] For example, an air conditioner is only an option in a car; it is an optional object in the pattern of parts we call a car.

Conversely, a subtype obtained by *adding* information will always be mutable with its supertype (but not vice versa) because the subtype will convey the information content of the supertype and then some; if the supertype carries a part of the essential pattern, so must its subtypes (like *Trailer Park* and *House* both conveyed "*Living Space*"). This is known as Liskov's Substitution Principle.[55]

(A word of caution: Remember that the added information may be attributes, effects, or constraints that an attribute, effect, or value is barred or restricted.)

If we remove or change immutable parts of a composition, the composition will cease to exist. It may be transformed to a new and different composition or cease to be considered as a composition at all. It all depends on the law that makes the pattern a pattern. The law is the pattern, and the pattern the law. They are indistinguishable shades of the other. Subtypes and supertypes of patterns are subtypes and supertypes of the law, even if they are patterns of unknown values. Patterns can carry meanings even if they are compositions of "Unknowns."

Preserving the essential meaning of a pattern—the composition—as its parts mutate is the key to product and process innovation; to do things differently as we strive for excellence is to find new mutations that will better serve our purpose—the purpose of the essential pattern.

## Mutability and Innovation

Innovation often involves replacing mutable parts of compositions without losing the essential pattern—the information conveyed by the composite object. In Figure 5.6b, we could replace *House* with *Trailer Park* and not lose the meaning of *Person lives in Town*. The behavior of each kind of *lives in* may differ; each may have different cost, tax, and mobility implications, but the essential pattern, the meaning of the composite, *Person lives in Town,* will stay the same.

Innovation usually involves mutability of this kind—to alter the composition without changing the essence of the composite object. Objects may be reconfigured into new patterns inside the composite, as mutable compositions are replaced or removed. Objects may even be exchanged for new objects with new properties—features[56] and effects, and if these objects are processes, then dependencies, costs, cycle times, controls, and resources may change.[57] Through all these changes, the essential relationships and meanings of the composite must be preserved.

Sometimes, innovation springs from paradigm shifts. A paradigm shift redefines the meaning of a pattern—its very essence. In the example of the house we discussed earlier, if we changed the criteria that make a house a house, it would be a paradigm shift—can a house without outside walls but with a roof be living space be a house? It might for some. Similarly, the essence of a process is in its work products. Changing the work product of a process is a paradigm shift.

A subtype adds its own meaning to that of its parents. One can redefine the essential meaning of the subtype without necessarily altering the essential meaning of its parents; there are levels of paradigm shifts. The larger and more complex the composition is, the more complex its meaning and information content can be—with commensurately larger opportunities for innovation through replacement or removal of mutable parts, as well as the commensurately larger risk of altering incompletely defined or unknown essential patterns. Therefore, the larger and more complex the composition is, the more abstract must be the corresponding supertypes that will support mutability and, through mutability, support innovation. This is the purpose of the Universal Perspective (described further in *Agile Systems with Reusable Patterns of Business Knowledge: A Component Based Approach*). Large global businesses, for instance, may be complex—very complex. Opportunities can be vast, and the risks immense. They can leverage opportunity and manage risk only by timely deployment of knowledge and sharing of innovation. The patterns in the Universal Perspective can be their pipeline, as we will see next.

If the repository of knowledge artifacts contains information on mutability of components, the configuration of components to meet a given goal subject to mutable criteria could be automated. When the cost of labor is low, a manual process could replace an automated one (and vice versa). Each process would be assembled from components in the repository of knowledge artifacts that will know what is mutable with what, and what their costs, cycle times, and constraints are. The metaphor will be preserved, even as its constituents and configurations change.

For instance, a new kind of accounting invoice or bill created to support one business environment will not only reuse the behavior it inherits from a supertype called *Bill*, but it will also be mutable with the supertype in every composition that contains the supertype *Bill*. The repository of knowledge artifacts can make it a consideration in all business environments that deploy these compositions. Whether to use it or not may depend on local criteria and local management, but it will be knowledge automated, automatically deployed, and knowledge automatically shared—the need of the hour for large, globally dispersed businesses that must excel in an unrelentingly competitive and unforgiving marketplace where customer loyalty and success depend on sheer excellence supported by information.

Meanings can be subtyped and refactored (see Appendix II on refactoring) as new learning sweeps away the old, and unknowns become known, and as new unknowns join the ranks of the old. Laws and compositions themselves may flit between states, subtypes, knowns, and unknowns as change runs riot through flickering perspectives of reality and its perceptions.

## THE CAPACITY FOR RELATIONSHIPS

Relationships connect objects, and objects return the favor, so which is the relationship and which is the object? The answer is a matter of perspective—relationships after all are object classes too.

Just as relationships could limit the numbers of objects they involve, objects too may limit the number of relationships they may have with other objects. Just as constraints on order, degree, and cardinality ratios could be imposed on relationship classes as well as on individual instances of relationships, so too may the same constraints be imposed at both classes and instances of objects.

Business rules might dictate that a person, an instance of an object, may participate (a relationship) in only one project (another object) at a time. This is an upper bound on the cardinality ratio of *Participate*, a dyadic relationship between object classes *Person* and *Project*. Assume we change the rule. We allow a person to divide her time between at most five projects. The upper bound on the cardinality ratio of *Participate* has just become five instead of one.

Along with special projects inside the firm, the individual may spend time with the firm's customers. Then, his time must be divided between customer care and internal projects. The total number of feasible relationships that employees may have with projects *and* customers may then be in question. The model may require that the upper bound cap the total cardinality ratio, rather than the cardinality ratios of relationships between employees and projects, and employees and customers separately.

So far, *participate*, the relationship, has conveyed only nominal information on a person's participation in projects and customer care. At the instance level, it has only told us whether a person is, or is not, associated with a specific project and/or a specific customer. It has not said how much of the resource (person) will be consumed by the project or customer, nor if all projects and customers will consume his time and effort equally.

The relationship can be more informative than this. For instance, it could tell us that one project might consume twice as much time as another, as might a customer. The time an individual can devote to projects and customers may be limited. Hence, there are two interdependent items of information involved—an individual's capacity to participate in relationships and the quantum of that capacity depleted by each relationship. The capacity for participation is an attribute of the object and normalized by it, and the capacity consumed is an attribute of each relationship and is normalized by the relationship. Each relationship between instances of objects may not only convey the fact of association, but also how much of an object's capacity for association with other objects it consumes. Just as cardinality ratios could vary at class or instance levels, the capacity for association locked up by a relationship may vary by relationship class or by relationship instance[58] (or even by combinations within a high order of higher degree relationship—combinations of the kind shown in Figure 5.4).

## TRANSITIVITY, ATRANSITIVITY, AND INTRANSITIVITY

The detail in a composition may be hidden from view. All we see may be a relationship (or an object). We might not even be interested in peeling the cover off an object to search for compositions within it—our interest might be only focused on the manifested behavior if the object. The black box has returned to haunt us again, but in a different form—clearer and more precise—precision in terms of information content, cardinality, ordinality, subtyping, and other properties.

Consider information content first. It is manifested in transitive relationships—a term for relationships that implies other relationships. Transitive relationships are merely alternative expressions of the same meanings.

Take a composition of relationships. Every composition implies the relationship it composes. It follows that we will replicate information if we articulate both the relationship and its composition(s) independently in our model. For instance, in Figure 5.6b, two assertions, a *person lives in one house* and *house is located in one town, implies* the third—that a *person lives in one town*.

When two or more relationships imply another, they are said to be transitive (with respect to each other). One must be dropped in order to normalize information because the others imply it. For instance, had we dropped "*located in*" between *House* and *Town* in Figure 5.6b, it will still be implied by the two assertions that we would have retained:

1. Person lives in House, and
2. Person lives in Town

Which relationship we drop is a matter of choice. Both perspectives will be equivalent regardless of our decision (if we assume homelessness is outside our scope).

Sometimes, relationships carry information on intransitivity—that they are *barred* by other relationships of the same kind. For example, consider parenthood and grandparenthood. A person may be the child of a parent, who, in turn is the child of another. The "*parent of*" relationship in *Person* may be *parent of Person* is recursive and irreflexive. It is also intransitive. We know that if three or more individuals are related via a chain of "*parent of*" relationships, the individual at the beginning of the chain cannot be the parent of the person at the end of the chain. (This also *automatically* applies to its inverse, the "*Child of*" relationship.)

The irreflexivity of "*parent of*" prohibits cycling back to the same individual but lets us cycle back to different individuals each time we go round the irreflexive loop that joins individuals into a daisy chain. However, this composition, made of identical repeating components, cannot co-exist with an identical component that joins the first and the last objects in the chain directly. This is the property of intransitivity.

When a relationship is intransitive, the composition and the direct relationship are mutually exclusive. They cannot coexist. The degree of intransitivity gives us the length of an intransitive composition that preserves intransitivity. It could be infinite.

Transitivity, on the other hand, implies the opposite. A recursive irreflexive relationship can be transitive. If it is a daisy chain of components, even identical components, and implies a connection of the same kind between the beginning and the end of the chain. Consider that a person may be a descendant of another person. "*Descendant of*" is an irreflexive, asymmetrical, recursive relationship on object class *Person*. If a chain of individuals are linked together by *descendant of*, it implies that the individual at the beginning of the chain is also a descendant of the individual at the end. Contrast this with *child of*.

"*Child of*" is an *intransitive* relationship that is asymmetrical, irreflexive, and recursive. "*Descendant of*" is a *transitive* relationship that is asymmetrical, irreflexive, and recursive. "*Child of*" was obtained by adding information to "*Descendant of*"—by making it more specific and reducing the degrees of freedom of its meaning. Using the principle of subtyping by adding information, "*Child of*" is a subtype of "*Descendant of*." Just as asymmetrical relationships crystallized from symmetrical relationships as we added information to their meanings, so too do intransitive relationships crystallize from transitive relationships when we add information to them.

Nontransitivity is a weaker condition than intransitivity. Consider the daisy chain of relationships we just discussed, in which "*child of*" "friend of" has replaced. The chain of "*friend of*" relationships between persons does not imply that the person at the beginning of the chain is a friend of the person at the end of the chain. It does not bar it either. Such a relationship may or may not exist independently of the composition represented by the chain of friends. This is the property of nontransitivity, also known as *atransitivity*.

Atransitivity tells us that the relationship is not transitive with another (or a composition). One relationship does not imply the other but may coexist with it and may articulate an independent atomic rule. It tells us that even if the same relationship connects multiple objects in a daisy chain of repeated relationships, the composition will not convey the same meaning as joining the objects at the beginning and the end of the daisy chain directly via the relationship.

## Cardinality Ratios of Composites

Consider the cardinality ratios of composites. A composite consists of daisy chains of objects and relationships. It follows that the cardinality ratio of a composite relationship will be determined by the cardinality ratios of relationships inside the daisy chain as follows:

1. A one-to-one relationship in tandem with another one-to-one relationship results in a one-to-one composite. It does not matter which end of an on-to-one relationship is joined to which end of another one-to-one relationship.
2. A one-to-one relationship in tandem with a one-to-many relationship (or vice-versa) yields a one-to-many composite.
3. A many-to-one relationship in tandem with a one-to-one relationship (or vice versa) yields a many-to-one composite.
4. A one-to-many relationship in tandem with a one-to-many relationship yields a one-to-many composite.
5. A many-to-one relationship in tandem with a many-to-one relationship yields a many-to-one composite.

One can easily visualize the above ideas by laying relationships like those in Figure 5.1 end-to-end. However, when we glue one-to-many or many-to-one relationships together end to end, we end up with a more complex kind of cardinality—a many-to-many composition. A many-to-many relationship may map a single instance of an object in the domain of the relationship to several object instances in its codomain (like Figure 5.1b), *and simultaneously its inverse may do the same in the opposite direction* (like in Figure 5.1c). The result is total ambiguity if one tries to retrace a relationship through its inverse.

Many-to-many compositions occur when:

6. A one-to-many relationship is joined in tandem with a many-to-one relationship (or vice versa).
7. A pair of one-to-many relationships is joined at their common source.
8. If any one (or both) of the relationships joined together is optional, the composite is also optional.

When many-to-many cardinalities occur, we can only resolve ambiguity by opening a window into the composition and resolving the many-to-many relationship into its injective and surjective components. We will now describe how this is done. The process is mechanical and may be automated.

## Resolving Many-to-Many Relationships

Consider the relationship *Person* is *employed* by *Organization*. Its inverse is *Organization employs Person* (the relationship and its inverse have been underlined for your convenience). It is possible for a single individual to hold multiple jobs in different organizations. For example, an individual may have a day job with one company and an evening job with another. As such, the employment relationship from *Person* to *Organization* is a one-to-many relationship; its inverse too is one-to-many. Most organizations employ several individuals. When a one-to-many relationship has a one-to-many inverse, it is called a many-to-many relationship. Figure 5.7 illustrates the many-to-many employment relationship between *Person* and *Organization*.

Many-to-many relationships are actually two relationships mediated by a Cartesian product. Hidden within the many-to-many employment relationship in the example above is the Cartesian product of *Person* and *Organization*. The object class *Person* has an optional one-to-many relationship with *Person Employed in Organization*, as does object class *Organization*. *Person Employed in Organization* is a Cartesian product of *Person*

*Figure 5.7. A many-to-many relationship*

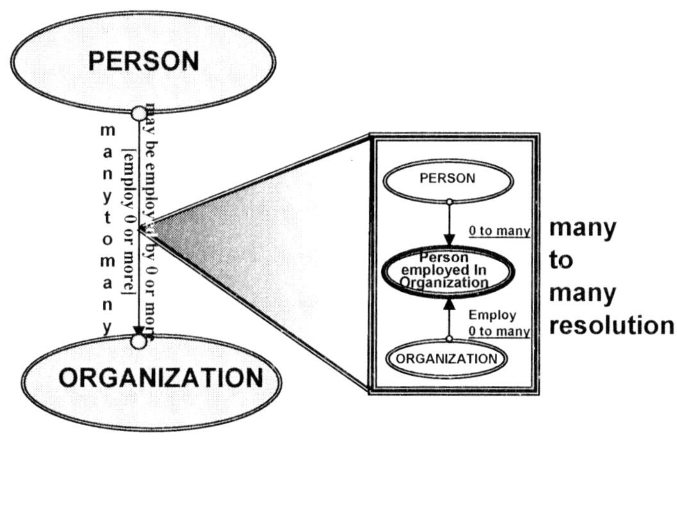

and *Organization*. Indeed, it is the employment relationship itself, an object in its own right. The many-to-many employment relationship between *Person* and *Organization* is merely a composition of two different relationships, one from *Person* to *Person Employed in Organization*, and the other from *Organization* to *Person Employed in Organization*—two relationships glued together end-to-end, in tandem, by the Cartesian product *Person Employed in Organization*. Figure 5.7 illustrates this.

Each many-to-many relationship may be resolved into two (or more) one-to-many or many-to-one relationships with an object that is the Cartesian product of the objects related by the many-to-many relationship. The choice of direction—an arbitrary choice—determines whether the relationships inside the composition are one-to-many or many-to-one (when one direction is chosen, the other is automatically implied by the inverse of the relationship that was chosen). Automated tools can resolve many-to-many relationships like the relationship in Figure 5.7. Indeed, many do.

## COLLECTIONS OF OBJECTS AND THE STATE SPACE OF RELATIONSHIPS

A relationship is an object. Figure 5.3 shows how the objects it relates determine the state space of a relationship: Each axis of this nominally scaled state space will represent an object class the relationship involves, and each tuple, a point in this state space, represents an instance of the relationship. The very identity of the relationship, an object, is the conjunction of the identities of the objects it relates, and is dependent on them.

The complete state space represents all possible relationships, regardless of whether they exist or not, or even if they are "lawful" or not. Regions in this state space represent collections of relationships. Slicing and dicing this state space groups and regroups relationship into different categories (Figure 5.8).

## SLICING AND DICING ASSOCIATIONS BETWEEN OBJECTS

Consider the object called "Sale" in Figure 5.8; it is a third order relationship. Figure 5.8a shows

*Figure 5.8. State spaces of relationships*

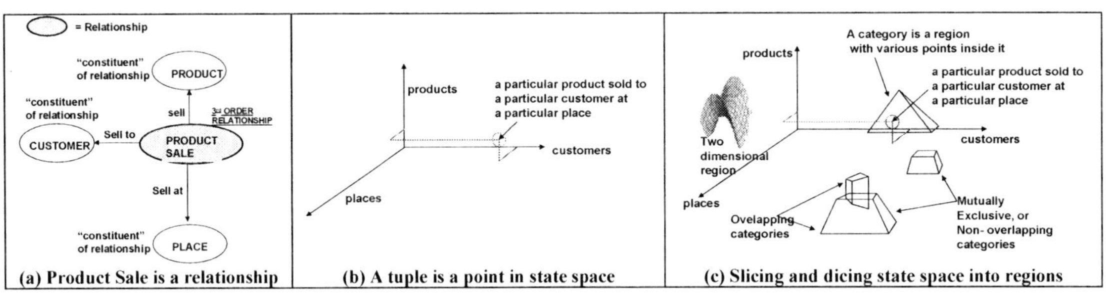


*Reproduced by permission from Mitra, A., & Gupta, A., Agile Systems with Reusable Patterns of Business Knowledge, Norwood, MA: Artech House, Inc., 2005. ©*

this in entity-relationship format, and Figure 5.8b in state space format. Figure 5.8c shows how this state space may be sliced and diced. Regions may be mutually exclusive or not. Even disjoint regions can be considered a part of a single collection. These arbitrary collections represent market segments based on what products (or product ranges) were sold to which kinds of customers in which places. These regions need not be three-dimensional volumes. They could be any subspace—lines, surfaces, patterns that may twist and turn,[59] patterns that are bounded, finite, unbounded, or even infinite. They may be any kind of pattern. If we only cared about products sold to a specific customer and were required to analyze which products the customer bought where, our market segments would be two-dimensional regions of state space—patterns of points on a plane. These points will be located in a vertical plane, parallel to the product-place plane of Figure 5.8c. The plane on which these regions are located will intersect the customer axis at the point that represents the customer in question.

*Box 5.3. "Don't care," the source of all values*

Just as the unknown domain (Chapter IV) was the supertype from which all domains emerged, the "Don't care" value is the supertype from which all other values flow. It asserts only that a value exists. It does not matter what that value is, not even if it is known or unknown. Every domain—even the unknown domain—has a "Don't care," that is, "All" value (equivalent to "everything in Figure 4.1) from which its values emerge as meanings of specific magnitudes are added to them.

Consider how the "Don't care" value is different from the "Unknown" value. Assume we make and sell graphic design software through intermediaries such as retailers and distributors. We may have information on identities and usage patterns of only some end users because they have registered the software they bought. There may be others who have not registered, so we do not know who they are, but they call in, requesting support on an ad-hoc basis. We may want to segment the market by known and unknown users—a distinction based on the "Unknown" value. We may also be interested in our pattern of sales regardless of whether we know or do not know the end user. Then we will segment the market based on the "*All*" or "*Don't care*" value—the collection of end users both known and unknown. This kind of segment is very different from the segmentation that made distinctions based on the "Unknown" value.

"Don't care" conveys less information than "Unknown"; it does not even tell us whether we do or do not know a specific value; it only tells us that values exist. Therefore, based on the principle of subtyping by adding information, "Don't care" is the supertype of all values, even "Unknown." It is identical to "Not null." "Null" represents meaninglessness and impossibility. See the section on the metamodel of relationships further on in this book.

**Representing State Spaces Graphically**

In a nominally scaled state space like that in Figure 5.8b (and Figure 5.8c), each axis represents a domain. The axes intersect at the origin; the origin is a point common to each axis. The "Don't care" value is common to all domains. Therefore, if the origin represents the "Don't care" value graphically, each facet of state space such as product-place, product-customer, and customer-place will represent state spaces in which respective values of customer, place, and product do not matter—that is, are (respectively) "Don't care." This is just one kind of origin. It is one way of representing a value shared by all domains that frame that space. There may be other kinds of origins as well because other kinds of values may be shared across domains.

All ratio scaled domains share the "nil" value. A ratio scaled state space may impute the nil value to its origin (see Figure 4.2). The origin of a state space may represent any value common to the domains that frame it. Sometimes it may be neither "Nil" nor "Don't care"; it could be a natural lower bound shared by the domains involved, or even an arbitrary point (as in difference scaled state spaces). The choice is ours—the geometrical representation of state space is just that—a graphical, albeit incomplete way of representing a more complex reality. Domains may share more than one value, but geometrically we can have only one origin—a point where the lines that represent each domain intersect.

On the other hand, if we only cared about products and where they were sold, regardless of customers, we would need a "don't care" value on the customer axis. ("Don't care" is identical to "all." This value will subsume both known values, as well as the Unknown Value.) Assigning this "don't care" value to the customer will be equivalent to reducing the relationship in Figure 5.8a to a second-degree relationship by eliminating *Customer*. Note that "don't care" does not bar the relationship with *Customer*, nor does it assert its non-existence (like the null value would). It merely asserts that the information is irrelevant or unavailable.

Based on the principle of subtyping by adding information, this relationship is a supertype of the relationship in Figure 5.8a. The state space of the supertype will be a two-dimensional state space defined only by *Product* and *Place*. Each instance of *Product Sale* will become a 2-tuple in the state space of the supertype. Similarly, if we were only interested in segmenting the market by product, the relationship would become monadic, and the state space would be left with only a single axis—the product axis.

As such, the kind of state space in Figure 5.8 cannot, by itself, represent *Market Segment*, the object. *Market Segment* is a collection of state spaces. One state space for each possible combination—combinations like those in Figure 5.4. It is a power set.

However, it is clear from Figure 5.8 that the existence of the three-dimensional state space *implies* the existence of its two-dimensional facets—the product-place, product-customer, and customer-place planes in Figures 5.8b and c. Indeed, we have just discussed how these second order relationships are supertypes of the relationship in Figure 5.8a. The existence of the subtype implies the existence of its supertype (but not vice versa). Therefore the three-dimensional state space in Figure 5.8b implies not only existence of regions of three-dimensional space, but also the existence of regions of its one- and two-dimensional supertypes—members of the power set we just discussed. As such, even though the state space in Figure 5.8b will not represent all market segments by itself, it can do so by implication. No new information need be added. Indeed, adding information already implied would only denormalize and duplicate knowledge.

The state spaces segmented in the examples above were nominally scaled. Points in each region (segment) were discrete collections of objects, unrelated, with no sense of continuity, no definition of closeness (beyond the fact that each is unique and distinct from others in the region) nor of any concept of ordered arrangement within the segment. There were no ranges or intervals between points involved. What if we had to slice and dice ordinal or quantitative state spaces or mixed spaces, in which different dimensions are scaled differently? In partially or totally ordered spaces (see Box 4.5), we must recognize ranges, intervals, and bounds—shapes and patterns like those in Figure 5.8c. For instance, market segmentation may depend on the sale price of the product, a quantitative attribute of *Product Sale*. If this happens, *Sale Price* will be an axis of the state space that we must segment. Market segments must now consider the set of all possible *intervals* along ordinal or quantitative dimensions. (To make it easier to visualize geometrically, consider a three-dimensional state space in which *Product Sale* is a binary relationship that only involves *Place* and *Product*, two axes of this state space, and the third axis is *Sale Price*, an attribute of the relationship[60]—see Figure 5.9.)

## Borel Objects

The set of all possible intervals opens the door to a very special object class called the *Borel Set*. A Borel set is the set of all possible intervals on an axis of state space, or when multiple axes are involved, the set of all possible regions in that space.[61] These intervals (regions) may or may not overlap. Each region in Figure 5.8c is an instance

*Figure 5.9. Instances of Borel Sets*

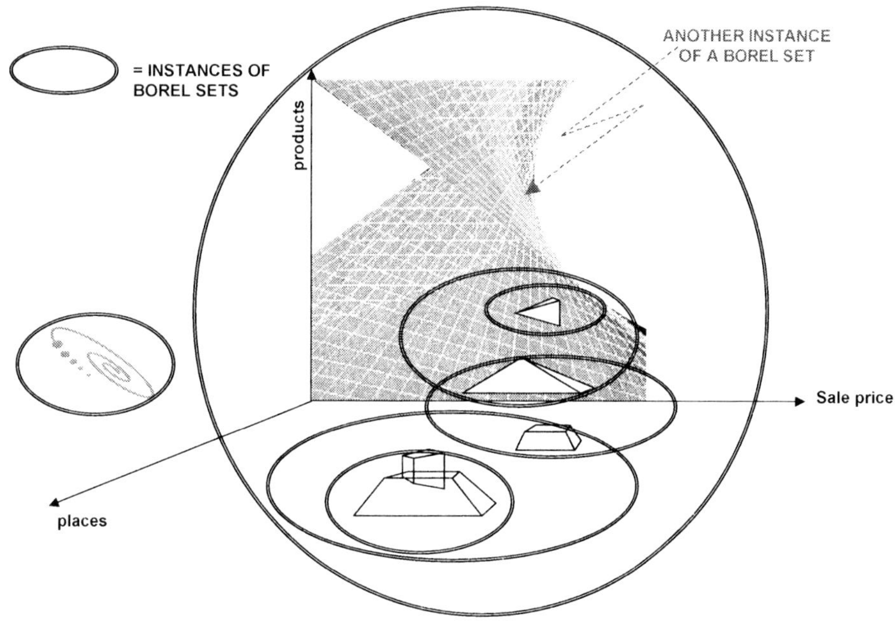


*Reproduced by permission from Mitra, A., & Gupta, A., Agile Systems with Reusable Patterns of Business Knowledge, Norwood, MA: Artech House, Inc., 2005.* ©

of a Borel set in the state space therein. If we recognize the "Don't care" value, the Borel set will include all intervals in state space, as well as intervals in the state space of its supertypes—the facets it implies.

Although a Borel Set is hard to visualize graphically, an instance of a Borel Set is easier to understand and visualize—at least in one-, two-, and three-dimensional spaces. Every region in space, whatever its shape, size, or extent is an instance of a Borel Set, and so is every collection of regions, overlapping or disjoint, finite or infinite, bounded or unbounded, open or closed. Figure 5.9 illustrates this simple truth.

When segmentation involves ordinal, difference, or ratio scaled axes, regions will depend on gaps between values, and hence Borel Sets, will be involved. When segmentation is in terms of nominally scaled axes, segmentation will involve collections of points in state space—the power set we discussed earlier. Intervals are also collections of points in state space. We will call the union of these intervals and collections as the *Borel Object* or the *Power Borel Set*. The Borel object generalizes the concept of the class of all possible segments, regardless of how the space is scaled, and regardless of whether it has any null values—"holes"—in it (see Figure A in Box 4.6). It is the class of segments.[62]

Every relationship class is associated with a Borel object; indeed, every relationship class automatically implies the existence of its Borel object. The rules are:

The Borel object of a relationship is related to the same object classes as the relationship.

Relationships between individual object classes and the Borel object are optional (to support the "all" value we discussed above).

*At least one*, perhaps more, of these individually optional relationships must exist in order to instantiate a Borel object. In other words, the degree of the combination of relationships between the Borel object and its constituent object classes must be one or more.

*Figure 5.10. Borel objects and relationships*

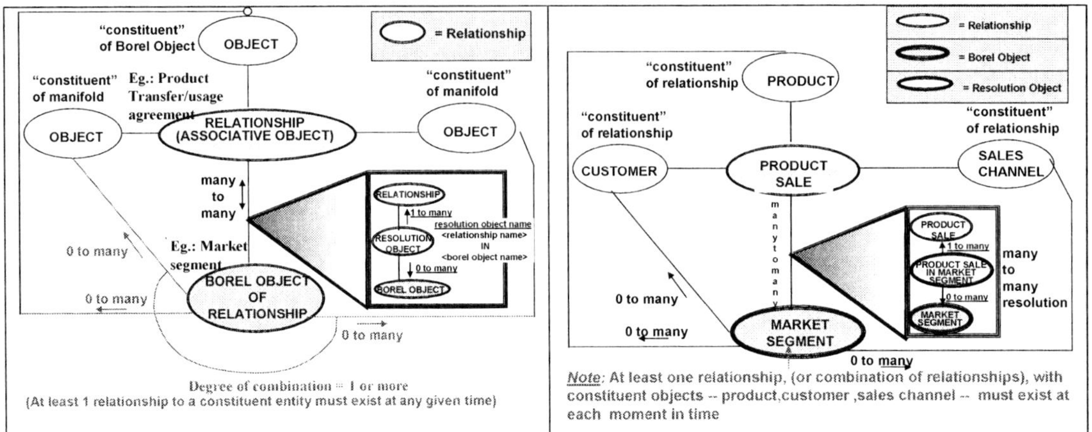


(a) A relationship class implies a Borel Object

(b) An example of a relationship and its Borel Object

A relationship and its Borel object have an optional many-to-many association between them. Note the cardinality ratios inside the many-to-many composition between the relationship and its Borel object in Figure 5.10. The relationship must necessarily be contained in some region of its state space, hence the composition is mandatory in that direction; but other regions of state space can be empty, and the composition is optional in the other directions. In compliance with Rule 8 for joining relationships, the overall many-to-many relationship is optional.

The rules we just articulated are illustrated in Figure 5.10.

The Borel object helps to analyze the information content of a relationship class by slicing and dicing it to look for patterns (just as Candu Compoot did in the tale reproduced earlier from our Web site[63]). Indeed, Borel objects provide a key to the analysis of business behavior and the search for patterns. This approach is a tool that supports management decision-making and process innovation rather than one that provides support for the day-to-day transactions of an operating business.

Borel objects are containers of analytical patterns that normalize a higher order of non-procedural knowledge about the businesses than transactions do. Take the thought a step further. What if we wished to segment the market by slicing and dicing information that the associative object—the relationship—does not normalize, but its constituents do? For instance, we want to segment the market by list price of product (an attribute of *Product*[64]), customer revenue (an attribute of *Customer*), and mean temperature of the place (an attribute of *Place*), all taken together, and look for patterns across these segments. To segment the market in this manner, we will need to consider the entire composition of objects in Figure 5.8a. This leads us to a kind of information space we have not discussed yet.

Since we are interested in *combinations* of information across constituent objects, we have implicitly recognized that a relationship binds them, and hence implicitly recognized the corresponding Borel object. However, we must enhance the state space of the relationship (and hence the Borel object it implies) by including additional axes—dimensions—one for each item of information normalized by its constituents.[65]

This enhanced state space of the relationship will support the kind of segmentation we require. In the example above, the enhanced state space of the relationship will include points that represent tuples of individual list prices, mean temperatures and customer revenues. We can slice and dice this space, and each region will represent a collection of points—a segment (which might or might not be empty). This kind of space is like no space we know. Each point on the axis bears more information than the mere existence of an object. It is also a token for an object that bears information on its state. Each axis is a token for a stateful object class and may unfold into a full-blown state space of its own.

Of course, treating the composite as a single object will denormalize information. For instance, the same place may be repeated in several distinct tuples that represent distinct points in the state space of Figure 5.8b,[66] and each will have the same mean temperature because mean temperature belongs to the place alone, not the *combination* of place, customer, and product.[67] However, when we look for patterns, we are synthesizing and combining information. We are looking at differences and similarities between *combinations*. The Borel set lets us do so. The fact that the mean temperature of a place belongs to place alone has already been normalized by the *Place*, a constituent of the state space of the three-way relationship between *Place*, *Product*, and *Customer*. Place has merely lent this information to the Borel object to allow it to be grouped with other tuples. The Borel object does not normalize the same information as its constituents; this would be repetition. Instead, it normalizes information about groups, patterns, and aggregates. It gives identity to an aggregate object.

Aggregate objects have emergent properties, patterns that the Borel object normalizes. Aggregate objects also subsume Borel objects. The Borel object is just one role of the aggregate object, as are object compositions, object classes, subclasses, and other collections of object instances. Even an object instance is a collection of attributes and hence an aggregate object.

## ENDNOTES

1. [88] in Appendix III describes relationships and their properties in mathematical terms.
2. [188] in Appendix III describes the inverse of a relationship in mathematical terms.
3. Readers interested in more mathematical rigor may refer to Function, Domain, Codomain, Image, and Range in Appendix II under the Theory of Categories. [232], [233], [234], [235], [308], and [309] in Appendix III have more information.
4. If A1 in set A is mapped to C1 in set C, C1 is called the ***image*** of A1.
5. Nominal attributes only establish the *existence* of values. They carry no information on *magnitude*. Therefore, in Figure A of Box 5.1, if attribute C is a nominal attribute, the mapping rule can only be a rule about existence of a value (i.e., an inclusion or exclusion rule). Relationships between nominal attributes will always be inclusion or exclusion sets.
6. See [211], [212], [214], [215], and [251] in Appendix III for the theoretical foundations of ordinality.
7. See [240] and [251] in Appendix III for the theoretical foundations of the richness of relationships between attributes.
8. Ron Ross, in [294], Chapter VII, calls these objects calculators. Ross does not distinguish the rule meaning from its possible expressions(s) (see [243] in Appendix III). He identifies type 1 rules as those that involve attributes, and type 2 rules as those that only involve values. [294] in Appendix III contains several examples of joint constraints and rule expressions acting in concert with inclusion and exclusion sets. Ross identifies the following rule expressions as those used frequently in business processes: *Summation* over a set of values, *subtraction*, *multiplication*, *division*, identifying the *largest item*

in a set, identifying the *smallest* in the set, *average* over a set, determining the *median* of a set, determining the *mode* (the most frequently occurring value in a set), determination of a *rate* per unit (usually time), determining a *percentage* and determining a *percentile*. In addition to the list in [294], *enumeration* is used commonly in business processes. Box 28 on our Web site discusses rule constraints in detail (the rule may be a simple "*or*," that is, the constrained value must/must not take a value from the value set, in which case *Rule Constrain* reduces to the inclusion/exclusion constraint (object B of Box 28 on our Web site). Refer to [294] for more information about the use of recursion in rule expressions.

9 Constraining values are those inside the value set in Figure C.

10 Here is an example of how the metamodel provides automated agents an opportunity to automatically adapt software to changes in scope by aligning with the metamodel of knowledge. When an attribute is an argument of a rule expression, its value is assigned to a value set and the link between the domain and the value is automatically instantiated by implication, i.e., rules associated with domain may be physically inferred by the software application (or automated agent) via the attribute in Figure C. However a value might not always be the value of an attribute. It could be a parameter of the rule expression, and independent of any attributes of objects in the business model. Often this happens because the scope of the model is limited and might exclude the attribute that the value could belong to. Since the value is a parameter that is not associated with any attribute in the scope of the system, the (automated) agent must establish a (physical) relationship between the value and the domain to inherit rules linked to the domain. If a subsequent scope change brings the corresponding attribute into the business model, the agent must recognize it, delete the physical relationship to domain, and switch the software strategy for accessing the domain and rules stored therein so that it inherits these rules via the attribute. Accordingly, the agent would automatically consolidate rules specific to the attribute with those it has inherited from the domain, eliminating redundancy and identifying conflict. This is only one of several kinds of adaptations that may flow from changing the scope and rules of business. However, it *is* an instance of how software can adapt to the new rules and scopes. It reflects the kind of intelligence that software must acquire to change its own configuration, with minimal or no human intervention, as it adapts to changes in scope and aligns with evolving business processes.

11 Refer to Chapters VI and VII of [294] (in Appendix III) for more information about recursive rule expressions.

12 Refer to Appendix II on Lambda Calculus and the Church Rosser Theorem for more detail on the implications of the fact that the terms of a rule may consist of other terms.

13 The fact that the same rule may be expressed in different *terms* is analogous to the fact that the same value may be expressed in different *formats*. In neither case does the *meaning* change the rule or the value. *Meaning* is the focus of the metamodel of knowledge.

14 To understand the rigorous, mathematical basis of why a single rule may have many expressions, refer to the abstract mathematics of Lambda Calculus. Appendix II has a nonbrief, nonmathematical description of Lambda Calculus. [240] in Appendix III has more mathematical detail. Appendix III also has other publications on Lambda Calculus: [239], [241], [242], [244], [245], [246], [247], [248], [249], [250] (all in Appendix III). [251] in Appendix III deals with the mathematics

of rules. Appendix III contains publications on mathematical functions that discuss the mathematics behind rule expressions.

15 Just as interfaces may pass values (of attributes) between systems, they may also pass rules. Both rules and values are information and the interface is where the contract for information exchange resides (see the discussion of SOA in Chapter III). Just as this contract describes formats for data exchange and presentation at the interface when passing data, it must describe the *expression of the rule* being passed when passing a rule to another actor. The rule is then, like data, just another parameter being exchanged between actors. Therefore, rule expressions (as opposed to meanings) reside in the interface rules layer of Figure 3.4. This concept, where both values and rules are generalized parameters of rule expressions, which may in turn be parameters themselves, are supported by the mathematics of Lambda (λ) Calculus. Mathematically inclined readers may refer to the publications on λ-calculus in Appendix III to understand how rule expressions may be manipulated. Nonmathematicians who are interested in the concept may refer to the note on λ-calculus in Appendix II. A new style of programming called *functional programming*, based on λ-calculus, is emerging in support of these concepts. Functional programming tools can turn these concepts into practical, working automation. Refer to Appendix II on functional programming, and [242], [254], and [306] in Appendix III for more information.

16 See [250] and [240] for reasons why there is no general algorithm to show the equivalence of different rule expressions. This is not in conflict with the Church Rosser Theorem ([245], [246], [247], [248], [249], and [307] in Appendix III) because the theorem does not imply that a normal form is reachable by the reduction procedure in it for rule expressions. It only says that *if* reduction of terms terminates, it will end in a term that is a unique normal form, and all *equivalent* rule expressions that *can* be reduced will always reduce to the *same normal form*. The normal form of all equivalent rule expressions are unique to them and can be used to anchor their unique meaning but may not always be easy, or even possible, to identify. Warning—nonmathematical readers beware!

17 The Church Rosser Theorem in mathematics describes the confluence property: that a rule expression may be evaluated in two or more different ways, and both will lead to the same result (See [243], [246], [247], [248], and [307] in Appendix III). [243], [244], and [246] in Appendix III describe methods of reducing two or more rule expressions to their common, normal form. Appendix II describes the Church Rosser Theorem and Normal Forms for nonmathematicians.

18 Some rule expressions may normalize meaning: "A lambda expressions which does not allow any function application reduction is called a normal form. Not every λ expression is equivalent to a normal form, but if it is, then the normal form is essentially unique.... Furthermore, there is an algorithm for computing normal forms. This algorithm halts if and only if the lambda expression has a normal form. This is the content of the Church-Rosser theorem."—[240] in Appendix III. Readers interested in the Church Rosser Theorem may refer to Appendix II and the several publications in Appendix III on this topic.

19 Readers interested in a more mathematically precise description of how objects may be "joined" in a sequence to create new configurations of knowledge will find additional information in Appendix II, in the note on gluing objects together.

20 "Two functions are equal by *Extension* if they have the same meaning: they give

the same result when applied to the same argument"—Andrew Myers of Cornell University on Lambda Calculus in [243] in Appendix III (see Appendix II on Lambda Calculus).

21 The relationship between *Rule Meaning*, *Rule Expression*, and *Computational Algorithm* (for the *Rule Expression*) is analogous to the relationship between *Domain*, *Unit of Measure*, and *Format* in [337] in Appendix III. Each *Rule Meaning* must be expressed in at least one, and perhaps more, *Rule Expressions*, each of which in turn, must be implemented with at least one, and perhaps several, *Computational Algorithms*. Most student programmers come across algorithms that involve blocks of instructions inside iterative loops. Often the algorithm might require a parameter be initialized each time the algorithm is invoked and be left unchanged thereafter, independently of any logic inside the iterative part of the algorithm. Every programmer learns not to put such initialization commands inside the iteration so that it is executed only once, and computing cycles are not needlessly wasted in iteratively restating the same value. Just as there are several formats for expressing values, there are multiple computational algorithms that could implement a single rule expression; of course, some could be more computationally efficient than others and therefore preferred by the designer of the automated system.

22 "*Any function that can be evaluated by a computer can be expressed in terms of recursive functions, without use of iteration*"—[237] in Appendix III.

23 [337] in Appendix III discusses value constraints. It describes simple constraints in which attribute values must/must not assume values in a set of values, called a "value set." The book also discusses "rule constraints" which are more complex. Values are permitted or not depending on interactions between values in a value set. An attribute might be permitted to take a value or not depending on a rule that might involve the values of one or more values in a value set. Finally, a magnitude constraint is defined as a special kind of value constraint, in which values and interactions in a value set might constrain quantitative values of ratio or difference scaled attributes.

24 Exhaustivity is an attribute of *Class*, an object in the metamodel of knowledge. An exhaustive class, or set contains every possible member. A non-exhaustive class (or set) contains fewer than all possible members. [337] in Appendix III discusses the impact of exhaustivity on value constraints in detail.

25 See inverses, *bijection*, *injection*, and *surjection* in Appendix II under the theory of categories and also [234] (in Appendix III).

26 Mathematically, when an inverse can be inferred from a class level relationship or rule expression alone, it is said to *exist*, and when it cannot, mathematicians say it *does not exist*. Mathematical existence implies that the inverse is completely determined by the relationship it reverses; it carries no additional information. Mathematical non-existence of inverses implies the opposite—that we need additional information if we need to map back to the original objects from the target because the original map does not have this information. In this book, we call such inverses "unknown," instead of non-existent because we can resolve ambiguity and map back to the original object instances given this information. The information must be explicitly associated with each instance of the relationship reversed.

27 *Homogenous fact* and *Unary Relationship* are NIAM terms. [297] in Appendix III describes NIAM (a methodology).

28 These are also examples of asymmetrical subtypes of symmetrical relationships.

29 When a relationship is both irreflexive and antisymmetric, it becomes asymmetric. Asymmetry follows from using the Boolean "and" to join irreflixivity with antisymmetry, that is, by the (set) intersection of these two properties. Each is an item of information—knowledge about a relationship. [165] in Appendix III discusses antisymmetry and its interaction with ordinal domains.

30 Cartesian Product: see Box 19 on our Web site.

31 These are NIAM terms for relationships. See [297] in Appendix III.

32 "Many" implies a finite value. Infinite cardinality leads to mathematical complications. See [202], [203], and [206] in Appendix III.

33 Cardinalities (and other properties of objects) may have upper and lower bounds, permissible and impermissible ranges, permitted or barred lists of values, and all the other value constraints in Chapter IV.

34 Chapter 5 of [297] (in Appendix III) has algorithms for breaking the tuple into equivalent patterns of objects and relationships.

35 If the numbers of customers and retailers is individually constrained, the number of customer-retailer combinations will also be constrained. As such, the populations of combinations in Figure 5.4 are interdependent. Each may be constrained by limitations on populations of other members of the power set. Constraints on cardinalities naturally imply these constraints. We do not have to explicitly assert these implicit constraints for every impacted combination. This also normalizes knowledge—explicitly asserting a truth implied another denormalizes knowledge. Independent constraints may make these constraints more, but not less, restrictive.

36 NIAM is a fact modeling methodology described in [297] in Appendix III. It provides more details on cardinality and interaction.

37 [337] in Appendix III discusses clashing constraints in more detail.

38 Figure 36 on our Web site represents the instance identifier of a relationship in a visual manner.

39 Limitations on cardinality will be framed by value constraints ([337] in Appendix III discusses these constraints in detail).

40 A list distinguishes between multiple occurrences of an object. Sets and classes do not. Thus a list conveys more information than a set and may be considered its subtype. Box 7.10 describes the difference between a set and a list.

41 Readers can find more information in [297] in Appendix III.

42 Barring an object is equivalent to constraining its instance identifier to *null.*

43 Constraining the degree of a tuple to exactly zero is equivalent to forcing its cardinality to zero. Both bar the relationship (i.e., create the null relationship).

44 [337] in Appendix III discusses validation of constraints.

45 [337] in Appendix III discusses mergers of constraints in detail.

46 Subset: see Box 19 on our Web site.

47 Figure 35 on our Web site shows the relationship between a domain and an attribute

48 A subtype may restrict or match the cardinality/cardinality ratios of the supertype, but cannot violate constraints inherited from supertypes.

49 [173] in Appendix III describes object compositions mathematically.

50 [173], [188], and [193] (all in Appendix III) mathematically prove that compositions are relationships, even compositions that loop back to the same object.

51 [173] in Appendix III shows compositions of relationships are associative (Appendix II, in the note on category theory, describes associativity in mathematical terms).

52 Based on the principle of subtyping by adding information, a perspective that adds detail to relationships or objects constitutes a subclass of the perspective it is detailing. The superclass can then be considered to be a reusable subassembly of configured components.

53 See Essential Patterns in Chapter IV.

54 An object that can be removed from a composition without affecting its meaning is mutable with the "null" object of Box 5.3.

55 Liskov's Substitution Principle asserts that it must be possible to substitute any object instance of a subclass for any object instance of a superclass without affecting the semantics of a program written in terms of the superclass. Although articulated for computer programs, this principle also applies to business meaning. See The Substitution Principle in Chapter 2 of [333] (in Appendix III).

56 Ownership, locations, technological capabilities, and other business properties are also features of objects.

57 The work products of a process are tied to its essential meaning. (The essential meaning is the same as the essence of a pattern, described in Chapter IV.) A paradigm shift, that changes the essential meaning of a process, will also change its work products.

58 This chapter extends XML sharability concepts. (See [54] and [55] in Appendix III).

59 If the choice of any one of the related objects (three in this example) is determined by the others (the other two in this example), we will get subspaces like these—lines, surfaces, and patterns that may be "flat" or may twist in higher dimensions.

60 An instance of product sale is a tuple identified by the conjunction of *Product* and *Place* in this example. *Sale Price* joins the product-place tuple to form a sale price- product-place 3-tuple. This is implied through the transitive relationships *Sale Price* has with *Product* and *Place*, via the instance identifier of *Product Sale* (see Figure 36 on our website).

61 [310], [281], and [282] (all in Appendix III) discuss the application of Borel Sets. [310] Chapter 4, Section 1 defines Borel Sets mathematically; Chapter 7, Section 5 discusses Borel Sets of tuples and multidimensional spaces.

62 The Borel object generalizes the concept of arrays. It implies the existence of not only the cells of a multidimensional array, but also of *collections* of cells. The "Don't care" value implicitly summarizes an array into its lower dimensional facets, which are also arrays. Borel objects subsume and extend the multidimensional arrays supported by XML ([54] and [55] in Appendix III).

63 The Borel object, the model in Box 14 on our Web site and Figure 4.5 all support the time series analysis mentioned in [54] and [55] in Appendix III; time can be a dimension of a multidimensional array.

64 The list price is an attribute of *Market Segment*, whereas the sale price is an attribute of *Product Sale*. *Product* is one way of segmenting the market.

65 An instance of product sale is a tuple identified by the conjunction of *Product*, *Place*, and *Customer* in this example. Compositions of relationships—relationships glued end-to-end by objects—are also relationships. The fact that *List Price* is an attribute of *Product*, *Customer Revenue* is an attribute of *Customer* and *Mean Temperature* is an attribute of *Place*, implies *List price*, *Customer Revenue*, and *Mean Temperature* of a place form a 3-tuple equivalent to the *Product*, *Place*, and *Customer* tuple. They

form the state space of the composition we segment (see Figure 36 on our Web site).

66 The points that represent the same place will lie in a plane parallel to the page you are reading. The place axis of Figure 5.8b will pass through this plane at the point that represents the place that is being repeated.

67 [297] and [304] (in Appendix III) discuss the normalization of repeating groups of data. The Universal Perspective bases normalization on meanings.

# Chapter VI
# Object Aggregation

## ABSTRACT

*This chapter describes the information and meanings that emerge from aggregates. It shows how the concepts like containment and subtyping are configured from the concept of location.*

Classes, subclasses, compositions, and relationships are collections of object instances. So are systems, cars, and households. They are all examples of *aggregate objects*. Aggregate objects are collections of parts—parts that are also objects—structured, unstructured, or collected into sets based on a multitude of criteria. These collections have properties that are distinct from the properties of the members that constitute them.[1] We have found these collections everywhere in the metamodel of knowledge—in perspectives, in relationships, in domains of values, in patterns of things; they are found even in the concept of object class itself, the root from which the tree of knowledge grows.

Let us start by recapitulating what we already know about aggregate objects:

1. Aggregate objects are also object instances. This implies that each instance of an aggregate object must have a unique identifier and history (except in the case of a domain, which may not have history). The class of insurance claims is a collection of claims. An instance of the collection is an instance of an object, and the many instances of insurance claims in it are also instances of objects. Further, aggregate objects may themselves be aggregations of aggregate objects.
2. Aggregate objects can be any collection of objects, structured or loose. Some examples are:
   - Patterns:
   - Perspectives: Perspectives are topoi[2]—consistent, self contained, complete structures of knowledge. They are compositions of components, relationships, and rules valid within a scope (see Box 2.5).
   - Sets and lists: Sets do not distinguish between multiples of the same object among its members; lists do.
   - Object classes: Members of object classes share attributes and effects. Object classes do not distinguish between multiples of the same object among its members.

- Domains and value sets: Domains and value sets are aggregates of values.
- Compositions and other aggregates of objects.

3. Aggregate objects have emergent properties (see Box 4.1), which are different and distinct from the properties of their constituent objects, but are derived from them on the following basis:
   - The enumeration of its members is a universal emergent property of all aggregate objects.
   - Enumeration is an attribute of the aggregate, not of its constituent members. Indeed, each combination in Figure 5.4 may be considered to be an aggregate, and it is clear that some of these combinations can contain others. For example, the combination of three represented by the lowest double headed arrow in Figure 5.4, implicitly contains all the other combinations, and the combinations of two in the same Figure implicitly contain two object classes.
   - Enumeration constraints on aggregates may also include enumeration constraints on combinations of aggregates—cardinalities, degrees, and the order of a combination. Constraints on the order of an aggregate are constraints on the number of different object classes from which instances may be aggregated at any given moment.
   - Order, degree, and cardinality are emergent properties of aggregate objects; relationships inherit them from aggregates. Relationships are subtypes of aggregates—subtypes with added information on structures and meanings of structures.
   - The overall state of the aggregate is determined by the states of its contents.
   - Objects inside aggregate objects may be events. Aggregate objects may change state spontaneously if invisible internal events or events beyond the scope of the model change the state of the aggregate object.

Emergent properties are often distinguished from resultant properties of aggregates.[3]

An emergent property is a property of the aggregate that is independent of the properties of its parts, whereas a resultant property is derived from properties of the parts of an aggregate. The horsepower of an engine belongs to the engine alone and is not directly derived from attributes of its parts, whereas the weight of the engine is the sum of the weights of individual parts and is therefore derived from them. As such, *Horsepower* would be an emergent property of *Engine*, whereas its weight would be a resultant property.

However, in this book, we will not make this distinction. We will not distinguish between emergent and resultant properties because both are items of information conveyed by the existence of the aggregate. The only difference between them is that a resultant property conveys information on its derivation, whereas the emergent property does not. The emergent property seems to pop up magically because the structural details of the composition within the aggregate are unknown. The aggregate is a pattern. We may not know the pattern in its entirety (and are at liberty to discard even what we do know).

The only reason the horsepower of the engine seems to pop up magically from the aggregate of its parts, rather than being logically derived from known properties of those parts, is that we have ignored the structure—the pattern of parts that make the engine. Resultant properties may convey more information than emergent properties (information about their derivation from parts), but distinguishing between resultant and emergent properties when we recognize the "unknown" value is redundant. Therefore, unless it is explicitly stated otherwise, emergent and resultant properties (of aggregates) will mean the same in this book.

## EMERGENT PROPERTIES OF AGGREGATE OBJECTS

Attributes may mutually constrain each other with value constraints. These constraints were relationships between attributes. In Chapter IV, we discussed operations that are valid in each kind of domain. These operations were relationships between values. We have seen how attributes of an object instance may be derived from other attributes. Derived attributes are related to other attributes via joint constraints that consist of valid operations between domains and/or inclusion and exclusion sets.

The perimeter of a triangle is the sum of the lengths of each side. *Perimeter*, as well as the length of each side, is a distinct attribute of *Triangle*. The summation is a relationship—a rule constraint valid only in ratio scaled domains. Similar operations may also relate attributes of the aggregate object with one or more attributes of objects that are contained in it.

The impact of operations such as summation, multiplication, and sequencing acting across the contents of an aggregate gives birth to an attribute of the aggregate—a derived attribute—derived from attributes of its contents. In an object class such as *Insurance Claim*, the total of all claim amounts is an attribute of the class, derived from individual claim amounts, which are attributes of individual instances of the class of insurance claims.

Just as attributes of the aggregate may be derived from the contents of an aggregate, so too may object classes. These may be considered derived classes rather than derived attributes. For instance, the largest insurance claim is a derived class with a single member—itself—because it is derived by a ranking operation that operates *across all instances* of the class of insurance claims (an operation valid in quantitative as well as ordinal domains[4]). Similarly the class of five largest customers is a class derived from the class of customers (both examples are also subsets of *Customer*, the class[5]). Rule constraints, like those in Box 5.1, may select, map, and transform the contents of an aggregate. The resultant collection will be a derived aggregate object[6]—derived because it not only contains information on its contents, but also information on rules about how it was derived from another.

We have seen how operations across attributes of an instance of an object create instance level derived attributes. Remember that the aggregate too is an instance of an object and therefore aggregates may also have derived attributes. These derived attributes are emergent properties like the number of objects the aggregate contains or the total weight of its parts. An object class is a kind of aggregate. For instance, if we are considering insurance claims, the number of individual claims is an attribute of the class. Therefore, the average claim amount—the total claim amount (an attribute of the class) divided by the number of insurance claims in the class (another class level attribute)—is also an attribute of the class. It is an attribute of the class because class (aggregate) level attributes may be derived from joint constraints with other class level attributes (attributes of the aggregate), just as instance level attributes were derived from other instance level attributes.

Data modelers sometimes argue that derived attributes are derived from others and therefore do not provide *additional* data; hence, derived attributes have no place in the data model. However, it is clear that derived attributes do convey additional *information*—the information conveyed by the operation(s) that they are derived from. Therefore, they *do* have a place in the object model. Derived attributes of contents of aggregates, as well as derived attributes of aggregates themselves, carry information about operations. These operations and the information they convey are often inherited from domains.

The use of the word *derived* might give an impression of a temporal sequence of calculation. This is not so. These joint constraints merely constrain values of attributes mutually. They tell us what values are valid with others in a pattern of attribute values. There is no before and after in these constraints.

## THE INFORMATION CONTENT OF AGGREGATE OBJECTS

In Figure I.4 of Appendix I, we can see how domains acquire structure, meaning, and behavior as we add information, a small step at a time. So too does the pattern of object instances—aggregates and compositions of objects.

At one end of the information spectrum, we have an aggregate object that has very little information—just that a bunch of objects belong to a pattern and that patterns are aggregate objects. On the other end of the spectrum, we have full information about the pattern—its meaning, structure, and detail. For instance, at one end of the information spectrum, we may merely know that a house consists of walls, and therefore instances of walls are members of an aggregate object called house; and at the other end of the spectrum we may have full information on the appearance, smell, and feel of a house and will know exactly where and how walls are connected into the structure, a pattern we call *House*.

### Connecting with Compositions: The Power of Inference

Until we open a window into an aggregate, we have no information on its composition—the structures and rules between objects in it. Indeed, we may not even know or care about the contents of an object—not even whether it is an aggregate or not. When this happens, the aggregate stops being an aggregate and becomes a simple object of the kind we have discussed throughout this book. Objects have relationships with other objects (or recursively with themselves). That is the only information of interest to us when the aggregate is hidden from view.

However, if we try to peer into the internal structure of an object, we may find that it consists of other objects. That is all we might know. We may know nothing about the structures that connect its contents or which external relationships connect to which object(s) inside it. As we gain information about the aggregate, we will know more about its internal structure and the objects inside it that give rise to various external relationships, that is, where external relationships connect to structures within the aggregate. Each object is a port that objects outside the aggregate can plug into. Remember, relationships are objects too and are therefore also ports of this kind. Objects may "plug into" relationships as illustrated in Figure 5.3. If objects plug into relationships, they increase the order of the relationship.

When we do not know about an object within an aggregate, it is hidden from us. The word "hidden" is a misnomer. It suggests that we know of its existence but cannot see it. That kind of rule belongs to the interface layer of Figure 3.4, not the business layer we have focused on. In the business layer, it is more appropriate to say that we have no information about where a relationship connects with a structure inside an aggregate because the information is missing from the aggregate—it is the same as saying that we do not know what the relationship connects to because we do not know the entire structure inside the aggregate and may not know all the objects in it; therefore, we cannot say which object an external relationship connects with. Both articulations are the same. They convey the same information—the internal connection is "unknown."

When objects in a composition are unknown, all we can say is that a relationship connects to the aggregate. When they are known, we can be more precise; we can say that we are certain that the relationship connects to the aggregate and not a component within, for the aggregate too is a repository of normalized information, or that it connects to precisely one or more objects within the aggregate.

The aggregate *consists of* its contents. The relationship "*consists of*" connects the aggregate to its contents. When another relationship touches the aggregate from the outside, the composition of that relationship and what it "*consists of*" connects the external object to the objects within the aggregate. If a *Person* owns a *Car*, and the *Car* consists of parts, a composite relationship will link *Person* to *Part* through *Car* (just as *Person* was linked to *Town* through *House* in Figure 5.6). Sometimes the composite relationship may be transitive, and sometimes not. If a person owns a house, he also owns its walls, which demonstrates that "owns" is transitive with "consists of" (Figure 6.1a). On the other hand, if a person lives in a house, it would be hard to believe that she also lives in its walls!—a fact that shows that "lives in" is nontransitive with "consists of."

Note that "lives in" is *nontransitive*, not *intransitive*. An intransitive relationship is mutually exclusive with a composition of relationships. To understand why "lives in" is nontransitive and not intransitive, think of termites in a house. If the termites live in the walls of a house, they also live in the house because the walls are a part of the house (the house *consists of* its walls), but to live in the house, the termites do not *have* to live in its walls (they could be abnormal termites which prefer living in rooms like people do). Hence, both "live in" and "consists of" can simultaneously and independently coexist (see Figure 6.1b—"live in" and "consist of" form a daisy chain from *Termite* to *House* to *Wall*, and "live in" also simultaneously connects *Termite* to *Wall* directly).

Note also that "live in" is transitive with "*part of*," the relationship that is the inverse of "consists of," from which you can infer that if you live in a part, you certainly live in the whole. This demonstrates an important rule—if a relationship is transitive with the inverse of another, it cannot be *intransitive* with the relationship in question—a law buried in the metamodel of knowledge and one that can be useful in automating inference, reasoning, and validating compositions of relationships.

You are absolutely correct if you think that the "*live in*" relationship between *Termite* and *Wall* in Figure 6.1 is a subtype of the "*live in*" relationship between *Termite* and *House* in the same figure. "*Live in*" between *Termite* and *Wall* is an inclusion polymorph of "*live in*" between *Termite* and *House*. The two relationships are not only nontransitive, but one is also a subset of the other, like the relationships in Figure 5.5c were. This will always happen when transitive inverses and nontransitive relationships are configured as they are in Figure 6.1b, because a subtype always implies and instantiates its supertype, but not necessarily vice versa.

*Figure 6.1. "Consists of" is transitive with some relationships, but not with others*

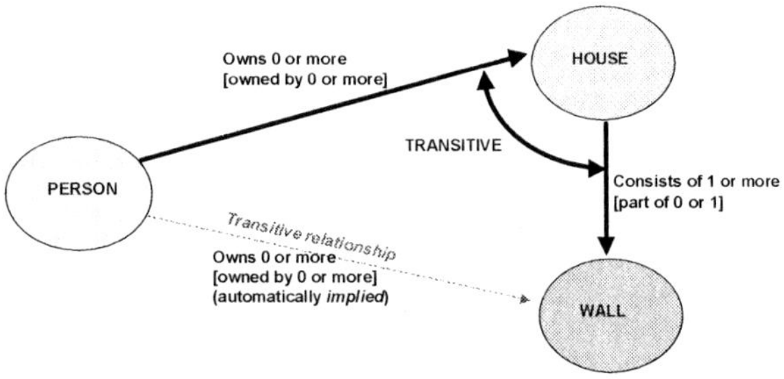


*a) Example of transitivity with Consists of*

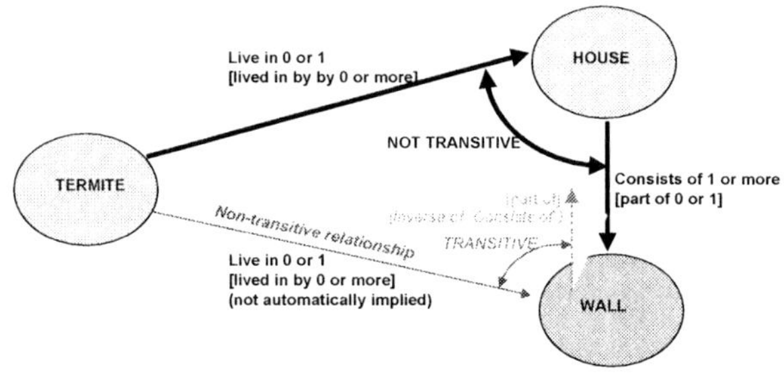


*b) Example of non-transitivity with Consists of*

This leads to a common pitfall when we integrate multiple perspectives and processes. It is one way in which knowledge may be unintentionally denormalized by the unwary. If we were working in a limited scope that was restricted only to termites in the walls of a house, we might have only modeled the relationship between *Termite* and *Wall* in Figure 6.1b. Later, if our scope shifted to include the entire menagerie that might occupy a house, including people, we might add *Occupant* and *House* to our model, and connect the two with the same "*live in*" relationship. Without the metamodel, knowledge would begin to fragment and denormalize; the fact that termites live in walls is *implied by* the relationship between *Occupant* and *House*, and it is restated again because a termite is also an occupant. Our metamodel however, recognizes that the "*live in*" relationship between *Occupant* and *House* implies the relationship between *Termite* and *Wall* because the wall is a *part of* the house (see the transitive pair in Figure 6.1b). It will be instantiated the moment a termite lives in a wall (or any other Part) of the house. The metamodel can coordinate knowledge without denormalizing it; it has the power to reason.

Relationships that are transitive with "*consists of*" also give rise to an important class of polymorphic relationships between the external object and its contents—polymorphic relationships that can help automate inference and reasoning. Owning the walls and the basement of a house are implied by the fact of ownership of the house; both relationships are examples of polymorphic variants of owning the house. Similarly, *Succeed* and its inverse *Precede*, which place objects on a timeline, are also transitive with *consists of*. This has profound ramifications on how the metamodel of knowledge infers and reasons.

Occurrence and connection constraints may also be imposed on relationships that touch an aggregate. Relationships of this type help to normalize constraints like:

- Whether the relationship must connect only to the aggregate.
- Whether the relationship must connect to at least one object within the aggregate (when the object becomes "known").
- Whether it must connect to every object within the aggregate as they turn from "unknown" to "known" (remember the "all" value of Box 5.3).
- How many objects of what kind within the aggregate the relationship may connect with.
- Other kinds of more complex constraints on occurrence obtained by constraining the degree, order, and cardinality of the relationship.

These relationships and constraints are the glue that can bind different compositions and aggregates into an integrated whole. They are the metaobjects behind the integration of behaviors, business processes, and the systems that support them. These systems, which are aggregations of objects, are sometimes still, but more often not; they flow, twisting and changing in step with the flow of time. They are then temporal compositions that we will discuss in Chapter VII. The key to reengineering is to keep these relationships and rules normalized as we integrate compositions by ensuring that they are attached to the information they truly normalize and are propagated where required by subtyping, inheritance, transitivity, and refactoring.[7]

## Existence Dependency

Sometimes the very basis, the identity of the aggregate, may depend on one or more constituents. If a house has no doors, it is just a house without a door, but still a house; however, without walls, it ceases to be a house. Walls and doors are different from House, the aggregate structure made of walls, doors, and other parts. A house can exist without a door, but without walls, there is no house. When this happens, the aggregate object is said to have an existence dependency on one or more constituent objects—in this case, on its walls.

The Borel object in Chapter V was another example of existence dependency. It depended on its constituents for its very existence; a market segment could exist even if it were empty (nothing was sold into it), but it could not exist unless at least one of its parameters (constituent objects like those in Figure 5.10b) also existed.

Note how existence dependency may involve properties of relationships like cardinality ratios, order, and degree:

- Take an example from the insurance industry: In the insurance industry, a fleet of cars is defined as a collection of at least five cars. In this case, the existence of the aggregate, the fleet, depends on the cardinality ratio of its containment relationship ("at least five") with its constituent object class, *Car*.
- Consider Market Segment: In Figure 5.10, the existence of Market Segment did not depend on the joint or individual existence of *Customer*, *Product*, and *Sales Channel*; instead it depended on the *degree* of its relationship ("at least one") that involved the *combination* of these objects.
- Consider the existence dependency between a house and its defining walls: We may assert that a house can exist only if its outer walls do. The problem is that houses come in different shapes. Houses may have several outer walls, be four walled, three walled, or houses with even fewer defining walls—perhaps even one curved cylindrical wall we call its outside surface. An upper bound of "many" on the relationship between a house and its defining walls will not capture this existence dependency. After all, "many" can also imply an existence dependency on fewer than *all* its defining walls, whereas we know that the house can only exist if *all* its defining walls do. Only if the cardinality ratio of the relationship is "all," the value we discussed in Box 5.3, will it accurately articulate existence dependency between houses and their defining walls (and customize the cardinality ratio for each instance of *House*).
- *Can a part be inseparable from the whole, that is, depend on the aggregate for its very existence?* Yes, indeed it can.[8] Consider a pattern, say a sphere. The sphere has a surface. The surface of the sphere is a part of the sphere—it might be considered an item in the composition that makes the sphere. However, without the sphere, there is no surface. As such, the surface, an item in the pattern called a sphere, depends on the whole pattern for its very existence. This fact of existence dependency—total inseparability of the part and whole—is an irreducible fact that is independent of other irreducible facts like shareability (see the discussion of an object's capacity for relationships) and mutability.
- A point on the surface may be shared by two spheres if they touch, but the existence of that point is dependent on the existence of the surface of the sphere—at least one of the two spheres—which in turn is dependent on the existence of the sphere for its very existence. The point may exist if at least one of the compositions it belongs to does. The spheres are even mutable. They may be deformed into other objects (or replaced by other objects) that have the same surface. The surface will continue to exist as long as it belongs to *some* shape.
- These examples illustrate that existence dependency between a component and the aggregate may have the same properties as that between the aggregate and the component. It all depends on the information content of the pattern—the composite inside the aggregate. We may not have full information on the pattern but may have just enough to say that a specific part depends on the whole for its very existence—especially if that part is pure information in a pattern of information.

It becomes a meaning[9] rather than a physical object that can be peeled off or physically removed like the walls of a house or the partitions of a cubicle in the office. For instance, a platoon cannot exist unless the army it belongs to does.

- Obviously, a composition cannot have an existence dependency with an optional object. That would directly contradict the very meaning of existence dependency.[10]
- On the other hand, the composition could be existentially dependent on one or more mutable objects. If this were so, the composition would exist if the mutable object existed and could continue to exist even if the mutable object were replaced. A house will continue to be the same house even if you replace its roof, but without a roof, it might not be considered a house because it will cease to be living space.

Relationships are metaphors for compositions and these examples demonstrate that existence dependency between aggregates and their contents is a relationship subject to the same rules as other relationships, rules that flow from properties such as cardinality, degree, and mutability. These properties are derived from properties of patterns.[11] Relationships, aggregate objects, and compositions are all patterns of association.

"*Aggregation of*" and "*composed of*" are relationships too. An aggregate object contains other objects. These objects are its contents. The aggregate might also consist of compositions of its contents. Existence dependency, mutability, and other properties of compositions that we have discussed earlier emerge from the information content of the "*aggregation of*" or "*composed of*" relationships—how much information each relationship conveys on internal structures and compositions inside the aggregate. We will discuss this next.

## THE INFORMATION IN AGGREGATION VS. THE INFORMATION IN COMPOSITION

A subtle difference exists between "*aggregation of*" (the same as "consists of") and "*composed of*." "*Aggregation of*" conveys less information than "*composed of*" (and therefore, by the principle of subtyping by adding information, it is the supertype of "*composed of*"): "*Aggregation of*" merely tells us that an object belongs to a collection. It conveys no information on structure. The collection is the "bag," and the object aggregated is an item in the "bag." *Aggregation of* tells us nothing about relationships, interactions, or other information within the bag. The "bag" might even be empty. A collection may have an identity independent of its contents, just as a warehouse has an identity independent of the goods that fill it.

"*Composed of*," on the other hand, may have varying amounts of information on the internal structure of the bag and the objects in it. It might have just enough information about structure to tell us that there is a structure of some kind, but not what it is. It might even add bits of information that give us partial information on the compositions inside the bag—bits and pieces about what connects to what, even bits and pieces about cardinalities, order, and degree.

As we leach the information from "*composed of*," its meaning starts approaching "*aggregation of*"; when all information on structure is gone, the two meanings become identical. However, even if "*composed of*" stops short of becoming "*aggregation of*," its information content can sometimes be very sparse indeed. It might only tell us what objects must exist for the composition to be meaningful. For example, "*composed of*" might only tell us that a market segment cannot exist without its constituents or that a house cannot exist without walls and a roof. When this happens, the result is the kind of existence dependency prevalent in UML and XML.[12]

Instead of removing information, if we keep adding information to "*composed of*" and dive deeper into its subtyping hierarchy, the meaning of the aggregation becomes clearer and more complete. It tells us more about the composition: its internal structures, cardinalities, cardinality ratios, capacities for association, sequences, and measurability; each property we have discussed starts crystalizing in step with the information we add. In the example of the house, we could go all the way up to full information including the image, feel, and smell of the house. The complete pattern tells us exactly where each component of the house, such as its walls, roof, doors, and windows fit, which items connect to what, where, and how, and what the emergent properties of the composition, a pattern, are.

Based on the above, "*composed of*" cannot be neatly subtyped into a finite hierarchy of subtypes. Compositions may be complex, and the quantum of information available on a composition may vary on a broad continuum, depending on the (possibly very large) multitudes of ways components in an aggregate may be configured into compositions of objects. Standards such as UML and XML address some of the most common subtypes of aggregations (see Box 6.1).

Figure 6.2 shows that "*composed of*" is a subtype of "*aggregation of*" because Object Composition is a subtype of Aggregate Object. Aggregate objects include compositions. This is why "*composed of*" is an inclusion polymorphism of "*aggregation of*" (Inclusion Polymorphism: see Box 4.8).

*Box 6.1. Existence dependency and share ability in object aggregations*

UML[13] recognizes two kinds of aggregation relationships (see the discussion of UML syntax in Box 5.1)—relationships that merely convey information on what items are in which collections (and upper and lower bounds on the cardinality ratios of these aggregation relationships) and relationships that assert existence dependencies with object classes. UML also recognizes, for aggregation relationships, a nominally measured, yes/no form of the capacity constraint on association we discussed in Chapter V. With UML, we can express the fact that an aggregate object may depend on another object for its very existence, and we may also assert that once the object is engaged in one collection, no other collection may have it (at the same time)—that is, the object cannot be simultaneously shared across aggregate objects.

These patterns of associations are the patterns we find frequently in business. However, the concepts we have developed in this chapter are broader. They subsume and extend UML and XML concepts. Unlike UML and XML, the intent of the metamodel in this book is to articulate the structure of knowledge—all deterministic temporal and nontemporal rules that may be configured into components of knowledge—rules that express different behavior depending on how they are glued, where, and in what subtyped form.

*Figure 6.2. "Composed of" is a subtype of "Aggregation of"*

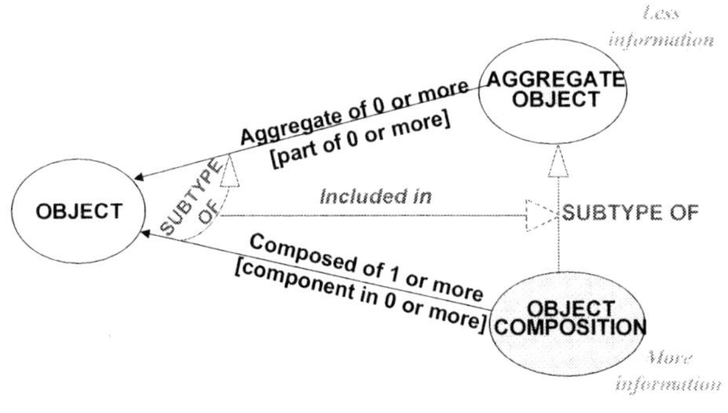

For a composition to exist, it must possess *at least* one object (and obviously, that object cannot be an optional object[14]). Therefore, although *"composed of"* is a subtype of *"aggregation of,"* the cardinality ratio of *"composed of"* is not the same as the cardinality ratio of *"aggregation of."* The cardinality constraints on a subtype may be the same as, or stricter than, the cardinality constraints of its parent(s).[15]

Of course, *aggregation of* is an asymmetrical relationship (and therefore *"composed of,"* its subtype, is also asymmetrical). It would be absurd to suggest that the constituent of an aggregate may contain the aggregate that contains it.[16] In Figure 5.6, if a town contains a house, the house, obviously, can never contain the town.

An aggregate object is a pattern of object instances just as a domain was a pattern of values with common meanings, and an object class was a pattern of object instances with common properties. Both domains and object classes were special kinds of aggregate objects. An aggregate object is a more general term than either—it could be any pattern of object instances—even patterns by decree.

The aggregate object is a hidden composition about which very little, or a great deal, might be known. At a minimum, we must know that it consists of other objects. Otherwise, it cannot be an aggregate. At most, it may blossom into a rich and complex composition of objects, connections, interactions, and emergent properties that can rival the reality that makes the aggregate its metaphor. Often, our knowledge lies between these two extremes, and we may only know what combinations of objects are mandatory for the mere existence of the pattern we call the aggregate object. Very often, much is unknown and hidden from view.

## LOCATION, CONTAINMENT, AND INCORPORATION

"Contains" may conjure a mental picture of a dream home furnished with rich furniture and a kitchen replete with your favorite food or of Santa Claus bearing a bag of gifts—gifts *contained in* his bag. "Contains" may also conjure a mental picture of an aggregate object with its contents inside it—inside the perimeter of its picture—a diagram that represents the *idea* of aggregation, like the diagram of subprocesses in Figure 7.21. Our mental pictures might make it seem most reasonable to equate the aggregation relationship that makes one object a part of another with the "contains" relationship, in which one object resides within another. However, our mental picture is not quite correct; "contains" is subtly different from "aggregate of."

The fact that "contains" is not the same as "aggregate of" becomes clear when we consider the inverses of the two relationships. The inverse of "aggregate of" is "part of" and the inverse of "contains" is "contained in." You may own a dream home, but a friend might have lent you the furniture and also asked you to stash some of the food in the refrigerator until she returns from a chore in the neighborhood; you may also have done your bit for Christmas and lent poor Santa the bag because Santa had none to spare. You own the home and Santa's bag, but alas, not the gifts *contained in* the bag; neither do you own your friend's food *contained in* your kitchen, nor the rich furniture *contained in* your house. However, you do own the walls of your home because you own the home. The house is an *aggregation* of its walls while it merely *contains* the food and furniture. They are not a *part of* the house (like the walls are). The *part of* relationship is stronger than *contained in*; it conveys more information. *"Part of"* means *"contains"* and then some; it conveys additional meaning over and above *"contained in."* That meaning is information on what it means for one object to *consist of* a collection of others. Based on the principle of subtyping by adding information in,[17] "aggregate of" is a subtype of "contains." "Consists of" it the same as "aggregate of"; they are synonyms. Therefore, "Consists of" is also a subtype of "contains."

"Location" merely locates a pattern in state space relative to another (it is synonymous with "located relative to" in Figure 7.27a and Figure 7.29). The location of an object is only meaningful relative to the location of another object. Location is a symmetrical relationship because location is mutual. There must be at least two objects involved. To locate an object in terms of itself conveys no information and is therefore meaningless. Therefore, no instance of "locate" may loop back on the same object instance. Object instances that locate each other may belong to the same or different classes. If object instances in the same class locate each other, "locate" becomes a recursive relationship, but it must be irreflexive because the object cannot locate itself.

"Contained in" is an asymmetrical polymorphism (subtype) of "locate"[18] that describes a special kind of relative location of *the limits* of a pair of patterns; it tells us that one pattern encapsulates another, without necessarily incorporating it—that the limits of the encapsulating pattern surround the limits of the enclosed (encapsulated) pattern.[19]

You might ask why we have labeled "Contained in" asymmetrical instead of antisymmetrical. Can an object or pattern be considered to contain itself? Isn't a pattern its own, largest, and most complete part? Yes, we could have labeled "Contained in" antisymmetrical, but remember that "Contained in" is a polymorphism of "Located relative to" (a relationship we can simply abbreviate to "locate"). As we have seen, a meaningful location must always reference another pattern; otherwise, it conveys no information. "Contained in" inherits this fact. To say a pattern contains itself begs the argument; it conveys nothing. This is why "Contained in" must be asymmetrical to convey any meaning. This is how we will use it in this book and in the repository of knowledge.

"Consists of" (its inverse is "Part of") is a stricter, more constrained condition. It tells us that the contained pattern not only lies within the boundaries or limits of the containing pattern but is also *incorporated* into the containing pattern. The containing pattern does not merely envelope the contained pattern in this case but makes it an integral part of itself. The two join as one pattern with its own unique identity.

"Locate" has several other polymorphisms. Mutually exclusive special meanings like "on," "under," and others may also be added to *"locate."*

*Box 6.2. Location vs. origin*

In the section on the architecture of pattern, we saw that a ratio scaled space has a natural zero. In Chapter IV, we saw that this added information turns difference scaled domains into ratio scaled domains. The origin of a ratio scaled space is fixed. All objects in a ratio scaled space will be located relative to a single fixed location that we have named their "origin." The origin does not locate itself; the origin adds information. It tells us that it is the reference point for locating all objects in a space. It is an object—a special object and meaning that conveys this information. As an origin embeds itself and becomes a part of a space or domain without a natural origin, it adds its meaning to the meaning of that space or domain and creates a new polymorphism—a new meaning built upon the old. The new meaning has a natural point of reference—usually a nil value or a natural limit of some kind. We have seen several examples of this in our discussion of patterns and domains. The origin in State Space, or the natural nil (or limiting) value of a domain, is a special pattern of information and an object. Indeed, all patterns of information are objects, and so is an *Origin*.

Each implies the general sense of "*locate*" (and elaborates on relative location) but may or may not be "part of" the object it is in, on, or under. "Part of" adds a different and an independent meaning to one of these polymorphisms—*contained in*—and hence is its subtype.

All subtypes of "*Contained in*," including "*Part of*," share the properties of asymmetry and transitivity that they inherit from "*Contained in*"—if one object contains others, which in turn contains yet others, the objects at the end of the chain will also be contained in the objects at the beginning of the chain. This is also true for the inverse relationships. Every subtype of "*contains*," including "*aggregate of*," will inherit the properties of asymmetry and transitivity from *contains*.[20] This gives the metamodel the power of reason—the ability to infer what objects are contained in which aggregations and what kinds of aggregations are subsumed in which others, and that the meaning of "*contained*" is not absolute; there are nuances within "*contain*," each with the power of inference it has inherited from "*contain*."

## ENDNOTES

1. [89] in Appendix III discusses aggregates and emergent properties.
2. The Oxford reference dictionary calls a topos a "stock theme." A mathematical category binds abstract structures and relationships into a consistent set of laws. A topos is a category with a complete set of laws in a given scope. See [173] and [183] in Appendix III.
3. Emergent properties were discussed in (Forsbak, n.d.), which is item [89] in Appendix III
4. Atomic rules that derive or constrain attribute values are relationships between attributes. The validity of a rule depends on the domain of the attributes bound into the rule (see [337]: Chapter III and Figure 48). When related values are all ratio scaled, relationships normalized by ratio scaled domains (e.g., arithmetic addition), and relationships inherited from parent domains (e.g., ranking) will be valid (Figure 68 on our Web site); when all related values are all quantitatively scaled, relationships that are valid in quantitative domains (e.g., arithmetic subtraction), along with those inherited from parent domains, will be valid; when related values are quantitatively or ordinally scaled, but not nominally scaled, relationships that are valid in ordinal domains (e.g., ranking) and those inherited from nominal domains will be valid; and if any value in the relationship is nominally scaled, only operations valid in all domains (e.g., association) will be valid.
5. See Box 19 on our Web site.
6. A derived aggregate object is the codomain of a rule of derivation (Box 5.1, Figures A and B) with a business meaning; it belongs to the business layer of Figure 3.4 (example: "the class of top ten customers"). Contrast this with *View* in Figure 33 on our Web site, which resides in the business process automation layer. A view adds information on presenting information to actors. It takes objects from business meaning to the Interface Layer and may also involve selection criteria. As such, *Selection Criteria* is a component of knowledge reused in different contexts for different purposes.
7. See *refactoring* in Appendix II. Refactoring is also discussed under Variation Inheritance in Chapter II of [337] (in Appendix III).
8. [89] in Appendix III discusses existence dependency between parts and wholes, their share ability, and their mutability.
9. Existence dependency implies that the very *meaning* of a pattern is contained in the *meaning* of another. The dependent pattern depends on another for its identity.

Mutual existence dependency implies that each pattern contains the meaning of the other. If the two patterns are distinct, this seems counterintuitive—how can an object (a meaning) that contains another be contained in the object (another meaning) that contains it? Mathematically, it can be shown that parts can contain wholes when we deal with infinitely large cardinalities. Indeed, we can see this even without abstract mathematical analysis. Consider Figure 5.9. The twisting surface in Figure 5.9 is a part of a three-dimensional space. Yet, because it twists and folds in three dimensions, the surface also implies the existence of the volume of which it is a part. The volume too admits the existence of the twisted surface, just because it is a volume, and the surface is one of its infinitely many parts. [202], [203], and [206] (in Appendix III) mathematically describe how parts may contain the whole and yet be a part.

10 An optional object in an aggregation is mutable with the null object (see the discussion on mutability in Chapter V). A null instance identifier asserts that the object does not exist. This is a more constrained pattern than not knowing if the object exists.

11 Cardinality relates to object counts in a pattern. Degree maps to extent. Mutability maps to the variability we will tolerate before we say it is a different pattern.

12 [55] in Appendix III describes XML standards. See the discussion of UML syntax in Box 5.1. UML and XML are discussed in Box 10 on our Web site.

13 UML is an acronym for the Unified Modeling Language. See Box 22 on our Web site.

14 Optional objects are mutable with "null" (see Box 5.3) because they do not convey the *essential meaning* of the composition (see Chapter IV).

15 The rule that asserts that a subtype cannot violate constraints imposed on its parent(s) was discussed in [337] in Appendix III, under Figure 42. That discussion demonstrates that cardinality ratios of subtypes may be different from, albeit constrained to lie within the limits imposed by their supertypes.

16 At first glance, it would seem "*aggregation of*" is asymmetrical: Common sense dictates that a constituent of an aggregate object cannot contain the aggregate it belongs to. In Figure 5.6, a town might contain a house, but it would be absurd to suggest that the house may contain the town. It is absurd to suggest that parts may contain the whole when we deal with object classes of finite population, but common sense breaks down when cardinalities (populations) are infinitely large. For example, the cardinalities of some domains are infinite (e.g., length). In such cases, an item that is a part of another may also contain the item it is a part of. [172], [202], [203], [206], and [212] (all in Appendix III) discuss this kind of containment. Some fractal patterns are examples of patterns that are created by repeating the same pattern endlessly so that each component and each spot on the pattern contains its own image; and we could drill down into points in the pattern to find itself forever (see [281] in Appendix III). The metamodel of Pattern in Appendix I also supports this. However, this book will assume that "*aggregation of*" is asymmetrical. If objects are permitted to contain themselves, it would become anti-symmetrical, but the idempotent instance of aggregation conveys no information and may be ignored (see Location, Containment, and Incorporation).

17 Box 4.3 discusses the principle of subtyping by adding information.

18 Asymmetrical polymorphisms of symmetrical relationships are discussed with the metamodel of relationship.

[19] See place, location, and containment in the Universal Perspective (Box 72 on our Web site).

[20] See Figure 7.27a. Box 72 on our Web site also elaborates on containment.

# Chapter VII
# Processes, Events, and Temporal Relationships


## ABSTRACT

*A process is a relationship that involves the flow of time. It is an irreducible fact about sequences in time. Processes are objects that cause change. Change involves time, and time involves events. Events have effects—effects that change states of objects and relationships. This is how processes are agents of change.*


*"The past not only contains, in its depths, the unrealized future, but in part the realized future itself"*
- Tagore, Nobel laureate and Bengali Poet

In order to understand Process, we must understand the temporal nature of relationships and the properties that flow from the place where time and event meet relationships and objects.[1] The scope of our metamodel is restricted to discrete change; all relationships, temporal or not, must relate not just object instances to object instances, but also time slices of object instances to time slices of object instances. Figure 7.1 shows this concept and the distinction between temporal and nontemporal relationships.

The time slices in Figure 7.1 are identical to those in Figure 4.5. Relationships may not only exist between object instances but may also occur between time slices of object instances. Figure 7.1 shows this fact. A temporal relationship is between time slices at different points in time; a nontemporal relationship is a relationship between contemporary time slices. Temporal and nontemporal relationships may be between the same or different object instances, and these object instances may belong to the same or different object classes.

The sweep of time makes temporal relationships special. Time cannot reverse itself. The direction of a temporal relationship carries more information than the nontemporal relationships of Chapter V. It carries information about the flow of time, about cause and effect. Temporal relationships are a subclass of relationships—a

*Figure 7.1. Temporal and nontemporal relationships*

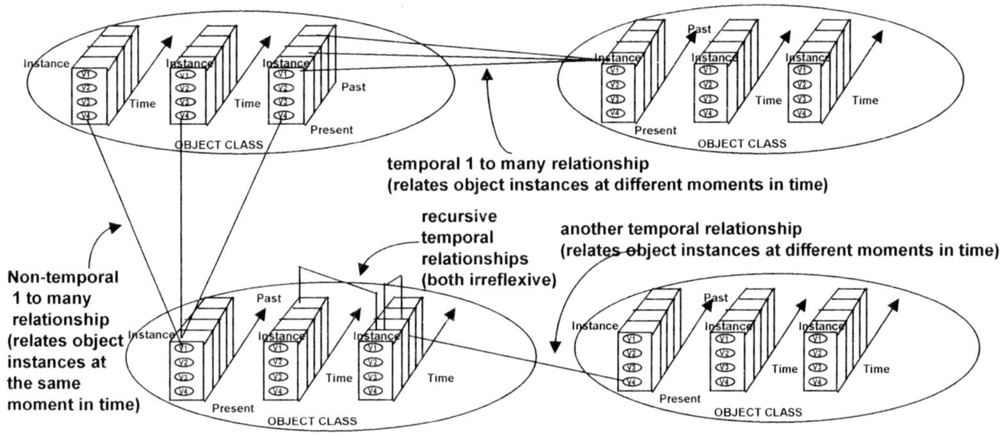


subclass that recognizes the flow of time and its irreversibility. They inherit the properties of nontemporal relationships and add temporal properties. They add the tide of time.

"Having written, the moving finger moves on"; no effect may change the past. States of time slices past are cast in stone, as are relationships between time slices in the past. However, the past can affect the present—and the future. Relationships between time slices present and past are mutable by events and effects, like any other relationship we have discussed thus far, but we must now consider their temporal dimensions as well. Taken together, they are properties of processes because temporal relationships are processes.

A temporal relationship is a process because it is a bridge across time built on causality.[2] Causality connects causes (objects) in the past to consequences (objects) in the present (or future); a process connects resources in the past to products in the present (or future). Processes are a polymorphism of causality. The meaning of Process conveys a little more information than cause and consequence. It also tells us that resources are used to produce products. Both resources and products are objects, but resources precede products, and processes are the causal link across time that connect them—processes like Bake Cookie that turn dough into cookies.

## RESOURCES AND WORK PRODUCTS

*Bake Cookie* is a temporal relationship between *Dough* and *Cookie* (ignoring the request for fresh cookies for the moment). *Dough* and *Cookie* are object classes. *Dough* comes first, and *Cookie* follows. *Bake Cookie* connects *Dough* in the past to *Cookie* in the present. *Dough* is a resource and *Cookie* is its work product. The objects that come before in temporal relationships are resources, and those that come later are products; they could be byproducts and waste products as well, which we will discuss later in this chapter.

Resources may be consumed by the process (as dough is) to make cookies or may only be needed for reference (or for other purposes that do not consume the resources). Resources that are not consumed are *catalysts* for the process. For example, the recipe for baking cookies is a resource (although it has not been shown in Figure 7.2a) that it is not consumed by the process, like the dough was. Similarly the cook is a resource

*Figure 7.2. Baking a cookie and the metamodel of resource use*

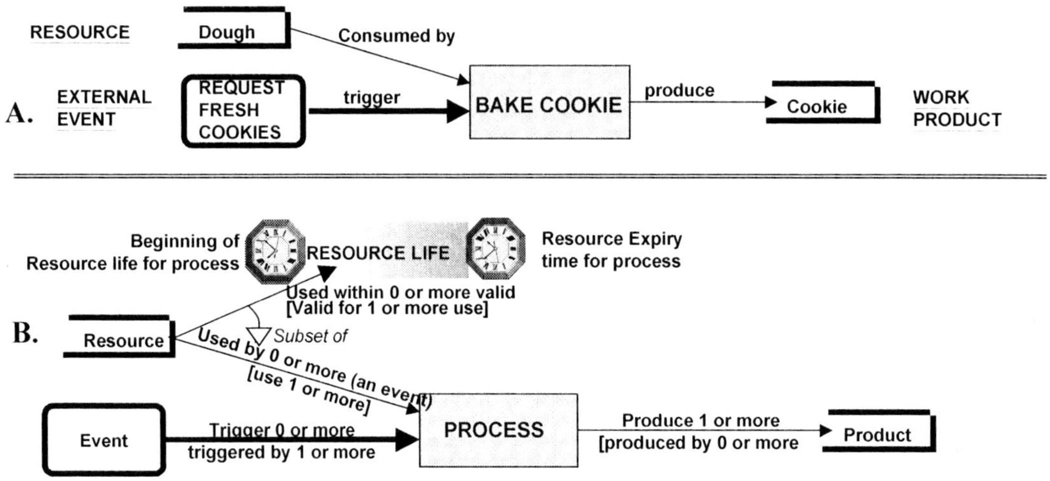


that is not consumed by *Bake Cookie* but is nevertheless needed by the process.[3]

Also note that a resource may have a life in the context of the process it is a resource for; that is, it may only be usable by the process provided it is used within a window of usability. For instance, the dough may harden and become unusable for baking. Similarly, most pharmaceutical products may only be consumed within a time slot after they are made—they have expiry dates. Figure 7.2b is the metamodel of this kind of behavior. The consumption and reference (or use as a catalyst) of a resource by a process are all polymorphisms (subtypes) of the generic *Use* relationship in Figure 7.2b. The process itself may have a window of time in which it is enabled. This is accounted for by the fact that an event is an interval of time and, like any other resource, may have a life or may expire at a certain time.

*Box 7.1. Inquiry, reporting, and observation*

Sometimes the work product of a process is pure information—an observation. This is where queries, reports, and observations fit in. We know that even the non-existence of an object is inseparable from information about it; non-existence can be considered to be a state—the null state we have discussed earlier. Hence, an object and information about it are as inseparable as light and shadow.

When information is the work product of a process, it is almost always in the form a report of some kind—an *observation.*[4] The report may be formatted in plain text, graphically, audibly, or in full audiovisual format. The report may even specify what data sources must be used. Reports, queries, and observations lie in the business process automation layers of Figure 3.4. Obtaining and reporting this information does involve the flow of time in those layers; there is a before and an after—the information comes before and the report comes after. These queries and reports are processes in the interface and information logistics layers of Figure 3.4.

These processes might not always be automated; they could be manual. You could ask a resident for driving directions in a new locality. This is manually done. The information exists because the locality does, but you still have to get it from someone, something, or somewhere—a source and a store for that information. The processes in the interface and information logistics layers of Figure 3.4 could be manual or automated, but information logistics and interfaces there

*continued on following page*

*Box 7.1. continued*

will always be. Inquiries are processes, but they are processes in the information logistics and interface layers, not in the Business Rules layer of Figure 3.4.

The trigger for a process that gives us information—a report or observation of some kind in some format—could be an explicit request for information or an internal trigger like a state change or the occurrence of an internal condition. For instance, a stock alert—a report—might be triggered when the inventory of an item falls below a critical level. Indeed, the trigger and the process are two different objects; the same process may be triggered by several different conditions. Each is a component of knowledge that we may assemble and configure into composite business processes. Each normalizes different kinds of information.

Can an inquiry change the state of a business object? Usually not. However, it is conceivable that the state of an object may change merely because we have asked about it. Many seasoned managers will testify that just asking about business operations can improve them. Indeed, that happens even in the physical world. An entire branch of modern physics—quantum mechanics—is based on the premise that merely knowing the state of a physical object or ensemble of objects may alter it. However, processes like these are beyond the ambit of both this book and our metamodel. Readers can refer to the additional information in Appendix II, under the note on the locale of matter and energy, and the generalization of distance. Items [284], [285], and [286] in Appendix III provide further reading (Note on Hilbert Space, n.d.; Hilbert Space Explorer, n.d.; and Sarfatti, n.d.).

When we must represent this kind of irreducible fact—a business rule that asserts that the state of an object emerges only when we ask about it, the inquiry would be an event like any other, an event with an effect that turns unknown values of attributes into known values (see the discussion on the unknown value in Chapter IV). The event is a trigger for a state change—a trigger that can perturb values of attributes, values unknown, or even known. The inquiry process puts an object into the "observed" state.

## CYCLE TIME

The time lapse between the two ends of a temporal relationship is the cycle time of the process. In Figure 7.2, it is the time it took to bake the cookie—to turn *Dough*, the resource, into *Cookie*, the product, by baking it. Cycle time is a universal attribute of all temporal relationships (processes). Cycle time maps to the time-lapse domain; it distinguishes temporal relationships (processes) from nontemporal relationships. *All processes must begin and end (except Sagas—see Box 7.2). The beginning moment and ending moment are events that occur at well defined times* (even if the beginning and the end are unknown, they are still presumed to be distinct moments). Temporal beginnings and ends map to the date-time domain. The cycle time is a derived attribute; it is the elapsed time between the beginning and end of the temporal relationship (the process).

The work products of a process follow from its resources; they *succeed* the resources that made them. *The process locates its products, relative to its resources, in time. Cycle Time* is the temporal distance between the products and resources. Succession is a temporal relationship; in fact, it is a temporal polymorphism of the "*locate relative to*" relationship we discussed in the section on *Location, Containment, and Incorporation* in Chapter VI. *Locate* turns to succession when we add the flow of time to its meaning. We will discuss this in detail later in this chapter.

## TEMPORAL INVERSES, REVERSIBILITY, AND REVERSION

The flow of time adds a new dimension to the inverse—the concept of reversibility of a process. Consider *Bake Cookie* in Figure 7.2 again. Once the cookie is baked, we cannot unbake it to reproduce the dough we baked; *Bake Cookie* is an irreversible process. On the other hand, we can freeze ice into ice cubes and melt the cubes to get the same water we had frozen. Therefore, *Freeze Water* is a reversible process.

A reversible process is an inverse that goes forward in time. It converts products back to the same instances of the resources that they were created from. All processes are not reversible. Reversibility is an attribute of *Process*. Without time, a relationship and its inverse would be one inseparable whole. Time adds information. This information separates a process from its inverse, or rather its *Reversion*. We must articulate which part of a relationship will go forward in time—the relationship in question, or its inverse. Moreover, we must distinguish processes that may be reversed from those that may not. The sweep of time brings forth the meaning of *Reversibility*.

Reversibility may not always be absolute. Reversible processes may not always recover all the resources that were consumed. *How much* of the original resources a reversible process may recover can be a consideration. When more than one resource is involved, reversibility may be unequal for each resource. The measure of reversibility may vary by resource, and partial reversibility, like any other metric, may be nominally, ordinally, difference, or ratio scaled. *Therefore, reversibility may be measured by resource* and the measure of reversibility is a measure of efficiency of the *reversion* of a process.

Each reversible process has one or more *reversion* counterparts. Each may be considered to be a mutable subtype of the generic reversion process (generic for the process being reversed). The efficiency of each alternative could be different. Cardinality constraints of inverses can constrain the number of object instances in an object class. Similarly, when the object class is a process, cardinality constraints can limit the number of times a process may be reversed (see the discussion under *Temporal Cardinality*).

Temporal relationships will also have ordinary inverses that go back in time, retracing the resources transformed into the product. These inverses can be very useful in quality assurance and in diagnosing the impact of resources and processes on products.

## TEMPORAL RECURSION, TEMPORAL REFLEXIVITY, AND TEMPORAL IDEMPOTENCY

When we include information on the flow of time in a recursive relationship, it enriches the repertoire of all three kinds of recursive relationships: irreflexive relationships, reflexive relationships, and idempotent relationships. The repertoire expands because recursion, reflexivity, and idempotency may apply independently to an instance of the object, to a time slices of an object, or simultaneously to both (see Figure 7.1). Time creates novel and exotic kinds of recursion, reflexivity, and idempotency from nontemporal parents.

A nontemporal recursive relationship loops back to the same object class. When the flow of time is considered, a relationship may or may not loop back to the same time slice. If it does, it cannot be a process because processes always involve the flow of time. Causality is implicit in a process. Resources come before products. Thus, when time is considered, we obtain strange and exotic relationships that may be processes or not, depending on how they are constrained:

- A *class recursive* temporal relationship also loops back to the same class, usually with different time slices of the same or different object instances. If it is also time slice reflexive, it may (but does not always have to) connect the same time slice; if time slice is irreflexive, it cannot do so. On the other hand, if the recursive relationship is time slice idempotent, then it *must* do so.
- A *class irreflexive* temporal relationship cannot loop back to the same object instance.
- A *time slice irreflexive* temporal relationship cannot loop back to the same time slice.

- An *idempotent* temporal relationship loops back to the same object instance but may be time slice irreflexive—it may *have* to connect different time slices of the same object instance. It could also be time slice reflexive; that is, it may be permitted to connect the same time slice of the same object but is not required to always do so.
- A totally idempotent temporal relationship must always connect the same time slices of the same object instance.
- A time slice idempotent temporal relationship *must* always relate concurrent time slices of object instances. The object instances could belong to the same or different object classes.
- A reflexive nontemporal relationship may loop back to the same instance of an object, but a temporally reflexive relationship may also loop back to the same *time slice* of the same object instance. However, unlike its idempotent counterpart, it does not *have* to do so (for example, a person may be his own counsel in a court of law or may ask someone else to fill the role).
- A nontemporal antisymmetric relationship is a relationship that is asymmetric unless it loops back to the object instance, and a temporally antisymmetric relationship is a relationship that is asymmetric unless it loops back to the same *time slice* of the same object instance.
- When a relationship loops back to the same time slice, there is no passage of time; it cannot be a process because there is no "before" and "after." Therefore, *totally or time slice idempotent temporal relationships are not processes, and neither are instances of reflexive relationships that loop back to the same time slice*. They fall under the category of the nontemporal relationship of Chapter V.

Hence, if a person is to represent herself in a court of law in future, the representation is a process. It may consist of compositions of subprocesses like preparation and planning. However, the irreducible fact that she is currently representing herself at the court, at this very instant, cannot involve the flow of time, and hence it becomes a nontemporal relationship.

As you leach a process of its temporal information, it fades into a nontemporal relationship because processes are relationships with information added—information on which end of the relationship (temporally) precedes which.

## TEMPORAL ASYMMETRY

The flow of time is asymmetrical. It always flows from past through the present, into the future. It can never flow the other way. Therefore, processes are all asymmetrical relationships. If they were not, causality would break down. We know that the physical world is causal. Business too must be causal because business must be done in the physical world of cause and effect. It is a part of the Universal Perspective.

The property of symmetry (and its opposite, asymmetry) of nontemporal relationships is replaced by the property of reversibility (and its opposite, irreversibility) of temporal relationships.

Figure 7.1 makes clear that cardinalities, orders, and degrees of temporal relationships must also consider the irreversible sweep of time. Nontemporal constraints may be placed on occurrences of concurrent combinations of objects in tuples, as they were in Figure 5.4 and Figure 5.5. Temporal constraints are similar, but they are constraints on occurrences across time slices. Constraints that cross time slices may cross time slices of a single object instance or time slices of different object instances of the same or different object classes.

Based on the above, Figure 5.4 cannot represent a higher order or higher degree temporal relationship. It must be adapted to include the time dimension. In Figure 5.4 (and Figure 5.5), one-dimensional chains of object instances are strung into tuples. Adding the time dimension turns the one-dimensional chain into the two-dimensional sheet of Figure 7.3.

Figure 7.3 is just like Figure 5.4 except for the fact that the tuple has been stretched along the timeline into the past and has been sliced each time it changed state. The one-dimensional combinations of Figure 5.4 may now extend across cells of the two-dimensional matrix in Figure 7.3.

Cardinalities, degree, order, mutability, symmetry, inverses, and the other properties we discussed in Chapter V are now expressed in terms of combinations of cells of this matrix of time slices. It stretches tuples into the past, slicing each as it changes state. New kinds of orders, degrees, and cardinalities can crystallize from this matrix, and no process may ever traverse this matrix from the future to the past. A process may only reverse the effects of another process but only as it spins into the future. A process and its reversible counterpart must always go forward into the future. *The moving finger, having written moves on*, but because it moves; it adds new meanings to concepts such as mutability, order, and degree as we will see next.

## TEMPORAL MUTABILITY

Consider a new car and its temporary license plate as you drive it away from the dealer. For a limited time, the temporary and permanent license plates will be legally mutable. After that, you must have the permanent license plate. The car has changed state. In its new state, the permanent license plate is not mutable with the temporary license plate. In its old state, it was. This example shows that mutability may be time sensitive.

The example of the car and its mutable license plate is simple. It depends on a single cell in Figure 7.3, a time slice of *Car*. Other rules are more complex; combinations of cells may be mutually mutable—combinations like those in Figure 5.4, extended into temporal dimensions as they are in Figure 7.3. Mutability, like the other properties of temporal relationships, may normalize a fact about a single cell or about combinations of cells in Figure 7.3. As such, mutability may be made contingent on the overall state of a system, which might change as processes forge ahead in time, creating, changing, and deleting objects and states.

*Figure 7.3. A temporal relationship is a two dimensional matrix*

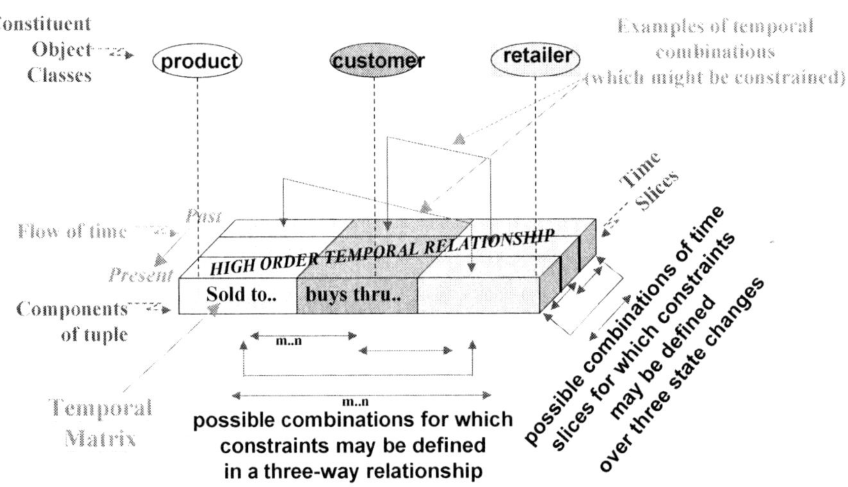

## TEMPORAL ORDER

Nontemporal order is the number of distinct object classes that a relationship binds, as elaborated below:

- When we consider temporal order, we must consider the remoteness of history bound into the relationship. How far back into the history of each object class does the relationship reach in order to articulate the rule about a change of state at present? We must know, by object class, how many time slices a relationship spans. This gives us the temporal order of the relationship by object class.
- The instance recursive relationship in Figure 7.1 is a relationship of second temporal order; the class recursive relationship is of third temporal order; the temporally injective relationship at the top of Figure 7.1 is also of third temporal order. It does not matter that the relationship connects with the current time slice of its target object, as well as the first past time slice (counting backwards from the present). It goes back to the third time slice in the past (the first time slice was in the present) and temporal order measures how far back a relationship reaches. Therefore, it is a relationship of the third temporal order.[5]

Among all time slices of all objects bound by a relationship, the time slice farthest back in the past is special. It tells us how remote a time period can influence the present (for a specific temporal relationship class). This is the overall temporal order of the relationship. The points on your driver's license earned three years ago may influence your insurance premiums today; this is a temporal relationship that spans three years in addition to the current year. Each year is a time slice for this purpose; hence, it is a relationship of the third temporal order.

The influence of the past usually fades with the passage of time. Temporal order tells us how far into the past we must go to account for present behavior. If an event five state changes old is a guard condition for a state change today, in a process that uses only one kind of resource to produce only one kind of work product, it is a second order process (because it relates only two object classes, a single resource to a single work product). However, it is a second order process of the fifth temporal order. *It is a temporally fifth order process* even if events one, two, three, and four time slices old have no influence on state changes at present *because events five time slices old influence state changes that can occur now.* When state transitions depend only on contemporary events, the processes that effect those transitions have no memory—they are processes of temporal order zero.

Although unlikely, it is possible that the remote past may influence some kinds of behavior more than the recent past can. The constructs in Figures 7.1 and 7.3 can support this scenario.

## TEMPORAL DEGREE

The degree of a relationship is the number of instances that may be glued into a tuple. Just as temporal order could be specified in terms of the temporal order of an object in a relationship, as well as the overall temporal order of the relationship, so too can the temporal degree:

- The temporal degree of a relationship with respect to a participating *object instance* is the number of distinct time slices of that object instance the relationship involves. It is therefore also the degree of an idempotent relationship—the number of times a process loops back to the *same* product or reuses the *same* resource—a process in which the resource and product are the same object (in perhaps different states. Example: the loop from *Check* to *Check* in Figure 7.24b).

Can distinct time slices ever be concurrent?—The answer might seem to be an obvious no, but there are subtleties that could turn it into a yes when polymorphisms are considered. Consider an electronic check that must be signed by two individuals. The check becomes payable when both have signed. We therefore have three states of the check—one for each individual's signature and the third which tells us it has both signatures and is therefore payable. The check may be signed electronically, independently by each signatory; therefore, the signatures may be obtained simultaneously or not. The signature process loops from check back to the *same* check, in a different state. Indeed, the process itself changes the state of the check; it is idempotent with respect to the check. If each signatory signs at a different time, the signature process connects two different time slices of the check, and clearly the process will be a second degree, idempotent relationship. However, if both polymorphisms of the process—each signature event—occur concurrently, the process has repeated both its polymorphisms simultaneously and is complete in a single time-period instead of two. Is this a first or second degree process?

It is a second degree process because two processes of the same kind (the signature process); a 2-tuple are inextricably joined together to produce the final product—the end state—a payable check. The relationship puts no constraint on temporal sequence or concurrency of the two polymorphisms of the signature process.

From the perspective of each polymorphism of the signature process—a classification based on *who* signs, it is a second order relationship—two different kinds of processes (objects) are involved, but from the perspective of their common supertype, the signature process, both are the same kind of object; hence the signature process is a first order process. It loops back to the same instance of check, so it is also a first degree, idempotent process. However, when we give it a temporal dimension, each signature being put on the check becomes an event, and thereby, paradoxically, a temporal, idempotent relationship may be a higher degree process, even if it loops back to the same time slice because the time slice may contain multiple polymorphisms of the same process in an aggregate object that also joins them into a tuple. The aggregation of subtypes is also a subtype of the generic signature process. We will elaborate objects of this kind under process engineering.

- The temporal degree of a relationship with respect to a participating *object class* is the number of distinct *time slices* of all object instances of that object class that an instance of the relationship involves (ties into a tuple). Compare this with the nontemporal cardinality ratio of an object in a relationship. The nontemporal cardinality ratio of an object in a relationship is the number of distinct target object *instances* that instances of the relationship associate with a single source object (see Figure 5.1 and the discussion under Figure 5.3).
- The overall temporal degree of a relationship is the total number of time slices of all objects that the relationship involves.
- Constraints on temporal degree constrain the length of the temporal tuple; they are occurrence constraints on numbers of time slices in a tuple; each cell of the temporal matrix is a time slice of an object instance of an object class. It is the occurrence of these cells, individually and in combination, that may be constrained—combinations like those in Figure 7.3. This constraint may limit the length of the tuple, put a floor under it, or both. Complex constraints may dictate several ranges of valid and invalid lengths. Just as multiple objects could be involved in the combinations in Figure 5.4, multiple

cells might be involved in the combinations of Figure 7.3. For example, the lowest double-headed arrow of Figure 5.4 is a three-way combination.

## TEMPORAL CARDINALITY: CONCURRENCY, REPEATABILITY, AND BATCH PROCESSES

The cardinality of temporal relationships must describe not just the cardinality of combinations, but also the cardinality of combinations across different time periods. Cardinality constraints may involve combinations of cells in the matrix of Figure 7.3. Implications of the temporal nature of cardinality include:

- **Batch processes:** The cardinality ratio of a single cell describes how many items of an object class were simultaneously involved in an instance of the relationship at the time. If the object class is a resource, the cardinality ratio of the cell that represents the contemporary time slice tells us how many items of the resource are required at a time by an instance of the process. If the object class is a product, it tells us how many items of the product a single instance of the process produces at a time. Remember that the process may consume resources or produce products in batches, and there may be several instances of the resource or product in a batch. (Figure 7.11c has examples of batch processes. Box 7.5 also has more information.)
- **Concurrency and repeatability:** A process is an object class, and like other object classes, counting the occurrence of instances of a process measures its cardinality. However, a process has a time dimension. It occurs over a time period and has a beginning and may have an end. Therefore, the scope of the cardinality of a process must be defined in terms of occurrences in time. Extending cardinality into temporal dimensions results in three kinds of cardinality:
    - **Concurrency:** The concurrency of a process is the number of instances of the process that are running in parallel (see Figure 7.4). It is a form of temporal cardinality because we count number of instances of the process *at a given time*.
    - **Repetition:** Repetition is the number of times the process repeats *across* time slices (Figure 7.4). It is a form of temporal cardinality because we count number of instances of the process *across time slices*. (*Repeatability* is a constraint on Repetition). The scope of repetition may be described in terms of one or more time slots—that is, we may care about repetition in only some time periods.
    - **Nontemporal cardinality:** Nontemporal cardinality does not care about the flow of time. It is "unknown" to the process. Nontemporal cardinality is the total number of instances of the process—the sum of those running in parallel at each time slice *and* those repeated across time slices. (In the example shown in Figure 7.4, the nontemporal cardinality is 3+4+2=9.) Although nontemporal cardinality does not care about the flow of time, when applied to a process that *does* care about the flow of time, it may be described in terms of one or more time slots—that is, we may not care about the flow of time only in certain time periods.
    - The *nontemporal* cardinality of an *idempotent* process must also be its *temporal* degree—the number of times it must repeat and/or occur concurrently.

Cardinality ratios, on the other hand, articulate somewhat different rules. In Figure 7.4, assume that the end of *Bake Cookie* in the preceding time

*Figure 7.4. Temporal cardinality: Concurrency vs. repetition*

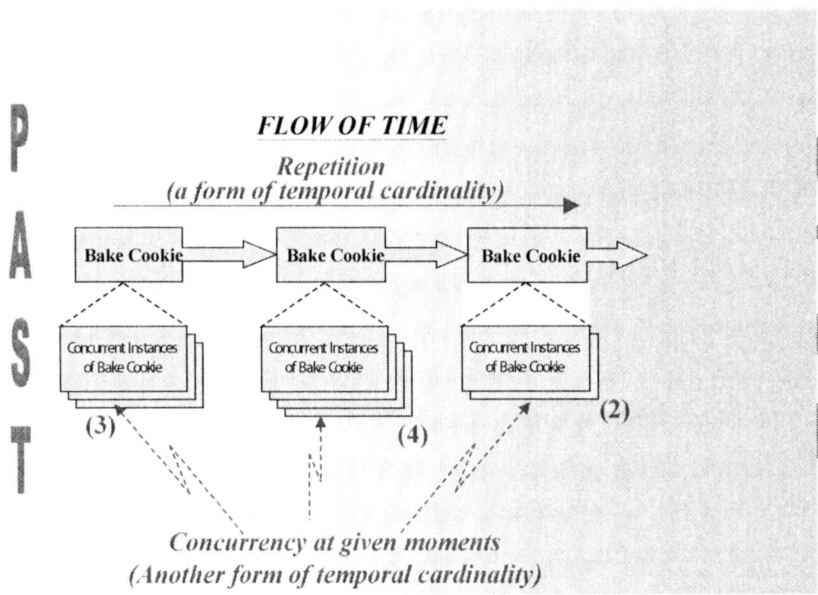


slice triggered each repetition of *Bake Cookie* in the following time slice. This implies that every instance of bake cookie in a time slice was related to its predecessor by a temporal relationship that reads "*succeeded by,*" one can think of each connecting arrow between successive *Bake Cookies* in Figure 7.4 as this relationship. The concurrency ratio (a kind of cardinality ratio) of this relationship tells us the number of successors in the following time slice that each instance of *Bake Cookie* may trigger.

Constraining the concurrency *ratio* of this temporal relationship at a given moment will limit the number of successors of each *instance* of *Bake Cookie* in the next time period, whereas limiting the concurrency of the *Bake Cookie* object class in the next time period will limit the total number of instances of *Bake Cookie* that can concurrently occur in that period, regardless of how it was triggered, or by which instance of possibly multiple instances of preceding processes. This is the difference between concurrency and concurrency ratio.

Naturally, the number of instances of the Bake Cookie process that may actually occur will be limited by *both* constraints if they occur simultaneously. The two constraints will then be merged subject to the laws of merger of constraints.

The difference between repeatability and repeatability ratio is similar—one constrains repeatability of processes triggered by a single instance of an event, and the other constrains the number of instances of the class that may be repeated over time. If a poor quality toner is a resource in a copying process, the repeatability of that process may be less than another similar process that uses high quality toner; that is, the repeatability of the process triggered by an instance of a toner cartridge in the copying machine may be different from the repeatability of the same kind of process triggered by a different instance of toner cartridge in the copying machine. This is different from the total repeatability of the process, which might depend on the overall life of the copying machine.

Constraining concurrency will cap (and/or put a floor under) the number of processes of that class that may run in parallel. (Constraining concurrency to nil in one or more time slices will bar the process from executing at those times.) Repeatability may cap (and/or put a floor under) the number of times the process may be repeated. Constraining nontemporal cardinality will cap (and/or put a floor under) the total occurrence of the process, parallel or repeating.

Constraints on the cardinality of a process could also be across a range(s) of time slices. A process may be barred at certain times but forced to occur at others with different limitations on concurrency and repeatability.

If there are several ovens used to bake cookies, several instances of *Bake Cookie* could occur simultaneously. The concurrency of *Bake Cookie* would be capped by the number of ovens available for baking cookies at the time. Some ovens might be shut down from time to time for maintenance. As such, constraints on the concurrency of *Bake Cookie* could change over time (Figure 7.4).

Like any other object, a process may consist of an aggregation or composition of processes. By constraining the cardinality of the aggregate, we can constrain the number of times the aggregation or composition may be repeated (or run concurrently). Constraining the repeatability of an aggregate that consists of a reversible process and its reversion will constrain the number of times a process may be repeatedly executed and reversed. It is the aggregate that will normalize this rule, not the individual processes in it.

Just as we could limit cardinalities of *combinations* or single objects in an aggregate, we can limit cardinalities of *combinations* of events in an aggregation or composition of events. These limitations may constrain concurrency, repeatability, or nontemporal cardinality, individually or in combination.

The occurrence of the aggregate may also be constrained in the same way. Constraining the occurrence of the aggregate is different from constraining independent occurrences of its parts. Constraining the aggregate ensures that the *aggregation* of parts is limited—not the independent occurrences of parts that may be members of the aggregate. We could limit the number of times *Bake Cookie*, the aggregate in Figure 7.5b occurs, but its constituent, *Arrange Dough Glob on Cookie Sheet*, will not be bound by this limitation if it occurs by itself, outside the composition in Figure 7.5b. Even if we do not bake cookies, we could still arrange dough globs if it pleases us to do so.

## EFFICIENCY AND PRODUCTIVITY

Efficiency is derived from cardinality ratios of resources and work products. It is a measure of the quantum of production per unit of resource consumed or used. The efficiency of a resource is the cardinality ratio of the product divided by the cardinality ratio of the resource. Temporal efficiency is the cardinality ratio of the product divided by the cycle time of the process—the number of units produced per unit time per (instance of) process. When the resource is human, we might call it productivity.

## CAPACITY FOR TEMPORAL RELATIONSHIPS

Just as objects could have a limited capacity for nontemporal relationships, they can have a limited temporal capacity for temporal relationships. Further, just as the number of object instances it could relate to measured an object's capacity for nontemporal relationships, the temporal capacity of an object for temporal relationships is the capacity of a time slice (of the object instance) for relating to time slices of other (or the same) object instances. Finally, just as an object's nontemporal capacity for relationships could vary at class or instance levels, so too may its temporal capacity for temporal relationships vary by class, instance, time slice, or even combinations thereof.

A razor used for shaving might use a single detachable blade at a time. The blade is a resource used by the shaving process. At any given moment in time, only a single blade can be a resource for a single instance of the shaving process, and while it is thus engaged, no other process can use the blade as a resource. Hence, its nontemporal capacity for use in processes like shaving, scraping, and cutting is limited to one.

On the other hand, the blade has a life. It gets blunter with each use and must be discarded after repeated use. Therefore, there is a cap on its capacity for repeated use.

The blade may be a resource for only one process at a time, but may be used multiple times. The cap on its simultaneous availability as a resource (its nontemporal capacity) is different from its capacity for repeated use (temporal capacity) as a resource. This example illustrated how temporal and nontemporal capacities are different properties of a temporal object (an object like the object in Figure 4.5 that exists for a period of time). One is the blade's capacity for simultaneous relationships and the other its capacity for repeated relationships.

Like nontemporal capacity, temporal capacity may be different for different object instances. Some blades get blunt more easily than others. Just as there could be instance level constraints on cardinality ratios, there may be instance level constraints on temporal and nontemporal capacities. Each instance level temporal or nontemporal relationship may consume a part of this capacity. How much it consumes is an attribute of the relationship (just as it was for instance level cardinality ratios). Indeed, we can extend the concept so that relationships at different times, as well as across different combinations of time slices like those in Figure 7.3, may deplete different amounts of an object's capacity for relationships.

An object instance's capacity for relationships might even change over time. The capacity of a time slice of an instance of an object for relationships will be the capacity for relationships at that point in time for that object instance.

## GOVERNANCE AND NONSTATIONARITY

When a relationship is mutable, that is, can change over time, it is a nonstationary relationship. When *any* property, such as capacity, cycle time, or efficiency, changes over time, it is nonstationary. Stationary relationships are frozen for all time and so are stationary properties. They do not ever change.

The properties of a stationary process are fixed for all time. When the properties of a process change over time, it is called a nonstationary process. Processes that change properties of other processes are called higher governance order processes. A second (governance) order process changes the properties of a first (governance) order process, a third (governance) order process changes the properties of a second (governance) order process, and so on. Higher governance order processes govern lower order processes, just as higher order patterns governed lower order patterns. Relationships are patterns too.

This terminology might be somewhat confusing, considering that processes are temporal relationships, and the order of a relationship has a different meaning (Chapter V). To avoid confusion, the term "order" of a relationship, be it temporal or not, will have the meaning of "order" in Chapter V, and this book calls the governance of one process by another as the *governance order* of the process (or pattern).

A process that *defines* another is also a higher governance order process. Defining a process is different from triggering a successor; triggers initiate instance(s) of a process, whereas process definition describes process classes. Box 7.4 provides an example.

## EVENTS

Temporal relationships are processes because they convey cause and effect information—information on resources and products. What if we do not have this information but know that *something* happens over a period of time or even at an instant in time? The occurrence is then an object—a temporal object but not a relationship. It is an event.

Events are independent objects. When we leach cause and effect information out of events, they stand on their own—temporal objects in their own right that, unlike processes, are not bridges between other objects. Based on the principle of subtyping by adding information,[6] every process is also an event.

We will expand on this concept soon, but for the moment bear in mind that *events are processes, or processes shorn of information on resources, products, and causality (the very information a process conveys on transformation of resources into products). Because processes are subtypes of events, they will inherit all properties of events—the properties we have discussed thus far and the properties that we will discuss going forward.* Processes may, of course, also possess additional properties that are not universal to all events.

Every event must have a start time and usually an end time. Events, like any other object, may be resources used and products produced by processes. In Figure 7.2, a request for fresh cookies is an event. It is also a resource that triggers *Bake Cookie* and starts the process rolling. *All processes must be triggered by some event*, even if it is the beginning or end of another process. Other examples of events that might trigger processes are the arrival of a particular time of day (for instance, the end of a trading day may trigger trade reconciliation processes) and the beginning or end of another event (for instance, the start of a production run for a batch of chemicals may be triggered by the end of the reactor loading process).[7]

Unlike processes, events may have no end and no duration[8]—its cycle time may be infinite or nil. For instance, the beginning and the end of a process are events with no duration. We will call an event of nil duration a *moment*.

When the cycle time is nil, the start time equals the end time. Bridging start and end times of an event with an equality constraint reduces it to an event of no duration like the flash of a camera. A question for the thoughtful reader—do the beginning and the end of a process of nil duration have implicit start and end times? Is this kind of process any different from a nontemporal relationship? Why?

Events may even occur spontaneously; they may be caused by processes beyond the scope of the model or by the inherent uncertainties we have ignored in our deterministic metamodel. These spontaneous events too can trigger, suspend, or terminate processes.

Processes are events of finite duration (or of infinite duration as shown in Box 7.2) with information on resources and products added.

*Box 7.2. The saga of processes that never end*

Some events may never end. They are patterns of infinite extent. Processes are polymorphisms of events. Processes that never end, like long stories, are called *Sagas*. However, if we assume that change must always occur in discrete steps, *instances* of processes must always begin *and* end; a resource must either be transformed (change its state) or not. A train of processes like the perpetual cycle of production runs in a factory are a saga when considered together: we know that a process may also be a composition of subprocesses. Subprocesses are not *subtypes* of the aggregate process (discussed under *the essence of a Process and the goals of Business*); they are members of the aggregation. Some compositions of

*continued on following page*

*Box 7.2. continued*

processes may be an unending sequence of discrete processes that goes on forever; the aggregate never ends after it starts, even if its parts do. This is how an aggregate can become a perpetual process. Although the scope of our metamodel is limited to the consideration of discrete change, it must include sagas.

The idempotent loops in Box 7.12 could be aggregate processes that perpetually cycle through sets of states, always returning to the state they started from before beginning their endless cycle afresh. Processes that cycle in this fashion resemble the finite, but unbounded, patterns that we discussed in Chapter IV. However, time flows remorselessly from the past to the future. The moving finger of time can never go back and neither can a process be undone (its effects may of course be *reversed* by another process, but the occurrence of the process is cast in stone or, more appropriately, in time). Time unravels these otherwise finite patterns to make them infinite and undelimited along the time axis in state space (like an infinitely long helix wound around the cylinder in Figure 4.5c—if the cylinder had not been delimited above).

The term *saga* conforms to the Business Process Markup Language (BPML) standard from the Business Process Management Initiative (BPMI) consortium, which is now a part of OMG, the Object Management Group.[9] [63] in Appendix III (Arkin, 2001) describes BPML in detail. An event of finite duration conveys more information than a saga. It tells us when the event must end. Based on the principle of subtyping by adding information, a process that ends is a polymorphism of *Saga*, the metaobject.

A generic *Saga* has no information on when it will end, if it ends at all. Its end time (and duration) is unknown and may even be infinite. On the other hand, we might know for sure that an event might be endless. This kind of endless event is a subtype of the generic saga. We will call it an *Endless Saga*. A process that we know will end, even if we do not know when, is also a polymorphism of the generic saga but we will not call it Saga. Rather, we will call it a discrete process. A process with a well defined, known end is a subtype of a discrete process. It is the "ordinary" process that we have been discussing here.

Therefore, they are subtypes of events. Processes *must* relate resources to products. Therefore, they are also relationships—temporal relationships, a subtype of *Relationship*. As such, *Process* is a subtype with two parents—*Event* and *Relationship*.

## SUCCESSION CONSTRAINTS: TEMPORAL RELATIONSHIPS BETWEEN EVENTS

Events are objects. Relationships between them will inherit all the properties of relationships we have discussed so far, even the temporal properties that we discussed in this chapter. However, events are not ordinary objects. They are temporal objects that occur in time and have a beginning and often an end. That makes temporal relationships between them special. The special characteristics that temporal relationships acquire, over and above those we have discussed thus far, is the property of temporal dependency—that the occurrence of one event might be contingent on another and that this contingency implies that one event may temporally succeed or precede another. ("*Precede*" is the inverse of "*Succeed*." The relationship is obviously asymmetrical.)

Shorn of information on its resources and product, *Bake Cookie* is an event. When we peel back the covers, we find that it is a composition of successive events; first we must arrange dough globs on a cookie sheet, then bake the cookie, and finally unload cookies from the oven. (If we added resource and product information to each event, the composition would become a process map like that in Figure 7.11c—a map of how cookies are baked.)[10] Indeed, events may even be contingent on beginnings and ends of other events. Temporal succession implies not just existence of states but also constraints on which states may succeed which. We will consider the mere occurrence of contingent events before we consider more complex dependencies in which events are contingent on beginnings and ends of other events.

## States of an Event

From Figure 7.5, each event in the composition is a state of the *Bake Cookie* process, and the different states represent a strict progression, tracking the extent to which Bake Cookie has progressed after it was started.

Every event (and therefore every process) of finite duration has at least three possible mutually exclusive states: *Not Started*; *Started* (the same as "in progress"); and *Finished*. *Not Started* and *Finished* are equivalent to *Not Occurred* and *Occurred*. For events of infinitesimally small durations, *Started* merges into *Finished*, both of which therefore imply *Occurred*. Sagas will never finish, although they may start (see Box 7.2).

For all events (and therefore all processes too), two more states must be added, *Suspended* and *Cancelled*. *Suspended* implies partial completion. Implicit in partial completion is the assumption that there are intermediate states, known or unknown, between *Started* and *Finished*—a progression, and therefore a composition of events, known or unknown, linked by a Web or chain of succeeds (precedes) relationships, also known or unknown. "*Suspended*" implies that this temporal progression was halted and may continue from where it stopped. We may not even know where it stopped, especially if we do not know the composition implicit in *Suspended*, but we do know that it stopped *somewhere*—in an *Unknown* state of an *Unknown* composition, supported by the *Unknown* value that we discussed earlier.

*Cancelled*, on the other hand, implies that the progression was halted and must be restarted from the beginning. *Cancelled* implies no intermediate states or compositions.

The more information we have about the composition, the more states we can add to the event. Each event in an aggregate event is a possible state indicator—an event started, finished, suspended, or cancelled. Events too, like other objects, have histories of state changes. States have temporal relationships with other (or the same) states, such as state transitions and succession rules. These rules and relationships, like all others, will be framed by the properties of temporal relationships. However, time always flows forward. "The moving finger, having written, moves on." Common sense tells us that temporal succession cannot cycle back to the same or previous time slices. Temporal succession is an asymmetrical relationship that is temporally irreflexive even if it loops back to the same object instance.

"*Suspended*" and "*Cancelled*" are two extremes in the spectrum of a halted progression of states of an event (and therefore its subtype—a

*Figure 7.5. A composition of events*

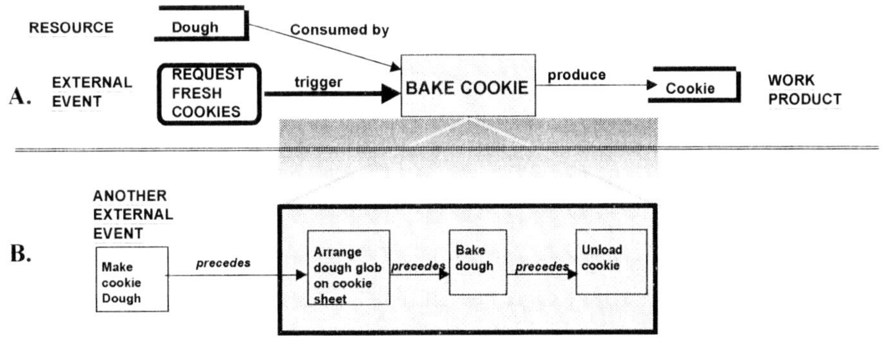

process). Business rules might dictate that the event (or process) be restarted from a past state. Any past state can qualify (and past states can also influence which past states qualify via temporal properties like order, degree, mutability, and others we have discussed). These kinds of rules about suspending and rolling back processes could not exist if the succession constraint did not. Temporal compositions carry more information than their nontemporal counterparts—they carry information on the flow of time.[11] Temporal rules of succession, suspension, and cancellation crystallize from the temporal information within *Event*—from temporal compositions known, unknown, or only partially known.

*Box 7.3. Plan, start, stop, and occur*

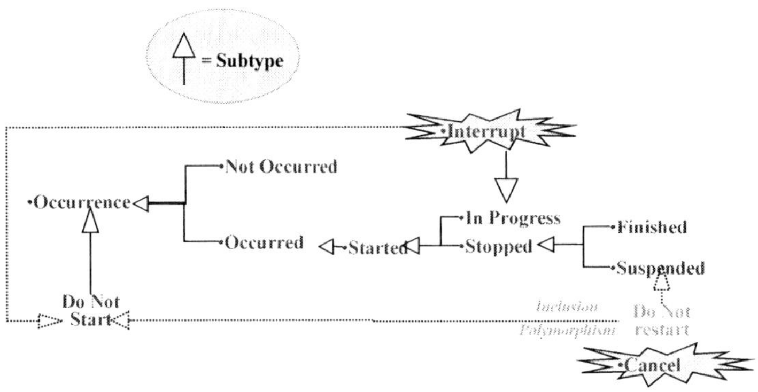


*Figure A. The topos of occurrence*

Is "Start" the opposite of "Stop"? It might come as a surprise to many, but "Stop" is not opposed to start; it actually extends the meaning of "Start." In information space, "Stop" is a polymorphism of "Start," and both are polymorphisms of occurrence as discussed in the following paragraphs.

Beginnings and ends can be distinguished in ordinal space. Unless there is a beginning, there can be no end. However, an end is not always mandatory. An occurrence like a process may begin but may have no end. It could be a pattern of infinite extent in the forward direction. An end constrains this infinite pattern and makes it finite. As such, we can have beginnings without ends, but all ends must have beginnings. Therefore "End" becomes an extension of the pattern called "Begin"; further, "End" is a polymorphism of "Begin."

"Start" and "Stop" occur when time sequences are considered. They are inclusion polymorphisms of "Begin" and "End" respectively. "Stop" is a polymorphism of "Start."

Moreover, we could attach a "do not start" constraint to the theme of occurrence so that the event cannot start. Additional polymorphisms of occurrence emerge when we consider the flow of time within this constraint. If the process had already started when the constraint is activated, it will interrupt the process. The meaning of interruption is assembled from "do not start" and "In progress."

The concept of Latency is also formed in a similar manner. Consider conditional polymorphisms of "do not start." If the occurrence of the event is contingent on the occurrence of other events, some of these predecessor events might occur, but the successor event will stay latent until all its predecessors have occurred. A latent event is in a suspended state. "Suspend" is a polymorphism obtained from "Stop," when we know that a process is not complete. When it is complete, we consider it "Finished." "Suspended" and "Finished" add information to "Stopped" and are therefore its polymorphisms.

An unconditional "do not start" constraint attached to "Suspended" creates the meaning of "cancelled," which is therefore a polymorphism of "Suspended." These are the universal states of process.

The power of reason resides in this ontology. Suspension and cancellation not only imply stopping but also the act of starting. Latency and interruption are transmitted down causal chains, which are sequencing constraints (relationships)

*continued on following page*

*Box 7.3. continued*

between events. An automated system can become "aware" of rings and cyclic causal chains of deadlocked processes (which we have discussed under load balancing), each waiting in deadly embrace for a predecessor to finish, which in turn, might be waiting for successors to finish. "Aware" processes may use some of the strategies described under load balancing to break the deadlock.

All processes inherit another universal state from the primal object. When we add intent on a future state to an object, it becomes a planned state. This universal state is normalized by the primal object and is inherited by all objects, including relationships and processes. There may also be planned and unplanned relationships and processes. This state is independent of the existence of the other universal states of Process. Hence, we may have planned or unplanned cancellations, suspensions, and occurrences.

## Events in Parallel

Compositions of events need not always be daisy chains like the composition in Figure 7.5b. Compositions could be networks of succession rules, like the task dependency diagrams in a complex project or business processes in a corporation.[12]

A firm might take an order, pick items from inventory, and ship the items to a customer. The events represent a natural progression of states of the order fulfillment process. No event in the daisy chain may occur unless the event before it has occurred. On the other hand, invoicing is contingent on taking the order, but it is independent on picking items from inventory (if we assume that all items are always available and we need no credit or payment check on customers). Therefore, invoicing may occur in parallel with picking stock to fulfill the order. Assume that the invoice is shipped with the order. Then the shipment event is contingent on completing both the stock picking and invoicing events. Figure 7.6 shows how this order fulfillment process is a network, not a daisy chain, of succession rules.

In Figure 7.6, the event at the arrowhead may only occur if the event at the tail of the arrow has occurred. Neither Pick Items nor Raise Invoice can occur unless an order is taken (obviously!), but once an order is taken, neither depends on the other, and both are free to happen in parallel. The shipment event, however, depends on both and cannot occur unless both *Raise Invoice* and *Pick Items* have occurred.

Figure 7.6 illustrates two alternative conventions for diagramming event dependencies; there are several others as well. The Project Manage-

*Figure 7.6. A network of event succession rules*

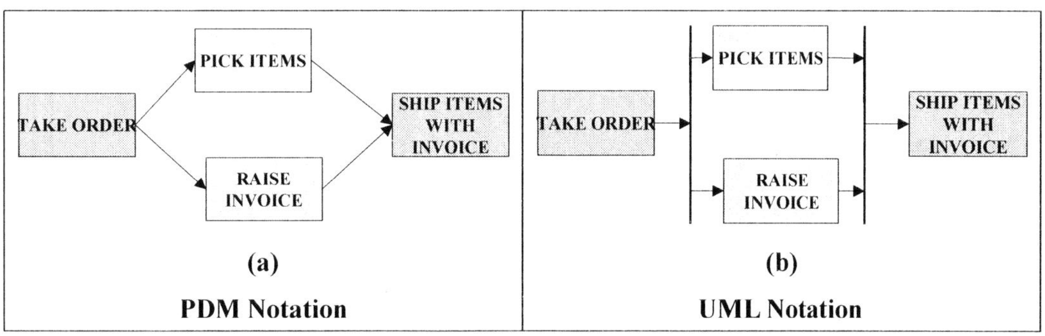

ment Institute (PMI)[13] prefers the notation in Figure 7.6a and the Object Management Group prefers the notation in Figure 7.6b. PDM is an acronym for Precedence Diagramming Method and UML for Unified Modeling Language. A detailed discussion of PDM and UML is beyond the scope of this book.[14] It is the pattern of rules about event interdependencies that we are interested in. The figures help us to visualize these patterns embedded in our metamodel.

## Conditional Events

Rules of succession can be conditional. Consider Figure 5.5 again. The relationships were conditional. Each relationship was contingent on another. Succession might be a temporal relationship between temporal objects, but it is still a relationship. Succession is subject to the same contingencies as the relationships in Figure 5.5 (and also the more complex contingencies that flow from constraints on order and degree). Let us consider the three simplest cases first and understand how the flow of time adds to each:

1. Mutual inclusion (Figure 5.5b)
2. Mutual exclusion (Figure 5.5a)
3. Subsetting (Figure 5.5c)

### Mutual Inclusion

When one event occurs, the other must too, and both are triggered by the occurrence of their common predecessor. In Figure 7.6, *Take Order* triggers both *Pick Item* and *Raise Invoice*, and, if items are picked, the invoice must be raised and vice versa.

If the relationship between *Take Order* and *Pick Item* were optional (the lower bound on its cardinality ratio would then be zero), *Pick Item* might or might not occur after *Take Order* occurs. *Raise Invoice* would occur only if *Pick Item* occurred, and *Raise Invoice* would not occur if *Pick Item* did not. Conversely, *Raise Invoice* might or might not occur after *Take Order* occurs. *Pick Item* would occur only if *Raise Invoice* occurred, and *Pick Item* would not occur if *Raise Invoice* did not. Processes inherit these constraints from relationships.

This is the most common form of succession between events with common predecessors. Diagramming conventions like PDM in Figure 7.6a support it. Indeed, we may have many mutually inclusive successor events after Take Order (such as *Check Customer Credit Rating, Check Customer Payment Status*, and *Check Stock Availability*). Each branch of the succession relationship is contingent only on the event at the root of the arrow and the occurrence of the other branch(es). Figure 5.5 highlights that the mutual inclusion constraint is on the cardinality of the *combination* of events, not individual events.

The usual convention in PDM is that succession is mandatory (implying that the cardinality ratio of the succession relationship is *at least* 1). Business processes and events are usually contingent on predecessors, and mandatory succession is the most frequent pattern of succession. If any one relationship in a mutually inclusive set (of relationships) is mandatory, all the others must also be mandatory. Most diagramming techniques like those in Figure 7.6 imply mandatory succession. We will also follow this convention.

So far, we have discussed succession in terms of events occurring (or not). We know events have beginnings and may have ends. When predecessors or successors are events of finite duration, succession must necessarily involve their beginnings and ends. Frequently, it is the beginning of the successor that follows the end of the predecessor. Unless we say otherwise, this will be our assumption; successors start only after predecessors end (although we will discuss complex rules under beginnings and ends of events).

The differences between temporal and nontemporal cardinality were described with Figure 7.4. Constraints on the concurrency of *Pick Item* will tell us how many items we may pick in parallel, regardless of whether they were triggered by one order or several. Constraints on its repeatability will tell us how many times we may repeat "pick item" over a set of time periods, regardless of what events might trigger each repetition. If the lower bound on the cardinality of the period 1–period 4 combination is two, it implies that *Pick Item* must happen at *least* twice in both time period 1 and time period 4. Their triggers and causes are irrelevant. In contrast, the cardinality *ratio* of the succession relationship between *Take Order* and *Pick Item* will tell us how many items we may pick in parallel for each *Take Order* event (after it occurs).[15] Their common trigger is an instance of *Take Order*.

The succession relationship is temporal. It can also specify different cardinality ratios in different time periods that follow *Take Order*. The incidence of *Pick Item* that follows a single *Take Order* event may differ in different time periods. For instance, concurrency ratios may dictate that three concurrent *Pick Item* events follow in the period immediately after (a specific instance of) *Take Order* and two more follow two time slices later.

Constraints on temporal cardinalities of combinations across the cells of the temporal matrix of Figure 7.3 lead to even more complex rules for triggering successive processes.

**Mutual Exclusion**

Succession of mutually exclusive events implies that one event cannot occur if the other does, even if both are triggered by the occurrence of a common predecessor. Consider a recruitment process. We interview the candidate and either offer him the job or not. If the candidate is offered a job, he is issued an offer letter; otherwise he gets a letter of regret; the event *Interview Candidate* will be succeeded by either *Make Offer* or *Express Regret*, not both. If the candidate is offered a position, the letter of regret must not be issued and vice versa. Figure 7.7a articulates this:

Assume the mutually exclusive pair is mandatory (like it usually is). The succession of events must proceed through one of the two mutually exclusive paths. What decides which path will be taken, and which excluded? Conditions and events do. The decision to reject or accept a candidate is an event (perhaps of zero duration). Conditions that occur in time are also events (as are all temporal occurrences[16]). Mutually exclusive events may trigger mutually exclusive successions of events. Figure 7.7b shows this. It is the decision to hire or reject the candidate, both of which are events that were buried inside the succession relationships in Figure 7.7a. Each has been shown explicitly in Figure 7.7b. Each is a part of the composition

*Figure 7.7. An example of mutually exclusive succession*

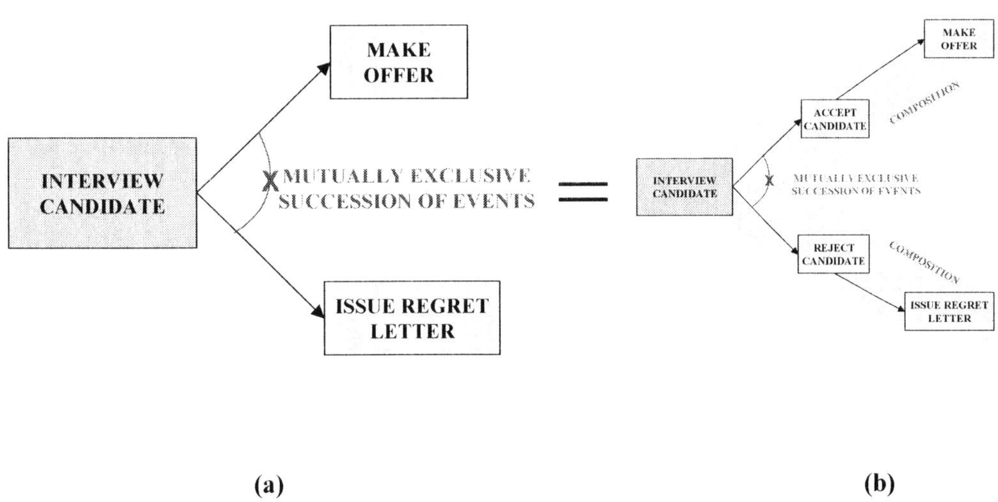

of events inside the succession relationships in Figure 7.7a.

These kinds of mutually exclusive triggers are found frequently in business.[17] Bill payment often follows this kind of pattern. If the total amount of a vendor's bill exceeds a threshold, a senior manager might have to approve payment. Otherwise, it might be paid routinely. The condition that the bill amount has exceeded the threshold is an event. That it is at or below the threshold is another mutually exclusive event. These events will determine which path is taken. They are guard conditions. How many such situations do you know of in the business you are in?

A mandatory pair of mutually exclusive succession relationships mandates that one of the mutually exclusive events in the pair must succeed their common predecessor. An optional pair implies that neither event may succeed their common predecessor. We have seen how mandatory mutual exclusion implies equating the degree of the mutually exclusive combination to one, and optionality implies a lower bound of zero and an upper bound of one. Similarly, a lower (upper) bound on *temporal* degree will mandate *at least* (at most) a prescribed total number of instances of the successor events be repeated over *any* of the prescribed time periods (a combination of time slices). If the lower bound on the degree of the period 1–period 4 combination is two, it implies that the process must succeed its predecessor at *least* twice in either time period 1 *or* time period 4, or *both considered together*.

(Contrast constraints on the degree of a relationship with the "and" constraint implied by limitations on temporal cardinality. Constraints on degree generalizes the inclusive "or" rule, whereas constraints on cardinality generalize the Boolean "and." "Not" is implied by Nil.)

Mutual inclusion and exclusion can occur together when we consider the flow of time. Two or more processes may be mutually inclusive but *concurrently* exclusive. With reference to Figure 7.6, in order to fulfill an order, we may need to pick items and raise an invoice, but a (somewhat foolish!) business rule might bar us from doing both concurrently. Therefore, either *Pick Item* may need to follow *Raise Invoice* or vice versa—we do not care which goes first—but the rule is that both cannot occur together at the same time (perhaps because resources are limited). Thus, temporal inclusion can coexist with temporal exclusion, provided they do not address the same time slice concurrently or are not in conflict if they do.[18] Indeed, as we saw in our example, constraints on temporal degree and temporal cardinality can interact in complex ways.

**Subtyping of Succession**

Consider a service center for a software manufacturer. They take calls and log customer issues. Many issues are minor, such as forgotten passwords and compatibility with printers. The customer service representative helps the customer to resolve these issues on the telephone. However, bugs and defects may surface from time to time. The service center logs and tracks these separately as outstanding software problems. The service center coordinates their resolution with the development, maintenance, and operations departments until they are closed to the customers' satisfaction. Some problems may be severe. Senior managers must be alerted when this happens. A part of this chain of events has been shown in Figure 7.8.

In Figure 7.8a, only software bugs are opened as problems; other issues might be logged, but that event stream is beyond the figure's scope. *Open New Problem* succeeds *Analyze Issue* only when a new software problem is found. Often no bug is discovered, or the problem was discovered earlier, and *Open New Problem* will not succeed *Analyze Issue*. Therefore, the succession of *Analyze Issue* by *Open New Problem* is optional (and the lower bound on the cardinality ratio of the succession relationship between *Open New Problem* and *Analyze Issue* is zero).

*Figure 7.8. An example of a succession subtype*

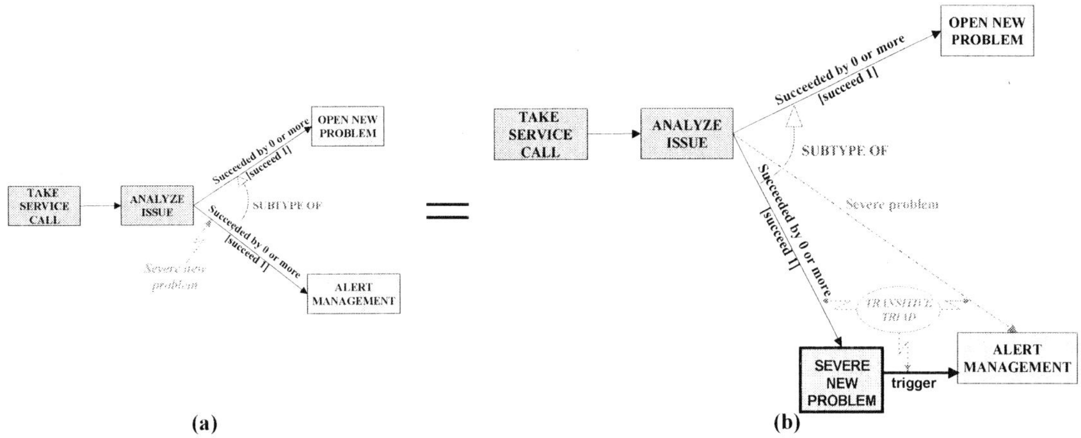


New problems must be logged regardless of how trivial or severe they might be. Whenever a new problem is deemed severe, senior managers must be alerted, and of course, it must be logged (like any other new problem); that is, whenever *Alert Management* succeeds *Analyze Problem*, *Open New Problem* must also succeed *Analyze Problem*. However, the converse is not true. *Open New Problem* may succeed *Analyze Problem*, but *Alert Management* might not because the problem was minor. A subtype always implies its supertype, but the supertype does not imply the existence of its subtype(s). The *Analyze Problem–Alert Management* succession is a subtype of the *Analyze Problem–Open New Problem* succession. It is like the relationship in Figure 5.5c, with facts about temporal succession added. Subtyping of temporal succession implies that when the subtype occurs, its supertype(s) must also occur (but not vice versa) at the same or different time(s). If the supertype has to occur concurrently, we must attach this constraint, which will then be a separate component connecting the subtype to its supertype.

The example in Figure 7.7 shows that it is events that trigger each successor and that compositions of events are transitive with respect to the relationships they replace. Figure 7.8b also shows this. The occurrence of *Severe New Problem* is an event. *Severe New Problem* is also a product of the *Analyze Problem* process. However, it does not *have* to occur each time *New Problem* occurs, but it may because *Severe New Problem* is a subtype of *New Problem*. This is implied by its succession being a subtype of the succession of *New Problem* (see Figure 7.8b). A successor event can also be considered the product of the process (a kind of event) it succeeds. Products and resources, including events and processes, may be subtyped like any other object.

When three relationships are mutually transitive, like they are in Figure 7.8b, they form a *transitive triad*. In order to normalize the information conveyed by the triad of three relationships, we must always leave one relationship out; the others imply it. Explicitly showing it would replicate the information. In a nontemporal triad of transitive relationships, it does not matter which relationship we drop to normalize the information in the ensemble. However, a triad of temporal relationships conveys more information than a triad of nontemporal relationships; it conveys information about the flow of time. In a transitive triad of temporal relationships, it is the relationship that has the longest duration that should be deleted because the others will imply it before it ends.

In Figure 7.8b, we would delete the direct link between *Analyze Issue* and *Alert Management*, and in Figure 7.11c, it is the direct link between *Request for Fresh Cookies* and *Arrange dough glob on Cookie Sheet* that would go. As we open windows into events and temporal relationships to show compositions within, it is important to remember this interrelationship. This principle is useful in designing workflow and creating process maps too.

We highlight an area of caution about subtyping of events. When two or more events share a common predecessor, and one or more successive events are mandatory while the others are optional; the mandatory relationship(s) may, in one sense, be considered supertypes of the optional relationship(s). The reason is that mandatory events always occur; they will happen when optional events do and also when they do not. Remember that a subtype always implies its supertype, but the supertype does not imply the existence of its subtype(s). If we had no other information on the meanings of these events, we might (fallaciously) conclude that the optional events imply mandatory events, but not vice versa. Showing an optional event as the subtype of a mandatory event is meaningful in a process map only when the subtype adds information to its supertype beyond the fact that it is optional, and the supertype is mandatory. The subtype must imply the supertype because it conveys additional meaning—just as *Severe New Problem* in Figure 7.8 added meaning to *New Problem* by qualifying it.

## Complex Constraints and Conjunctions of Events

Conjunctions of events are also events. Consider *Ship Items* in Figure 7.6. Neither *Pick Item* nor *Raise Invoice* triggered it. It was triggered by their conjunction. *Ship Item* could only occur when both *Pick Item* and *Raise Invoice* occurred. This is the meaning of several arrows converging on a single event in PDM or several arrows converging on a single bar in UML (see Figure 7.6). Convergence of arrows implies that tuples of events (tuples like the combinations in Figure 5.4) trigger the common target of converging arrows (for example, the last event of Figure 7.6). The combinations in Figure 5.4 were subject to constraints on order and degree, and so too are the triggers of events. Triggers are events that initiate others.

Since succession of events is a temporal relationship, and events are temporal objects, we may constrain both temporal and nontemporal properties (such as cardinality, degree, order, etc.) of these triggers. Both simple and complex rules of succession will flow from constraints on temporal and nontemporal properties. Here are a few scenarios:

- Each instance of the successor will be triggered by a single conjunction of its predecessors (the usual meaning of arrows converging on a target event): The cardinality *ratio* of the *tuple* of predecessors *with respect to* the successor will equal one (Figure 7.9)[19]:
- The target event will be triggered by any one of its predecessors (the inclusive "or"): The *degree* of the tuple of *predecessors* will equal one or *more*. For example in Figure 7.16, either *Collaborate and Resolve Exceptions*

*Figure 7.9. A single conjunction of predecessors triggers the successor*

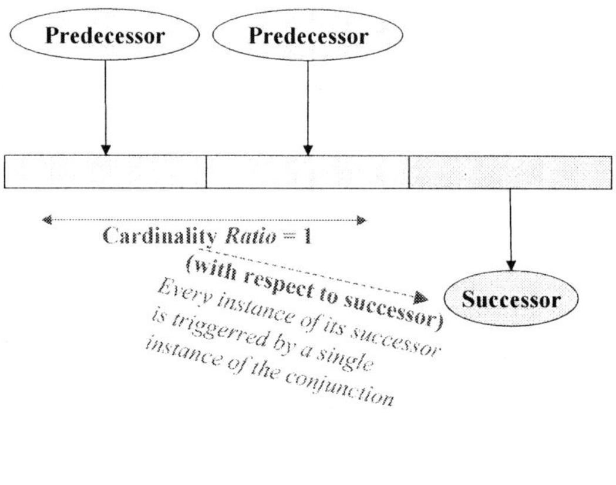

or *Identify Order Forecast Exceptions* may trigger *Create Order*.

- The target event will be triggered by the occurrence of any two of its predecessors: The *degree* of the tuple of *predecessors* will equal two or *more*.
- The target event will be triggered by the occurrence of any one predecessor if the other(s) does (do) not simultaneously occur (the exclusive "or"): The *degree* of the tuple of *predecessors* will equal *exactly* 1.
- The target event will be triggered by the consecutive repetition of a predecessor: The repeatability of the predecessor must be two or more over successive time periods—see Figure 7.4.
- The target event will be triggered by the repetition of its predecessor (exactly) once each at two specific times. Each qualified repetition will trigger exactly two parallel instances of successors. However, if multiple instances of the trigger occur in parallel at both times, they will not trigger the target event:
  There is a temporal relationship between predecessors and successors that captures this complex rule. The relationship combines constraints on concurrency with constraints on concurrency ratios as follows:
  - "*The target event will be triggered by its predecessor*": Two types of events are involved; one type is the successor and a different type the predecessor. Therefore, the triggering relationship is a binary relationship between predecessor and successor—its order is two.
  - "*The target event will be triggered by the repetition of its predecessor (exactly) once each at two specific times ...However, if multiple instances of the trigger occur in parallel at both times, they will not trigger the target event*": The concurrency of the trigger is mandated to be exactly one at those two times.
  - "*Each qualified repetition will trigger exactly two parallel instances of successors*": The concurrency ratio between the successor and predecessor is two in each time slot.

  If we needed to make the triggering condition even more stringent by asserting that the triggering event must repeat only in the specified time slots in order to trigger the successor, we could further constrain the nontemporal cardinality of the trigger (in the triggering relationship) to equal exactly two.
- The target event will be triggered by at least two repetitions of the predecessor at two different times; it does not matter when the predecessor was repeated as long as it fell into one of the specified time slots: The temporal degree of the *combination* of triggers in those time slots will be two or more.

As an exercise for the reader, how should one constrain the cardinality of succession if the successor must occur only if the predecessor does *not* occur at a specific time? For instance, if no customer calls occur over a period of one day, one might make random calls to customers to confirm that no call center or communication problem exists.[20]

Mutual inclusion, subtyping, and mutual exclusion constraints can transcend across time slices to bind similar or different kinds of relationships across time into a rule. When we consider the flow of time, conditional succession can express complex "if-then-else" rules that frequently occur in business—rules like "*if a review occurs today, it cannot occur for the next 30 days*," or "*if a review occurred last month, it must be followed up next month and the month after by similar reviews*," and "*a follow up session cannot be held if the initial review was skipped*."

Mutual inclusion, mutual exclusion, and subsetting relationships of Figure 5.5 are special cases that emerged from special constraints on cardinalities and degrees of combinations of the kind in

Figure 5.4. In the same way, succession relationships across time—mutually inclusive, mutually exclusive, and subtype succession—emerge from constraints on degrees and cardinalities of combinations across time. All occurrence rules are built on this foundation, be they simple or complex. They may even be rules about when and under what conditions how many resources are required, and when, depending on what, how many items are produced.[21] These rules are irreducible facts about occurrences of events that are contingent on occurrences of other objects—rules about processes that create, temper, and mold.[22]

## Successions of Compositions: Information in Time

Event succession is a temporal relationship.[23] Relationships are objects, which may grow attributes and behavior in step with new learning as their information payload becomes larger than a mere semantic link between objects. This is also true for succession relationships. As we add information to a succession relationship, the latter can grow into a full-blown process. It must be a process because the flow of time is already embedded in the fact of temporal succession.

This process (or event) will naturally occupy a time slot between the two events that it connects, like the discovery of *Severe New Problem*, an event in Figure 7.8, did between *Analyze Issue* and *Alert Management* (which were also events in that figure). We can always insert an event between two successive events by adding information to the fact of succession. The new event will always be *automatically* located between the two successive events it connects and the facts of succession will not be disrupted (as we did in Figure 7.8 by inserting the discovery of a *Severe New Problem* between "*Analyze Issue*" and "*Alert Management*"). Conversely, we can remove information from an event in a process map until it only carries information on its position in time relative to the other events in the composition. Then it will become a mere event succession relationship between the events it connects. *We could "remove" a process (or event) from a composition, and the succession relationships will automatically "heal themselves" by merely going "through" the missing process to the objects that event connected them to.* As illustrated in Figure 7.8, a relationship that goes "through" another event or process in this manner is transitive with respect to the relationships that were "removed."

Indeed, just as relationships could grow into full blown multiobject compositions as we added information, a succession relationship can grow into a full blown process map as we add information to it; and just as an entire composition could shrink into a relationship as it lost information, so too may full blown process maps shrivel into mere assertions of temporal succession if all information, save the flow of time, seeps out. (If the assertion loses all temporal information, it will cease to be an event; instead it will become the nontemporal relationship of Chapter V.)

Event succession is a relationship, and process maps are compositions of events. With the passage of time, an entire composition could succeed another. Indeed, that is how we integrate processes—processes like the baking of cookies integrated with the making of dough as we have done in Figure 7.5 and in Figure 7.11, or even entire integrated supply chains that sweep products and services from businesses to business to customer, which we will discuss in this section.

Chapter VI described how each known object (and relationship) in a composition or aggregate object is a "port" to the world outside the aggregate. When objects in the composition were unknown, all we could say was that a relationship connects to the aggregate. When they were known, we could articulate:

- Whether the relationship must connect only to the aggregate.

- Whether the relationship must connect to at least one object within the aggregate (when the object becomes "known").
- Whether it must connect to every object within the aggregate as they turn from "unknown" to "known."
- How many objects of what kind within the aggregate the relationship may connect with and other kinds of more complex constraints based on the degree, order, and cardinality of the relationship.

When the relationship in question is temporal succession, rules can become even more complicated for we must now articulate what comes before what and under what conditions. Paradoxically, this complexity can actually simplify and anticipate requirements of business processes. Remembering that event succession is a Cartesian product is the key that makes the complex look simple.

Asymmetrical relationships are Cartesian products and so are event successions. Event succession is an asymmetrical relationship between events because time cannot be reversed—what is done is history and cannot be undone. It follows (from the discussion in Box 5.2) that event succession is a Cartesian product of the events it connects with added meaning—the meaning of succession in time. Event succession is transitive with "consists of," the relationship that makes a composition an aggregate and connects every constituent to this aggregate.[24] *When a succession relationship connects an object to a composition or aggregate object, it potentially connects it to every object within the aggregate.*

Consider the composition in Figure 7.8. *Analyze Issue* was an event that preceded both *Open New Problem* and *Alert Management*. Consider an aggregate object that contains both *Open New Problem* and *Alert Management*. Not only did *Analyze Issue* precede the aggregate, but subtypes of *Analyze Issue*—*Analyze "Open New Problem" Issue* and *Analyze "Alert Management" Issue*—were automatically implied. (Note that the subtypes are at a level of detail not shown in the figure.) They were implied because *Analyze Issue* preceded the aggregate object that contained both.

We also know that succession can be conditional. Whether the event that precedes a composition precedes every object in it, or only some, is an irreducible fact normalized by the succession relationship (these relationships are temporal polymorphisms of constraints on connections with aggregate objects). Sometimes, we may not have full information; we may know that the event must precede at least one object in the composition (and perhaps more), but we may not know which one(s). If we do not know, all we can say is that it connects to the composition as a whole; we cannot tell more because we have no information.

*When a composition succeeds an event, not only must the event precede one or more objects inside the composition, but a polymorphic subtype of the event may also precede objects in the composition (just as Analyze "Alert Management" Issue preceded Alert Management)—one subtype for each object. Each such subtype will be a case of inclusion polymorphism (see Box 4.8), and each will be a specialized event relevant to only its "own" object within the overall composition, an object it will always precede. Whether we recognize these polymorphic subtypes or not, they are implied for every object in the composition (unless a relationship is specifically barred for a particular object in a composition, it is implied by the "all" value of Box 5.3). Recognition of these implicit events is only a question of how much detail we must have to satisfy our business requirement. These polymorphic implicit events anticipate requirements; they were always there in the metamodel of knowledge, emerging only when we need them from the timeless engagement of meanings within.*

## Beginnings and Ends

So far, we have considered only the occurrence of events, not their beginnings and ends. We had discussed how occurrence involves beginnings and ends, but we have ignored these beginnings and ends of events. It is now time to consider them; rules of succession cannot be complete unless we also consider beginnings and ends of events in the sweep of time. A renowned American poet has said:

*What we call the beginning is often the end. And to make an End is to make a Beginning. The End is where we start from.*

- T.S. Elliott

Beginnings and ends of events are events too and all we have said for succession between events will also apply to their beginnings and ends. Of course, when we resolve events into their beginnings and ends, the end of an event (if it occurs) must always succeed its beginning, but this need not be true across different events. Across events, we can treat each beginning and end as an occurrence—an event by itself. Let us start by considering the succession of a pair of events:

- One event may not begin before the other does
  - Delays may be involved
  - Events will be constrained to begin together when delays are forbidden
- An event may not end before another does
  - Delays may be involved
  - Events will be constrained to end together when delays are forbidden
- The beginning of one event must follow the end of another
  - Delays may be involved
  - The beginning of one event must immediately follow the end of another when delays are forbidden

The first two succession constraints are independent and may be put in place simultaneously. We could have events that must begin and end together. The last constraint leads to a daisy chain of successive events or processes that trace a path through a PDM or UML activity diagram in Figure 7.6. It excludes either of the first two succession constraints above and can support complex rules of delayed succession (see Complex Constraints and Conjunctions of Events in this section). Table 7.1 summarizes possible interactions between the beginnings and the ends of successor–predecessor pairs:

The concepts in Table 7.1 may be generalized to cover cases where multiple events are joined into a single successor–predecessor relationship. We have recently discussed the joining of multiple events and how these conjunctions are higher order temporal relationships. What we have not

*Table 7.1. Begin-End interactions between a successor-predecessor pair of events*

| SUCCESSOR / PREDECESSOR | Begin | End |
|---|---|---|
| **Begin** | Optional time gap (may be nil or *unknown*) | Optional time gap (may be nil or *unknown*) |
| **End** | Optional time gap (may be nil or *unknown*) | Optional time gap (may be nil or *unknown*) |

discussed is the issue of delayed beginnings and ends of conjoined events. We will do so now.

Every instance of an event has a beginning and perhaps an end on a timeline. What we mean by the term "event conjunction" becomes complicated when we involve the passage of time. In Figure 7.6, consider the completion of events *Pick Item* and *Raise Invoice* that trigger *Ship Item*. *Ship Item* was triggered by the conjunction of the *ends* of *Pick Item* and *Raise Invoice*. If one of the two predecessors to *Ship Item* finished, how long would we have to wait for the other to finish before the conjunction "timed out," that is, was not considered a conjunction? In other words, the question of temporal delay is implicit in the concept of "conjunction" when the conjunction is between events—the question is, in what windows of time will the conjunction be considered a conjunction? (Of course, we could even wait forever.) The value constraints[25] may assert simple or complex temporal windows.

Temporal windows could be sets of specific times or ranges framed by inclusion or exclusion sets. When inclusion sets are involved, the window will assert the conjunction. When exclusion sets are involved, the window will deny it.

A conjunction is a relationship. When events in a conjunction belong to different classes, the conjunction is a higher order temporal relationship; when events in a conjunction belong to the same class, the conjunction is a higher degree temporal relationship. Constraints on temporal and nontemporal cardinality and degree (discussed earlier) may make these conjunctions even more complex. However, the timing of conjunctions is our topic now. It will suffice to remember that these conjunctions will inherit the rules we have discussed for temporal relationships, and that these may in turn interact with the timings and occurrences of events in a conjunction. Complex rules of business may emerge from complex interactions between properties of processes and events in conjunctions like these.

Consider the collection of beginnings and endings of events in a conjunction (the union of the set of "begin event" events and the set of "end event" events). When we consider rules and constraints on event succession, every distinct pair in the set may (optionally) be time lagged with respect to every other. Beginnings of events may follow each other subject to timing constraints, as may ends of events, or even beginnings and ends of events. These beginnings and ends may be beginnings and ends of the same or different events.

The time lag between the beginning and the end of the *same* event will be its cycle time, whereas time lags across different events will be considered delayed beginnings or endings; however, both are conceptually identical—both are time lags between beginnings and ends of events and may be parameters in rules about event succession.

Time lags and leads are ratio scaled. They can be subject to constraints on ratio scaled values. When multiple events are related, windows of time may even mutually constrain each other via joint constraints such as those in Box 5.1.[26] These rules about time lags and timings of beginnings and ends could become as complex as necessary but will always be subject to two constraints. We will call them the Golden Rules of Event Succession in this book:

- The common-sense constraint that the end of an event cannot precede its beginning.[27]
- The fact that a successor cannot start until all its predecessors have started. If it did, the successor would be anticipating a future event and thus violate the laws of cause and effect. This is the principle of causality. All causal processes are subject to it.[28]

High order/degree (and binary) event conjunctions may involve not only predecessors but also all events in the succession relationship—predecessors and successors. As such, when time delays are involved:

- There may be time delays in triggering successors.
- There may be time windows within which successors must (or may) occur (or time windows that constrain cycle times).
- Exact time delays between triggers may be mandated (or exact cycle times may be mandated).
- There may be time delays between triggers, and these delays may be time windows in which the conjunction of triggers is recognized (or denied).[29]

When conjunctions of multiple events trigger a successor, the occurrence of a predecessor is said to "enable," but not necessarily trigger the successor. "Enabling" a successor changes its state by readying it for execution. Processes may be only temporarily enabled. The enablement may be annulled after a time. If the other triggering event(s) does(do) not occur in the requisite time period, the successor reverts to the "disabled" state. The state of an event (or process) may change to various stages of "enablement" even before it starts. When processes are enabled, but not triggered, we call them latent processes. The property of being latent is called process latency.

The opposite may also happen. Processes may be disabled by events (or conjunctions of events, which, as we have discussed earlier, are also events). Processes disabled in this manner will not fire even when all other prerequisites have been satisfied.

In general, enablement and latency may involve complex rules about time lags and leads. Moreover, there may be multiple types and stages of latency and enablement (and disablement) corresponding to the occurrence of multiple events in the conjoined trigger of a process (or event).

In the case study with the check payment example in Module 5 at our Web site, the CFO and CEO signing the check are two distinct events (processes that produced corresponding signatures—see the discussion on process engineering under Figure 7.24 later in this chapter) with clear beginnings and ends. Assume that a business rule dictates that the signatures must be obtained within three months of each other. The end of each signature event (process) would enable the check payment event, but check payment would stay latent until both predecessor events ended—*provided no more than three months elapsed between the ends of the two events.* Unlike nontemporal relationships that mutually relate "derived attributes," such as "price per piece," "Quantum of Money," and "Number of pieces" (Box 4.6, Figure A), these kinds of temporal rules are normalized by workflow, which are temporal relationships between events and capture the *dynamics* of derivation based on the flow of activities in time.

We have seen how cycle time is a special case, a subtype, of time lags between events. Figure 7.10 shows examples of delayed event conjunctions. Note how the principle of causality ensures that time lags (delays across events and cycle times of conjoined events) are constrained in each event conjunction so that the successor always begins after the predecessor starts.

Enablement and latency may involve not only timings of beginnings and ends of different events but may also involve cycle times of the events in the conjunction. *The term "Timing of an event" generalizes both concepts.* ("Timing" means specific times or windows of time relative to an absolute time, such as a specific date, or relative to another event, such as the beginning or end of a process.) The timing of an event is the key to event conjunction.

Note that an event conjunction is also an event in its own right, and all we have said about events in general will also be true for their conjunctions. Each conjunction will also have its own beginning and perhaps an end, as Figure 7.10 shows. Figure 7.10 also shows that the cycle time of a network (or conjunction—a special part of the network where events converge into a conjoined relationship[30]) of successive events cannot be obtained

*Figure 7.10. Examples of delayed succession (Delays across events and cycle times are both examples of time lags)*

**(a)**

1. **Predecessors must follow each other with a finite delay.**
2. **Successor is delayed relative to the *end* of the <u>last</u> predecessor.**

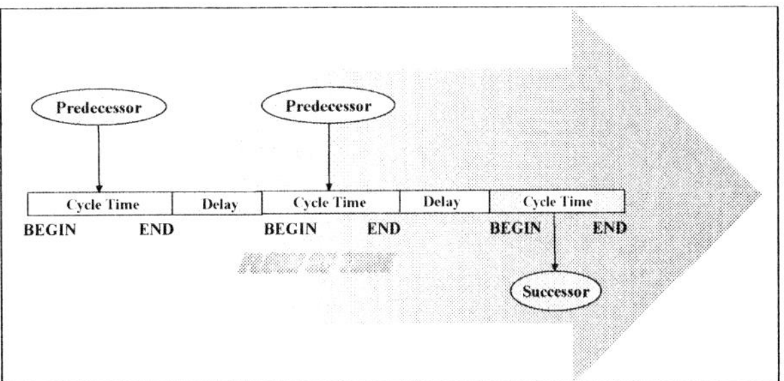


**(b)**

1. **Predecessors must follow each other with a finite delay.**
2. **Successor is delayed relative to the *start* of the <u>last</u> predecessor**

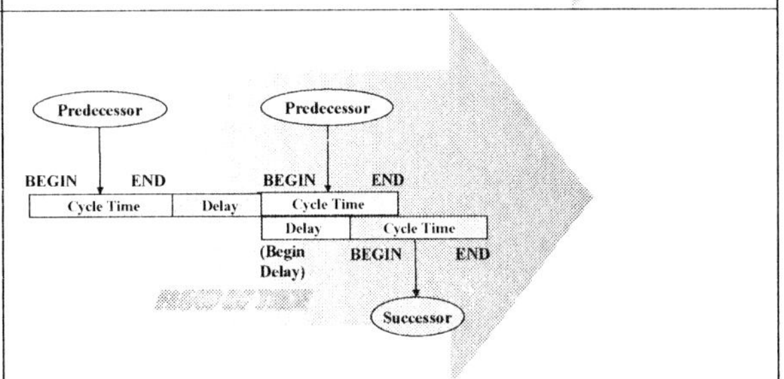


**(c)**

1. **Predecessors must follow each other with a finite delay.**
2. **Successor is delayed relative to the end of the <u>first</u> predecessor**

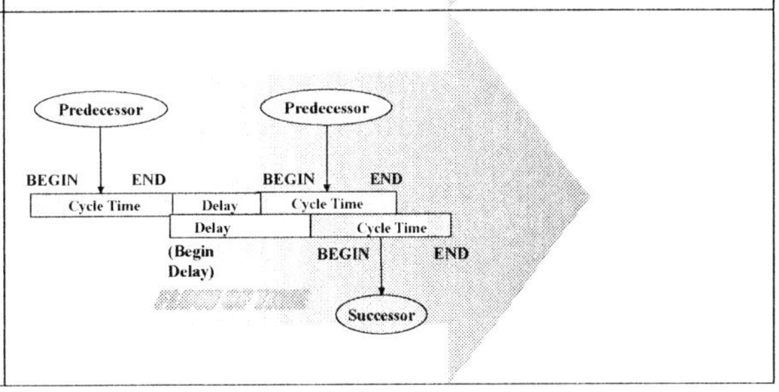


by a simple summation of all delays and cycle times of processes in the network. Instead, *this cycle time depends on the critical path*—the path with the longest duration going forward in time through the network.[31]

A network of events linked by succession relationships is also a composition of events. The cycle time of the composition is the cycle time of the critical path through the composition. For instance, the cycle time of the composition in Figure 7.6 is the cycle time of *Take Order*, plus the cycle time of the *longer* of the two parallel events, *Pick Item* and *Raise Invoice*, plus the cycle time of *Ship Item with Invoice*. The longer event is the bottleneck because its successor cannot start until it finishes.

When a network of events has conditional events in it, its cycle time will be conditional. We have discussed how a composition may represent a single relationship. Processes are temporal relationships. Event succession is a temporal relationship between events. As such, a network of events (even a part of a network) may also be considered an event in its own right, and the cycle time of an event may thus be conditional. Often process reengineering and innovation involves discovering compositions that will reduce cycle times in order to speed up a process. Speed is becoming the key to prosperity, and even survival, in the dawning economy driven by knowledge, ideas, and innovation across the globe. The rules described herein are the basis for management of speed under different conditions.

We can reduce any part of a succession network to a single high level event if we are not interested in the detail within it, and conversely, any node (event or process) in a succession network may be expanded into a network.[32] A rule in Chapter VI said that every object in the composition is a potential port for connecting to objects outside the composition. If we expand an event into a composition, at least one event, and perhaps more, in the composition must connect to the event(s) it connects. Indeed, we might even formulate rules that will constrain compositions by constraining the number, type, and identity of events within a composition that may be ports to events outside it.[33] However, the fewer the constraints, the richer our choices, and the easier it will be to innovate.

As we increase the number of events involved in triggering or constraining other events, the possibilities grow explosively—even more explosively than the possibilities described under Figure 5.4 because each event has a beginning *and may also have an end.*[34] (Scheduling techniques in PDM, PERT, and GERT focus on techniques that identify these critical paths and calculate cycle times of the network as a whole under various assumptions).[35]

Conjunctions of events are relationships, which in addition to constraints on timing and latency may be subject to constraints on temporal and nontemporal cardinalities and degrees discussed earlier. Processes must also have goals and purposes. A work product tied to an event makes it a process. Businesses have goals they strive to achieve and events of interest to business must serve its objectives. This is the essence of *Business Process.* We will discuss this next.

## The Essence of a Process and the Goals of Business

Every process must have a work product. This product is its essence—its purpose and goal. It could have several work products. Each would be a purpose. For instance, a process that separates wheat from chaff produces both wheat and chaff. Wheat is food and chaff may burn as fuel. An event (process) may have multiple goals. It may also have byproducts, waste products, and coproducts that are produced in the act of producing the work product(s). What is considered a work product or coproduct and what is considered a byproduct or waste product is a business decision—a decision about the goals, priorities, and purposes of the process and hence of the business. If the intent were to produce wheat, chaff would be a waste product. If the overwhelming priority was to pro-

*Box 7.4. Goals and governance: Processes for making processes*

The aim of a business is an item of information. It is information implicitly attached to an unknown process. The process is a process for realizing a goal or achieving an objective.[36] If the objective of a business is to make cookies, this purpose is a goal implicitly attached to the *bake* process (Figure 7.11a). This composition of Work Product and unknown process is the businesses' chosen purpose—its aim and intent. We may subsequently add information to this "unknown" process, as we have done in Figure 7.11, to flesh out *how* cookies will be baked, but the initial composition tells us *what* we must make—what the objective is. However, neither composition tells us *why* we must make cookies. For this, we must turn to a higher governance order process, a process that sets the purpose, the initial composition of goal and unknown process. This governance process is different from the process that *realizes* the purpose set by the governance process. The process that sets the purpose also tells us *why* it is the purpose of the business. This purpose or goal setting process is a higher governance order process because it creates another process, even if the process it creates is only implied and even though this implied process conveys no information beyond its work product at this point.

Its purpose results from the interaction of the enterprise with its external business environment. This purpose is formulated from interactions of four kinds of factors. Two are internal to the business, and two are external:

*continued on following page*

*Box 7.4. continued*

- Internal factors:
  - Internal strengths of the business
  - Internal weaknesses of the business
- External factors:
  - Opportunities in the business environment
  - Threats in the business environment

The core value of the product and service propositions a business offers to its markets lies in the interaction of these four kinds of factors. Since value emerges from the interaction of a business with its external environment, at least one factor in the interaction must be internal, and another must be external. It follows that the goals of a business will follow from this foundation; the rationale for a goal is a relationship between at least one internal and one external factor. However, there could be many factors in a single interaction as long as at least one factor is internal and another is external. Thus, the goal setting process will be a second or higher order relationship. Its degree too must be two or *more* (several strengths, several opportunities, several weaknesses, and several threats might participate in the interaction). This relationship is a process because the factors in its rationale temporally precede the goal. The purpose and objectives of the business are work products of this process that answers *why*.[37]

Figure A shows an instance of the goal setting process for a local telephone services provider after barriers to local and long distance telecommunications services were legislated away. Strengths, weaknesses, opportunities, and threats *precede* the firm's purpose Therefore, their mutual higher order relationship with the objective that follows is a process:

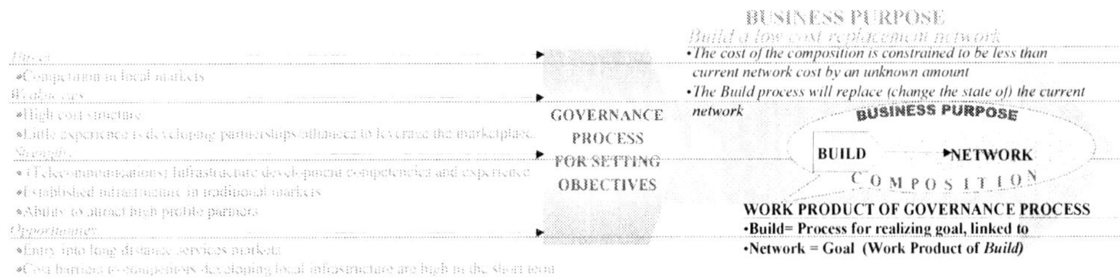


*Figure A. Example of a process for setting corporate objectives*

Note that the relationship between *Business Purpose*, the object class, and *Rationale*, another object class (a process of the kind shown in Figure A, with or without its temporal information) may be a many-to-many relationship. Several purposes may emerge from each rationale, and several rationales may lead to the same purpose. The rationale is the interaction between Strengths, Weaknesses, Opportunities, and Threats that leads to *Purpose*. We will call it the SWOT interaction.

Process engineering starts when we start identifying the means by which we will realize our goals: only when we add information to a purpose, which is a composition of a goal and an unknown process on how the unknown process will realize its goal, will waste and byproducts (or side effects) emerge. It is only then that we will know if two or more goals of the business can be coproducts realized by a single process—an irreducible fact, like the separation of wheat and chaff that produced both wheat and chaff—or if each is a separate subprocess, a separate irreducible fact in an aggregation. That information is added only when the process for *realizing*, not deriving, the corporate purpose is designed.

Sometimes the goals of a governing process are confused with the goals of the process it governs. Take a process called *Ship Item* that ships an item from a warehouse to a customer. Like all other processes, it normalizes information like cycle time (shipment time in this case), latency, efficiency, and others that we have already discussed. Assume the objective is to shorten shipment cycle times by an as yet unknown amount. The goal is a value constraint attached to the cycle time attribute of the shipment process. The constraint is a goal because it was the work product of a governing process—it is a governance goal. Strictly speaking, the shipment process normalizes the constraint, not the goal. Even if the governance process is not in scope, or unknown, it is implied the moment we call the constraint a goal[38]; the limitation on cycle time is an object that is a constraint when it relates to the shipment process and a goal when it relates to

*continued on following page*

*Box 7.4. continued*

> the process that governs the shipment. Indeed, a smart governance process might even assemble both into a conjoined, irreducible fact as it designs *Ship Item*.
>
> (As an exercise for the reader, how would you model a goal that requires that each shipment meet its delivery commitment?)

duce wheat, but production of chaff for fuel had a marginal priority, chaff would be a byproduct. If the priority given to chaff were comparable with that for wheat, chaff would be a coproduct.

Let us consider a business that bakes cookies. This is its goal. The purpose of a *Bake Cookie* process is to produce cookies. Figure 7.11a shows this.

Figure 7.11a shows how *Bake Cookie* is triggered by an event, *Request for Fresh Cookies*, and how *Bake Cookie* consumes a resource, *Dough*, in order to produce cookies. Resources and triggers are pieces of information added to business goals. They are information on *how* the goal will be achieved, not *what* the goal must be. There may be other ways of achieving the goal with other resources and triggers. Based on the principle of subtyping by adding information, the process that identifies resources and triggers (triggers are also resources) is a subtype of the

*Figure 7.11. An example of how a process map follows from business objectives*

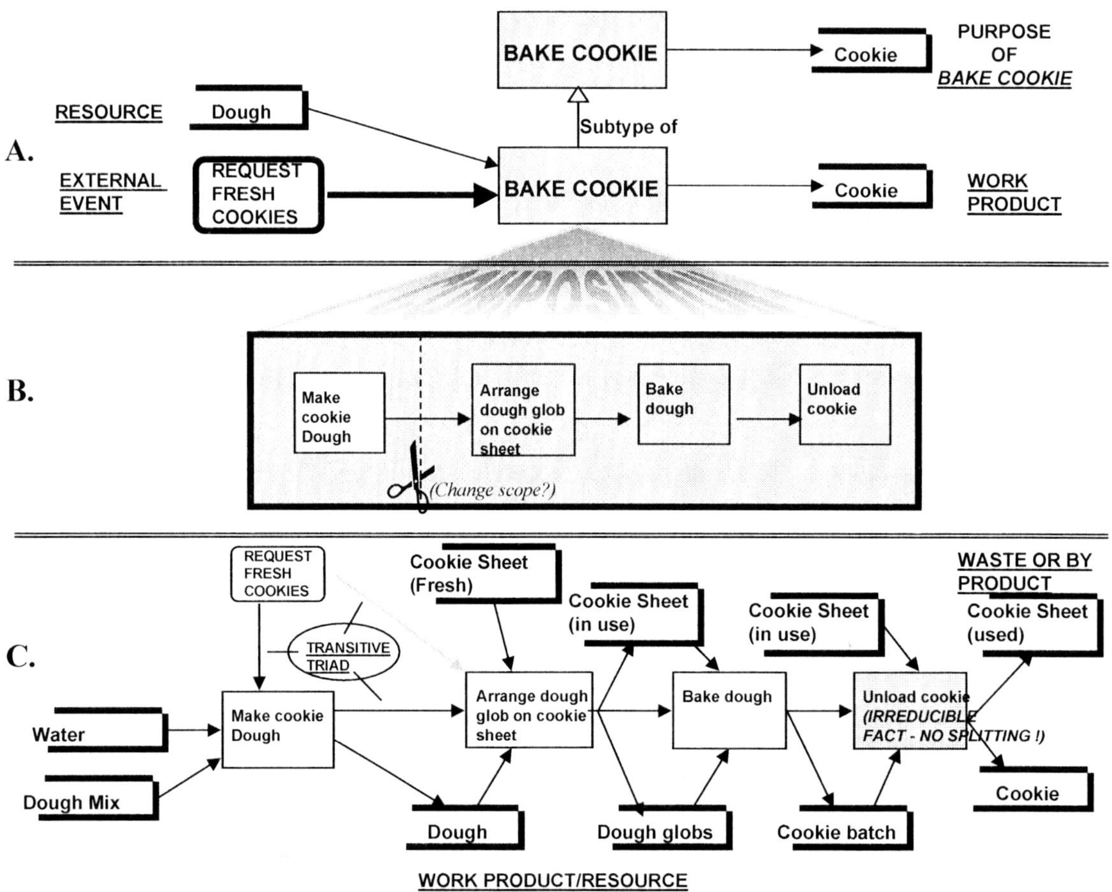

process that realizes the goal. The goal is a work product (*Cookie* in this case).

Contrast this kind of subtype of a process from a subtype that elaborates on or integrates business purposes by adding information, and detail, only to the goal. Assume that the cookie factory does some strategic thinking and repositions its business as a multiproduct bakery instead of a cookie factory. It decides to produce other baked products, such as cakes, bread, muffins, and others in addition to cookies. *Cookie* will then become a subtype of *Baked Product*, and *Bake Cookie* will be a subtype of the more generic *Bake* process (remember *Inclusion Polymorphism* from Box 4.8).

Indeed, each process for baking the different kinds of products the bakery decides to bake will be a subtype of the generic "*Bake*" process. These subtypes are based, not on adding information on resources and triggers, but on subtyping the work product itself. The strategic objective of the business now is to manufacture *Baked Product*. Manufacturing Cookies, Cakes, Bread, Muffins, and other subtypes of *Baked Product* are tactical objectives towards this end—each is a subtype of the strategic goal; each is also an irreducible fact made specific by adding meaning.[39]

Sometimes, business objectives will be less homogenous. They may not always neatly fit an obvious process based subtyping hierarchy of the kind we just described. When this is the case, the business will consist of a collection of processes that may have little in common beyond the generic "Make" process (under supply chains). The collection will be an aggregate object. This object is a composition of processes, in which processes may or may not be interdependent and the products of a process in the composition may or may not be used as resources by others. (A composition could be a network of connected objects, a collection of isolated objects, or a collection of isolated networks of objects, with no connections between these isolated "islands.")

Consider how a business might see opportunity in heterogeneous products—products that do not belong to a subtyping hierarchy. Contrast the composition in Figure 7.11b with the subtype in Figure 7.11a. Figure 7.11a shows how one irreducible fact may be a subtype of another based on the principle of adding information. Figure 7.11b is a collection of successive processes that constitute a temporal composition. Some work products of processes in the composition are subtypes of Baked Product, while others are not (see Figure 7.11c). The composition is an expression of *Bake Cookie*. The first process in the composition, *Make Cookie Dough*, produces *Dough*. The bakery could also position itself as a supplier of dough (in addition to baked products). Whether dough is a coproduct, a byproduct, or intermediate product (work in progress) is a business decision. This is the essence of the SOA framework, that the process for producing each s considered a "service", and it is a busincess decision as to what these service offerings will be, and the availability of these choices will not only make the business agile, because it will enable it to seize new opportunities that it can identify in the market place, but will also identify services it can outsource or provide to its business partners in an extended enterprise. The processes that serve the objectives of a business, and indeed, the objectives themselves, might be subtypes of strategic goals or mere collections of irreducible facts in connected or unconnected temporal compositions, as they are in Figure 7.11b.

Processes that produce disparate products may even merge into one irreducible fact—a conjoined high order temporal relationship. Separating wheat from chaff was an example of this. It was an irreducible fact. The very act of separating the wheat from the chaff produced both the wheat and the chaff. Based on the principle of subtyping by adding information, this process was a subtype of two processes—one that produced wheat and another that produced chaff. The process for separating wheat from chaff was aligned with the goals of a business that asserted that its objective was to produce wheat, a business that asserted that its primary purpose was to produce chaff, or a business that asserted its twin objectives were to produce both. Note that the two parent processes were inseparable in their common subtype. The two parents were glued into an irreducible fact by a process that supported either or both business objectives—the production of wheat and the production of chaff.

We cannot represent the process that separates wheat from chaff as a *composition* of two separate business processes, one that outputs chaff and another that outputs wheat. It would be meaningless to decompose the process in this way. The very act of separating wheat from chaff produces both wheat and chaff. The process was not a composition of two separate subprocesses. Rather, it was a subtype with two parents, each of which described a distinct (potential) goal. Thus, the process itself was a single irreducible fact. Business could prioritize these goals and even declare that one has no priority and hence was a waste product of the process, but two products there would always be.

These examples demonstrate how, when the multiple individual objectives of a business are subtypes of a single higher level strategic objective, each process will be a subtype of a single higher level strategic process (remember inclusion polymorphism in Box 4.8). However, when a business has multiple disconnected objectives, the supporting process may be a collection of distinct processes, an aggregate object (perhaps parts of a composition), or be a subtype of multiple parents. It all depends on business process engineering and the difference between a subprocess and a subtype of a process.

*A subprocess is different from the subtype of a process. A subprocess is a part of an aggregate object, which may be an event or another process. A subtype of a process is exactly what it says it is—it is a subtype, subject to rules such as inheritance, mutability of subtypes, enumeration of subtypes and others we have discussed (subtyping is a much stricter polymorphism of the "Part of" relationship—see Location, Containment, and Incorporation and Figure 7.27). Substates are not states of the subtypes of a process or event; they are states of events within a composition inside an aggregate event (or process).*

*Although individual subprocesses are not subtypes of the process they collectively express, based on the principle of subtyping by adding information, the composition as a whole is a subtype of the process it expresses because it was obtained by adding information to the process.*[40]

## Process Maps, Supply Chains, and Business Process Engineering

A process map is a composition of processes. To be meaningful, it must express a business objective or, more accurately, *support* it. A composition expresses a relationship, and a composition of processes or events expresses a process or event. Processes within compositions are called subprocesses.[41]

Figure 7.11b shows one possible expression of Bake Cookie. The processes in this composition are subprocesses; these subprocesses are by no means subtypes of *Bake Cookie*. They are steps towards that goal, and each is a process in its own right with its own purpose and products. Each is also a step in time towards the end of *Bake Cookie*. Each must be a temporal step because Bake Cookie is a process, and a process is a temporal relationship. The expression of a process must therefore be a temporal composition, and each subprocess in the composition is the repository of a substate of the process it expresses—a substate in a temporal progression.[42]

Other temporal compositions could also achieve the same goal. We might not make the cookie dough ourselves. We might buy the cookie dough from a vendor. Then we would insert a *Buy Cookie Dough* process between *Make Cookie Dough* (now the responsibility of a supplier) and *Arrange Dough Glob on Cookie Sheet*. This composition would be another expression of *Bake Cookie*. Indeed, *Make Cookie Dough* might now be considered beyond the boundaries (scope) of the Bake Cookie composition. This is how processes are reengineered. This is also how the same process may be expressed differently without deflecting its purpose.

(It is not that we do not need dough anymore, and *Make Cookie Dough* must still occur before *Arrange Dough Glob on Cookie Sheet*, only the ownership of the process has shifted so that it is not the firm's responsibility. The scope of Bake Cookie has changed from one perspective, but not from another, larger perspective that includes the complete supply chain.[43] The discussion on process mutability in Box 7.6 describes the principles involved. We will discuss this kind of scope change when we discuss process ownership and supply chains.)

Both *Make Cookie Dough* and *Buy Cookie Dough* are subtypes of a generic *Obtain Cookie Dough* process and hence are mutually mutable in the composition. It is the shadow of *Obtain Cookie Dough*, their common supertype that lies hidden in the composition making *Make Cookie Dough* and *Buy Cookie Dough* mutable. The supertype facilitates creative process reengineering. If we recognize this, we can be even more creative and flexible and look for other subtypes of *Obtain Cookie Dough* that might give us an edge over our competitors. (Of course, we can only outsource *Make Cookie Dough* if we agree that making dough is not a business goal of the firm.)

Compositions like these, that describe the subprocesses within a process, are called process maps. They are expressions of the processes they map. The process map in Figure 7.11b conveys information on temporal succession of subprocesses. Figure 7.11c is a more detailed process map. It adds information on resources and products to the events of Figure 7.11b. Unlike the composition in Figure 7.11b, the composition in Figure 7.11c is mixed. It is a temporal network of processes and "ordinary" objects that have nothing to do with the flow of time.

In Figure 7.11c, these "ordinary" objects are shown as open-ended rectangles. Processes are closed rectangles. Arrows pointing from the "ordinary" object towards a process (input relationships) show that the object is a resource to the process. Arrows emerging from the process (the output relationships) show that the object is a product. Arrows between processes show succession relationships. Indeed, when one process triggers another in succession, the trigger in one sense is a resource to the process it triggers—a triggering resource.

*Dough, Dough Globs*, and a *Cookie Sheet* are "ordinary" objects, whereas *Arrange Dough Globs on Cookie Sheet* is a process. *Dough* and a *Fresh Cookie Sheet* are also resources used by *Arrange Dough Globs on Cookie Sheet*, which then produces *Dough Globs* and a *Cookie Sheet In Use* (the process changes the state of *Cookie Sheet* from "*Fresh*" to "*In Use*").

Figure 7.11c bears an uncanny resemblance to a dataflow diagram. It is no accident. We have deliberately chosen a technique that is familiar to many information systems analysts to represent the flow of resources and products through a chain of processes.[44] However, unlike the dataflow diagrams in information systems design, the open-ended rectangles do not represent data stores or files. They represent real world objects in our object model. We are still in the uppermost layer of Figure 3.4. Later, we will study the transforms that take us from this layer into the layers of business process automation and information logistics.

## Input and Output Processes

The "input" relationship between resource and process, as well as the "output" relationship between process and product can also be temporal relationships. These relationships too will have the properties of processes we have discussed in this section. The cardinality of input and output relationships will tell us how many instances of each resource are required and how many instances of each product is produced by a single instance of the process. This cardinality may be temporal or not, that is, resources (instances of resources) may be required sequentially or simultaneously, and products (instances of products) may be produced sequentially or simultaneously by a single instance of a process. When the flow of time matters, temporal properties must be considered, when it does not, nontemporal properties will suffice. The transformation process at its core is a temporal relationship between the inputs and outputs of a process. Therefore the availability and acquisition of resources, and the outflow of the product, are events in time. This is why input and output relationships have been shown as processes in Figure 7.12.

Input and output processes may interact and be constrained in complex ways, like the other higher order or higher degree process we have discussed. We may slice the input process in Figure 7.12 horizontally into independent processes (one for each input) only when the rules within the input process for a single resource

*Box 7.5. Batch processes*

A single instance of a process may produce multiple instances of a product. Then the nontemporal degree of the temporal relationship, the process, is two or more with respect to its product; it is a batch process. In Figure 7.11c, cookies were baked in batches (when we consider the *Bake Cookie* composition without the last, unloading process, the baking of cookies is done in batches). The batch is an aggregate object—the collection of a single class of work products that is produced by a single instance of a process. Members of the aggregate may be traced back to the same instance of the process that made or changed them.

When a single instance of a process uses (consumes, refers to, or uses as a catalyst) multiple instances of a single resource, that is, its degree is two or more with respect to the resource, it is said to use the resource in batches. Indeed, the input process may then be said to be a batch process. For instance, the input of cookies into the *Unload Cookie* process in Figure 7.11c was in batches.

Sometimes the use of the term Batch Process does not make clear whether its products are produced in batches, its resources used in batches, or both. In this book, the term will mean that batch processes produce in batches, regardless of how they pick their resources.

Batch processes are frequently found in manufacturing operations. Pharmaceutical products, confectionary, bottles and cans, and many other items are made and packed in batches. The World Batch Forum (WBF) is a nonprofit industry consortium dedicated to the management, operation, and automation of batch process manufacturing. We will discuss their standards later in this section[45] (see http://www.wbf.org/world_batch_forum.htm).

*Figure 7.12. A composition of input, output, and transformation events*

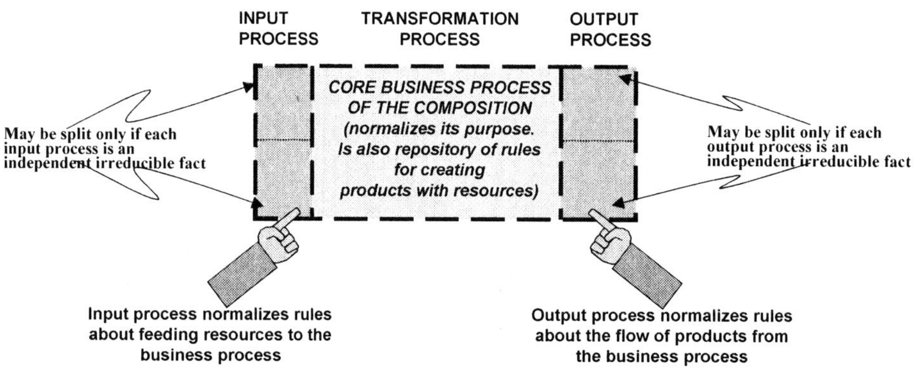

(type) are independent of other resources or output processes. Otherwise, like the separation of wheat from chaff in the discussion on Figure 7.11, the input process will tie several objects into an inseparable irreducible fact. (This reasoning is equally valid for the output process.)

Consider the last process in Figure 7.11c. It unloads cookies from the sheet they were baked on. The resources are the cookie sheet (in use—a state of the cookie sheet, in which it is loaded with cookies), and the batch of cookies that were just baked on the cookie sheet. Before the batch of freshly baked cookies is unloaded, when it enters the unloading process, the batch of cookies is still on the cookie sheet that it was baked on. Both resources are input to the process together. There is no other way they may be input—it would be meaningless for a cookie sheet to be fed into the unloading process without its cookies and vice versa. The separation of wheat from chaff was a process that bound the production of two products, wheat and chaff, into one irreducible fact. Similarly the *Unload Cookie* process of Figure 7.11c binds the feeding of two resources, cookie sheet and cookie batch, into a single irreducible fact. The two resources interact. The input relationships are mutually inclusive and temporally synchronized. The input process presumes it is so and ensures that cookies are fed to the unloading workstation arranged on the cookie sheets they were baked on. It cannot be split into separate input processes—one for cookies and the other for the cookie sheet any more than the process for separating wheat from chaff could be split into a process for producing wheat and another for producing chaff. Figure 7.12 articulates these rules.

The transformation process in Figure 7.12 is the event that normalizes rules about how resources are turned into products. The transformation process will bake the batch of cookies and separate cookies from the cookie sheet. In the Unloading subprocess inside "bake cookie", the production of cookies and the waste product, used cookie sheets, are also inseparable, but once it is done, separate processes could convey the cookies and the used sheets away. As such, even though the input process and the transformation process cannot be split, the output process may be split after the cookies have been peeled off the cookie sheet.

Input and output processes will also normalize any constraints on the temporal rate or speed with which resources are fed to the process (for example, from a hopper to the machine that consumes the inputs) and output from the process (after they are produced). Sometimes the entire composition might be an irreducible fact. In a chemical factory that produces hydrocarbon based resins, the kind of resin produced depends on the rate at which raw materials are fed to the reactor, and the rate at which the product is taken out. However, this kind of complexity is normally absent in the discrete and deterministic business processes that are the ambit of our metamodel (as opposed to continuous engineering processes like those for producing hydrocarbons).

Input and output relationships may sometimes carry no information on the flow of time. They will then cease to be processes. A person may be responsible for overseeing the operation of a process, but not actually operating it. He is a resource needed by the process, even if he does not actually work it (see *Process Ownership*). Oversight responsibility is an irreducible fact, an item of information and a relationship that has nothing to do with the flow of time. It is an "ordinary" relationship between a process and a resource it utilizes.

On the other hand, consider input processes for individuals who actually work a process and hence are also resources used by the process. The process we will consider is a meeting that is expected to articulate and finalize a strategy. The meeting will be held in a specific conference room. The participants will all have to physically travel to the meeting (perhaps only walk across a hall, but walking too is a mode of transportation). The participants are resources used by the meeting, a process, to create a work product, a strategy. Their transportation to the meeting place is the input process.

Contrast this kind of meeting with a teleconference. That too is a meeting that might use the same resources to create the same products; only the mode of transportation to the meeting, its input process, will be different. Both kinds of meetings will be subtypes of the process that creates a strategy. Indeed, both subtypes even use the same resources. They will differ only in terms of the input process—how participants are conveyed to the meeting. The composite process in Figure 7.12 is therefore a subtype of the process at its core; input and output processes are information added to the transformation process. The transformation process is at the heart of the temporal relationship. Without it, there are neither resources nor products, neither inputs nor outputs.

When the result of the transformation depends on the method of input or the method of output, such as rates of flow, the composition becomes a single irreducible fact. Otherwise it may be divided into subprocesses. In either case, the input process and the output process are components of process knowledge that may be "snapped on" to the transformation at the heart of a process.

## Load Balancing

Load balancing ensures that limited resources are optimally allocated. When resources have a limited capacity for relationships (Chapter V), the issue of critical paths and cycle times of the composition can become very complex. If a process (or another object) engages a resource,[46] the resource may be unavailable or only partially available for use by another process: its capacity for relationships may be completely or partially consumed.[47] For instance, a person may be unavailable or only partially available as a resource for a project if she is engaged in other tasks.

When this happens, the process may:

- Be cancelled.
- Wait for the resource to become available (be "enabled" but not triggered, as we had discussed under beginnings and ends of events[48]).
- Use a substitute resource (a resource mutable with the resource that is engaged). The substitution may fully or partially substitute for the quantum of the resource that was engaged.
- Acquire the engaged resource, totally or partially, and proceed. The other processes that had engaged the resource will then either be interrupted or might extend their cycle times commensurately (since the resource will either become unavailable to them or its availability will diminish). Interrupted processes may be cancelled or suspended until requisite resources are available in sufficient quantity.

Which of the four options actually happens will depend on business rules. These rules might depend on (and hence be normalized by) only the resource (such as a first-come-first serve rule) or the process. They might even depend on the interaction of resources and processes (events). Hence, complex rules may be normalized by relationships between processes (such as relative priorities), relationships between resources, or relationships between processes, events, and resources—including processes of a higher governance order.[49] When 3 or 4 is the case, acquisition of the resource may also depend on similarly complex business rules.

The interactions that normalize rules of acquisition and mutability of resources may be simple or complex relationships—sometimes higher degree and high order relationships, sometimes temporal and sometimes not. They will conform to the laws of temporal and nontemporal relationships we have discussed previously. These relationships are containers for rules about interactions—containers that can normalize if we generalize.

The issue of cycle time and critical path through a process map can become complex when many processes that share common resources occur in parallel. Load balancing ensures that limited resources are optimally shared subject to business rules. The criteria that determine what is optimal are business decisions. Frequently, it is minimal cycle time, minimal cost, or priority for critical products, customers, and services. However, there are several other kinds of criteria that management may use to determine optimality and resolve resource (and goal) conflict (such as equal treatment for all customers—often a regulatory requirement for public services).

Unless care is taken, chains of complex processes may deadlock; that is, a process might wait for a resource that is not available because it has been engaged by another process (or processes), which in turn is (are) waiting for a product of the first process,[50] which they also use as a resource (for example, two programmers who must change the same item of code—each might wait for the other to finish so that they do not overwrite each other's modifications). Each process might even have engaged an insufficient quantum of the resource and might be waiting for more before it can complete. Neither process can therefore finish and release enough resources for the other to finish. Thus, deadlocked processes will wait forever unless a governing process or time-out breaks the deadlock. Indeed, in long and complex causal chains, the product the deadlocked processes are waiting for might occur far down the chain. Processes stalled thus are sometimes said to be in a "deadly embrace."

Temporal networks (process compositions) could become chaotic when complex rules and shared resources are mixed with massively parallel processes.[51] This may lead to deadly embraces that paralyze the network (entirely, or in parts). Parallelism, however, is often the key to speed. This is why speed is sometimes traded for risk in the design of business processes. Greater accuracy (especially temporal accuracy) and higher order governance (see Nonstationarity discussed earlier on) can sometimes reduce risk, when cycle times are compressed, by promoting greater reliability at high speeds.

(Most scheduling and workflow management software resolves resource conflict by allocating scarce resources first to high priority processes, and then, if priorities are equal, on a first-come-first-serve basis. These priorities are usually ordinally scaled. However, as we have seen, priorities may be conditional, and rules could be far more complex[52,53]).

## Cycle Time, Activity Cost, and Process Value

Even when a business has sound vision, sound products, and a robust strategy, the cycle time, cost, and net value of its processes are often of critical concern. Together, they can determine the ability of the business to compete. *Event* normalizes the cycle time of a process; *Process* normalizes its activity cost. The metacomponent that normalizes value is more complex. The value added by a process is its contribution to the value of the supply chain that it is a part of. The supply chain is its context and its contribution to the value of the supply chain is its contribution to the value of products and services produced by the aggregate. The aggregate, as we know, is a composition of processes that form the supply chain. Therefore, the value of a process is normalized by the aggregation relationship between the process and the composition. We have discussed how membership in one composition does not necessarily preclude membership in others. *Therefore, the total value added by a process is normalized by the aggregation of aggregate relationships it participates in.* The net value added by a process is the difference between its added value and its activity cost.

## Added Value

The only reason for the existence of a process is the value it adds to the product *despite* its cost and cycle time. The products in question are the products and services that the overall supply chain delivers—its ultimate goal(s). Because it is derived from interactions beyond the immediate scope of the subprocess, the value added by a subprocess is often harder to quantify than its cycle time or activity cost. For this reason, it is sometimes ignored, or given short shrift, when processes are reengineered. The cost of a process is easier to measure, and measurability may tilt the balance when a more judicious approach might be called for. The question is how might we measure the value added by process. It is a question we must answer with a question.

The answer to this question lies in the answer to another question: "what would we lose if we eliminated this process?" Added value of a subprocess in a composition is an opportunity cost that must be measured in terms of the *entire* composition—the supply chain that provides its context. The opportunities lost by eliminating a subprocess may be measured in terms of changes in parameters of the overall composition, such as cycle time and product quality, as well as the impact of these changes on consequential opportunity costs of products and services produced by the composition. Opportunity costs may be measured in terms of opportunities and risks of different kinds, such as revenues, market share, competitive position, and others. Like cycle time, the value of a composition cannot be obtained by the arithmetic addition of values of individual subprocesses in it. It is perhaps paradoxical that the entire value of a composition might be wholly contained in more than one subprocess at the same time. In Figure 7.11c, eliminating even one subprocess would bring the entire composition to a grinding halt. That is the opportunity cost of each subprocess; each has a value equal to the entire composition.

While eliminating a subprocess will not always bring all compositions to a halt, it could have other impacts on product quality, cycle time of the composition, and its cost. If this happens, we must measure the consequences of losing or replacing the subprocess in terms of impact on items such as market share and revenue. That will be its opportunity cost.

The value of an *instance* of a process is the value it adds to each instance of compositions it participates in *simultaneously*. An object (and therefore a process) may simultaneously participate in several compositions. When we compute the total contribution of a process to the goals of the business, we must be careful not to double count its contribution to processes and products in overlapping compositions that also contribute to the same goals. This makes estimation of value even more difficult when the process contributes to several close knit similar compositions with many common processes and products that are work in progress.

Supertyping and subtyping—abstracting common components by generalizing them, can sometimes make complex compositions simpler, and untangle uncontrolled proliferation of overlapping processes. (We will see examples under supply and demand chains.) However, in large businesses, the estimation of the value of every activity, or even only critical activities, may be a daunting task. Subprocesses may be too many, and compositions too complex, with not enough information to allow accurate and reliable estimation of the value. Analysts may be overwhelmed. Hard data on monetary value might be impossible to obtain and soft estimates might have to suffice ("Soft" information: see Box 4.4).

Often monetary value added may only be nominally or ordinally measurable, yet it is the key to competitive advantage. Even when estimates have wide margins of error, value can exceed cost by orders of magnitude. Even when it cannot be quantified, even when estimates are subjective, even if they are intuitive, value must be considered.

## Activity Cost

An activity has a cost. The activity cost is the cost of each instance of the process. It may be the direct or indirect cost of the activity that includes overheads such as governance costs or costs that truly belong to, and are normalized by, a composition to which the activity belongs (such as facilities costs). The *Direct Line Activity Cost* is the direct cost of the activity. It does not include indirect costs such as allocations and overheads.[54] The *Indirect Line Activity Cost* includes indirect costs such as allocations and overheads and is the cost of ownership of the activity.

The activity is an event. It may be a composition of input, output, and transformation events (the transformation event uses resources to create products—see Figure 7.12). Each event in Figure 7.12 will have a cost (even if the cost is nil or "unknown"). In addition, resources consumed may have costs. The activity cost is the sum of the entire composition of resources consumed, input and output events, as well as the transformation event that corresponds to a single occurrence (instance) of the activity. Unlike cycle times, the activity cost of a composition of processes (or events) is the total cost of all activities (processes or events) in the composition.

However, when a composition contains conditional events, conditional activities may or may not actually fire. An activity cost is incurred only when an activity occurs—once for each instance of the activity that actually fires. Therefore, conditional compositions may have conditional activity costs—just as they may have conditional cycle times. The purpose of reengineering processes and products is often to reduce the activity cost and/or cycle time of the entire composition.

Marginal cost—the change in cost—is key when the purpose of process reengineering is to reduce cost. Fixed costs might have been normalized by the composite process but allocated to subprocesses to support accounting requirements. These costs will not change if an individual subprocess in a composition is altered or even eliminated (for instance, fixed overhead costs like facilities and oversight costs for the entire composition considered as a whole will not change unless the entire composition with *all* its subprocesses is eliminated). Therefore Direct, rather than Indirect Line Activity Costs, are often the key to cost minimization.

This argument does not rule out the fact that sometimes the direct line activity cost of a process may also have fixed cost components. These fixed costs could flow from subprocesses within the activity. In Figure 7.11, cleaning the vat in which dough is made might be a subprocess hidden inside "*Make Cookie Dough*," and the cost of cleaning the dough vat each time we make dough might be fixed. Eliminating the making of dough would eliminate this subprocess as well. Consequently, the cost of the subprocess, fixed or not, would also go away if we eliminated the making of dough.

When we consider the marginal cost of a composite subprocess, we must *not* consider the cost components normalized by the composition(s) the subprocess belongs to, but *must* consider costs normalized by other subprocesses that belong to it. When we eliminate entire compositions as a part of process reengineering, we may eliminate the activity costs of a subprocess in them completely only if we eliminate *all* compositions that own the subprocess. If some such compositions remain, instances of the subprocess will no longer be triggered as a part of compositions that *are* eliminated. This will reduce the frequency with which instances of the subprocess are triggered but will not completely eliminate the subprocess. Therefore, the frequency with which the activity cost of the subprocess is incurred will be reduced, but the activity cost will still be incurred (albeit less often). That in turn will reduce, but not eliminate, the aggregate activity cost of the subprocess. This aggregate cost will be the activity cost of the subprocess aggregated over the compositions it still belongs to.

In complex cases, governance costs could also be impacted by the existence of subprocesses, and some "fixed" governance costs might even interact with a process merely because it exists. In such cases, the model may become complex. Fortunately, this level of complexity is usually not necessary. Simpler models may often be almost as effective. When interaction of marginal cost with governance costs cannot be ignored, the composition under consideration—the scope of the cost model—must also include higher (governance) order processes—see the discussion of nonstationary processes early in this section. ([83] in Appendix III (Jones, 1998) provides details of compositions that mix governed processes with governance processes.)

## Cycle Time

We have seen how, unlike activity cost, the cycle time of a composition of processes (or events) is not obtained by summing up cycle times of individual events in the composition; rather, it is obtained by summing cycle times and delays along the critical path through the composition. However, cycle times, like activity cost, may be fixed or may depend on the quantum of resources used by the process. The relationship may be simple; the cycle time might decrease inversely in simple proportion to the cardinality of the resource. Two persons may finish digging a ditch in half the time it would take one person to dig it, or it might be more complex—a team of 50 programmer analysts might take more than one fiftieth of the time it would take one programmer analyst to finish a project.

Cycle time could even depend on interactions between different kinds of resources and events. The quantum of workspace, numbers of workers, and availability of tools might jointly determine productivity.[55] Joint dependency implies that the contribution of each resource or event to overall productivity might depend on properties of the other resources, events, and even products produced. Measuring the marginal contribution of each resource or event to cycle times of others in the composition (and hence to the cycle time of the overall composition) may not be meaningful in isolation; in very complex situations, we might have to consider the entire composition of resources, input, output, and transformation processes as one indivisible unit—a single irreducible fact.

And finally, cycle time, activity cost, and added value will all depend on the scope of the composition—what subprocesses we will consider in arriving at the cycle time, activity cost, and value of the whole. The scope of the composition is often determined by process ownership (as it was in the example in Figure 7.11b, when *Make Cookie Dough* was outsourced). Naturally, changing scope or ownership may also change activity costs, cycle times, and value. Reliability, accuracy, and quality may also be impacted.[56]

## Process Ownership

A person or organization must be responsible for every business process—even automated processes. Responsibility for a process is different from doing the work of a process. Sometimes it is called "ownership" of the process. The "owner" is responsible for the overall quality and relevance of the process, its issues, and coordination requirements. Usually the owner of a process will also oversee its operation. However, in large organizations, the supervision of the process might be delegated to another organization or person (through formal and informal internal "contracts"). The owner will still be responsible for the process, but its supervision and immediate authority for proper operation may be the responsibility of a different person or organization. We will therefore distinguish between the Responsibility (R) and Authority (A) dimensions of process ownership.

The individual who actually executes or operates the process might also be different from those who are responsible for it or have supervisory authority over its operation. Although a supervisor may have oversight responsibility for the manufacturing process, a workman might actually operate a machine on the shop floor; although an operations supervisor may be responsible for the operation of an information system, an operator might actually key data into a screen to operate it. We will call this responsibility for "working" the process the "Work" (W) dimension of ownership.

Processes frequently require collaboration or consultation before or as the work is done. We will call this the "Consultative" (C) dimension of process ownership. All processes will be RW processes, and some may be RWC or RAWC processes. Of course, there is no bar on a single individual filling more than one of roles for the same or different tasks; if C and W merge, the

*Box 7.6. Automatic mutability of roles and resources in a process*

W replaced C when the two roles were played by the same person or organization because, based on the principle of subtyping by adding information, W is a subtype of C, and when the two roles converged on the same person (or organization), we replaced the supertype with the subtype as follows: C is responsible for providing information to facilitate operation of the process, whereas W is responsible for operating it and applying his or her expertise to ensure its proper operation. When we merged C with W, we added information on who does a special kind of work—operation of the process itself. This is why W is a subtype of C. Conversely, a W role may also be split into C and W roles played by different individuals.

Unlike the convergence of C and W, R replaced A because A was a subtype of R that we removed when the two roles were merged in the same person or organization. Consequently, only the supertype was left as follows: Based on the principle of subtyping by adding information, A is a subtype of R because it carries information on the contract that delegated authority for process oversight. When we merged the two roles in a single resource, delegation had no meaning. Therefore, the subtype became meaningless and was automatically replaced by the supertype as a resource for the process. (In terms of the metamodel we are building, delegation is a special kind of representation—an irreflexive subtype of the reflexive representation relationship.[58] When that irreflexive relationship is attached to the owner of a process instead of a symbol, it is called delegation.)

*In both cases, the metamodel automatically adjusted the roles when responsibilities were realigned. If the metamodel can automate the merger of roles, so can automation. These rules are a part of the algebra of process reengineering and they may be automated in the electronic repository of knowledge artifacts—automated in support of process reengineering.*

When we remove information about a resource without changing the transformation process of Figure 7.12, a supertype implicitly replaces the resource we removed. It happened when R and A converged. It also happened when we divested dough making in our introductory discussion on process mapping. In that discussion, a supertype, *Acquire Cookie Dough*, automatically replaced its subtype, *Make Cookie Dough*. Subsequently we added information to the subtype to make it more specific.

*This principle of mutability is at the heart of process reengineering. Whether we recognize it or not, whether we realize it or not and whether we know it or not, the supertype exists within a broken supply chain. Supporting information systems may ignore this law only at their own peril. Conversely, adding information to resources may refine a supply chain (or part thereof).*

An event or process that triggers a successor process is also a resource for the successor. Based on Liskov's principle, a subtype of a resource is mutable with its supertype, but not necessarily vice versa. The implicit supertype hidden in a broken temporal composition is a special supertype—a supertype mutable with the subtype it has replaced. If a process was lost, the supertype is a process that produces the resource that was lost or produces a mutable supertype of that lost resource. In terms of patterns, the supertype is the home of the essential pattern—the information that is essential for the resource to stay a resource of the transformation process (see The Essence of a Pattern in Chapter IV). This law will govern all governing processes that declare that their objective is to integrate or divest parts of a supply chain—it is embedded in the metamodel of knowledge. It is integral to what makes a process a process. It is a law that governs the making and breaking of processes.

C role will be lost. W will replace it. Similarly, if R and A merge, R will replace A.[57] It is common sense, but someone has to tell the computer that.

People or organizations with R, A, C, and W level responsibilities are also resources used by processes. High-level processes are implemented by compositions of subprocesses. As we descend through successive levels of detail in a composition to individual tasks in a workflow, we will assign W-level role responsibilities.

Although a task may have several C resources, it is usually good management practice to have only one each of R, A, and W resource. However, this is not always possible. Just as the separation of wheat from chaff was a task that could not be broken into separate subprocesses for producing wheat and chaff, some tasks need multiple W level resources. A tug-of-war game in which two teams pull a rope from opposite sides needs at least two people—one on each side. The cardinality of the input relationship may be two or more for a W resource, or the process might even be an irreducible fact that binds different kinds of resources to each other inseparably.[59]

On the other hand, it is always possible for a task to have unique R and A resources by *design*. It must happen by design; nothing stops us from assigning multiple managers responsibility and authority for a single task—if we do not mind them tripping over each other. Also remember that, from a purely mechanical perspective, tasks may be arbitrarily grouped into a composition, and each subtask may have a different owner. The composition, a process, may have several owners unless it is a special composition in which all processes have been assigned the same owner.

Several process mapping techniques such as the Activity Dependency Diagramming technique of UML and the process mapping technique by Hammer superimpose one of the three RAW dimensions on process maps with "swim lanes"[60] (as opposed to joining the resource to each process with a line as the dataflow diagramming technique

*Figure 7.13. Swim lanes in a process map*

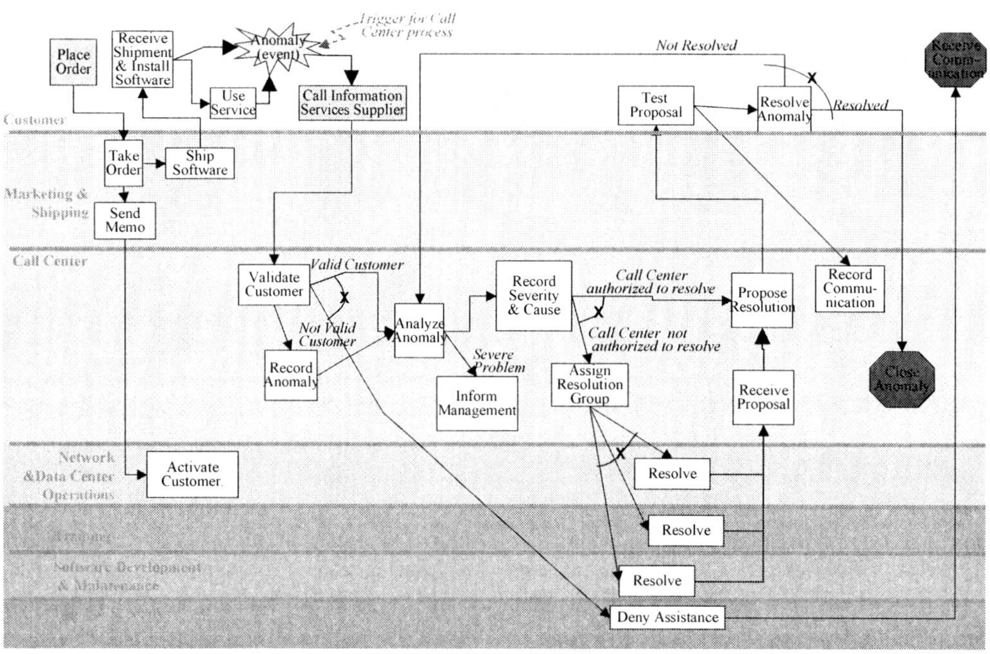

does). Figure 7.13 shows the R dimension in swim lanes for the call center process of an information services provider. Note how the customer is uppermost, and the other swim lanes are the supplier's internal organizational units (or supply chain partners). Note also how the supplier's swim lanes are arranged in terms of their "distance" from the customer. Those dimensions that interface directly and most frequently with the customer come first. This helps us understand the value of each process owner in terms of her contribution to the value of the service delivered to the customer. It also facilitates process design and simplicity from the customer's perspective.

Technology is creating a new economy of rapid and unrelenting change on a global scale. It is changing our paradigms of what can be, what should be, and the very image of what a business process is. The age of knowledge is not only an age of rapid and unrelenting change driven by competition, but also an age of rapid and unrelenting change served by collaboration. Product life cycles are being rapidly compressed. Risks are large and success is handsomely rewarded. Experience and expertise must be rapidly pooled in order to innovate and bring ideas, products, and services to market in compressed time frames.

The old sequential paradigms of isolation built in the age of mass production are being replaced by paradigms of speed, simultaneity, and collaboration. Tasks in which workers would throw their work products over the wall to individuals tasked to perform the next task are being rapidly replaced by collaborative tasks in which multiple and diverse knowledge workers simultaneously collaborate to rapidly and iteratively produce a finished product in a compressed time box. It is the age of the high order relationship. In this age, more and more, we find several individuals playing W and C roles in a single, indivisible, time-boxed process. In these collaborative processes, a new role, "Facilitator" or "Coordinator" is replacing "Authority" (A). We could call it "F."[61]

## Objectives of Subprocesses

Each subprocess has work product(s) and hence has its own objectives. Collectively, subprocesses express the goals of the process they compose in concert, but each has its individual goal(s). In very large and complex compositions, prioritizing, reengineering, and realigning subprocesses can become very complex indeed.

Although each work product in a process map is a step towards the larger purpose of the composition as a whole, we have seen how it is not the goal of the overall composition, and it may not even be a subtype of this larger goal. The goals of processes they own become the goals of individuals and organizations that own them. How individual work products orchestrate steps towards the overall goal of the composition may get lost in the "wiring" of large and complex compositions. Goals of subprocesses may become paramount to their owners. Many seasoned managers have experienced how this can lead to resource conflict and even conflicting objectives in organizations. Conflict resolution and organizational effectiveness are complex subjects that have spawned professional experts and specialized branches of knowledge. It is beyond the scope of this book. It will suffice if we recognize that the golden rule of process design is "keep compositions simple—as simple as possible."

As we will see under supply chains, the concept of subtyping facilitates simplicity by recognizing commonality. When process compositions are complex, high order (governance) processes are needed to prevent chaos by regulating these complex compositions.

## Integrating Businesses

Business integration often implies business process integration. Business processes are integrated to realize synergies between the integrated parts. Synergies might be in terms of value delivered to customers, reduced cost, reduced cycle time, less risk and greater reliability, or enhanced product and process quality. Product, customer, or process imperatives may drive the perceived benefits of integration.

- Customers may buy or use a cluster of related products and services together, or different products may be sold in similar markets to similar customers. Therefore, there may be benefit in managing their marketing, distribution, and sales in an integrated way.
- Products may be similar. Therefore, there may be benefit in designing, manufacturing, and marketing them in an integrated way.
- Processes may be similar. Therefore, there may be benefit in managing them in an integrated way.
- Some processes may use products of others as resources. Therefore, they may also benefit from being managed in an integrated fashion. Benefits of scale, quality, reliability speed, cost, and responsiveness are only some of the benefits an integrated process might reap.

Information, telecommunications services, and entertainment are each distributed to similar customers electronically with public communications networks; hence, the concept of ICE (Information, Communications, Entertainment) businesses. Indeed, telephone, television, and entertainment firms have sought to acquire and integrate their businesses on this basis.

Similarly, Manufacturing, Transportation, Retail, and Distribution businesses also build strategic relationships or otherwise try to integrate their processes because the product of the processes of one is often a resource for the processes of another, and together, they are a supply chain delivering value to the user (ultimate customer) of the product produced by the overall supply chain. The user of the product is the very reason for the existence of the supply chain and therefore the very reason for the existence of each business in the supply chain.

There are two kinds of process integration—*horizontal integration* and *vertical integration*. In *horizontal integration,* subtypes are integrated so that economies are realized by integrating management of common components. These components may be components of products or processes. The bakery that decided to produce variations of baked products or an automobile manufacturer who decides to produces variations of similar models of cars are both expanding and integrating their business horizontally. In *vertical integration,* the processes in a supply chain are integrated so that the products of one process are used as resources of others. These products may be work products, coproducts, byproducts, or even waste products. When a firm integrates its business with a supplier, it is integrating vertically.[62] Indeed, horizontal integration, driven by the need to manage common components of products, services, and processes may also benefit from vertical integration. The two kinds of integration are not mutually exclusive; they may even be complementary.

As collaboration wraps itself around competition in the age of the World Wide Web, a Web of information backed by expertise and global capabilities, it is supply chains more than individual firms that have begun competing for their place in the sun.

## Supply and Demand Chains: Compositions in Time

A supply chain is a succession of events, resources, and intermediate products that deliver end products and services to consumers or end users. Customers in a supply chain need not always be end users. For instance, customers of a confectionary manufacturer may be the distributors or retailers, whereas the end users of confectionary are *their* customers. Figure 7.11c was an example of a part of the supply chain for cookies. Figure 7.14 is an example of a full supply chain.

*Figure 7.14. An example of a basic supply chain*

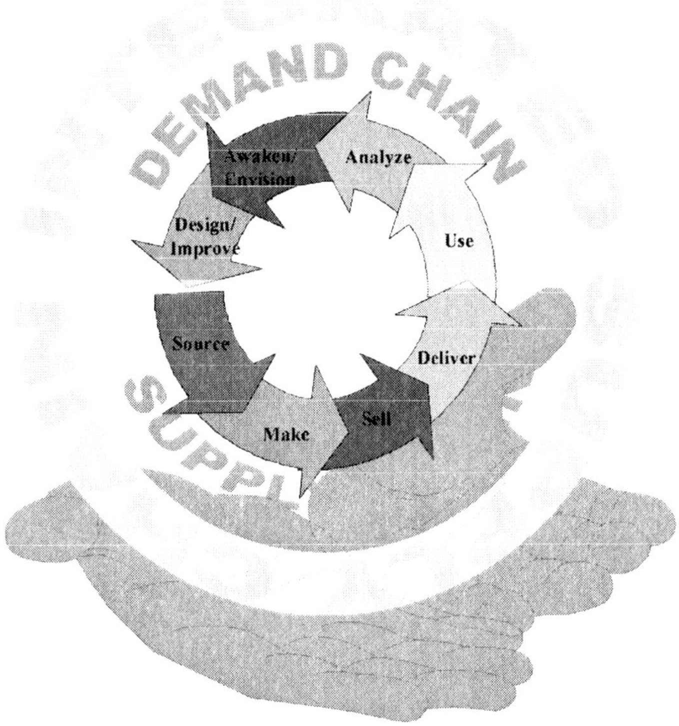


*Reproduced by permission from Mitra, A., & Gupta, A., Agile Systems with Reusable Patterns of Business Knowledge, Norwood, MA: Artech House, Inc., 2005. ©*

The supply chain in Figure 7.14 consists of two parts. The upper half is a composition of processes that add value to the product or service in order to generate customer demand, whereas the lower half focuses on making and getting products and services to customers.

The upper half of the integrated supply chain is where new products, services, and business propositions are developed based on market needs. This is where customers' needs and product–service use is analyzed to create new product–service propositions and specifications. The upper half addresses the satisfaction of customer needs that creates the demand for products and services. That is why it is called a *Demand Chain*. The demand chain is where providers of products and services awaken to new opportunity, embrace their vision of business, articulate missions, state their objectives, and assert their intent in product markets of their choice.

The lower half of the integrated supply chain in Figure 7.14 produces and delivers products and services conceived and designed in the upper half: Resources are sourced and staged; the products and services are produced and delivered to their users ("delivery" might involve physical transportation or merely giving users access to services, software, or information). The Demand Chain creates demand, and the Supply Chain fulfills it.

Consider how a distribution channel consisting of several supply chain partners is typically found in the lower half of the supply chain in Figure 7.14. Consider a candy maker. The candy maker may sell candy to distributors, who in turn sell their stock of purchased candy to retail outlets, from where the end customer buys candy. The manufacturer's customer is the distributor, not the consumer (user) of candy, and the distributor's customer is a retailer who is also not the consumer of candy. The manufacturer, distributor, and retailer are all a part of the supply chain to the consumer of candy. They are owners of processes in the supply chain that make them owners and customers of candy on the way to its consumer—the end user of candy. This is why "customer" is an ambiguous term. To remove ambiguity, we will call the user "end customer," "end user," or "consumer."

(A point to ponder for the thoughtful reader: if a customer buys a box of candy as a gift for someone else, who is the consumer and who the end user? What if the recipient of the gift shares the candy with someone else? Where should we stop and why?)

Although the upper half of Figure 7.14 is called a demand chain and the lower half the supply chain by many, the industry does not universally agree on these terms. It is broadly accepted that the upper half will be called a *Demand Chain*, but there is no agreement on whether only the lower half or the entire cycle will be called the *Supply Chain*. Unless we qualify it otherwise in this book, we will call the full, integrated cycle the supply chain. However, regardless of the tyranny of words, each half is a value chain wedded to the other.[63] Together, the cycle creates value for the consumer, the producer, and the intermediaries between them. Their mutual interdependence is thus completed.[64]

Hidden inside the high level processes in Figure 7.14 may be subprocesses like ordering, planning, and purchasing that describe how different products are made, sold, and designed. Also, hidden in the "wiring" of Figure 7.14, are succession rules, input processes, and output processes that bind the value chain into a composite whole. Each subprocess normalizes information of a different kind. However, at this highest level, they are all *unknown*—hidden but not necessarily *null* in the integrated supply chain.

With markets driving the need to collaborate and innovate across corporations and with technology making it ever more possible to do so creatively and quickly, collaboration across corporate and functional boundaries is becoming increasingly important to the survival and prosperity of firms; often the highest returns are obtained by addressing cross-enterprise issues. Processes are being integrated and redesigned in support of these needs—even across corporate boundaries. Since the late 1990s, there has been a quickening of interest in creating supply chain standards to facilitate process integration and improvement across corporations. These standards must unify, yet they must also support diversity. This can be challenging.

The chain of events in Figure 7.14 fits a mass produced product more than a custom-engineered product. Consider the supply chain for mass-produced candies. The manufacturer must produce the candy before he can sell it. This conforms to the chain of events in Figure 7.14. Contrast this situation with the supply chain for a highly customized product developed in close collaboration with the customer. Consider a custom-built home. The customer and the architect might envision and design it together, and the home may be sold, on this basis, before it is made and delivered to its owner. If this happens, the "sell" process would migrate to the upper half of Figure 7.14. This supply chain does not conform to the chain of events in Figure 7.14. As such, the supply chain in Figure 7.14 cannot be a universal standard.

This was an example of the difficult and delicate challenge that standard supply chain models must overcome—competitive advantage often lies in distinguishing the firm's products, services, and processes from competition in order to pull ahead, whereas collaboration presumes a common interface, supported by a common process. The two business imperatives are diametrically opposed and standard models must support both, or at least not compromise either—a difficult proposition.

As automation speeds time to market, produce, and deliver, as rapid and continual innovation overwhelms older products, shortening life cycles and making customers ever more fickle and harder to satisfy, as the cycle in Figure 7.14 whirls faster and faster squeezing some into oblivion, the following have become the key to survival and prosperity:

- **Change:** The demand chain is becoming critical, as is its integration into the overall supply chain. Changes to products and processes are fraught with risk, but change is also the very basis for survival and growth; change avoidance has become the larger, more strategic risk. Changes to products and processes distinguish a firm and give it custom advantages over its competition in the eyes of its customers. Custom built supply chains can steal a march over competition with custom processes and improved products that satisfy end users better, faster, and cheaper than competition.
  *(The term "product" means the entire package of products and services that constitute the business proposition offered to customers, and this is how we use the term in this book.)*
- **Automation:** Automation has become an integral part of the business process. Automated enablers reduce cycle time, manage the scale of operations, increase reliability, widen the window of availability, and reduce operating cost. However, setup costs for automation, such as software development, training, and infrastructure, can be significant. The time taken to develop and deploy improved automation can adversely impact the cycle time of supply chains very significantly. The impact on business can be severe if it increases the time taken to implement innovative ideas and market improved products. This delay is often a major disincentive for innovation, and innovation is vital to business in this age of knowledge. It is change and new learning that sustains business. Reuse of automated components will reduce setup costs, speed the process, and reduce "teething trouble" each time changes are made, this is the basis of service oriented architecture, also known by its anronym SOA. Therefore, done right, it can make the business; done wrong, it can break it.
- **Process:** Changing a process requires realignment of automation with the new process. Not only can change be hampered by the need to alter and reconfigure automated support, but the process can also be adversely affected for the same kinds of reasons as automation was—setup costs, the cost of process definition, training, infrastructure, deployment, testing and tuning, and so forth.
- **Process integration:** Processes, integrated and automated across a supply chain, speed its cycle time. They can also reduce cost, improve reliability, and improve the quality of service. The key to success is integration across the enterprises that are partners in a supply chain, shortening, simplifying, standardizing, and removing process redundancy, giving each partner visibility into the processes and information of the other.

Hence, it is a delicate balance that must be struck between change vs. stability, competitive strength through difference, vs. interoperability through common standards—a balance between customization and standardization. It is this balance between uniqueness and conformity that is becoming ever more precarious, even as it becomes the key to survival and success. Figure 7.15 makes the point.

The most broadly reusable components of knowledge are those that configure the meaning of business. That is the outer rim of Figure 7.15. These components are best practices all busi-

*Figure 7.15. The delicate balance between competitive advantage, commonality, and distinction*

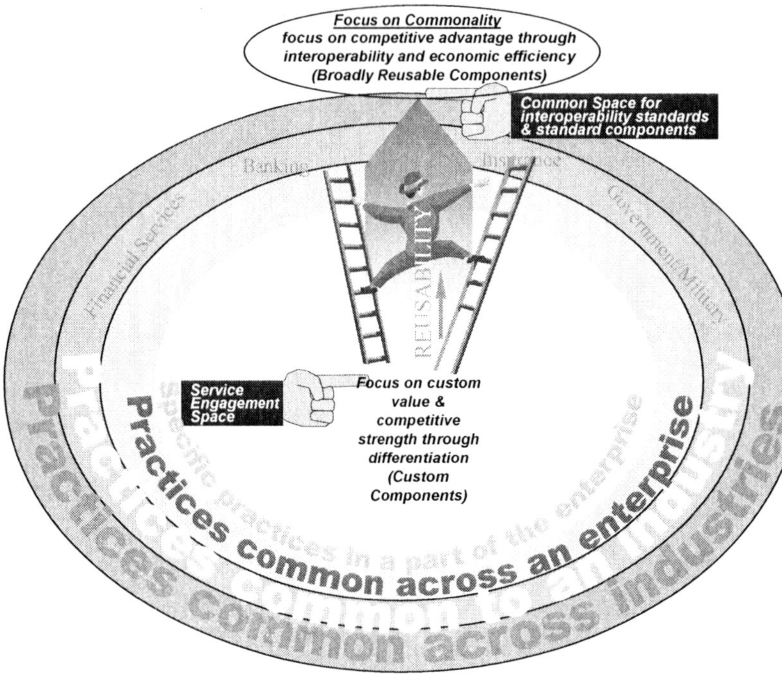


nesses follow. They are the configurations of knowledge that integrate the diverse partners in a supply chain. It is these components that make interoperability possible. They are relatively few but the key to every business. Naturally, they are also the components of knowledge most often denormalized, fragmented, and repeated across businesses, business systems, departmental systems, and low-level operations. They are replicated uncountable times in uncountable forms and formats. It makes their numbers seem vast and their nature impossibly diverse. It makes integration of processes seem difficult and integration of supporting software sometimes impossible. Identifying and normalizing this knowledge must be the ultimate goal of every supply chain. These componenets should therefore also be the basis for identifying services in SOA. They are described in item [338] of Appendix III.

Snapped on to these broad components in the outer rim of Figure 7.15 are components that differentiate one industry from another. This is typically the space occupied by vendors of Enterprise Resource Planning (ERP) solutions such as ORACLE, SAP, PeopleSoft, MAPICS, and others. However, ERP and supply chain management are rapidly converging under the pressures of driving competition and shortening time frames. To merge the ERP of the twentieth century into the spinning supply chains of the twenty-first, we must identify the broader components in the outer rim of Figure 7.15. Only then will we be able to extract the common cross industry knowledge embedded in the multitude of ERP systems in operation today. Only then will we know what normalized industry practices may be snapped on to which cross-industry components to normalize the entire ensemble of knowledge, which will make our processes and systems incredibly agile.

Users of ERP may then snap custom knowledge from the inner rings of Figure 7.15 on to the common knowledge at the rim. Thus, they can quickly differentiate their firms from competition in a way that will facilitate process and product innovation as well as standardization—the three survival imperatives in the turbulent age of knowledge.

Understanding and normalizing this knowledge in the outer rim of Figure 7.15 is not only the key to its reuse but also the key to interoperability, innovation, and a strong competitive position under the immense pressures of global change. Recognizing these facts embedded in the common sense, Figure 7.15 provides the key to normalizing knowledge, its customization, and reuse. This is the key to the kinds of creativity and cost control that lend a corporation its competitive cutting edge. It is also the key to managing change in order to speed it. To survive and prosper, the whirling supply chains of our time must be reconfigured even as they whirl ever faster, flexing nimbly with opportunistic and strategic business practices; Opportunity may be lost forever if not grasped in time.

In business and in software, it is separating the shared and identifying the unique that presents the biggest challenge. This challenge must be won if we must create standards that will wrest integration and interoperability across the diverse work products and services in supply chains (see Figure 7.19). Industry standard supply chain models have tried to address the outer rim of Figure 7.15. They have had only limited success. These standards are not mutually integrated and do not refer to each other. The Universal Perspective, summarized on our Web site, ties them together. It addresses the outer rim of Figure 7.15. *Agile Systems with Reusable Patterns of Business Knowledge: A Component Based Approach*, another book by the same authors, elaborates further on the Universal Perspective and has the unifying patterns from which all supply chains and their standards must emerge.

The Universal Perspective flows from the Metamodel of Knowledge. It adds normalized business information to the already normalized meanings in the Metamodel of Knowledge. Supply chains are polymorphisms of the Universal Perspective. Supply chain standards derived from the Metamodel of Knowledge, and the Universal Perspective will normalize and integrate information in complex, global supply chains of the kind in Figure 7.19.

*The State of the Art in supply chain standards is discussed in Supply Chains and the Metamodel of Knowledge, a supplementary section on our Web site.*

*Reviewing standard supply chain model standards will help the reader to understand how these standards help and what their limitations are.*

*Figure 7.16. The high level CPFR supply chain model*

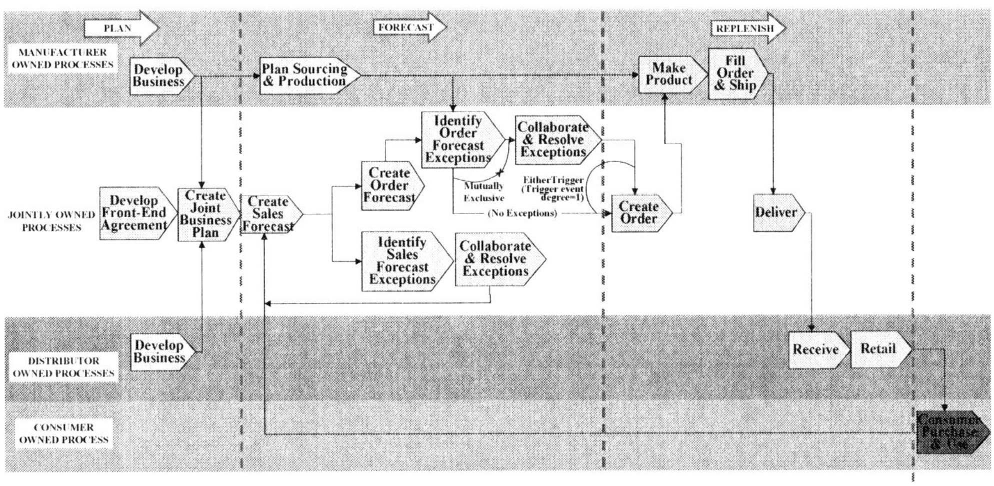

*Figure 7.17. The basic ARIS business process model*

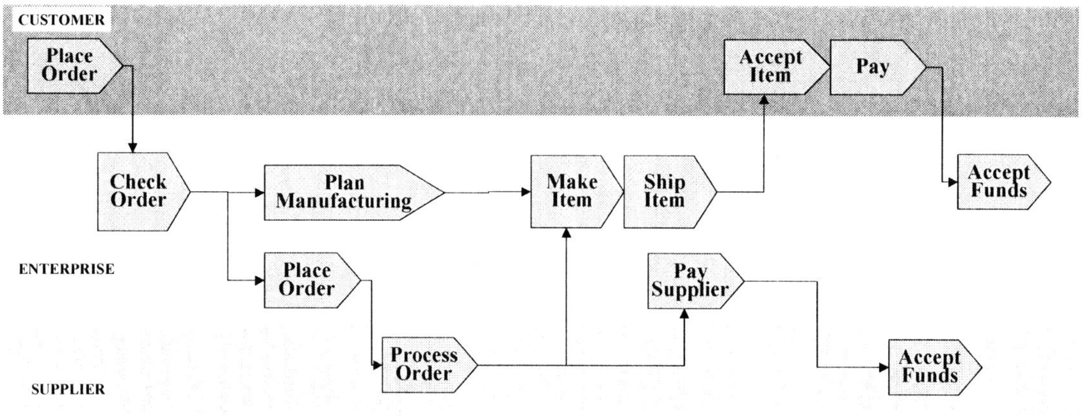


*Figure 7.18. The netmarket supply chain*

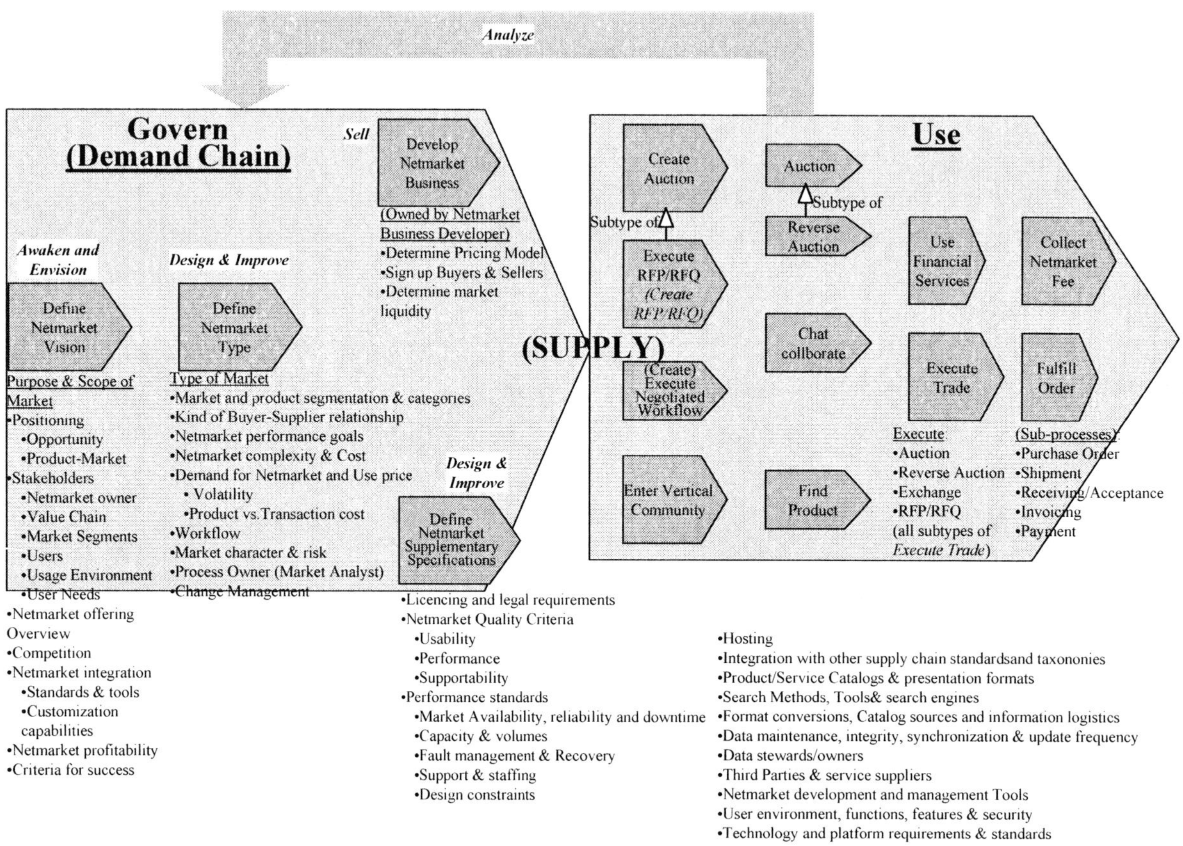

*Box 7.7. Collaboration and agility with unstructured processes and soft information*

You must have personally experienced ad-hoc and unstructured processes; they are even desirable under some circumstances. Sometimes they can speed things up, handle difficult exceptions, or even make business agile in turbulent times when plans and assumptions become obsolete even before they are articulated. Under these conditions, good governance can break down in a storm of change and complexity. Most of us intuitively understand and have personally experienced processes that are ad-hoc and lack the kind of structure prescribed for baking cookies in Figure 7.11. It would be an exercise in futility to attempt to structure a meeting for brainstorming new ideas in fine detail by attempting to anticipate every detailed event that can occur at the meeting, the conditions for it, its work products, interactions, resources, and ownership. Business has room for ad-hoc and unstructured processes. Does the metamodel we are building have room for unstructured or semistructured processes? The answer is a resounding yes.

The structure of a process, or the lack thereof, is based on its information content. There are four dimensions—kinds of information that lend a process structure:

- Ownership dimensions
- Triggering rules (rules of process succession and process prerequisites)
- Resources and work products (Although they have been shown together in the cube below, resources and work products are separate dimensions in the structure of a process)

When any of this information is unknown, the process loses some structure. When nothing is known about the process, it becomes the metaprocess. The metaprocess only tells us what a process is—its meaning and properties. On the other end of the information scale, when everything about a process is known, we cannot only draw deterministic process maps like that in Figure 7.11c, that show each resource, product, and flow, but also assign ownership in terms of the RAWC and F roles we discussed earlier. When some of this information is unknown, the process is semistructured. The larger the quantum of missing information, the more unstructured the process will be.

For instance, consider the rambunctious exchange of information in a brain storming session. It lacks almost all the information above. All we know is who the participants are (the resources), the facilitator (if indeed one exists), and the kind of work product we expect (but not a great deal about it). Indeed, sometimes even the resources and roles are unknown. There is no team. Then the process is truly ad-hoc (when governance processes fill in or change the information dynamically, the process cannot be called ad-hoc or unstructured. It might only be nimble. Only when information is truly missing—it is unknown and ungoverned until the process occurs—is the process unstructured).

Consider the following figure. It is busy, but it describes exactly where structured and unstructured processes sit in the metamodel of process and how it is the inherent lack of information that makes a process unstructured. As we leached a domain of information, it lost measurability; as we leach a process of information, it loses structure—provided we do not remove the temporal information that makes a process a process (if we do, it ceases to be a process and becomes a nontemporal relationship). This is how processes become "soft" information. (The characteristics of "soft" information are described in more detail in Box 4.4.)

*continued on following page*

*Box 7.7. continued*

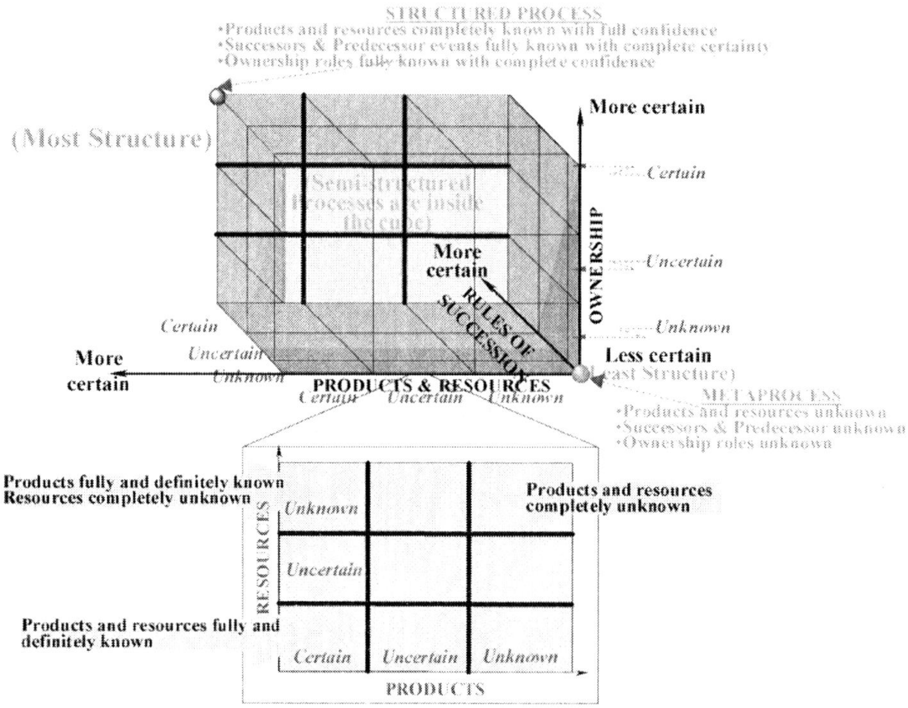


*Figure A. The information content of structured vs. unstructured processes*

Each edge of the cube in the upper half of the figure represents a dimension of process structure. The corresponding information may be missing (unknown), uncertain or known (certain). The metamodel in this book is deterministic. It does not admit chance. Information is either present or absent; it is either certain or certainly missing. Therefore, for our purpose, each kind of information is either unknown or known. The "uncertain" position was only included for illustrative purposes—to show that information content of each dimension is actually a sliding scale in a continuum of uncertainty in the real and uncertain world; we are going to wish away uncertainty in our discussion here but uncertainty that cannot be wished away from reality.

Moreover, the cube has only three dimensions—length, breadth, and height. We need four, one each for ownership, triggers, resources, and products. We are one dimension short. That is why products and resources share a single edge of the cube (at the bottom). That edge has been expanded into a grid in the bottom half of the figure to show separate dimensions for resources and products. Together, the grid and the cube show that processes are structured in four dimensions.

(If we became bloody minded about detail, we could insist on a dimension for each kind of responsibility, for each resource, each product and each kind of trigger; however, such detail would contribute little to this discussion on the meaning of process structure or rather the lack of it.)

The process on the top left hand cell of the cube is a completely structured process in which all resources, products, triggers, and responsibilities are completely known. We could map it like the processes in Figure 7.11c. Diagonally opposite it is the process in which none of these are known; it is only known that these will occur. This is the metaprocess of our metamodel. Inside the cube, between these two extremes, are processes in which some of this information is known, but some is missing. They are the semistructured and unstructured processes. The ad-hoc process, in which only the work product is known, would lie inside the bottom edge of the cube. Within that edge, it would be in the top left hand cell of the grid in the lower half of the figure.

Consider how unstructured and structured processes can orchestrate a composition of processes together. An aggregate process that consists of subprocesses without full information on succession, ownership, resources, or work products, is an unstructured process. Unstructured aggregate processes may well be a subprocess in a structured process map, and

*continued on following page*

*Box 7.7. continued*

conversely, parts of an unstructured process may be structured. For instance, Figure 7.13 described a structured process, but the subprocess that assigned responsibility for resolution may have been unstructured in its internal operation. The analysis of the problem and assignment of responsibility for resolving the problem might have been a collaborative process between the call center, operations, training, and software development departments.

We may have completely ad-hoc processes, collaborative processes in which the team and resources are known, but not any chains of subprocesses in a composition or a fully structured process of the kind in Figure 7.11 or Figure 7.13, or even a mix of each in a complex composition. Indeed, in a deterministic model like ours, that does not support partial certainty, each item of information will either be known or unknown. Four dimensions lend a process its structure. Thus, processes may be structured in 2 x 2 x 2 x 2 = 16 ways. Of these, one is the completely structured process we have discussed at length and the other is the metaprocess in the metamodel we are developing. That leaves 14 kinds of unstructured processes in a deterministic metamodel (excluding the metaprocess). The ARIS supply chain model, which we will soon discuss, describes five kinds of unstructured processes in Figure 46 of Scheer.[65]

The 14 unstructured processes in our metamodel include, subsume, and extend the five processes in ARIS.

Adding structure (information) to an unstructured relationship or process creates more structured polymorphisms. A Saga is also a kind of unstructured process. It has no information on when it will end, if it ends at all. An Endless Saga is a subtype of Saga that we know for sure will not end. A process that we know will end, even if we do not know when, is also a polymorphism of the generic saga, but we will not call it Saga; we will call it a discrete, or "ordinary," process (Box 7.2).

(Points to ponder for the thoughtful reader: This book describes more than four properties of processes. If some of these other properties, like cardinality, degree, or the operating instructions that turn resources into products, are missing, might the process be considered unstructured? Would we be justified if we considered some of these properties, such as degree, order, and cardinality, extended information on process succession and subsumed them under that item? What if we know who has responsibility for a process, but not who actually works it? For example, the responsibility for producing and delivering a management report might be fixed, but the choice of the person who physically delivers the report to preordained recipients might be ad-hoc. Does this make report delivery a semistructured process? Does it imply that the process ownership dimension lacks structure and the process itself is therefore semistructured? How do we distinguish between structured and unstructured processes?)

*Some of these standards address unstructured processes. This section discusses how the Metamodel of Knowledge addresses unstructured and loosely structured processes. It shows how the lack of structure does not imply lack of clarity or an unmanaged process, but a flexible process, which determines the values of its parameters, its owners, responsibilities, and goals at execution time. It discusses the governance of unstructured processes to ensure that they foster flexible responses, not chaos.*

*The purpose of these standards is to support interoperability between partners in a supply chain and to foster flexibility, integrity, transparency, and diversity of products, services, and processes. The following standard models are widely referenced and have been discussed in this section.*

*Figure 7.19. A dynamic, semistructured, flexible, any-to-any supply chain*

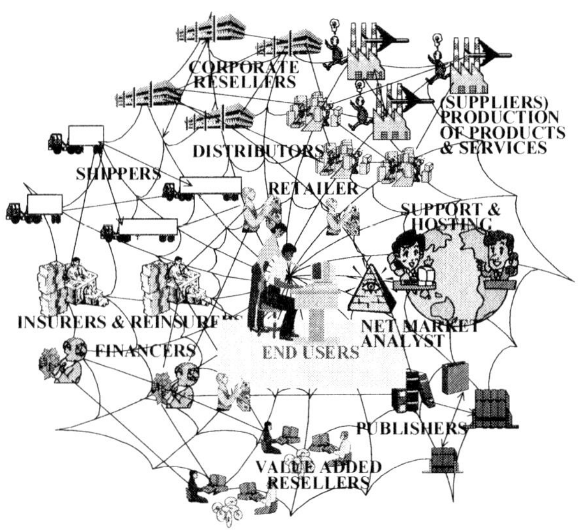

**The CPFR Model from the Voluntary Inter-industry Commerce Standards Association**

*CPFR is an acronym for Collaborative Planning Forecasting and Replenishment. The CPFR model in Figure 7.16 is a model of collaboration between buyers and sellers that primarily targets the retail industry. Its intent is to facilitate collaboration between manufacturers and intermediaries in the supply chain that ends with the consumer.*

*Figure 7.20. The SCOR supply chain model*

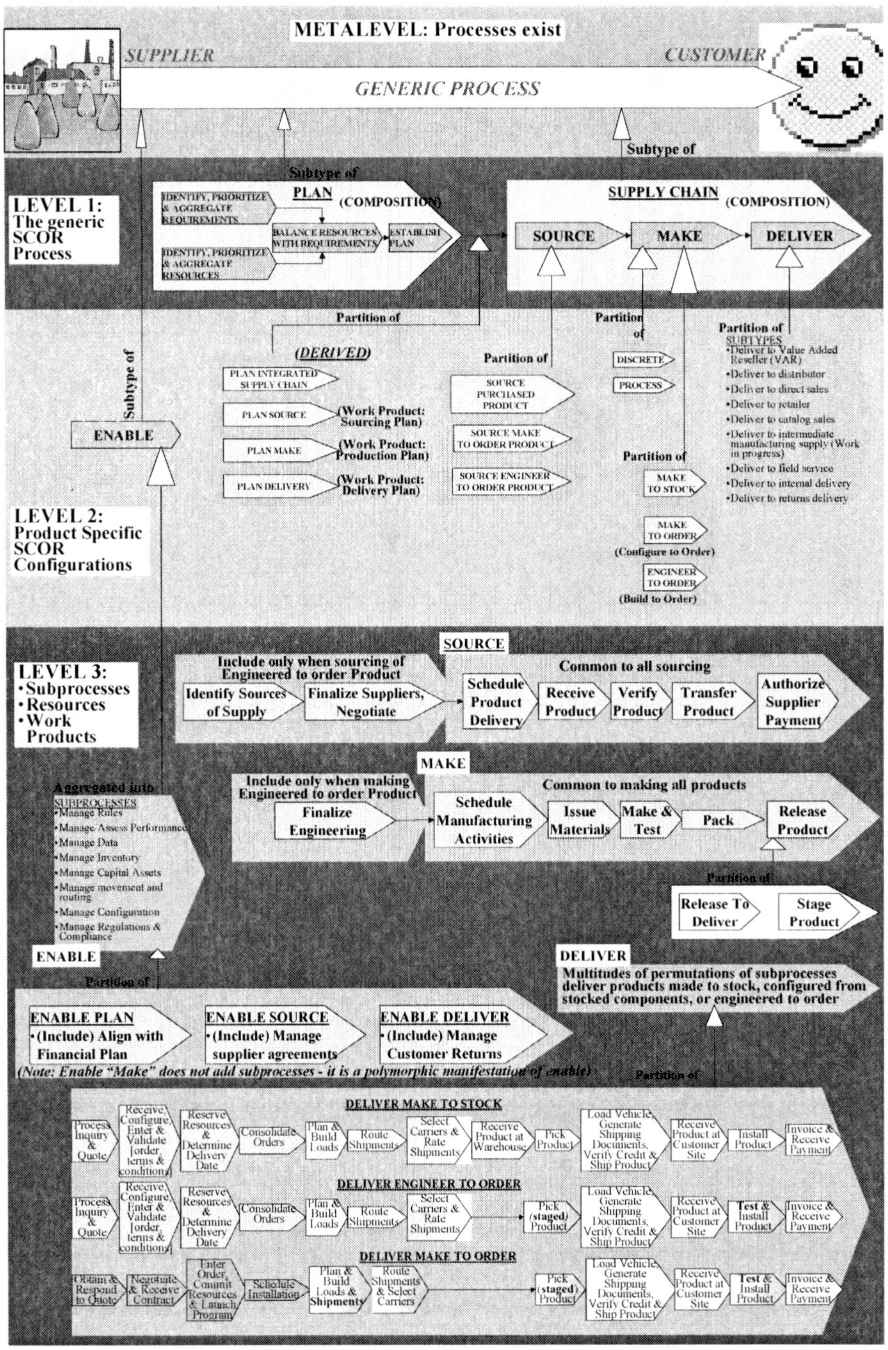

### The ARIS Model

*ARIS is an acronym for Architecture of Integrated Information Systems. The backbone of the ARIS supply chain is shown in Figure 7.17. It is an input-output model with the enterprise at its center. ARIS focuses on inbound and outbound logistics between customers and the enterprise and, separately, between suppliers and the enterprise.*

### The Netmarket Model

*Like CPFR, and unlike ARIS, the netmarket model from Rational Software Corporation in Figure 7.18 is an intensely collaborative set of unstructured processes that are reusable within a limited scope, primarily for trading through the Web. This section on the Web describes the flexibility, governance, utility of these unstructured processes, and what the lack of structure means to automation.*

*Figure 7.21. Examples of SCOR Level 3 processes with resources and work products*

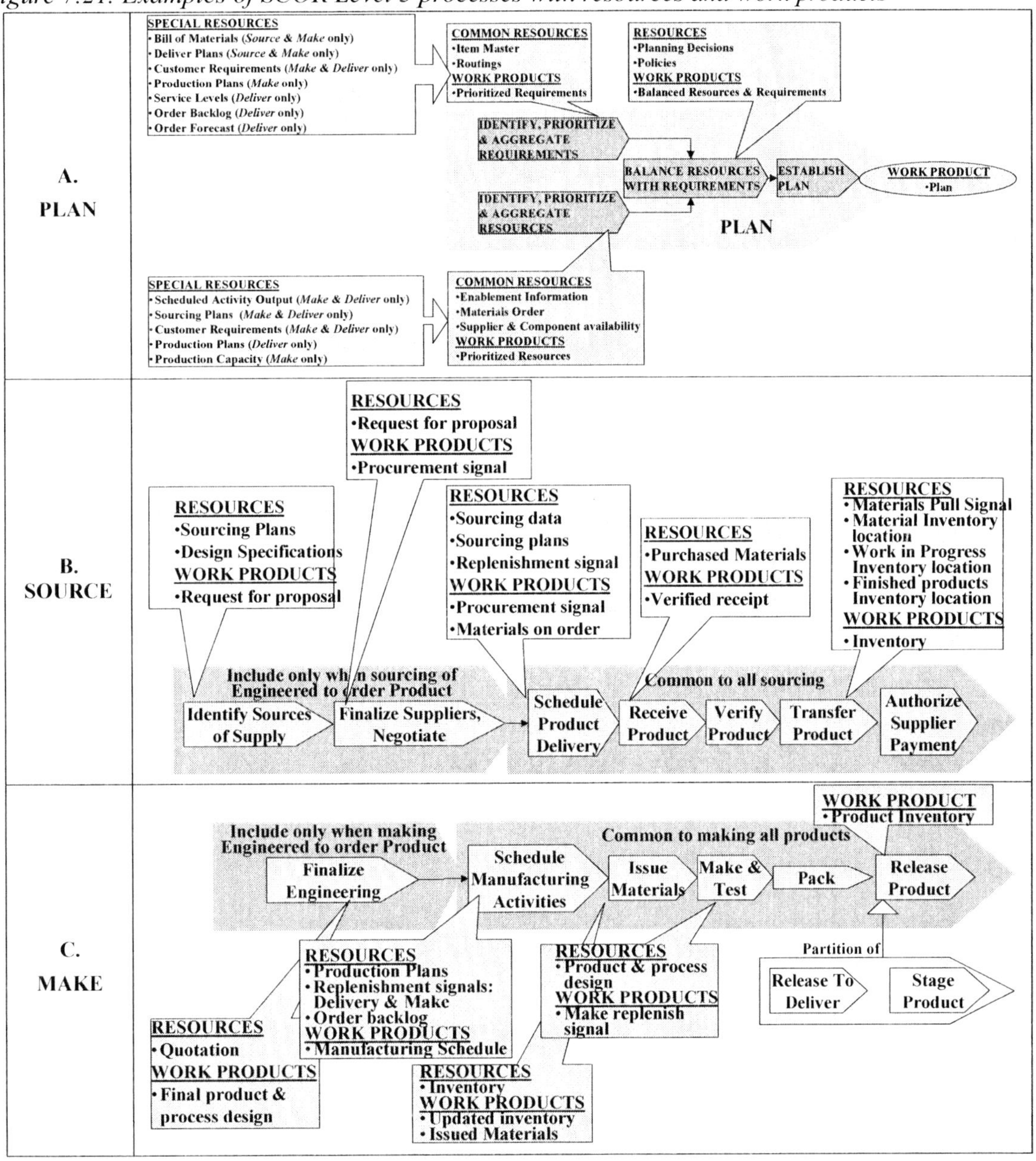

*Figure 7.22. Examples of the SCOR Enable process*

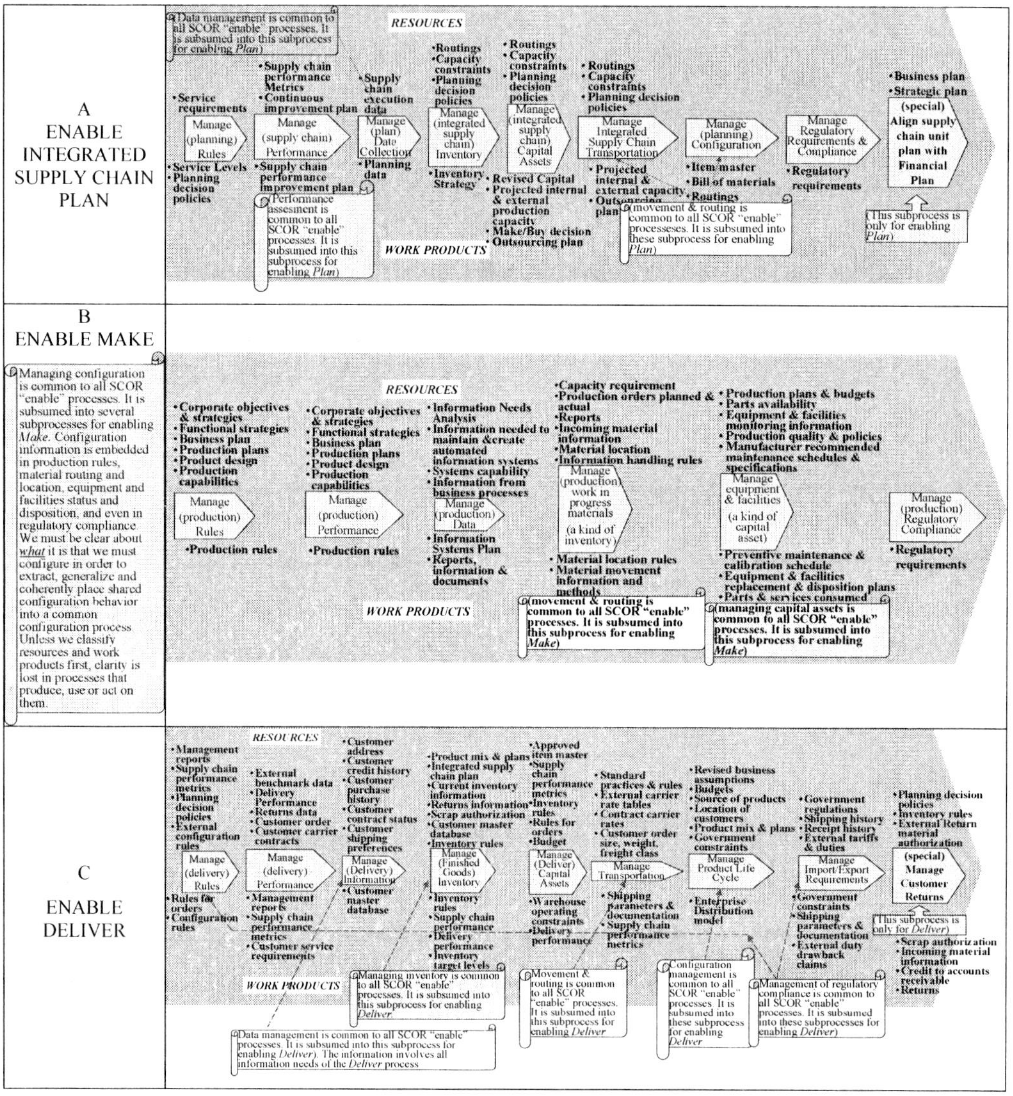


*(Note that the subprocesses in the figure do not necessarily occur in sequence)*

**Rosettanet**

*Rosettanet is a consortium of over 400 major Information Technology, Electronic Components, and Semiconductor Manufacturing companies. The intent of Rosettanet is to create and promote business process standards that will help integrate global supply chains driven by the Web. Rosettanet supply chains may be global, dynamic, and flexible, flexing to seek new opportunities even as they reduce cost and time. Rosettanet emphasizes the "supply" side of dynamic supply chains in electronic space.*

**The SCOR Model from the Supply Chain Council**

*SCOR, the Supply Chain Operations Reference Model, is a generic, multilevel supply chain model that was developed in 1996. The Supply Chain*

*Figure 7.23. The S95 hierarchy model*

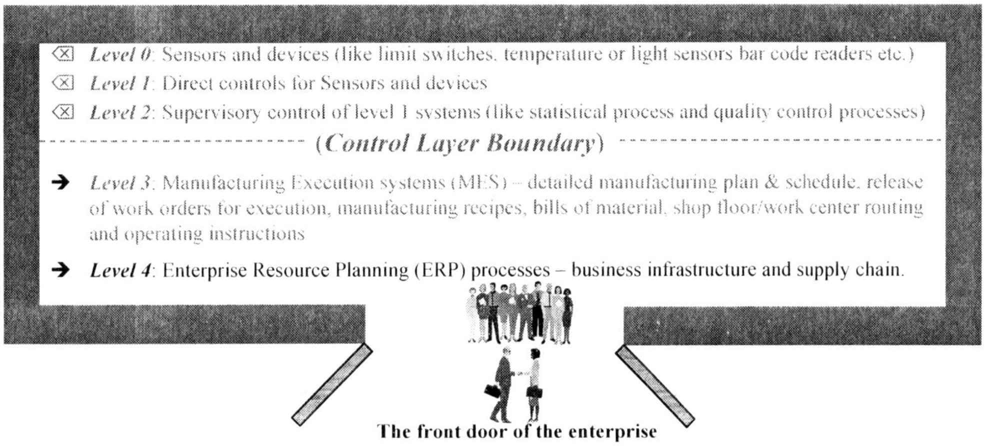


*Council (SCC), a rapidly growing global trade association of several hundred major firms, has adopted it as a standard. Figures 7.20 through 7.22 describe SCOR at different levels of detail. SCOR is also a polymorphism of the generic process model in Figure 7.12: The Source process in SCOR is a polymorphism of the Input process in Figure 7.12; the Make process of SCOR is a polymorphism of the Transformation process of Figure 7.12, and the Deliver process of SCOR is a polymorphism of the Output process of Figure 7.12. The merits and demerits of SCOR are discussed in detail in Module V on our Web site. This discussion will show that:*

- Generic processes are reusable, and we can customize them through the subtyping mechanism.
- Subtyping and polymorphism give us a great deal of flexibility in configuring and customizing processes.
- Temporal compositions are both like and unlike the nontemporal compositions because a temporal composition is a polymorphism of a nontemporal composition.
- The limitations of obtaining reuse by generalizing and subtyping processes, rather than the objects these processes use, create, and change.

**S95 from the World Batch Forum (WBF) and Related Standards**

*The purpose of S95 is to seamlessly integrate manufacturing operations on the factory floor with the logistics of business. The World Batch Forum (see Box 7.5) and ISA (Instrumentation Systems and Automation Society)[66] sponsor the S95 standard. S95 divides manufacturing operations into the five conceptual layers in Figure 7.23, starting from sensors and devices deep inside the machinery of production and ending at the Enterprise Resource Planning Level. Our Web site has more detail.[67]*

The reason for forging supply chains is the meeting and melding of processes—their integration and optimization across corporate and national boundaries in support of innovation, speed, responsiveness, and most of all, in support of customers. Therefore it is important to understand how the metamodel will help us integrate and reengineer the business process itself. That will be our focus in the sections that follow.

## Expanding, Integrating, and Divesting Chains of Processes

Businesses integrate across supply chains through partnerships, acquisitions, mergers, strategic arrangements, and a plethora of other formal and informal business relationships. However, the benefits of integration will only flow if business processes are integrated and information flows smoothly. Requisite products must be available where they are needed, when they are needed, and at the right price in supply and demand chains, and so must information. Experience shows that integrating information systems is difficult and risky unless the processes they support are also integrated and conform to a core of common standards. The age of collaboration is also the age of unity in infinite diversity.

When we integrate compositions of processes, there is every chance that information and business rules will be replicated and denormalized. They must be coordinated and merged. In other words, knowledge must be normalized if synergies must be realized. The components described in this book and rules we have discussed for assembling and mutually engaging these components will facilitate normalization of knowledge and realization of process synergy.

Consider Figure 7.11. Assume that one organization makes cookie dough and another bakes cookies. The two processes are a part of the supply chain that eventually delivers cookies to customers. Assume that they decide to integrate their processes. Before integration, *Arrange Dough Glob on Cookie Sheet* was triggered by a request for fresh cookies (the transitive succession relationship in Figure 7.11c). After integration, we must decide when we will initiate *Make Cookie Dough*—should we start making the dough when a request for fresh cookies is made (the "make to order" polymorphism in SCOR), or should we keep replenishing the dough each time it falls below a critical level (the "make to stock" polymorphism in SCOR) and not change the trigger for *Arrange Dough Glob on Cookie Sheet*?

Assume we decide to trigger the making of dough only in response to a request for fresh cookies (as we have done in Figure 7.11c). In order to keep information normalized, we must *move*, not add, the triggering relationship to *Make Cookie Dough*. We discussed the rules and reasons for this under Figure 7.8b. When we expand a temporal composition and add objects and relationships to it, some temporal relationships might be transitive with respect to others; we have discussed why we must exclude the transitive relationship with the longest duration in order to normalize temporal information.

Conversely, these kinds of considerations are equally true when we divest parts of a process. In a temporal composition, downstream triggers, relationships, events, and constraints derived from upstream objects must be replaced if they are broken off as a part of process divestiture or reengineering. Not only will these replacements repair and refurbish the divested and retained parts of the process and make them operational but will also articulate the functional requirements for making supporting information systems operational for the separated parts of the composition. Indeed, with the transforms in Chapter VIII, some of the changes could even be automated.

In the turmoil of global markets and the converging pressures of opportunity and competition, driven by new learning, technology, and innovation, businesses must continually flex to prosper, or even to merely survive. In this tumult, continual divestiture and acquisition of products and businesses, with supporting processes, is becoming more the norm than the exception. In this age of information, the information infrastructure that supports a process has significant value. It is not just the process, but also its supporting information systems that add value to a divestiture or acquisition. Information systems must be divestible with processes, or conversely, acquiring the information system with the process will add significant value to the acquisition. The rules we will discuss next will facilitate all three: divestiture, acquisition, and integration.[68]

## Process Reengineering and the Mutability of Compositions

A process has a purpose. We understood this purpose is the essence of the process. If the purpose changes, the process loses its identity and its essence—the essential temporal pattern and rule it represents. We also understood that a rule might have many expressions (Box 5.1). A process is a temporal rule. Like any other rule, it may be implemented (*expressed*), in many different ways without losing its identity or purpose. We saw this when we discussed subprocesses. We saw processes could be reengineered in four ways without losing their purpose:

- Subprocesses may be added to (or deleted from) a process map (same as adding or deleting substates).
- Rules of succession between subprocesses may be changed (same as changing permitted state transitions).
- Resources (and role responsibilities) may be changed, merged, or split.
- Processes may be made more or less structured.

Through all four kinds of changes, the work product of the process must remain inviolate. Its essence and purpose will then be preserved. Even as it keeps its work products and purpose intact, all four kinds of changes will change the process map—the composition that represents the process. It will be the same rule—the same essential pattern—only the expression of the rule will be different; the temporal composition will have changed, but not its work products. These temporal compositions are knowledge machines that engage elemental meanings to create the process, and each meaning is a part—a component of knowledge. The essence of a process can only be preserved when change parts of these compositions are mutable. Thus, mutability of components—of Knowledge Artifacts—lies at the heart of process reengineering.

*These change parts are subprocesses, resources, rules of state change and succession of substates, and the information that lends a process its structure—three of the four dimensions of Box 7.7 (the work product is not negotiable). The states of events within events, the events in compositions hidden within aggregate events (and processes), are often called substates of the aggregate (discussed in The Essence of a Process). They are change parts too. Process reengineering involves discovering those compositions that match our improvement criteria—our process objectives—more than current compositions do.*

## Adding and Reusing Subprocesses

Processes may be reengineered by adding subprocesses (substates) to the original process. For instance, in Figure 7.11, we could have inserted an "*Inspect Dough Glob*" process between "*Arrange Dough Glob on Cookie Sheet*" and "*Bake Dough.*" It would change neither the work product nor purpose of *Bake Cookie*. The process would remain a bake cookie process, but the process map would now have an additional subprocess and an additional substate, "*Dough Globs under Inspection.*" The process was changed without changing the product.

Process reengineering often involves inserting new subprocesses that will add value to the process or product in some way or removing subprocesses of doubtful value. Inserting processes into a sequence is identical to adding information to the sequence and turning a succession relationship into a full blown process, whereas deleting a subprocess will merge it into the succession relationship, which will consequently "heal itself" (discussed under successions of compositions).

The new composition of subprocesses will be a subtype of the old composition. It must be; we added a substate and changed nothing else. We know it must be a subtype of the old composition because adding a new state is adding information. and we know that subtypes retain the information in their parents and add their own information to this inherited information. Liskov's substitution principle also tells us that subtypes are mutable with corresponding supertypes in a composition but herein lies a trap: the composition is a temporal composition; some objects occur before others, and the work product occurs last. In the following discussion, we will see that process subtyping does not necessarily imply subtyping its work products nor does subtyping the work product always imply that a subtype of the generic process can produce it. Moreover, compositions may be subtyped in bewilderingly different ways, which can make their reuse extremely complicated.

We could decide that we will introduce colored cookies into the market and modify the composition in Figure 7.11b to make colored cookies. To make colored cookies, we might insert an "*add color*" event between "*Arrange Dough Glob*" and "*Bake Dough.*" However, that would change the work product. Thus, that change would be a case of product engineering and expansion of product markets. In this case, both the process and the product were changed; the process was changed to make and support a new product. Process engineering followed product engineering. It was a consequence, not a cause. We will discuss that under Product Reengineering. Our present focus is the new process.

The new process will produce colored cookies. It will also add a new state to *Bake Cookie* (which supports our intuition that *Bake Colored Cookie* is a subtype of *Bake Cookie*). The new process is a subtype, an inclusion polymorph (see Box 4.8) of the old process because *Colored Cookie*, its work product, is a subtype of Cookie, the work product of the old process—provided we did not know nor care about the color of cookies the old process produced. If we did (and we probably did care about their shade of brown or white, even if we did not call those cookies "colored," and did not think of them as such in business parlance), then the old cookies had a color. In that case, neither kind of cookie would be a subtype of the other; both would be subtypes of a generic class of cookies.

A completely different process may produce the same work product as the following example shows. When this happens, the process is a subtype of the same service. A service may be considered to be the composition of product and the generic process that produces it:

Consider two processes that make potable water—one from fuel cells by combining oxygen and hydrogen and the other from seawater by desalinating it:

1. The fuel cell burns hydrogen. The chemical reaction releases energy and water is a coproduct.
2. Seawater has salt; it is unfit for drinking. A different process uses energy to distill seawater to produce purified, potable water for drinking.

Resources and processes are different between the two processes for making potable water, but both make drinking water; they have the same purpose. If we had no information on resources or transformations within the process, the two would be indistinguishable "black boxes." The differences are internal—different compositions for producing the same work product, with different resources, transformation rules and probably cycle times and activity costs as well. Each is a subtype of a service for production of water.

## The Trap of Reusability and the Paradox of Knowledge Reuse

Mathematically, the problem with subtyping compositions (or aggregations) is that each is a combination of parts, and each might share its parts with others. Thus, there could be an enormous number of ways of partitioning the composition—every possible part and combination within the combinations within the composition

*Figure 7.24. An example of a polymorphic process in a process map with nontemporal relationships*

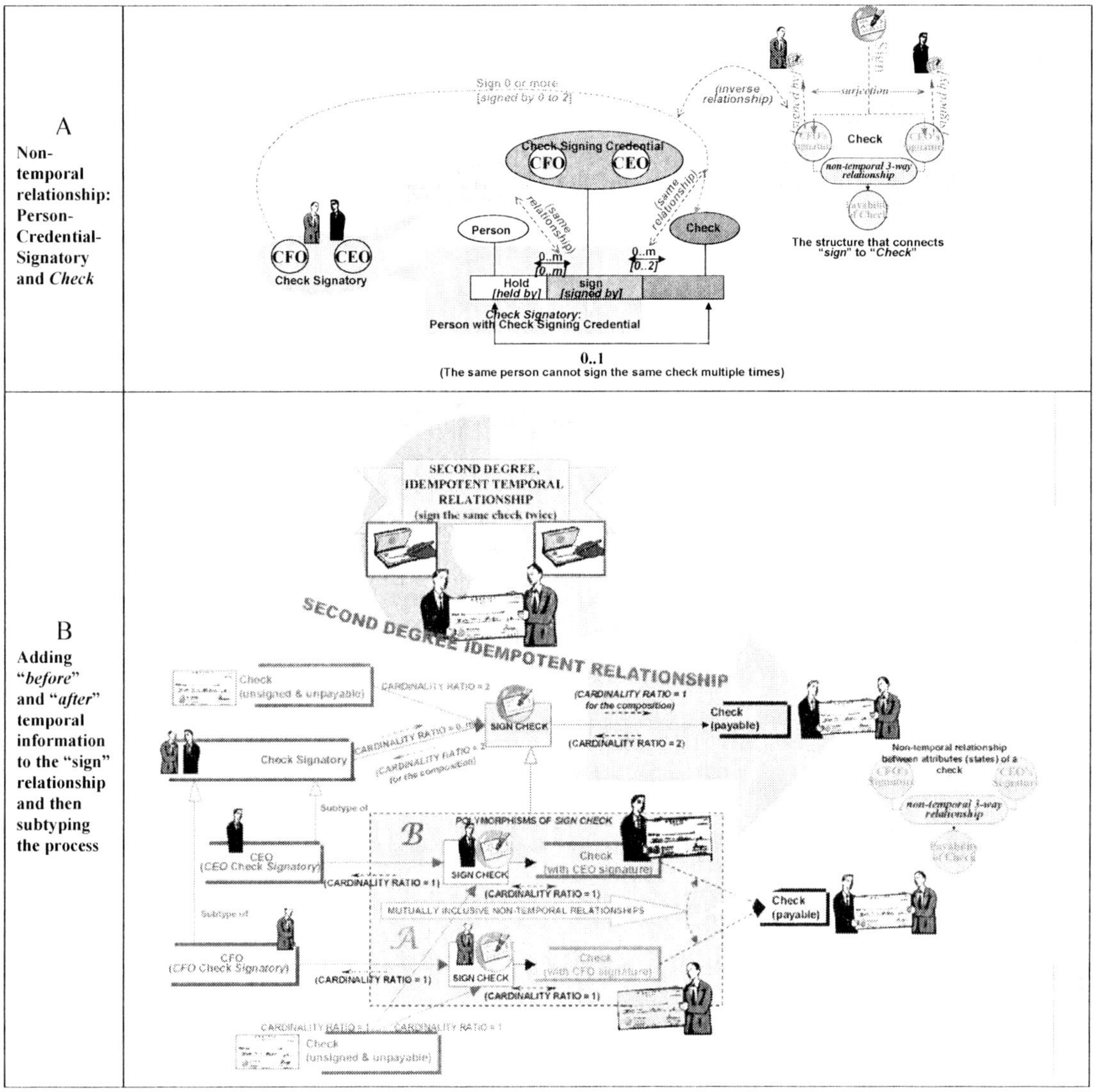


is a possible criterion for partitioning it (see the Borel object in Chapter V).

The only object shared by the two processes for making water was their work product—potable water, the object at the end of the composition. The work product is the single stable object that anchors alternative compositions, but it occurs last. The universe of mutable compositions means every possible composition that leads to that single object at its end. The possibilities could be immense and even infinite. The subtypes of these compositions may be equally bewildering and prolific. Indeed, if we change a few succession relationships in this possibly immense variety of subtypes so that a different object takes the last place, what was a resource may become a product and the product a resource. A subtype of the composition that produced one product may even be said to produce the resource that produced the product—a very confusing situation indeed!

Nontemporal compositions are different. No one object or a group of objects can be said to occur before or after others. All objects in the composition are equal. However, subtyping even nontemporal combinations can lead to the same problem of a confusing profusion of subtypes of bewildering variety.

We discussed the problem of perspective in Chapter II. It is also process decomposition come back to haunt us again and to tell us why it will not work when scope is too broad, operations too diverse, or systems too complex—the very characteristics of the global large-scale businesses and supply chains of the post-industrial era. To slay the problem of perspective, subtyping must start with products, resources, and processes—not with compositions. This is the hidden trap we must step around.

Paradoxically, reusing process knowledge *is* reusing knowledge of subprocesses and compositions of subprocesses that express a process, produce a product, and conform to performance criteria. It is knowledge of what works, what works well, and what does not, in terms of what and under what conditions—parameters that are often the goals of the process that *governs* the composition (see Box 7.4). Thus, the heart of the paradox is that extracting the common parts of a composition involves subtyping the composition and attempting to subtype compositions with even a few change parts can be bewildering—a trap we must step around.

The solution to this paradox lies in the fact that reuse of the composition is not based on subtyping compositions per se. Rather, it is based on either using the work product of the composition as a resource in a larger composition, or it is based on subtyping the work product itself—just as "colored cookie" was a subtype of generic cookies, and generic cookies were a subtype of *Baked Product*. The basis for adding processes was the requirement for creating the new attributes (or behaviors) of the subtype. The composition for producing a generic product may be reused on this basis, and new subprocesses added to create specific properties. When we do this, the generic product becomes an internal, possibly notional resource in the composition, just as a generic cookie was a notional resource in the process for making colored cookies; the new process becomes an inclusion polymorph of the old. The old process may then be reused as a supertype, just as *Chat-*

*Box 7.8. The information content of concurrency and sequencing constraints*

Each person may sign the check at different times, but we have not *constrained the concurrency* of the polymorphisms of "Sign Check" in Figure 7.24b. If it is a paper check, two persons cannot sign concurrently, and the two polymorphisms in Figure 7.24b will be mutually exclusive at a given *moment*, but mutually inclusive *over* a given time period. On the other hand, if it is a check that must be signed electronically, the two subprocesses in Figure 7.24b will not be barred from occurring at the same time. Our discussion assumes that the constraints on concurrency are not known. The check is just a paper or electronic check. We discuss concurrent check signatures under product engineering (see Box 7.9). Note also that we have not constrained the *sequence* in which the two checks must be signed. There is no procedure that insists that the CFO sign before the CEO or vice versa. If there were, the two polymorphisms would be sequenced—a daisy chain in a process map inside the aggregate. Naturally, if such a sequence *was* mandated, the subprocesses could not be concurrent, but the converse is not true—barring concurrency does *not* mandate a sequence. Sequencing a set of processes carries *more* information than a bar on concurrency does. Sequencing not only tells us that events cannot occur concurrently but also tells us which events must *follow* which. Therefore, *a succession relationship is a subtype of a bar on concurrency.*

*Collaborate* was reused in the Netmarket supply chain of Figure 7.18. Module 5 on our Web site has a case study on reusing and modifying process knowledge with the check payment example in Figure 7.24, in which both the CEO and the CFO's signatures are needed to pay a check. It shows how compositions of processes can emerge from the need to subtype a generic process based on its work product. The case study also shows how process design may be automated with reusable components of normalized knowledge.

## Changing the Succession of Processes

Even if no new subprocesses are added, and substates stay the same between temporal compositions, we can still change sequences of activities to produce new compositions that will produce the same end product. The only difference between the two compositions will be that state transitions will differ—Rules for state transitions and process roll backs emerge from what may succeed what. In the example on making colored cookies that we just discussed, the "*add color*" subprocess would be situated between "*Arrange Dough Glob on Cookie Sheet*" and "*Bake Dough*" in Figure 7.11b. Subsequently, our process engineers might discover that the taste and quality of our cookies will not be affected, but process costs will be trimmed if we use colored dough instead of coloring each dough glob individually before we bake it. We might then transfer "*Add Color*" to its new position, between *Make Cookie Dough* and *Arrange Dough Glob on Cookie Sheet* (in Figure 7.11b). The new composition will have the same parts as the old, but it will be a new configuration and both configurations will be mutable. Both configurations will be mutable because both configurations are subtypes of a composition in which *Add Color* is included in *Bake Cookie*. Therefore, conforming to Liskov's Substitution Principle, they are mutually mutable. Neither composition will change the meaning of *Bake Colored Cookie*. *Bake Colored Cookie* will have the same states as before, but rules for state transitions, process interruption, and rollback will change because the pattern of succession of events within the composition has changed. The composition normalizes these kinds of rules.[69]

Neither the meaning of *Bake Colored Cookie*, nor the meaning of its work product, *Colored Cookie*, has changed, but the activity cost of one composition is less than that of the other. Different temporal compositions may retain the purpose of the composite process and yet have different activity costs, cycle times, use different resources (usually subtypes of a more generic resource), and differ in other vital process parameters we have discussed previously. The composite process will retain its meaning, for its meaning is determined by its work product, not by its constraints or its parameters. The work product is the purpose and the reason for its very existence; if the work product does not change, neither does the process or its purpose. This is the heart of process reengineering.

(Each variant is just a different mutable subtype of a supertype in which only the purpose is known. Each variant is therefore automatically mutable with others; see Liskov's Substitution Principle.)

We could also change sequences of processes by making them parallel to successors. The process in Figure 7.6 may have been the result of reengineering an older version of the process in which *Take Order*, *Pick Items*, *Raise Invoice*, and *Ship Items with Invoice* were all serially strung together in a sequential daisy chain. The parallel implementation of the reengineered process reduced its cycle time without affecting its work product—its purpose and objective.

Rearranging subprocesses or their succession within a process is thus no different from adding subprocesses to a composition—*if we maintain the constancy of its work products*. We are merely creatively reconfiguring the subprocesses within. The succession relationship too is a process; it is a temporal relationship, albeit one that is starved of information (see Successions of Compositions).

## Alternative Resources: Alternative Processes

Reassignment of responsibility is arguably the most common form of process reengineering we will find. It happens when a manager assigns (or reassigns) roles of employees; it happens when organizations restructure and reassign roles and responsibilities of organizational units such as departments and profit centers; it happens when an organization outsources its processes and services, when supply chains are made or broken, and even when organizations merge or divest parts of their business.

People are a resource processes use. People fill roles, and roles impose responsibilities. People who fill these roles must discharge the responsibilities we discussed under Process Ownership. Thus, roles are resources; each role is a class of resource that is instantiated by individuals before a process occurs. Thus, role is a resource class, and the individual is a resource instance. A person may fill one or more roles, and in doing so, may have to merge the responsibilities of each role. Box 7.6 discussed the merger of roles and responsibilities. Roles may also require credentials and skills of different kinds of the individuals who fill them—credentials and skills needed to discharge the responsibilities the role demands. Just as the merger of responsibilities subsumed some roles into their supertypes (see Box 7.6), so can skills and credentials be subsumed into supertypes.

The "A" role for manufacturing operations on the shop floor of a factory might require that the person discharging the responsibility have an engineering degree; the engineering specialization and degree might be irrelevant, the person must be an engineer. The person could be a mechanical, civil, electrical, or electronics engineer, or any other. The engineer might have a bachelor's degree in engineering, a master's degree, a PhD, or something else, provided it is a recognized degree. This credential is a supertype of more specialized credentials, such as degrees in different engineering specializations (mechanical, civil, electrical, electronics, etc.), at different levels (bachelor, master, PhD, etc.). Liskov's substitution principle (and common sense!) tells us that each of these kinds of specialized credentials is mutable with the others in this role. The example demonstrates that in order to normalize process knowledge, the most generalized resource, that is, the resource that carries the least information, which is also, *the least specified or constrained resource the process can use*—can be specified as the requirement for the process. We will call it the Principle of Parsimony (see Appendix II).

The Principle of Parsimony will apply equally to any resource,[70] even resources that are not people—resources like materials, information, and the like. In Figure 7.11, if dough of any kind would do when we bake a cookie, asking that dough be a resource used for baking cookies is the right thing to do. On the other hand, if only cookie dough, a special kind of dough with special properties is needed, then only cookie dough the resource must be.

Let us assume this is the case; that baking a generic "*Baked Product*" requires a generic kind of dough, whereas baking a cookie needs special cookie dough. Then the process—the temporal before-and-after relationship between *Cookie Dough* and *Cookie* would be an inclusion polymorph, a subtype, derived from the similar generic *Bake* relationship between *Dough* and *Baked Product*. As we have seen under reusing compositions, when this happens, we can reuse the process map for baked products as a basis for the new process, and add information to this generic map to derive the process map for the more specialized process. Process knowledge and the wisdom that comes with experience can thus be reused to create new processes and meet new challenges that grow out of the old.

Subprocesses in process maps like these—maps that are polymorphic subtypes of more generic process maps—could use the same generic resources as corresponding subprocesses in their parents, or they may add information to resources in one of two ways: Subprocesses that are inherited from the parent process could add information to the parent subprocess by (1) subtyping its resources or (2) by including additional kinds of resources. A generic *Bake* process might use a generic resource—*Dough*, whereas *Bake Cookie,* its subtype might use a subtype of *Dough—Cooke Dough;* similarly, each check signing process in Figure 7.24b used a different kind of signature. On the other hand, subtypes of the planning process in Figure 7.21a added information by including new resources of different kinds in each of its different polymorphic manifestations (even as it retained the resources used by its parent). Of course, a subtype could also do both.

Naturally, different resources imply that the rules for transforming resources into products will also be different. Additional resources, or subtypes, of generic resources could impact guard conditions or even the elementary operations within the process that transform resources to products—operations as elementary as the Production Segments of standard S95, which we discussed under *Supply Chains*.

Inclusion polymorphs, subtypes of a more generic relationships between generic resources and products, could also impose more stringent constraints on order, cardinality, degree, and other properties of corresponding subprocesses than the parent relationship does, provided they violate no constraints set by the parent. We saw how subprocesses may even be added or resequenced in polymorphic relationships of this kind.

However, through all this, to normalize knowledge and retain flexibility, the composition, as well as the subprocesses within, should only specify the bare minimum of information required to produce the requisite work product. The key consideration is that subprocesses obtained by adding information to sparse parents will reuse the information in their more generic parents and add only the information needed to transform specialized resources into specialized products. Naturally, this must take into account the constraints imposed on the process and also the product by its governing processes (if any)—governing processes like those in Box 7.4. No constraint (like constraints on cycle time, activity cost, or others we have discussed) may be violated just because we neglected to include this information. These constraints could be inherited, if they were generic constraints normalized by the supertype, or added on, if they are specific to a subtype.

Process and product reengineering may also involve assessing the net value and opportunity costs of these constraints and sometimes even acting on the assessment by obliterating or altering constraints based on prior assumptions (and sometimes even presumptions). When processes change, so could resource requirements; even roles and requirements for skills and credentials might have to be creatively reengineered. This will be our next topic. The metamodel we are building does not constrict creativity; rather it creates room for it with its laws—these laws, after all, are the laws of reason; we could even call them laws of common sense.

## Processes That Gain or Lose Structure

Let us return to a process snapped in two for some reason. The reason may be a divestiture, an organizational restructuring, a disrupted supply chain or any other reason. From Box 7.6, we know that even if we neglect to repair the process, the ghost of the divested process, a supertype that carries its essence, will still lurk in the shadows. If we do not consciously repair divested processes, unstructured processes will take their place, or the process will cease—it will lose its essence and simply disappear.

Unstructured processes may keep the process going in some form because it is a supertype of the lost process and hence mutable with it (conforming to Liskov's Substitution Principle); from Box 7.7 we know that unstructured processes carry less information than structured processes but can preserve their essence (see Unstructured Collaboration). For instance, consider Figure 7.11b. If we divested the making of cookie dough but neglected to say how we would get the dough to make dough globs, someone (unspecified) would somehow (unspecified) beg, borrow, or steal dough to make dough globs each time we made cookies. The process for getting dough would become unstructured and ad-hoc with no articulated values for parameters like cycle time, activity cost, and the others we have discussed. Each would only be instantiated at the moment an instance of the ad-hoc process actually occurs and could swing wildly and unpredictably without constraint over any conceivable range. This is the penalty an unstructured process imposes; it may not necessarily be more nimble than a structured process but will certainly be less constrained and hence risky (unreliable) and less stable. Poor quality may be the penalty we must pay for the lack of governance.

Poor quality might mean product or process quality, the process in terms of the properties that relate resources to work products, including the temporal properties of processes we have discussed, and the product, in terms of its attributes and behavior.[71] The term *quality* subsumes both—it is an aggregation (not a subtype!) of the information conveyed by both the process and the product. Both have to be interpreted in the context of the domains of information quality described in Chapter IV. However, quality need not always be the price of agility. Unstructured processes may or may not be nimble, but they can be *made* more nimble as we will now see.

Parameters for structured processes are established by governing processes—processes of higher governance order of the kind described in Box 7.4 and elsewhere. In the century we have just left behind governing processes were more like the processes in Box 7.4; parameters were static and preordained, prescribed by slow moving governance, for a broad class of processes, and reviewed infrequently (if that). Governing processes in the century that we are entering must be different. They must be different because businesses, nay, entire supply chains must be agile *and* reliable in order to survive, respond, and win a prize as fickle as it is precious—the customer for whom they exist. It is the fickle but fractious customer they must serve in order to prosper and grow.

In the previous century, parameters of processes—their desired values and prescribed subprocesses—were usually set in stone and preordained for every instance of a class of processes. In the century future, governing processes may have to set these values from instance to instance,[72] even as the supply chains beyond the enterprise spin on at blinding speed, driving the processes within—processes of the kind in Figure 7.20—at an equal pitch so that they can be in harmony. This is not an ad-hoc process. It is a governed process and can even be a well-governed process, but it is an unforgiving process. It is also a process that must be governed at blinding speeds. Some business managers compare it to changing the tires of a car even as it belts down the highway at 60 miles an hour.

(Even if governing the parameters of, and creating subprocesses for, every instance of a process is an extreme situation, parameters and subprocesses may have to be reviewed much more frequently, much faster, and at more granular levels than before. Automation leveraged by qualified, motivated, and creative people will help.)

What it implies for business is convergence of governance and execution—a sea change from the work ethic of the industrial age where workers repetitively and, often mindlessly, followed instructions with little thought and no creativity. That approach, applied to the needs of the new century will also divorce plan from action and governance from process. Obliterating governance is not the solution. It will not always speed processes; it can even slow them down, and it will always increase risk. The result can be inconsistent or invalid and ad-hoc processes—perhaps even a slower, blundering process. The solution is to change the style and substance of governance.

The solution is to drive responsibility and authority down to the lower levels of the chain of command; to make them converge at the point where a process meets the person who executes it. Each person with W level responsibility (see Process Ownership in this chapter) should also be responsible for at least first order governance of agile processes. In extreme cases, the governance process might even allocate individual responsibilities each time an instance of a process occurs. (For example, the most qualified person available in a network of workers may, by mutual consent, volunteer to take responsibility for doing the task.[73])

The workers of the knowledge-age must be qualified, creative, self-driven, and able to exercise relatively sophisticated judgment compared to those of the age just past. The focus of management must shift commensurately upwards—towards processes that govern the governance processes—upwards on the scale of governance order. The age of knowledge has arrived, and with it the age of the trained knowledge worker *and* the age of the trained knowledge manager.[74]

## Product Reengineering and the Mutability of Compositions

So far, our focus has been on a process and its given purpose. It has been *on doing things right.* Product engineering is more strategic. The focus must be *on doing the right things* for the right reasons and matching the right purpose to the needs of the market and all the other constituencies the business must serve. When we reengineer products, the purpose of the process that makes it shifts—*the purpose is not inviolate any more.*

The purpose of the process, its work product, has remained a constant unshakeable anchor for a process even as it flexed, changed, and morphed to wrap itself around constraints and objectives dictated by governance. Now that anchor will

*Figure 7.25. The community of stakeholders*

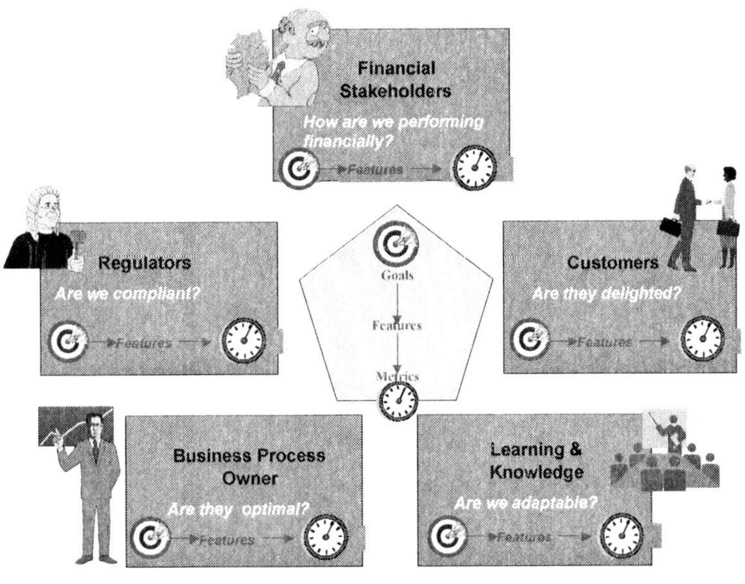

have to move. Product reengineering can even obliterate it. It can shake the process to its very foundations. The purpose of the process is no longer inviolate; it is violated. The purpose shifts usually in response to shifting needs. Shift it may, but we cannot let the purpose drift, for that would cast the process adrift. When it lifts anchor, a process can move purposefully only if it knows what others need. The process, bereft of its anchor, will need a guiding star.

The work product is this guiding star. It must be; even when it is not an immutable anchor, it is the work product that connects the process to the needs of the world beyond: The process will chart a course only when its work product matches the requirements of the world beyond its boundaries, either as a resource for another process or as a solution that satisfies customers—partners in a supply chain—or even the end user at the very end of the chain. Figure 7.25 describes the different kinds of stakeholders—communities of interest—that work products must satisfy. They can be communities with complex stakes in the business.

The features in Figure 7.25 are qualities of the product or process that each community may be interested in and may assess formally or informally, quantitatively or qualitatively, methodically or intuitively; even impressions might count. These "features" are features in the broadest sense. They are attributes, relationships, costraints, and behaviors at class or instance levels that impact each community in Figure 7.25.[75]

(A single feature of a product might be of interest to a single community in Figure 7.25 or to several. For instance, a guaranty of performance might be of interest to every community in Figure 7.25.)

The community of financial stakeholders may be internal stakeholders like accountants and profit center managers, or external, like the financial analysts and stock traders who fuel financial markets. Similarly, regulators may be internal, like internal auditors, or external, like external auditors, government regulators, public interest groups, and others. Customers may be partners in a supply chain or the end user who is the target of the chain. The community of learning and knowledge may be trainers, researchers, teachers, and other specialized communities interested in the information content of the product and its potential for reuse and absorption. Process owners are those interested in the product meeting its specification in order to match a mandate; a mandate dictated by either a governing process or a process downstream that will use the product as a resource. Perhaps both the process that produces the product and the processes that use it belong to a larger composition—a process that is being reengineered for the kinds of reasons we have discussed before.

The work product is a bundle of features, sometimes tied together by complex rules of inclusion

*Figure 7.26. The structure of a product or resource*

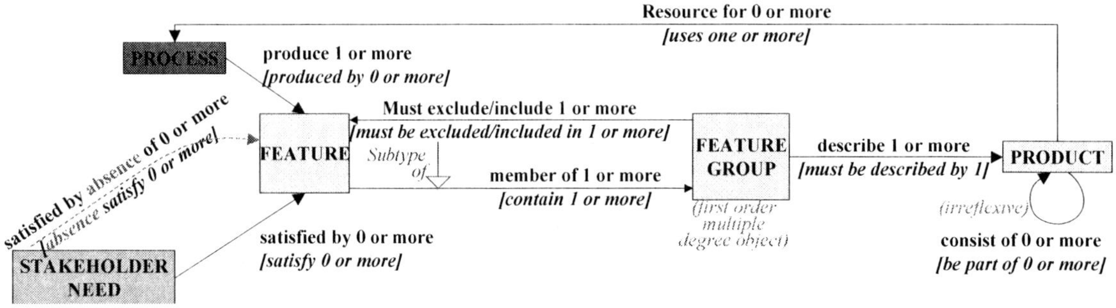

or exclusion. For instance, attributes like product color, footprint, shape, warranties, guarantees, insurance, service options, financing options and others will all be features of products. Sometimes inclusion of one feature might automatically imply inclusion of others. For instance, coverage against theft may automatically include coverage against fire when cars are insured. Features may be bundled into feature groups that describe a product, as illustrated in Figure 7.26.[76]

Figure 7.26 is the metamodel at the root of all product engineering. It is the summarized metamodel of Object, and hence of all products and resources. Note how mandatory inclusion or exclusion of features in a group restricts membership of the group. It tells us what features may or may not be bundled together in the product. A restricted group has fewer degrees of freedom than an unrestricted group. Therefore, a group that restricts membership is a subtype of a group that does not. The inclusion or exclusion constraint, the relationship between *Feature* and *Feature Group* in Figure 7.26, adds this information to the membership relationship in that figure. Therefore, based on the principle of subtyping by adding information, the inclusion/exclusion relationship is a subtype of the membership relationship between *Feature* and *Feature Group*. Indeed, on this basis, the *Feature Group* itself is a subtype of *Feature* and therefore a feature with an identity of its own.

Note also that some stakeholder needs may be insatiable or unsatiated—there may be no features that address them. Conversely, a feature may have little value; it may satisfy no stakeholder need. It will then be a candidate for reengineering or a target of obliteration. The many-to-many relationship between *Feature* and *Stakeholder Need* also implies that many features may address a single need, and some features may therefore be redundant. Those too could be targets of product reengineering.

Sometimes, a feature may be of worse than marginal value. It might actually *reduce* the utility of the product for the constituencies it serves; its *absence* will then add value to the product. Consider the check in Figure 7.24. It needed two signatures: the CEO's signature and the CFO's signature. If it was a paper check, both the CEO and the CFO could not sign the check simultaneously. That is information. Constraints add to the information content of the check and may therefore be considered its features.[77] However, those features are inconveniences. The business community had to accept these constraints because there were no alternatives until information technology made electronic money transfers and electronic signatures possible. Both individuals may sign an electronic check simultaneously or separately; it does not have to be physically conveyed from one desk to another. The absence of these constraints of the paper check—features with information payload—actually increases the utility of an electronic check; it becomes more valuable to the community than the paper check was. Thus, losing features—information—can sometimes add value to the product.

The relationship in Figure 7.26, represented by the broken-lined arrow between *Stakeholder Need* and *Feature* articulates this negative synergy between features and stakeholders. That relationship, a negative articulation, will be a subtype of the other relationship, the positive articulation between *Stakeholder Need* and *Feature*, only when it is a constraint. Otherwise it will be an equal and independent relationship (see Box 7.9).

The process in Figure 7.26 is also worth noting. It is a business or engineering process that is not necessarily restricted to the production of a single feature; it may produce many. Conversely, there may be different processes that can all produce the same feature; we saw examples of this earlier—how different processes may produce the same product. This is why the relationship between a *Feature* and *Process* is many-to-many in the figure. It tells us that there may be many different ways of producing the same feature—an issue we have discussed at some length under process reengineering. The cardinality of that relationship also tells us that a process need not always produce a feature; for instance, the concurrency constraint on signing the paper check was not produced by a process.

(Could we consider the concurrency constraint a byproduct of the engineering process that printed the check? Why or why not?)

Each such process is also a subprocess in a composition that makes the product. "Color" was a feature of "cookie" (in the recent example of colored cookies), and "add color" was the subprocess that produced it. This is similar to the relationship between product segment and production segment in the S95 standard (under supply chains), except

*Box 7.9. Product engineering, features, added value and information content*

A feature may add value to the product and it might also detract from it, but a feature will always add information. A product with more features is loaded with more information than one with less; in terms of the pattern that represents the product in information space (state space), its degrees of freedom are fewer. A feature may be desirable or undesirable from the perspective of the stakeholders in Figure 7.25. When it is undesirable, the *absence* of the feature will address their needs. The absence of a feature is as much an assertion as its presence. It conveys information about the product and is different from being ambiguous (not knowing) about it. A product with a feature is as much a subtype of a product in which the presence of the feature is indeterminate (unknown) as a product without it is—provided that the feature we have removed is not a constraint. When a feature is a constraint, removing the constraint removes information. A constraint restricts the degrees of freedom of the pattern of information that represents the constrained object. A constraint is information, and it adds information. Therefore, a constrained object is a subtype of a similar unconstrained object.

For instance, a paper check has a feature in common with all physical objects; it can only be at one physical location at a time. It is a constraint. On the other hand, an electronic check is not constrained thus. Therefore, it conveys less information (it lacks information on its precise location in space and, more importantly, locations it is *excluded* from) and is consequently less restrictive—it has more degrees of freedom (see Chapter IV). Product reengineering often involves *removing* features like this—features and constraints that are undesirable or otherwise reduce the value of a product. The unconstrained product has less information than the constrained product and fewer features but more value.

The following metamodel illustrates the constraints a paper check adds to the process in Figure 7.24. It is these constraints that an electronic check targets with smart product and process reengineering.

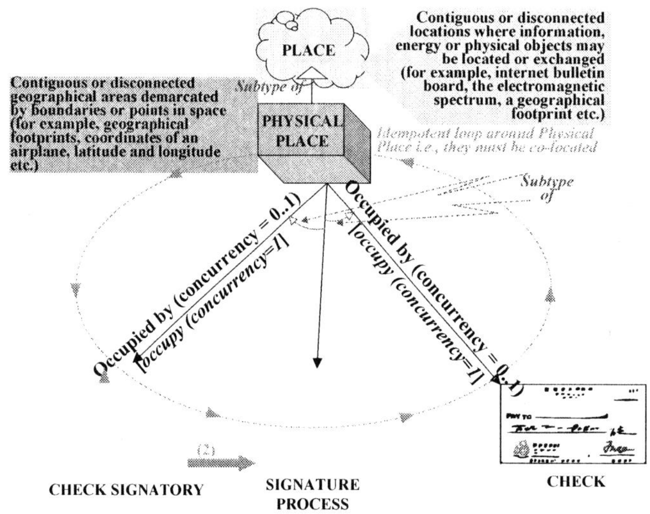


*Figure A. Multiple inheritance of the same relationship type ties the signatory of a check, the check, and the check signing process to the same physical space*

*continued on following page*

*Box 7.9. continued*

Figure A tells us that a check must be signed where the signatory is located, and only one signatory may sign at a time because both signatories cannot be at the same place at the same time—a place of signature can hold only one signatory and check at a time. The *Occupied by* relationship in Figure A is a subtype of the *Contain* relationship we have discussed in this book. The same kind of relationship relates each instance of check signatory, the check itself, and the signature process to *Physical Place* in Figure A.

We hardly need to elaborate on the fact that the signature has to happen where both the check and its signatory are placed. It is perhaps less obvious that this bit of common sense makes the relationship between *Physical Place* and the signature process a subtype of both the relationship between *Physical Place* and *Signatory* and the relationship between the *Physical Place* and the check. The relationship between *Physical Place and the process* is a derived relationship. It is derived from both parents, to which it adds information about the occurrence of the process at that place. We can see that the relationship between *Physical Place and the process* is a subtype of its twin parents because it is contingent on both parents, but not vice versa. The parent relationships, *Physical Place to Signatory* and the *Physical Place to Check*, stand independently; a signatory must occupy *some* place and so must the check. However, the check can only be signed where both these locations coincide. (See the discussion on the subsetting constraint in Figure 5.5c—the subtype cannot occur unless the supertypes do, but the supertype may occur without the supertype.[78])

All three are also polymorphisms of *Occupied by*, and in Figure A, the relationship in the middle is also a polymorphic subtype of the relationships on either side. It is also idempotent with respect to place: if we followed the relationship around the loop from an instance of physical place occupied by the signatory, the signature process and the check, we would end at the same instance of physical place we started from. We must because all three objects—the signatory, the process, and the check—must be collocated. The cardinality constraints imposed on the quaternary relationship of Figure B are just a different format for expressing exactly the same rules as Figure A. Figure B shows the cardinality constraint that makes the relationship in Figure A idempotent with respect to *Physical Place*. The format in Figure B is useful for showing complex cardinality constraints—also components of knowledge—that occur in high order relationships.

In Chapter V, we saw how constraints on degree, cardinality and order are at the root of the behavior of relationships and their interactions. These constraints on occurrence can manifest themselves in uncountable variations and interactions as properties of mutual inclusion, mutual exclusion, subsetting, reflexivity, idempotency, and even more complex constraints on occurrence. The cardinalities in Figure A show that a signatory, a process, a check, or any combination of these objects may optionally occupy a place, but the inverse is mandatory—each object, singly or in combination, must occupy a place (obviously!). Figure B elaborates on the cardinality of this inverse:

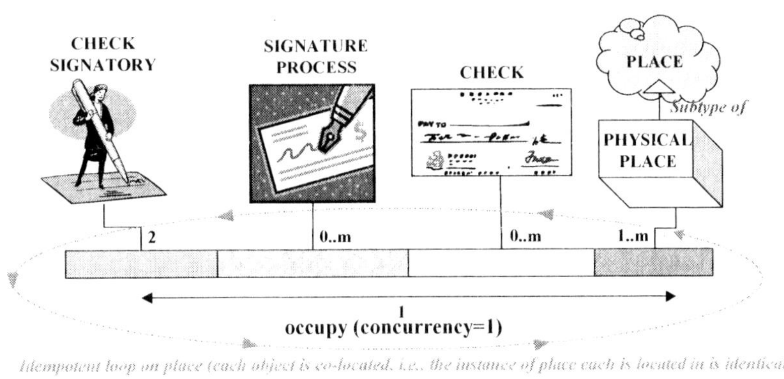


*Figure B. Idempotency can be interpreted as a cardinality constraint*

Figure B tells us that there are exactly two signatories to a check, that there may be no checks or several, and that there are several places to hold them. Figure B also tells us that a check may only be signed where the signatory is (naturally!)—that is, the signatory, the signature process, and the check must occupy the same physical place at the same time. Moreover, this combination of signatory, the signature process, and an individual check at a given time and place is unique. It distinguishes one signature process from another. Idempotency is established by this limit on the cardinality of the signatory-process-check-place tuple. (The cardinality of *Occupied by* relationship (not shown in Figure B) for this

*continued on following page*

*Box 7.9. continued*

combination ranges from 0 to 1 and provides for the contingency that there may be quiescent periods when check signing does not occur.)

However, unlike Figure A, Figure B by itself does not tell us that a person may occupy a different place than a check does (it does not bar it either). To articulate these rules, we would require distinct Signatory–Physical Place and Check–Physical Place relationships—separate relationships, 2-tuples not shown in Figure B, with (binary) cardinality constraints that would tell us that at a given time a check or person may only occupy a single place. The three relationships would each normalize three different irreducible facts. Figure B shows only fact 3 below:

- A check must always have a physical location.
- A signatory must always have a physical location (not necessarily the location of the check).
- The location of the signatory and check must be identical when the check is signed (Figure B).

The fourth irreducible fact, also not shown in Figure B, is the inverse relationship between the signatory and physical space—that an instance of physical space cannot hold more than one signatory at a time. It is a cardinality constraint imposed by this inverse, an assertion that articulates an independent irreducible fact. It forces the two polymorphisms of the signature process in Figure 7.24b to become nonconcurrent. They cannot occur at the same *time*, even if they are mutually inclusive.

Our reengineering focus will be Rule 1—a feature of the check. We will change it so that the check *can* be in several places simultaneously. Then each signatory can have simultaneous access to the check, and the signature process may then occur concurrently. To understand how we can do this, we must understand the subtyping relationship between *Place* and *Physical Place*.

*Place*, in Figures A and B, is a more generic concept than the three-dimensional physical space we live in (or its subspaces like a two dimensional geographical area); it is any venue in which information or physical objects may be exchanged or stored. It subsumes both physical and virtual space; a place could be a virtual location like a Web site or the electromagnetic spectrum. Indeed, the FCC (Federal Communications Commission, a government organization for regulating telecommunication businesses in the U.S.) auctions parts of the spectrum to telecommunications companies like others might auction real estate. Unlike an object in physical space, an item of information in the virtual world may not be tied to a single place at any moment in time; the same information may concurrently exist at different locations—Web sites, frequencies, electronic bulletin boards, and the like. Information about the check can be available to both the CEO and CFO wherever and whenever they access the Web (or virtual space in general). This is the key to reengineering not only the check but also several other kinds of products which, stripped of their tangible form and format, are pure information.

*Physical Place*, unlike its more generic parent, is a special kind of *Place*. It is a constrained place occupied by physical objects. *Physical Place* is a subtype of *Place* in which an object may occupy only one place at a time (different instances of *Physical Place* also have different capacities for "containing" different objects—see the discussion on an object's capacity for relationships).[79] The paper check is stuck in this paradigm. That is why all the signatories who must sign it cannot concurrently sign it. To release this constraint on *Check*, we must recognize that it is not a physical object; it is information, and it can reside in a virtual place. The moment we switch the relationship between *Check* and *Physical Place* in Figure A from *Physical Place* to *Place*, it loses its concurrency constraint; it is a different product, less constrained, with fewer features.

Figure C breaks physical *Place* into two subtypes to show the two places the check must be signed—one place for each polymorphism in Figure 7.24b. Figure C also shows each polymorphism of Sign Check, as well as each signatory, separately. The cardinality ratio of each signatory with respect to each signature process is shown in parenthesis between the signatory and the process in Figure C. It is the same as in Figure 7.24b because it is the same process:

*continued on following page*

*Box 7.9. continued*

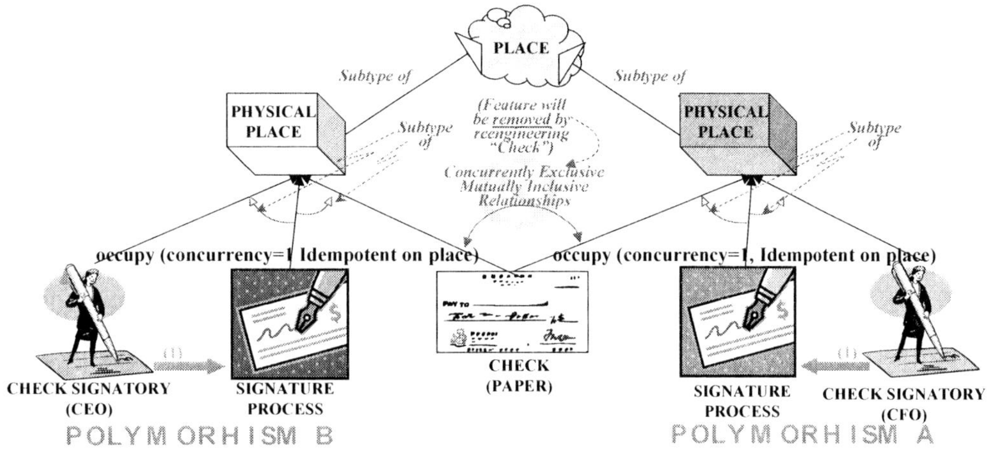


*Figure C. Polymorphisms of "Sign Check"*

In Figure C, the fact that the check cannot be in two places at the same time is shown by the concurrency constraint on the mutually inclusive relationship between the check and the two places where it is signed. It is this feature of check we will remove as we release it from its *Physical Place* into a more generic *Place*. Figure D shows how this happens as we relocate the check from *Physical Place* to *Place*. We do this by switching the "occupy" relationship between the *Check* and *Physical Place* from *Physical Place* to *Place*. The check is now pure information stripped of its physical medium—its paper form. Figure D illustrates the effect of this switch.

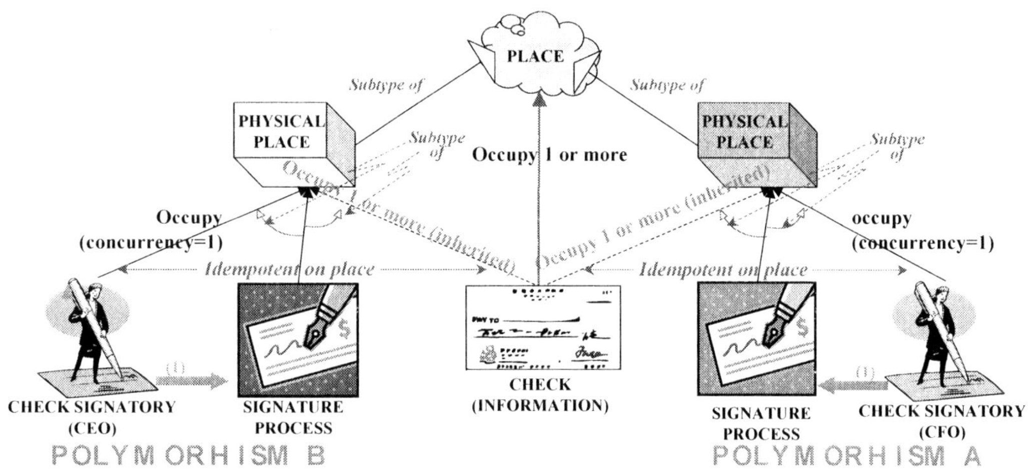


*Figure D. The reengineered check and its signature process minus undesirable features*

Before the check was reengineered, it was a paper check. The two polymorphisms of Sign Check in Figure 7.24b were constrained. They could not occur concurrently. After reengineering the check, the two different polymorphisms of the check signing processes in Figure 7.24b may occur concurrently. The process will be faster, with less latency. It will adapt the moment it loses this burdensome feature, a constraint on concurrency. The process will thus become more valuable to those with stakes in the business.

*continued on following page*

*Box 7.9. continued*

This example demonstrated not only how a product may be reengineered but also focused on a frequent source of reengineering opportunities and a common source of business rules—subtypes of the "contains" relationship that relates objects of different kinds to *Place* and *Physical Place* and how *Physical Place* can inherit these relationships from *Place*, imposing concurrency constraints of its own. A companion book by the same authors, *Agile Systems with Reusable Patterns of Business Knowledge: A Component Based Approach*, elaborates on patterns in the Universal Perspective, which describe several other universal and frequently reused patterns like this. These generic patterns are the basis for product and process reengineering. They are used frequently in different and disguised forms, like the electronic check was. The patterns stay disguised, hidden behind their polymorphic masks. Designers and analysts focus on the mask (like *Check* was a mask—a manifestation of *Information*); knowledge remains unshared and imprisoned in specific reengineering applications—we keep re-inventing the wheel every time we make a change. The Universal Perspective unifies shared knowledge and unmasks its fragmented multitudes to show them up for what they truly are: polymorphic hordes with a single face and a single form. In *Agile Systems with Reusable Patterns of Business Knowledge: A Component Based Approach*, we will see them crystallize out of their uncountable disguises. We can then reuse the wheel, unmasked.

Sometimes features may be even more complex than we have shown in this example. Some features may add value for some stakeholders but detract from the product for others. The needs of the communities shown in Figure 7.25 sometimes diverge to the point of conflict. Then a feature that is useful for some may become worse than worthless for others. Reducing the order-to-payment cycle time might be a desirable feature for a seller but undesirable for a cash strapped buyer. Business strategy often involves formulating the optimal balance of features for the community of stakeholders. However, that discussion is beyond the scope of this book. It belongs to the realm of game theory ([313] in Appendix III and Chapter 11 of Gillett, 1976, has additional reading on game theory. Readers who are interested in the business aspects of product and process reengineering may read [295] of Appendix III—Hammer & Champy, 1993).

For us here, it will suffice to understand that the concept of feature and the structure in Figure 7.26 provide the hooks that connect product planning and business strategy, disciplines at the heart of any well run business, to business process engineering. Processes produce features, and features require processes; the line between process and product reengineering is indeed very thin.

that the structure in Figure 7.26 is not confined to products and processes of the manufacturing industry alone. The products in Figure 7.26 could be individual services like an insurance policy, individual physical items like a car, packages of several services or physical items bound into a product, or even services packaged with tangible physical items like a car with a warranty and 24x7 customer service (that is, customer service at any time on any day), information on upgrades or new features, membership of chat rooms or communities of interest, and so on.

Note also that it is the inclusion of temporal information in the composition of relationships that loops back from *Product* to *Feature* that turns it into a process—the process on the top left hand corner of the figure. Every nontemporal relationship is a potential process if we add temporal information to it. It can instantiate how, and with what resources, the product at the other end of the relationship may be produced.

For now, it will suffice to understand that subtyping and reuse of components cannot happen in a vacuum. That, as we saw, could easily trap us into a meaningless and confusing mechanical exercise that interminably juggles complex combinations with no clarity or precision about what may be reused where. Rather, inclusion and exclusion of features based on stakeholder's needs, will help us identify and reuse compositions of processes—processes that produce a product via its features. Subtypes of products and polymorphic variants of processes may thus be driven by stakeholder need channeled through features—the features that make a product and lend it an identity. Random walks through fields of abstract and meaningless permutations of subprocesses and their mutual interdependency can neither be productive nor meaningful. It is unlikely to result in creative reuse of process knowledge across large scopes in complex situations.

Indeed, the line between product and process engineering is very thin. Reengineering a process may alter substates of the process and features of intermediate products within the process—an aggregation of subprocesses. Reengineering the features—states—of the end product is product reengineering—a subtype and a special case of process reengineering, in which the features of the *last* product in a temporal composition are reengineered. We may cross the thin red line in either direction as we strive to please the stakeholders in Figure 7.25. In this, we strive to excel. It is a search for excellence driven by global competition and striving that will never end.

## THE METAMODEL OF RELATIONSHIP

Generalizing relationships is the key to normalizing interactions between objects. Relationships are objects that convey information about interactions, strong and weak, quantitative and qualitative, information rich and information sparse. The inchoate information in the gulf between objects crystallizes around a Web of relationships.

A relationship is an object. It is also a pattern of objects, sometimes sequenced, sometimes not.[80] Sequenced, it can be a Cartesian product; unsequenced, it is still a pattern of object instances (see Box 5.2). It could also be a pattern of the same object instance, for example, reflexive or idempotent relationships, but it must always be always a pattern with a meaning.

This meaning might convey minimal information: that some unknown relationship "involves" or associates object instances in some unspecified way. As such, "*involves*" is the basic thread, a bare relationship that is the foundation and parent of every relationship in this book. If it had a lighter information payload, it could not be a relationship. "*Involves*" only tells us that the objects it connects are associated. "*Involves*" is the essence of the pattern called "*relationship.*"

Meanings of relationships crystallize and grow around this central thread shared by every relationship. If this thread breaks, relationships vanish into *null space*—a place of nonbeing for things that are not and the things that cannot be. It is this place, in the bottomless gulf between objects in information space, that holds the meaning of nonexistence—nullity—and within it lies an even darker region—the nullity of the impossible, the home of things that *cannot* be. That which cannot be is a subtype of that which is not. It adds information to nullity—the meaning of impossibility. Null space denies existence, and its darker regions deny even the possibility of existence.

Processes that cut relationships or delete objects send them into null space. Constraints that clash send objects and relationships even deeper—into the region of impossibility. Effects that create bring objects into existence from the darkness of null space, a change of state. Effects that delete constraints can make even the impossible possible. They can pull objects out, even from the darkness of impossibility at the heart of null space into the band of possibility. Other effects may then make the possible exist.

Any relationship that denies existence describes the impossible relationship in the depths of null space. A relationship that asserts that a person cannot contain another person bars containment and, in so doing, sends that which it denies into null space. "*Involve*" is the shared meaning that makes a relationship possible. "*Involve*" could declare the existence of an association, and "*Involve*" could also bar it. In either case, "*Involve*" conveys information about an association. It is a thread shared by all relationships.

The primary channel for propagating shared meaning is the subtyping relationship. The metamodel in Figure 7.29 shows how the common behaviors of relationships filter down to the bottom of the hierarchy there. A subtype adds information. The added information manifests meaning by making a general meaning more specific, like "*composed of*" makes "*aggregation of*" more specific by describing the structure of the composition. Subtyping also propagates constraints. Subtypes inherit the lawful state space of their supertypes and may restrict it even more by adding constraints—also information—of its own. A subtype may add features that increase the dimensionality of the state space it inherits. The inherited state space will then become a subspace within the state space of the subtype, but even as it adds information, the subtype must stay within the constraints it has inherited. A subtype cannot violate the constraints and lawful state space it has inherited from its parent but may add information to the parent relationship in the following ways:

- Like any other object, a relationship will have its dual in null space—a rule that says that the relationship (or object) in question does not (or cannot) exist. These will all be

*Box 7.10. List vs. relationship vs. set*

A set has no information on replication of its members. Multiple instances of the same member are considered to be one. Different members are considered different instances, even if they are identical in every way because the individual instance identifiers of each member are then considered a symbol of all things (states) that are different between the members and therefore distinguish one member from another nominally identical member of the set. A list, on the other hand, has information on the multiplicity of membership of instances of the same object instance.

A relationship is like a list of object instances, but there are differences: A list may be empty, without any items, whereas an instance of a relationship must list *at least* one object instance (perhaps more). If the relationship has only one object instance, it is idempotent because it relates the instance to itself. Therefore, it must list the instance at least twice. A relationship is a more constrained pattern than a list, with less freedom and more information: a subtype. Figure 7.29 makes this clear.

An empty list is a zero degree, zero order aggregate. A list with only one occurrence of a single object instance is a first order, first degree aggregate. A relationship *must* be *at least* a second-degree list of at least first order. Its order and degree could be higher, and as we have seen, enumeration constraints of various kinds may capture interactions between members of this list.

Unlike an aggregate object or list, an instance of a relationship cannot occur unless the objects (instances) it relates also occur. Thus, *Aggregate Object* and *List* have more degrees of freedom than *Relationship*.[82]

A list is a kind of aggregate object. An aggregate object may contain nothing: It may be the empty set, and so may a list be empty. A list or aggregate object (instance) thus has an existence independent of the actual occurrence of instances of the aggregation relationship; their potential to occur suffices. However, the converse is not true. An aggregation relationship cannot exist without its aggregate object—the object that will hold the constituents aggregated. The aggregation relationship fuses a constituent with an aggregate object. The aggregate object only signifies this potential.[83] The aggregation relationship adds the meaning of "fusion" to the sparse "involve" relationship. Simultaneously it mandates the occurrence of an aggregate object, but the aggregate object does not mandate the occurrence of the aggregation relationship—it may be an empty set. Thus, the aggregation relationship is richer in information than either *involve* or the aggregate object. It is a subtype of *involve*, thrice removed from the aggregate object of Figure 7.29.

A list could also be an arbitrary, meaningless pattern by decree. (Indeed, this is why it may even be an empty list—it may even exist by decree, without any constituents.) A relationship, on the other hand, has a tad more information. It must *always* have a meaning. At a minimum, this meaning must be that it is a list of interacting objects that *involve* each other. Even if we do not know precisely what this interaction is, we know that there *is* an interaction—a set of rules that binds the members of the list to each other in some unknown way. This makes *Relationship* a subtype of the more generic concept called *List*.[84]

subtypes of the generic relationship that bans (or nullifies) its target object. In Figure 7.29 it is labeled "Bar." Some of its more common synonyms are also shown in parenthesis next to this label.

- A relationship is similar to an aggregate object. It is a kind of *List*. An instance of a relationship is a collection of object instances like an instance of an aggregate object is. The same object instance may occur several times in an aggregate object, as it may in a list, and in a reflexive relationship. However, the *aggregate* (not the aggregation relationship) conveys less information than a relationship: Even when several object instances are interrelated with a bare higher order or higher degree "*involve*" relationship, we know that they are inextricably joined into one irreducible fact. An aggregate is more nebulous. We have no information on the junctions between individual objects—we only know that they have a common envelope—the aggregate. The aggregate may be a collection of objects with no relationships between them, or even if some are related, the relationships may not be fused into one irreducible fact like those in Figures 5.3 or 5.4.[81] An aggregate may even be empty. A relationship, on the other hand, must have at least one object, and if it has only one, the relationship must repeat that object instance at least one more time (see Box 7.10). It is a more constrained pattern of information than the aggregate. Constraints add information. Thus, the aggregate is on the other side of the thin line of information that makes a relationship a relationship. It is a pattern like a relationship but with a tad less information than "*involve*." Therefore "*involve*" is a subtype of an aggregate object even though, paradoxically, "*aggregation of*" is a subtype of "*involve*" (see Box 7.10).
- The aggregation *relationship* is a special subtype of the "involve" relationship. Aggregation implies the existence of a collection. The collection is the aggregate. Objects are members of the aggregate. The aggregate is related to each member with a "*consists of*" relationship ("*Aggregation of*" is a synonym. The inverse is "*aggregated by*," or its synonym, "*part of*").[85] *Consists of* conveys only a little more information than *involve*, but unlike *involve*, it does not negate existence; it always asserts it. Aggregation tells us that the objects involved are members of a group. Little else is known. We know neither rhyme, reason, nor basis unless we elaborate on this basic "*consists of*" relationship, which will add meaning and turn it into a subtype or polymorphism of "*consists of*." In this threadbare form, aggregation is a pattern by decree.
- Set membership is also a subtype of the aggregation relationship. An aggregate could be a *list* or a *set*. The same object instance may occur several times in an aggregate when it is a list, but when the aggregate is a set, multiple occurrences of the same object are not

*Box 7.11. Subtypes, sets, lists, and polymorphisms*

A list has more information than a set; it distinguishes between occurrences of identical parts, whereas a set does not. Based on the principle of subtyping by adding information, it follows that a list is a subtype of a set, and therefore *listed in* is a polymorphism of *set of* Figure 7.27a makes this distinction.

Figure 7.27a shows that subtypes are polymorphisms of subsets—they are proper subsets (proper subsets: see Box 19 on our Web site) with constraints attached to features of the parent object. This includes the case where the value of a feature of the parent might be "unknown" to the extent that it is not even known if the feature may exist, whereas its value in the subtype is "does not exist" (i.e., *constrained* to be null) or *constrained to exist (with a non-null value)*. Therefore, Figure 7.27a shows subtypes and lists as different polymorphisms of set membership and hence also of the Aggregate Object.

*Figure 7.27. The subtyping relationship is its own creation.*

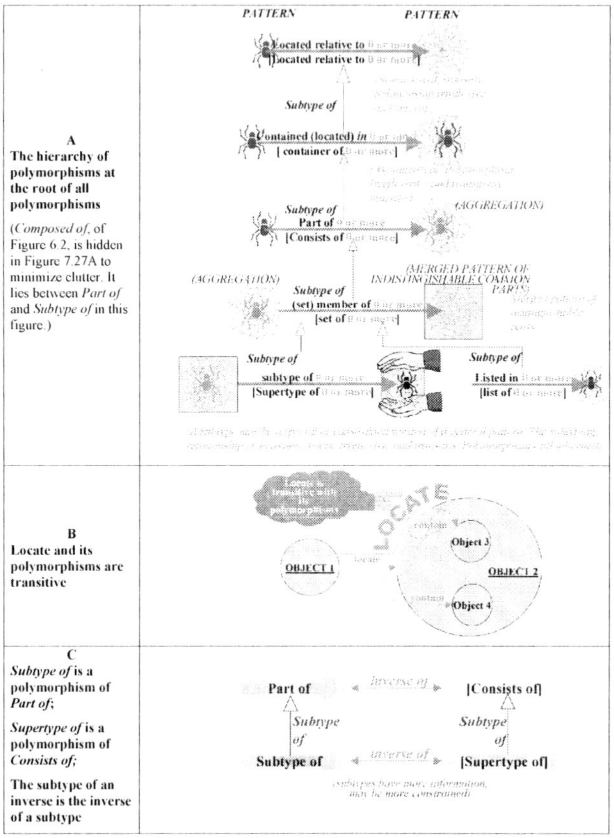


distinguished from each other. Each member of a set is considered only once in the set. Therefore, a list conveys more information than a set does—it distinguishes between separate occurrences of the same object. An aggregate could be either. Thus, based on the principle of subtyping by adding information, both "*list of*" and set membership are subtypes of "*consists of*," and *Set* and *List* are subtypes of the generic aggregate object. This kind of subtyping is called *polymorphism*. It is a form of subtyping wherein new meanings are obtained by constraining other meanings to become more specific. *Polymorphisms are meanings obtained by adding information to other meanings.*

- A relationship and its inverse are one integral whole, representing the same pattern in information space. *Thus, the inverse of a polymorphism of a relationship is also a polymorphism (subtype) of the inverse of the parent relationship.* (See Figure 7.27c: we may substitute any relationship for "*Part of*" and any polymorphism of that relationship for "*subtype of*," and the relationships between inverses and subtypes in Figure 7.27c will still hold true.)
- We have just seen that set membership is a polymorphism of "*Consists of*." The implications are profound. It implies that "*Subtype of*," the fount of inheritance and reusability, is a polymorphism of "*Part of*." Consequently,

"*Supertype of*," the inverse of the subtyping relationship is a polymorphism of "*Consist of*," the inverse of "*Part of*."[86] Figure 7.27c makes this clear. Figure 7.27a summarizes our earlier discussion on location, containment and aggregation, and adds to it the fact that subtyping is a polymorphism of "part of."

The impact of these polymorphisms is so profound and universal that we barely stop to think about it. We take these polymorphisms of "*locate*" for granted; we consider them common sense, but we must tell automation that. Only then can we instill automated common sense in our processes. The impact of the hierarchy in Figure 7.27a will be our next topic of discussion.

- The locate relationship is the root of the concept of Place—physical or virtual.[87] Location is relative: an object can only be located by another object, and an idempotent location conveys no information. It starts as soon as we have enough information to distinguish a pair of objects (see Chapter IV) and becomes firmly established with the concept of neighborhood in the ontology of Figure 4.1. The ontology in Chapter IV also tells us that when we have enough information, location can become absolute (in domains with nil values). However, the concept of relative location is still valid in spaces that support absolute location. These features are inherited down the ontological hierarchy in Figure 4.1).

*Locate* flows from the concept of the Proximity Metric described in Chapter IV. As we add information to the domain that describes *Locate*, it becomes progressively more quantitative (see the discussion in Chapter IV). Polymorphisms of Locate also inherit this behavior. For example, *Contained in* can be a yes/no relationship, or it could describe the exact quantitative position of the contained object relative to the envelope that defines the containing object. Thus, the exact position of a chair in a room may be specified relative to the walls of the room, or we may only know that the chair is inside the room, but not exactly where in the room. This would apply to *Part of* as well. For instance, we may know that salt and water are parts of a salty solution, and we may also know the exact concentration or quantity of salt in the solution. *Subtype of* also inherits this property, but it is harder to conceive of quantitative subtypes. A quantitative subtyping relationship would convey information on how *much* one object may be considered a kind of another. For instance, consider a class of objects called "sharp knife." How sharp a class of knives is would determine how much they fit into the category of sharp knives.

The relationships in Figure 7.27a are polymorphisms of location. They are common relationships we use all the time. The hierarchy in the figure implies that relationships deeper in the hierarchy may be more constrained but cannot violate constraints imposed on relationships above them.[88] This information gives us a ready template for normalizing several kinds of rules and constraints associated with *Place*. If we assert that a Mountain is a kind (subtype) of Terrain, it also implies that a Mountain must be a part of a Terrain, that it must be contained in a Terrain and that the mountain is smaller than the terrain that contains it. We can also infer, from the hierarchy in Figure 7.27, that a Terrain locates a mountain (and vice versa). (However, it does not imply that a mountain is a terrain if we merely assert that a terrain locates the mountain or it contains it or is a part of it.)

A *Place* might also be a virtual place. For instance, a television show might be located on a (television) channel. A television channel is a part of in a *Medium* (television), which implies that the location of the show is the medium. A medium is a class of places. Thus, location in a place also implies location in a medium, which makes Medium a kind of *Place* (for example, the channel).[89]

If we constrain the information carrying capacity, or the size of a virtual place, the constraint will be inherited by all channels in that place and will constrain all items *Contained in*, *Part of*, or *Subtypes of* that medium (place). Similarly, if we constrain the size of a physical location, all items *Contained in*, *Part of*, or *Subtypes of* that place will inherit that constraint.

The hierarchy in Figure 7.27a is a template that we can use to normalize constraints; it tells us where and at what level we must attach what constraints and rules to have them automatically filter through the hierarchy of Figure 7.27a to all the objects the rule must constrain.

Thus common sense flows from the power of reason, and the power of reason flows from the Metamodel of Knowledge. Both may reside in a repository of Knowledge artifacts if we can identify the patterns of information, like the hierarchy in Figure 7.27a, that are a *Part of* it. That hierarchy is a component, a part, a pattern of information, and a meaning.

- Figure 7.27a also tells us that an aggregate is a kind of *Place* because objects may be parts of an assembly (or subassembly). For instance, gears are parts of the transmission of a car and the car itself is made from its parts. For this reason, both the car and the transmission can be legitimately called a *Place* that locates (and contains) its parts. Indeed, the fact that a Car can *contain* people (who are obviously not car parts!) also makes it a place for people. It could even be inferred from this that people must be smaller than cars. On the other hand, if we told it that people may also be *located* on a bicycle, it would not know which the larger object is—a person, or a bicycle, all it could infer is that a bicycle is a kind of place.
- Constraints on size are instance level caps on the cardinality ratios of *contained in* or its polymorphisms (the *live in* relationship between Person and House in Chapter V was a polymorphism of containment).[90] Size and other constraints/rules will filter down the hierarchy of Figure 7.27a. We will discuss constraints on cardinality ratios next. This discussion will demonstrate how the structure in Figure 7.27a can help normalize behavior and automate the power of reason.
- Figure 7.27c shows that a subtyping relationship between a pair of objects will inherit the same cardinality constraints as a *Part of* relationship between the pair and could crimp the cardinality between the pair even more, but *Subtype of* may never violate the cardinality of *Part of*. The same line of reasoning

will also apply to *Supertype of* and its parent, *Consists of.*

- The hierarchy in Figure 7.27 asserts that *Part of* is a subtype of *Contained in,* and hence *Consists of,* the inverse of *Part of,* is a subtype of *Contains*, the inverse of *Contained in.* This fact combined with Liskov's principle tells us that when items like cars, homes, and machinery are assembled from other items, *a part that is declared to be mandatory must be a part of the assembly, but may be substituted by variants, which may be optional subtypes.* For instance, consider a car being manufactured. A rule tells us that every car must have one steering system. It is a mandatory *part of* a car. Steering systems may be of different kinds. Say we have two, Power and Manual, steering systems. Each kind of steering system is a non-overlapping subtype because a power steering system can never also be a manual steering system or vice versa. The fact that a car must have a steering system automatically implies that a car must *consist of* a steering system, which in turn implies that a car may or may not *consist of* a power steering system (the same logic also applies to the manual steering system or any other mutually exclusive kinds of steering systems). This example demonstrates that *the subtype of a part can be optional if the supertype of the part is mandatory*—common sense, but someone has to tell the computer that! Indeed, this fact is inherited from "Locate," which is where it is normalized.
- There are two rules about summation of populations in partitions, which lead to more complex kinds of inference when combined with the subtyping hierarchy in Figure 7.27. They are as follows:

1. The sum of populations of individual subtypes in an exhaustive partition will equal that of the parent object. In a non-exhaustive partition, the sum may be less but cannot exceed the population of the parent object. The units of measure of the sum will be inherited from the enumeration domain.
2. Adding to (subtracting from) the population of a subtype will add to (subtract from) the population of its parents but not necessarily vice versa.

These rules also tell us other things about parts, assemblies, and subtypes. For instance, they tell us that if at least two (or more) of an item is mandatory in a group or assembly of items, some non-overlapping subtypes of the item may be mandatory, while others could be optional. On the other hand, if a group or assembly of items cannot consist of more than three of an item, the group cannot have more than three of any non-overlapping subtype of the same item. Also, cardinalities of specific (non-overlapping) subtypes of the item could be capped at three, two, one, or none, provided the total cardinality of all subtypes, taken together, are capped at three. All this is common sense. This kind of common sense and reasoning flows from the rule in Figure 7.27c, combined with rules about domains in the Metamodel of Knowledge, which assert that the cardinality (number of instances) of a subtype is limited by the cardinality of its supertype(s), and the cardinality of the supertype adds up to the sum of cardinalities of its (non-overlapping) subtypes in an exhaustive partition. The following example clarifies and illustrates this bit of common sense embedded within the metamodel of knowledge:

Consider which objects in the hierarchy of Figure 7.27a normalize this logic. At first glance, it might seem that this kind of common sense is normalized by a composite relationship in which *Part of* acts in tandem with *Subtype of.* However, we will be mistaken if we think so. The hierarchy in Figure 7.27a contradicts this seemingly simple and intuitive conclusion, as the following arguments show:

*Locate* is a transitive relationship; if a chain of objects are connected by a string of *locate* relationships, the object at the beginning of the chain locates not just its immediate neighbor in the chain but also every object in the chain. Polymorphisms of *locate*, namely *contains*, *part of*, and *subtype of*, also inherit this property of transitivity (see Figure 7.27a).

Keeping this in mind, consider the *locate* relationship between the pair of objects in Figure 7.27b, one of which envelopes (contains—but not necessarily as its parts) other objects. Naturally, Object 1 will also locate the contents of Object 2 (Objects 3 and 4) as it locates Object 2 in Figure 7.27b. Objects 3 and 4 will be located by a relationship that is also *locate* but that *locate* is a composition of the original *locate* joined with *contain* (Figure 7.27b). The composition is transitive with respect to *locate*. Therefore the composite relationship also boils down to *locate*.[91]

However, the composite *locate* carries a tad more information than the *Locate* between Objects 1 and 2; it tells us that it is a composition of *locate* and *contains*. *Contains* has more information than *locate*, hence so too must its composition have more information. This makes the composite *locate* of Figure 7.27b a polymorphism of *locate* between Objects 1 and 2 in that figure. This implies that the composite locate will inherit any constraints imposed on the relationship between Objects 1 and 2, including cardinality constraints. Moreover, it could crimp these cardinality constraints even more (but it cannot relax them). This property is normalized by the composition of *Locate* and *Contain*. *Lower level polymorphisms of these relationships, like compositions of Part of and Subtype of, will also inherit this property.* Indeed, in the examples we discussed, we have seen that they do.

The rules in our example above about the occurrences of subtypes, derived from rules of occurrences of parent parts in an assembly or aggregation, was normalized not by the composition of *Part of* acting in tandem with *Subtype of* but by the composition of *Locate*, acting in tandem with *Contain*.

Without the hierarchy in Figure 7.27a, it might have been much harder to derive this. Un-normalized, the rule would have been replicated polymorphism by polymorphism, in each polymorphism of the composite locate of Figure 7.27b. The composition is a permutation of relationships; possible variations are many. Behavior would fragment and replicate, and its impact would spin uncontrolled through these variations into business processes or at best be manually controlled and coordinated by the common sense of process designers or programmers. Experience has told us that that approach has its limitations; coordinating, developing, testing, correcting, and deploying processes will take longer. The bottom line: a negative impact on time to market which might be intolerable in the age of innovation backed by information.

The rules normalized by Figure 7.27, in tandem with the other rules we have encapsulated in our model, instill common sense and the power to reason in artifacts of knowledge. This kind of common sense can help tune and transform cardinalities of relationships as perspectives shift in step with new learning, new technology, and new options. Perspectives shift as new learning and new options let us generalize or specialize parts and components of items (like cars or books) in new contexts. This common sense flows from the metamodel of knowledge and is normalized within it.

- Note how the hierarchy of Figure 7.27a turns into a process as we infuse temporal information into it. It is clear that if we infuse a bare modicum of temporal sequence into the subtyping relationships in the hierarchy of Figure 7.27a, we will get generic processes like *Locate and then Contain*, which locates an item and then envelopes or acquires it without incorporating it as a part (envelope and acquire are also polymorphisms of contain); *Locate and Contain*, followed by *Incorporate*, which make the acquired item a part; *Locate, Acquire, and Incorporate*, followed by *Absorb (or Ingest)*, which make the acquired part lose its independent identity so that the composite becomes one integral entity rather than a composition made of distinct parts. As we have seen, the composition, considered as a whole, will then be a subtype of the object that absorbed it. These are examples of how universal patterns and processes flow as polymorphisms from the Metamodel of Knowledge. These processes are universal patterns used in manufacturing, mergers, targeting, or salvage operations and much more.

- Aggregates and compositions that add information to an object are its polymorphisms. We must consider the aggregate (or composition) as a whole. Each object in the aggregation adds information to the overall aggregate. This is also true when the objects in the aggregation (or composition) are relationships. Thus, aggregations and compositions of relationships, considered in *Toto*, are subtypes of the aggregate (or composite) relationship they represent.

Let us now analyze how this impacts idempotency. An idempotent relationship is an object. As we obtain more information about its composition, we might find the idempotent relationship is an aggregation of objects.

We might then find that it is an aggregation of idempotent relationships like a bunch of looping strands of wire that circle back to a common origin (like the edges of the petals of a sunflower loop back to the calyx in the center), or we might find that the idempotent relationship breaks up into a chain of distinct objects connected in a looping ring (see Box 7.12). However, we might have added just enough information to an idempotent relationship to clearly say that it consists of distinct object classes, but not enough to say that these object classes are linked in a loop like the cycle of states in Box 7.12. The information we have might only tell us that the idempotent relationship is an aggregate of three or more object classes and that one object class anchors the idempotent polymorphism as follows:

Each object in the aggregate will be related to the object that anchors the polymorphism in a pattern like a wheel with spokes. The anchoring class will be at the hub of the wheel, and the other classes will lie on the rim, with relationships from each converging on the hub (like the spokes of the wheel). Moreover, instances of these relationships will converge on the same *instance* of the object at the hub, much like the pattern in Box 7.12.

To understand this polymorphism of an idempotent composition in business terms, consider a negotiation. The negotiation negotiates the terms and conditions of an agreement. A renegotiation is called a renegotiation only because it renegotiates the *same terms and conditions* as the original negotiation. Thus, the negotiation and its renegotiation are idempotent with respect to *Terms and Conditions*, an object class:

The relationship between *Negotiation* and *Terms and Conditions* not only requires that *Negotiation* and *Renegotiation* be related to instances of *Terms and Conditions*, but requires that they be related to the same instance of *Terms and Conditions*. Only then may an instance of *Negotiation* to be considered a renegotiation and only then may we pair an instance of negotiation with an instance of renegotiation and vice versa. Thus, the pattern of *Negotiation* and *Renegotiation* is idempotent with respect to *Terms and Conditions*.

It follows that the idempotency of the aggregation must be demonstrated with respect to *at least* one object class in the aggregate—the class that anchors the idempotent hub of the pattern. The aggregate may also be idempotent with respect to more than one object class. Instances of relationships could converge on the same instance of different objects in different classes. Then the aggregate will be idempotent with respect to two or more object classes (the wheel will then have multiple hubs).

Consider the mutually inclusive pair of relationships in Figure 5.5b. It tells us that the owner of a car must also own insurance. Thus, the composition in that figure is idempotent with respect to *Person*. The rule also tells us that it is the owner's car that the insurance policy must insure (a relationship not shown in the figure). It follows that the composition must also be idempotent with respect to *Car*. As such, this composition has two idempotent hubs, *Person* and *Car*.

Indeed, if we did not have enough information to distinguish cars from people, we would not be able to separate cars and people into distinct object classes; we would only know that a car is a different instance of an object than a person and would perforce club both instances into a single object class (we might call the class *Physical Object*). The composition we just discussed would still be idempotent, but now it would be idempotent with respect to two instances of *Physical Object*, a single object class. The order of the relationship was reduced by the loss of information, but not yet its degree (as we lose even more information, distinctions between object instances too may be also be lost; see Chapter IV). *Thus, an idempotent relationship may be idempotent with respect to several object instances or several object classes.*

Consider the difference between relationships that are merely mutually inclusive and those that are also idempotent. Common sense would

*Box 7.12. Idempotent processes: State vs. object*

We have seen how an idempotent loop was a composite relationship that strung several subtypes of a Check—different states—via another object, the signatory of the check, into a composite loop to articulate a rule that said that they must all sign the *same* check. We have also seen how the class of signatories was glued to the class of checks with a relationship between attributes—a relationship and composition that was a port of connection between the check and objects that were not checks—objects beyond the boundaries of the class. We know that we can consider a path that loops back to a given object through multiple objects, tracing relationships in-between, a single, unified, composite relationship—a recursive a loop from an object back to itself—if we ignore the objects buried within the loop. This is how a composition that loops through several objects can be considered a recursion on one member of the group (Figure A, Part d). The loop is idempotent with respect to a member when the relationship must always loop back to the same *instance* of that object class.

We know that these relationships between attributes need not always loop back through different object classes; they may even connect an instance of an object to others in its own class. The relationship then becomes a recursive relationship. It becomes an idempotent relationship when it *must* always connect to the same *instance* of the same object. Indeed, a relationship between states may even cycle back to the same state of the same object instance via intermediate states. It can only do so when each state is separated from the others by the flow of time. The composition must connect states of the *same* instance of the object across the time slices shown in Figure 7.1. Naturally, the relationship cannot loop back in time, but it *can* loop back to the same state—a loop in state space as the following figures show. If the object is always condemned to loop back to the same state, it is an idempotent relationship between states.

*Box 7.12. continued*

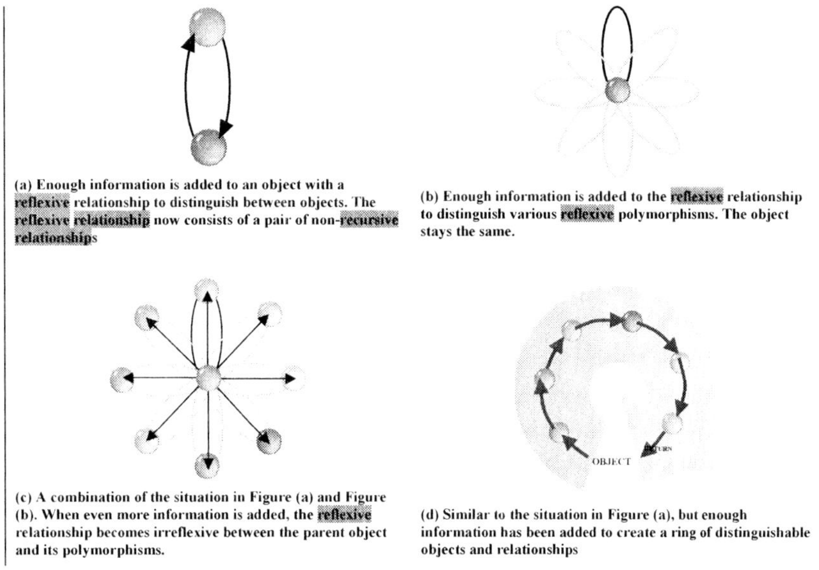


*Figure A. Some polymorphisms of reflexive relationships*

A business rule that articulates a loop in state space is an idempotent relationship. Such loop will be a path in state space through intermediate states that always cycles through the same set of states. There might even be several loops that cycle back to the same state—each loop a different path through a different set of states; some might even share states in common, but each path will have a distinct identity if even *one* state in it is unique to it. Each loop like this, with or without states in common, is a process because it involves the flow of time; it cycles through states, moving forward in time.

Loops of this type are idempotent relationships, but they are not idempotent relationships between object instances; rather they are idempotent with respect to a given *state* of a single instance of an object—an even stricter, more constrained form of idempotence than the relationships we have discussed earlier. The patterns we had discussed were idempotent with respect to a single instance of a single class of objects; the pattern we are discussing now is idempotent with respect to a single *feature* (or a combination of features) of a single instance of a single class of objects.[92] When only two states are involved, the relationship becomes a "toggle" that can respond to events by switching to the state it is *not* in. This kind of toggling or looping between states will be familiar to many analysts and designers: a watch may toggle between displaying the date in Gregorian vs. military format each time a stud is pressed. Naturally, if we add a daisy chain of intermediate states to this idempotent loop, as we have seen, that loop will become a composition and a subtype of the original pair. The behavior and the rules involved will be exactly the same, regardless of whether the process or relationship in question is between object instances or between features of an object instance. It is the *relationship* that we are dealing with and the rules that a *relationship* will normalize.

dictate that the mutually inclusive relationship in Figure 5.5b is idempotent with respect to *Person* as well as *Car*, that the owner of a car must also own insurance for the car she owns. Contrast this rule with a somewhat nonsensical rule that might mandate that if a person owns a car, *somebody* must own car insurance (and vice versa). The rule need not require the owner of the insurance to also be the owner of the car or even the owner of *a* car. It might not even require the owner of the insurance policy to insure the car owner's car—any car might do. Hence, mutual inclusion may be idempotent or not.

A strictly constrained pattern of information that mandates mutual inclusion of the same object instance, not just an object instance of the same object class, is a polymorphism of its less constrained parent. In the same way, the other relationships in Figure 5.5 may be idempotent or not. As such, idempotency with respect to an object instance is independent of mutual inclusion, mutual exclusion, or subsetting constraints. Each is an irreducible fact which may be joined to create new, more restrictive irreducible facts, which attach to the same object instance.

- It is perhaps not immediately clear that the subtyping relationship too may have special polymorphisms—subtypes that convey special information or constraints even as they subtype an object class. Figure A of Box 7.12 shows this can happen:
  - The fact that an aggregate, considered in Toto, adds information to an object even as it expresses its meaning is the source of one such polymorphism. It is a key polymorphism—the *expressed by* relationship in Figure D of Box 5.1 reproduced earlier in this book. As we have seen, this relationship is the cornerstone for innovation, process reengineering, and much else. In Box 5.1, in the discussion on rule expressions, we show how a single meaning may be expressed in multiple ways. Each expression is a composition of terms. In Chapter VI, we learned that a relationship may be expressed by a composition of objects, and there may be several compositions that may boil down to the same relationship. In this chapter, we have seen how a process or service may be implemented in several ways and how these can be compositions expressing a relationship. The *expressed by* relationship is a special case—a polymorphism and subtype of the subtyping relationship itself. Figure 7.29 articulates this.
  - Picking a single member, an object instance from an object class is also a polymorphism of the subtyping relationship. This polymorphism is frequent in business. It is the parent of business rules that select a special item for attention from a group of *similar* items.
  - Its parent relationship, "*Part of*" in Figure 7.29, is more generic. It singles out one item from a collection. The collection does not have to be an object class. It could be an aggregation of like or unlike objects. A class of objects is a collection of like object instances. Thus, "*instance of*" is a polymorphism of "*Part of*," and a subtype of the subtyping relationship itself.
  - *Part of* singles out one item as a member of a collection, but that item may also be a collection. Thus *Part of* has the freedom to pick multiple items. *Instance of* is different. *Instance of* is a special polymorphism of the subtyping relationship. In this polymorphism, the cardinality of the subtype is restricted to a single member. All aggregate objects are not object classes. Even though *Part of* focuses attention on one item among those in any kind of aggregation or composition, that item might be a collection of objects, an object instance in a class of similar objects, or a single item in a collection of dissimilar parts of a composition. When the collection is a class, we can make finer distinctions. The subtyping relationship is based on shared information. We have recently seen how this makes the subtyping relationship a specialized polymorphism of *Part of*, one that applies only to object classes. That *Instance of* is also a

polymorphism of *Part of* is thus a fact inherited from its parent—the subtyping relationship itself. That *Instance of* restricts the subtype to only one member is an irreducible fact added to the subtyping relationship. It would replicate information to reassert that *Instance of* is a polymorphism of *Part of* when we have already asserted that *Subtype of* is a polymorphism of *Part of*. This is why the relationship between *Instance of* and *Part of* is a broken line in Figure 7.29. The broken line merely reiterates the fact without reasserting it. The purpose is to remind and clarify, not replicate.

  - "*Instance of*" fuses with a temporal parent, a process, and manifests itself as the "Pick" production segment in the S95 standard model we described under supply chains. Figure 7.29 shows this. "*Pick Item*" tells us when and under what conditions an item will be picked for processing. *Instance of* restricts the subtype to only one member. *Pick* to picks one item of a class. The process selects only one item, just as *instance of* does. Of course, the item picked could be a collection and aggregate object in its own right. Then each would be a member of a batch based on the instance of *Pick* that picked them. Thus, the concept of a batch process is implicit in the concept of picking items from a collection.

- Higher order and higher degree relationships are polymorphisms of their lower order counterparts. It is a special case of a composition being a subtype of the aggregate; adding an object to a relationship adds information to the relationship. For instance, take a second order relationship: *Product* is sold to *Customer* (both *Product* and *Customer* are objects; sold to is the relationship between them). We can attach a third object, *Retailer*, to this relationship to make it the third order relationship in Figure 5.3. That third order relationship adds information to "*Product* is sold to *Customer*" and is therefore a subtype of its second order counterpart. Similarly, *Feature Group* in Figure 7.26 was a relationship between features and also a subtype of *Feature*.

Thus, we can add new objects to relationships and include fresh detail on their interactions each time we do so. It will add detail to the meaning of the relationship and build new atomic rules by adding components of knowledge—meanings—to the old. Thus, we may iteratively detail and enrich our business model and the business rules it represents. We can do so as we iteratively cycle through increasing levels of detail in a prototype on its way to becoming a full-fledged information system. ([144] in Appendix III, Kruchten, 1995, has more on iterative systems development).

However, we must judiciously sidestep the problem of perspective when we peel back layers of detail. As the order (or degree) of a relationship increases, there may be enormously large numbers of combinations of relationships that may be supertypes of a given subtype. Conversely, given a high order or high degree relationship, it may be subtyped in an enormously large number of ways. A relationship between any combination of two of the objects in Figure 5.3 would be the supertype of the third order relationship in Figure 5.3, and the possibilities will increase explosively as the order (or degree) of the relationship increases. When scope is broad, and interactions complex, it is easy to get lost in information space if we have no mooring. This is why we need the Universal Perspective; it is our anchor (on our Web site).[93]

*The Universal Perspective will not have the fine detail and granularity of the final model but will articulate common rules and shared objects. Systems definition can then proceed in rapid iterative steps. Each iteration will add functional detail to the Universal Perspective by enriching it with new information—objects, features, effects, rules, aliases, and so forth. As we add detail, we should apply Liskov's Substitution Principle (see Mutability of Compositions) and the Principle of Parsimony (see Alternative Resources—Alternative Processes) to ensure that we add only information essential for the business function. The shared information in the Universal Perspective will help ensure that information stays normalized and that the mutability of objects and processes are optimized. The Universal Perspective will also help untangle the tangled inheritance hierarchies that might have been inherited from legacy systems and opportunistic designs of the past.*[94]

The Universal Perspective will anchor the outermost layer of Figure 7.15 and lead to the layers beneath. It can be the starting point for iterative development and the basis of the initial prototype from which development of all information systems and business processes can proceed.

- Constraints on the upper and lower bounds of the cardinality of a subtype might be identical to the supertype or be constrained to lie within the bounds imposed by the supertype. These rules also apply to the degree and order of subtype relationships.
- A relationship between specific attributes, states, or features of objects is a subtype of a more generic relationship between objects; it adds information to the more generic relationship by elaborating on the features it relates and becomes a subtype of the relationship it elaborates on (see the examples in Box 5.1).
- Like any other object, a subtype of a relationship may add features of its own. For instance, we added an attribute, sale price, to the product sale relationship in Figure 5.8a. A subtype may thus add attributes, effects, constraints, and relationships. (A relationship may add relationships by involving more objects, that is, increasing its order or degree.)

  A relationship may also be subtyped by adding new meaning to it, like *part of* added meaning to *contained in*. Making a meaning more specific adds information to the relationship as much as new features and effects do. It is equivalent to changing its state by adding constraints that restrict it (the meaning) to make the relationship more specific. Thus, "*mother of*" is a subtype of "*parent of*." It adds meaning to "*parent of*" and makes it more specific—a change of state and a polymorphism of "*parent of*" that resulted from elaborating on, and thereby constraining, its meaning. (As we have seen, all relationships are polymorphisms of the generic "*involve*" relationship).
- A relationship may also be subtyped by subtyping one or more objects it binds together. Subtyping objects makes them more specific and increases their information content, which then flows into polymorphisms of the generic relationship between the generic objects it ties together. Box 4.8 has examples. The *composed of* relationship in Figure 6.1 was another example of this kind of polymorphism.

  Each object a relationship binds may potentially be subtyped. Thus, each object carries within it the potential to add meaning. Each is potentially a parameter of the polymorphism (see Inclusion Polymorphism in Box 4.8). Idempotent relationships bind only one object, so they may have at most one parameter.
- An asymmetrical relationship may be a polymorphism of a more generic symmetrical relationship (see Box 5.2). An asymmetrical relationship constrains its inverse to have a different meaning from the relationship. The constraint is a business rule—an item of information.

  For example "*Involves*" is a generic relationship that only tells us that two objects are associated, that is, "involved" with each other, but conveys little meaning beyond that. It is symmetrical because it has the bare minimum of information—just enough to make it a relationship. Similarly, the relationship "relative of," in "*Person* is relative of *Person*" is a symmetrical relationship between persons. On the other hand, a more specific kind of relationship like "*ancestor of*," which adds meaning (the meaning of "ancestor") to the generic concept of relative, is an asymmetrical relationship between persons; a person cannot be the ancestor of his own ancestor. "*Ancestor of*" (and its inverse "*descendant of*") is an asymmetrical subtype derived from a symmetrical relationship, "*relative of*."

- An antisymmetrical relationship is also a polymorphism of a symmetrical relationship (for the reasons cited above). It is also a reflexive relationship. We have added just enough information to make every instance of the recursive relationship asymmetrical *except* the instances that loop back on the same object (instance).

Consider the subtraction relationship between two ratios or difference scaled values. Subtraction is an antisymmetrical relationship. Subtraction is also a subtype, a polymorphism of a generic reflexive *involve* relationship. A reflexive *involve* relationship only tells us that there is some unknown interaction between object instances that belong to the same object class. "Involve," we know, is a symmetrical relationship; if one object instance involves another, it naturally implies that the involved object must also involve the object that involves it. The meaning of arithmetic subtraction is more specific. Subtraction too is a kind of involvement, but it is an involvement that is asymmetrical unless a value is subtracted from itself; then it becomes symmetrical. Constraining the meaning of involvement to "subtraction" will make the relationship antisymmetrical. The arithmetic subtraction is an antisymmetrical polymorphism of the symmetrical, reflexive "*involve*" relationship (between quantitative values).

(If we added even more information to the meaning of an antisymmetrical relationship, it could become a true asymmetrical relationship.)

Note that an *instance* of a relationship that loops back to the *same object instance* must always be symmetrical, but there is a caveat. The state of the object instance at each end of the relationship must be identical. This will make them indistinguishable. (This is automatically the case when it is the same time slice of the same object instance—see Figure 7.1.) Since the object instances the relationship connects are the same, and in the same state, they will be indistinguishable.[95] It will therefore be meaningless to say that one precedes the other in a relationship. This implies that the instance of the relationship is symmetrical. *Self Help* is a symmetrical relationship because *Helped by* and its inverse, *Help*, are indistinguishable when a person helps herself. When this is not the case, *Help* is asymmetrical—*helped by* is not the same as *help* unless the person who is helping and the person being helped are the same person. *Help*, as in *Person* helps *Person*, is an antisymmetrical relationship, and *Self Help* is its idempotent polymorphism.

This is one way an idempotent relationship may be a polymorphism of an antisymmetrical relationship. The idempotent "fibers" (symmetrical instances) of an antisymmetrical relationship loop back to the same object instance, whereas the other "fibers" (asymmetrical instances) of the antisymmetrical relationship are both irreflexive and asymmetrical. Therefore, if we segregate the two kinds of instances of the relationship into distinct subclasses, one subclass will be a symmetrical idempotent polymorphism, and the other will be an irreflexive *and* asymmetrical polymorphism of the antisymmetrical relationship we have partitioned. The two subsets will exhaustively partition the antisymmetrical relationship. Figure 7.29 makes this clear.

- A recursive relationship conveys less information than a nonrecursive relationship. It does not distinguish one object class from another; its source and target object classes are indistinguishable. A recursive relationship, with no further information except that it is recursive, does not even tell us if there are constraints on it that will prevent it from being reflexive. Even the existence or nonexistence of the constraint is unknown. The constraint carries even less information than the "*Don't care*" value of Box 5.3; it could even be null.
  A reflexive relationship conveys a tad more information. It tells us that there are *definitely no constraints* that will bar the relationship from looping back to the same object instance that the "value" of the constraint is definitely *null*. A reflexive relationship is a subtype of a recursive relationship, a fact that is both intuitive and logically sound in Figure 7.29.

Moreover:

- An irreflexive relationship is also a subtype of a recursive relationship; an irreflexive relationship asserts that there *is* a constraint that bars reflexivity in a recursive relationship (the value of the constraint is *at least* "not null," a value that is identical to the "*Don't care*" value of Box 5.3. It implies that, at a minimum, we know that the relationship is irreflexive even if the rest of its meaning matters little or is unknown. Of course, we could add meaning to irreflexive relationships to obtain even more specific irreflexive meanings, which will be irreflexive polymorphisms of irreflexive relationships. The "*parent of*" relationship we cited recently was an irreflexive polymorphism of another irreflexive relationship, "*ancestor of*." All recursive relationships, including irreflexive relationships, may have irreflexive polymorphisms. This is why the irreflexive polymorphism is a direct subtype of a recursive relationship in Figure 7.29. Every other recursive relationship inherits this fact.
  An irreflexive relationship can be a polymorphism of its reflexive parent because irreflexivity constrains a recursive relationship and hence adds information. The information it adds is an irreducible fact: that the relationship cannot loop back to the object at its other end. It cannot look like a snake eating its own tail.
  Consider the generic *represent* relationship.[96] It is a reflexive relationship. Conversion or encryption of formatting symbols is a polymorphism of this generic representation. Conversion of a symbol to itself has little value if we are encrypting it. If we impose a constraint that denies this kind of meaningless encryption, the reflexive *represent* relationship will open out to become an irreflexive *encrypt* relationship. The constraint is the added information that makes encryption an irreflexive polymorphism of *represent*. Encryption may apply not only to symbols but also to meanings: Although no eagle has ever touched the moon, the first manned spaceship to land on the moon announced, "The Eagle has landed," when it completed the journey.
- An idempotent relationship is also a polymorphism of its reflexive parent. Idempotency also constrains a reflexive relationship and adds information. It adds the fact that the relationship *must* loop back to the object at its other end. It *must* look like a snake eating its own tail.
  Consider people helping people. A person may help himself or other people. Thus, *help* is a reflexive relationship on object class *Person*. *Self Help* is an idempotent polymorphism of the generic *help* relationship: *Self Help* is a subtype of *Help*, in which the help relationship *must* loop back to the same person; it is con-

strained to do so. This constraint is the extra information *Self Help* adds to the meaning of *Help* that makes *Self Help* idempotent.

The example also makes it clear that any reflexive relationship may be partitioned into mutually exclusive irreflexive and idempotent subsets. Indeed, the antisymmetrical relationship inherits this constraint. However, the idempotent subset is more restricted when it is applied to an antisymmetrical relationship. We have recently discussed why this subset must be a class of symmetrical relationships. Figure 7.29 clearly articulates these irreducible facts.

Readers might find it puzzling that in Figure 7.29, the class of reflexive relationships has not been partitioned into two mutually exclusive subsets—one idempotent and the other irreflexive. Moreover, the irreflexive polymorphism of a reflexive relationship is not even directly shown as a subset of the reflexive relationship in that figure (the polymorphism is inherited from a supertype). This is because an irreflexive relationship may be a polymorphism of any recursive relationship, be it idempotent, antisymmetrical, or even another irreflexive relationship. We have seen how this can happen to an antisymmetrical or reflexive relationship. It is also true for idempotent relationships. An idempotent relationship can also "open out" into an irreflexive polymorphism when we add information. The reasons are subtle. They are buried deep within the laws that carve objects out of the inchoate information swirling through information space as the following example will show:

Consider a nation. Nations may be at war with other nations. A nation may even be at war with itself. When a nation wars with itself, we call it a civil war. *Nation* is a class of objects. Thus, *War* is a reflexive relationship between nations, and *Civil War* is its idempotent polymorphism that loops back to the same instance of *Nation*. If we add information to the nation to discriminate between its warring parts, the idempotent relationship will open out to show which part is at war with which. The idempotent relationship normalizes the fact that an entity is at war with itself, and its non-idempotent polymorphisms normalize the fact that the war is between distinct parts of an intrinsically whole entity.

A reflexive relationship may have irreflexive or idempotent polymorphisms, and idempotent polymorphisms in turn may have irreflexive polymorphisms. The indirect and direct routes to an irreflexive polymorphism of a reflexive relationship are subsumed by the fact that a reflexive relationship may have irreflexive polymorphisms, as Figure 7.29 implies it may. It may because this feature is inherited from the generic recursive relationship.

As we add information to a recursive relationship, it may resolve into nonrecursive or recursive relationships of various kinds, in step with the information and meanings we add. Polymorphisms of a recursive relationship are subtypes of the relationship that may take up different positions in the subtyping hierarchy for recursive relationships in Figure 7.29. Eventually, after enough information has been added, the recursive "loop" may "open up." The recursive relationship may distinguish between object classes it connects and "straighten out" into a nonrecursive relationship. The "*parent of*" relationship in Figures A and B of Box 4.8 was an example of this. Figure 7.29 highlights that *any* recursive relationship—all its polymorphisms (subtypes)—may have nonrecursive polymorphisms.

The objects a polymorphism connects may not all be subtypes of the generic objects connected by the parent relationship. Polymorphisms may also connect supertypes to subtypes. The "*parent of*" relationship in Figures A and B of Box 4.8 was an example of this. The "*composed of*" relationship in Figure 6.1 was another example of this kind of polymorphism.

Thus, we may obtain a nonrecursive polymorphism of a recursive relationship by seeding it with extra information through its parameters, but we can never obtain a recursive polymorphism by adding information to a nonrecursive relationship. For similar reasons, we may obtain irreflexive polymorphisms of reflexive or idempotent relationships by adding information to them, but not vice versa. Indeed, relationships of different kinds in Figure 7.29 may have polymorphisms that are beneath them in the subtyping hierarchies there but cannot have polymorphisms *above* them.

- Polymorphisms of relationships may even be obtained by adding a parent from another partition. The parent will contribute information to create new meanings. With reference to Figure 7.29, adding temporal information to "*part of*" would create a process that changes the parts of an aggregate over time. The process would tell us when, and for how long, a component will be a part of the aggregate object. Of course, the component could also remain a part of the aggregate indefinitely after it is assembled into it. The process for assembling an item from its parts will be a subtype of this process.[97] "*Assemble*" is a process and a polymorphism of *consists of* because it now contains temporal information, that the parts are resources that exist before the assembly that consists of those parts. Thus *Assemble* is a process that has two parents, the *Part of* relationship, and the generic process. Figure 7.28 shows that *Assemble* connects the same generic objects *part of* did, but the relationship now has added a nuance to its meaning. As such, *Assemble* is a polymorphism that has elaborated on the meaning of "*part of*."
If the work product of the *assemble* process (the target of the *part of* relationship) is a car, then the process will tell us when which part is assembled into the car being manufactured. *Assemble Car* is thus a polymorphism of *Assemble*. *Assemble Car* is a step deeper into the subtyping hierarchy of Figure 7.28, a step that increases information content. It adds the information that the aggregate object in question is a car. It constrains the generic aggregate by making its meaning more specific. It is a subtype of *assemble*. It adds meaning

*Figure 7.28. An example of a polymorphism between subtypes*

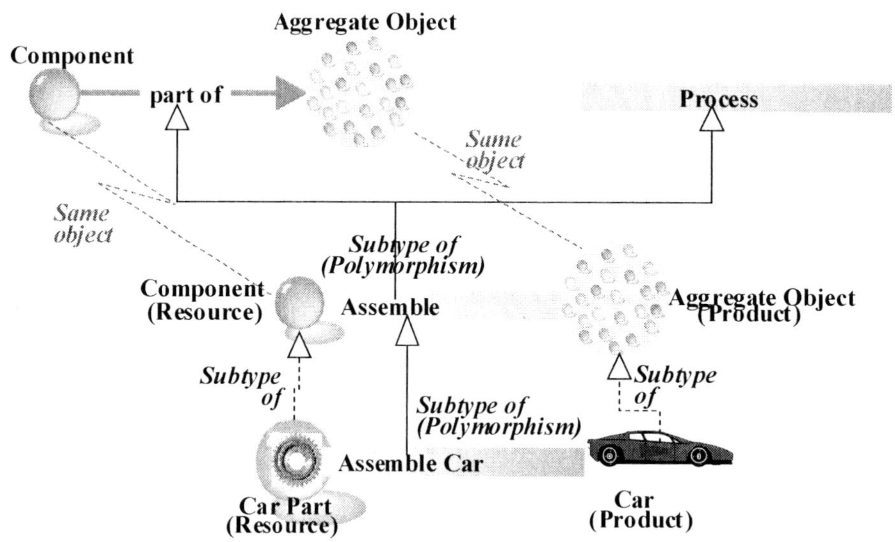

to *assemble* and makes it more specific. It is also an example of a polymorphism that relates subtypes of the objects the parent relationship binds together. Note how the objects bound by the parent relationship in Figure 7.28 (the generic *assemble*) have become parameters: If the aggregate object is a car, it automatically implies that the resources (components) are car parts, which are now subtypes of *Component* in Figure 7.28.

Figure 7.28 shows how *Assemble Car* normalizes the fact that it connects a subtype to a subtype and thus becomes a subtype of a more generic *Assemble* relationship. The subtyping operation embedded in *Assemble Car* is thus *implied* by the subtyping operations on either side of it. Thus, the triad of subtyping operations is not independent irreducible facts: The polymorphism in the middle implies the subtypes on either side. This is why the subtypes on both sides have been shown with broken lines. If we articulate all three as independent irreducible facts, we will denormalize information. The information we will replicate will be that *Assemble Car* binds specific subtypes of the same object classes its generic parent binds. This is the information *Assemble Car* has added to the generic assemble process.[98] This is how *Assemble Car* made the objects it involved more specific. The relationship constrained the degrees of freedom of *Component* and *Aggregate Object* because it was a constraint—a stricter constraint than its parent. It created a pattern of objects, as did its supertypes. It carved new patterns from the patterns created by its supertypes. These patterns were not the patterns of tangible symbols but patterns of abstract meanings—information in information space shaped by constraints. Thus, constraints that constrain patterns become polymorphisms of the patterns they constrained, and both could be abstract meanings.

- The concept of transitivity and intransitivity is only meaningful in a composition. A relationship may be said to be transitive, intransitive, or atransitive with respect to others in a composition. The following arguments will show that an intransitive relationship is actually a subtype of an asymmetrical relationship in a composition:
Consider *relative of*, and its subtype, *ancestor of*, again. We discussed both relationships recently. *Relative of* was a transitive relationship in the composition we had discussed. It was also a symmetrical relationship. On the other hand, *ancestor of*, also a transitive relationship, was asymmetrical. This demonstrates how the property of transitivity is independent of symmetry or asymmetry of relationships in a composition.
However, the property of **intransitivity** is different; if a relationship is intransitive with respect to a composition, the relationships in the composition must be asymmetrical. Consider what would happen if we made *ancestor of* even more specific and turned it into and *parent of*. Parent of is a subtype of *ancestor of*. It constrains the ancestor to be a parent. The composition we had discussed would become intransitive if we constrained ancestor of thus. An ancestor twice removed from a descendant remains an ancestor but cannot be a parent. We added information—meaning—to a transitive composition and turned it into an intransitive composition by constraining it further.
We did this by constraining an already asymmetrical relationship even more. *Parent* of made *ancestor of* even more specific than it was. Unless we leach meaning from the composition, it will remain intransitive. Adding meaning will plant it even more firmly in the camp of intransitive compositions. Thus, if we constrained *Parent of* even more and turned it into *Mother* of or *Father of*, the composition would stay intransitive because we crossed a critical threshold when we made *ancestor of* into *parent of*. The threshold we crossed

was in terms of information content—the richness and specificity of meaning. Only asymmetrical relationships that are patterns of information with little freedom may be assembled into intransitive compositions.

Asymmetry does not always imply intransitivity, but the converse is not true; intransitivity always implies asymmetry. Thus, intransitivity conveys more information—meaning—than mere asymmetry. It adds information to asymmetry (like parent of added information to ancestor of by telling us what kind of ancestor we meant). An intransitive composition is therefore a subtype of an asymmetrical relationship.

An intransitive relationship will never be symmetrical. The information payload of symmetrical relationships is too light to automatically imply the nonexistence of another relationship. (Of course, we could do so by including additional constraints, but this information will then be normalized by the constraint added explicitly, not implicitly, by the relationship.) This is why an intransitive composition must always describe an asymmetrical relationship. Figure 7.29 makes this clear. It shows that an intransitive composition is a subtype of an asymmetrical relationship.

- A symmetrical composition is a subset of the set of transitive compositions. A symmetrical composition always implies transitivity (like the *relative of* composition we recently discussed), but we have seen that the converse is not true; a transitive relationship may or may not be derived from a composition of symmetrical relationships. It could also flow from compositions of asymmetrical relationships (like *ancestor of* did in our recent example). The set of symmetrical compositions is therefore a subset of the set of transitive compositions. Symmetrical compositions also express symmetrical relationships; they let us peek into the guts of a symmetrical relationship by adding information on its components. Therefore, the composition, *considered as a whole*, is a subtype of a symmetrical relationship. It follows that a symmetrical composition is a subtype of a symmetrical relationship, *even as it is a subset of transitive compositions.* Figure 7.29 makes this clear.
- An intransitive relationship is a polymorphism of a transitive relationship for the same reason that made an asymmetrical relationship a polymorphism of a symmetrical relationship; enriched meanings may also add constraints—information—that bar transitivity. If a chain of three or more persons is related via the "*ancestor of*" relationship into a hierarchy of ancestors, the person at the beginning of the chain will also be an ancestor of the person at the end of the chain. That relationship is implied by, and is therefore transitive with, the others in the chain. On the other hand, when we add meaning to "*ancestor of*" to make it a more specific relationship like "*mother of*," we know that the person at the beginning of the chain cannot be the mother of the person at the end of the chain. Thus, the "*mother of*" relationship is intransitive. It was obtained from the "*ancestor of*" relationship by adding meaning (information) to it. "*Mother of*" is thus an intransitive subtype of a transitive relationship, "*ancestor of*."

*Transitive Composition* in Figure 7.29 is in a different partition from symmetrical (and asymmetrical) relationships. The metamodel in Figure 7.29 will permit a transitive composition to be either a symmetrical or asymmetrical relationship (as it should). On the other hand, an intransitive composition is always constrained to be an asymmetrical relationship in Figure 7.29 because *Intransitive Composition* is a subtype of *Asymmetrical Relationship*. It is perhaps less obvious that this structure also implies that an intransitive composition is a subtype (polymorphism) of its transitive parent.

To understand why this is so, consider that a transitive composition may be asymmetrical or symmetrical (for instance, *relative of*, a symmetrical relationship, and *ancestor of*, an asymmetrical relationship, were both parts of transitive compositions in examples cited recently). Therefore, if we only know that a composition is transitive, we cannot tell whether it is describes a symmetrical or asymmetrical relationship. On the other hand, an intransitive component must always be asymmetrical; if we know that a composition is intransitive, we *can* tell with complete certainty that the composition describes an asymmetrical relationship. Thus, the intransitive composition has a larger information payload than a transitive composition. It adds meaning and is therefore a subtype.

That an intransitive composition is a subtype of a transitive composition is thus implied in Figure 7.29 by the subtyping relationship between asymmetrical and symmetrical relationships, together with the fact that a transitive relationship may be symmetrical or asymmetrical, whereas an intransitive relationship is always asymmetrical. The subtyping relationship between *Symmetrical Relationship* and *Asymmetrical Relationship* in Figure 7.29, together with the subtyping relationship between *Asymmetrical Relationship* and *Intransitive Composition* in that figure, thus *implies* the subtyping relationship between *Intransitive Composition* and *Transitive Composition* in the same figure. This is why it is shown with a broken line in Figure 7.29.

Note also how subtyping and subsetting operations are distinct and different in Figure 7.29. If we ignore their common information content, transitive and intransitive relations may be segregated into mutually exclusive subsets in the set of all compositions, but when we consider the information conveyed by their *meanings*, one is a subtype of the other, based on their generic and shared meaning (just as *mother of* was a subtype of *ancestor of*, in the example above, because a mother is a kind of ancestor (but obviously not vice versa). It tells us that, although we may group transitive and intransitive compositions into mutually exclusive sets, we may also obtain an intransitive relationship from a transitive relationship by constraining or adding to its meaning. Thus, polymorphism and subsetting need not always be aligned. Whether polymorphism equates to a subset depends on the criterion for partitioning the object class.

(For the same kinds of reasons, we could also segregate symmetrical and asymmetrical relationships into mutually exclusive subsets even though one is a *subtype* (polymorphism) of the other and similar arguments will hold for the rule expressions in Figure 7.29.)

- Adding information on the flow of time to a relationship creates a subtype—a process. This temporal information flows into relationships from *Event*. Thus, a process has two parents, *Relationship* and *Event*.
- "*Succeeds*," the succession relationship (and its inverse "*precede*"), adds the bare minimum of information on the flow of time to "*involves*." It is the thread from which all processes emerge. "*Succeeds*" is asymmetrical because *time* is asymmetrical. "*Succeeds*" is therefore a subtype of "*involves*" that has become asymmetrical with the addition of temporal information on the flow of time from the past to the future—*the moving finger, having written, moves on*.
- Every process is a subtype of "*Succeeds*" (or its inverse "*precede*"). Every process is derived from "*Succeeds*" by adding meanings, work steps, or resource transformation information to it. "*Succeeds*" (and its inverse, "*precede*") is the parent of every process. "*Succeeds*" is an asymmetrical relationship and so is every process. They have all inherited this information from "*Succeeds*."

*Figure 7.29. The metamodel of relationship*

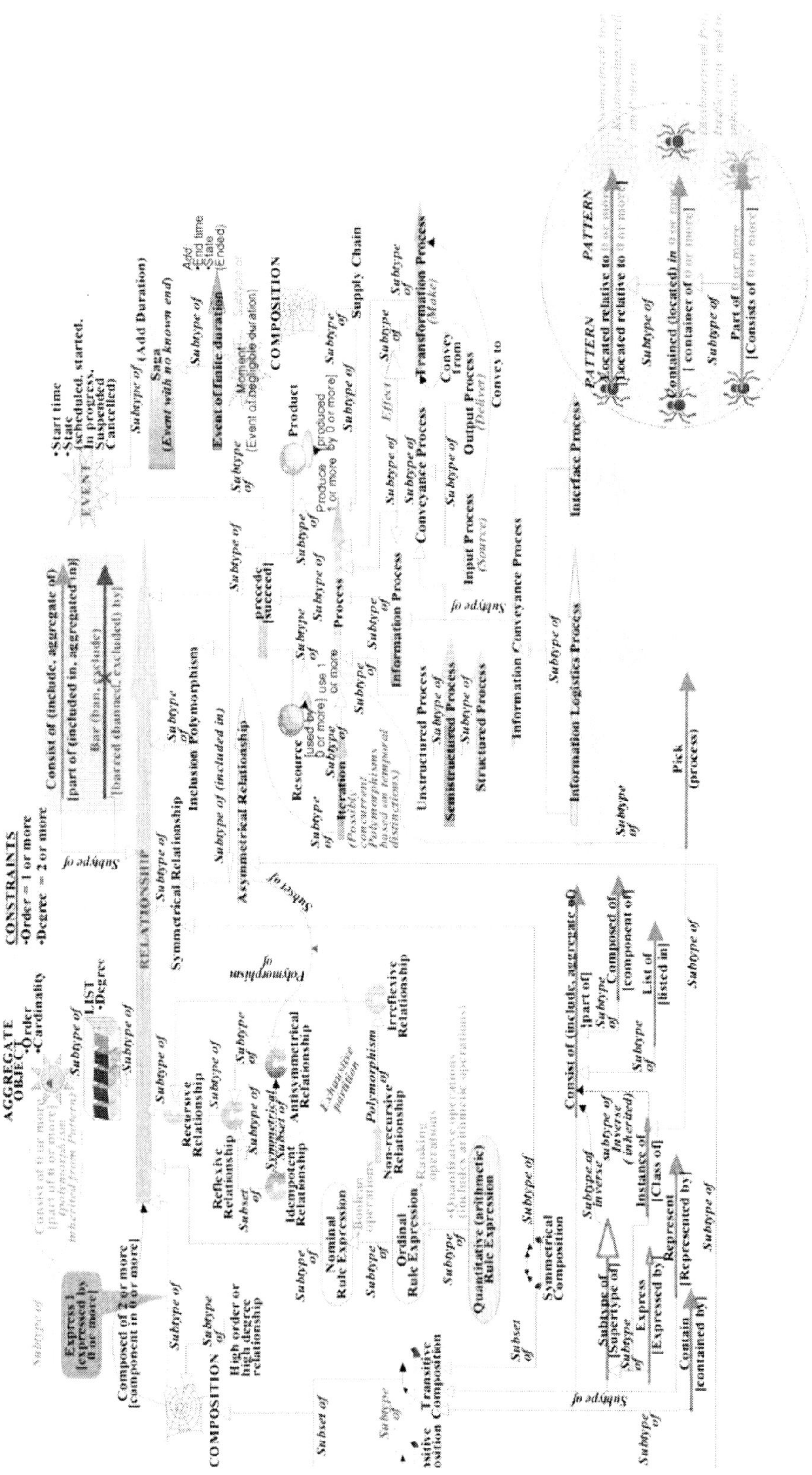

- Every process must use at least one resource and may use more. It must also produce at least one product and perhaps more. On the other hand, every object need not be a resource for a process or a product of one (although all polymorphisms of the primal object are potential resources and also potential products of some unknown process).
- Adding information on the flow of time can also result in temporal distinctions between similar relationships that lead to new kinds of subtypes. These subtypes distinguish one iteration of a process from another (even when the iterations are concurrent). They divide processes into different polymorphisms and new subclasses of the original relationship. We discussed this early under temporal degree. In Box 7.12 and the case study in Module 5 at our Web site, we also saw how instances of an idempotent relationship could split into different subclasses as we added information on the flow of time to the signature process. The object labeled "iteration" in Figure 7.29 articulates the existence of these kinds of polymorphisms.
- Adding structure (information) to an unstructured relationship or process creates more structured polymorphisms. We discussed this in Box 7.7 and under unstructured collaboration. Indeed, processes added 16 new conduits for adding information to those created by nontemporal relationships. Moreover, the information added in any of these 16 ways may lie in a continuum that goes from nil to a lot. Each dimension in Box 7.7 can be a basis for partitioning a process. A *Saga* is also a kind of unstructured process. It has no information on when it will end, if it ends at all. An *Endless Saga* is a subtype of *Saga* that we know for sure will not end. A process that we know will end, even if we do not know when, is also a polymorphism of the generic saga, but we will not call it *Saga*; we will call it a discrete, or "ordinary," process (Box 7.2).
- A *Moment* is even more constrained than a definitive discrete event. It is a moment in time, an event of nil duration in which start and end times coincide. It is therefore a subtype (polymorphism) of the "ordinary" event.
- Constraints are also relationships. Just as a composition is a subtype of a relationship, a *Rule Expression* adds information on the steps by which the value of a rule may be derived (and its meaning expressed). Thus, rule expressions are polymorphisms of rule meanings. Computational algorithms are the link between the business and informa-

*Box 7.13. Subtypes, features, polymorphisms, and constraints*

In Figure 7.29, "Subtype" and "Polymorphism" are synonymous. You could substitute one for the other without changing any meanings. This happens because, when we consider subtyping a relationship, we must consider its shared features. The features it has in common with other relationships stem from the shared information payload of a relationship. We discussed features and their relationship with constraints under product engineering. There we saw how constraints bear information and add to the information content of objects. These are the features inherited by subtypes. Subtypes will also add features of its own to those it inherits. Thus, the conduit of shared information is the subtyping relationship, which will convey a progressively larger information payload down a subtyping hierarchy. Relationships also share information in the same way. Constraints may also be shared thus. These constraints sculpt meanings from the inchoate information swirling through information space. A subtype retains inherited meanings and makes it more specific by constricting it with stricter constraints of its own. Thus, "ancestor" is more specific and more constrained than a "relative," and "mother" or "father" is even more specific and constrained than "ancestor."

tion logistics layers of the Architecture of Knowledge.

- As rule expressions descend the hierarchy from occurrence to Boolean to ordinal to ratio scaled rules, they add information on magnitude and measurability to the meaning of the rule. This is yet another way relationships may be subtyped.

Interactions, information, rules, and meanings lead us from aggregation to *Relationship.* As we plunge down through this hierarchy of meaning, relationships get richer and more meaningful but always more constrained. Meanings, as we have understood, flow from constraints. A constraint is information.

Figure 7.29 describes the semantics of Relationship. It shows how meanings are shared, constrained, and how the information percolates through patterns normalized by relationships of different kinds. The left half of Figure 7.29 focuses on nontemporal relationships, whereas the right side is the metamodel of *Process*. Figure 7.29 shows subtypes of relationships can be more complex than most. They are polymorphisms based on shared information. We have discussed each in this chapter.

An object or relationship is a pattern of information. The pattern conveys meaning, and that meaning conveys behavior. Patterns need not be patterns of tangible symbols; they may also be patterns of abstract information. The pattern and the meaning it conveys is a component, which may be combined with others and reused to create new meanings.

Meanings may be combined across the plethora of partitions and subtypes in Figure 7.29 to yield a rich harvest of relationships. Figure 7.28 was one example. Figure 8.3 has another. In Figure 8.3, adding temporal information to "Consists of" produces "invoke." "Invoke" tells us when to invoke effects in the control process of Figure 8.3, the contol process is called an orchestration Service in the lexicon of SOA. These are two examples of the myriad meanings that lie hidden within the metamodel in Figure 7.29. These meanings lurk as possibilities we can call forth and instantiate in reality. There are an immense number of ways objects may combine and specialize as they spin their webs of meaning in information space—webs that continually tie and sculpt more objects of different kinds. These webs sunder kind from kind, the existent from the possible, and the possible from the impossible. Thus, the Web of reality is spun by rules that constrain.

Each relationship in Figure 7.29 is a starting point. These starting points are abstractions at the heart of multitudes of nuanced meanings conveyed and normalized by the uncounted hordes of business relationships, which express business meanings, needs, recommendations, requirements, policies, and rules of various kinds. The subtypes and partitions in Figure 7.29 provide the templates and guidelines for normalizing the essential information conveyed by these rules about interactions between objects. Each parent parts one essence of a pattern from another, peeling it away from the essence of its subtype. Each subtype is also a relationship and a pattern of information. Each enfolds, encapsulates, and normalizes a meaning. Each meaning is a rule that different polymorphisms of a relationship will inherit even as they enrich it with meanings added. Each is a vessel of normalized behavior. We can create richer, even more complex vessels by combining them across the partitions of Figure 7.29. Each such vessel will be a more complex pattern that will enfold and normalize a more complex rule. The example in Figure 7.28 was but one such instance.

A constraint adds information to a pattern and reduces the freedom of the pattern to be the pattern it is. Constraining a relationship in any way will subtype it. Subtyping is the channel through which common behavior flows and spreads into information space. Constraints flow through this channel, attaching themselves to objects and relationships in myriad polymorphic disguises.

A constraint turns the inchoate information at the gray border of existence into objects. These objects are the relationships, categories, perspectives, and symbols we can sense and understand. They may be also be conduits of pure and abstract information, meanings devoid of form that exist as timeless concepts in information space. The concept of constraint subsumes and extends beyond relationships. We will now turn to constraints to conclude our journey into the metaworld of knowledge.

## REFERENCES

Arkin, A. (2001, March 8). *Business Process Management Initiative Consortium.* Retrieved October 14, 2007, from http://www.bpmi.org

Jones, R.L. (1998, August). *NASA technical paper.* Retrieved October 14, 2007, from Design Tool for Multiprocessor Scheduling and Evaluation of Iterative Data Flow Algorithms: http://www.iis.sinica.edu.tw/JISE/ 2000/200005_07.pdf

Kruchten, P. (1995). The 4+1 view model architecture. *IEEE Software* (Canadian version), pp. 42-50.

## ENDNOTES

1 To understand the nature of the temporal information added to an object or relationship by the flow of time, see the note in Appendix II on the flow of time.

2 A process is the Cartesian product of two aggregate objects—the aggregation of resources and the aggregation of products. Resources come first, and products come afterwards.

3 [116] in Appendix III has more information on resources of different kinds and frameworks for using and assigning them.

4 Like any other resource, an observation may have a life (period of validity for a process). (See [299] in Appendix III.) The interaction between a process and its resource normalizes this behavior.

5 When we considered nontemporal order, we were counting the occurrences of purely nominal information—the participation of object classes in relationships; each class must be counted. Time on the other hand implies a natural progression. Counting back to the past implies the passage of all time slices until the present. One can derive the temporal order of a relationship across time by counting back to the most remote time slice that influenced the present.

6 Box 4.3 describes the principle of subtyping by adding information.

7 [331] in Appendix III classifies events into *Call Events* (requests that must be responded to); *Change Events* (conditions, or changes, in the value of a Boolean expression); *Signal Events* (receipt of explicit communication—a message); *Time Events* (arrival of an absolute time, or the passage of a relative amount of time).

8 Events with no duration are called delta functions in mathematics. Processes of negligible duration also occur, but change that denies the passage of time also denies causality. The explosion of a firecracker produces smoke and uses resources (such as the oxygen in the air and the energy consumed in triggering it), but cause and effect—before and after—are implicit in a process: The resources come first, and the products come afterwards; a process must have a finite duration, even if it is negligibly small.

9 The Business Process Management Initiative (BPMI) consortium is a consortium of diverse firms across the industrial spectrum. BPMI asserts that its purpose is to standardize business process definitions "that span multiple applications, corporate departments

and business partners, behind the firewall, and over the internet" to facilitate collaboration across supply chains. BPMI standards also facilitate integration of information systems assembled from best-of-breed components provided by diverse vendors who might excel in their respective niches. See http://www.bpmi.org.

10 The objects in Figure 7.5b are events. They convey no information on transformation of resources to products. Their names imply work products and make them look like processes, but they become explicit processes only when information about resources, products, or both are added (see Figure 7.11). Based on the principle of subtyping by adding information, a process is a subtype of an event. It is a subtype of an event that is also a relationship between resources and products; therefore, it is a subtype with two parents—*Relationship* and *Event*.

11 Temporal compositions carry more information than nontemporal compositions (rules of event succession). Based on the principle of subtyping by adding information, temporal compositions are subtypes of nontemporal compositions. Temporal compositions inherit the properties of compositions we discussed earlier and add special properties that flow from the tide of time and event.

12 [61] in Appendix III (*A Guide to Project Management Body of Knowledge*, n.d.) has further reading on the task dependency diagramming technique. The sections on process algebras, UML, and Petrinets have additional reading on other techniques for modeling business processes.

13 The Project Management Institute is a cross industry international organization dedicated to developing and standardizing best project management practices. The PMI publishes, owns, and maintains the Project Management Body of Knowledge (PMBOK). The PDM diagramming technique helps to schedule project tasks and to determine the critical path. (The acronym for the Critical Path Method is CPM.) PDM is also the basis of PERT (Project Evaluation and Review Technique), GERT (Graphical Evaluation and Review Technique), and SPREM (Software Project Evaluation and Review Model). GERT, SPREM, and Petrinets of various kinds also support conditional branching of processes. See Appendix II on Petrinets and items under Process/Task/Schedule Management and Models and Process Algebras and Techniques in Appendix III.

14 The diagram in UML is called an activity dependency diagram. Both PDM and UML help to describe event (and process) dependency. (See [61], [86], [329], [330], [331], and [332] in Appendix III.)

15 What if the two constraints clash? What if no orders are taken, but *Pick Item* is mandated? [337] in Appendix III discusses consistency of constraints.

16 [331] in Appendix III classifies events into *Call Events* (requests that must be responded to); *Change Events* (conditions, or changes, in the value of a Boolean expression); *Signal Events* (receipt of explicit communication—a message); *Time Events* (arrival of an absolute time, or the passage of a relative amount of time).

17 PDM does not support conditional branching; GERT, SPREM, Hierarchical Time Extended Petrinets (H-EPNs), and UML do. In UML, the branch will occur at a diamond icon, and each branch will be associated with a guard condition (usually written in plain English). An arrow from the preceding synchronization bar would terminate in the decision diamond, from which all mutually exclusive branches would flow on to other successor events and synchronization bars. H-EPNs support the semantics of event dependencies described here. They support

event compositions (via the subnet concepts), temporal delays, and complex branching decisions. (See [72] in Appendix III.)

18 When two or more event succession rules are in conflict, the result is *null* succession (meaningless, nonexistent succession). When subassemblies of knowledge are assembled from knowledge artifacts, the knowledge repository should bring these conflicts to the attention of analysts or repository managers and insist on their resolution before the subassembly can be released for use.

19 Multiple instances of events may occur simultaneously and the number of event conjunctions that trigger a successor may be different from the number of successors a conjunction triggers. The relationship we considered in the example is a conjunction that triggers a single successor. The cardinality ratio of the inverse of this third order relationship (with respect to the *conjunction*) is the number of successors each instance of the conjunction (of predecessors) triggers; in this case, it will be one.

20 The non-occurrence of service calls on a given day is also an event. It would trigger the Make Random Customer Call event. Conversely, the occurrence of an event may ensure that a successor is not triggered, even if the other triggers occur; that is, an event may disable a successor. A special kind of connection in the succession network, called an "inhibitor arc," between the event that bars and the event barred is used to represent these "negative" succession relationships. See Petrinets in Appendix II and section 2.5 of [72] in Appendix III. Mutually exclusive sets of events are also inhibitors (of the excluded event). "Inhibitor arcs" assert a negative temporal relationship—a constraint on event succession.

21 Petrinets, a technique developed in 1962 by Carl Petri, implements cardinality and event conjunctions with the artifice of passing "tokens" to successor processes. The successor begins only after its predecessors have provided the requisite tokens. See Appendix II on Petrinets.

22 This book supports the standards published by the BPMI consortium (see [63] in Appendix III). BPML supports the kinds of conditional branching and event triggering described here. [63] also supports conditional mutability of resources and products (which our metamodel supports via subtyping and polymorphisms). However, this book emphasizes the layer of business meaning in Figure 3.4 and interfaces to the business process automation layers more than [63] does. Conversely, [63] emphasizes the business process automation layers and its interfaces with the technology layer more than this book does. (See http://www.bpmi.org for information about BPMI.)

23 Triggering events and predecessor processes are resources in the before and after relationship a process articulates. Successors are products produced by predecessors: when one process spawns another, the spawned process is clearly a product of the process(es) that spawned it either singly or in combination.

24 Every constituent may be a constituent of one or *more* aggregates; unless constrained by a capacity constraint, physical aggregates are an important class of aggregate objects discussed in the Universal Perspective (see [338] in Appendix III): The physical world naturally constrains physical objects to one physical location. Consequently, their membership in physical aggregates may be constrained. However, in general, the "*part of*" relationship (the inverse of "*consists of*") does not necessarily constrain the membership of a constituent to a single aggregate.

25 [337] in Appendix III discusses value constraints in detail.

26 Business rules that involve mutual constraints between time slots are consistent with the metamodel of *Value Constraint* in Figure 49 of [337] in Appendix III.

27 If a convoluted rule ever places the end of even a single event before its beginning for any combination of time lags or timings, the process will never execute; it will be the impossible "null" process. The repository of knowledge artifacts should pre-empt this by alerting users.

28 The principle of causality states that no event may be influenced by an event that has not yet occurred (else cause and effect will break down). An exercise: Is risk a measure of how the future might influence the present? Consider the distinction between current anticipation and future occurrence.

29 UML draws heavily on Petrinet and State Charts. (See State Charts on page 55 of [337] of Appendix III and Appendix II on Petrinets.) The vertical bars in Figure 7.6b are called synchronization bars. UML does not explicitly recognize and structure time delays between triggers or windows of opportunity for successors. Other techniques like Petrinets, SPREM (see [87] in Appendix III), LOTOS (see [78] in Appendix III), and ARIS (see [118] in Appendix III) do. In UML, they could be written in unstructured text near the synchronization bar as guard conditions). See bibliography items under Process Algebras. [69] in Appendix III provides a succinct overview and links to additional resources. LOTOS, an acronym for Language of Temporal Ordering Specifications, was declared a standard by the International Standards Organization (ISO) in 1988 (ISO standard 8807). However, LOTOS did not support complex rules such as those that involved delayed responses to events. Subsequent extensions to LOTOS, including Real Time LOTOS (RT-LOTOS), do. RT-LOTOS supports time delays, restrictions, and process latency, wherein a process may have been enabled by one event but will not be initiated unless another occurs. LOTOS supports mutually exclusive processes, parallel processes, processes that must synchronize on an event, as well as the "normal" sequence, wherein the beginning of a process is contingent on the end of another. LOTOS also supports interruption of processes. RT LOTOS adds the concept of delays, windows in time when processes may be latent, and "hidden" internal events. [78] in Appendix III provides more information on LOTOS and RT-LOTOS.

30 Although it is not the intent of UML, the vertical synchronization bars in UML activity diagrams could represent event conjunctions—relationships of various, degrees, orders, and possible latencies between events (also see Figure 7.6b).

31 Temporal networks cannot loop back on past events; that is, the future cannot influence the past, but the past may influence the future (the principle of causality). Networks like this are called *acyclic networks* because they cannot cycle (loop back) to previous instances (nodes). Critical paths apply to acyclic networks.

32 See the mathematics of Hierarchical Time Extended Petrinets in [72] in Appendix III.

33 Rules that constrain connections to ports within a composition will be higher order rules of governance. They will not be higher order *processes* unless they change constraints over time, but they will be higher order *patterns* because they will constrain other patterns.

34 A branch of mathematics called Pi-Calculus deals with concurrent interactive processes, in which dynamic interaction may change the flow of events in a process. See [75], [76], and [77] in Appendix III and Appendix II on Pi-Calculus and Petrinets.

35 UML could, but does not, use the activity dependency diagramming technique (Figure 7.6) to address process cycle times; it focuses on interpreting requirements for computer programmers. Also see Appendix II on Petrinets, [312] and other publications on Petrinets and scheduling in Appendix III.

36 Management literature sometimes distinguishes a goal from an objective. In some strategic planning methodologies, goals are quantitative and objectives are not. However, the distinction is not universally accepted. In this book, we will not make fine distinctions between "Goal" and "Objective." The "Purpose" of a business is very similar to both goal and objective. It is the goal attached to an unknown process for meeting the goal. The process, being "unknown," does not add information to its goal.

37 This process is called SWOT analysis in management literature—an acronym for Strengths, Weaknesses, Opportunities, and Threats analysis. In SWOT analysis, it is often easy to show linkages between objectives and their rationale in a table, a column each for strengths, weaknesses, opportunities, threats, and objectives.

38 An object may play several roles simultaneously. (See [337] in Appendix III.)

39 See the discussion in Box 4.3.

40 Different compositions of a process are different ways of obtaining the same end results. Each will be mutable with the others because compositions, as a whole, are subtypes of the process they compose (see Liskov's Substitution Principle).

41 A process may be a relationship of any order—an irreducible fact that connects several resources and work products into a single relationship. For instance, *Unload Cookie* in Figure 7.11c is a fifth order temporal relationship that glues three resources (including its trigger) and two products into a single irreducible fact.

42 The state of the composition is the *combination* of states of components in it. It is called a *superstate*. See [79] in Appendix III and the section on state charts in [330] in Appendix III.

43 A supply chain is a chain of events that uses resources to create and deliver products. Figure 7.11c shows a part of a supply chain.

44 Information systems analysts are familiar with data flow diagrams. This is why we have adapted them for process mapping. There are other more robust techniques, which also show flow rates, cardinalities, and other rules. (See [6] and [10] in Appendix III.)

45 See batch processes in [100], [103], and [104] in Appendix III. Our metamodel supports the requirements for batch processes articulated at CAPE-21 (a process engineering forum). (See [104] in Appendix III.)

46 The "lived in by" relationship between *House* and *Person* (see The Capacity for Relationships in Chapter V) demonstrates how an "ordinary" object may engage another so that it becomes unavailable as a resource to a process: The house, a building, will not be available as factory for memory chips while it is a home. As such, it cannot be a resource for a process that produces memory chips while people live in it.

47 In 2001, the BPMI (Business Process Management Initiative) consortium aimed to standardize business process definitions "that span multiple applications, corporate departments and business partners, behind the firewall, and over the internet" (see http://www.bpmi.org). BPMI published the BPML standard for business process modeling (See [63] in Appendix III)). Our metamodel extends BPML: BPML recognizes that a process may engage resources. Our processes inherit this behavior from relationships. Our relationships also recognize that they may partially engage the capacity of an object. Moreover, processes also inherit the property

of cardinality from relationships. We have seen how this translates to the quantum of resources required by a process.

48 The succession of a process may depend on the occurrence of a predecessor object (this object could also be an event or another process). An object becoming available as a resource is a temporal occurrence and, therefore, an event. This is why the metamodel makes succession contingent on events. The events could be input events.

49 [116] in Appendix III articulates governing principles for resolving resource conflicts. Resolution of resource conflicts may depend on objectives. (See [72], [83], [85], [86], and [153] in Appendix III.)

50 In a deadlock, the process may be waiting for an item produced one or more steps down the causal chain of events.

51 Complexity leads to chaotic behavior. This occurs when small differences in rules, timings of responses, and values of variables lead to unpredictable, unmanageable, and large differences in end results that cascade through the composite process. It then becomes hard to foresee every exception and contingency. Chaotic behavior is a major field of mathematics. Experience chaos interactively in [293] in Appendix III, or see [292], [323], and Box 18 on our Web site.

52 If it can be inherited from the metamodel, process modeling, task, or project management functions do not need to be re-analyzed and rebuilt each time software is developed. Rules that acquire or substitute resources and resolve resource conflicts are relationships. With temporal information added, they become processes, their behavior inherited from relationships and processes in the metamodel.

53 The complex behavior of temporal networks, their optimization, and load balancing is a subject in its own right and is addressed in the recommended reading in Appendix III, under Process/Task/Schedule Management and Models. [72], [83], [86], [305], and [312] in Appendix III provide additional information on this topic. [83] (in Appendix III), a NASA paper, describes an automated optimization algorithm that resolves resource conflicts and complexity with governing processes (called "control edges" in the publication).

54 [7] in Appendix III has illustrative examples and more information on activity cost. It includes a calculation worksheet.

55 Joint constraints are discussed with Figure 43 in [337] (in Appendix III), Figure 44 in [337], and Figure C of Box 5.1 (in this book).

56 [295] in Appendix III discusses methods of business process redesign and the business rationale driving change and scope creep.

57 Sometimes the "I," or "keep informed" role, is included in the RAWCF dimensions of process ownership. However, "I" gives us little information on the purpose of the role. At the meaning level, we need to know that the information is being shared for consultation, facilitation, tracking, or governance. Tracking and governing processes are considered to be distinct from processes they track and govern. Thus, we believe the RAWCF categories are more precise and action oriented. The "I" dimension belongs to the information logistics layer, more than the business meaning layer in the architecture of knowledge. It describes information flow.

58 Box 36 on our Web site discusses representation in more detail. Representation must be irreflexive because every component of knowledge must convey some information; it is a pattern in information space. An object representing itself conveys no information. Therefore, representation must be irreflexive. Unlike representation, a relationship like "self help" does convey information and hence is a component of knowledge. [338] in

Appendix III describes several key business polymorphisms of representation.

59 [116] and [153] in Appendix III discuss resolution of resource conflicts, interchangeability of resources, work allocation, and derivation of work hierarchies.

60 The section on Activity Diagrams (see [333] and [331] in Appendix III) discusses UML swim lanes.

61 A facilitated workshop in which management and information systems specialists design a service architecture or a collaborative session in which designers, production specialists, and product managers jointly design a product (e.g., a car) are examples of intensely collaborative processes. The resolution processes in Figure 7.13 may be an intensely collaborative process between the departments involved. The section on supply and demand chains has more examples. [36] in Appendix III provides examples of intensely collaborative, reusable e-commerce use cases. Also see [115], [116], and [120] in Appendix III.

62 [295] in Appendix III has more on business engineering.

63 The Value Chain Markup Language (VCML) from Vitria Technology, Inc., describes a value chain as "a network of all of the business partners and transactions in a supply and demand chain from raw materials and subassemblies to the consumer." It asserts "*A value chain spans vertical and horizontal relationships within and across industries. It addresses relationships with all parties participating in designing, manufacturing, financing, marketing, delivering, and supporting a product or service.*" See [65] in Appendix III and http://www.vcml.net/. Note the subtle but important difference between this definition and that in this book. In this book, the value chain is the chain of interdependent *processes* that deliver value. These processes might be owned and managed by the kinds of process owners mentioned in the VCML definition, but our definition focuses purely on the process regardless of ownership; our *Value Chain* is the chain of *processes* that deliver value.

64 Items in Appendix III under Demand and Supply Chain Standards discuss supply and demand chains, the value chain of Figure 7.14, and the imperatives that drive their integration.

65 [118] in Appendix III provides further reading on the ARIS patterns published by Dr. Scheer.

66 The Instrumentation Systems and Automation Society (ISA) is a nonprofit trade association of measurement and control engineers. Founded in 1945, ISA has over 39,000 members spread over more than 110 countries. In its own words, ISA "fosters advancement in the theory, design, manufacture, and use of sensors, instruments, computers, and systems for measurement and control." See http://www.isa.org/.

67 [100] and [102] in Appendix III describe the S95 process standard.

68 [295] in Appendix III discusses business redesign, reasons, and methods.

69 State charts articulate rules about permitted and barred state transitions. See [79] and [333] in Appendix III.

70 [153] in Appendix III discusses subtyping of mutable resources for processes.

71 [337] in Appendix III discusses features of objects such as attributes and behavior.

72 The BPML standard, recently published by the Business Process Management Initiative consortium (http://www.bpmi.org), is one of the very few that support dynamic assignment of resources and products as instances of processes occur. BPML, like the metamodel in this book, recognizes that loss of structure may make a process unreliable. The metamodel model in this book also tells us that this will happen unless unstructured

processes are dynamically governed. [63] and [64] in Appendix III discuss BPML.

73 [116] in Appendix III expands on how needs may be identified and matched with available resources in different business environments. [153] in Appendix III expands on subtyping hierarchies of roles that can facilitate assignment of mutable human resources.

74 Automated actors are assuming W responsibilities, and individuals are moving up to A (see Box 7.6 and the discussion around it). As W and A start converging in the same individual, the value added by individuals at the W level is being replaced more and more their value at the A level.

75 The "features" of Figure 7.25 are called "attributes" by the Balanced Score Card methodology, a framework that is used to identify measures of success for a business. It is a broader concept than the "attribute" of this book.

76 *Agile Systems with Reusable Patterns of Business Knowledge: A Component Based Approach*, a companion book by the same authors, elaborates on the metamodel of "Feature." Chapter IX in this book describes the metamodel of feature at a high level.

77 The information added to the check are temporal cardinality constraints: the concurrency ratio between the resource that signs a check and the check signing process must be 1 or less (i.e., a signatory may sign only one check at a time), and the concurrency of the aggregate process, the two polymorphisms in Figure 7.24b considered together, must be one or less (i.e., the same check cannot be signed by more than one person at a time).

78 If the signature process *always has* to happen whenever the check and signatory are collocated, the relationship between the place and the process would be *implied* by the relationships on either side of it in Figure A. That relationship would then become transitive with respect to the other two, instead of being their common subtype. Obviously, that is not the case. Therefore, the relationship between the place and the process is *derived* from the other two, but as a subtype, not as a member of a transitive triad.

79 These patterns of information—rules and relationships of objects with Place and Physical Place—are discussed in the Universal Perspective in *Agile Systems with Reusable Patterns of Business Knowledge: A Component Based Approach.*

80 The metamodel of Pattern in Figure I.3 and Figure I.2 of Appendix I is a detailed description of the semantics of "Object." Figure 31 on our Web site summarizes the concept. [337] in Appendix III discusses the semantics of pattern in detail.

81 See Appendix II on gluing objects together: The connectives between objects in a threadbare "involve" relationship are not null. A null operator implies no operation, no relationship, no interaction, and *assured* independence between objects. We could call a "value" that subsumes both "*Don't care*" and "null" "*Any*." "Any" conveys no information. There is no element of surprise, it distinguishes nothing and subsumes everything. It is always expected. Its information content is zero (see Appendix II on Shannon's information theory). The *Exclude* relationship in Figure 7.29 is also a connective (a single connective could connect multiple objects). It is an interaction between that which exists and that which cannot. This exclude relationship is subsumed by *involve* (Figure 7.29). All relationships are interactions, and all interactions are connectives. Involve is the "*Don't care*" relationship. It does not care what the interaction is, only that there is one. This is different from "Any" and "Unknown" (see Box 5.3).

82 Chapter IV discusses degrees of freedom.

83 An aggregate object is a supertype of the aggregation relationship. The object not only conveys less information than the relationship, but the relationship cannot exist without the object, whereas the object may occur without the relationship.

84 Figure 31 on our Web site summarizes the semantics between *List* and *Object*.

85 Some kinds of aggregation may be symmetrical (relationships): when classes of infinite cardinality are considered, a part may even contain the whole. Thus, a class that is a part of another class may also be a part of the class it is a part of. The metamodel in Figure 7.29 supports this because it tells us that asymmetrical relationships are subtypes of their symmetrical counterparts but does not make this arcane and surprising symmetrical supertype of asymmetrical aggregation explicit.

86 A set is a kind of mathematical class, but we have used *Set* and *Class* interchangeably in this book.

87 [337] and [338] in Appendix III discuss place and location in detail.

88 *Composed of* (Figure 6.2) has been hidden in the hierarchy of Figure 7.27a. *Part of* does not distinguish between structure and the lack of it, whereas *Composed of* does. Hidden to avoid clutter, *Composed of* lies between *Part of* and *Subtype of* in Figure 7.27a.

89 The Universal Perspective in [338] in Appendix III elaborates on the concept of Place. Also see Box 72 on our Web site.

90 Size is a polymorphism of capacity. *Capacity* stems from relationships (Chapter V) and *Size* from the containment relationship. Size can have different polymorphisms. Each polymorphism of containment is a potential polymorphism of *Size*. For example, a constraint on how many people can live in a house is a polymorphism of size that stems from the *Live in* relationship (Chapter V), which in turn is a polymorphism of containment. The floor space of a house is another polymorphism of size that stems from a containment relationship with the area domain.

91 The precision with which Object 1 locates Object 2 in Figure 7.27b will be greater than the precision with which it locates Objects 3 or 4; the contents of Object 2 could lie anywhere within its limits. Object instances are patterns of information, and patterns have limits and degrees of freedom. Precision increases as degrees of freedom are reduced.

92 A generic relationship between instances of objects that tells us only that the objects are related ("involved" in some unspecified way) conveys less information than one between attributes of objects. You could consider generic occurrence relationships between object classes relationships between instance identifiers. Instance identifiers may also be considered attributes of objects, albeit special attributes that lend an object its very identity. Occurrence information like cardinality, ordinality (order of the relationship) degree, and idempotence add information to this generic and vague involvement between objects. They make the relationship more specific. An occurrence relationship between object classes conveys less information than a quantitative relationship, or even a relationship that tells us *which* specific attributes of what objects are related and bound by what constraints on values. This is why an idempotent loop on the states of an object instance conveys more information than an idempotent relationship that generically relates the object instance to itself. The relationship tells us specifically which state of the object must cycle through what other states to return to the original state.

Indeed, if the cycle involves states of other objects, it becomes an idempotent composition—a composite process with resources and products that cycles back to restore the object at the beginning back to the state it started in. If the cycle is not idempotent with respect to the other objects in the loop, the original object may be considered a catalyst for the composite process; it is a resource that facilitates change without being altered.

93 [338] in Appendix III describes the Universal Perspective in detail.

94 The Universal Perspective is useful for new systems/process designs and also for the integration and reengineering of diverse legacy business processes, supply chains, information systems, and databases.

95 Idempotent relationships between different states of the same object may or may not be symmetrical. The "*shatter*" relationship from a whole to a shattered glass pane in Figure 20 in [337] in Appendix III is idempotent, asymmetrical, and irreversible: it involved whole and shattered states of the *same* glass pane. State transitions involve processes. Processes involve time. Time is asymmetrical. Therefore, processes, idempotent or not, are asymmetrical relationships (which may or may not be reversible).

96 Box 36 on our Web site and Chapter IV discuss representation.

97 *Assemble* is a polymorphism of *Make* in the SCOR supply chain of Figure 7.20.

98 *Assemble Car* normalizes the intelligence about how car parts are assembled into a car: Given any two members of the triad in Figure 7.28, "*Car Part*," "*Assemble*," and "*Car*," the third is implied and adds no new information.

# Chapter VIII
# Crossing the Chasm: Business Process to Information Systems


## ABSTRACT

*This chapter describes the bridge between business meanings and automated information systems. It describes the information architecture that interfaces computational processes to the business semantic.*


We have seen how an object is a pattern of information (see Chapter IV and Box 7.9). It is an abstract pattern in an abstract place that can be called *information space*. This pattern of information is the *essence* of the object—its "spirit" in one sense; it lends meaning to the object. This information manifests itself in physical space only when it is attached to a format. A physical object could in the same way also be considered to be a "format" of an object in physical space, a manifestation of the information it conveys. This information makes it what it is. In crossing the chasm from business process to information systems, our focus must shift from format to meaning.

The meanings glue the physical world of business process, tangible objects, and mechanisms

*Figure 8.1. The bridges from business process to information system*

to the world of tangible information systems that automate and track the information content of the real world. As we have seen, these meanings engage each other to produce new, compound meanings that support both simple and complex behaviors in multitudes of possible configurations. Changing or reconfiguring a meaning will automatically change the meaning and behavior of the business process or object that manifests it in the world of business and, simultaneously, without pause, will also change the information content and configuration of information systems that tangibly manifests *information* about that behavior. The meanings unify, but we must know what bridges we must cross and how to transform meanings into the behavior of information systems. The transforms in this section are those bridges.

These bridges too are components of knowledge—great sweeping bridges that connect the physical world of business to the vast universe of meanings beyond—meanings that are pure information—and then sweep back from abstract meanings to the tangible world that gives pure information a shape and form that we can sense, store, and manipulate.

The primary focus of this book has been the bridge that links the tangible world of business to the abstract world of meanings beyond. Box 4.1 and Equivalence of Patterns in Chapter IV contained transforms that gave intangible meanings tangible form—formats and measures we could manipulate. In this section, we will dwell on translating business processes to information systems. The design of the technology, interface, and information logistics layers of Figure 3.4 are discussed where they touch layers of business meaning. We will see how the design process may be automated by special transformation logic.

The key to the first bridge in Figure 8.1—the bridge from the tangible world to the world of abstract meaning—is simple. Tangible objects and processes convey information that we must abstract, normalize, and focus on. Every object and every process in the real world must be mirrored by a pattern of information—a model that abstracts its essence. Its counterpart in information space, a simple reflection, will reflect every object, resource, product, and process. Unfortunately, rules that are simple at the beginning seldom retain their simplicity as we peel back layers of meaning to reveal the complexity that lies beneath.

A real life business object—a resource, a product, or both—must map to an information object, but it must also be generalized and classified in order to normalize information. This, as we have seen, can be complex, but the patterns in the Universal Perspective, in tandem with our metamodel and the various algorithms for reducing data to normal forms can help (see Appendix II on normalization). Liskov's principle and the Principle of Parsimony must be applied to the Universal Perspective, so that the business semantic is an generalized as possible, without being ambiguous. This will facilitate agility and resuse across different contexts in support of innovation.

A real life business object will interact with other objects. These interactions will be reflected in information bearing relationships in information space. The interactions too must be normalized. We have discussed them at length. It is the same with processes. They are relationships that carry information on the flow of time. We have discussed them too. However, as we will see, the behavior of these reflections is subtly different from the reality they mirror.

## TRANSFORMING BUSINESS PROCESSES INTO EFFECTS OF EVENTS

The reflection of processes in information systems is relatively simple when the process produces (or changes) only one product: Events normalize temporal information, and objects respond to events; events have effects on objects through processes. Such effects bridge the chasm between information space and information system. When a process produces or alters a single product, the process maps directly to the effect. The information process will then be a direct reflection of the business process and is also the effect of an event. The event it is an effect of is the businesses process itself or, transitively, the effect of the event that triggers the business process.

When a process produces multiple products, the rules become more complicated; the system must know how information in an individual information object must be changed to reflect the changes wrought by processes that act on several objects. If we can decompose the process into subprocesses that have only one output, we can map each process to an effect of an event, but the map between process and effect becomes complicated when the process cannot be resolved into subprocesses with a single output—when the process is an irreducible fact like the process for separating wheat from chaff was (under The Essence of a Process) or like the unloading of the cookie sheet was in Figure 7.11c. Unloading the cookie from the cookie sheet separated cookies from the sheet they were baked on and, in a single operation, created each cookie in its final form even as it created the used cookie sheet. It was done in one stroke as a single inseparable irreducible fact. There is no *business* process that will produce the cookie separately from the used cookie sheet in this operation—but, as we will see next, its reflection in information space will.

An information system deals in information, not the real and tangible objects that are the manifestation of that information. A process in an information system must update both the information about the cookie sheet and the cookie to reflect the changes the business process has made. Updating the state of the cookie sheet is the effect of "*Unload Cookie*," an event on *Cookie Sheet*. *Cookie Sheet*, the information object, conveys and normalizes information about the real cookie sheet. It normalizes this effect—an item of information on the behavior of cookie sheets used for baking cookies. On the other hand, the production of the cookie in its final, unloaded form is the effect of the same "*Unload Cookie*" event on *Cookie*, the information object that reflects information about real world cookies. If we cut the *Unload Cookie* process in two as we have done in Figure 8.2 so that each piece of the process has only one output, we will have the two individual effects—one for *Cookie* and the other for *Cookie Sheet*.

*Figure 8.2. The bridge from Process to Effect: Cutting a process with two products into effects of events*

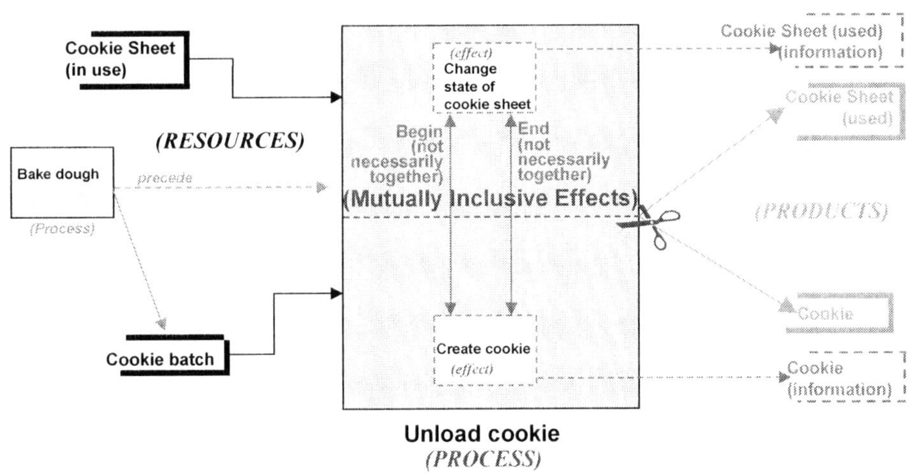

However, we know that we cannot cut the meaning of the *business* process thus. As we have seen, that will be meaningless. This transform has taken us beyond the world of business into the world of information *about* the business. Each effect will drive the logic at the heart of the process that updates information, a process that information systems will use.

If the information system is synchronized with the real world, both effects will begin and end together with the process in the real world but a process and its reflection do not *have* to be synchronized. Indeed, even the two effects do not have to be synchronized. All we know is that they are mutually inclusive; if one occurs, the other too must occur—even if they do not occur concurrently.

Technology constraints might bar them from occurring concurrently or even simultaneously with the processes they reflect, but they must both occur because the business process, reflected in the universe of information, has no meaning unless they both occur (in the terminology of service oriented architecture the pair would be called a "short running" or "ACID" transaction). If some technical glitch in the information system prevents one of the two effects from occurring when the other has, we must restore the information system to the state it was in *before* either one occurred—it is the source of roll-back and recovery rules many designers of information systems are familiar with. (There may also be other causes for rollback and recovery that are internal to the design of the process automation and technology layers of Figure 3.4, but those are not our focus here.[1])

Note how this kind of roll-back and recovery is different from a business rule (discussed under Transforming Business Processes into Effects of Events), in which the chef asserts that if the *Bake Cookie* process (in Figure 7.11c) is interrupted for more than an hour after making dough, then it has to restart from the beginning—by baking fresh dough and starting the process all over again. That is a business rule, a fact that stands on its own. On the other hand, rolling back the information carrying reflection of a business process because both effects could not complete and therefore compromised the integrity of the process, was a rule of information systems *derived* from, and dependent on, the transform in Figure 8.2. It did not stand on its own as a rule of *business*. (As an exercise for the reader, how would you model the chef's rule? In the terminology of service oriented architecture, rules like these are called "long running" transactions.)

If a business process has more than two products, the transformation in Figure 8.2 will slice the business process once for every product in order to derive the effect that applies to *that* product. The business process will then be mirrored by a collection of information processes—effects—that have a single output in information space.

## TRANSFORMING BUSINESS PROCESSES INTO INFORMATION SYSTEMS CONTROL PROCESSES

The effect is how an event touches an object. The junction can be a many-to-many relationship (see Figure 5.7). If we group all effects for a given event into an aggregate object, that aggregate can sometimes be a module in an information system—it will contain a complete set of instructions on how objects must be changed when the event occurs, or rather, when the information system gets word of its occurrence.[2] However, the order in which effects are applied to a system to change its state must not violate the sequence of effects mandated by business processes. Ignoring this sequence is a common source of defects in information systems. We can prevent these defects from occurring by using the transform in Figure 8.2 to derive effects and then sequencing effects in sequences dictated by *business* process maps.

Control processes in information systems sequence effects. To keep the state of information consistent with the state of the business process, these control processes must be derived from business processes. Just as business processes were transformed into effects in information space, process dependencies, timings, latencies, and sequences may be transformed into control processes in information space. When two or more effects in information space are derived by the transform in Figure 8.2, the control processes in information space will only specify that they are mutually inclusive and have the same process dependencies and timing constraints as the business process each was derived from.

*The actual implementation of this abstract control process will only crystallize when it crosses the bridge to information systems in Figure 8.1. It is then that rules about synchronization will be added. These rules will tell us whether the implementations of effects are timed to occur in parallel, in sequence, synchronized with the occurrence of the physical business process (in real time systems), within what tolerances and with what accuracy, reliability and completeness. The augmented control process in Box 8.2 has these rules.*

The implementations of the abstract control process will also incorporate information on interfaces to mechanisms that convey information about the occurrence of real world events to the control process. Similarly, information on interfaces that convey information *from* the control process to interfaces used by the actors who use the system will be a part of the control process—information about states of objects, control events, exceptions, and substates within the control process. We will call this the *augmented* control process.

We will return to transforms that produce this interface under navigation interfaces and again under information input-output processes. Now we will focus on the sequencing of effects. Figure 8.3 illustrates how control processes sequence effects of events on objects (the term "*I/S*" in the figure is an acronym for "Information System"):

*Figure 8.3. Control processes and the sequencing of effects*

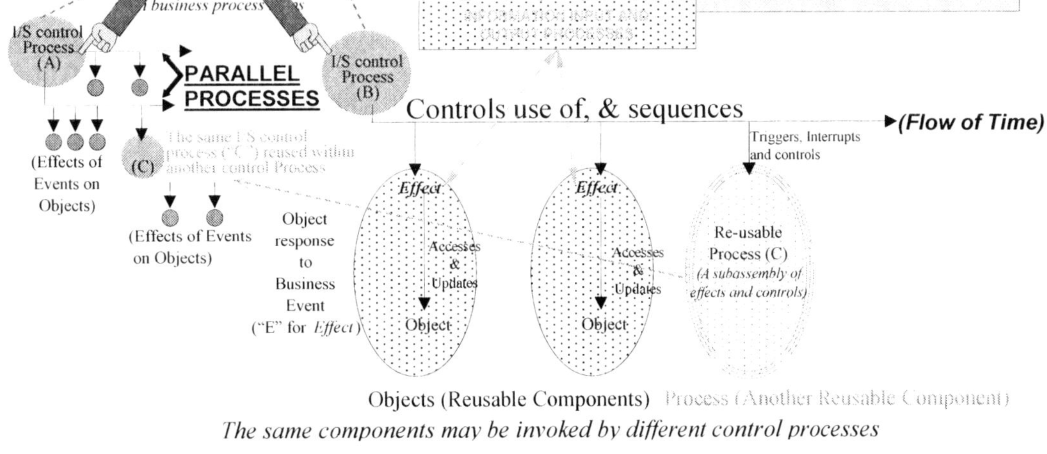


*The same components may be invoked by different control processes*

Automation can be blindly mechanical and totally reliable if it is told *how* to transform resources into products. If we automate the transform in Figure 8.2, as well as the creation of control processes from business process maps, defects of the kind that flow from incorrect sequences of effects will be few. Control processes thus created will reflect business process dependencies.

Control processes sequence and coordinate effects of events. Information objects that are reflections of their real world counterparts encapsulate these effects. These objects normalize or inherit the effects that control processes sequence. Control processes reflect the sequence of business events described by business process maps. (Control Processes are called "Orchestration Services" in SOA lexicon, and the effects they invoke are called "Services" that compose business processes.) The object, and through it, the effect, both become reusable components of knowledge that can be referenced by different control processes. Under process engineering, we saw how business processes may be reengineered by changing process dependencies, sequences, or inserting new processes in process maps (sometimes in support of new features). Corresponding control processes will reflect these changes by resequencing the same effects differently (in tandem with new effects when new processes are inserted). For instance, each variation of the "*Sign Check*" process in Box 7.9 referenced the same effects of the same signature events on the check, but the temporal sequences in which these effects were invoked were different. Similarly, the Bake Colored Cookie process we discussed under process engineering resequenced effects by inserting a new effect into the process map for baking cookies (in support of a new feature—the color of the cookie).

In Box 7.9 (and under Process Reengineering), had there been two variations of the check signing process favored by two different subsidiaries, one in which the CEO had to sign before the CFO, and the other in which the CFO signed before the CEO, it is the control process that would change, not the computer code or information structures that reflect the effects of signature events on the check. In this manner, change has been isolated and contained in information space by normalizing different kinds of information in the right objects in the metamodel of knowledge.

Control processes could also be reusable knowledge (components) in information space. Control processes normalize information about sequencing effects. They are the direct reflection of the sequencing information contained in process maps that describe business process dependencies, sequences, and latency. In our discussion on supply chains, we have seen how one business process may reuse another. In the same way, one control process may invoke another, and there is no bar against other control processes invoking it as well. As such, control processes themselves may be shared components of information—subassemblies of knowledge in information space.

Control processes are also called 'Orchestration Services' in the lexicon of Service Oriented Architecture. Figure 8.3 illustrates how a control process may not only invoke an effect of an event but may also invoke another control process that itself is a subassembly of parts—a sequence of effects and events—a shareable component of knowledge in the repository of knowledge artifacts, referenceable (invokable) by several control processes. Figure 8.3 shows how these sequences may even execute in parallel if the business process they are derived from may also do so.

A control process could also encapsulate rules about process interruption, process suspension, and roll-back, like the chef's rule about restarting the baking process if it is suspended for too long (described in our discussion of the states of events). To these rules of business, control processes also add rules about effects of events that are not strictly *business* events. They are events that flow from things that happen in the business process automation layers of Figure 3.4—rules like the roll-back rule in our discussion of Fig-

*Box 8.1. The metamodel of "invoke"*

> Note that this recursive "invoke" relationship on the class of control processes is a subtype of the "*composed of*" relationship. It is an optional many-to-many relationship in our metamodel. "*Invoke*" tells us *when* a part of the composition must fire because we have infused information on sequences of effects in time into "*composed of*." It is a synonym for "select" and "Pick."
>
> We have seen how an object may optionally contain other objects or be contained in several others. *Contains* is a generic many-to-many, recursive, optional relationship on a generic object. Both "*invoke*" and "*composed of*" inherit this recursion and cardinality from "*contains*."

ure 8.2 for effects that fail to occur. Eventually, when the information system is adapted to a specific technology platform, control processes will also add effects of events in the technology layer of Figure 3.4 (see Box 8.2). However, these events, effects, and even objects that reside in the technology, interface, and information logistics layers of Figure 3.4 are beyond the scope of this discussion. For us, it will suffice to understand how control processes are derived from business process maps and how they reflect rules of process dependency, latency, and roll-back that sequence and control the execution of *business* effects on information objects—objects that are derived from business objects.

Information about business events is conveyed to the information system via an interface with an *Actor* (the interface will also provide information to the system about events that have occurred in the other layers of Figure 3.4, but those events are not the focus of this discussion). The *Actor* executes the control process and could be either a person or automation (see the "W" dimension of process ownership in the section on Process Ownership). The actor's interface with information objects lies in the business process automation layers of Figure 3.4. We will discuss the transforms that produce these interfaces later this section.

The metamodel does not restrict a control process to a single interface or a single actor. There may be several. Different technologies and mechanisms may support different interfaces and actors, and each may reuse the augmented control process of Box 8.2. This augmented process is how the process in Figure 8.3 is implemented in information systems. It resides in the interface layer of Figure 3.4. The augmented control process was derived from the control process in Figure 8.3, which may be reused in several implementations. The control process in Figure 8.3 and its augmentation in Box 8.2 are both components of knowledge, but not components of *business* knowledge. They are components of business process automation. They carry information on how the information system will synchronize and time effects, without violating the constraints imposed by the business process.

(All possible implementations of control processes may not be realized. This is why the injective relationship in the metamodel above is optional. Also note that the injective relationship between control processes in the different layers of Figure 3.4 and the augmented control process is "*composed of*" rather than its less restricted form, "*consists of.*" This is because the effects and events in the lower layers of Figure 3.4 are *added* to on the structure in Figure 8.3. Thus, when the unaugmented control process of Figure 8.3 is augmented, it tells us exactly when and under what conditions the augmented control process in the metamodel above will invoke the nonbusiness effects embedded in it.)

Different footprints of large businesses and supply chains often subscribe to different standards and technologies in support of different needs, legacies, and business environments. A

*Box 8.2. The injective relationship between a control process and its augmentation*

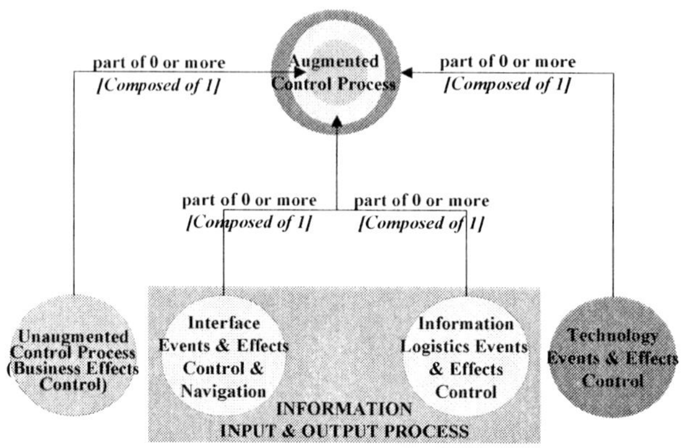


*Figure A. The metamodel of an augmented control process*

A control process may have several augmentations. Indeed, the control process at the core of an augmentation will not change when new technology drives changes in interfaces with new or old actors or information systems reengineering drives changes in information logistics. (The unaugmented control process will only change if the product or business process is reengineered. We have discussed how this can be automated under process and product engineering.) The distinction between a control process and its augmentation separates business process knowledge from its technological implementation. Designers of information systems will thus be free to reuse the unaugmented control process even as they leverage new technology innovatively, creating new and innovative interfaces in step with the growing potential of advancing technology platforms. Indeed, the same unaugmented control process may even be at the heart of processes that support diverse legacy technologies, in diverse legacy environments, in different business footprints (like it was in Box 3.1). Thus, we will be able to support swift change through reuse of business process knowledge even as change rides in on the wings of technology and diversity.

For example, a business unit or supply chain partner in a less technologically advanced footprint might support only old IBM 3270 interfaces without GUI (Graphical User Interface), whereas another footprint might support Microsoft Windows. The interfaces, and even source and destination files, may be different, but the unaugmented control processes at the heart of equivalent business applications for both actors will stay the same. Only the interface and information logistics processes will be different. These may be "snapped on" to the unaugmented control process to produce the different configurations that will execute in each environment. Together, the interface control and information logistics control processes will constitute the information input or information output process. This process is identical to the input and output process in Figure 7.12, except that it applies only to processes that use information to produce information; it is a subtype, an inclusion polymorphism of the input/output processes of Figure 7.12 (inclusion polymorphism was discussed in Box 4.8. The polymorphic behavior of the generic check signing process in Figure 7.24b was another example of inclusion polymorphism). We will discuss information input and output processes later in this section. Now it will suffice to understand that the injective relationship between a control process and its augmentation is the reason why a business rule may have multiple implementations (see Box 3.1).

large and complex global corporation or supply chain must coordinate its policies across this diverse and fractured world. It must leverage shared knowledge and draw the line between centralization and autonomy very carefully to optimize the synergy of its parts without losing its agility and ability to compete in diverse communities. It must walk a very narrow divide between reuse and replication, between standardization and customization, between stability and innovative change and, most of all, between bureaucratic morass and uncoordinated chaos.

This is getting harder and harder to do as corporate footprints and supply chains stretch to transnational and even global scales in support of integrated businesses and the enormously diverse supply chains. These supply chains must be coordinated. It is hard to coordinate these large and diverse chains because change flies swiftly on the wings of new technology bolstered by ruthless competition. The fact that a control process may have several augmentations gives each footprint the agility it needs to serve the fractured global communities of Figure 7.26 (see the business example in Box 3.1). The transforms we have described will isolate and normalize change to foster reusability. Components of shared business practices may be welded to custom interfaces and different technologies appropriate for different footprints. We can then innovate without losing the standard and create without losing the legacy of appropriate practice. It will become easier to navigate the middle path—the narrow divide that is becoming ever narrower and harder to walk. Automation can help us race while we keep our balance.

*However intricate the rules of business or automation might be, the key to creating the control processes in Figure 8.3 is the realization that an effect is derived from a process—a temporal relationship—and therefore the sequence in which effects are applied must be the same as the sequence of the processes they were derived from. Changing the sequence can compromise the integrity of the system. The system might then diverge from the reality it must reflect.*

Of course, business process maps themselves may be created from reusable components (discussed under Process Engineering, Product Engineering, and Supply Chains). However, that is not the focus of *this* transform. Here our sole intent is to turn business processes into information systems processes.

## TRANSFORMS THAT IMPLEMENT NONTEMPORAL RELATIONSHIPS

Information systems processes also mirror static constraints. Consider the relationships in Figure 5.1. In an information system, a bidirectional navigation process may implement each kind of relationship in Figure 5.1. Each kind of relationship can also be the basis for a presentation format—an interface. The process will support and implement the interface:

### Navigation Interfaces

Take the injective relationship in Figure 5.1b. It charts a navigation path from a single instance of object class A to possibly several instances of object class B. This information may be presented to a human actor as tables, pull down windows, drop down lists, information bearing graphics, and multimedia formats of the kind we discussed in Box 4.1. For nonhuman actors, it will be information bearing files and feeds such as indexed tables, sequentially batched files, queue files, random access files, and so forth. The only constraint imposed by the relationship is that it be possible to list several instances of object class B for each instance of object class A.

Interfaces of this kind will be objects in the interface layer of Figure 3.4,[3] and an injective relationship may be supported by any presentation interface that can show several values associated with a single value. Relationships may be navigated in both directions; hence the same kind of interface will also apply to surjective relationships. Thus, any presentation interface including tables, drop down lists, or other presentation formats that permits the presentation of several associated objects, given a single target object instance, will suffice.

Given a source object (an instance of object class A in Figure 5.1), the interface for the surjective relationship should have the capability of navigating to, and presenting any instance of, the target object (an instance of object class B in Figure 5.1) that the source object might be related to, and conversely for an injective relationship, given a target object that is an instance of object class B, the interface should be capable of navigating back to the related instance of the source object in object class A.

Many-to-many relationships are surjective or injective relationships joined end-to-end (Figure 5.7). Thus, the interface for a many-to-many relationship would involve the same one-to-many (or many-to-one interface) we just discussed, except that they will be joined end to end into a composite interface. Each many-to-many traversal will involve stepping through each injective–surjective component of the composite interface every time we step from an instance of a source object to an instance of a related target object.

Higher order or higher degree relationships implemented in a relational database will typically present related object instances as joined tables. Each row of the table will be the union[4] of all features and effects normalized by each object in the relationship and the relationship itself. The selection criterion object[5] will give actors access to some or all of these features, depending on who the actor is.

Information on sequences, visibility, and accessibility may be added to the navigation process. Value constraints are special kinds of relationships. Also, all objects, including relationships, will inherit formatting rules, sequencing rules, inclusion and exclusion sets, and displays, which are all components that mediate a view of an abstract object. (Figure 33 on our Web site describes the semantics of *View*). A View links abstract meanings to the interface layer of Figure 3.4 to make them tangible. Then, with style guides, the design of the interface layer may be automated (see [154] and [155] in Appendix III). A View is one of several bridges between the business and interface layers of Figure 3.4.

*Note that the sequencing object attached to a View[6] does not necessarily imply a temporal sequence. It implies the generic sequenced pattern. It could be a temporal sequence, a sort sequence in a report, a sequence in one or more directions in space relative to one or more delimiters, or any other dimension mapped from state space. Sequences in a report or display do not necessarily imply that the displayed items must be produced in the same temporal sequence. An information systems process could fill the slots in any temporal sequence or even simultaneously if the technology permits it.*

## The Navigation Process

Each component of View will be supported by a process in either the business process automation layers or in the technology layer of Figure 3.4. A process that implements an interface may be an inquiry process that merely presents information to an actor or a process that also changes the state of an object (Box 7.1). Information systems processes that change the state of an object must pick the object instance they will update via a View. The process that implements the interface will reside in the lower layers of Figure 3.4. This *interface* will also be an object. The *process* that implements it may be in either the interface layer or the technology layer of Figure 3.4 (it will depend on the degree of automation of the technology platform—see Chapter III). This process will seek, select, and gather information, navigating from object to object, traversing relationships as it and composes information, and building compositions of information objects in the information system.[7] The relationships it traverses may be subtypes or not, temporal or not (if they are temporal, they will be processes), inherited or not. Remember also that subtypes of objects will inherit the navigation process itself.

These processes are the bridge between control processes and the presentation process (P) in Figure 8.3. These interface processes, objects, and events add to and augment the list of business objects and effects in Figure 8.3. They round out and complete the control process. They implement the information system in tangible form. Thus, these processes and interfaces turn intangible meanings into tangible information. They are the transforms that sweep abstract meanings over the chasm in Figure 8.1, across the bridge from abstraction to information system. We will describe how this information, produced by each transform, is normalized when we discuss Information Input-Output further on in this chapter. Now it will suffice to understand that the interface to an object may be automatically created from business objects and their mutual interactions—the relationships and processes that bind them to each other.

## Implementing Nontemporal Relationships with Processes

Sometimes static constraints can be more complex than the relationships in Figure 5.1, or even Figure 5.2. For instance, the state of a check (an object) made payable when it has the CEO and CFO's signature is derived by a nontemporal relationship between payability (a state of the check) and the presence of each signature (also states of the check). On the computer system, however, a process implements the nontemporal relationship because derivation takes computer time (however short).[8] This applies not just to relationships between attributes but can also apply to relationships between objects. It takes time to create, update, or remove information about real world relationships, that is, a real world technology constraint.

When these relationships are transformed into processes in the technology or business process automation layers of Figure 3.4, these processes may create multiple outputs. Slicing the process into effects, as we have done in Figure 8.2, will augment the control process by adding these information systems effects to the business effects they invoke.[9] The triggers for these process implementations of nontemporal relationships are derived from the nontemporal relationship they implement. The trigger is the occurrence of a state that leads to changes in one or more derived states.

For example, in Figure 7.24b, a check becomes payable when it has two signatures. A process can implement this rule by changing the state indicator of the check to signal that it is payable *after* state indicators for signatures show that the check has obtained the requisite signatures. Effects of internal events like these (information systems events internal to the information object) are transitive with external business events (like signing the check). The control processes in Figure 8.3 must also manage them. The control process will ensure that the state of the information system remains consistent with the state of the real world process it reflects.

Sometimes information systems processes will merely validate the consistency of the information system and raise alarms when there are exceptions. These alarms may apply to temporal or nontemporal constraints—alarms that are raised when rules like mutual inclusion, mutual exclusion, subsetting, concurrency, value constraints, and the like are violated. Some of these alarms would be business exceptions, whereas others will be exceptions triggered by faults within the technology, information logistics, or interface layers (for example, a computer or a program may be defective, a file might be missing, or data might be in an unexpected format or transported too slowly or too rapidly). Exceptions require exception processes. Only some of these exceptions are violations of business rules. Exceptions may also be faults and anomalies within technology, information logistics, or interface layers.

This discussion has shown us why information systems process maps may not always faithfully reflect business process maps. Moreover, automated process flows must reflect business process dependencies augmented with information systems dependencies that implement nontemporal rules and relationships in the business model. The purpose of the control process in Figure 8.3 is to ensure that the state of the information system remains consistent with the state of the real world business system. The information systems process map is derived from the business process map. However, the information systems process map must also account for nontemporal business rules and orchestrate interface processes, information flow, and technology rules, as well as potential faults, failures, and anomalies in all of these layers

The business process and the information systems maps are coordinated by operations that constitute the effect of an event—operations on information objects. Understanding these operations—the most granular of all components through which time sweeps into, through, and beyond an object to record the steady drumbeat of its history—will be our next step into the metamodel of knowledge. These operations are simple and few, yet they rivet effects to objects, and by doing so, they seamlessly weld information system to business process.

The heart of the information system, the transforms that make the state of the information system consistent with the states of the business, can then be produced by automation. Business will thus be seamlessly and automatically reflected in the information system that supports it. The business process will thus create its own information system, an information system that is its shadow. Like all shadows, it will be an information system that will flex in step with the business process. It will adapt, as the business process continually adapts to serve the communities in Figure 7.24 in their eternal search for excellence. It is a restless search, a perpetual striving, a flexing and reshaping that can never end.

## THE OPERATION OF EFFECTS

Effects fundamentally make change; they create, delete, or update objects. Strictly speaking, creation and deletion are also subsumed into the concept of updating the state of an object; they are subtypes of the update effect in which the value of the instance identifier of the object is either changed from "*null*" or to "*null*."[10] Processes (and therefore effects) may also change relationships; relationships too are objects. For example, a person or organization becomes a *Customer* when a business process ties the buyer with a product and a seller via a purchasing relationship. Thus, effects may create, delete, or update relationships, like they may update, delete, or create any other object. In terms of the *operations* that constitute an effect:

- An effect might create an (information) object.
- An effect might delete an (information) object.
- An effect might update the state of an (information) object.
- The object may also be a relationship, attribute, or an effect.
- If the object is a relationship, the effect might switch the relationship from one instance of an object to another.

The state of an object is the combination of values of its attributes, constraints, and relationships with other objects. The effect[11] changes the state of an object by changing its features. A process could also be a relationship between attributes. Corresponding effects will then alter specific attributes—one attribute for every distinct effect. Effects like these are operations. The same event may trigger several operations. Indeed, the fact that an attribute has changed may also trigger cascading changes, all stemming from the same root cause—the event that started the chain of cascading changes.

All operations triggered by a single event on a single object will be the effect of the event on the state of the object (see the example in Figure 8.4). These attribute (and feature) level effects[12] are the elementary operations that collectively constitute the object level effect of the event. As we have also discussed, some of these operations may even stem from nontemporal relationships between attributes. These operations will keep attribute values mutually consistent with business rules, updating attribute values as needed, or flashing alarms if they are validation operations (sometimes they may do both). Thus, at the object level, the effect of an event on an object may consist of the following kinds of operations:

An operation may replace the value of a feature (data attributes, relationships, effects, and constraints). Replacing a feature could imply switching a relationship from one instance of an object to another.[13] An input process will provide the replacement value (discussed this later in this section).

- An effect may delete or create an object (remember relationships are objects too).[14] This too is an operation.
- An effect may replace, create, or delete another effect. These too are operations.

  For example, the terms and conditions of an agreement under negotiation may be updated several times, but once the agreement is sealed, the update effect is deleted. It is recreated again if the agreement is reopened for renegotiation.

This kind of behavior can be modeled by barring the update effect *if* a state indicator shows that it is a sealed agreement—a guard condition on a state change that is contingent on another state indicator. Thus, the combination of a guard condition and a state indicator conveys information on the applicability (and hence, the very existence) of the effect that would change the terms and conditions of the agreement. Updating the state indicator referenced by the guard condition is thus tantamount to an operation on the effect. Thus, state indicators that establish the presence or absence of an effect and guard conditions contingent on these values of the state indicator can model effects of this kind.

(See Figure 8.4 for another example of an effect like this. This is only one of several techniques for implementing effects that create, delete, or change other effects. Can you think of other techniques for implementing effects like these?)

- An operation may determine the value of an attribute (feature) from the values of other attributes (features)—perhaps even states of *other* objects. These operations flow from relationships between attributes (features). They are attribute (feature) level effects that capture information on cascading changes that flow from an effect that changes *any* attribute (feature) in the relationship. It might even change several attributes (features) simultaneously, but each will be a distinct operation. The operations will collectively constitute the effect.

The payability of the check in the section on process engineering was implemented in the information system by an effect that was contingent on other state indicators of the check. Similarly, a quantitative rule like "Amount = price x Quantity" may be implemented by an effect that derives the value of one of the attributes in the relationship from values of the other attributes. These kinds of effects typically implement second or higher degree (and order) quantitative or qualitative relationships between attributes. Attribute value constraints and relationships between attributes are identical in the metamodel of knowledge.[15]

For example, any event that changed either Price or Quantity would change the Amount. The Amount will be fixed the moment we know the exact values of both Price and Quantity. However, the converse is not true. Fixing the Amount will not fix the Price and Quantity. Their degrees of freedom will be limited, but not zero. A value is fixed only when its degree of freedom is nil; that is, the attribute (feature) has no freedom to take any other value. The inverse relationships from Price and Quantity to Amount do not have this information. Thus, if an event changed the Amount, we would be at a loss to make corresponding changes to the Price and Quantity unless at least one of them was also known.[16] If not, the best we could do would be to set the price and quantity to "*Unknown*" and fix all three values when any two become known. (Does this kind of "*Unknown*" value carry more information than a completely unconstrained "*Unknown*" value? Hint: Consider its degrees of freedom and the discussion on the ratio scaled domains in Chapter IV.)

*If we have an event that will change values of all three attributes simultaneously (Quantity, Price, and Amount), that is, an effect constituted of operations that update all three values without reference to the constraining relationship between them, the constraining nontemporal relationship[17] would translate to a process that validates all three for consistency. Setting state indicators to flag the object for inconsistency (or consistency) will record the result of such validations. These attribute level validations and changes to state indicators will also be operations on the check. You could think of these operations as being effects that are mutually inclusive, or transitive, with the effect that changes any one of the attributes in the relationship. Since they must always go together, the operations may all be packaged under the effect that occurs first but all must occur if any one occurs—even if they happen at different times in the information system.*

The example in Figure 8.4 shows the operations that constitute the effect of an event on an object. Note also how operations have been aggregated into the effect based on how a single event (class) will change the state of a single object (class). Note also how the guard condition establishes the presence or absence of an attribute level effect, which is an operation within another effect.

Thus, an event may trigger a series of one or more operations on an object. These operations collectively determine the state of the object *after* the event has occurred. Taken together, these operations constitute the effect of the event, and like any other process, the temporal order of these operations may be significant: Executing these operations in different sequences may result in different states of the object. To keep the state of an information object consistent with its real world counterpart, the order of operations must be consistent with business processes in the business process map. These operations are the most granular of information systems processes needed to keep the state of an individual information object consistent with the real world object it reflects.

An operation may *set* the value of an attribute (or the occurrence of another effect) in information space but will *store* it in an information system. *Store* in an information system reflects *Set* in information space. *Store* is also a subtype of its more generic counterpart, *Set*, because it conveys more information; It tells us *how* the value in question is set in an information system.

*Operations* in information space are thus reflected in information systems by their subtypes. However, *attributes* (or features) in information space may be reflected in information systems by their supertypes because the information system might drop some real world information. For example, in Figure 8.4, the information system might set a nominal "yes/no" flag instead of the full signature to show that the check is signed. Then, the information system would have less information than the real world on the signature

*Figure 8.4. An example of an effect with guard conditions and operations*

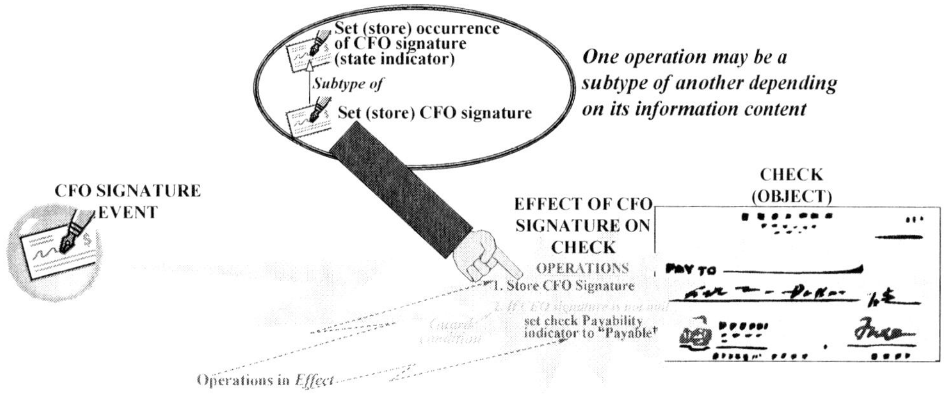


on the check. Hence, the state of the check in the information system would be a supertype of its counterpart in the real world. This could happen because input or output mechanisms have limitations or because the input process or the output process filters information.

It depends on business process automation: interface and information flow. For instance, if the check is signed on a pad that senses the signature and stores it automatically, then the actual image of the signature may be faithfully stored in the information system with no information loss. Electronic signatures may also be used and stored without losing information (see Box 7.9). On the other hand, if only the information about the *occurrence* of the signature (a *Yes* or *No*) is input by an operator via a simple IBM3270 or GUI interface, from a workstation equipped with a simple CRT (Cathode Ray Tube) terminal hitched to keyboard or a touch screen, we might only be able to capture information about the *occurrence* of the signature, but not its real world form or format. The implementation of an attribute in information space will climb the subtyping hierarchy in Figure 4.1, depending on how much information is filtered as it maps to the information system. Information input-output processes also convey and filter the real world value of the attribute. Naturally, this will impact the choice of possible formats in which the attribute can tangibly manifest itself in an information system (see the information carrying capacity of Format in Box 4.1). Units of measure information could become invalid when quantitative information maps to qualitative domains in an information system.

The feature being mapped to an information system may also be value constraints. If the value constraint loses information as it maps to an information system, its implementation will climb the subtyping hierarchy from quantitative rule expression, through ordinal rule expression, to nominal rule expression. Note that occurrence relationships between objects are also value constraints. They are nominal value constraints between object identifiers. Thus, information rich, real world value constraints may even be reduced to information sparse occurrence relationships in information systems.

Automating the transform that carries a feature over the bridge in Figure 8.1, from abstraction to concrete information system, can facilitate *automatic* adaptation to a technology environment. When an interface or mechanism can convey more information, an automated agent[18] could sense it and adjust the feature, its formats, and operations in the information system (including value constraints). The scope of adjustment may include guard conditions that might bar input or output formats because the information content of an object does not support them. Information conveyance processes will normalize these effects. In the same way, the navigation interfaces (discussed recently) can also become sensitive to the technology that will (or will not) support them.

Each time an event affects an object a transform sweeps a feature over the chasm in Figure 8.1 from abstraction to concrete system. If an automated agent could adapt this transform to its technological environment, the information system could become a chimera that flexes with the reality it mirrors.

Then, a change in information acquisition technology will also become an event that has an effect—perhaps different effects on different objects. These effects will collectively, transparently, and seamlessly rewrite and reconfigure the information system each time it updates the state of an information object. The augmented control process of Box 8.2 would incorporate these interface events into the structure in Figure 8.3. The information system would then automatically adapt, leveraging interfaces and mechanisms that convey information to it each time it triggers an effect. This information would filter through operations and effects to corresponding objects.

The shadow of reality will be cast through the prism of technology, and these shadows will flex and move when input and output processes flex in response to shifting technology. The same effects may be manifested by a choice of interfaces supported by a choice of platforms in support of the choice of business process automation appropriate for environments in vastly different footprints. Indeed, the same information may even be simultaneously acquired or presented in different formats and styles by different interfaces supported by different input and output devices.

This is how the information system can move, adapt, and change in step with business in its eternal search for excellence. This is also how we can fulfill the promise of seamless integration between business processes and information systems and support businesses striving to serve the diverse global community of supply chain partners and other stakeholders.

## INFORMATION INPUT-OUTPUT PROCESSES

Input and output processes may also be snapped on to information systems processes (like in Figure 7.12; joining transformation processes with input and output processes is generic. This is inherited by both business and information systems processes from their generic parent). When the process was a business process, the input processes described how resources are conveyed to the process that makes the product, and the output process describes how products are conveyed from the process that makes them.[19] The resources and products of information systems processes are information. The input process snapped onto an effect or any process that uses information to produce information must describe where the information will be sourced from, subject to what rules (like sequence, format, speed, etc.). These are rules of information logistics and the protocols for interfacing with other processes and actors. Input and output processes may be divided into information logistics processes and interface processes (Figure 8.5).

Input and output processes are analogs of the sourcing and delivery processes we discussed under supply chains (the transformation process at the heart of Figure 7.12 is the analog of "*Make*"). The information that information sourcing and delivery processes normalize was discussed in Chapter III under Information Logistics Layer and Interface Rules Layer. Snapping input and output processes onto an effect or operation identifies from where (which files, records, and so forth), when, and under what conditions information will be fed to the effect and where the results will be recorded, for how long, and in what formats.

Figure 8.5 shows subtypes in two distinct partitions. It is these components that isolate and connect business meaning to the technology platform that implements a business process. Typically, in a large and diverse corporation, similar information is fragmented and replicated in several files managed by a colorful legacy of multiple systems used in different business footprints by different subsidiaries and organizational units for different or similar purposes. Different input processes may be snapped on to the same transformation process to support different business units. They might refer to similar data stored in different files, formats, units of measure, storage media, and so forth. Thus, business and systems knowledge will be segregated and normalized in different metaobjects. An automated repository of knowledge artifacts can then facilitate reuse in different parts of the firm.

Information input and output processes are not reflections of the business input and output processes of Figure 7.12. Business input and output processes are business processes (for example, the feeding of dough to the oven in Figure 7.11c), which will have their own information input, transformation and output processes.

The input and output processes in Figure 7.12 were processes that conveyed resources to, and products from, a transformation. They were business processes. Each business process might also have exceptions—what action must the process take when the unexpected occurs—conditions like missing resources or broken conveyance mechanism. Exceptions like these lead to exception processes. Each process in Figure 7.12—the transformation process, the input process, the output process, and corresponding exception processes may be transformed from information space to information systems by the transforms we have described. The products of these transforms will also be the effects, operations, control processes, and interfaces of the kind in Figure 8.3 (P). These effects and control processes will also be implemented by information systems processes and will all have *information* input and output processes "snapped on" to either end (like the process in Figure 7.12 had *business* input and *business* output processes snapped on to the transformation process at its core).

These *information* input, output, and transformation processes may, in turn, have their own exception processes—exceptions that deal with unexpected conditions in the business process automation layers of Figure 3.4—exceptions like missing files, corrupt data, and unexpected or unknown formats.

The information input or information output process is not a reflection of a business input or output process, but it is a polymorphism of it—a polymorphism derived from processes that use information to produce information. All input processes must source and transport resources

*Figure 8.5. Kinds of information conveyance*

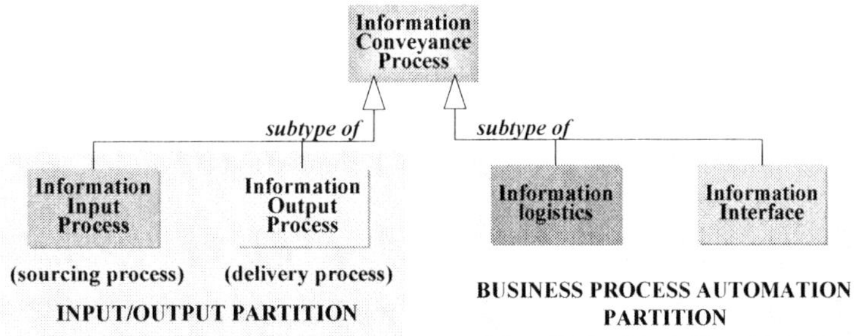

to the transformation process in Figure 7.12 and so must the information input process source and transport *information* resources to the *information* transformation process; it is a subtype of the transformation process in Figure 7.12. All input processes must time sequence and prepare the resource and feed it to the transformation process in the required form and orientation; so must the input process feed the information to the *information* transformation process in the required form and format at the right time and in the right sequence. These factors apply equally to the output process that receives the product(s) of the transformation. Overall, information input and output processes will consist of an *information logistics layer* that normalizes information transportation, source, and destination information and an *interface layer* that formats, times, and prepares information in the tangible form expected by the *information* transformation process.

### Transforms from Business to Interface Layers

Thus, the transform from information space to information system *adds* information about the form, format, timing, sequence, quality, and security of tangible information in the information system (see the examples in Chapter III). *This transform is the contract for information exchange between information space and tangible information systems* (Figure 8.1).

### Transforms from Business to Information Logistics Layers

The transform from information space to information system also *adds* information about the sourcing, delivery, and transportation of information in the information system. The transportation of information includes calculations and algorithms, which are all expressions of meanings. There may be several ways of expressing a meaning, and several algorithms may produce the same result (see Box 5.1). *This transform describes how the availability of information, implicit in information space, will be implemented by its physical transportation and storage in information systems*, as it sweeps requirements over the bridge in Figure 8.1.

Information input and output processes in an information system are assembled from the interface and information logistics components in Box 8.2. They wrap themselves around pure business meanings that cast their shadows from abstract information space and connect these abstractions to technology platforms lending them tangible form and substance. We discussed how, if these transforms are automated and transformation events are considered every time information crosses the bridges of Figure 8.1, these forms could become context sensitive formats. The form will flex with the shadow, input and output processes will add to the effects, events, and objects in the control process of Box 8.2. When this happens, it will be hard to distinguish the shadow from substance.

*"...the self was not the same;*
*Single nature's double name*
*Neither two nor one was call'd.*
*Reason in itself confounded,...*
*Simple were so well compounded,*
*That it cried 'How true a twain*
*Seemeth concordant one!'"*

William Shakespeare
*The Phoenix and the Turtle*

## WHEN RULES ARE VIOLATED

The chef's rule about restarting the baking process for cookies if it was interrupted for too long was an example of the fact that a rule—any rule—may be violated. In other words, there may be exceptions. This is our penalty for ignoring the uncertain nature of the real world. We have seen how a process is a container of special kinds of rules. No rule is absolute, and therefore neither is any process. Exceptions are our hook into the world of chance we have ignored.

What would we do in Figure 7.11c if there were no cookie sheets even though the dough globs were ready for baking? What would we do if the input process had no exceptions but the oven did not produce cookies of the right consistency, taste, or color? What would we do in Figure 7.24b if a check without both signatures were accidentally paid? Exception processes will describe the procedures that must be followed when rules are violated—when the unexpected happens. These exception processes will be subprocesses within "*Bake Cookie*" or "*Pay Check*." To account for possible mistakes, or violation of rules, we must have exception processes—also triggered by events—events that must *not* happen.

## The Risk Management Transform

We can account for these events by "cutting" (partitioning) a business process into the expected and the exception. This is our first "cut" in Figure 8.6a—the horizontal cut right through the "middle" of the process. The exception process in Figure 8.6a is the contingency process that describes the procedures that must be followed when an exception occurs.

Figure 7.12 showed how input and output processes can be "snapped on" to the transformation process at the core to produce a composite process. The input and output processes in the composition normalize input and output rules (for resources and products respectively), separating them from the rules of transformation. We have also discussed how exceptions will apply equally to the components in Figure 7.12. The aggregate in Figure 8.6a is the collection of the core business process and corresponding exception process(es). The vertical "cuts" in Figure 8.6a separate transformation processes from input and output processes. The vertical cuts follow the first horizontal "cut." Thus, we obtain not only the input and output processes for the "normal" business process but also the input and output processes for business contingencies—how contingency resources will be sourced and how products of contingency procedures will be produced and registered.

Each partition in Figure 8.6a will be a subprocess of the aggregate process. The aggregate process in Figure 8.6a itself will thus be a composition of interdependent processes—a process map. This composite process will also be a subtype of the process that was partitioned. Subtypes add information. This subtype will add information on exceptions.

The business process and its exception(s) are transformation processes like the transformation process in Figure 7.12. Each has input and output processes snapped on to either end (like the transformation process in Figure 7.12 did). Each "normal" and "exception" transformation process also has its counterpart in information space. Figure 8.6b expands the composition in Figure 8.6a to include these information processes from information space. These reflections of business processes in information space also consist of processes for input, output, and transformation of *information*. These too are included in Figure 8.6b. The aggregate in Figure 8.6b has been sliced into business and information segments to make these distinctions clear.

Each information transformation process, in turn, may be partitioned into "normal" and "exception" segments. Each segment will be a subprocess, and each will have corresponding information input and output processes. They too are members of the composition in Figure 8.6b. The "diagonal" slices of input and output processes in Figure 8.6b distinguish input or output of "mainstream" information from exception information—information like missing files, unexpected formats, unreadable data, and the like.

Figure 8.6 represents a transform that takes a business process and "cuts" (segments) it into

*Figure 8.6. Exception processes*

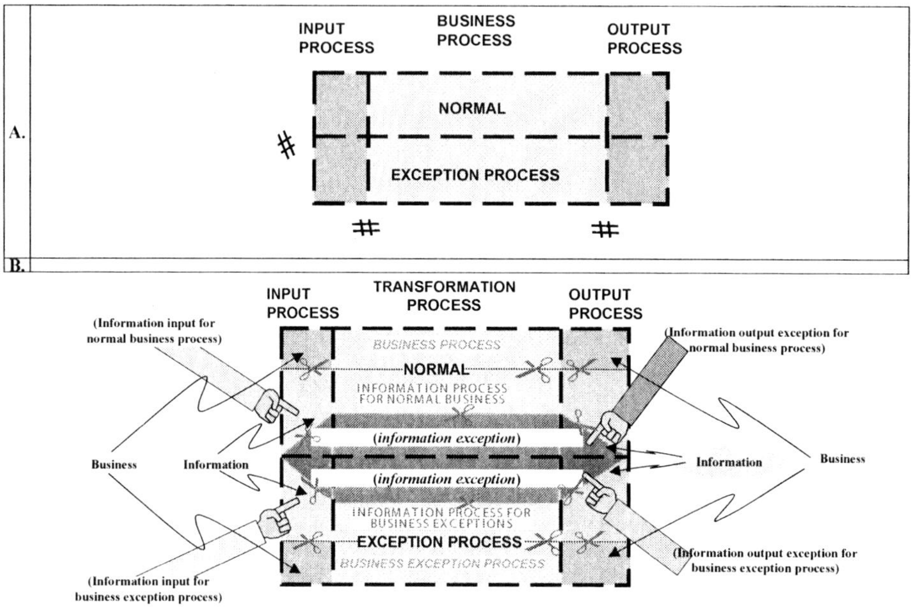


subprocesses by *adding* information. Each segment (subprocess) adds and normalizes a different kind of information. Missing from Figure 8.6 (to avoid clutter) is the fact that each *information* input and output process for each information systems process, exception, or otherwise, will be further subdivided into information logistics and interface processes.

Remember that effects, also not shown in Figure 8.6 to reduce clutter, are embedded in each subprocess. The transforms we have discussed for producing additional information systems processes, like effects, control processes, process implementations of static rules, and others, will also apply to each subprocess of Figure 8.6b. The composition in Figure 8.6b will integrate these control processes, effects, navigation objects, and derived processes into a composite whole. It will cement the business layer in Figure 3.4 to the business process automation layers in that figure. The two business process automation layers in Figure 3.4 will thus mediate between abstract business meaning and its physical implementation on a computing platform. They will glue abstract meaning to its technology implementation even as they decouple and isolate each (Box 8.2).

We also know that a single meaning may have several expressions (see Box 5.1). This is also true of meanings and their implementations in information systems; a single business process ("normal" or "exception") may have several polymorphisms in information systems. Each polymorphism will be a variation that has different input or output processes, possibly implemented on different technology platforms (see Box 3.1). We have also seen how different successions of subprocesses in a process map, or different sequences of effects in an information system, can also implement the same process. These too may be considered polymorphic variations of the same single theme—a process and a meaning.

Note how our discussion of the transform in Figure 8.6 has conveniently ignored exceptions in the technology layer—the computing platform itself. We have ignored them, not because they do not happen, but because the scope of this book is restricted to the layer of business meaning in Figure 3.4. The interface and information logistics layers mediate between business meaning and its instantiation in technology. We have described this meeting ground—the grand confluence that gives form to the shadows of pure meaning cast from information space.

## The "Unknown" Exception and Unstructured Processes

It is not only the business process that can suffer exceptions; any business rule may be violated in the real world. For instance, the cardinalities of an "ordinary" nontemporal relationship may be violated, a value constraint may be violated, a conversion rule may be violated, or more generally, *any* rule mandated by *any* pattern may be violated. Objects only change state in response to an event. Even if the state in question is an initial state, it is an inquiry event that will discover the violation (see Box 7.1). Therefore, the occurrence of the exception will always be an event, and the event will trigger its exception process. *If no exception process is explicitly specified, the process will not be null; it will be "Unknown."* An automated agent[20] would treat it as such and might alert users if exceptions without prescribed exception procedures occur.

*Indeed, the exception process might trigger a facility for creating exception processes "on-the-fly" when the exception procedure is unknown. The facility will let a user make the unknown exception process known. A facility of this kind might assist in implementing the kinds of unstructured processes we discussed under net markets and in Box 7.7. Note also that based on the principles in Box 4.3, an unknown process, be it an exception or mainstream process, is a supertype of a known process in the metamodel of knowledge. Thus, the metamodel of knowledge requires that an unknown exception process automatically trigger this facility if it is implemented and available. It will be a reflection of the logic, naturally and timelessly embedded in the metamodel of knowledge, casting its shadow from information space (see Unstructured Collaboration under Supply Chains).*

## Information Exceptions

*Business exception* processes will manage violations of *business rules*, and corresponding information processes will manage information about these violations, such as the issuing of alerts, alarms, the tracking of exceptions, changing states of exceptions, and the like. *Information exception* processes will manage violation of *information systems rules* as follows:

- The interface layer within the *output process* snapped on to the *information systems* exception processes would perform formatting functions like highlighting *information* exceptions (missing files, corrupt data, and so forth). Outputting alarms about *information* exceptions in the form expected by a device that displays, sounds, or shows the alarm, navigating and displaying *information* exceptions and the like will also be the responsibility of the *information exception* output process. The information logistics layer in the *information* exception output process would manage the storage and transportation of *information* exceptions after they are created or updated.
- The interface layer within the corresponding *input process* would accept corrections or other information that might change states of *information* exceptions. Its information logistics layer would manage the storing, staging, and transportation of this kind of input data into the process that changes the state of information exceptions.

*(The information normalized by interface and information logistics layers has been listed in Chapter III.)*

- States of *information* exceptions would only be set and changed by the *information* exception (transformation) process between the information input and information output processes in Figure 8.6. The information exception process would simultaneously signal the *existence* of any associated alarms and set their states and magnitudes. (Box 4.1 has several examples.) The corresponding information output process would *interpret* these states, magnitudes, and alarms, and format them in appropriate forms for actors who will then sense them. These formats may be different and may depend on the kind of output device and style guide being used.

Given an exception style guide and the transformation in Figure 8.6, an automated agent may create exception processes and its counterparts in information systems.

May we also snap (reuse) the input and output processes for "normal" transformation processes onto exception processes? Absolutely!—it is a process design decision. Inputs like corrections could be fed to the input process through the same interface as normal data (for example, a screen). Many information systems designers do this intuitively. Output interfaces as well as information transportation and staging rules may be similarly shared by both "normal" and "exception" streams. It is up to the information systems designer (or the style guide) to determine how information exceptions will be stored, segregated, and displayed in tangible form. The transforms in Figure 8.6 identify the processes that normalize and hold this information in information space.

## Referential Integrity Exceptions

Referential integrity rules are rules of interdependence between states of a system—business, information, or automation. When the lawful state space[21] of any object depends on, that is, "*refers to*," states of other objects, the states in question are said to be mutually constrained by *referential integrity constraints*. The objects in question may even be compositions, attributes, features, or relationships and processes. The states in question may even be the mere occurrence or absence of the object.

The relationship between the payability of the check and the presence of signatures, and the relationship between price, amount, and quantity were examples of referential integrity constraints. Some relationships between objects also impose special kinds of referential integrity constraints—constraints that make the occurrence of one object contingent on the occurrence of another. That the existence of an order is contingent on the existence of the customer is one such referential integrity constraint.

Referential integrity must be addressed in all but the simplest information systems. Most analysts are familiar with referential integrity issues. Exception processes resolve these issues. For example, consider the issues raised by the relationship between a customer and her open orders when the customer must be deleted: Should the request to delete the customer be honored if the customer has outstanding orders still pending delivery? Typically, there would be three different solutions to an issue like this:

1. **The automatic cascading delete solution:** The customer will be deleted without further ado and so would all outstanding orders for that customer.
2. **The optional cascading delete solution:** The customer will be deleted and so would all outstanding orders for that customer after the user is warned, and a response elicited, in which he (or an inanimate actor—it) confirms that this is indeed what is required. In this implementation, the user also has the option of canceling the request if orders are still outstanding for the customer.
3. **The prohibited delete solution:** The user has no choice. He (or it) cannot delete a customer if the customer still has open orders pending. The user must delete every outstanding

order before he (or it) is allowed to delete the customer. (There may also be variations on this theme. For example, confirmation may be sought for each outstanding order, and the user given the option of deleting each. The customer would be deleted only after the user deletes every order outstanding on that customer.)

Each solution lies in the exception layer of the deletion effect, and each is a different "snap-on" component. These differences give the effect the variability needed across different footprints that might require different implementations of the deletion effect. The first solution is an event that affects two objects—the customer and orders attached to the customer via the ordering relationship. The other two are guarded effects: The second solution creates the deletion effect depending on a business process automation event—the confirmation (or lack of it) flashed from the interface with the actor in Figure 8.6. The third solution simply bars the effect—deletes it—if an instance of customer shows a connection to pending orders via the ordering relationship (or its subtypes). Each implementation of the deletion effect is a polymorphism of the basic deletion request. We obtained each variation by snapping on a different exception process to the deletion effect.

The deletion effect was only one of several kinds of referential integrity issues that information systems designers must address. Typically, referential integrity issues involve mandatory relationships between objects (we must also create its mandatory relationships if an effect creates an instance of an object with mandatory relationships), subtyping relationships (we must delete the subtype if the supertype is deleted, but not vice versa) and mutual exclusion (mutually exclusive objects cannot simultaneously coexist. Either the creation of a mutually exclusive object must be barred by a guard condition, or the effect must delete an object as it creates its mutually excluded counterpart). Earlier we saw how even more complex referential integrity issues can emerge from constraints on degree, order, and cardinality of relationships between objects. The approach here will also resolve these complex issues. It will also solve referential integrity issues that involve more than mere occurrence information—issues like violations of magnitude constraints such as Amount = Price x Quantity, ranking constraints, and the like. The transform in Figure 8.6 will stay the same; only the exceptions fed to it will change. The transform will always cut the process into the subprocesses in Figure 8.6—once for each business exception.

The transform in Figure 8.6 isolates change and encapsulates variations. It permits reuse of common knowledge even as it creates the space for diversity and exception. Overall, it facilitates agility, innovation, excellence, and customer satisfaction in the face of diversity, change, competition, *and the unexpected.*

## Automating Adaptability

Adapting to the unexpected is the key to new learning. Learning is the key to adapting successfully. The information poor "unknown" process, as we have seen, is the key to both. It creates room for things without structure—things beyond our experience—and the room for improvisation (see unstructured collaboration under supply chains and Box 7.7). Adaptation, improvisation, and learning converge for us and also for information systems.

Each time the "unknown" exception process for a hitherto unanticipated contingency is specified (possibly with the facility for creating exception processes that we have recently discussed), that particular exception will have a known solution. That solution may be instantiated and recorded by the facility for creating exception processes "on the fly"—the facility we discussed under the risk management transform. The next time a similar exception occurs, the same solution could be optionally presented to an actor (who may or may not use it), or it might fire automatically. (A governing process will determine which implementation is chosen.) The key to reusing experience in this way is similarity—the similarity of exceptions, as well as those of solutions. The key questions are how similar must the exceptions be, and more importantly, how do we determine what similarity is before we can fit our past experience to it?

Similarity is indistinguishable from proximity in state space. Relationships, processes, and constraints are patterns of information. Similarity flows from their parameters and properties—properties like those we have discussed under each kind of metaobject—enumeration, reliability, validity, cardinality, degree, kind of constraining rule, the kind of domain it maps to, and several others. Objects may be subtyped depending on their information content (Box 4.3); so too may exceptions and exception processes. Matching an exception process to an exception boils down to matching the right patterns of information—to find and match the *essence* of the exception with the *essence* of the exception process.

Pattern recognition techniques may be used to match an exception to the right exception process.[22] Often this process will be adequate to respond to subtypes of the exception also. Pattern matching is still an area of active research beyond the scope of this book. It will suffice to understand that the pattern of information in an exception may be matched to the pattern of information in the corresponding exception process, which might then be applied to subtypes of the exception. This is our hook to the universe of systems that adapt through experience—experience of exceptions and the processes for managing them.[23]

Pattern recognition in tandem with *the Principle of Parsimony* (discussed under alternative resources, under process reengineering) may be useful in generalizing exceptions, which could then be matched with corresponding processes. Sometimes we may have to add operations, guard conditions, and other information to subtypes of these exception processes to respond optimally to subtypes of exceptions (that is the subtype might be an inclusion polymorphism).

The exception process is a relationship. The key to generalizing the process depends on the parameters of relationships, which we have discussed. This is how we integrate it all into the Metamodel of Relationship, and thus complete it. As we jave seem meanings are relationships and objects carved by patterns of information shaped by constraints in information space. The time has now come to understand how constraints shape meanings and features of ojects. That will be our last step as we close this discussion on relationships and the bridges they build in information space.

## ENDNOTES

1. BPML ([63] in Appendix III) maps roll-back recovery requirements in the information logistics layers of Figure 3.4 to rules of technology.
2. Events may be represented by the rows, while objects by the columns, of a matrix. Each cell of the matrix may then hold the effect of the event in the row, on the object in the corresponding column of the matrix. Each row of the matrix would then contain all effects of the event in the row, and each column, the effects that a single object suffers from all the events that affect it. A matrix like this facilitates grouping effects by event or by object.
3. [154] and [155] in Appendix III have more information on presentation formats.
4. See Box 19 on our Web site.
5. The semantics of selection criteria are in Figure 33 on our Web site.
6. Figure 33 on our Web site describes the semantics of View.
7. The navigation process resides in the interface layer of Figure 3.4. As navigation processes step from object to object

through relationships, subprocesses in the information logistics layer gather and store information by accessing and updating files. (See information input-output processes.)

8 We have discussed why computers need processes that take time to execute, even when implementing nontemporal relationships. We speculate that quantum computers of the future may speed response times by implementing nontemporal relationships with "quantum entanglement," in which the passage of time is irrelevant. Quantum entanglement is the phenomenon described by the Aspect Experiments discussed in Appendix II in the note on messages between objects.

9 Processes in the lower layers of Figure 3.4 have the same characteristics as the business processes of this section.

10 Box 5.3 elaborates on the Null value.

11 The *Law of Demeter* [IEEE Software in 1989] asserts that a method associated with an object should invoke only methods associated with the following kinds of objects: (1) itself, (2) its parameters, (3) any objects it creates/instantiates, and (4) its direct component objects (in case it is an aggregate object). The Law prohibits invocation of the methods of an object that is returned by another method. See the Demeter/Adaptive Programming home page at http://www.ccs.neu.edu/research/demeter/ or "The Demeter Method with Propagation Patterns," a book by Dr. Karl J. Lieberherr of Northeastern University, published by PWS Publishing Company, ISBN: 0-534-94602-X.

12 Effects may act on individual properties (attributes, relationships, constraints, and even effects. (See Box 10 on our Web site).

13 *Null* and *Unknown* are also values. Replacing any value with *Null* removes information and turns an object into a supertype. Conversely, replacing *Null* with any other value subtypes the object. If the feature is a relationship, nullifying it is equivalent to cutting (deleting) the relationship, and replacing the null value is equivalent to tying the objects involved into a relationship (creating a relationship between them).

14 Creating an object is equivalent to replacing the *Null* value of its instance identifier with a different value. Deleting an object is equivalent to making its instance identifier *Null*.

15 [337] in Appendix III discusses attribute value constraints in more detail and shows why they are relationships between attributes.

16 Chapter 4 of [311] (in Appendix III) discusses degrees of freedom. [312], [313], Chapter 8, section 6 of [309] and Chapter 7, section 7.5 to 7.8 of [314] (all in Appendix III) discuss determination of constrained values.

17 Figure 44 on our Web site is a graphical representation of a three-way constraint between check amount, monthly rental, and energy charges, in which the three-way relationship may become a validation process if an event changes all three simultaneously.

18 Agents are discussed in Box 36 on our Web site.

19 BPML, a process modeling language from BPMI (http://www.bpmi.org), calls the generic conveyance process the *assignment* process. See [63] in Appendix III.

20 Box 36 on our Web site discusses agents.

21 [337] (in Appendix III) and Appendix II on the BWW model discusses Lawful and Conceivable state space.

22 [337] (in Appendix III) describes the semantics of Pattern and discusses pattern recognition.

23 [298] (in Appendix III) provides an overview of expert systems, artificial intelligence, and pattern recognition.

# Chapter IX
# The Nature of Constraints

## ABSTRACT

*This chapter wraps up the discussion by describing how normalized components of information are carved out of inchoate information by constraints, and manifested as objects with specific properties and meanings. It describes the essential identity between a law and its outcome.*

*"The very small is the very large when boundaries are forgotten;*
*The very large is the very small when its outline is not seen"*
- Seng ts'an, 6$^{th}$-century Zen patriarch

A constraint is like a prism through which we can view the inchoate and bring order to it. Constraints split the clear light of information into the rainbow shards of objects and meanings we have discussed earlier and those we will discuss ahead. We have seen how constraints add information and metamorphose into objects of different kinds—objects and relationships we have discussed throughout this book. Now we will unify them into an integral whole by subsuming them into the ultimate constraint—a generic concept that will sunder information space to make the inchoate choate.

## THE SHAPING OF OBJECTS

Usually when we think of constraints, we think of constraints on attribute values.[1] However, "Constraint" is a broader concept; it subsumes value constraints and more. Constraints surge through information space, sculpting and shaping islands of meaning, sundering and merging as they ebb and flow through patterns of information. They fashion all that is, all that is not, and all that cannot be from the inchoate information shimmering through information space. To understand how this happens, put this book down on a clear night, go out and look up at the sky.

On a clear night, the sky is full of stars, each an instance of a star. How do you tell one instance from another? By its position, of course. The position of each star distinguishes it from its neighbors. The position of an object is one aspect of its state. To the naked eye, each star is distinguished by its state in physical space. Look for Jupiter. Your newspaper may contain a star chart that will show you where it is. Some stars twinkle and others burn steadily in the night sky. If Jupiter has risen, it will be the brightest star burning steadily in the sky. If you have a powerful telescope, look at Jupiter through the telescope. Jupiter is a single spark seen with the naked eye—a single instance of an object. Seen through a good telescope, you will see Jupiter resolved into many sparks. Each new spark is a satellite of Jupiter—each a distinct and different instance of an object.

Seen with the naked eye, Jupiter was a single spark, a single instance of a star because of its unique position—its state—in the night sky. This location—a state—was the pattern of information that made Jupiter a unique instance of an object. The telescope made finer distinctions than the unaided eye could. It added information. It resolved smaller differences in positions to make them distinctly different. It could make finer distinctions between states. Thereby, the telescope split what appeared to be a single object into distinct object instances. The resolution of the telescope was far finer than the resolution of the naked eye, and it resolved a single instance of an object into many instances by adding information on the state of an object. It reduced the degrees of freedom of the pattern—the region of the sky—that a spark could occupy and still be considered a single occurrence of an object. It constrained the law that made the pattern a pattern and made it more restrictive. That is how a single instance of an object was resolved into several distinct instances of objects and a single state split into many. The pattern sculpted stars from amorphous and inchoate information. That law was a constraint.

In previous chapters, we have seen how an instance of an object is a unique pattern of information that captures its essence—a meaning. The state of a pattern of information determines its unique identity and distinguishes it from others of its kind. The instance identifier represents this identity; the law that makes the pattern a pattern also shapes an instance of an object in information space. This law creates the pattern by constraining its degrees of freedom.

The law that makes a pattern a pattern is indeed a constraint. We may resolve a pattern into additional distinct patterns by making the constraint even more restrictive. Each pattern may be an instance of an object, a relationship, an object class, or any of the other metaobjects we have discussed so far. The spark seen with the unaided eye subsumed the sparks seen with the telescope. If we considered the original spark an object class, the sparks through the telescope would be its subtypes. If the original spark was an object instance, each spark resolved by the telescope would be its polymorphism.

Conversely, if we remove information, boundaries of patterns may blur. Patterns may then lose their identities and become indistinguishable from each other. They may merge into one pattern that will subsume them all. Thus, many sparks may become one; object instances could lose their distinct identities and merge into one, an object that subsumes them all.

It can happen to any object instance—any pattern. Even object instances like colors and values could blur and melt into each other or split into distinct object instances just as the spark of Jupiter did (see Box 4.4). Consider the impact of this on polymorphisms of idempotent and antisymmetrical (or reflexive) relationships. An instance of an idempotent relationship loops back to an instance of an object (as an instance of a reflexive relationship also might). If we add information to this object, it could resolve into multiple objects, just like the single spark of Jupiter did. Some subtypes (polymorphisms) of the original relationship would then connect distinct objects. These polymorphisms would not be idempotent or antisymmetrical (or even reflexive). In this way, *polymorphisms of idempotent or antisymmetrical relationships could be irreflexive relationships.* Figure 7.29 makes this clear. Moreover, the relationship could even "open out" into a nonrecursive relationship between object classes. This is why polymorphisms of an idempotent relationship may be idempotent, irreflexive, or even nonrecursive, in step with the information it adds through its parameters—the objects it connects.

The instance identifier in the discussion of Figure 4.5 was a token for the essential pattern that makes the instance of an object what it is. When the boundaries of this essential pattern start blurring, object instances start losing their identities. Some models permit multiple object instances to be in the same state. For instance, there may have been several whole red glass panes or several shattered blue panes of identical thickness, which are therefore considered to be in the same state. Two or more object instances may be in the same state, only because we have not represented the complete state space that gives the instance its identity. Very often, the unshared aspects that lend an object—a pattern of information—its identity are not explicitly stated in the model; rather they are intuitively understood. The object class is based only on shared dimensions of state space. When we permit two or more object instances to occupy the same point in state space and still retain their distinct identities, we are implicitly using their distinct object identifiers as tokens for all that is *not shared* so that each has a distinct existence—an unshared *meaning* in state space.

Hence, constraints on the instance identifier, a nominal, albeit special attribute that signals the existence of a distinct instance of the object, will force or deny the existence of a specific instance of an object.

Thus, information content distinguishes one instance from another. When this happens, the implied relationship is that the instances related these objects to the same class. Adding information to a class distinguishes one class from another—remember that a class is also an instance of an object. Thus, as we add information to an inchoate object, it acquires meaning, first in terms of a distinct identity, and then, as its information content grows, in terms of different classes and categories. Thus, membership of a class is a type of relationship between instances of that class. We have also seen how classes may be subtyped based on their information payload. Instances may also be subtyped based on information content. When the relationship between instances is not sufficient to provide a distinct identity to each object, but enough to distinguish between them in terms of subtypes, it leads to the concept of temporal distinction on a timeline: An instance of a temporal object is distinguished from its past states by the fact that it "knows" about its past; that is, it has that information, whereas instances of past states do not have information on the states that succeeded them (see Appendix II on the flow of time).

## PATTERNS OF PERSPECTIVE AND THE METAMODEL OF CONSTRAINT

*At first was neither Being nor Nonbeing.*
*There was not air nor yet sky beyond.*
*What was its wrapping? Where?..*
*There was no death then, nor yet deathlessness;*
*..Then that which was hidden by the void,..emerging, stirring, through the power..came to be.*

- The Rig Veda, 10, 129, the third millennium B.C., one of the oldest treatises known to man

The recursive second degree "*involve*" relationship is the most information sparse of all relationships. It is the border that marks the point where relationships crystallize from the generic concept of a list (Box 7.10). Every relationship is a polymorphism of this phantom milestone in information space. Figure 7.28 showed us its key polymorphisms. These polymorphisms may flow from its parameters—the objects it connects—or should we say that the objects get the information from the relationship?—that the relationship is special, and therefore the objects it connects are subtypes of the object its generic parent connects? The information content of the relationship is actually the information content of the entire ensemble—the composition of objects connected by relationships—a pattern.

Note the difference between the two polymorphisms of the *part of* relationship in Figure 7.28. The generic *assemble* was obtained by adding information to the *part of* relationship independently of the objects it connected (actually it was obtained by fusing it with a third object—the process—via the subtyping relationship). On the other hand, *Assemble Car* was obtained by adding information to the aggregate object by making it more specific—by constraining and restricting it to specifically be only a car and nothing else. The "*assemble*" relationship obtained the extra information that turned it into a polymorphism, "*assemble car*," from one of the objects that had been previously bound by it. No *new* object was assembled into it. Was the meaning added to an object it bound, to make that object a subtype, or was it implied by the connection between objects?—Did the information flow from "*car*," to turn "*assemble*" into "*assemble car*," or was "*car*" the result of "*assemble car*"? It is impossible to say. In its most generic and abstract form, both formulations are equivalent. They are polymorphisms of the same concept—an amorphous, abstract constraint lurking at the boundaries of conception.

We understood how the information in "*assemble car*," a relationship, carved the subtypes on either side of it in Figure 7.28. What if a subtype was given *a-priori*? What if it were given to us that we must only be concerned with cars when we consider aggregate objects and all else is out of scope? Then we would also know that every aggregate object—a car—is linked via the *Assemble Car* relationship to *Car Part*. As such, that *role* of *Aggregate Object* (car), in conjunction with the *Assemble Car* relationship would identify those components that were car parts (this is called *Backward Chaining* in Artificial Intelligence—King & Hamon, 1985).[2] Similarly, Car Parts, a role of *Component*, in conjunction with *Assemble Car*, a relationship that contains the instructions for assembling car parts into cars, would map only to those aggregate objects that are cars (this is called *Forward Chaining* in Artificial Intelligence—King & Hamon, 1985).

Thus, the law that sculpts the pattern contains the pattern within it. The law cannot be separated from the pattern or the pattern from the law. The pattern and its law are identical, both are constraints, and that constraint is information (see Appendix II on Lambda Calculus).

How do we obtain these patterns? We obtain them with relationships—interactions of various kinds. An attribute may constrain the value of others via value constraints. Value constraints are relationships (between attributes—Mitra & Gupta, 2006). The value of an attribute may also be constrained, independently of any other attribute, by a relationship between the attribute and a value in a domain. Indeed, a constraint on attribute value is a feature, and a single value associated with an attribute in merely a special case of the value constraints, in which the upper and lower limits of the range of a value constraint on a quantitative attribute have converged to the same value, or for a nominally scaled attribute, the inclusion set has been reduced to a single value (value constraints have been described in detail in [337] of Appendix III). We have also seen how attributes themselves emerged from relationships between domains and instance identifiers,[3] and even how domains emerged from the junction of value (measurability) with shared meaning. We saw how domains themselves lie hidden between domains, in relationships. Even rule expressions were constraints and composite relationships,[4] as were bounds, ranges, and patterns of every kind. Every metaobject we have discussed thus far is a pattern of information—a constraint and a polymorphism of a relationship. Some conveyed more information, and some less, but all were patterns—relationships between metaobjects.

We saw how relationships between instance identifiers are polymorphisms of occurrence or existence constraints and how relationships between attributes may be magnitude constraints, also polymorphisms of constraint. We saw how magnitude constraints reduce to existence constraints in their most information sparse form. Ultimately, we saw how an instance identifier was only a token for a pattern of information—an instance of an object. A pattern is the ultimate object. Every instance of an object is a pattern of information, and every pattern is an instance of an object. They are one meaning, identical and indistinguishable, in information space.

Even object classes were patterns based on relationships between an instance identifier and various domains. Each kind of relationship grouped information into classes. Each group was therefore valid in a perspective. Perspectives themselves emerged from relationships that tied these groups to them. Only the universal object—a specter that only tells us that a group exists—subsumed them all. It could even be the empty set.

The universal object was a gray ghost that contained within it not only the potential to be, but it is also the potential to be anything and everything, even null space—the place for that which cannot be—an emptiness and a paradox in information space at the very edge of all that is and that which can be.

They all are patterns built with constraints, which classify, segregate, sunder, and bind. Each constraint is information. Information is meaning. A meaning may not only be expressed but may also be subtyped—turned into new meanings and made more specific by constraining it further; each meaning is a pattern of information and that pattern is a constraint—an abstract law of information.

Moreover, each expression of a rule, and there may be several, are its polymorphisms. Thus, we arrive at the metamodel of *Constraint*, the most general and abstract of all that we have surveyed, and yet an integral part of them—a part that subsumes the whole; every metamodel we have seen thus far is subsumed in it. None could exist without it, yet some of these polymorphisms are as complex as the metamodel of constraint is simple. We have generalized them, and generalizations, although often hard to conceive, tend to be simple when we finally articulate them. This generalized constraint is the ultimate feature. It subsumes all

*Figure 9.1. The metamodel of object property*

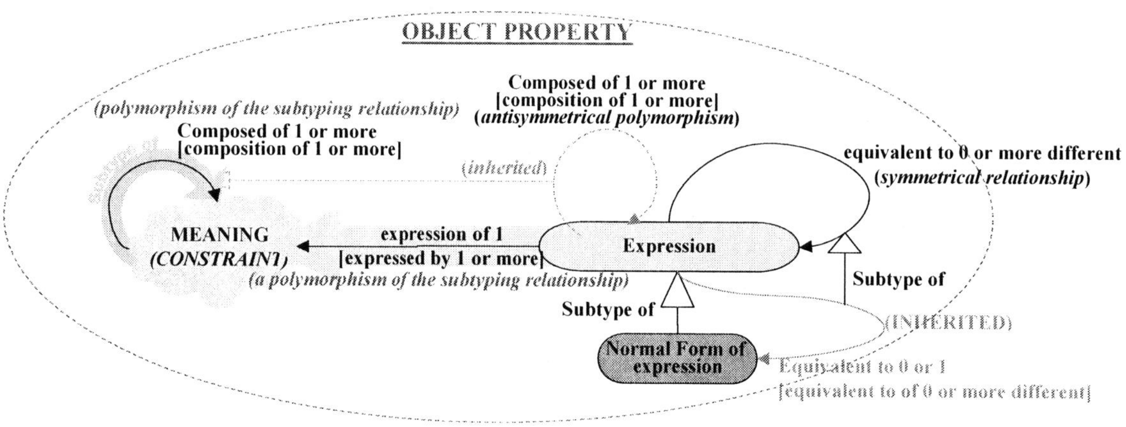

other features. It lends an object its very meaning and behavior to match. It is the metamodel of Object Property.

We have discussed how a single meaning might have several expressions. Figure 9.1 adds to this; it tells us that meanings may add to meanings, and each time a new meaning or nuance is added to a meaning, it makes the meaning more specific, further restricting the freedom of the pattern, reducing its degrees of freedom and thereby subtyping it. We have seen several examples in Chapter IV. Box 5.1, under rules, their meanings, and expressions, discusses how meanings and expressions may be qualitative or quantitative, and that many expressions may be reduced to a unique "normal" form. If the meaning is a conjunction of meanings, this normal form will contain conjunctions of other normal forms—one for each conjoined meaning.

Meanings, quantitative or qualitative, and their expressions may be combined with other meanings. The area of a face of a cube is a meaning that can be quantified (length of one side multiplied by the length of another). The volume of a cube is also a quantifiable meaning, which may be expressed in several ways: area of a face multiplied by the length of one side or its equivalent expression, the length of a side multiplied by itself thrice and others. Thus, volume may be derived from area, and the meaning of *Area* is embedded in the meaning of *Volume*. Both are quantifiable patterns of information, and one is a component of the other. We can use the concept of area as a constraint on its own or to constrain a volume. For instance, a term that expresses the area of a face of a cube will constrain the area of a painting on a face of the cube and also the volume of fluid that the cube will hold. In this way, the real world lets us reuse meanings to create new meanings, expressed in different formulae.[5] The recursive relationship on *Meaning* in Figure 9.1 represents this *natural* atomic rule.

When meanings may be combined with meanings to create new meanings, their expressions may also be combined into an expression of the new meaning (Figure 9.1). The expression inherited this rule from the meaning it expresses because it is a subtype of that meaning. If the meaning is the volume of a cube, it contains within it the meaning of the area of a face of the cube. Then the normal form of the formula for computing the volume—an expression of its meaning—will also contain a term that is the normal form of the formula for computing the area of the face of the cube, as it does.

We saw how this was a step towards lending the metamodel the power of reason. The law and the pattern were one inseparable object, a meaning. Such meaning could be qualitative (like "ancestor" or "friend"), a quantifiable concept (like area or volume), a formula, a bound, a range, a visible, audible, or tangible pattern like a picture or a signal, or even a physical law like the path of a ray of light through a prism. The meaning of *Meaning* in Figure 9.1 subsumes all of these meanings. This Meaning is a generic constraint—a pattern of information. The law and the pattern are one.

Figure 9.1 is a model of this ultimate generalization. We have merged the concept of patterns, processes, interactions, information, objects, meanings, their expression, and constraints into one unified whole. However, this merger, considered in isolation, is only another step towards the ultimate flexibility and adaptability we seek. We have seen that we must not only generalize but also normalize these constraints to automate and facilitate their reuse. Only through reuse of meanings and their configurations can we make our business processes and information systems adaptable *and* scalable. It is only through normalization that we can automate the propagation of constraints and meanings, even as we control their risk of their uncontrolled replication and the consequent risks of cascading, uncontrolled, and unintentional side effects. As such, it is the normalization of constraints that holds the key to flexibility, adaptability, and reuse of information. The normalization of constraints is the focus of the next section.

## NORMALIZING CONSTRAINTS

*Who knows what is the truth or who may declare it? What is the path that leads to the place of forces? Only the inferior abiding places are perceived, not those in mysterious superior locations*

The Rig Veda 3.54.5

The key to normalizing information is to attach the right constraint at the right place so that it is inherited, rather than replicated. Only then may we make a change and have it automatically radiate through a system of meanings—objects and relationships—changing behavior where it must and *only* where it must. If we can do this, new learning will seep into the system, through it, and the system will adapt in step.

Consider the concept of size in physical space. Length is a primary domain, and domains such as area and volume emerge from relationships the length domain has with itself.[6] Consider the size domain. The meaning of size subsumes length, area, and volume because it is a supertype of length.[7] *PhysicalSize* is an ordinally scaled domain that has lost all quantitative information, save the nil value and ranking information. (Remember how quantitative domains fade to qualitative domains as they lose information.) We could impose a constraint on physical size, which cannot fall below nil, and the constraint will be inherited by every kind of (physical) size domain. If we did not, we would have to replicate this information for every attribute that measures physical size, be it the size of an ant or of an elephant.

Based on the above, the constraint, that the smallest possible physical size is nil, should be attached to the physical size domain. It is a *feature* of the domain. Nil physical size implies the absence of physical size of any *magnitude*, not the absence of the *meaning* of physical size. Ants, elephants, and all other objects that map one or more attributes to domains like length, volume, and others we discussed, will inherit this constraint. We will not have to replicate it for each. It will even be inherited when we do not quantify size—when it is a nebulous, qualitative concept. This is how generalization and normalization must go hand in hand to facilitate adaptability through reuse of meaning.

Every metaobject we have discussed so far generalized shared behavior. Each was a pattern of universally shared information, the meanings shared and reused most often. From these patterns of sharing, the world of business is shaped. These metaobjects are information poor compared to the objects and processes familiar to business. They must be because they are the information sparse containers of the few critical rules that are always used and reused to lend meaning to the universal behaviors that shape our understanding of the world around us. They are skeletal structures of information—patterns that frame new learning even as they support the old. As we fill them with meaning, they swell with information and manifest themselves as the information rich objectives, goals, resources, products, and processes that enrich, and indeed create, the meaning of business.

Perception flows from their expression, their formats, and measures, and reason from their tight embrace. Configured and attached to each other with the right relationships, metaobjects create the logic of business. In this book, we have seen how backward and forward causal chains of metaobjects, in the right configuration and ontology, can not only seek goals but also the means for achieving objectives. Hence, the right metaobject ontology can infuse the power of reason into the model.

So far, we have studied each metaobject in isolation. We discussed configurations in the isolated chapters. Now they must be combined. We can only normalize their interaction if we can rise above the minutiae of each metamodel to see how each interacts with the others, configuring and synthesizing knowledge, and normalizing behavior.

The next chapter will integrate the Metamodel of Knowledge. The purpose of the integrated model will be to attach features—the meanings in Figure 9.1—at the right places to the right metaobjects, which themselves are patterns of meaning. They are constraints that surge through patterns in information space, rendering, creating, sundering, melding, and morphing meaning. The integrated metamodel of the next chapter is the overarching structure that rules the rest.

## REFERENCES

King, D., & Hamon, P. (1985). *Artificial intelligence in business.* John Wiley & Sons.

Mitra, A., & Gupta, A. (2006). *Creating agile business systems with reusable knowledge.* Cambridge University Press.

## ENDNOTES

1 Value constraints and "joint constraints," in which several data items mutually constrain their values, have been discussed in depth in [337] in Appendix III. The scope of this discussion includes the "unknown" and "null" values.

2 In *Backward Chaining*, a chain of reasoning may traverse several relationships backward from a purpose to resources and means. In *Forward Chaining*, a chain of reasoning may traverse several relationships forward, from resources and means, to purpose.

3 How attributes emerge from relationships between domains and instance identifiers is described in Chapter IV; see Figure 35 on our Web site.

4 The fact that rule expressions are composite relationships is explained in Figure 45 on our Web site.

5 See [337] in Appendix III (Chapter IV, section 3). This describes how quantitative and qualitative meanings may be reused and formulated in units of measure and expressions of meanings they are a part of.

6 Described in more detail in [337] in Appendix III (Chapter IV, section 3). See Rule 10 under the metamodel of domain and Rule 2 under The Risk and Benefit of Domain Analysis.

7 See [337] in Appendix III (Chapter IV, section 3).

# Chapter X
# The Whole Shebang:
## The Integrated Metamodel of Knowledge


## ABSTRACT

*This is the final chapter of the book. It describes the overarching structure of knowledge. This chapter provides an overview of the interactions between the fractured meanings normalized by each metaobject. It shows how the entire scheme is integrated into one unified context, which leads to the concept of Knowledge itself. Wherever knowledge and meaning exist, we will find their generic components configured in this manner.*


*"...impose thine awe upon all thy works and thy dread upon all that thou has created...that they may form a single band to do thy will with a perfect heart"*

-extract from a Jewish prayer at Rosh Hashanah

## WHAT IS THE MODEL OF KNOWLEDGE AND WHY IS IT USEFUL?

Knowledge is the understanding of meanings, reasons, and rules. In preceding chapters, we have seen how it starts with the recognition of *Pattern* and is based on reasoning, inference, understanding, and predictability. It is coordinated information that has a structure. The concept of a pattern is the cornerstone of Knowledge, and recognizing this helps us integrate reasoning, business rules, business processes, and ontology into one holistic pattern we have called the Metamodel of Knowledge in this series of books.

Each pattern in this book and its companions describes the components from which knowledge is assembled. These patterns are not isolated islands of meaning. Each is only a window into the overall pattern of information that describes the very meaning of Knowledge. The overall pattern would be impossible for a single human mind to grasp in its entirety unless it is presented piecemeal—a few concepts and relationships at a time. Thus, each is also a window into the whole. Although every concept may not be present in every diagram in this series of books, each affects the others through relationships and interactions that are hidden in that figure. Figure 10.1 shows, at a high level, the overall interaction between these parts. The behavior of the entire structure, its complex interactions, and configurations is best stored in electronic Knowledge Artifacts and managed by automation. These Knowledge Artifacts will facilitate the operation of the 24 Hour Knowledge Factory we described in Chapter I.

The objects and semantic models in this book can help identify irreducible facts. They are the shared, generalized patterns that provide templates for mapping the irreducible facts of knowledge and meaning and can thus assist in the parsing of knowledge (the patterns in its companion book from Artech House Publishers can help parse business rules to identify its atomic components). The ontology and the semantic models in this book also lend the model power to reason. For instance, Figure 7.27 describes the ontology of location and containment. That chapter described why containment relationships are transitive when joined together. Thus, if it is known that a person lives in a house and the house is located in a town, it may be automatically inferred that the person lives in the town. Box 7.9 had another example of pattern based automated reasoning. Thus, the patterns in this book and its companions can be a cornerstone for the Semantic Web.

Sometimes, this reasoning defies human intuition. However, it is always mathematically correct and logically consistent. For instance, consider the question: can a part equal a whole? The intuitive answer is that it cannot. However, we have seen that when we deal with infinite numbers, a part may equal the whole. Consider Figure 7.27b. If the envelope that contained Objects 2 and 3 were infinitely extended, containment would be meaningless, and the asymmetry of "part of" could become "unknown." In some situations, it could behave symmetrically like "locate" does (see the notes at the end of Chapter VI. This is consistent with the fact that an asymmetrical relationships may be derived from symmetrical relationships by adding information, and "part of" can lose its asymmetry as we increase the freedom of the pattern and reduce its constraints and information content by extending the pattern to infinity in information space). The following example shows one instance of how this could happen.

Consider a triangle like that in Figure 1.2. Imagine it is cut in two by a horizontal line like one of the boundaries between the segments in the figure. This line is shorter than the base of the triangle. The side of the triangle connects the one end of the shorter line to the one end of the base. Take a point on the shorter line that is close to this end. You can draw a line from that point to a point on the base that is close to the end of the base. Repeat this until you reach the other end of the shorter line and the base. Now do this for the points in between those you have connected. You can continue the procedure an infinite number of times because there are an infinite number of points on each line. You will always find a point on the base that corresponds to a point on the shorter line. However, if you superimposed the shorter line on the base, it would only be a part of the larger line that represents the base of the triangle. This implies that the points on the shorter segment are only a part of the points on the full base. On the other hand, we have also shown that every point on the base has a corresponding point on the shorter segment. This has happened because containment and "part of" may become symmetrical relationships like "locate" when patterns of infinite extent are considered, and an infinite part of an infinite pattern may contain the whole pattern. This is not intuitively obvious to us because we cannot easily understand the infinitely large or infinitesimally small. However, the semantics of knowledge implied and anticipated it.

The objects and their features in the semantic models in this book can also be the basis for identifying the most granular services that knowledge management and process modeling tools should provide (remember that relationships are also objects). Each object also implies three effects, which are also services: creation of the object, and change of state (changing to a null state implies deletion, similarly, changing from a null state implies creation). Relationships also imply services that may switch instances of relationships between values and adding temporal information to relationships, or compositions will create processes. In the same way, the patterns in a companion book, *Agile Systems with Reusable Patterns of Business Knowledge: A Component Based Approach* from Artech House Publishers, can be the basis for creating the components of business services and business processes.

For example, the patterns in this series, working in unison, may even lead into an intelligent "wizard" for analyzing functional requirements. Consider the semantics of buying and selling. We know that the process of selling may be automatically inferred from the effect that creates the Negotiation/Agreement object (called NAG in Figure 2.18 of *Agile Systems with Reusable Patterns of Business Knowledge: A Component Based Approach*). The work product of this process is the transfer of rights to a business product (which could be a physical product, money, information, a place, a task (service), an organization or some aggregation of one or more of these items, a pattern described in the companion book). The semantics of the pattern described in that book also imply that a buyer and seller must be involved in creating the "NAG," and optional intermediaries may be involved. The process "wizard" could require the mandatory information and ask about the optional information. The user would have the option of saying that the information is unknown and could fill it in later. The wizard would "know" that optional items, like intermediaries, may be "null" (does not exist), but mandatory information (e.g., the buyer and seller) may be "unknown," but cannot be "null." Moreover, the wizard could infer from the ontology in that book that the buyer and seller are either individual people or organizations and would inherit their features and behavior. Thus, it would automatically present the appropriate forms to capture this information for each sale. It may ask about the distribution channel, and if this consists of intermediary persons and organizations, it would capture the same information, along with their interrelationships, if any. It would also "know" that the distribution channel is a network of relationships and therefore can have restructuring behavior associated with it. Beyond this, it would know that the sale process must have the RAWCF parameters described in Chapter VII and that the sale must be executed by a person. It may therefore automatically present the requisite forms to capture this information. The semantics of tasks and resources would also lead into asking about requisite credentials and qualifications for the individual executing the sale (for example, real estate sales require that the realtor be certified). Semantics like these would be inferred from the fact that adding temporal information to the sale turns it into a process, which has the same semantics as a task and the task-resource pattern in Figure 2.16 of *Agile Systems with Reusable Patterns of Business Knowledge: A Component Based Approach.* This example describes only a tiny slice of the reasoning abilities inherent in the integrated pattern of knowledge. We leave it to the reader who has read the entire series to see how even terms of sale, like provisioning of products, billing, and payments may be inferred by the integrated model of knowledge.

Moreover, these patterns distinguish the semantics of meanings from how they are rendered. Thus, these services also permit a business or knowledge service to interface with others through a multiplicity of Service Level Agreements (SLAs); that is, the SLA also becomes a service that is invoked by the core services which operate at the plain of meanings. Such SLAs will render information in different physical forms with different degrees of precision, which can all tie back to a single unified meaning. For example, alternative algorithms for computing the same quantity with the same or different levels of precision (for example, the surface of a sphere) or alternative representations of the same item (for example, a mountain as a contour map or a hologram) would render the same meaning differently by attaching different SLAs to the core meaning being represented. Thus, the patterns in this series identify the core meanings that must underpin the Semantic Web (the semantics of patterns that render information were outlined in Chapter IV and have been described in more detail in a companion book from Cambridge University Press: *Creating Agile Business Systems with Reusable Knowledge*).

## METHODOLOGY

We could speed systems integration and requirements analysis with the patterns in this series as we discover new information on the behavior of a complex, large scale business system in iterative steps. We can start with the generalized semantic patterns in this series and use them as-is (with perhaps only cosmetic name changes and synonyms to fit the business domain). This would help with the difficult task of abstracting generalized patterns to help integrate and coordinate information. This kind of model is time consuming and risky to build, but nevertheless, is critical for coordinating information across broad scopes and creating reusable services in SOA. The patterns in this series give us a prepackaged starting point and would save the time required to build abstract models while mitigating the risks inherent in developing the right abstractions. We would add information to these patterns only when we must, in the form of constraints, data, relationships, and behavior specific to the business domain. We would add this information only if it does not exist in the generalized models articulated in this series.

We could speed process modeling, integration, and reuse by using the patterns in this series as a starting point and adding temporal information to create processes. The patterns in this series can help identify generic processes (relationships would become processes when temporal information is added). Key resources and work products could also be identified from these patterns. For instance, a relationship between Fund Amount and Calendar may help identify a process for applying funds to specific time periods in a spending pattern (Pattern in Figure 2.19 of *Agile Systems with Reusable Patterns of Business Knowledge: A Component Based Approach*) and a mutually inclusive relationship (Figure 5.5b of this book) may require that two processes be mutually inclusive. Thus, buying a car should trigger buying car insurance and vice versa.

When integrating diverse semantic models, such as those commonly found in different systems or different collaborating businesses, the patterns in this series can broker the translation of information between them. Each semantic model, object model, or data model would be mapped to the objects in model of normalized knowledge in this series. This would help normalize and coordinate information much faster, and with less risk, than if these abstractions were built from scratch each time. Thus, *Employee* in a Human Resources system and *Citizen* in a Homeland Security system would both map to Person. Moreover, Person would convey additional behaviors like consumption of goods and services, the behavior of becoming a customer through purchases and so on. The Universal Perspective, described in *Agile Systems with Reusable Patterns of Business Knowledge: A Component Based Approach*, is a polymorphism of the model in this book, which would be especially useful in this regard.

Sometimes the problems that flow when these patterns are not used may be more instructive than abstract discussions on how to use them.

For instance, one of the authors (Mitra) was dealing with a complex fund management system. It was important to know the locations that were impacted by actions taken on various funds and grants, as well as the location of the action. The latter capability had been omitted during requirements analysis and was difficult to update the design to include this information. The patterns in this book determine that location is a universal property normalized by the fundamental metaobject. It is created by the Locate relationship we discussed in Chapters VI and VII. We also know that a Task is a kind of object and therefore inherits the location property from the Fundamental Object (Chapter VII). Therefore, the patterns in this book would always permit easy incorporation of location information for a task. This location could be a physical or virtual location, and it may be "unknown" until it is given a specific value. However, the location of a task would never be "null" (does not exist). Thus, had the designers of the fund management system used the patterns in this series of books, this important fact would not have been overlooked during requirements analysis and the fund management system would have been easily extensible.

In this book, we have described the *information* that is required to model complex and simple business rules and processes. How this information can facilitate, and even automate, process design is illustrated by several examples. Some of the more complex processes that were optimized, automated, or made more resilient may be found in examples under Processes That Gain or Lose Structure, Product Reengineering and the Mutability of Compositions, Box 7.9, and the complex example on the Web referred to in Figure 7.24.

This series of books identifies the information that is required to model business knowledge. It is a complete model because it is derived from the semantics of Pattern, which is the foundation of all knowledge. What constitutes knowledge, behavior, business rules, process, and reasoning must be identified before we can discuss *how* the information should be collected: whether it should be done iteratively, or in a waterfall, which roles should do what tasks, the skills required, and the work breakdown structure of these tasks. Traditionally, we have relied on intuition to identify information needs. However, if we wish to automate the process, create the Semantic Web, or even design tools that will describe the process in a standard, computing platform independent form for automation, we must formalize this information and ensure its completeness. That is the intent of this series.

The right process for collecting the information will depend on the state of each organization—its size, complexity, skills, and culture. There may be many ways in which this information may be collected and managed. The complexity and volume of information required to cover diverse business environments suggests that a separate book be dedicated to the *process* of collecting the information identified in this series (tasks, roles, responsibilities, skills, sequence, format, and so forth).

Figure 10.1 binds the models in this book and its companions into one integrated meaning: the meaning of knowledge and how it is configured. It is a concise view; each object and interaction in Figure 10.1 is rich with the semantic information we have already described. Together, they weave a mighty tapestry of information that creates the very concept of knowledge.

## THE INTEGRATED MODEL OF KNOWLEDGE

Figure 10.1 shows how domains mediate between objects, the corresponding meanings and physical representations they create. As seen in Figure 10.1, meanings may be represented by different patterns of symbols in different formats, and each will then be a synonym for the others.

*Figure 10.1. The integrated metamodel of knowledge*

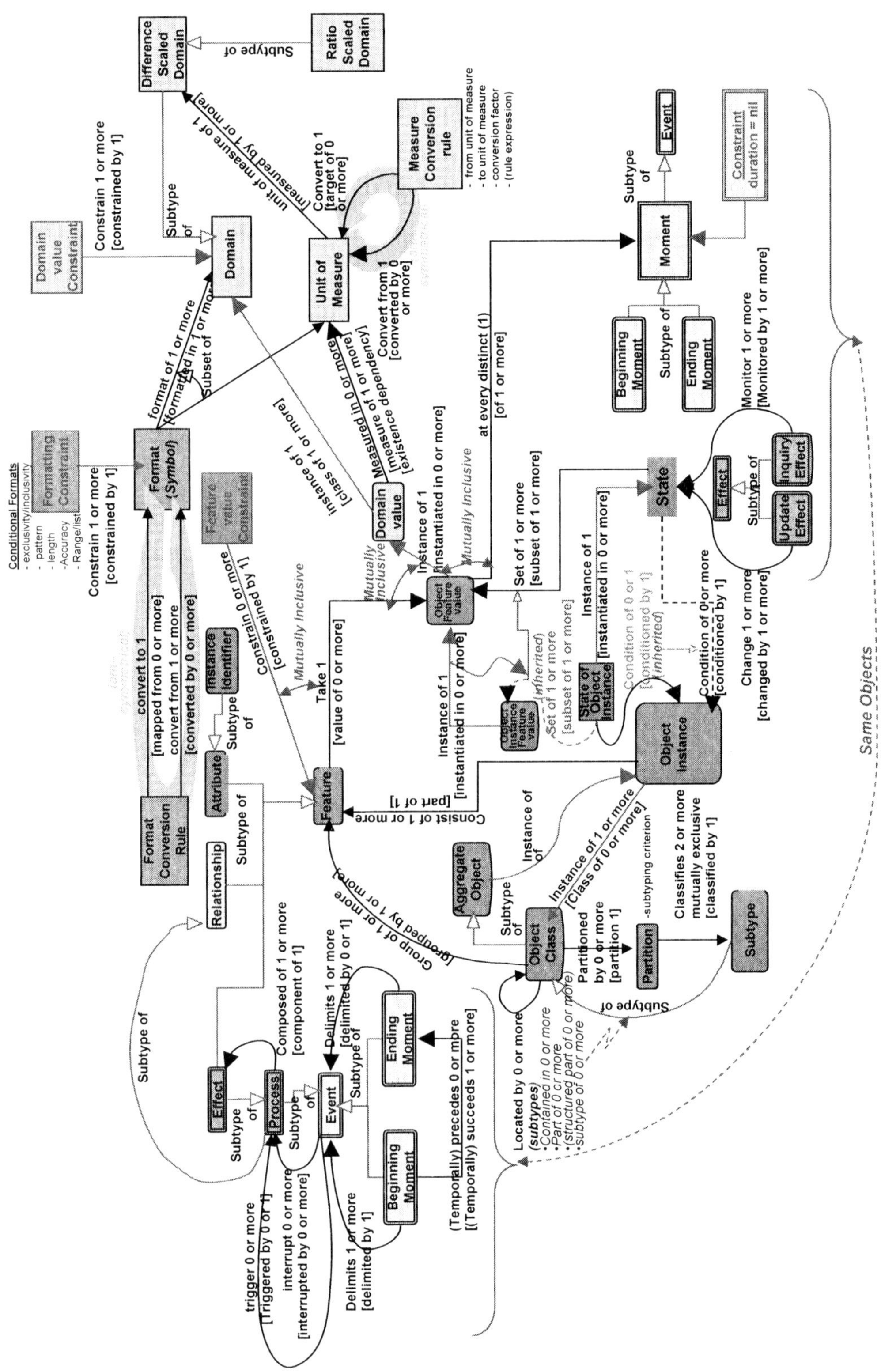

Note how domains normalize measurability and numerical expressions of magnitude. Figure 10.1 shows that a magnitude may be articulated in different units of measure, which in turn may be stated in different formats. Further, ratio scaled domains will inherit the fact that they must articulate magnitudes in units of measure from difference scaled domains. Many common codes of a business organization will be found in the top righthand quadrant of Figure 10.1.

Note also how *Event* normalizes the passage of time. The beginning and the end of an event are attributes of *Event* that map to the Date Domain (not shown in the figure). *Process* links meanings to Time through *Event*, *State*, and *Effect*, the portals through which time flows into objects from *Process*. Some implications may not be obvious. Remember processes have owners. Effects will inherit this information. Processes always end unless they are *sagas*—see Box 7.2.[1] The end of a process is the beginning of an altered state of an object (processes that only monitor information also make subtle changes—that the object has been/is being monitored. However, note that for an inquiry process, its *beginning*, not end, signals the fact that the object is under observation. This fact is also a state of the object. As such, an inquiry (i.e., monitoring) process changes the state of an object as it begins[2]). It follows that every instance of state in Figure 10.1 will convey information on not only the meaning and value of the state of an instance of an object, but also on:

- Who made the change (All the dimensions of process ownership: R, A, W, C, and F).
- When the change was made.
- The instance of the process that caused the change and the instances of resources that were used.
- Why it was made (the causal chain that led to the process).
- How long it took to make the change (cycle time of the process).

This information is useful for auditing the process. Therefore, we call them the *audit attributes* of *State*. They are naturally associated with every time slice in Figure 4.5. How much of this information the computer system actually records is a design decision in the business process automation layers (of the Architecture of Knowledge), but regardless of what is filtered in or out, in what form or format, the information is naturally available and resident in the meanings of things—in the metamodel of knowledge of Figure 10.1. This information is also critical for satisfying the Sarbanes-Oxley Law that corporations in the United States must satisfy.

Figure 10.1 conveys the semantics of *State*. Remember that "*instance of*" is a polymorphism of the subtyping relationship. If we consider the entire composition from "*Object Feature Value*" through "*Domain*" in Figure 10.1, the structure in this figure shows that a feature must assume a single value from a single domain at a moment in time. This value could be a constraint.

Since the value of a specific feature of a specific object instance is an *instance of* the value of object features in general (Figure 10.1), and *State* describes a collection of values of features in Figure 10.1, it follows that the state of an object instance will be a collection of values of corresponding features for that object (instance). This relationship between "*Object Instance Feature Value*" and "*State of Object Instance*" is inherited from their generic (class level) parents in Figure 10.1. Figure 10.1 articulates this fact.

Several object instances could be in the same state. The relationship between *State* and *Object Instance* in Figure 10.1 articulates this (when different object instances are considered to be in the same state, the fact that they are different instances is the sole differentiator of their states, which is represented by the differences in value of the instance identifier). The corresponding relationship between *State of Object Instance* and *Object Instance* is an inclusion polymorphism of this relationship. The state of an object instance is an instance of (and therefore a subtype of) *State*.

Figure 10.1 shows that an object class is an aggregate object based on common features. It tells us that object classes may be partitioned into subtypes and that there may be several such partitions but that subtypes in a single partition will always be mutually exclusive. It is true that even if we show only one subtype in a partition, its dual, the class that is *not* that subtype, implicitly exists. A partition will always have at least two subclasses, and it could have more. Moreover, Figure 10.1 generalizes attributes, effects, constraints, and relationships into *Features* and maps features to domains.

An instance identifier is an attribute, albeit a special kind (subtype) of attribute. It is a token for the unknown (unspecified) pattern of information that lends an instance of an object its unique identity. The instance identifier distinguishes one instance (of an object) from others in its class. It tells us that this object (instance) is *different* from another object (instance) of the same class. It is a token for the information that makes them different. It is therefore a kind of classifier, a nominally scaled attribute only because we might find it difficult to articulate its state, which we know is different from the footprint of another object with a different identity. If both objects have exactly the same footprint (state) in information space, they become mutually indistinguishable. It follows that all instance identifiers must map to the nominal domain.

An "ordinary" relationship between objects is a relationship between instance identifiers. It only tells us that a specific interaction occurs (or does not). It too conveys only nominal information. The Involvement Domain is thus a polymorphism of the nominal domain.[3] All relationships are defined on the involvement domain.

Some relationships can convey more information than the mere occurrence. For instance, attributes are a kind of object. We have seen how nominal relationships between attributes can swell into ordinal and quantitatively scaled rule expressions. This happens as we fill them with information on measurability and magnitude. They do so in step with the hierarchy of rule expressions in Figure 7.29. Relationships between attributes, like the attributes themselves, may also map to quantitative domains. For instance, the enumeration relationship maps a collection of instance identifiers to a quantitative domain of enumeration. These maps will be rule expressions that mutually constrain values of attributes. Relationships may also map to *Ordinal Involvement* and *Quantitative Involvement* domains. Quantitative involvement domains in turn may be domains of ratio scaled involvement or difference scaled involvement in which the strength of the interaction only quantifies *differences* in magnitude, not absolute levels of involvement (see Chapter IV).

The hierarchy of domains of involvement mirrors the hierarchy of domains in Figure 4.1, each a subtype of a domain in Figure 4.1. Every domain of involvement is thus an inclusion polymorphism of a corresponding domain in Figure 4.1. This is why relationships, like other kinds of features, also emerge from maps between objects and domains; only in this case, the domains are domains of *involvement*.

*Effect* is also a kind of feature. What kind of domains might effects map to? Effects hold the winds of change. Remember that they are a kind of process (albeit not *business* processes), and processes are relationships. Processes are also the conduits of information about temporal changes. Therefore, effects map to temporal polymorphisms of the involvement domains we just discussed—polymorphisms that convey information on how qualitative or quantitative involvement has changed with the flow of time.[4]

An effect may cut an "ordinary" nominally scaled occurrence relationship between objects or tie objects together into this kind of nominally scaled involvement. However, the domain of changing involvement can be more complex when we focus on quantitative involvement. A quantitative rule that involves two or more objects normalizes the magnitude by which the value of one object will change if the magnitudes, or qualitative involvement, of the others change. In Figure A of Box 4.5, we know that the total amount (*money*) is the arithmetic product of unit price (*money per piece*) and number of units (*number of pieces*). We can compute the change in the magnitude of total amount, given changes in magnitudes of unit price and units. This information is normalized by the quantitatively scaled arithmetic relationship between the three items (total amount, unit price, and units). If an effect changes one, it must also convey information on how *much* the *magnitude* of the other(s) will change.

This effect will flow from a process. The process is information about changes in time. The effect maps changes in time to the object. It will tell us how quickly or slowly, at what tempo and to what drumbeat of effects, do changes in magnitude occur. Therefore, the effect will inject information about the temporal rate of change of magnitudes into the objects it involves. In the example we just discussed, it would tell us how quickly, at what temporal pace, units, prices, and total amounts might change. (Clearly, the sensitivity of one attribute to changes in the others differs in different regions of the sail-like surface in Figure A of Box 4.5. If we introduce time into this equation, so that one or more involved attributes start changing, how quickly or slowly the others will respond will depend on where we are on that surface.) The quantitative relationship maps to the generalized domain of changes in involvement over time. These are domains of growth. They are frequently used secondary domains.[5]

The audit attributes, discussed earlier in this chapter, flow into objects from processes through effects—especially information on cycle time—the time taken to make a change. However, effects also convey an additional polymorphism of this temporal change domain. Remember that an effect is not a business process; it is an information systems process. *Therefore, an effect normalizes the time when the information system, not business process, made the change and the time it took to do so* (as opposed to the real world timing and duration of the business process). For instance, in the process in Figure 7.6b, the shipment may have been made at 10 p.m. and completed (unloaded at its destination) by midnight but may have been actually entered into the information system only at the start of business on the following day. The effect would only occur the next day, even though the corresponding business process may have occurred the day before (see Figure 8.2).

The start, end, and duration of an effect are *systems* audit attributes that may also be associated with the state of an object, but unlike the audit attributes we have discussed earlier in this section, they will lie in the business process automation layers of the Architecture of Knowledge. These are also attributes that map to domains of temporal involvement—the Date (date-time) domain and the Time (time-lapse) domain. Indeed, we may use this information to compute and balance the load on the information system. We would do this in much the same way we balanced resources and load on the business system.

The metamodel of knowledge is a container for common sense. It normalizes common sense even as it creates room for constructive creativity. It is flexible and generic; its polymorphisms are many, almost uncountable. These uncountable polymorphisms manifest the creativity and innovation latent within the Metamodel of Knowledge. This metamodel is key to integrating and reusing the knowledge that lies in our amorphous collective experience—experience that gives the businesses we work for the competitive edge they must constantly seek, sharpen, and hone in order to survive and prosper in the Age of Knowledge.

Our next step must therefore be to bring order to the infinite possibilities that lie within this metamodel—to fill this container of meaning with business sense. This business sense will be normalized patterns of business meaning—the patterns most often used, which are also the patterns of business that integrate business processes, supply chains, information systems, databases, and even business knowledge itself into the elusive, but real Universal Perspective. The Universal Perspective is a shared understanding that is the basis of our shared communication of meanings and their mutual engagement in the shade and light of human thought. It is the enabler of the 24 hour Knowledge Factory and the steps beyond.

As we add business information to the Metamodel of Knowledge, a new framework, the *Universal Perspective* bubbles up. The *Universal Perspective* captures the essence of business from which the tree of knowledge grows. Within the Universal Perspective hide simple rules that join businesses—common rules, disguised. They are used again and again in a million masks, each a generalization that hides the substance within. The Universal Perspective is where abstraction and substance meet, and in that meeting, shadow and substance transform themselves into the knowledge machine, where logic, inference, and information combine into one indistinguishable whole at the beating heart of the machine. That, however, must be the topic of a different book ([338] in Appendix III).

*"There came a lady clad in grey*
*in the twilight shining:*
*one moment she would stand and stay,*
*her hair with flowers entwining,*
*He woke, as he had sprung from stone,*
*and broke the spell that bound him:*
*he clasped her fast, both flesh and bone,*
*and wrapped her shadow around him.*
*...when caverns yawn*
*and hidden things awake,*
*they dance together...till dawn*
*and a single shadow make."*
-from the Shadow Bride in The Adventures of Tom Bombadil by J.R.R. Tolkien

## REFERENCE

Mitra, A., & Gupta, A. (2005). *Agile Systems with Reusable Patterns of Business Knowledge.* Artech House.

## ENDNOTES

1 Must a monitoring process end? States of some objects could be continuously monitored, over an infinite time horizon after some business event triggers the process. The triggering event may even be the creation of the object that must be monitored. For example, consider radioactive decay: the half life of an isotope is the time it takes for one half of (the mass) of the isotope to spontaneously change into another isotope or chemical element. Thus, at the end of its half life, one half of the original isotope is left; at the end of two half lives, one quarter (½ x ½) is left; at the end of three half lives, one eighth (½ x ½ x ½) is left; and so on. The amount of the changing isotope left keeps decreasing, but the process cannot consume the entire quantity of the isotope in a finite time. Thus, radioactive decay is a saga which may trigger its own monitoring and also be continuously monitored forever.

2 Information dissemination activities are polymorphisms of the monitoring process of Figure 10.1. The inquiry (monitoring) process in Box 7.1 makes an object "aware" of the state of another (or even the same) object. Whether this is done by "asking," "sending," or "publishing" are business process automation issues. The inquiry process in Figure 10.1 (and Box 7.1) belongs to the business rules layer of the Architecture of Knowledge (see Chapter III). "Asking," "sending," "disseminating," "publishing," and "broadcasting" information are poly-

morphisms that implement it in the information logistics layer of the Architecture of Knowledge. They address information conveyance. However, if the scope of the process—its meaning—goes beyond mere *communication* of information and also involves the creation of a document of some kind, such as a newspaper, a magazine, a Web page, or an electronic file, it ceases to be an information inquiry process. It has a physical work product—a document that it creates or updates, and is therefore an update process.

3 An interaction (relationship) between objects may be a matter of chance in a stochastic model. If there is no chance of an interaction, the validity of the relationship is Nil. If the interaction is certain, its validity is *Total*. The involvement domain could become ratio scaled in a nondeterministic model if we measure the validity of involvement. [337] (in Appendix III) discusses validity in more detail.

4 Effects hook the metamodel to analytical calculus and differential equations in mathematics: If we allowed continuous change, changes in involvement would map to time derivatives of various orders, which are domains of growth.

5 [337] (in Appendix III) discussed domains of growth in more detail.

## APPENDIX I
## SEMANTICS OF PATTERN

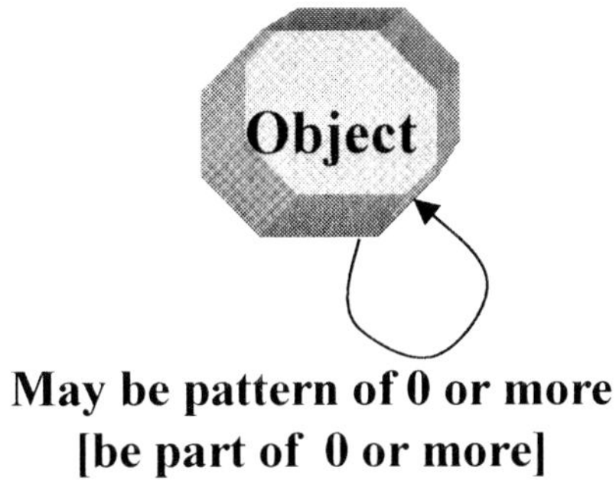


*Figure I.1. An object may be a pattern of objects*

The *Pattern of* relationship in Figure I.1 summarizes the semantics of Pattern, which we discussed briefly in Chapter 4. Mitra and Gupta (2006) discuss the semantics of Pattern in detail. The following figures convey the semantics of location, dimensionality, proximity, freedom, order, sequence, delimitation, extent, and the other properties of Pattern that are discussed in Chapter 4.

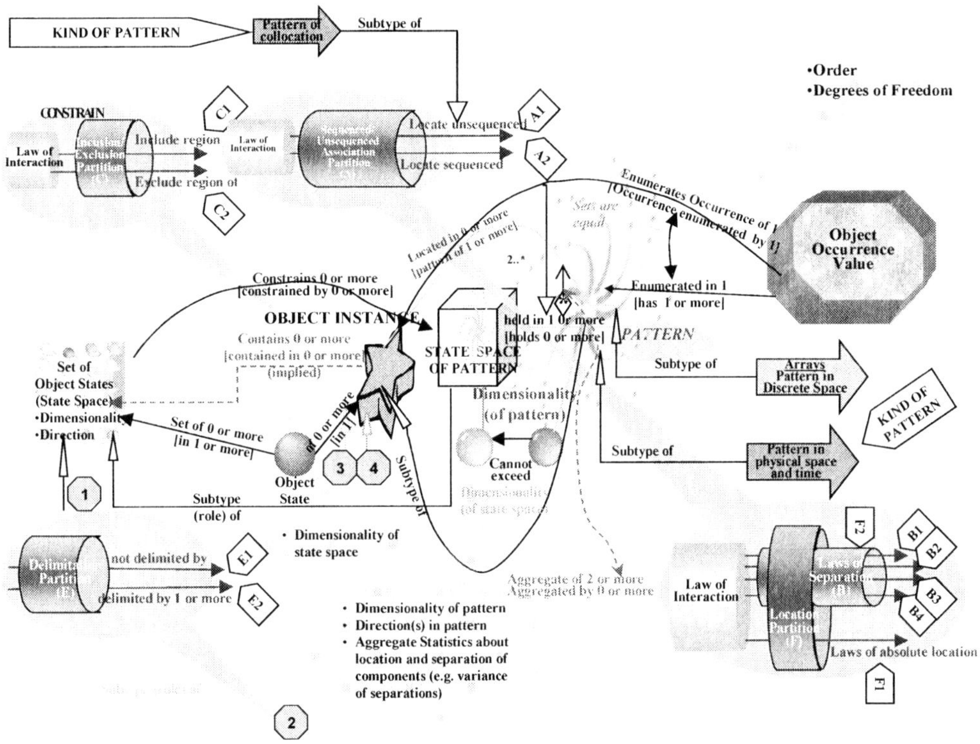


*Figure I.2. Top: Semantics of partitions and subtypes of Pattern: The structure of the "Pattern of" relationship*

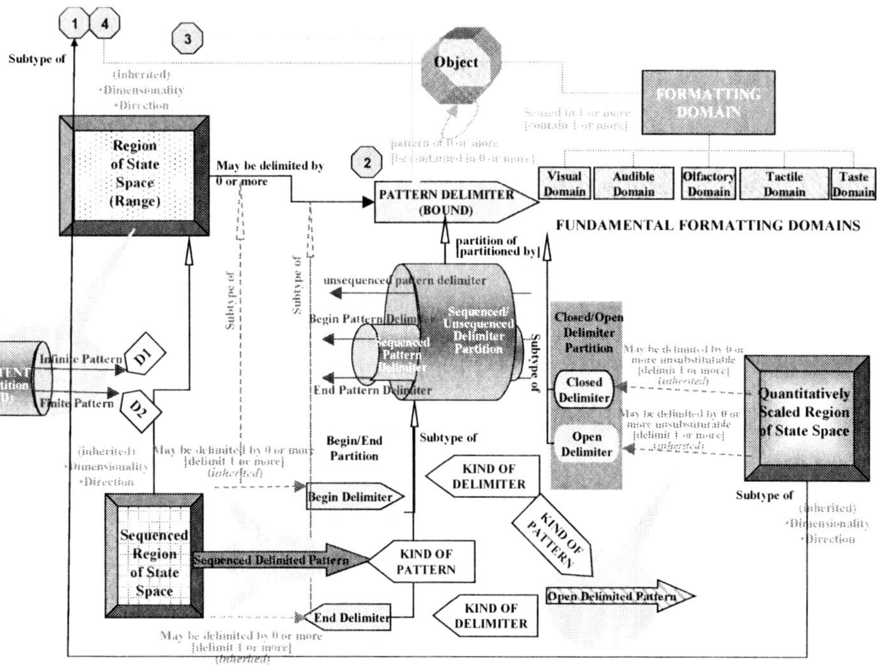


*Figure I.2. Bottom: Semantics of partitions and subtypes of Pattern: The structure of the "Pattern of" reationship*

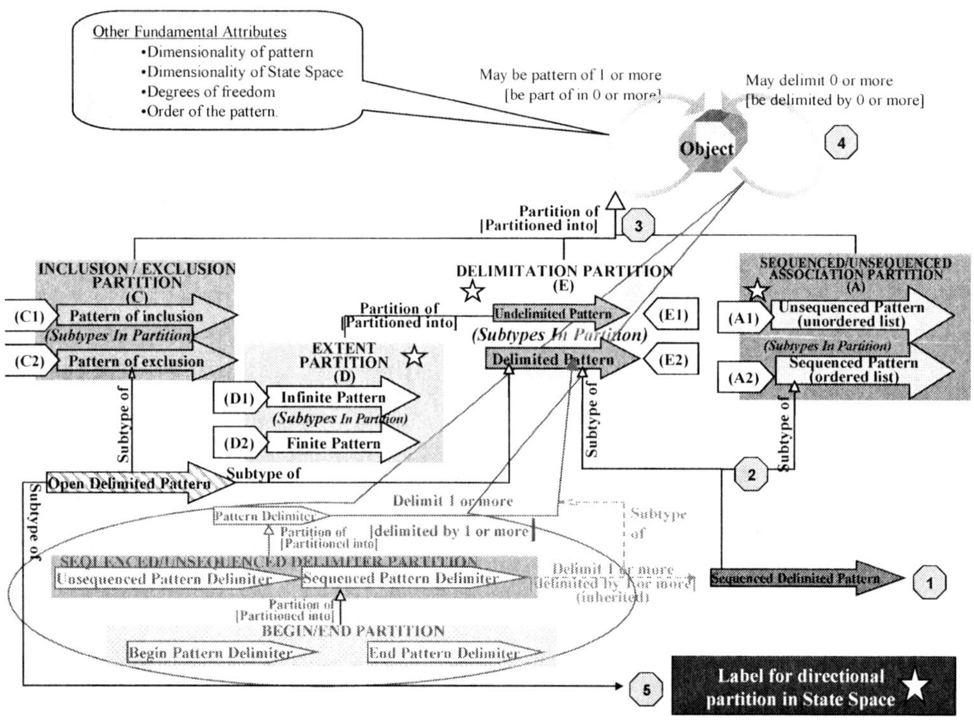


*Figure I.3. Top: Metamodel of Pattern*

*Reproducted by permission from Mitra, A., & Gupta, A., Creating Agile Business Systems with Resusable Knowledge, New York, NY: Cambridge University Press, 2006. ©*

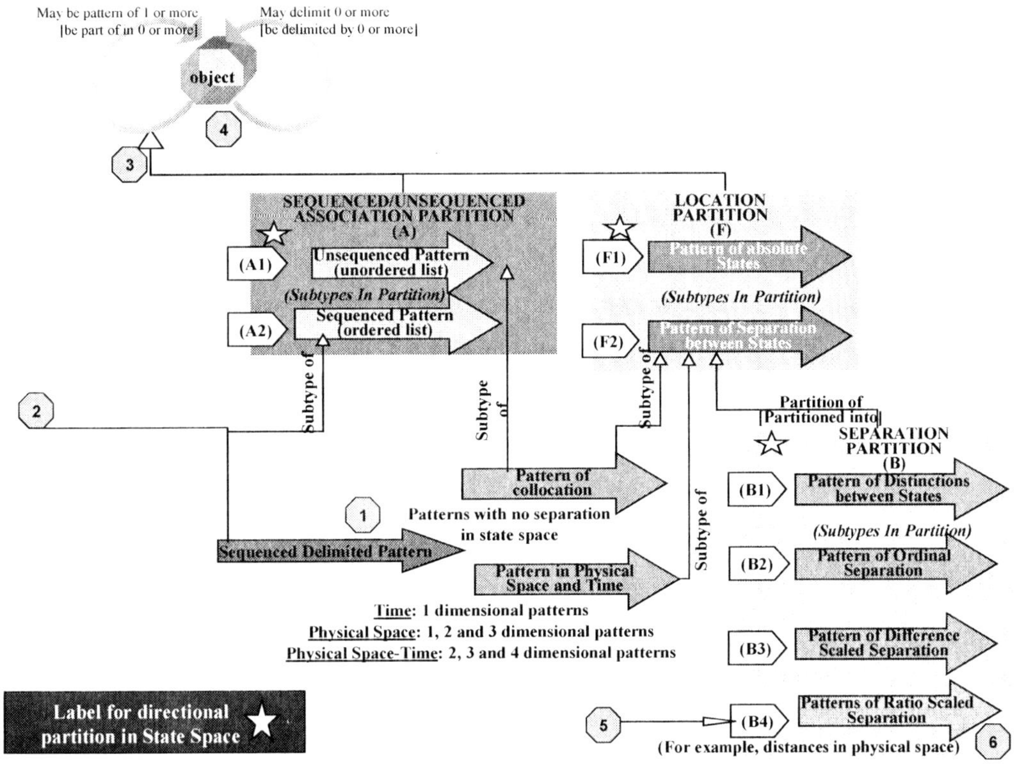


*Figure I.3. Bottom: Metamodel of Pattern*

*Reproduced by permission from Mitra, A., & Gupta, A., Creating Agile Business Systems with Reusable Knowledge, New York, NY: Cambridge University Press, 2006.©*

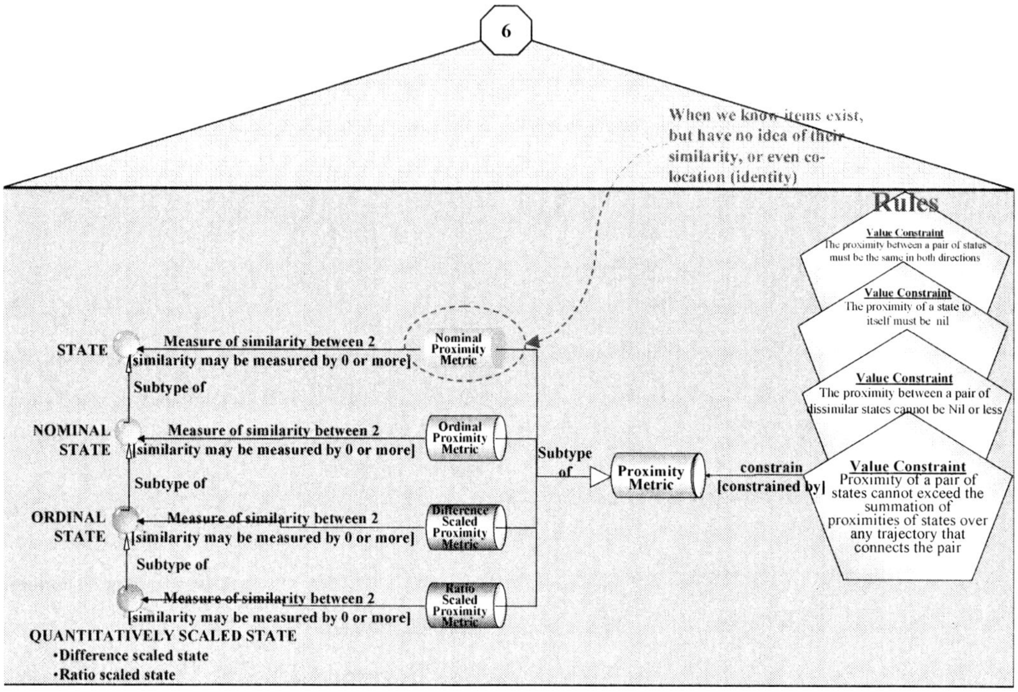


*Figure I.3. Continuation: Metamodel of Pattern*

*Reproduced by permission from Mitra, A., & Gupta, A., Creating Agile Business Systems with Reusable Knowledge, New York, NY: Cambridge University Press, 2006.©*

The concepts of information, meaning, and measurability start with the semantics of Pattern. Domains are based on the information content of patterns and encapsulate the concept of measurability, from which the properties and behavior of temporal objects emerge.

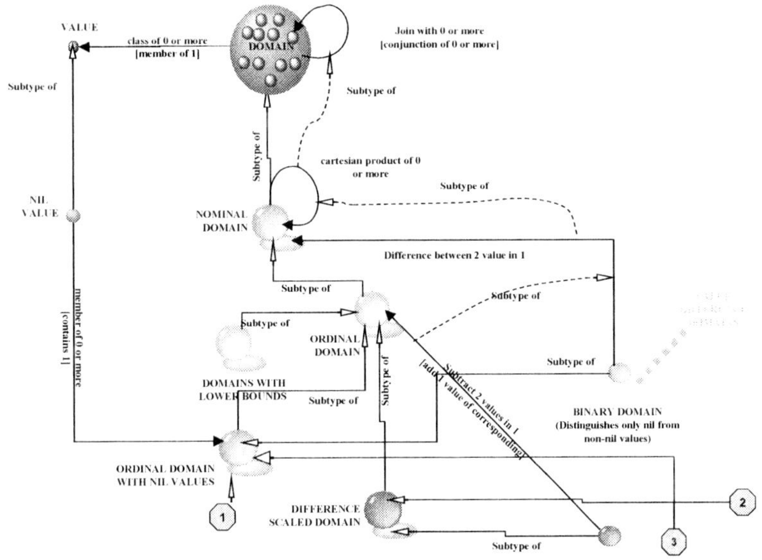


*Figure I.4. Top: Metamodel of Domain*

*Reproduced by permission from Mitra, A., & Gupta, A., Creating Agile Business Systems with Reusable Knowledge, New York, NY: Cambridge University Press, 2006.©*

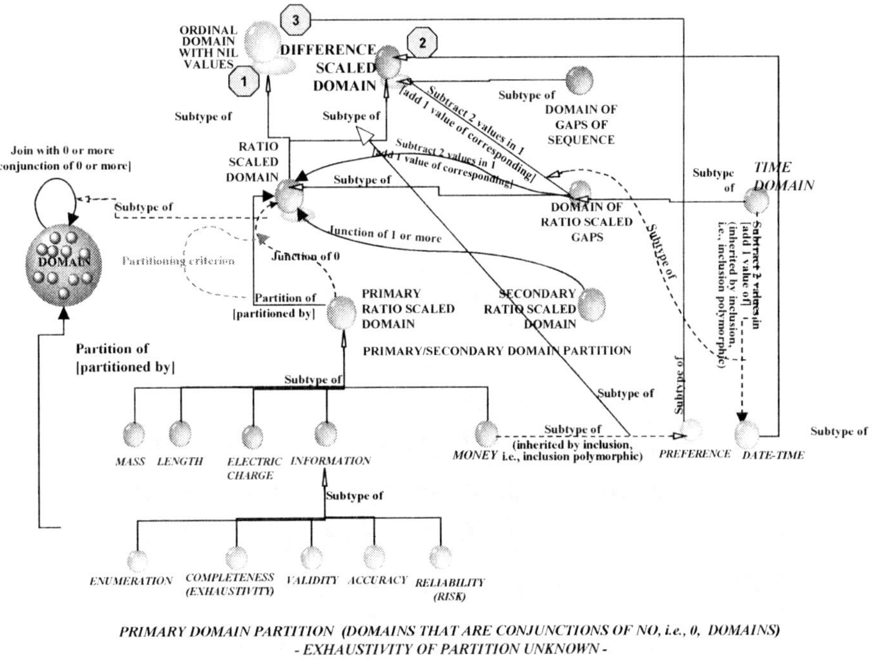


*Figure I.4. Bottom: Metamodel of Domain*

*Reproduced by permission from Mitra, A., & Gupta, A., Creating Agile Business Systems with Reusable Knowledge, New York, NY: Cambridge University Press, 2006.©*

# APPENDIX II
# NOTES

*The text in this appendix is based on portions of material from Agile Systems with Reusable Patterns of Business Knowledge: A Component Based Approach, published by Artech House Press, Norwood, Massachusetts, USA. The URLs provided in this book may have changed since it was written. Readers may use the Wayback Machine at http://www.archive.org/index.php to locate the following publications. Searches should go as far back as the year 2000.*

## A. Normalization

The process of removing redundancy in information is called Normalization. When normalized, each unique item of information is stated only once. The benefit of dealing with normalized information is that when information changes, it may be changed only once (at source) to effect the change wherever that item is used. However, to optimize computer performance, information is often denormalized in automated systems; that is, the same items of information are repeated redundantly. This, however, comes at a cost—inflexibility under the pressure of change and new learning.

As a natural consequence of advances in database technology in the 1960s, Dr. E.F. Codd of IBM proposed the first rules of data normalization in a research paper, "A Relational Model for Large Shared Databanks" in 1970. The paper turned out to be a decisive definition of rules for removing redundancy in data. Influenced by President Nixon's attempts at normalizing relations with China, Dr. Codd called the process "normalization."

Modern relational databases consist of two-dimensional tables of columns and rows. These tables are termed relations, hence the name "relational database." The columns and rows are known as attributes and tuples, respectively.

The process of normalization is incremental and can exist at several levels of completion. Redundancies have to be removed in stages by decomposing relations into smaller, simpler tables.

1. **First Normal Form:** Breaking up rows so that they do not contain any repeating groups of data brings it to the First Normal Form. For example, a row containing customer data with concatenated customer information, such as name, address, and billing details, is not in the First Normal Form because there will be several rows with the same customer name/address data, each associated with different billing data. In order to bring it to First Normal Form, the name-address pair needs to be placed in a separate table and the billing information in yet another table; both tables should be referenced by the same unique identifier, such as a customer ID.
2. **Second Normal Form:** When all data are not only unique in each row (first normal form), but also all of the attributes (columns) are dependent on the full primary key, then the data are supposed to be in the Second Normal Form. By dependent, we mean that only by knowing the full primary key, one can uniquely identify the value of each attribute. For example, if the primary key in a parts order table is the vendor ID and order combined, we cannot identify an order by knowing only the order ID or the vendor ID. All the data for that order are dependent on knowing both IDs (i.e., the full primary key).
3. **Third Normal Form:** A table is said to be in Third Normal Form when each non-key column (attribute) is unique, is dependent only on the primary key and nothing else, and is independent of

other columns. For example, if state name and state abbreviation are both non-key columns in an address table, the value of one column is dependent on the value in the other. Thus, only one of them needs to be present in the address table; the other should be placed in a state table, in order for the data to be in Third Normal Form.

4. **Fourth Normal Form:** A table is in Fourth Normal Form when there is at most one many-to-one relationship in the table. If a vendor has many office locations and each location supplies certain unique parts, then inputting the location and part information in a single vendor table would not render it in Fourth Normal Form. The locations need to be in one table and parts (dependent on location ID) in another table—thus ensuring one 1:M relationship in each table. The first table would have many locations for one vendor. The second table would have many parts for one location.
5. **Higher Normal Forms:** There are more normal forms; they occur when an object has three or more parents.

As a result of normalization, tables get broken up into many independent tables. A highly normalized database is easy to maintain due to the nonredundancy of information. In real life, data are *denormalized* to speed automated processing. If it is needed, denormalization should be controlled and tracked by automation in order to facilitate impact analysis if changes are required, while simultaneously improving computer efficiency.

Although Codd enunciated a well-defined set of rules for normalization, which have been further developed over time, it should be noted that these refer only to *data*, not their *business meaning*. However, it is possible to store not only data but also business rules (knowledge) in a nonredundant fashion such that change made at a single source automatically takes effect in corresponding business processes. This series describes the concept in detail.

## B. Messages Between Objects

Objects, in computer systems, interact with each other by passing messages between them. In real life, objects can interact with each other without passing messages. The Process Algebras and Techniques section in Appendix III describes concepts such as Petrinets, SPREM, and other formal techniques. These techniques, which deal with sequencing and conditional branching, all implicitly or explicitly use the concept of passing messages between objects. However a message is only one kind of interaction. Interactions between objects may not involve the flow of time or the passing of messages, as we have discussed in this book. They may be rules about how these objects are semantically related to each other or about shared information. Interactions of this kind (as well as those that involve the flow of time or messages) may also be considered objects. Recent experiments in physics have demonstrated it is not just semantic concepts that relate to each other without message passing; physical objects can do so too. The Aspect experiments at the end of the twentieth century demonstrated that physical objects separated in physical space in the real world may also influence each other without physically passing information or messages to each other. Refer to the "Aspect Experiments" performed by Philipp Grangier, Alain Aspect, Jean Dalibard, and Gerard Roger at the Instut d'Optique Theoretique et Appliquee, Orsay, France in 1981/1982 (these experiments are described for laymen in *The Meaning of Quantum Theory* by Jim Baggot, published by Oxford University Press in 1992 and in *The Conscious Universe* by Menas Kafatos and Robert Nadeau published by Springer-Verlag in 1990 on pages 9 and 71-72).

## C. Background: How the Concepts "Energy and Matter" Were Established

A Greek philosopher named Thales (638-548 B.C.) first developed the theory of matter. Centuries later, Antione Lavosier defined the first law of the conservation of matter in 1777. For further information, please visit http://www.nidlink.com/~jfromm/chem201/history.htm, http://atomhistory.homestead.com/timeline.html, and http://www.nidlink.com/~jfromm/chem201/history.htm.

One hundred fifty years later, in the second half of the seventeenth century, the concept of energy was first developed when Huygens stated that the "capability of a system to do work is called energy which can be measured (in ergs). It possesses no mass, shape, size or inertia." Julius Robert von Mayer and James Joule independently discovered the universal law of conservation of energy in 1842 and 1843, respectively.

For detailed information, go to: http://zebu.uoregon.edu/~js/ast121/lectures/lec06.html, http://zebu.uoregon.edu/~js/glossary/huygens.html, http://www.science.urich.edu/~rubin/pedagogy/132/132notes/132notes_18.html, and http://www.nidlink.com/~jfromm/chem201/history.htm.

Just as Huygens formalized the existence of energy, Shannon produced a revolutionary paper on information content. Shannon's original paper, called "A Mathematical Theory of Communication" was a watershed in information theory (see the note on Shannon's theory).

## D. How Physical Objects and Information Relate

We know that several physical objects can be applied to or governed by a single physical law. This law is just an item of information. Many objects can express this law. For example, the mathematical calculation of gravitational force between two objects is a piece of information conveyed by each and every pair of possible objects. The mathematical formula has *information,* which is as real as the matter that constitutes the objects. Taking this further, one can say that it is the *information content* of objects that allow us to sense them through our own senses or artificial sensors.

## E. Location of Matter and Energy

In the book, matter and energy are presumed to be determined in absolute terms. Quantum principles are not relevant to business situations. However, quantum theory demonstrates that not only are even physical objects and energy stochastic rather than deterministic concepts, but so are space and time themselves. They are all manifestations of information. For those who are interested in further reading on the topic, several impressive books exist on quantum phenomena such as *The Meaning of Quantum Theory* by Jim Baggot published by the Oxford University Press in 1992, *The Nature of Space and Time* by Stephen Hawking and Roger Penrose (1996) published by Princeton University Press, and *Quantum Mechanics and Experience* (1992) by David Albert published by Harvard University Press.

The only difference between physical objects and energy on one hand and pure information or concepts on the other is that physical objects and phenomena are constrained to exist in one region of physical space at a given moment in time to the exclusion of all other physical places. Information is physically sensed or recorded in the physical world by physical objects or energy. As we have described in this book, the same information may have multiple expressions in the physical world. Indeed, as we have discussed in this book, pumping information into objects creates distinctions between them so that they acquire distinct identities in information space. This concept may also be extended to physical space, which is merely one aspect of information space.

## F. Measure of Information: Shannon's Information Theory

Claude Shannon of Bell Laboratories, in his epic paper titled "A Mathematical Theory of Communication" (1948), created a new postulate using Statistics, Probability Theory, and Communication Theory. He stated that both information and uncertainty are technicalities of choosing one or more items from a set. Shannon provided the means to *measure* this information in a real system. His premise was that the amount of information in a message or observation was directly correlated to the average amount of "surprise" contained within. To use Shannon's words, the postulate says that uncertainty is the average "surprisal for the infinite string of symbols produced by a device." In other words, the less the message content, the more the information content in it. The unit of information content was called *bit*.

If a system possesses an identical probability of being in one of "M" possible states or if a message has "M" equiprobable possible values, the amount of information in that system or message can be expressed as:

**Amount of Information = $\log_2(M)$, where M denotes the number of possible states or values.**

In situations where the chances of outcomes are uneven, the amount of information can be computed by:

$$H = -\sum_{i=1}^{M}[P_i Log_2(P_i)]$$

where H is the amount of information, and $P_i$ is the probability of the $i^{th}$ of M possible outcomes

A twentieth-century mathematician, A.N. Kolmogorov, showed that the amount of information contained in ordinal, nominal, difference scaled and ratio domains increases in consonance with Shannon's measures.

For example, consider the quantum of information conveyed by the nominal domain "gender." It is equally possible that a person is a man or woman. Since there are only two possibilities (M=2 in the formula), Shannon's formula would yield:

**Amount of Information = $\log_2(2)$ = 1 bit of information**

We can now compare this with the information content of a two-valued ordinal domain—say an individual's preferences for two types of activities—indoors and outdoors. In the following example, all outcomes are deemed to be equally possible. The possibilities include:

1. The individual likes indoor activities more than outdoor activities;
2. The individual likes both of them equally;
3. The individual likes outdoor activities more than indoor activities.

There are three equally possible answers; therefore, Shannon's formula states:

**Amount of Information in the Domain = $\log_2(3)$ = 1.585 bits of information**

This is obviously more than the amount of information conveyed solely by gender. Since gender is in a nominal domain, whereas activity preference is in an ordinal domain, we can say that the latter is richer in information than the former. This is consistent with our model of knowledge.

The purpose of elaborating on Shannon's theory is to show that his perspective on laws of data compression and data transmission are consistent with our metamodel. Our focus is on normalizing knowledge through discovery of its natural laws. Shannon's law focuses on the quantum of information. It says nothing about the structure of information or the meaning the information conveys. This is the void that we address in this book and in the two companion books.

There are many remarkable publications on the subject of information theory. The *Information Theory Primer* by Thomas D. Schneider, although geared towards molecular biologists, is an introduction that explains information theory very concisely to mathematically inclined readers. The publication is located at http://www-lecb.ncifcrf.gov/~toms/paper/primer/latex/index.html. Lecture notes from *A Short Course in Information Theory*, a set of eight lectures on information theory (January 1995) by David J.C. MacKay of Cavendish Laboratory, Cambridge, Great Britain has links to Mr. Schnieder's primer as well as to other relevant publications. This publication can be found at http://wol.ra.phy.cam.ac.uk/pub/mackay/info-theory/course.html. Advanced material can be found in the paper "Entropy and Information Theory" (1990) by Robert Gray of Information Systems Laboratory, Stanford University (publisher by Springer-Verlag); this publication can be found at http://ee.stanford.edu/~gray/it.pdf. In "Fifty Years of Shannon Theory" by Sergio Verdu, Fellow, IEEE, published the details of Shannon's work and its extension by other researchers in *IEEE Transactions on Information Theory*, Volume 44, No. 6, October 1998. Verdu describes how the theory is also applicable to diverse fields of knowledge beyond data transmission and compression; this publication can be found at http://www.ehb.itu.edu.tr/~devrim/shannon.pdf.

## G. Mathematical Theory of Categories (or Types): Domains, Functions, Groups, Functors, and Morphisms

In mathematics, a set of objects is a *category* and their related transformations (*morphisms*). They are the building blocks of set theory. Saunders McLane, one of the creators of the Theory of Categories, explains that categories are created to describe natural transformations. This theory forms the basis for much of information systems, as well as for this book.

When applied on a successive basis, a total set of transformations will leave the original objects; in addition, one will have a *Group*. (Items subject to transformation may constitute any number of things—objects, numbers, rules, relationships, state spaces, attributes, or anything else.) Mathematically, a *group* is a category with one object in which all transformations (morphisms) are isomorphisms (i.e., after all transformations occur the *net* change applied to the object is zero). For a more complete definition of a group and other information, see:

Group: http://www.math.niu.edu/~beachy/abstract_algebra/study_guide/31.html
Isomorphism: http://www.math.niu.edu/~beachy/abstract_algebra/study_guide/34.html, or
Isomorphism from Wikipedia at http://www.wikipedia.com/wiki/isomorphism

*("An isomorphism is a bijection from one set of a mathematical object to the set of another mathematical object such that the structures defined upon these sets in these objects, such as orderings and operations, are preserved.")*

Order isomorphism from Wikipedia: http://www.wikipedia.com/wiki/order+isomorphism

*(Useful for ordinally scaled values: An order isomorphism is an isomorphism between a pair of partially ordered sets that preserves the order of elements in each set when the elements of one are mapped to the other.)*

Each group (of transformations) is characterized by mathematical rules that have no preference as to *what* will be changed. A mathematical operator such as addition is easy to understand, as it does not matter what is being added. As such, group theory can be applied to many types of objects and is very helpful when an analysis of the laws governing sets and their relationships needs to be performed; it is a powerful tool for deducting and analyzing the properties of metaobjects and constitutes a robust theoretical foundation for the metamodel of knowledge.

For readers who are mathematically inclined, key concepts in category theory are as follows:

A *category* is a collection of objects and a collection of *morphisms* (shown as "arrows" below) such that

1. Each morphism f has a "typing" on a pair of objects A, B written f:A→B. This is read 'f is a morphism from A to B'., A is the "source" or "domain" of f and B is its "target" or "codomain"
2. There exists a partial function on morphisms called composition. A composition is shown with the infix ring symbol, o as follows: A "composite" U o V : A→ C occurs when U:B→C and V:A→ B (this is the mathematical basis of process decomposition and traversal of relationships in object models).
3. This composition is associative: h o (g o f) = (h o g) o f (this is the mathematical basis for transitive relationships).
4. Each object A has an identity morphism id_A:A→A associated with it. This is the identity under composition, shown by the equations id_B o f = f = f o id_A (this is the mathematical basis for reflexive relationships).

At times, the composition ring is not included. A common, but not universal, mathematical convention is to use uppercase letters for objects, lowercase letters for morphisms, and script font for categories, which may also be considered mathematical variables.

Usually, the morphisms between two objects need not form a set (to avoid problems with Russell's paradox described at the end of this note). *2-morphisms* are transformations between morphisms, 3-morphisms are transformations between 2-morphisms, and so on to *n-morphisms*. *N-categories* are the number of categories with n-morphisms. These types of morphisms serve as the foundation for metarules such as sociopolitical laws.

*Isomorphism*: An isomorphism is a *bijection* (see *bijection* further on in this note) from one set of objects to another, such that the structures defined on these sets of objects (like orderings and operations) are preserved, that is, fA→B = fB→A.

*Homomorphism*: A homomorphism (commonly referred to as a morphism) is a copy of an original transformation.

A *domain* of a function is the set of values for which a function is defined. A *codomain* is the set of values consisting of all the possible results of a function. The codomain of a function f such that fD→ C is C. A function's range (defined below) is a subset of its codomain.

***Suggested additional reading:*** Items [166], [167], [168], [232], [233], [234], [235] , [308], and other publications listed under "Set Theory" in Appendix III.

The *range* of a function is the class of values attained by applying the function to each element within its domain. So, if f : X→ Y then the class g(X) = { g(x) | x in X } is the range of X under g. The range is a subclass of C, the codomain. The image of a function is defined in the same way but usually pertains to an individual member of the class of values.

Thus, for a class of values x and any function g(x), x is the domain and g(x) is the range, and the mathematical expression g: X→ Y implies:

A *function* maps an object from one value in its domain to one and only one member in its range. It is a special kind of relationship and a subtype of the more generic mathematical concept of a *morphism*. A morphism is a transformation that can make one set equal to another. As such, a function can be formally defined as:

If X and Y are sets where X is the domain and Y is the codomain, then a function g from X to Y, normally written as a subset of X x Y such that:

1. For each x in X, there exists some a in A such that (x, a) is an element of the function g. It means that the function is defined for every element of X.
2. For each x in X, a1 and a2 in a, if both (x, a1) and (x, a2) are elements of the function g then a1 = a2; that is, the function is uniquely defined for every element of X.

## Inverse of a Function:

For function, f : X→ Y, the function g : X→Y is a left inverse if for all y in X, g (f y) = y. g is a right inverse if, for all x in X, f (g x) = x. g is called the inverse of f without the "right" or "left" qualification, if both conditions are true. Only an *injection* (when no pair of different inputs will result in the same output) has a left inverse (it cannot be a many-to-one relationship). Only a *surjection* (every member of the codomain maps to a member of the function's domain) has a right inverse. Only a *bijection* (there is one and only one element of the domain that maps to one and only one element of the codomain) possesses an inverse. The mathematical convention is that $f^{-1}$ denotes the inverse of a function f.

These mathematical axioms also serve as the basis of cardinality ratios and inverse relationships between objects.

Consider a *class* of mappings between two objects, X and Y, of a category. A mathematical *morphism* is an instance of the class.

*Map* is a function that yields a list. A Map uses its first argument as a parameter for each element of its second argument (a list) to return the list of results.

*Functors* are generalizations of the "*Map*." Classification may be thought of as using a special mathematical operator on its arguments to create a "Type." If we call the operator T, it returns a type "list of T." The difference with the map function is nondescript: *Map* takes a function and applies it to each element of a list separately; however, it does not return a single item called *List*, which would be a container of individual items. This container is the *list* and is the shared mathematical basis of aggregations and relationships. A *functor* F is a mathematical operator. It operates on types. Functors are polymorphic operators on functions with the type:

F : (x→y) → (F x→F y)

## Ring:

A ring is a commutative group (R, E) and a binary operation ⊠ that satisfies the following constraints for all a, b, and c in R such that there exists a multiplicative identity or unity for all a in R:

a ⊠1 = 1⊠a = a     (This "unity" is a generalization of the number 1)

when:

a ⊠ (b E c) = (a ⊠b) E c
a⊠ (b E c) = (a⊠b) E (a⊠c)
(a E b) ⊠c = (a ⊠c) E (b⊠c)

Sometimes, the term "unitary ring" is used for these kinds of rings because they possess a multiplicative identity. The term "Ring" is then generalized to mean mathematical groups with or without this kind of multiplicative identity.

A ring is a system that possesses a set R of elements and two binary operations. The first binary operation is commutative, while the second is associative. The second operation distributes over the first. (Also, see notes on commutative operators, associative operators, and distributive operators.)

In a *commutative ring*, the commutative law will hold true for both the associative and the commutative operations. One example of a commutative ring is a set of real numbers.

## Commutative Operators:

A binary operation combines two items. A binary operation is commutative if the of order of items being operated on is irrelevant to its result. When adding two numbers, the order in which the numbers are added does not matter. Therefore, we can conclude that addition is commutative. Certain operations, however, such as subtraction and division are not commutative. The fact that 4 divided by 2 is 2, whereas 2 divided by 4 is 0.5, is an instance of the noncommutativity of the division operator.

## Associative Operations:

An operation is associative when it combines three or more items, two at a time, and the initial pairing of the items is irrelevant to the result. For example, addition is associative because (a+b)+c = a+(b+c). Because (a÷b)÷c does not equal a÷(b÷c), division is not associative. It follows that the parentheses indicating which quantities should be combined first are not needed when an operation is associative.

## Distributive Operations:

Take an operation, "*" and another we will call "E." * is called *left distributive* over E when

a * (b E c)=(a * b) E (a * c) for every possible value of a, b, and c.

Similarly, *right distributivity* over E occurs when
$(a * b)\ E\ c = (a\ E\ c)\ *\ (b\ E\ c)$ for every value of a, b, and c.
For instance, multiplication is left distributive over addition because $a\times(b+c) = (a\times b) + (a\times c)$.

## Polymorphism:

Christopher Strachey first conceived of *polymorphism* in 1967. Hindley and Milner then developed and extended it. Polymorphism is when context specific behavior is normalized by subtyping and generalizing objects. These objects may also be relationships and interactions. For example, a word and a room have length, but the exact meaning of length is ambiguous. It depends on whether we are discussing the length of a word or the length of a room. As such, "word" and "room" can be seen as parameters of length that fix its meaning by adding contextual information to the generic concept of length. Therefore, the length of a word may be measured by the amount of letters in it, whereas the length of a room may be any real number. This is also an example of subtyping by adding information (constraints), in which the context constrains the meaning of length, pegging it down more precisely than in an "unknown" context.

*Box II.1. Kinds of polymorphism*

Polymorphism describes the shared behavior of objects and helps normalize the behavior common to different classes of objects. Polymorphism may be categorized as follows (additional reading in [90], [91], and [239] of Appendix III). [91]

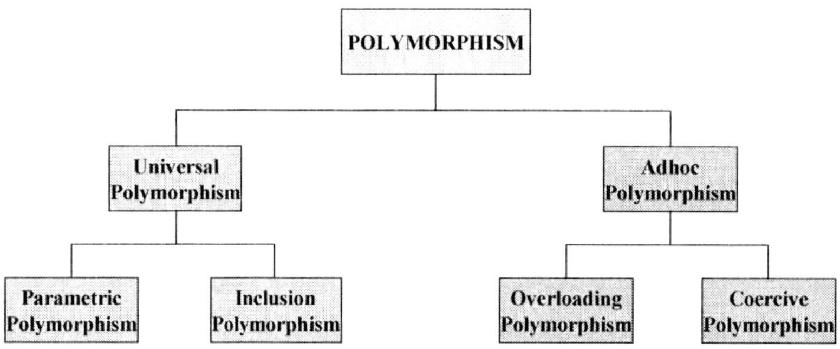


*Figure A. Kinds of polymorphism*

*Reproduced by permission from Mitra, A., & Gupta, A., Agile Systems with Reusable Patterns of Business Knowledge, Norwood, MA: Artech House, Inc., 2005. ©*

**Universal, or "true" polymorphism:** In this book, we are concerned mainly with Universal (true) polymorphism. Universal polymorphism is a uniform type in which behavior has been generalized over an infinite number of types into a common feature as follows:

***Parametric polymorphism*** is when common behavior is generalized in abstract classes. Subtypes add information by constraining these classes to provide more precise forms of the generalized behavior. For instance, movement is generic behavior shared by all physical objects. A wheel rolls. Rolling is a more constrained and precise form of movement added by a subtype called "wheel" of physical objects. Parametric polymorphism lends an ontology the power of inference. Thus, the parameter "wheel" helps infer that the object will roll, whereas the parameter "frog" would infer that the object moves by hopping. Parametric polymorphism also flows from domains and their interrelationships. For example, the age of different kinds of objects such as individuals, documents, ideas, or buildings may be calculated by:

*Box II.1. continued*

*Age = Current Time - Time of creation*

Current time and time of creation may be considered parameters of the function called "Age." This is why this kind of polymorphism is qualified as *Parametric*.

***Inclusion polymorphism*** is when subtypes inherit behavior. For example, a human may walk, which means both male and female humans may walk.

***Ad-hoc polymorphism*** is usually "unnatural" in that it is a construct that acts over a finite number of possibly unrelated types. It usually flows from some kind of ad-hoc assignment of items to object classes as follows:

***Overloading*** assigns the same syntax for behaviors of different types. For example, the symbol "+" may stand for arithmetic addition of integers, the separate arithmetic additions of the real and imaginary parts of complex numbers or concatenation of strings of symbols. Unlike parametric polymorphism, which will use the same procedure to derive the behavior of every subtypes, overloading reuses the name of the function but, depending on the context, uses different procedures to handle the different subtypes. Thus, the function name is really a homonym (two different meanings with the same label) in this case.

***Coercive polymorphism*** is when an object instance is arbitrarily declared to belong to a subtype (usually for computational convenience or efficiency. For example, symbols such as periods, commas, asterisks, and other "special characters" in a computer system are assigned a sort sequence, even though, unlike numbers, they do not convey any magnitude or sequencing information. Similarly, in a nominal domain, values may be arbitrarily assigned an order or magnitude. In an ordinal domain, coercion happens when differences or ratios between values are arbitrarily assigned a magnitude or ratios of values in any but ratio scaled domains are compared. It is also common in object-oriented programming: sometimes programmers will use the same variables to refer to objects of different classes at run-time.

## Infix Rings and Infix Notation:

- When functions are placed between their operands, this designation is called "infix notation." For example, "1+2" is an instance of infix notation.
- A function that is not defined for all possible values of its arguments is called a partial function. For example, f(x) in the following equation is a partial function:

$f(x) = 1/x \text{ if } x \neq 0.$

A partial function on morphisms is called a *composition*. The infix ring symbol, o, stands for a composition. A composition may be denoted by a symbol. Let us consider a composition Z= x o y. Z is the "composite."

$Z: A \rightarrow C, \text{ if } x: B \rightarrow C \text{ and } y: A \rightarrow B.$

## Russell's Paradox and the Axiom of Regularity:

Russel's paradox pertains to set theory. It is a logical contradiction, first discovered by Bertrand Russell (1872-1970), a British mathematician. The contradiction can be stated as: If R is the set of all sets which do not contain themselves, is it possible for R to contain itself? If R contains itself, it cannot do so because a set cannot contain itself, and if it does not, then by definition, it contains itself. This happens because sets may only have members of a single type (e.g., integers or sets of integers) and no type is allowed to refer to itself so no set can contain itself. This principle is called the *Axiom of Regularity* of the *Axiom of Foundation*. The formal assertion is that for every set S, there is an element in it that is disjointed from S. As such, no set can belong to itself. The concept of mathematical classes resolves this contradiction because classes may refer to themselves.

## H. Natural Zeros for Temperature and Time (Date)

Although a natural zero was established for temperature and more recently for time/date by cosmologists, this concept does not apply to the metamodel for *business* rules. We are only concerned with the fact that there are domains of information that convey information on differences or gaps between objects but do not have any information on ratios, which makes them difference scaled rather than ratio scaled.

Those interested in further reading on the natural zero in the date domain may refer to almost any article on modern cosmology. The following publications have a more narrative, as opposed to a mathematical, approach to the issue:

- *A Brief History of Time* by Stephen Hawking published by Bantam Books
- *The Whole Shebang* by Timothy Ferris, published by Simon & Schuster
- *The Elegant Universe* by Brian Greene, published by W. W. Norton and Co
- *The Nature of Space and Time* by Stephen Hawking and Roger Penrose, published by Princeton University Press
- *The Inflationary Universe* by Alan H. Guth, published by Addison-Wesley Publishing Co. Inc.
- *Principles of Physical Cosmology* by P. J. E. Peebles, published by Princeton University Press
- *Before the Beginning* by Martin Rees, published by Addison-Wesley

The first three of these books also explain the natural zero of temperature in their glossaries.
(Also see the note on the flow of time as an emergent property of information in this appendix.)

## I. Positivism

Positivism postulates that concepts exist only as "quantities" that can be observed. This concept is divergent from our focus in this book, which is to develop a metamodel that will facilitate normalization of knowledge—a very real and tangible outcome for information systems.

## J. Definition of the State Machine and How It Relates to Service Oriented Architecture

A state machine may be described mathematically as a 6-tuple: its inputs, outputs, and internal states are as follows:

Let
**I** be the set of input events

**O** be the set of output events

**S** be the set of internal states

**f** be the function that maps **I** and **S** to **O**, such that the outputs will result from inputs to the system in internal state **S**, (i.e., **O**= **f** (**I** x **S**)). **f** is called the *transfer function* or *transform* of the black box that describes the state machine.

**g** be the function that maps **I** and $\mathbf{S}_{\mathbf{current}}$ to $\mathbf{S}_{\mathbf{next}}$, $\mathbf{S}_{\mathbf{next}}$ being the internal state of the system *after* it has received inputs **I** in its current state $\mathbf{S}_{\mathbf{current}}$, (i.e., $\mathbf{S}_{\mathbf{next}} = \mathbf{g}\ (\mathbf{I} \times \mathbf{S}_{\mathbf{current}})$. Note that in the nomenclature of knowledge this book, **g** is the set of effects of events in set **I** that changes the state of an object).

$\mathbf{S}_0$ be the set of possible initial states (it follows that $\mathbf{S}_0 \subseteq \mathbf{S}$).

The state machine is then described by:

State Machine = $(\mathbf{I}, \mathbf{O}, \mathbf{S}, \mathbf{f}, \mathbf{g}, \mathbf{S}_0)$

The cardinality of **S** could be infinite (i.e., the set **S** may have an infinite number of members). When **S** is finite, the 6-tuple is called a *finite state machine*, also known as *finite state automata*.

Configurations of finite state automata, composed of parts that do not change their internal states are less prone to chaos when its parts or configurations are changed. The concept of assembling business processes by coupling such "services" is a cornerstone of service oriented architecture and reuse of services. These services may be shown as a 3-tuple:

Service = (**I**, **O**, **f**)

Services are then said to be "loosely coupled" because they have no information on the internal states of other services (the 6-tuple represents "tight" coupling between components).

Services interface with each other through a published "contract," which determines what outputs, in what formats and precision the service will return in exchange for inputs provided in the "contracted" format and precision. This kind of architecture can facilitate concepts like "business on demand," in which services mutually "call" on each other via a messaging network (usually the Web), as they are needed (on demand). Thus, an accounting service (system) may choose which of several possible currency exchange services it will use at run time when it finds the need to convert foreign exchange. These services may have been made available on the Web by different foreign exchange brokers, and the accounting service may "fail-over" to another vendor if its preferred service is down.

Although loose coupling facilitates and simplifies service reuse, loose coupling does not guarantee reusability. Identifying reusable components is a major issue in the current state of the art in Service Oriented Architecture (SOA). This book and its companions in the series develop the models and patterns that assist in identifying reusable services. We do this by identifying the ontology of concepts from which deterministic knowledge is configured.

## K. The Question of Gender

Gender is a complex domain, rich with meaning. It is much richer than many of us may think and provides a good example of how behavior and systems can flex and adapt in step with new learning. The following excerpts and references show how the meaning of gender expands and flexes in step with our biological knowledge of living species. The other books in this series use these examples to show how knowledge may be refactored. As an exercise, readers of this book may use the following to construct examples of how processes and scopes of systems may shift as the simple biparental concept of gender gives way to more complex constraints:

*General discussion on gender* (from http://pages.ripco.net/~barbarian/archive_08NOV00.html).

Living creatures may be male, female, or hermaphrodite. Hermaphrodites may be of two kinds: those that can procreate by mating with themselves and those that must procreate by mating with another individual of its species. Do we count hermaphrodites as a single gender or are there two hermaphrodite genders? Some sea creatures exhibit more complex genders: There are a number of species that have "intersexual" genders. Intersexual animals have both male and female organs without being hermaphroditic. There are also many transsexual species: individuals of transsexual species change their gender in the normal course of their life. Most changes are just variations on the male/female theme, but some are not. For example, the striped parrot fish has five genders derived from biological sex, genetic origin, and "color phase": (1) genetic female, born female—each of these fish will become male and change color; (2) transsexual male, born female. These individuals become male before they assume their terminal-phase color; (3) terminal-phase transsexual males, born female. These fish become male and change color at the same time; (4) genetic male, born male. Most of these individuals change color but do not change gender; (5) terminal-phase genetic male, born male. They start as males, change color, but not gender, while they are still young.

Thus, the concept of gender can be fluid and may depend on the criteria we use to differentiate between genders. Here are more examples:

*Earthworm Gender* (based on Nick Musurka's Earthworm Web Page http://members.aol.com/camusurca/earthworms/reproduc.htm):

Earthworms are hermaphroditic, meaning that each worm carries male and female sex organs. During mating, the worm produces tubes from its skin in which sperm is released and carried, and several eggs are released as well. Fertilization itself actually takes place inside of the capsule.

*Fish gender* (by Aaron Rice, Department of Biology, Davidson College, North Carolina, USA at http://www.bio.davidson.edu/Courses/anphys/1999/Rice/Rice.htm):

Most reef fish are characterized by sex change during the course of their life. Only a small part of the population stay the same sex their entire lives (gonochoristic). Some fish will change sex only once, while others will switch sex multiple times, and some even have both sexes at the same time.

The University of Michigan, Museum of Zoology, Animal Diversity Web article by Erin Wayman at http://animaldiversity.ummz.umich.edu/accounts/cirrhilabrus/c._exquisitus$narrative.html

The Exquisite Wrasse is a particular type of reef fish, in which only female fish can change its sex. When the female changes her sex, her appearance also changes into that of a male.

*Plant Gender* (an article by Rachel Clark, August 1, 2000, at http://www.earthsky.com/2000/es000801.html):

Almost all flowering plants have both male and female parts; some rely on animal pollination while others are self reliant. An interesting flowering plant, however, is known as Zuckia brandegei. Each half of the plant will open up with either the male or female parts and then, a few weeks later, they switch.

*Species with a single gender* (from Lizards Without Dads by Maryalice Yakutchik, Copyright © 2000):

The New Mexico whiptail is a half a foot long lizard with the ability to clone itself naturally. Therefore, a female can bear genetically duplicated offspring without a male counterpart.

Discovery Communications Inc at http://www.discovery.com/exp/lizards/wodads.html

Recently, it was discovered that Komodo dragons can sometimes, but not usually, also reproduce in the same way.

## L. The Bunge-Wand-Weber Model

Developed between 1990-1996, the Bunge-Wand-Weber model (BWW model) was based on a rigorous mathematical foundation in an effort to unify both natural and abstract reality (similar to the Theory of Categories). The BWW model has essentially been developed and can be used as an instrument for analyzing the redundancy, accuracy, and completeness of information systems methodologies.

The BWW model can check *completeness* and redundancies (called *overspecification*) in methodologies (see item [12]—Roseman & Green, 2000—in Appendix III for BWW ontological constructs) in order to characterize the behavior of information systems. The intent of this note is to give readers an understanding of the core concepts of BWW based on [21] in Appendix III (Opdahl, 1998).

According to this model, the real world is comprised of *things*. *Things* have properties (which are also *things*). Some *properties* may be shared by multiple things. These shared properties denote relationships between these *things*. A system is a composite *thing*. Composite *things* are comprised of component *things*, and may in turn be a part of a still larger system. The properties of a composite *thing* may be either hereditary or emergent. A hereditary property belongs to a component *thing*, whereas an emergent property does not. It is a property of the composite *thing*. A set of things with the same set of properties form a class. Things, properties, systems, and classes are the metaconstructs of the BWW model. *Things* and associated properties are the fundamental metaconstructs of the BWW model, whereas classes and systems are derived from these fundamental metaconstructs. (The BWW model asserts that these derived concepts be derived *only* from its fundamental metaconstructs and nothing else.) These concepts of the BWW model support static structures. "State," "Transformation," and "Stable state" support dynamic behavior. The BWW model asks that real world systems should be represented as completely and validly as possible. It also stipulates that problem analysis methods should support exploration of relations, both within and between each of these metaconstructs in as systematic a way as possible.

## M. Multiperspective Modeling and Facet Modeling

(This discussion is based on research in item [15] in Appendix III)

Every experienced analyst knows of the trials, tribulations, friction, and professional disagreements of modeling information in "the correct fashion." Projects are known to have stalled because of differences in professional opinions of "*the correct* model," given the same requirements. This happens because each stakeholder brings a slightly different perspective to the problem. Stakeholders possess different

*Box II.2. BWW model test criteria*

- A methodology is considered to be *incomplete* (i.e., there exists a construct deficit in BWW terms) unless it possesses at least one construct for each and every BWW ontology construct.
- The clarity of the methodology (in BWW terms) is calculated by a review of the following three criteria:
  - *Construct Overload*: If there exists more than one way to specify a BWW ontological construct, then the methodology is said to be affected by *construct overload*, an ultimate detraction from *clarity*.
  - *Construct Redundancy*: If more than one methodology construct specifies the same BWW ontological construct, then the methodology is said to be affected by *construct redundancy*, another detraction from *clarity*.
  - *Construct Excess*: If there exist constructs that fail to map to BWW ontological constructs, then the methodology is said to be affected by *construct excess*, yet another detraction from *clarity*.

BWW Model Constructs are cataloged in the following figure (for additional reading on the BWW model, see Appendix III for a detailed explanation of each one):

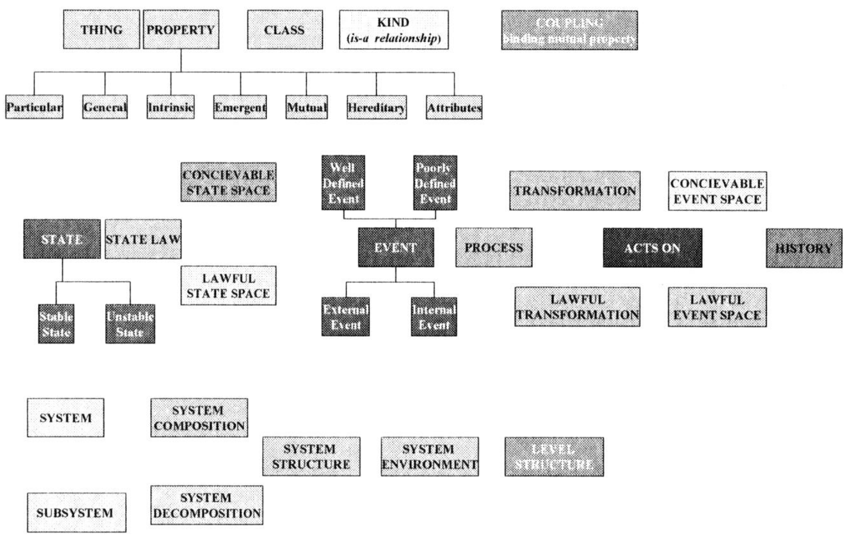


*Figure A. Bunge-Wand-Weber constructs*

*Reproduced by permission from Mitra, A., & Gupta, A., Agile Systems with Reusable Patterns of Business Knowledge, Norwood, MA: Artech House, Inc., 2005. ©*

experiences, training, and beliefs that shape their perspectives of the problem domain. The underlying assumption of multiperspective modeling is that a problem analyses endeavor should involve several stakeholders who bring different perspectives of the problem and the associated business processes.

By applying the BWW model, we can see that *perspectives*, made up of things and properties, are limited by the set of things and properties that a stakeholder is aware of. A perspective can therefore be seen as an abstraction of the problem domain. The BWW model defines a class as a set of things that holds a particular set of properties, and a perspective summarizes only a component of properties of each thing; therefore, the same thing may belong to different classes when viewed from different perspectives. Mutual properties correspond to interrelationships between things. Therefore, different perspectives of the same things will correspond to dissimilar dependencies between these things.

Hence, when viewed from different perspectives, the problem domain will appear as different systems of things, classes, and properties.

As observers, we constitute a part of the reality that we look at. We can, therefore, not regard observation of reality as distinct from the reality that is being observed. From the facet modeling point of view, perspective and conception hold just as much weight as things and properties in the problem domain. Does this mean that we have to be limited by perspective? Individuals perceive the world partly from their own unique point of view, partly from widely held generalizations implicit to the world of business, and partly from values that are imposed by the physical world. Due to the existence and applicability of these widely shared ideas, it *is* possible to define universal business classes as has been done in Part II of this book.

Four metaconstructs emerge as essential to multiple perspectives modeling:

1. Things: This is the elementary unit of the BWW model. The real world is comprised of things. A composite thing may be comprised of other things.
2. Properties: Things possess properties. Properties can be either intrinsic, mutual (shared in relationships), emergent (i.e., emerge when things are assembled), or hereditary (i.e., acquired through inheritance).
3. Conceptions: Conceptions emerge when things are perceived from a specific perspective. Conceptions are based on a subset of the properties of the underlying thing.
4. Perspectives: Perspectives are the views of stakeholders of the particular problem domain in a given context at a particular moment in time. A perspective comprises of a set of conceptions with properties and class definitions.

Object-oriented methods do not explicitly recognize perspectives as being fundamental metaobjects and rarely support explicit methodological steps to represent them; however, facet modeling does support multiple perspectives.

Facet modeling views the problem domain as consisting of phenomena (i.e., "things" in the BWW model), properties, aspects (i.e., "conceptions" in the BWW model), and perspectives, as follows:

1. Items represent phenomena. Items are durable categories, instances, and aggregations, but not events since events are not durable.
2. Facets of items represent various aspects of phenomena.
3. Primitive subfacets represent various properties of aspects. Properties are perceived only from an aspect; hence they belong to the aspect and not directly to the item. Sometimes the same property may emerge from two or more aspects. This is the key to reuse across aspects.
4. Perspectives are views abstracted from the facet model.

## N. Generalizing Concept of Distance: Metric Spaces and Metrics

The distance between objects in the physical world can be grasped intuitively. The physical concept of distance is specified in terms of the difference between two objects in terms of their positions in physical space. Distance can also be generalized to measure how different or similar two objects are in terms of other properties as well. This mathematically generalized distance leads to the concept of a *metric* (see [266] and [309] in Appendix III). A metric is calibrated in terms of similarities of positions in *metric space* (see items [265] and [266] in Appendix III). Physical space is three-dimensional. It is the space we physically occupy and is only one of several kinds of possible of metric spaces. We measure physical distance along a straight line. This is only one type of metric. State space exemplifies a whole different kind of metric space and may have different metrics. Mathematically, metrics and metric spaces are defined in the following manner where the function "m" possesses the characteristics of distance:

A metric on the set U is a real-valued function m on U x U that satisfies all of the following conditions (item [305] in Appendix III):

1. Positivity: m(u,u) = 0 but m(u, v) > 0, if u is distinct from v (common sense dictates that no separation must exist between identical positions because they are at the same location and a finite distance must exist between distinct places).
2. Symmetry: m(u, v) = m(v, u). In other words, the metric (distance) between a pair of locations is the same, regardless of the member of the pair used to measure from.
3. The triangle inequality: m(u, v) possesses the maximum value denoted by m(u,v) + m(w, v) for every w. "The direct metric," that is, the distance between a pair of locations, cannot exceed the metric (length of the path) via a third point. The direct metric is an analog of the length of a straight line in physical space.

In mathematical terms, a metric space is a set U with a metric defined on it. The metric space is a *discrete metric space* when the attributes of an object are nominally scaled as follows (item [267] in Appendix III:

A discrete metric, M, is:
M(u, u) = 0, and
M(u, v) = 1, if u is not equal to v

The discrete metric can only specify whether or not there is a difference in state between objects, but not the magnitude of the difference.

*Pseudometric spaces* are spaces in which m(u, v) = 0 for some u, v pairs, even if u and v are different. This is the basis of the concept of mutability between components. In this book, if a knowledge component replaces another in an aggregate, the aggregate is considered to have changed state. Thus, in our metamodel of knowledge, state spaces are metric, not pseudometric spaces. However, the Principle of Parsimony in our book and the ontology we describe makes subclasses mutable with superclasses. This is because objects (components) become mutually distinct in step with added information. Consequently, as we ascend ontological levels, one loses information and distinctions fade away. This is how mutability is derived in our model, even though the state space of knowledge is described by a metric, not pseudometric, space.

*Semimetric spaces* are those that do not satisfy the triangle inequality; that is, the direct metric between two points cannot be more than the metric via a third point. This may occur, for instance, when the cycle time of a business process making a direct state transition is more than the sum of cycle times of processes that pass through various intermediate states. For instance, a process of shipping packages via a direct route could be more expensive than routing it via several intermediary points.

Readers interested in more information about different kinds of spaces should read the section on *Spaces and their Properties* in Appendix III. [266] in Appendix III has succinct definitions of various kinds of spaces. [268] and [269] in Appendix III provide mathematical descriptions of the generalization of the concept of distance.

*Hilbert Spaces* are a type of metric space are used for modeling state spaces of stochastic systems (while this book focuses on discrete *deterministic* systems). They are difficult to visualize as analogs of the two dimensional planes, three-dimensional spaces, or even higher dimensional state spaces. Each axis of a Hilbert space is a complex number so that information can be arranged in Hilbert space. This means that the probability of a given state is represented by each coordinate, which is a complex number (unlike the spaces we have discussed thus far, where each coordinate is a real number, rank, or category). A Hilbert space is capable of having infinite dimensions. Each dimension of Hilbert space connotes a state of *potential* existence of the system. Objects in an undetermined state are said to exist in a convoluted pattern of a Hilbert space that is infinitely dimensional. These objects have incompletely defined potentialities. All possible states, even mutually exclusive states, coexist and add up provided they are not observed. (Observation turns unknowns to known values and changes the state of the system). Each object can then possess its own Hilbert space. When many objects interact, or for an aggregate object, the Hilbert space is the product of all the individual Hilbert spaces of their components. In this labyrinthine notion, components lose their identity and may be thought of as being in all possible states at all possible times but with differing probabilities.

Since the metamodel in this book addresses only deterministic discrete systems, Hilbert spaces would only be of interest if the metamodel is extended to include stochastic behavior, which is inherent in the uncertainty of information in the real world.

Although in our metamodel querying the state of a system will not change its state, such systems do occur in real life. For example, productivity increased in several factories when workers came to know that their productivity was going to be measured. This fact alone can cause improvements. However, such effects are difficult to calibrate. Accordingly, we ignore Hilbert spaces in this book. Individuals interested in more information may refer to Appendix III. In Appendix III, [266] has succinct definitions of various kinds of spaces, whereas [268] and [269] have mathematical descriptions of how the concept of distance can be generalized. [283], [284], [285], [286] in Appendix III provide additional reading on Hilbert spaces.

## O. Kinds of Inheritance

Bertrand Meyer, the creator of the object oriented language Eiffel and the president of ISE first described this scheme. Meyer took imperfection of modeling, programming and knowledge into account while building this scheme. Remember that polymorphism (described in the note on the Mathematical Theory of Categories) is also an inheritance mechanism. The inheritances in Meyer's taxonomy emerge naturally from the Metamodel of Knowledge. The metamodel unifies these concepts rendering extraneous distinctions unnecessary:

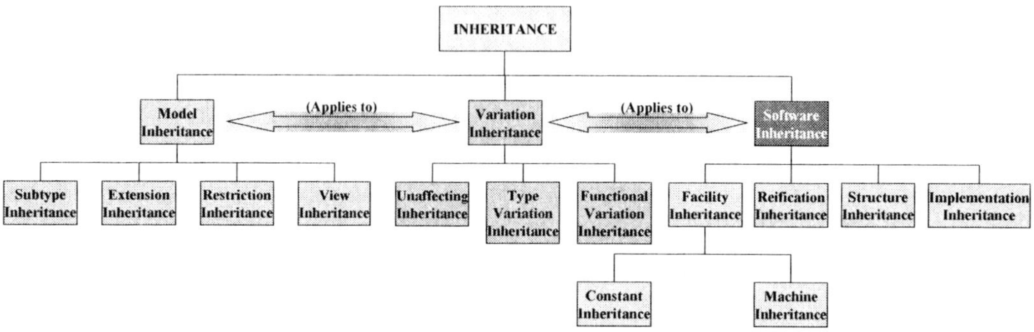


*Figure II.1. Kinds of inheritance*
*Reproduced by permission from Mitra, A., & Gupta, A., Agile Systems with Reusable Patterns of Business Knowledge, Norwood, MA: Artech House, Inc., 2005. ©*

**Model Inheritance:** When one object is related to another with an *is-a* relationship.

**Software Inheritance:** Inheritance used to express pure software issues, rather than external "real world" issues. This book focuses on business knowledge components and software inheritance is not in scope.

**Variation Inheritance:** When an object class is described by identifying their *differences* from another object class and may apply to either model or software inheritance.

**Model Inheritance:** Model inheritance describes the following kinds of inheritance and unifies them under one ontology:

- ***Subtype Inheritance*:** When mutually exclusive subtypes inherit the behavior of a class of objects. Subtypes *must* exist in the state space of their supertypes and hence share their attributes and effects. The mutual exclusivity, which leads to the concept of partitions as metaobject in our model of knowledge, is derived by adding a constraint that members are mutually exclusive between subtypes.
- ***Extension Inheritance*:** When a subtype adds features. These features may be attributes, relationships, and effects. Thus, the state space of the subtype extends of the state space of the supertype into additional dimensions. This is why it is called "extension" inheritance. The subtype will inherit properties of the supertype, which are the dimensions of state space that the subtype shares with its supertype.
- ***View Inheritance*:** This happens when the constraint that prohibits an object instance for being a member of two or more subtypes is omitted. Then the object instance may simultaneously exist in two or more subtypes, which will be subtypes in different partitions. The object will then "inherit" the properties it shares with its supertype and will also have special properties and restrictions, which is the information that the subtype adds to its members.
- ***Restriction Inheritance*:** Constraints add information. Thus, restricting the state space of an object class may create subclasses. This may involve constraining values of attributes or behavior. Restrictions on behavior are typically called "guard conditions" in UML. When restricting the state space of an object in this way creates the subclass, the state space of the subclass carves out a region *inside* the state space of the superclass. This region is shared between the subclass and superclass and is the information they share in information space.

**Variation Inheritance:** Reuse of knowledge implies that we gather common components and *add* to them, rather than *modify or override* them. A variation created by excluding or overriding some properties implies that a reusable component with common properties might have been overlooked or redundancies created. From a practical point of view, as Meyer points out, it might be expedient, even if not theoretically perfect. For example, it might be expedient to assume that deserts have sand and then declare exceptions for specific ice deserts. This may also be addressed by assigning different default values to different subtypes as described in other books in this series.

- **Unaffecting Inheritance:** Unaffecting Inheritance *excludes* specific features of the parent object(s); asserting that those features of the parent do not exist in the subtype. Excluding behavior is the same as declaring one or more features "null," that is, "meaningless" (as opposed to "unknown." In this, the Entity relationship diagramming technique commonly used for modeling is ambiguous. There is no clear convention about whether not mentioning a feature of an object implies that it cannot exist or if its existence is unknown). This is a constraint that asserts that something cannot be. Constraints are information added, and thus this basis for creating a subtype is valid and conforms to the principle of subtyping by adding information.
  Thus, implied constraints on these subtypes may be more restrictive than those on the supertype. A subtype may not violate the constraints it inherited from the supertype but may be denied some state transitions in order to keep it within the restrictions in *its* state space (this is one way of automating inference). Unaffecting inheritance and exclusion partitions can be convenient constructs for normalizing knowledge under these conditions.
  Meyer calls these implied constraints *Restriction Inheritance*. Restriction and unaffecting inheritance converge in our model of knowledge (see item [338] in Appendix III).
- **Type Variation Inheritance:** When one or more states (of an object) require definition of *additional* behavior(s). For example, athletic persons have lower resting pulse rates than the average person it requires definition of pulse rate to describe this type of person. It boils down to applying extensional inheritance in a restricted region of the state space of an object.
- **Functional Variation Inheritance:** When the subclass *overrules* some behavior(s) of the superclass. It boils down to combining "unaffecting" with Extension inheritance. The comments related to "unaffecting" Inheritance apply here as well. For example, nonflying birds such as ostriches override the flying behavior of the superclass, birds.

**Software Inheritance:**

- **Facility Inheritance:** When the supertype is an *arbitrary* collection of properties that other object classes may inherit from. These supertypes might be some composition of real world objects, tailored to optimize performance on specific software platforms, or perhaps the business model just did not do due diligence and designers find reusable facets on the fly and decide to use them in the interests of expediency. Reusable properties should naturally flow from the object classes in Part II and the metamodel of knowledge:
  - Constant Inheritance: When subtypes inherit attributes from the supertype.
  - Machine Inheritance: When subtypes inherit effects from the supertype.

- **Reification Inheritance:** "Reification" means making an abstract concept into a material thing. It is the actual structure that implements a concept. For example, Entity-Relationship of data models in relational databases use Reification Inheritance.
- **Structure Inheritance:** When subtypes inherit mathematical properties like addition, subtraction, and the like. Thus, they apply to domains that inherit properties because they are subtypes of other domains. For example, the set of integers is naturally ratio scaled because it inherits properties from ratio scaled domains.
- **Implementation Inheritance:** This deals with implementation of concepts in software. Software objects inherit properties from concepts and implement them in software with Implementation Inheritance.

## P. Lungfish

While it is a common belief that all fish are aquatic, it is less well known that some fish are amphibious. These facts were used in this series of books to construct examples of how new learning can reshape concepts and how models and computer systems must flex to accept new knowledge. Readers may use the following details to examine how systems based on the assumption that fish are always aquatic animals might automatically adapt to the fact that a class of fish, called Lungfish, are amphibious. Between 345-395 million years ago, most of the world was inhabited by lungfish. Today, only six known species of lungfish exist. All lungfish possess gills, for breathing water, and lungs, for breathing air. They live in swamps and small rivers in South America, West and South Africa, and Australia. When the water dries up, African and South American lungfish burrow into soft mud and breathe through their mouths. The African lungfish can survive up to four years outside water, while the Australian lungfish can be up to seven feet long and weigh over 100 pounds. This fish can also walk on dry land on its fins. For more information, see http://www.oregonzoo.org/cards/Rainforest/lungfish.african.htm or http://home.enitel.no/haraldseide/.

## Q. Refactoring

When it is first written, object-oriented software is usually not reusable. Systems designers experience problems when they attempt to reuse code written for one application in another. Reusable software slowly emerges after several modifications have been made, keeping reuse in mind, of course. This evolution may involve writing of new code or modification of existing code. Behavior must be preserved as code is added or modified in order to let existing applications continue to use the new code. Behavior-preserving manipulations that alter the design of such reusable code are called *refactoring.* The process is also termed "refactoring," however, it does not change behavior. Instead, *refactoring* redistributes and then reorganizes behavior among components of a system. If performed correctly, this can enhance the reusability of components, and the modification can become more simplified depending on the reusability of the components, even though reusable components emerge through a trial and error basis. This process helps to keep software well structured, even under the pressure of change. Changes follow typical patterns. Effects, relationships, attributes, and constraints are transferred from one class to another. Classes may be split into smaller components or subclasses, so that one part can be altered independently of another. At times, classes are generalized into a common superclass, followed by moving common functionality up into the new superclass. To date, refactoring is performed manually, making it time-consuming, resource intensive, and prone to errors. This laborious process allows reusable components to emerge in a slow and incremental fashion. The intent of the patterns and metamodel is to diminish the incidence of errors to provide guidance and template that could help to diminish the side effects of modifying code between design iterations and to enable refactoring to be performed with greater speed and reliability. Automated refactoring tools, like *refactory,* can greatly assist in this endeavor.

See Chapter 2 of [329] in Appendix III for further details on refactoring and when to use this approach. The University of Illinois has a research project on developing automated techniques to facilitate refactoring: details are available at http://cbl.leeds.ac.uk/nikos/tex2html/examples/concepts/node9.html and at http://losser.st-lab.cs.uu.nl/~visser/cgi-bin/twiki/view/Transform/SmalltalkRefactory or http://st-www.cs.uiuc.edu/users/brant/Refactory/.

## R. How Attributes Emerge from Domains

An attribute might be thought of as an overlap (set intersection) between the domain it is from, which is a class of values with shared meaning, measurability, and constraints, and a temporal object, with specific properties. Each distinct intersection of the object with a domain provides a distinct attribute of the object. Sometimes the same object and domain may have several distinct intersections. Each will be an attribute that maps to the same domain. For example, a sugar cube is an object with length, width, and height. Each is an attribute that maps to the length domain. Thus, the sugar cube has three distinct intersections with the length domain.

In general, each axis of an object's state space is an intersection of the object with an abstract domain: an irreducible fact that a distinct property exists.

## S. Lambda Calculus

Lambda Calculus, denoted as λ–calculus and developed by Alonzo Church in the 1930s, provides a mathematical system for specifying relationships between functions, expressions, and values. Each is considered to be a type of a mathematical object that exists on its own merit. Relationships between these objects are expressed in terms of *λ–expressions.*

In λ–calculus functions, values and λ–expressions can constitute arguments of λ–expressions. At the time when λ–expressions are evaluated, results can be λ–expressions, functions, or values. Further, expressions can operate on other expressions or be defined in terms of other expressions and objects, much like a string of beads that is used to form longer strings and even a necklace.

Based on the above, λ–calculus can serve as a theoretical foundation for the metamodel of knowledge, especially for generalizing and abstracting concepts related to meaning and expression. Since business rules, constraints, relationships, and objects are inherently equivalent in character, one can use λ–calculus to express all of these parameters as arguments of λ–expressions. Readers may refer to the publications listed in Appendix III. Automation implements λ–calculus using Functional Programming techniques. (See the note on functional programming.)

Germane within λ–calculus are the *Church-Rosser theorem* and the *Normal Form* (of λ–expressions); these deal with the issue of equivalence of λ–expressions. The fact that the same meaning may be expressed in different forms is a concept that is related to our metamodel of meaning. Readers can refer to the note on the Church-Rosser theorem and relevant publications in Appendix III.

## T. Church-Rosser Theorem and Normal Forms

The Church-Rosser theorem, discovered by Alonzo Church and J. Barkley Rosser, proves that a Rule Meaning possesses no more than one normal form and that this normal form is the value of a λ-expression if it exists. The Church-Rosser theorem further asserts that all equivalent rule expressions can be reduced to the same single normal form (see items [240], [241], [242], [250] in Appendix III).

Two strategies exist for reducing rule expressions to their normal forms. Applicative Order Reduction is similar to the "bottom-up" approach in systems analysis; while it is less computing resource intensive, it is not always successful in locating the normal form even when one exists. Normal Order Reduction, on the other hand, is a "top down" approach that uses more computing resources but is guaranteed to find the normal form if it exists. Unfortunately, not all lambda expressions have normal forms, and reduction algorithms may cycle endlessly when this happens (see λ–calculus in Lambda calculus, n.d.; A Brief description and history, n.d.; Larson, 1996; Entscheidungsproblem, n.d.).

## U. Gluing Objects Together

Operators configure components by gluing objects together to create new meanings. The theory of categories and Rings provides the mathematical basis for this (see the note on the theory of categories). Relationships flow from the concept of the generalized (generic) operator. The generic operator has different subtypes. In this note, we will describe the subtypes that are key to configuring knowledge from its components. It is worth noting that symmetry is based on commutative operators, whereas asymmetry is based on noncommutative operators (see the note on commutativity).

One subtype of the generalized operator is similar to arithmetic addition (indeed, arithmetic addition is a polymorphism of this operator when ratio scaled values are involved). For brevity, we will denote this operator with the symbol "&." A configuration, "C," of objects "A" and "B" is created by joining two objects, "A" and "B" with the operator "&" as follows:

C = A&B

We can further postulate an object "null" in our system, such that joining this object to another with "&" will not add information, and therefore will not create a new meaning. Symbolically, we show this as follows:

B = null & B

We may also postulate that "&" is commutative, that is, A&B is the same as B&A. This means regardless of the sequence in which the objects joined by "&," it will result in the same composite object "C." Imagine that "C" is a box. Only the *contents* of the "box" give the box its properties; the order in which items are arranged inside the box does not matter. In terms of knowledge, the order of arrangement does not *exist* because A&B cannot be distinguished from B&A.

Similarly, we could postulate a commutative operator, ⊠, which generalizes arithmetic multiplication and has the property:

null ⊠ B = null

Existence dependency between objects is the based on this operator. For example, an attribute cannot not exist if its value is null.

Some junctions between objects are not commutative (in this book, we have described why noncommutative operators are polymorphism of commutative operators). Let ⊘ be a noncommutative operator. Then, unlike the arithmetic plus operator A⊘B will not equal B⊘A (provided B and A are not equal); that is, the order in which two objects (or object classes) are joined will yield different and distinct objects (or object classes) with different properties. For instance, arithmetic division is an example of a noncommutative operator because swapping the divisor with the dividend results in a different quotient.

Operators join two or more propositions into a compound proposition. Therefore, operators are called *connectives*. Connectives are also objects. Connectives may be monadic. Monadic operators operate on one object at a time. Negation is an example of a monadic operator. Operators may also be dyadic. Dyadic operators operate on two objects at a time. Triadic operators operate on three objects at a time. In general, operators may be "p-adic" connectives that glue "p" objects together at a time. (Based on the principle of subtyping by adding information, the generic p-adic operator may be considered a polymorphism of the generic (p-1)-adic operator; an object that is not an operator, and does not depend on another for its existence may be considered a "zero-adic" operator.)

## V. Functional Programming

Functional programming is related to λ–calculus. Unlike algorithmic languages, which contain assignment statements, iterative loops, and variables, functional programming focuses on the computation of functions that may contain values, rule expressions, and mathematical functions in the form of arguments and return functions. Higher-order functions are capable of taking functions as arguments and return functions as results. Functional programming relies on recursion. Typically, a functional programming call to a function, with itself as its argument, can be computed without multiple calls.

Examples of functional programming languages are Haskell, Scheme, ML, and LISP. Haskell is an area of active research. Please visit http://www.haskell.org/ for further details.

## W. Dimensions of Color

Colorimetrics is the science of measuring color. The physical identity of color is based on the wavelength of light and its intensity as a function of this wavelength. The subjective sensation of color, on the other hand, is extremely difficult to quantify. Maxwell's Color Triangle theory gives us one of the systems for classifying color and describes the subjective sensation of color using three dimensions: Hue, Saturation, and Brightness.

Brightness is described as the "luminosity" of a color—a sensation that correlates with the intensity of light it reflects back to the eye compared to a white object similar to it. The Hue of a color correlates with its position in the electromagnetic spectrum and specifies the kind of color in terms of primary colors—red, blue, and green, up to *two at a time*. Maxwell's Color triangle specifies mixtures of *all three* primary colors and conveys information on hue, as well as the "richness" or saturation:

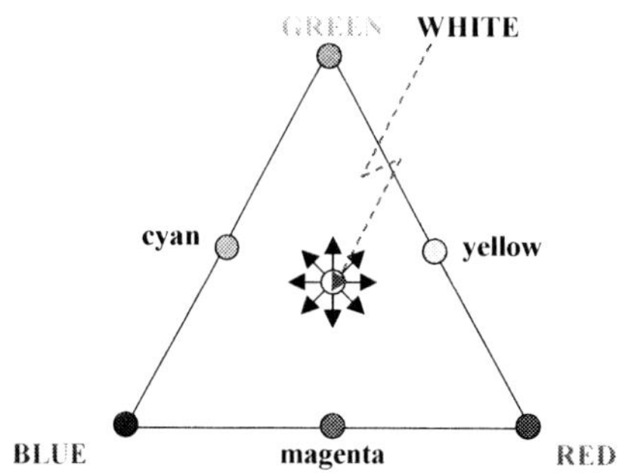


*Figure II.2. Maxwell's Color Triangle*

*Reproduced by permission from Mitra, A., & Gupta, A., Agile Systems with Reusable Patterns of Business Knowledge, Norwood, MA: Artech House, Inc., 2005. ©*

Colors at the periphery of Maxwell's Triangle are fully saturated and do not become "paler" with any shade of white. Colors at the three corners of the triangle are the three "pure" fully saturated, primary colors—red, blue, and green. In the middle, it is an equal mixture of all three primary colors, that is, pure white. Along its edges are fully saturated mixtures of two colors.

Item [324] in Appendix III provides further reading on colorimetry and Maxwell's Triangle. (See Chamberlin & Chamberlin, 1980 in Appendix III.)

## X. Number Systems and Radix

Multiple numbering systems exist—binary, octal, decimal, and even hexadecimal. The decimal system is our normal numbering system, composed of 10 digits, 0 through 9. The system is based on powers of 10; it uses 10 different numeric digits, hence its base, or *radix,* is said to be 10.

Within the binary system, there exist only two digits, 0 and 1. The base or radix is therefore 2. In the binary system, the number 10 is equal to 2 in our decimal system, 11 is 3, 100 is 4, 101 is 5, and so on.

The Octal system uses eight digits and, therefore, starting from 0, its count becomes 0, 1, 2, 3, 4, 5, 6, 7, 10, 11, 12…

The hexadecimal system utilizes 16 digits, six more than the decimal system. The extra digits beyond 9 are A, B, C, D, and F. As such, numbers starting from 0 are: 0, 1, 2, 3, 4, 5, 6, 7, 8, 9, A (same as 10 in the decimal system), B (same as 11 in the decimal system), C (same as 12), D (same as 13), E (same as 14), F (same as 15). Then we wrap around to 10 (same as 16 in the decimal system), 11 (same as 17 in the decimal system), and so on. We come to 1A, the same as 24 in the decimal system, and continue from there.

A number system may be based on any radix. The binary system is useful in computer technology when dealing with hardware and has found its way into software via that route. The Octal and hexadecimal systems condense the binary format since they are even multiples and exponents of the binary system.

## Y. Ordered Sets and Sequences

A *well ordered* set of symbols possesses a lower bound. A ranking scheme that commences with the lowest height of a human is an example of a well ordered set. The chapter numbers of a book is another example of a well ordered set. When there is no lower bound, but members of the set must still follow a sequence, we have a *totally ordered set*. Consider the set of integers. If we allow both negative and positive integers in our set, it will be an unbounded set of integers that are naturally sequenced from lower to higher magnitudes. This is an example of a *totally ordered* set. The only requirement for this type of set is that one must be able to position every member of the set in a sequence. *Mapping ordinal values to a totally ordered set of numbers suffices to convey the relevant information.* Naturally, all well ordered sets are also totally ordered, although the inverse is not necessarily true. Thus, well ordered sets are a subclass of totally ordered sets.

## Z. Pi-Calculus

Robin Milner developed Pi-calculus in the late 1980s as a formal language for the simulation and the analysis of complex interacting processes. It is a formal mathematical language that describes multiple concurrent processes that interact with each other. The feature called "mobility" caters to a network of interdependent events that can dynamically reconfigure the topology in step with interactions between events. Pi-calculus includes syntax to specify the behavior and interactions between processes. It contains a set of "laws of congruence" to determine the equivalence of syntactically different expressions and "reduction rules" to determine the timing and nature of the interaction in terms of a collection of states, an initial state, a set of transitions that describe a starting state, an action and a post-action state, and a set of accepting states.

Pi-calculus can deal with both deterministic and nondeterministic interactions. Apart from issues of timing, state transitions, and guard conditions, pi-calculus can cater to the location and the migration of processes from one place to another. The concept of *Place* in pi-calculus is an extension of the concept of a purely geographical place (as described in this book and its companions). Further reading on pi-calculus is provided in Appendix III, items [75], [76], and [77].

## AA. Petrinets

Petrinets are named after Carl Petri, the creator of this technique for graphically modeling processes. Processes are represented in a linked network of interdependent processes. Predecessor processes pass "tokens" to successor processes, through connections called "arcs," which enable the execution of these successors. The successor processes commence only after their predecessors have provided all required tokens.

Thus, a Petrinet can be visualized as a network like that in Figure II.3. Each node is an event, and each connection between them is a succession relationship (the *arc*). *Places* at the ends of each arc hold incoming and outgoing tokens. (Think of the area within a node in Figure II.3 as a "place.") A process starts by consuming its tokens, only after all requisite tokens are received. (The input and output cardinality of the arc determines how many tokens are added and removed from the places it connects.) Some kinds of arcs may convey tokens to stop state transitions. Transient latency (time-out) of a process is represented by allowing places to hold a token for a limited time.

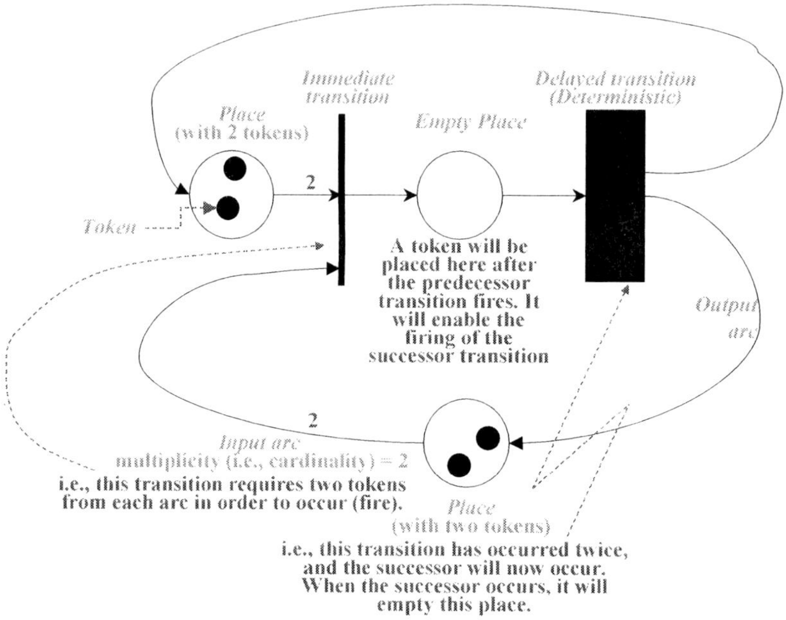


*Figure II.3. An example of a Petrinet*

*Reproduced by permission from Mitra, A., & Gupta, A., Agile Systems with Reusable Patterns of Business Knowledge, Norwood, MA: Artech House, Inc., 2005.* ©

In "color" Petrinets, tokens are associated with data, which may be related to guard conditions, time delays, and complex rules about triggering events. [69], [70], [71], [72], [74], and [78] in Appendix III provide further reading on Petrinets. Section 2.5 of [72] in Appendix III has an especially succinct description of various features and extensions of the technique.

## AB. The Law of Minimal Specification and the Principle of Parsimony

The law of minimal specification is a version of Occam's Razor, conceived by philosopher William of Ockham (1284-1347), stating that only the minimum assumptions needed, and no more, should be made when developing a model or theory (sometimes called the *Principle of Parsimony*).

This implies the omission of concepts, properties, features, and other constructs that are not truly needed to model or explain a phenomenon. This strategy simplifies the model and reduces the risk of inconsistencies, ambiguities, and redundancies within or outside the model. In terms of the ontology of information, Occam's Razor suggests generalization to the maximum extent possible, provided one does not generalize essential patterns away. (Essential patterns were discussed in Chapter IV.) It thus maximizes the mutability of resources and products, making a process or a model more resilient under the pressures of change.

The Principle of Parsimony is very important for universal models, such as those in this series because their domains are complex. Without the Principle of Parsimony, the chances of arriving at a manageable model are slim.

The English translation of Occam's words, "*Pluralitas non est ponenda sine necessitas,*" is "Plurality should not be posited without necessity"—in other words, "Keep it simple." Simplicity has various interpretations in different situations. In this book, we have interpreted it as generalizing patterns, concepts, and models, without compromising the essential pattern of information or behavior. These comprise the *Essential Features* of the model.

Aristotle's version of the Principle of Parsimony is "Entities must not be multiplied beyond what is necessary." Although Occam and Aristotle's principles predate us by three millennia, they are still useful to us today in formulating and utilizing the models in this series. It can also assist in guarding against analysis paralysis, which is arguably the biggest risk many complex projects face. This is why we call it "The Law of Minimal Specification."

## AC. The Nature of Time

The flow of time is universal. In this book, we have also seen how Time is a fundamental component from which the meaning of "Process" is derived. Can we derive the meaning of Time from other more fundamental components? We speculate here that we can. Consider the difference that time makes to the information content of a temporal object as it flows from the past to the future (see Figure 4.5). As the object progresses through time, it progressively acquires larger and larger amounts of history, which is nothing but information on past states of the object. Thus, it gains information and may be considered a subtype, or polymorphism, of its past identities. We have discussed in this book how the subtyping relationship emerges from the concept of location, which emerged from the concept of reference (when one object refers to another. Location is a polymorphism of this concept). If we add enough information to the subtyping relationship between objects to make it a dense, ordinal composition, the composite object will be time like. It will become a dense, sequenced domain, in which a value further on in the sequence will have information about all values prior to it but no information about its successor values. Moreover, because the class is dense, these values will be in a continuum. This implies that it will always be possible to find an intermediate value between every pair possible of values of time regardless of how close they are to each other. (Ordinal and dense domains were described under the ontology of domains in Chapter IV.) If we consider a stochastic, as opposed to a purely deterministic model, it will imply that values may have probabilistic information about successor values—a kind of "leakage" of information about future states. The further the future, the more the uncertainty, and the less the leakage will be (see soft information in Box 4.4).

Thus, we can speculate that the time domain may be configured as an aggregate object that consists of a dense, sequenced aggregation of the subtyping relationship and that the flow of time will be its emergent property. Seen thus, it can be deduced that the time domain must have a natural nil value when there is insufficient information to distinguish between objects as in the "all value" we discussed in Chapter IV. Similarly, we can speculate that the distinction between object instances is merely a result of the class acquiring enough information to enable distinctions between instances (see Chapter IX). It implies that if we track back in time to the point when there is no information, it will not be possible to distinguish between instances, or even classes, of objects, and this will be the natural nil value of the time domain. Since information content cannot take negative values, the Time domain will be a well ordered class, with a lower bound at nil information, or the "All" value. Moreover, the ontology in Chapter IV also implies that the time domain will lose the characteristics of a continuum and become discrete and even nominal as we approach this imputed nil value of time, and the ability to distinguish between distinct objects and instances in time will also increasingly become grainy and stochastic.

# APPENDIX III
# SUGGESTED READING

*(The URLs provided in this book may have changed since it was written; readers may use the Wayback Machine at http://www.archive.org/index.php to locate the following publications. Searches should go as far back as the year 2000.)*

## PAPERS

### Intelligent Agents

1. Mark Nissen, Professor BA248D, Naval Postgraduate School, Monterey, CA (http://web.nps.navy.mil/~menissen/) in Telecommunications and Distributed Processing: Intelligent Agents: A Technology and Business Application Analysis, Nov. 30, 1995
2. Shen, W., and Norrie, D.H. of Division of Manufacturing Engineering, The University of Calgary in Knowledge and Information Systems, an International Journal, 1(2), 129-156, 1999: Agent-Based Systems for Intelligent Manufacturing: A State-of-the-Art Survey at http://imsg.enme.ucalgary.ca/publication/abm.htm
3. Cetus Team: Distributed Objects & Components: Mobile Agents, 2001/03/17, Copyright © 1996-2000 at http://www.cetus-links.org/oo_mobile_agents.html

### Business Process (Re)engineering and E-commerce

4. B. de Vries, J.P. van Leeuwen, H. H. Achten of Eindhoven University of Technology, The Netherlands: Design Studio of the Future (1997) at http://www.ds.arch.tue.nl/Research/publications/bauke/CIBW78_97.htm *(Describes structures of Physical Object, Feature, Activity, and application of virtual reality to engineering design)*
5. Craig Standing, School of Management Information Systems, Edith Cowan University, Joondalup, Western Australia: Managing and Developing Internet Commerce Systems with ICDM © 1999 at http://www.vuw.ac.nz/acis99/Papers/PaperStanding-048.pdf *(Perspective of the full BPR process—Strategic planning through process design and rollout. Focuses on differences between business processes in a traditional vs. collaborative e-commerce environment)*
6. William J. Kettinger, James T. C. Teng, and Subashish Guha in Business Process Change: A Study of Methodologies, Techniques, and Tools, Appendices 4 and 5, in MISQ Archivist, March 1997 (Alphabetical list of major Business Process Reengineering Techniques and tools with brief descriptions) at http://129.252.51.247/bpr/aa-4.htm (you may have to access the paper from the MISQ Archivist site at http://www.misq.org/archivist/home.html)
7. Activity Based Costing and Management from QPR software at http://www.qpronline.com/abc/activity_based_intro.html (you may have to go there via http://www.qpronline.com)
8. The (U.S.) Department of Defense, 12/15/94: Framework for Managing Process Improvement
9. Ellen Gottesdiener, President, EBG Consulting, Inc: OO Methodologies: Process & Product Patterns © EBG Consulting, Inc., SIGS Publications. (All Rights Reserved) published in Component Strategies November, 1998 Vol. 1, No. 5 at http://www.ebgconsulting.com/OOmethodsArticleCS-mag.html

10. Wilfred van der Vegte, Assistant Professor, Delft University of Technology presented at EDIProd Conference, October 14, 2000, Dychow, Poland: Reflections on artifact related process modeling at http://www.ediprod.uz.zgora.pl/files/ediprod2000.html, http://dutoce.io.tudelft.nl/%7Ewilfred/WFvdVegte-EDIProd2000.htm, http://www.sdpsnet.org/journals/vol6-2/vegte1.pdf, http://dutoce.io.tudelft.nl/~wilfred/ *(Summary and assessment of different Process Modeling techniques and a process classification scheme)*

## Ontologies and Component Reuse Projects

11. Jose Vasconcelos, Department of Computer Science, University of York, UK and Multimedia Resource Center, University of Fernando Pessoa, Portugal, Chris Kimble, Department of Computer Science, University of York, UK, Feliz Gouveia, Multimedia Resource Center, University of Fernando Pessoa, Portugal, Daniel Kudenko, Department of Computer Science, University of York, UK: A Group Memory System for Corporate Knowledge Management: An Ontological Approach, September 2000 at http://www-users.cs.york.ac.uk/~kimble/ research/ECKM-2000-paper.pdf
12. Peter Green of Department of Commerce, University of Queensland, Australia and Michael Roseman of School of Information Systems, Queensland Institute of Technology, Australia: Ontological Analysis of Integrated Process Modeling: Some Initial Insights: a paper presented in the Proceedings of the Australian Conference on Information Systems (ACIS 2000), Brisbane, Australia, 6-8 December 2000 (Evaluates ARIS against BWW criteria)
13. Michael Rosemann of Queensland University of Technology, School of Information Systems and Peter Green of University of Queensland, Department of Commerce in the Proceedings of the Information Systems Foundations Workshop on Ontology, Semiotics and Practice 1999: Enhancing the Process of Ontological Analysis—The "Who cares" Dimension at http://www.comp.mq.edu.au/isf99/Rosemann.htm (A discussion of the BWW model applied to facets and Information Systems Analysis and Design) (Knowledge Reuse Algebras and Test Beds for Techniques)
14. C N G (Kit). Dampney and M. S. J. Johnson, Department of Computing, Macquarie University in Proceedings of the Information Systems Foundations Workshop: Ontology, Semiotics and Practice 1999: An Information Theory Formalization and the BWW Ontology at http://www.comp.mq.edu.au/isf99/DampneyJohnson.htm (Bunge Wand Weber (BWW) Framework - Rigorous algebra for testing the completeness of techniques/ontologies regarding Business Rule expression)
15. Andreas L. Opdahl and Brian Henderson-Sellers of School of Computing Sciences, University of Technology, Sydney in Proceedings of the Information Systems Foundations Workshop Ontology, Semiotics and Practice 1999: "Evaluating and Improving OO Modeling Languages Using the BWW-Model" at http://www.comp.mq.edu.au/isf99/Opdahl.htm (Bunge Wand Weber (BWW) Framework - Rigorous algebra for testing the completeness of techniques/ontologies regarding Business Rule expression)
16. Glynn Winskel and Mogels Nielsen, Computer Science Department, Aarhus University, Denmark: Categories in Concurrency (1997). See abstract at http://www.brics.dk/upd/EP/97/WN_CC/EP-97-WN_CC.bib, https://booktrade.cambridge.org/catalogue.asp?isbn=0521580579 (A comprehensive process algebra based on Category Theory and Functors)
17. David Rowe, John Leaney, Computer Systems Engineering, School of Electrical Engineering, University of Technology, Sydney: Evaluating Evolvability of Computer Based Systems Architectures: An Ontological Approach in IEEE International Conference on Engineering of

Computer-Based Systems (ECBS workshop 1997) at http://csdl2.computer.org/persagen/DLAbsToc.jsp?resourcePath=/dl/proceedings/&toc=comp/proceedings/ecbs/1997/7889/00/7889toc.xml&DOI=10.1109/ECBS.1997.581903 (Applies BWW to systems evolution trajectories and Architecture)

18. John Mylopoulos, University of Toronto in Information Systems 23 (3-4), June 1998: Information Modeling in the Time of Revolution (Compares various well known reuse, Modeling and Knowledge Representation algebras)
19. Julieanne van Zyl and Dan Corbett, School of Computer and Information Science, University of South Australia: Framework for Comparing Methods for Using or Reusing Multiple Ontologies in an Application, a paper presenred in the proceedings of the 8th International Conference on Conceptual Structures, Darmstadt, Germany. August, 2000. (Also lists and compares several major Ontology and Reuse projects/frameworks)
20. Urban Nulden, Department of Informatics, Göteborg University, Sweden: The Why, What, and How of Reuse in Software Developmentat the 20th Information Systems Research Seminar in 1997 at Scandinavia, Hankø, Norway at http://staff.cs.utu.fi/IRIS/y/1997.htm (Translates the set-theoretic BWW framework to a more easily understood metamodel and compares various modeling algebras in terms of BWW criteria. Also evaluates the BWW framework itself.)
21. Andreas L. Opdahl, Department of Information Science, University of Bergen: A Comparison of Four Families of Multi-Perspective Problem Analysis Methods (1998) (Analyzes the nature of multiple perspectives in BWW ontology for information systems and identifies principal differences between structured analysis, object-oriented analysis, faceted analysis, and viewpoints-based analysis)
22. Yair Wand, Management Information Systems, Faculty of Commerce and Business Administration, The University of British Columbia, Canada, and Richard Y. Wang, Sloan School of Management, Massachusetts Institute of Technology, Cambridge, MA Business: Anchoring Data Quality Dimensions in Ontological Foundations (1994) at http://web.mit.edu/tdqm/www/papers/94/94-03.html (Analyzes various modeling techniques in terms of their ability to satisfy information quality requirements)
23. Andreas L. Opdahl, Associate Professor, Department of Information Science, University of Bergen: Towards A Faceted Modeling Language (1997) in Proceedings of the Fifth European Conference on Information Systems 353-366, Cork Publishing Ltd, Cork (ISBN 1-86076-953-5)
24. National Committee for Information Technology Standards, Technical Committee H7: Object Model Features Matrix (document number X3H7-93-007v12b, May 25, 1997) at http://www.objs.com/x3h7/omfm12b.doc (Describes the Object Management Group core metamodel and compares it with various other metamodels and standards, such as Eiffel and CORBA. Information about Technical Committee H7 may be found at http://www.objs.com/x3h7/h7home.htm) *(Knowledge Reuse Projects)*
25. John Kingston AIAI, University of Edinburgh: Merging Top Level Ontologies for Scientific Knowledge Management (ref EDI-INF-RR-0171) in Proceedings of the AAAI Workshop on Ontologies and the Semantic Web, AAAI-02 Conference, Edmonton, Canada, 29 July 2002 at http://www.inf.ed.ac.uk/publications/report/0171.html (Lists, describes, and compares various major Knowledge Reuse and Ontology projects)
26. List of some key Domain Specific and Cross Industry Software Component Reuse Projects with links to each at http://marexpo.balport.com/Project-Navigator/project_navigator.htm and http://marexpo.balport.com/Project-Navigator/matrix12.htm

27. Peter Clark of Boeing: Some Ongoing KBS/Ontology Projects and Groups compiled at http://www.cs.utexas.edu/users/mfkb/related.html
28. Institut für Angewandte Informatik und Formale Beschreibungsverfahren links to worldwide Ontology and Knowledge use projects and researchers at http://www.aifb.uni-karlsruhe.de/ or http://www.aifb.uni-karlsruhe.de/Projekte/
29. COMMET & KREST Knowledge Reusability and Configurability Projects at http://arti.vub.ac.be/www/krest/information/commet-krest.html
30. TOVE (TOronto Virtual Enterprise) Knowledge Reuse project (as of 18, Feb 2002) at http://www.eil.utoronto.ca/comsen.html
31. TOVE ontologies at http://www.eil.utoronto.ca/tove/toveont.html
32. KACTUS Reusable Knowledge Modeling (1995) at http://www.swi.psy.uva.nl/projects/ Kactus
33. Wielinga, Schreiber and others. Project 8145 (The project partners were Cap Gemini Innovation (Jan. 94–Sep. 95), Integral Solutions Limited (Sep. 95–Sep. 96), CAP Programator, DELOS S.p.A, FINCANTIERI, IBERDROLA, LABEIN, Lloyd's Register, RPK Universität Karlsruhe, STATOIL, SINTEF Automatic Control, University of Amsterdam: KACTUS ESPRIT): Modeling Knowledge About Complex Technical Systems for Multiple Use: Several papers at http://hcs.science.uva.nl/projects/Kactus/Papers.html
34. PROJECTXML™, (Year: 2000) by Project.Net San Diego, CA. The firm's Web site is http://www.project.net/scripts/SaISAPI.dll/website/products/ProjectXML.jsp
35. The One World Information System (OWIS) General Enterprise Management (GEM), Engineering, and Improvement Framework at http://one-world-is.com/rer/owis/emeif.htm
36. Rational Corporation: Rational Requirements Framework: Net Market Edition (Year: 2000)
37. Simon Cox of Dublin Core Metadata Initiative: DCMI Box Encoding Scheme: specification of the spatial limits of a place and methods for encoding this in a text string (Date Issued: 2000-07-28) at http://dublincore.org/documents/2000/07/28/dcmi-box/
38. Simon Cox of Dublin Core Metadata Initiative: DCMI Period Encoding Scheme: specification of the limits of a time interval and methods for encoding this in a text string (Date Issued: 2000-07-28) at http://dublincore.org/documents/2000/07/28/dcmi-period/
39. Simon Cox of Dublin Core Metadata Initiative: DCMI Point Encoding Scheme: a point location in space, and methods for encoding this in a text string (Date Issued: 2000-07-28) at http://dublincore.org/documents/2000/07/28/dcmi-point/
40. Tim Menzies, Department of Artificial Intelligence, University of New South Wales: KBS Methodologies: KADS and Others in a technical report in 1995 (TR95-28, Department of Software Development, Monash University)
41. KADS: A development methodology for knowledge-based systems at http://www.mdx.ac.uk/www/ai/samples/ke/53-kads.htm
42. Philippe Martin, University of Adelaide (Australia) - Computer Sciences Department: KADS top-level ontology of concept types and relations types at http://meganesia.int.gu.edu.au/~phmartin/WebKB/kb/topLevelOntology.html, http://meganesia.int.gu.edu.au/~phmartin/WebKB/interface/hierarchyBrowser.html?objectKind=concept+type&top=Thing&relation=Subtype&minDepth=0&openNodes=Entity+Situation+Spatial_entity+Information_entity, http://meganesia.int.gu.edu.au/~phmartin/WebKB/interface/hierarchyBrowser.html?objectKind=relation+type&top=BinaryRel&relation=Subtype&minDepth=0&openNodes=BinaryRel_from_a_situation+BinaryRel_from_a_Process

43. A. Th. Schreiber, J. M. Ackkermans, A. A. Anjewierden, R. de Hoog, N. R. Shadbolt, W. Van de Velde, B. J. Wielinga: Knowledge Engineering and Management: The Common KADS Methodology at http://www.commonkads.uva.nl/frameset-commonkads.html and http://www.commonkads.uva.nl/frameset-commonkads.html
44. Kieron O'Hara, Artificial Intelligence Group, University of Nottingham, UK: A Representation of KADS-I Interpretation Models Using A Decompositional Approach (1993) in Proceedings of 3rd KADS Meeting at http://eprints.ecs.soton.ac.uk/4164/
45. John Kingston AIAI, University of Edinburgh Common KADS: Overview of Knowledge Engineering Methods at http://www.aiai.ed.ac.uk/~jkk/kadspubs.html
46. I. Laresgoiti and A. Bernarasl of LABEIN, Spain, A. Anjewierden, A. Th. Schreiber and B. J. Wielinga of University of Amsterdam, Department of Social Science Informatics, The Netherlands, and J. Corera of IBERDROLA, Spain: Ontologies as Vehicles for Reuse: A Mini-Experiment (1996) http://ksi.cpsc.ucalgary.ca/KAW/KAW96/laresgoiti/k.html
47. Knowledge Interchange Format (KIF) draft of proposed American National Standard (dpANS) NCITS.T2/98-004: A Framework for Comparing Methods for Using or Reusing Multiple Ontologies in an Application (Year: 1998) at http://logic.stanford.edu/kif/dpans.html
48. Rational Corporation: Rational Reusable Asset Specification (A 1999 technical report; major contributors Grady Booch, Catapulse, CTO Peter Eeles, Rational, RSO UK, Luan Doan-Minh, Rational, SSO US, Kelli Houston, Rational, A&AF Senior Architecture Specialist, Ivar Jacobson, Rational, VP of Business Engineering, Wojtek Kozaczynski, Rational, Director of A&AF, Philippe Kruchten, Rational Fellow, Grant Larsen, Catapulse, Senior Architecture Specialist, Jon Lawrence, Rational, A&AF Product Manager, Davyd Norris, Rational Software, RSO Australia, Jim Rumbaugh, Rational Fellow, Bran Selic, Rational, Methodologist, Jim Thario, Rational, A&AF Senior Software Engineer)

## Unified Modeling Language (UML)

49. Mike Lee, of Project Technology Inc: Object Oriented Analysis in the Real World (1992).
50. Rational Software Corporation: UML Quick Reference for Rational Rose (2001) at http://www.rational.com/uml/resources/quick/index.jsp

| |
|---|
| UML General Purpose Concepts |
| UML Class Diagram |
| UML Class Diagram Relationships |
| UML Collaboration Diagram |
| UML Component Diagrams |
| UML Class Visibility Notation |
| UML State Transition Diagrams |
| UML Sequence Diagram |

## Extended Modeling Language (XML)


51. XML Information Set W3C Working Draft 16 March 2001 and XML Information Set (Second Edition) W3C Recommendation 4 February 2004 at http://www.w3.org/TR/xml-infoset/#infoitem.element
52. XML Schema Part 1: Structures, W3C Candidate Recommendation 24 October 2000 of the World Wide Web Consortium and XML Schema Part 1: Structures Second Edition, W3C Recommendation 28 October 2004 at http://www.w3.org/TR/xmlschema-1/
53. XML Schema Part 0: Primer W3C Proposed Recommendation, 16 March 2000; editor David C. Fallside (IBM) at http://www.w3.org/TR/2001/PR-xmlschema-0-20010316/primer.html. Copyright World Wide Web Consortium (Massachusetts Institute of Technology, Institut National de Recherche en Informatique et en Automatique, Keio University). All Rights Reserved.
54. XML Core Metamodel at http//:www.omg.org-cgi-bin-docad-01-02-03.txt and ftp://ftp.omg.org/pub/docs/ad/01-02-03.txt
55. Extensible Markup Language (XML) 1.0 (Second Edition) Copyright © 2000 W3C® (MIT, INRIA, Keio), All Rights Reserved and Extensible Markup Language (XML) 1.0 (Third Edition) W3C Recommendation 04 February 2004 at http://www.w3.org/TR/REC-xml


## Process/Task/Schedule Management and Models


56. Veryard Projects: Process Management Workflow, Workload, Work Control (© 1995-2001) at http://www.users.globalnet.co.uk/~rxv/sebpc/workflow.htm
57. M. C. Tanuan, Software Engineering Manager of Waterloo EAServer QA, eBusiness Division, Sybase, Inc.: An Introduction to Workflow and Business Process Modeling (December 2, 1997) at http://se.uwaterloo.ca/~mctanuan/cs645/IntroBPMWF.htm
58. Stephen Russell Jernigan, M.S.E. and K. S. Barber, The University of Texas at Austin, 1996: Distributed Search Method for Scheduling Flow Through a Factory Floor at http://www-lips.ece.utexas.edu/~stevej/papers/thesis/masters.html
59. Various practitioners and academics: Diverse manufacturing process summaries of Refereed Conference Papers of ICME 2000, 8th International Conference on Manufacturing Engineering in Sydney, 27-30 August 2000. See http://www.unisa.edu.au/ame/pubs/2000.asp.
60. S. R. Jernigan, S. Ramaswamy, K. S. Barber, The Laboratory for Intelligent Processes and Systems, The Department of Electrical and Computer Engineering, The University of Texas at Austin: November 30, 1995: A Distributed Search and Simulation Method for Job Flow Scheduling at http://www-lips.ece.utexas.edu/~stevej/papers/simulation/simulation.html
61. Project Management Institute (PMI): A Guide to Project Management Body of Knowledge: PMBOK Guide 2000 edition. PMI Web page is at http://www.pmi.org/info/default.asp
62. Jürgen Sauer and Jain, L., Intelligent Techniques in Industry, CRC Press, 1998: Knowledge-Based Scheduling Techniques in Industry. (Excerpts available at http://www-is.informatik.uni-oldenburg.de/~sauer/paper/scheduling.html)

## Process Algebras and Techniques

63. Assaf Arkin of Intalio Inc. from the Business Process Management Initiative (BPMI) consortium: Business Process Markup Language (BPML) Working Draft 0.4 3/8/2001. (The BPMI site is http://www.bpmi.org) ("Business Process Modeling Language (BPML) is a meta-language for the modeling of business processes, just as XML is a meta-language for the modeling of business data. BPML provides a…model for collaborative & transactional business processes based on a…finite-state machine")
64. Vitria Technology, Inc.: Executive Overview: Value Chain Markup Language™ - VCML™: A Collaborative E-Business Vocabulary Copyright ©2001 (Vitria Technology Inc. home page at http://www.vitria.com)
65. Vitria Technology, Inc.: Downloads: Value Chain Markup Language™ - VCML™: A Collaborative E-Business Vocabulary Copyright ©2001 (Lists transactions in different industries—indicator of functions that are similar and different across industries. Visitors may download sample schemas and documentation)
66. Alexander James Cowie, School of Computer and Information Science, University of South Australia: The Modeling of Temporal Properties in a Process Algebra Framework (1999) at http://www.cis.unisa.edu.au/~cisajc/thesis.pdf (For the mathematically inclined reader, a comprehensive review of process algebras, their meaning, operation, utilization, and properties)
67. Deepa Pandalai, Honeywell Technology Center, Honeywell Inc. Minneapolis, USA and Lawrence Holloway, Center for Robotics and Manufacturing Systems, University of Kentucky, Lexington, KY, USA: Template Languages for Fault Monitoring of Concurrent and Non-Concurrent Discrete Event Processes (March 1997) at (An algebra that deals with the rules of single and multiple interleaved instances of identical concurrent processes)
68. Rajeev Alur and David Dill, Computer Science Department, Stanford University, CA, USA: A Theory of Timed Automata (1994). Abstract available at http://www.cis.upenn.edu/~alur/Icalp90.html and http://citeseer.ist.psu.edu/alur94theory.html
69. Petrinets at http://pdv.cs.tu-berlin.de/~azi/petri.html#pnresearch (Maintained by Armin Zimmermann Dr.-Ing., research assistant, Technische Universität Berlin)
70. Graph Theory: Color Petrinet at http://markun.cs.shinshu-u.ac.jp/learn/graph/cn7/colorPetrinet.html (Maintained by Shinshu University, Japan)
71. Graph Theory: CO Petrinet at http://markun.cs.shinshu-u.ac.jp/learn/graph/cn7/coPetrinet.html
72. Srinivasan Ramaswamy, Ph.D. University of Southwestern Louisiana: Hierarchical Time-Extended Petri Nets (H-EPNs) for Integrated Control and Diagnostics of Multilevel Systems (1994) (For the mathematically inclined reader, this is an excellent dissertation on the properties of processes, as expressed by Petrinets)
73. Vijay K. Garg, University of California, Berkeley, CA, USA and M. T. Raghunath of the University of Texas, Austin, TX, USA: Concurrent Regular Expressions and their Relationship to Petri Nets (1992) at http://citeseer.ist.psu.edu/garg92concurrent.html (For mathematically inclined readers only! Flexible way of specifying concurrent processes and also deals with interleaving, interleaving closure, synchronous composition, and renaming of processes)
74. C. Ramchandani: Timed Petri nets, Technical Report 120, Project MAC, Massachusetts Institute Technology, February 1974: A study of asynchronous concurrent systems. (An old but interesting

paper. Project MAC (MAC was an acronym for "Man and Computer") was one of the first visionary attempts to program common sense in the form of business rules into automation)
75. Calculi for Mobile Processes at http://lamp.epfl.ch/mobility/ (A set of links to research papers on Pi-Calculus. You may need permission from LAMP Programming Methods Laboratory, Institute of Core Computing Science, School of Computer and Communication Sciences, Swiss Institute of Technology, Lausanne at http://lamp.epfl.ch to access the site)
76. Marcus Lumpe at the University of Berne, Germany: A pi-calculus based approach to software composition, an inaugural dissertation (January 21, 1999) in Bern University, Germany at http://www.iam.unibe.ch/~scg/Archive/PhD/lumpe-phd.pdf
77. Lucian Wischik, University of Bologna, 30, August 2002: New Directions in Implementing pi calculus at http://www.newcastle.research.ec.org/cabernet/workshops/radicals/2002/ Papers/Bertinoro/18.pdf (A succinct, if mathematical, description of pi-calculus)
78. J-P. Courtiat, C.A.S. Santos, C. Lohr, B. Outtaj of LAAS-CNRS, France and Ecole Mohamedia d'Ingénieurs, Rabat, Maroc: Experience with RT-LOTOS, a temporal extension of the LOTOS formal description technique in Computer Communications 23 (2000) 1104-1123 at http://www.laas.fr/RT-LOTOS/doc-src/CompCom99/CompCom99/ and http://www.laas.fr/~courtiat/PAPERS/ComCom00.pdf (Real-Time LOTOS Process Algebra)
79. David Harel: On Visual Formalisms, Communications of the ACM, pages 521 to 523 and 527, May 1988, Volume 31, Number 5 (Algebra to simplify state representations in real world finite state automata)
80. Alan M. Davis: A Comparison of Techniques for the Specification of External System Behavior. Communications of the ACM, page 1105, September 1988, Volume 31, Number 9
81. David Harel and A. Pnueli, Department of Applied Mathematics, The Weizmann Institute of Science, Rehovot, Israel: On Development of Reactive Systems, pages 8 to 10; NATO ASI Series F, Vol. 13, Springer-Verlag, 1985
82. David Harel: On Visual Formalisms, Communications of the ACM, page 519, May 1988, Volume 31, Number 5
83. Robert L. Jones III of Langley Research Center, VA, USA: NASA Technical Paper 3491: Design Tool for Multiprocessor Scheduling and Evaluation of Iterative Data Flow Algorithms (August 1998) at http://www.iis.sinica.edu.tw/JISE/2000/200005_07.pdf (Although this paper focuses on distributed computer capacity and process efficiency, several concepts are also germane to real-world, distributed business processes)
84. Sergio Bandinelli, Alfonso Fuggetta, Sandro Grigolli at Proceedings of the Second International Conference on the Software Process: Process Modeling in-the-large with SLANG (1993) (Deals with evolution of large process models and high level Petrinets)
85. Mark E. Pitstick and William L. Garrison, Path Research Report UCB-ITS-PRR-91-7, Institute for Transportation Studies, University of California, Berkeley, USA: Restructuring the Automobile Highway System for Lean Vehicles: The Scaled Precedence Activity Network (SPAN) Approach, April 1991 (SPAN Process diagrams)
86. Klaus Neumann and Welf G. Schneider, Dokumenteserver der Universitätsbibliothek Karlsruhe, in a 1997 Technical Report, Heuristic algorithms for job shop scheduling problems with stochastic precedence constraints, describes GERT concepts at http://www.ubka.uni-karlsruhe.de/cgi-bin/psview?document=/1997/wiwi/6&search=/1997/wiwi/6

87. Bin-Shiang Liang, Feng-Jiang Wang, Institute of Computer Science and Information Engineering, National Chiao Tung University, Taiwan, and Jenn-Nan Chen of Samar Electronics Corporation Ltd, Taiwan: A Project Model for Software Development, a short paper in Journal of Science and Engineering, 16, 423-446, 2000 at http://www.iis.sinica.edu.tw/JISE/2000/200005_07.pdf(SPREM Process Algebra)
88. Workshop on Design of Algorithms, Dresden, Module 17 Design Algorithms Channel: A matrix calculus for the analysis and generation of binary relations generalizations and applications, Part 1(1996) at http://marvin.sn.schule.de/~inftreff/modul17/task17_e.htm
89. Oyvind Forsbak, University of Oslo, Department of Informatics: A Critical Review of Aggregation in Object Models and a Proposal for New Aggregation Concepts in UML, Graduate thesis
90. William Paul Rogers, Senior Engineering Manager and Application Architect, Lutris Technologies, in the April 2001 issue of Java World: Reveal the Magic Behind Subtype Polymorphism at http://www.javaworld.com/javaworld/jw-04-2001/jw-0413-polymorph_p.html
91. Eric Allen, PhD graduate student, Programming Language Technology Group, Rice University, in the February 2000 issue of Java World: Behold the Power of Parametric Polymorphism at http://www.javaworld.com/javaworld/jw-02-2000/jw-02-jsr_p.html
92. R. Armstrong, D. Gannon, A. Geist, K. Keahey, S. Kohn, L. Mc.Innes, S. Parker, B. Smolinski at CCA Forum (1999): Towards a common component architecture for high-performance scientific computing
93. Grady Booch (Rational Software Corp.), Magnus Christerson (Rational Software Corp.), Matthew Fuchs (Commerce One Inc.), Jari Koistinen (Commerce One Inc.) at the UML Resource Center: UML for XML Schema Mapping Specification 12/08/99
94. Dr. James Rumbaugh (a collection of papers on OMT, objects, and patterns): OMT Papers, September 1995
95. P. H. Aiken, 1998, IBM: Reverse engineering of data at http://www.research.ibm.com/journal/sj/372/aiken.txt

## Demand and Supply Chains and Standards

96. Bill Hakanson, Executive Director Supply Chain Council (SCC), December 2, 1997: Supply Chain Management: Where Today's Businesses Compete at http://www.ascet.com/documents.asp?d_ID=228 (Supply Chain meaning and process overview)
97. Gaps in Common Knowledge Between Professions (August, 2000), Copyright 2000 Kenneth Kmack Associates (Analysis of gaps between standard business process models and initiatives such as SCOR, CFPR, ARIS, XML, and others)
98. Gordon Stewart: Supply Chain Operations Reference Model (SCOR): The First Cross Industry Framework for Integrated Supply Chain Management in Logistics Information Management, Vol 10 No 2, pp 62-67 (Year: 1997)
99. QPR Software: SCOR Supply Chain Model from the Supply-Chain Council at http://www.qprportal.com/pg/scor_eng/ (you may have to access this publication via http://www.qpronline.com/)
100. S95 Standard (May 2001, ANSI/ISA S95.00.01-2000 Enterprise—Control System Integration Standard) at http://www.pera.net/Standards/Stds_S95.html

101. Dennis Brandl, Director, Enterprise Initiative Sequencia Corporation, NC USA, Peter Owen, Eli Lilly & Co: A Tutorial on the SP95 Enterprise/Control Integration Standard at http://www.iee.org/oncomms/sector/manufacturing/Articles/Download/EF5A16ED-3D3C-466F-BB4FB-D56A2FB90CB
102. Keith Unger of EnteGreat Inc: Integrate ERP with Control Systems Using the S95 Model, © 2002, Mountain Systems Inc, a presentation at the Mountain Systems Conference (May 13-17, 2002) http://www.entegreat.com/eg_downloads_presentations_mountainsystems2002.htm (An overview of S95 standard and its object model. You may have to access the site via www.entegreat.com)
103. Controls Definition & MES to Controls Data Flow Possibilities; MESA International White Paper Number 3 © MESA International, Pittsburgh, PA, USA at http://www.mesa.org
104. Paul Sawyer, PES Associates presented on 13 August 2001 at CAPE-21 (a conference on Computer Aided Process Engineering Tools and Techniques for the 21st Century): CAPE Tools for the Design & Operation of Batch Processes (information on CAPE-21 is at http://cape-21.ucl.org.uk/ and http://cape-alliance.ucl.org.uk/)
105. Brian A. Johnson, managing partner for strategy, research, and thought leadership in the Cross Financial Services Solutions Group, Accenture Corp: Fault Lines in CRM: New E-Commerce Business Models and Channel Integration Challenges, White Paper (1/15/1999) at http://www.crmproject.com/documents.asp?d_ID=706
106. Jagdish Sheth, Professor of Marketing, Goizueta Business School and Dr. Rajendra Sisodia Trustee Professor of Marketing, Bentley College, Waltham, MA: Marketing's Final Frontier: The Automation of Consumption 2000, accessible from http://www.jagsheth.net/pubs_articlesbytype.html and http://www.crmproject.com/documents.asp?grID=187&d_ID=709
107. Osman Turan (2000), Department of Industrial and Systems Engineering, Virginia Tech: Introduction to Supply Chain Management at http://hokies.ise.vt.edu/oturan/SCM/introduction.html
108. QPR Software (2001): Introduction to Supply Chain Management at http://www.qpronline.com/supplychainmanagement/supplychain_intro.html
109. Cyber M@rketing Services: Demand Chain Management: New Strategies for E-Business © IMA 1998, 1999, 2000. Cyber M@rketing Services, Teaneck, NJ, USA may be found at http://www.elsnet.org/orgs/1697.html, Information Management Associates, Inc. (IMA), Irvine, CA, USA may be found at http://www.elsnet.org/orgs/0770.html
110. Jan Holmström and Tiina Tissari, The ECOMLOG research program at the Department of Industrial Engineering and Management, Helsinki University of Technology: IT Value Capture: Creating an Effective Demand-Supply Chain for IT Solutions, presented at Logistics Research Network (LRN) 5th Annual Conference, Cardiff, UK, September 2000. The paper may be accessed from http://www.tuta.hut.fi/logistics/publications.html (Information Technology Value Chain)
111. REM Associates of Princeton, Inc: Supply chain move over, it's time for demand chain (March 2000) Copyright © 1999, 2000 at http://www.remassoc.com/news/demandchain.asp
112. Jim Noller, project consultant, Renaissance Worldwide: Integrating the Demand Chain and the Supply Chain: Technology and Trends (1999) at http://www.afsmi.org/journal/jun99/jun-003.htm. Register at http://www.afsmi.org/ to access this site ("There is an inherent difference between enterprise resource planning (ERP) systems and customer management systems. ERP systems measure financial transactions. Customer management systems measure customer contact events. However, to maximize the demand-chain value, processes and events need to be defined and systems implemented to reduce the demand cycle time.")

113. Jan Holmstrom, William E. Hoover Jr., Perttu Louhiluoto, and Antti Vasara, Mckinsey & Co., The other end of the supply chain, McKinsey Quarterly, 2000, Number 1, pp. 62-71
114. Roberto Michel, Manufacturing Systems (1997): Why Best Practices Make Perfect: CFAR and SCOR Initiatives Aim to Improve Supply Chain Operations, a paper in a 1997 issue of Manufacturing Business Technology. The paper can be accessed online by registering at http://www.mbtmag.com/Default.asp
115. Elgar Fleisch and Hubert Oesterle of Institute of Information Management, University of St. Gallen, Switzerland: A Process Oriented Approach to Business Networking, in Volume 2, Number 2 (year: 2000) Virtual Organization Net at http://verdi.unisg.ch/org/iwi/iwi_pub.nsf/wwwPublYearEng/9A080ADF5173DC38C1256FC600471E98 or http://www.ve-forum.org/Projects/264/Issues/eJOV%20Vol2/Fleisch%20-%202000%20-%20eJOV2,2-1%20-%20A%20Process-oriented%20Approach%20to%20Business%20Networking.pdf (access through http://verdi.unisg.ch/org/iwi/iwi_pub.nsf/wwwPublRecentEng /9A080ADF5173DC38C1256FC600471E98) (Maps supply and demand chain models to collaborative business networking models)
116. Kevin Crowston of School of Business Administration, The University of Michigan, USA in the MIT Sloan Center for Coordination Science (http://ccs.mit.edu/): A Taxonomy of Organizational Dependencies and Coordination Mechanisms (May 1999) at http://ccs.mit.edu/papers/CCSWP174.html (Task and resource coordination models)
117. R. Alexander Milowski, XML Architect, and Ray Waldin, Senior XML Engineer, © 1999 Lexica LLC: iLingo—The Language of Insurance e-Business at http://xml.coverpages.org/ilingowhitepaper19991218.html (Insurance Supply Chain)
118. Prof. A.W. Scheer, Instutut Fur Wirtschaftinformatik der universitat des saarlander: ARIS business process model at http://www.iwi.uni-sb.de/teaching/ARIS/aris-i/aris-e-i/index.htm and http://www.iwi.uni-sb.de/teaching/ARIS/aris-i/aris-e-i/
119. Lee, Hau, L., Billington, Corey; Managing Supply Chain Inventory: Pitfalls and Opportunities, in Sloan Management Review; Cambridge; Spring 1992; Volume 33, Issue 3
120. Ranier Alt, Elgar Fleissch, Hubert Osterle, Institute of Information Management, University of St. Gallen, Switzerland: Electronic Commerce and Supply Chain Management at ETA Fabriques d' Ebauches SA (2000) at http://www.csulb.edu/web/journals/jecr/ issues/20002 (Maps Complementary Relationship between the intensively collaborative processes that support Electronic Commerce and traditional Supply Chain process models such as SCOR)
121. Voluntary Interindustry Commerce Standards (VICS) Association: The CPFR Process Model at http://www.cpfr.org/ProcessModel.html and http://www.cpfr.org/Images/5.htm
122. Voluntary Interindustry Commerce Standards (VICS) Association: The CPFR Data Model (2002) at http://www.cpfr.org/Images/AppendixH.HTM or http://havinghadlunch.com:8080/ tamikin/GLS/matter/CPFR_Tabs_061802.pdf (also see links to current papers at http://www.vics.org/committees/cpfr/)
123. Collaborative Practices Research Initiative Sponsored by The Neeley Supply and Value Chain Center, Texas Christian University, November 15, 2004 at http://www.vics.org/committees/cpfr/academic_papers/academic_papers
124. VICS: Process and Results Metrics: Measuring the Success of a Process-Driven Value Chain at http://www.cpfr.org/Process-Results%20.html. See also http://havinghadlunch.com: 8080/tamikin/GLS/matter/CPFR_Tabs_061802.pdf

125. VICS CPFR XML Messaging Model standard draft dated Jan. 17, 2001 for public comment at http://www.cpfr.org/XMLMessageModel.doc
126. ICS/CPFR IDEF0 Format Model at http://www.cpfr.org/AppendixI.html. See also http://having-hadlunch.com:8080/tamikin/GLS/matter/CPFR_Tabs_061802.pdf
127. Rosettanet Standards at http://www.rosettanet.org/rosettanet/Rooms/DisplayPages/LayoutInitial?container=com.webridge.entity.Entity%5BOID%5B5F6606C8AD2BD411841F00C04F689339%5D%5D&expanded=com.webridge.entity.Entity%5BOID%5B5F6606C8AD2BD411841F00C04F689339%5D%5D (You may have to access the site via www.rosettanet.org)
128. Rosettanet PIP Directory at http://www.rosettanet.org/rosettanet/Rooms/DisplayPages/LayoutInitial?Container=com.webridge.entity.Entity%5BOID%5B9A6EEA233C5CD411843C00C04F689339%5D%5D (PIP is an acronym for Partner Interface Processes. The site has a list of standard Rosettanet PIPs—transactions exchanged by trading partners in a supply chain. You may have to access the site via www.rosettanet.org)
129. Rosettanet PIPs at http://www.rosettanet.org/rosettanet/Rooms/DisplayPages/LayoutInitial?Container=com.webridge.entity.Entity%5BOID%5B279B86B8022CD411841F00C04F689339%5D%5D (PIP is an acronym for Partner Interface Processes. The site classifies rosettanet PIPs—transactions exchanged by trading partners in a supply chain. You may have to access the site via http://www.rosettanet.org)
130. Rosettanet Fundamental Business Data Entities at http://www.rosettanet.org/rosettanet/Rooms/DisplayPages/LayoutInitial?Container=com.webridge.entity.Entity%5BOID%5B07C504EE1A96D411BD89009027E33DD8%5D%5D (You may have to access the site via www.rosettanet.org)
131. Rosettanet Business Data Entities at http://www.rosettanet.org/rosettanet/Rooms/DisplayPages/LayoutInitial?Container=com.webridge.entity.Entity%5BOID%5BF7C104EE1A96D411BD89009027E33DD8%5D%5D (You may have to access the site via www.rosettanet.org)
132. Rosettanet Business Properties at http://www.rosettanet.org/rosettanet/Rooms/DisplayPages/LayoutInitial?Container=com.webridge.entity.Entity%5BOID%5B62C104EE1A96D411BD89009027E33DD8%5D%5D (You may have to access the site via www.rosettanet.org)
133. David Sprott: Open Market Components: A CBDi Forum Report (January 2000) at http://www.componentsource.com/services/cbdiopen_market.asp (Analyzes the market and emerging supply chain standards in terms of how components must be defined)

## Financial Accounting

134. AccountingSTUDY.com$^{SM}$ Accounting Study Guide Copyright 1999-2002 at http://accountinginfo.com/study/index.html (Succinctly describes the key principles used in financial accounting)
135. AccountingSTUDY.com$^{SM}$ Accrual Basis vs. Cash Basis Accounting Copyright 1999-2002 at http://accountinginfo.com/study/accrual-01.htm (A succinct description of Accrual and Cash basis accounting with examples)
136. AccountingSTUDY.com$^{SM}$ Introduction to Adjusting Journal Entries Copyright 1999-2002 at http://accountinginfo.com/study/aje-01.htm (Describes reasons for accounting adjustment transactions, with examples)
137. Wikipedia: U.S. generally accepted accounting principles at http://en.wikipedia.org/wiki/U.S._generally_accepted_accounting_principles (Brief description of Generally Accepted Accounting Principles and related standards)

138. AccountingSTUDY.com.SM: FASB Statements, © by Financial Accounting Standards Board. ARB, APB Opinions, © (All Rights Reserved) by the American Institute of Certified Public Accountants, Inc: Generally Accepted Accounting Principles in the United States Index © 1999-2002 at http://cpaclass.com/gaap/gaap-us-01a.htm (A comprehensive source of U.S. GAAP information)
139. BookkeepersList.com, Copyright 1999-2003 at http://bookkeeperlist.com/gaap.shtml (A succinct description of the principles that guide Financial Accounting Practices)
140. CPAclass.com: Ratios for Financial Statement Analysis Web Site, Financial Ratios: Summary, © 1999-2002 at http://cpaclass.com/fsa/ratio-01a.htm (Succinct definitions of key ratios used for financial analysis and evaluation)
141. CPAclass.com: Ratios for Financial Statement Analysis Web Site, Financial Ratios: Index, © 1999-2002 at http://cpaclass.com/fsa/ratio-01.htm (List of common ratios used for financial analysis)
142. CPAclass.com: Annual Report Project Resources © 1999-2001 at http://www.cpaclass.com/arp/(A comprehensive source of information related to developing a corporate annual report)

## Software Process

143. David Chappell of Chappell & Associates: The Next Wave: Component Software Enters the Mainstream, April 1997, at http://www.mc.edu/campus/users/gwiggins/syllabi/csc320/papers/dynamic-3.html
144. Philippe Kruchten of Rational Software Corp. Canada in IEEE Software, November 1995, 12 (6), pp. 42-50: The 4+1 View Model of Architecture
145. D.E. Perry and A.L. Wolf, "Foundations for the Study of Software Architecture," *ACM Software Engineering Notes,* Oct. 1992, pp. 40-52
146. Capability Maturity Model for Software (version 1.1) Publication TR 25 from Software Engineering Institute (SEI)
147. Carnegie Mellon University: CMMI Models Copyright 2002, at http://www.sei.cmu.edu/cmmi/models/models.html (You may have to access the site through http://www.sei.cmu.edu/cmmi/)
148. Michael Paulk of Carnegie Mellon University: A History of the Capability Maturity Model for Software at http://www.dfw-asee.org/archive/cmm-history.pdf (An overview of how the CMM was sponsored, how it evolved, the other models it absorbed in the process, and its continuing evolution. You may have to access the site through http://www.sei.cmu.edu/cmmi/)
149. Carnegie Mellon University: Concept of Operations for the CMMI Copyright 2002, at http://www.sei.cmu.edu/cmmi/background/conops.html (Background and introduction to the Capability Maturity Model Integration project. You may have to access the site through http://www.sei.cmu.edu/cmmi/)
150. Bob Rassa of Raytheon Corporation and Clyde Chittister of the Software Engineering Institute © 2002 Carnegie Mellon University: State of the CMMI: Improving Processes for Better Products at http://www.raytheon.com/feature/stellent/groups/public/documents/legacy_site/cms01_042355.pdf
151. Sarah A. Sheard of the Software Productivity Consortium: The Frameworks Quagmire, a Brief Look, at http://www.software.org/quagmire/frampapr/frampapr.html (A brief descriptions of several quality and process maturity frameworks and standards, and their relationships with each other)

152. S. Bandinelli, A. Fugetta, and S. Ghezzi: Software processes as real time systems: A case study using high level Petri nets. In Proceedings of the International Phoenix Conference on Computers and Communications (Phoenix, AZ, April 1992, pp. 231-242)
153. Giancarlo Succi of University of Calgary, Canada, and Luigi Benedicenti, Paolo Predonzani, and Tullio Vernazza of University Di Genova, Italy: Standardizing the Reuse of Software Processes at http://portal.acm.org/citation.cfm?id=260564 (Develops a model for reuse of processes and contains some excellent references to other research in the area)

## User Interface Standards

154. Microsoft Inductive User Interface Guidelines at http://msdn.microsoft.com/library/default.asp?url=/library/en-us/dnwui/html/iuiguidelines.asp
155. CSS2 Specification: Cascading Style Sheets, level 2 W3C Recommendation 12-May-1998 at http://www.w3.org/TR/REC-CSS2/

## Agile Processes and Adaptive Software

156. Peter Norvig and David Cohn of Harlequin Incorporated: Adaptive Software at http://www.norvig.com/adapaper-pcai.html
157. Laura M. Meade of Automation & Robotics Research Institute's Enterprise Engineering Program, The University of Texas: Agile Process Design at http://arri.uta.edu/eif/lmmdis.html
158. Scott W. Ambler: Agile Software Development at http://www.agilemodeling.com/essays/agileSoftwareDevelopment.htm
159. Extreme Programming: A gentle introduction Copyright (c) 1999, 2000, 2001 Don Wells at http://www.extremeprogramming.org/
160. Jim Dowling and Vinny Cahill of the Department of Computer Science, Trinity College, Dublin: K-Component Architecture Meta-model for Self-Adaptive Software at http://www.cs.tcd.ie/publications/tech-reports/reports.01/TCD-CS-2001-50.pdf
161. Howard Smith, chief technology officer (Europe) of Computer Sciences Corporation and co-chair of the Business Process Management Initiative, and Peter Fingar, executive partner with the Greystone Group: The Next Fifty Years, an article in Darwin, December 2002 issue, at http://www.darwinmag.com/read/120102/bizproc.html (A discussion of how computers have been seen as record keeping machines for fifty years as opposed to adaptable management machines. The need is now to use computers to gain actionable insight. For this, the authors say, corporations must shift their focus from "systems of record" to "systems of process." Moreover, "data processing" must give way to "process processing." The basic unit of automated support will then become the process, not data or the application system. The concept of databases will thus give way to "process bases," which will record and track past, present, and future of business process structures because, in the words of the authors, "business processes are the business." The authors describe how business processes will be made the central focus and basic building block of all automation and business systems in support of agility and responsiveness, and assert that the manual development of supporting information systems will be eliminated.)

162. Peyman Oreizy, Ph.D candidate, University of California, Irvine; Michael Gorlick, Research Scientist, Aerospace Corporation; Richard Taylor, Professor, Department of Information and Computer Science, UCI and Director of the Irvine Research Unit in Software; Dennis Heinsbigner, Research Associate Professor, University of Colorado, Boulder; Gregory Johnson, Member of Technical Staff, Concept Shopping Inc.; Nenad Medvidevic, Assistant Professor, Computer Science Department, University of Southern California; Alex Quilici, Associate Professor of Electrical Engineering, University of Hawaii, Manoa; David Rosenblum, Associate Professor, Department of Computer Science, UCI; and Alexander Wolf, Associate Professor, Department of Computer Science, University of Colorado, Boulder: An Architecture Based Approach to Self-Adaptive Software at http://ftp.ics.uci.edu/pub/c2/papers/ieee-is99.pdf
163. Paul Robertson of Dynamic Language Labs, Andover, MA: Self Adaptive Software, a white paper for the Workshop on New Visions for Software Design and Productivity at http://www.hpcc.gov/iwg/sdp/vanderbilt/position_papers/paul_robertson_self_adaptive_software.pdf
164. Karyl Scott, InformationWeek, April 1, 2002: Computer, Heal Thyself at http://www.informationweek.com/story/IWK20020329S0005 or http://www.informationweek.com/story/IWK20020329S0005

## Mathematical Foundations: Set Theory, Number Theory, Category Theory, Theory of Functions, Lambda Calculus, Spaces and Their Properties, Borel Sets, and Tensors

165. Mathematical and Logical Vocabulary, © 1996, 1997, 1998 Cycorp. All rights reserved. Cycorp is based in Austin, Texas. The Cycorp home page is at http://www.cyc.com/cyc/company (Mathematical Sets, Categories, Topoi, Groups, and Rings)
166. Kyle Siegrist, Department of Mathematical Sciences, University of Alabama in Huntsville: Sets and Events (© 1997-2001) in Virtual Laboratories in Probability and Statistics. The tutorial is available at http://www.ds.unifi.it/VL/VL_EN/prob/prob2.html. Virtual Laboratories in Probability and Statistics is at http://www.ds.unifi.it/VL/VL_EN/index.html (Describes Set Theory and Sigma Algebra)
167. Set theory at http://www.wikipedia.com/wiki/Set_theory (describes the basic axioms of set theory)
168. Basic set theory from Wikipedia at http://www.wikipedia.com/wiki/Basic+Set+Theory
169. Axiom of choice at http://www.wikipedia.com/wiki/Axiom_of_choice (About creating sets by choosing elements from a collection of sets, even if they are sets with infinite members)
170. Power set at http://www.wikipedia.com/wiki/Power_set (The power set of any given set is the set of all possible subsets of the set)
171. Axiom of regularity from Wikipedia at http://www.wikipedia.com/wiki/Axiom+of+regularity ("no set belongs to itself, …otherwise [it] would violate the axiom of regularity.")
172. Mathematical class from Wikipedia at http://www.wikipedia.com/wiki/mathematical+class (Describes the differences between classes and sets, and how the mathematical concept of *class* subsumes the mathematical concept of *set*: "A class is a collection of sets that can be unambiguously defined by a property that all its members share.")
173. Category theory from Wikipedia at http://www.wikipedia.com/wiki/category+theory ("A category attempts to capture the essence of a class of structures, instead of focusing on individual objects... the structure preserving maps between these objects are emphasized.")

174. John Baez, Professor of Mathematics, University of California, Riverside (August 7, 1992): Categories, Quantization, and Much More at http://math.ucr.edu/home/baez/categories.html (Although it is written primarily for mathematical physicists, the paper is a good source of information on category theory, groups, and morphisms, including higher order morphisms and categories, as well as their application in diverse areas)
175. Chris Hillman, Ph.D., Mathematics, University of Washington: A Categorical Primer (July 2, 2001), a tutorial paper, available at http://www.di.uminho.pt/~lsb/mmc_ap/Hilmann.pdf (A reasonably simple mathematical introduction to category theory and topoi)
176. Goldblatt. Topoi: The Categorical Analysis of Logic at http://www.andrew.cmu.edu/~cebrown/notes/goldblatt.html (An introduction to categories and topoi, the need for them, and how categories and topoi generalize the concept of set)
177. John Baez, Professor of Mathematics, University of California, Riverside: This Week's Finds in Mathematical Physics (Week 68) October 29, 1995 at http://math.ucr.edu/home/baez/week68.html (A relatively benign discussion of topoi for beginners, and a nonmathematical description of how sub-objects emerge from commonalities based on the logic of topoi)
178. Steven Vickers, Department of Computing, Imperial College, London, UK, in Mathematical Structures in Computer Science (1995), Volume 11 © 1995, Cambridge University Press: Topical Categories of Domains at http://mcs.open.ac.uk/sjv22/TopCat.ps.gz ("a geometric form of constructive mathematics…enables toposes as 'generalized topological spaces' to be treated…in a...spatial way....it is quite in order to treat a topos as a 'space' whose points are models of the theory and to treat a geometric morphism...as a transformation of points of one such space to points in another…. a topos can be considered both as a 'generalized topological space" and as a 'generalized universe of sets.'")
179. Heyting Algebra at http://publish.uwo.ca/~jbell/HEYTING.pdf (A brief introduction to Heyting Algebra as a generalization of Boolean Algebra)
180. Masao Mori, Department of Information Systems, Interdisciplinary Graduate School of Engineering Science, and Yasuo Kawahara of Research Institute of Fundamental Information Science, both of Kyushu University, Japan: Heyting Algebra at http://www.i.kyushu-u.ac.jp/~masa/fuzzy-graph/node2.html (A mathematical, but brief, introduction to Heyting Algebra, without proofs)
181. Robert Goldblatt in Studies in Logic and the Foundations of Mathematics, Volume 98, North Holland, New York, 1984: Topoi, Categorical Analysis of Logic. Access the book via links at http://www.mcs.vuw.ac.nz/~rob/ or http://www.library.cornell.edu/math/digital-books.php#index
182. Andrew M. Pitts of Computer Laboratory, University of Cambridge, England: Non-trivial Power Types Can't be Subtypes of Polymorphic Types, a paper presented in Proceedings of the Fourth Annual IEEE Symposium on Logic in Computer Science, Asilomar, CA, July 1989, pp. 6-13 (IEEE Computer Society Press, 1989), downloadable from http://www.cl.cam.ac.uk/~amp12/papers
183. Mathematical topos from Wikipedia at http://www.wikipedia.com/wiki/mathematical+topos ("A topos (plural: Topoi) in mathematics is a type of category which allows to formulate all of mathematics inside it.")
184. John Baez, Professor of Mathematics, University of California, Riverside, January 3, 2001: Topos Theory in a Nutshell© John Baez at http://math.ucr.edu/home/baez/topos.html
185. Law of excluded middle from Wikipedia at http://www.wikipedia.com/wiki/law+of+the+excluded+middle ("The law of excluded middle states that for any proposition, either it or its contradictory obtains; for any proposition P, either P or not-P." This law may not be true for all Topoi)

186. Functor from Wikipedia at http://www.wikipedia.com/wiki/functor ("In category theory a functor is a mapping from one category to another which maps objects to objects and morphisms to morphisms in such a manner that the composition of morphisms and the identities are preserved")
187. Monoid from Wikipedia at http://www.wikipedia.com/wiki/Monoid ("the set of all morphisms from this object to itself, with composition as the operation [is an example of a Monoid]... categories [are] generalizations of monoids.")
188. Mathematical Group from Wikipedia at http://www.wikipedia.com/wiki/mathematical+group("G roups underlie other algebraic structures such as fields and vectors...also important..for studying symmetry")
189. Semigroup from Wikipedia at http://www.wikipedia.com/wiki/semigroup
190. Subgroup from Wikipedia at http://www.wikipedia.com/wiki/subgroup (the abstract mathematical theories that support the concept of subtyping by partitioning sets and show that subsets are subtypes of supersets)
191. Group Action from Wikipedia at http://www.wikipedia.com/wiki/group+action
192. Mathematical Ring from Wikipedia at http://www.wikipedia.com/wiki/Mathematical+ring (A kind of mathematical group that generalizes commutative and associative operations)
193. Fundamental Group from Wikipedia at http://www.wikipedia.com/wiki/fundamental+group (Mathematical structures that convey information on loops and the one-dimensional structure of space)
194. Group representation Lie Algebra from Wikipedia at http://www.wikipedia.com/wiki/group+representation
195. Abelian group from Wikipedia at http://www.wikipedia.com/wiki/abelian+group (the mathematics of commutative operators)
196. Lie Group from Wikipedia at http://www.wikipedia.com/wiki/Lie+group
197. Lie Algebra from Wikipedia at http://www.wikipedia.com/wiki/Lie+algebra
198. Ring Ideal from Wikipedia at http://www.wikipedia.com/wiki/ring+ideal (The mathematical theories behind "ideal," an abstraction and generalization of numbers)
199. Integral domain from Wikipedia at http://www.wikipedia.com/wiki/Integral+domain
200. Field from Wikipedia at http://www.wikipedia.com/wiki/field
201. Finite Field from Wikipedia at http://www.wikipedia.com/wiki/Finite+field
202. Countable at http://www.wikipedia.com/wiki/Countable(A set is countable if it is either finite or the same size as the set of positive integers, a set with infinite numbers of members)
203. Countably infinite at http://www.wikipedia.com/wiki/Countably_infinite (On countability in infinitely large sets)
204. Continuum hypothesis at http://www.wikipedia.com/wiki/Continuum_hypothesis (the set theoretic basis of a continuum based on the continuum of real numbers)
205. Cantors Diagonal argument at http://www.wikipedia.com/wiki/Cantors_Diagonal_argument (A logical argument that demonstrates that real numbers are not countably infinite)
206. Cardinal number at http://www.wikipedia.com/wiki/Cardinal_number (gauges the relative sizes of sets, even sets with infinite members)
207. Number from Wikipedia at http://www.wikipedia.com/wiki/number (describes numbers as abstract patterns and links to definitions of numbers of different kinds)
208. Dense from Wikipedia at http://www.wikipedia.com/wiki/Dense

209. Jens Blanch, University of Gavle, Gavle, Sweden (1998): Domain representation of topological spaces at http://www.sm.luth.se/~jens/pdf/top.pdf (describes Scott-Ershov domains and their properties; Scott-Ershov domains can facilitate approximation of the infinite continuum of numbers in finite state machines)
210. Pascal Hitzler, Universität Tübingen February 1998: Scott Domains, Generalized Ultrametric Spaces and Generalized Acyclic Logic Programs (now at University of Karlsruhe) ("...every object of interest can be arbitrarily closely approximated by [compact elements])
211. Guy Davies, in a seminar series at ITE; Decision Theory, Hösten 2000: Order and Value Assignment (A relatively benign discussion of ordinal value theory for those willing to brave it)
212. Ordinal at http://www.wikipedia.com/wiki/Ordinal (A set theoretic discussion of ordinalilty)
213. Total Order at http://www.wikipedia.com/wiki/Total_order (Mathematical basis of ordered sets and ordinal domains)
214. Well-founded set at http://www.wikipedia.com/wiki/Well-founded_set (The set theoretic basis of the origin in a coordinate system, especially in an ordinal domain)
215. Well-order at http://www.wikipedia.com/wiki/Well-order (A set theoretic discussion of lower bounds on ordinal domains)
216. Ordered field at http://www.wikipedia.com/wiki/ordered+field (describes the set theoretic basis of the "natural zero" of a domain)
217. Partial order at http://www.wikipedia.com/wiki/Partial_order (mathematical descriptions of subtyping and relationship to set theory, especially "posets")
218. Lattice from Wikipedia at http://www.wikipedia.com/wiki/Lattice (Numbers, Functions, and Number Theory)
219. Natural number from Wikipedia at http://www.wikipedia.com/wiki/Natural_number
220. Rational number from Wikipedia at http://www.wikipedia.com/wiki/rational+number
221. Irrational number from Wikipedia at http://www.wikipedia.com/wiki/irrational+number
222. Real number from Wikipedia at http://www.wikipedia.com/wiki/Real+number
223. Complex number from Wikipedia at http://www.wikipedia.com/wiki/complex+number
224. Transcendental number at http://www.wikipedia.com/wiki/transcendental+number
225. Hyperreal numbers from Wikipedia at http://www.wikipedia.com/wiki/hyperreal+numbers
226. Hypercomplex numbers from Wikipedia at http://www.wikipedia.com/wiki/Hypercomplex+numbers
227. Octonions from Wikipedia at http://www.wikipedia.com/wiki/octonions
228. Quaternions from Wikipedia at http://www.wikipedia.com/wiki/quaternions
229. Sedenions from Wikipedia at http://www.wikipedia.com/wiki/sedenions
230. P-adic numbers from Wikipedia at http://www.wikipedia.com/wiki/p-adic+numbers
231. Surreal numbers from Wikipedia at http://www.wikipedia.com/wiki/Surreal_numbers
232. Functions and Random Variables at http://www.math.uah.edu/stat/ (Elementary introduction to the mathematical theory of functions)
233. Function at http://www.wikipedia.com/wiki/Function (Another easily readable introduction to the mathematical theory of functions)
234. Injective, surjective, and bijective functions from Wikipedia at http://www.wikipedia.com/wiki/Injective,+surjective+and+functions
235. Cartesian product at http://www.wikipedia.com/wiki/Cartesian_product

236. Direct Product from Wikipedia at http://www.wikipedia.com/wiki/direct+product ("In mathematics, one can often define a direct product of objects already known, giving a new [object]"—focuses on mathematical groups)
237. Recursion definition at http://www.wikipedia.com/wiki/Recursion_definition
238. Transfinite induction at http://www.wikipedia.com/wiki/Transfinite_induction (Transfinite Induction is a technique of proving that a property applies to all Ordinals) (Lambda Calculus, Functional Programming, and Semantics)
239. Luca Cardelli of AT&T Bell Laboratories, Murray Hill, NJ, USA and Peter Wegner, Department of Computer Science, Brown University, Providence, USA in Computing Surveys, Volume 17, no. 4, pp. 471-522, December 1985: On Understanding Types, Data Abstraction, and Polymorphism at http://research.microsoft.com/Users/luca/Papers/OnUnderstanding.pdf (A mathematical treatment of polymorphism and inheritance based on λ-calculus)
240. Lambda calculus at http://www.wikipedia.com/wiki/Lambda_calculus (A brief informal discussion of λ-calculus, including emergence of functions, arithmetic operations, and recursion, as well as a discussion of equivalence of rule expressions)
241. The Lambda Calculus: A Brief description and history at http://www.kids.net.au/encyclopedia-wiki/la/Lambda_calculus#History
242. Jim Larson at the JPL Section 312: An Introduction to Lambda Calculus and Scheme, a talk in a Programming Lunchtime Seminar on 7/26/1996 at http://www.jetcafe.org/~jim/lambda.html (Describes how polymorphism emerges from λ-calculus and how λ-calculus is a universal model of computation. Also describes a programming language, Scheme, which facilitates application of λ-calculus.)
243. Andrew Myers of Cornell University: Advanced Programming Languages at http://www.cs.cornell.edu/courses/cs611/2000fa/slides/lec09.pdf (A brief presentation on normalizing rule expressions with Lambda Calculus. "Two functions are equal by *Extension* if they have the same meaning: they give the same result when applied to the same argument")
244. H. Zhang of Iowa University: Lambda Calculus at http://www.cs.uiowa.edu/~hzhang/c123/Lecture5.pdf (A simple but mathematical definition of lambda calculus and normal form with reduction algorithms and examples)
245. Church-Rosser theorem Copyright © 1999 M-J. Dominus at http://perl.plover.com/yak/lambda/samples/slide014.html (A brief presentation of the Church Rosser theorem that reduces rule expressions to a normal form)
246. Chris Clack, Senior Lecturer and MScCS Course Director, Department of Computer Science, UCLA: The Lambda Calculus, A Deeper Look at http://www.cs.ucl.ac.uk/teaching/3C11/HTML_Lectures/lecture3_3C11/sld011.htm (Another good presentation on the essence of the Church-Rosser Theorem)
247. Stephen Fenner (1996): Normal Forms and the Church-Rosser Theorem at http://www.cs.usm.maine.edu/class/cos370/handouts/lambda/node7.html (Describes when Rule Expressions can and cannot be reduced to normal forms)
248. Selinger, P., "Functionality, polymorphism, and concurrency: a mathematical investigation of programming paradigms," PhD thesis, University of Pennsylvania, 1997 (Both formal and intuitive descriptions of the normal forms and the Church Rosser Theorem)

249. Peter V. Homeier, U.S. Department of Defense, Ph.D. in Computer Science, UCLA, 1995: A proof of the Church Rosser Theorem for Lambda Calculus in Higher Order Logic at http://www.cis.upenn.edu/~hol/lamcr/lamcr.pdf
250. Entscheidungsproblem at http://www.wikipedia.com/wiki/Entscheidungsproblem ("Entscheidungsproblem" is german for "the Decision Problem." In mathematics Entscheidungsproblem addresses the issue of the same rule being expressed in different ways. It specifically proves that there is no general algorithm that will show that algebraic expressions that consist of different terms are equivalent)
251. First-order predicate calculus at http://www.wikipedia.com/wiki/First-order_predicate_calculus (Deals with symbolic logic that is the basis of set theory, values, relationships, arithmetic, and logical operators)
252. Manfred Kanka: A paper on Semantics © Manfred Krifka, Institut für deutsche Sprache und Linguistik, HU Berlin, WS 2000/2001at http://amor.rz.hu-berlin.de/~h2816i3x/SemanticsI-07.pdf
253. Anthony J. Roy, Department of Computer Science, University of Keele, UK in Technical Report TR99-11, June, 1999: A Comparison of Rough Sets, Fuzzy Sets and Non-monotonic Logic at http://pages.britishlibrary.net/aroy/ant/revigis/Comparisonpdf.pdf
254. Functional programming at http://www.wikipedia.com/wiki/Functional_programming (Functional programming expresses logic by combining functions instead of focusing on execution of computer commands. Arguments as well as results of functions can be functions.) (Spaces and Their Properties)
255. Eric W. Weisstein: Space from Eric Weissensteinn's Treasure Trove of Science at © Eric W. Weisstein at http://hades.ph.tn.tudelft.nl/Internal/PHServices/Documentation/MathWorld/math/math/s/s513.htm (Succinct but very abstract mathematical definitions of various spaces including metric spaces and state spaces)
256. Tensor from Wikipedia at http://www.wikipedia.com/wiki/Tensor
257. Tensor/Old from Wikipedia at http://www.wikipedia.com/wiki/Tensor/Old ("Tensors are quantities that describe a transformation between coordinate systems…in such a way that the physical laws [are described in a way that is]…independent of the coordinate system chosen….tensors were introduced as specific representations of the group of all changes of coordinate systems.")
258. Tensor at http://hades.ph.tn.tudelft.nl/Internal/PHServices/Documentation/MathWorld/math/math/t/t078.htm
259. Metric Tensor at http://hades.ph.tn.tudelft.nl/Internal/PHServices/Documentation/MathWorld/math/math/m/m217.htm
260. Vector space from Wikipedia at http://www.wikipedia.com/wiki/vector+space
261. Normed vector space from Wikipedia at http://www.wikipedia.com/wiki/normed+vector+space (description of mathematical "norm" and isometry)
262. Topology from Wikipedia at http://www.wikipedia.com/wiki/Topology
263. Pointless Topology at http://www.wikipedia.com/wiki/Pointless+topology
264. Topology Glossary from Wikipedia at http://www.wikipedia.com/wiki/Topology+Glossary
265. Dr. Paul Cairns (Principal Investigator) and Jeremy Gow (Researcher) of Interaction Design Centre at the School of Computing Science, Middlesex University, UK: The definition of a metric space based on lecture notes by Peter Collins in Elements of Euclidean and Metric Topology of the Interactive, available at the Mathematical Proofs research (IMP) project (January 2001 to June 2002),

funded by The Engineering and Physical Sciences Research Council (EPSRC), UK at http://www.uclic.ucl.ac.uk/imp/ (A simple definition of metric spaces)

266. Spaces with richer structures especially metric spaces in The Mathematical Atlas at http://www.math.niu.edu/~rusin/known-math/index/54EXX.html (A minimally mathematical definition of metric spaces and discussion of a metric as a generalized concept of topological distance)
267. Bruce MacLennan, Computer Science Department University of Tennessee, Knoxville: Discrete metric space (1996)
268. Manifold from Wikipedia at http://www.wikipedia.com/wiki/Manifold ("A manifold, in mathematics, can be thought of as a 'curved' surface or space which locally looks like Euclidean space and therefore admits the introduction of local charts or coordinate systems....Every manifold has a dimension, the number of coordinates needed in local coordinate systems.")
269. Hausdorff space from Wikipedia at http://www.wikipedia.com/wiki/Hausdorff+space ("A Hausdorff space is a topological space in which any two distinct points have disjoint neighbourhoods.")
270. Tychonoff space from Wikipedia at http://www.wikipedia.com/wiki/Tychonoff+space ("A Hausdorff space X is called a Tychonoff space if, for every nonempty closed subset C and every x in the complement of C, there is a continuous function f : X -> [0,1] such that f(x) = 0 and f(C) = {1}"; that is, a tychonoff space is a space of distinct points that may be partitioned into two mutually exclusive sets of points. This is the mathematical theory that supports partitioning objects and state spaces.)
271. Dimensional Analysis from Wikipedia at http://www.wikipedia.com/wiki/Dimensional+analysis (A description of how other physical domains emerge from fundamental physical domains and the use of this information in engineering sciences)
272. Fundamental Dimensions from Wikipedia at http://www.wikipedia.com/wiki/Fundamental+dimension (A description of fundamental physical domains of this book, called "dimensions" in this publication)
273. Hausdorff dimension from Wikipedia at http://www.wikipedia.com/wiki/Hausdorff+dimension (A mathematical description of the dimensionality of complex metric spaces that subsumes the "normal" Euclidean concept of dimension)
274. Infimum from Wikipedia at http://www.wikipedia.com/wiki/Infinimum (a type of lower bound. The Hausdorff dimension is related to this concept)
275. Hamel dimension from Wikipedia at http://www.wikipedia.com/wiki/Dimension+of+a+vector+spa ce (A mathematical description of the dimensionality of vector spaces that subsumes the "normal" Euclidean concept of dimension and accounts for the cardinality—see cardinal number—of the space)
276. Connectedness from Wikipedia at http://www.wikipedia.com/wiki/connectedness (Mathematically describes the concept of points in space being connected to points in their neighborhood, as well as the weirder concept of points being isolated from others)
277. Simply Connected from Wikipedia at http://www.wikipedia.com/wiki/simply+connected (A mathematical description of a path and connections in abstract spaces)
278. Eric W. Weisstein: Distance © Eric W. Weisstein at http://hades.ph.tn.tudelft.nl/Internal/PHServices/Documentation/MathWorld/math/math/d/d325.htm (A succinct description of a generalized concept of distance in a manifold)
279. Eric W. Weisstein: Metric © Eric W. Weisstein at http://hades.ph.tn.tudelft.nl/Internal/PHServices/Documentation/MathWorld/math/math/m/m213.htm (A succinct description of a metric as a generalized concept of distance)

280. Measure at http://www.wikipedia.com/wiki/Measure (gauges the relative sizes of sets)
281. Thierry Coquand: How to define Measure of Borel Sets at http://www.cs.chalmers.se/~coquand/riesz.pdf (A complex mathematical discussion of Borel sets and Cantor Spaces)
282. Borel Measure at http://www.wikipedia.com/wiki/Borel_measure ("The Borel Measure is the measure on the smallest set algebra containing the intervals which gives to the interval [a,b] the measure b-a.")
283. Koji Tsuda, Electrotechnical Laboratory, Japan, Machine Understanding Division: Subspace Classifier in Hilbert Space, Pattern Recognition Letters, Volume 20, Issue 5, May 1999, pp. 513-519.(Using Hilbert spaces to automate creation of classes and subtypes based on similarities between objects. The paper is a sophisticated mathematical discussion of how objects might be classified from a large number of samples using statistical methods.)
284. Prof. C-I Tan Department of Physics, Brown University: Notes on Hilbert Space at http://www.chem.brown.edu/chem277/Tan_on_Hilbert_Space.html
285. Hilbert Space Explorer, Copyright (GPL) © 2000 Norman D. Megill at http://us.metamath.org/mpegif/mmhil.html (A set of definitions, theorems, and explanations about Hilbert Space)
286. Jack Sarfatti: A Semi-Pop Nonmathematical Tutorial on Hilbert Space in Quantum Mechanics at http://www.qedcorp.com/pcr/pcr/hilberts.html (This paper focuses on representing quantum mechanical states with the help of Hilbert Spaces: "Hilbert space contains infinite dimensions, but these are not geometric. Rather, each dimension represents a state of possible existence for a quantum system. All possible states coexist." The book you are reading is about business systems, not quantum states, and the metamodel in this book focuses on purely deterministic systems. In contrast, the state of a quantum system is unknown, and merely querying it can change its state. However, mathematically astute readers will find interesting analogs that can be extended to describe the states of nondeterministic business systems in Sarfatti's paper—especially those that might change state by merely querying the information in them. This can happen in all real-world systems but is beyond the scope of this book. We can safely ignore Hilbert Space in this book.) (Buckingham's Pi Theorem—about the independence of physical laws from their units of measure)
287. Harald Hanche-Olsen, Department of Mathematical Sciences, Norwegian University of Science and Technology (NTNU), Trondheim, Norway: Buckingham's pi-theorem (Version 2001-09-15, 1998) (Describes Buckingham's pi theorem with illustrative examples of its use in finding solutions to physical problems. Includes a mathematical discussion of values, measurement, and units of measure—nonmathematicians beware!)
288. Buckingham's pi theorem from the Academic Press Dictionary of Science (Editor: Christopher Morris). Publisher: Elsevier Science & Technology Books, December 1991 (concise description of Buckingham's pi theorem)
289. Eric Weisstein: Buckingham's Pi Theorem from Eric Weisstein's World of Physics at http://scienceworld.wolfram.com/physics/BuckinghamsPiTheorem.html(Description and mathematical proof of Buckingham's pi theorem)

## Information Theory, Chaos Theory, and Miscellaneous Publications

290. Information Theory from Wikipedia at http://wikipedia.com/wiki/information+theory(A brief introduction to Shannon's Information theory and measures of information)

291. Sapir-Whorf Hypothesis from Wikipedia at http://wikipedia.com/wiki/Sapir-Whorf+hypothesis (An overview of the impact of language on meaning and perception)
292. Chaos Theory from Wikipedia at http://www.wikipedia.com/wiki/Chaos+theory(A succinct introduction to the theory of chaos)
293. Takashi Kanamaru, Dept. of Electrical & Electronic Engineering, Tokyo University of Agriculture & Technology, Japan, and J. Michael T. Thompson, Dept. of Applied Mathematics & Theoretical Physics, Cambridge: Introduction to Chaos and Nonlinear Dynamics, Sept. 1997 at http://brain.cc.kogakuin.ac.jp/~kanamaru/Chaos/e/. See Time Series of Logistic map at http://brain.cc.kogakuin.ac.jp/~kanamaru/Chaos/e/Logits/ (An interactive site that can give the reader a hands-on experience in chaotic systems)

## Books

294. Ronald G. Ross: The Business Rule Book: Classifying, Defining and Modeling Rules. Publisher: Database Research Group Inc, 1997.
295. Michael Hammer & James Champy: Reengineering The Corporation. Publisher: Harper Collins (1993).
296. Peter Herzum and Oliver Sims: Business Component Factory: A Comprehensive Overview of Component-Based Development for the Enterprise. Publisher: John Wiley & Sons, 1999.
297. G. M. Nijssen and T. A. Halpin, Conceptual Schema and Relational Database Design: A Fact Oriented Approach. Publisher: Prentice Hall (1989).
298. Paul Harmon and David King: Artificial Intelligence in Business, Chapter 4: Representing Knowledge, Chapter 5: Drawing Inferences. Publisher: John Wiley & Sons (1985).
299. Martin Fowler (1997): Analysis Patterns: Reusable Object Models. Publisher: Addison-Wesley Longman Inc.
300. Prof. August-Wilhelm Scheer: ARIS, Business Process Frameworks. Publisher: Springer-Verlag Ltd (August 1999).
301. Prof. August-Wilhelm Scheer: ARIS, Business Process Modeling. Publisher: Springer-Verlag Ltd (November 1996).
302. James Rumbaugh, Michael Blaha, William Premerlani, Frederick Eddy, William Lorensen at the General Electric Research and Development Center: Object-Oriented Modeling and Design, Publisher: Prentice Hall (1991).
303. Structured Systems Analysis and Design Methodology (version 4) from the SSADM College Ltd, 1996 (See http://www.comp.glam.ac.uk/pages/staff/tdhutchings/chapter4.html).
304. Candace C. Fleming and Barbara von Halle. Handbook of Relational Database Design, Publisher: Addison-Wesley (1989).
305. Maisell and Gnugnoli of Science Research Associates: Simulation of Discrete Stochastic Systems. Published in 1972.
306. Raphael Finkel: Functional Programming. Publisher: Addison-Wesley Publishing Co. © 1996; Chapter 4 at ftp://ftp.aw.com/cseng/authors/finkel/apld/finkel04.pdf
307. Paul Taylor: Practical Foundations of Mathematics, section 2.3 *Sums, Products, and Function-Types*, at http://www.dcs.qmul.ac.uk/~pt/Practical_Foundations/html/s23.html Publisher: Cambridge University Press, 1999.(A simple, physical explanation of lambda calculus and the need for it in

addressing practical real world problems: "[We] discussed how functions act, but they must also be considered as entities in themselves. Early...problems arose in which the unknown was a function as a whole, rather than its value at particular or even all points: the Sun's light takes that path through the variable density of the atmosphere which minimizes the time of travel; the motion of a stretched string depends on its initial displacement along its whole length.")

308. Daniel Finkbeiner II of Kenyon College: Matrices and Linear Transformations, Chapter 1. Publisher: W. H. Freeman and Co (1966).(Includes a mathematical discussion of sets, set operations, functions, mapping between sets, relationships, and domains)
309. George Thomas and Ross Finney, Calculus and Analytical Geometry. Publisher: Addison-Wesley Publishing Company Inc. 1996 (third edition published in 1960).(Has simple mathematical descriptions of functions, domains, ranges, existence, and continuity)
310. Emanuel Parzen of Stanford University: Modern Probability Theory and Its Applications. Publisher: John Wiley, 1960, 1992.
311. Sidney Siegel, research professor of psychology, The Pennsylvania State University: Nonparametric Statistics for the Behavioral Sciences. Publisher: McGraw-Hill, Kogakusha Ltd, © McGraw-Hill, 1956, 1988.
312. Harvey M. Wagner of Yale University: Principles of Operations Research with Applications to Managerial Decisions. Publisher: Prentice Hall, 1969, 1975.
313. Billy E. Gillett, Professor of Computer Science, University of Missouri-Rolla: Introduction to Operations Research, a Computer Oriented Algorithmic Approach. Publisher: McGraw Hill Inc. © 1976.
314. Erwin Kreysig, Professor of Mathematics, Ohio State University: Advanced Engineering Mathematics. Publisher: John Wiley and Sons, Inc. (1967, 1999).
315. A.W. Goodman, The University of South Florida: Modern Calculus with Analytic Geometry. Publisher: The MacMillan Company, New York © 1967, 1974.
316. Durell, William R. of Data Administration Inc: The Complete Guide to Data Modeling.
317. W. Durell: Data Administration: A Practical Guide to Data Management. McGraw-Hill, Inc., New York (1985).
318. Anastasia Pagnoni: Project Engineering: Computer-Oriented Planning and Operational Decision Making. Publisher: Springer-Verlag, Berlin, Germany. (Describes various techniques for modeling and managing tasks, including complex stochastic models of repetitive processes using techniques such as GERT and Petrinets)
319. Kenneth M. Dymond: A Guide to the CMM: Understanding the Capability Maturity Model for Software. Publisher: Process Transition International Inc., MD, USA, 1998. (Describes the dynamics of Best Practices and processes needed to institutionalize change based on the System Engineering Institute's [SEI] Capability Maturity Model [CMM])
320. Jeanie Daniel Duck, Senior Vice President, the Boston Consulting Group. The Change Monster. Publisher: Random House, 2002. (Excellent and very readable work on the social, emotional, and organizational dynamics of change)
321. Geoffrey Moore: Crossing the Chasm. Publisher: HarperCollins Publishers Inc., New York, USA, 2004. (On the acceptance of technological innovation in the marketplace)
322. W. H. Inmon: A Brief History of Data Base Design. Publisher: John Wiley, 1999. (Describes some changes in business environments and assumptions that have disrupted legacy systems)

323. Tom Mullins, Department of Physics, University of Oxford, David Holton, Department of Hydrogeology, Harwell Laboratory, Robert May, Department of Zoology, University of Oxford, J. M. T. Thompson, Center for Nonlinear Dynamics and Applications, University College of London, Peter L. Read, Department of Physics, University of Oxford, M. S. Child, Department of Chemistry, University of Oxford, and Jonathan Keating, Department of Mathematics, University of Manchester: The Nature of Chaos. Publisher: Oxford University Press, 1993.
324. G. J. Chamberlin and D. G. Chamberlin: Colour, Its measurement, Computation and Application. Publisher: Heyden and Sons Ltd © 1980.
325. Cybernetics A to Z by V. Pekelis, English translation. Publisher: Mir, Moscow 1974.
326. Maurice Aburdene of Bucknell University: Computer Simulation of Dynamic Systems Publisher: William C. Brown Publishers, Dubuque, Iowa, USA (1988).
327. Averill Law, President, Simulation Modeling and Analysis Company, Tucson, Arizona, USA and Professor of Decision Sciences, University of Arizona, and W. Kelton, Associate Professor of Operations Research and Management Science, University of Minnesota: Simulation Modeling & Analysis, second edition (1991). Publisher: McGraw-Hill, Inc.
328. Bertrand Meyer: Object-Oriented Software Construction Interactive ©1993-2001 Software Engineering, Inc (All rights reserved). Key extracts are available at http://www.eiffel.com/doc/manuals/technology/oosc/inheritance-design/section_05.html
329. Martin Fowler and Kendall Scott: UML Distilled. Applying the Standard Object Modeling Language: Publisher: Addison-Wesley Longman Inc.
330. Bruce Powel Douglass: Real-Time UML, Second Edition: Developing Efficient Objects for Embedded Systems. Publisher: Addison-Wesley Longman Inc, 2000.
331. James Rumbaugh, Ivar Jacobson, Grady Booch: The Unified Modeling Language Reference Manual. Publisher: Addison-Wesley Longman Inc, 1998.
332. Grady Booch, James Rumbaugh, Ivar Jacobson: The Unified Modeling Language User Guide. Publisher: Addison-Wesley Longman Inc.
333. Pierre-Alain Muller: Instant UML, published by Wrox Press Ltd. (© 1997), Birmingham, UK
334. Eugene Blanchard (Edited by Joshua Drake, Bill Randolph, Phuong Ma): Introduction to Networking and Data Communications. Copyright © 2001 by Commandprompt, Inc and Copyright © 2001 by Eugene Blanchard at http://www.linuxports.com/howto/ intro_to_networking/book1.htm
335. Howard Smith and Peter Fingar: Business Process Management: The Third Wave. Publisher: Meghan-Kiffer Press, 2002.
336. The New Encyclopedia Britannica, 15th Edition © 1988 Encyclopedia Britannica Inc.
337. Amit Mitra and Amar Gupta: Creating Agile Business Systems with Reusable Knowledge. Publisher: Cambridge University Press.
338. Amit Mitra and Amar Gupta: Agile Systems with Reusable Patterns of Business Knowledge: A Component Based Approach. Publisher: Artech House, 2005.
339. James Martin: After the Internet: Alien Intelligence. Publisher: Regenery Publishing Inc., 2000.

## OWL (Ontological Web Language)

340. OWL Web Ontology Language Use Cases and Requirements, W3C Recommendation 10 February 2004 at http://www.w3.org/TR/webont-req/#section-use-cases

341. OWL Web Ontology Language Overview, W3C Recommendation 10 February 2004 at http://www.w3.org/TR/owl-features/
342. OWL Web Ontology Language Guide , W3C Recommendation 10 February 2004 at http://www.w3.org/TR/owl-guide/#Datatypes1

## 24 Hour Knowledge Factory

343. Research on the 24-Hour Knowledge Factory, in which work proceeds round-the-clock with three teams of workers located in different continents at http://next.eller.arizona.edu/projects/24HrKF/ and http://next.eller.arizona.edu/publications/ssrn/index.aspx
344. Research on a pioneering example of off-shoring by a large multinational financial organization, and novel approaches for other industries at http://next.eller.arizona.edu/books/ and http://next.eller.arizona.edu/publications/ssrn/index.aspx

# APPENDIX IV
# MEANINGS, THE SEMANTIC WEB, ONTOLOGY, OWL, AND RDF

The Semantic Web is a vision of automation that operates on the plane of meaning. It envisions a future in which machines automatically process and integrate a World Wide Web of information, based on their meanings. A cornerstone of this vision is the concept of Ontology. An ontology is a semantic model of concepts and their relationships. It describes a formal vocabulary and grammar. In support of this vision, the W3C consortium recommended two modeling standards in 2004: RDF, the Resource Description Facility for metadata, and OWL, the Web Ontology Language for integrating information. This appendix summarizes the meanings in this book and its companions, and compares them with those in OWL and RDF.

In earlier chapters, we have shown how some meanings are derived from others by constraining the patterns of information they convey to create new meanings. These constrained patterns are subtypes of the meanings they constrain, and every meaning is a polymorphism of the universal object—an unknown pattern in information space that means everything and anything, and conveys nothing. It is a primal pattern of information at the bare edge of existence from which all meanings flow. Every object in our inventory of components is a polymorphism of this universal metaobject:

- **Activity (and other) Costs:** The direct cost normalized by a process. Overheads are normalized by the composition.
- **Aggregate Object:** A collection. A composition is a structured aggregate.
- **Array:** A multidimensional pattern of discrete points marking locations of objects and classes in information space.
- **Assemble, a Polymorphism of Process and the Part of Relationship:** Assemble emerged from a process that made an item a part of an aggregate in step with the flow of time. Similarly, disassembly cuts the relationship between an aggregate and its parts so that the part does not remain a part of the aggregate after disassembly has occurred. Disassemble is also a process, but it is a polymorphism of the Exclude relationship. Polymorphisms of Disassemble will tell us how an aggregate is picked apart—explosively, all at once, or in steps—perhaps even one item at a time.
- **Attribute:** A kind of object property that is also a subtype of Domain. It is a relationship between an object class and a subtype of a domain that consists of a single value at any given time.
- **Beginning:** A delimiter that marks the lower limit of a sequenced pattern in information space. **Start** is a temporal polymorphism of Beginning. It is a beginning in time.
- **Beginning and Ending Moments of an Event:** Both are subtypes of Moment.
- **Borel Object:** A generalization of the concept of Array, useful for categorization and segmentation of objects and state spaces—a power set of values or an infinitely large power set of ranges.
- **Bounds:** The limits of a pattern in state space.
- **Capacity:** A kind of cardinality constraint.
- **Cardinality:** The "size" of a class. Cardinality is a supertype of **Enumeration**.
- **Composed of:** A subtype of Consist of, wherein there is some information on the internal structure of the aggregate in terms of associations between its parts; its inverse has been labeled Component of.
- **Consist of:** The inverse of Part of and a subtype of Locate.

- **Contain:** A supertype of Consist of and a subtype of Locate, wherein Location is constrained within a delimited region of information space.
- **Cycle Time:** The time interval from the start to the end of a process (Chapter V, Compositions of Relationships—cycle time is a subtype of Event).
- **(Degree of) Freedom:** The quantitative measure of the variability of a meaning or pattern. When the meaning or pattern exceeds this, it changes its identity and is considered a different meaning or pattern. The meaning of "freedom" stems from this concept (Chapter IV).
- **Delimiters:** Patterns that mark the existence of a limit or boundary in state space. For instance, a circle delimits a disk.
- **Domain:** A domain is a class of values. The class may contain finite or infinite numbers of distinct values and lends its members a common meaning, such as "length." The meaning of Qualitative measurement is encapsulated in nominal and ordinal domains: Nominal domains only distinguish between values; Ordinal domains add information on sequences. The meaning of Quantitative measurement is encapsulated in difference and ratio scaled domains: Difference scaled domains add information on magnitudes; Ratio scaled domains add information on ratios and the concept of nil magnitude. The Metamodel of Knowledge infers that quantitative values must be expressed in units of measure, of which it may have several. **Domains are arranged in a subtyping hierarchy.** The most elementary business and physical meanings start with **Primary domains**: Enumeration (ratio scaled), Mass (ratio scaled), Physical separation (ratio scaled), Date/Time Lapse (difference scaled—includes date and time of occurrence) Electric Charge (ratio scaled), and Overall Information Content (ratio scaled), and Preference (ordinal). **Secondary domains** are derived from primary domains as polymorphisms or from relationships between domains. A few frequently used secondary domains are Domains of Information Quality (Validity, that we are measuring the right thing; Reliability, that the measurement is always consistent; Completeness and Accuracy, that the measurement is unbiased), Economic Value Added (Ratio scaled polymorphism of Preference), various domains of proportions, various domains of change/growth, and Gender. The cardinality of a domain is a measure of its size, which might be infinite. A dense domain has an infinite number of values between any ordered pair of values (for example, a difference scaled domain like temperature or a ratio scaled domain like mass).
- **Effect:** This is a kind (subtype) of process that changes the state of a single object. It is not always a business process, but effects always map directly to computer systems processes. Effects are a kind of Object Property.
- **Efficiency and Productivity of Processes:** Temporal polymorphisms of cardinality ratios between the work product of a process and resources used.
- **End:** A delimiter that marks the upper limit of a sequenced pattern in information space that also has a beginning. Although it is counterintuitive, **End** is a polymorphism of Beginning. It is obtained by adding information to beginning and thus creates a distinction via a constraint. **Stop** is a temporal polymorphism of End. It is an end in time (and thus is a polymorphism of Start).
- **Essence (of a pattern):** This is the information that gives the pattern its identity and distinguishes it from other similar patterns. It is closely tied to the freedom the pattern has to be that pattern. The meaning of "essential" is derived from "essence," and the meaning of "freedom" is derived from the degrees of freedom of a pattern—Chapter IV, Measure of Similarity, under Pattern.
- **Event:** A time interval. The time difference domain is a subtype of the Time domain.

- **Exception Process (Polymorphism of Process):** Processes triggered when constraints are violated. Exception processes are a mechanism for addressing the inherently stochastic nature of the real world with a model that permits only discrete, deterministic change. Exception processes are polymorphisms of Process in a different partition from input and output processes. Hence, there may be exception processes for inputs, outputs, and transformations.
- **Expression of/Express:** This relationship is a polymorphism of the subtyping relationship.
- **Extent:** The scope of a pattern in information space (Chapter IV, Properties of Patterns in Information Space).
- **Feature:** Any property of an object—an attribute, relationship, effect, or constraint.
- **Format:** A physical representation of information that may be sensed by an actor or observer.
- **(Generic) Constraint:** A generic Constraint is a generalized Meaning, synonymous with Object Property. Rule Constraint and Value Constraint are special subtypes of this generic constraint.
- **Governance (Applies to Constraints, Patterns, and Processes):** Governance instantiates parameters and features of processes. Governing processes are processes that set parameters of processes they govern. Governance processes often depend on tracking and exception processes to govern—another commonly used theme in business.
- **Governance and Nonstationarity (Applies to Constraints, Patterns, and Processes): Nonstationarity** is the property in which features and parameters change over time. Stationarity is a form of temporal symmetry, in which behavior and properties are constant and agnostic of the flow of time. Knowledge is configured from the meanings above and so are atomic rules and irreducible facts, which are also components of knowledge. The fabric of knowledge is woven from these components and their polymorphisms. These are the metaobjects and concepts that normalize rules of different kinds. Rules, embedded in these containers, are configured and assembled into the tapestry we call knowledge. When new learning flows into this structure, it radiates through the entire fabric, changing and reconfiguring it through the rules, polymorphisms, and dependencies we have discussed in this series of books. Figure 10.1 is an overview of their interaction. It tells us how the container of knowledge is woven.
- **Idempotent Relationship:** A relationship of an object instance with itself (for example, "self help").
- **Inclusion and Exclusion Sets (Mutually Exclusive Subtypes of Partition):** Items in an inclusion set are permitted, whereas items in an exclusion set are forbidden.
- **Incorporation:** A subtype of Consist of, wherein the object loses its identity as a member of a separate class of objects. It becomes a subtype.
- **Instance of:** A different polymorphism of the subtyping relationship in the same partition that imposes a constraint on a subclass that has only one member at any given time.
- **Intransitive Relationship:** When a composition of relationships disallows the existence of another relationship.
- **Involvement:** The fact that a relationship exists. It is the most fundamental relationship. All relationships are polymorphisms of involvement.
- **Joint Constraints:** When a value is constrained by an interaction between multiple objects. Joint Constraint is a polymorphism of Value Constraint; it is a relationship of a higher order, with more information in its Rule Expression and meaning.

- **Language:** A set of meanings and corresponding visual and audible symbols that point to the same meanings. The existence of both auditory and visual symbols is not mandatory for every meaning, but the existence of at least one of the two is mandated.
- **List of:** A subtype of Consist of, wherein there is information on multiple occurrences of an instance.
- **Load Balancing of Processes:** Balancing capacities of related processes.
- **Location (Locate):** When position in information space is fixed in relation to another object. **Origin** is a special location that contains a nil value or a value shared by multiple domains that create a manifold in information space.
- **Location, Containment, Part of, and Subtyping:** Location is relative. One object locates another and creates the concept of **Place**. A Place may be a physical place, a virtual place, or even an abstract meaning.
- **Magnitude Constraints:** Restricts the magnitude of a difference or ratio scaled value. Based on the principle of adding information, a magnitude constraint is a polymorphism of Value Constraint. Joint Constraints and Magnitude Constraints are subtypes in different, independent partitions of Value Constraint, so a constraint could simultaneously be both.
- **Meaning:** Meanings are patterns of abstract information—Chapter IV. Meanings include the meaning of a rule, as opposed to its expression. Polymorphisms of Meaning carve object instances and object classes from the primal object.
- **Metaobject:** A Metaobject is a generic and inchoate instance of an object. All objects are subtypes of this primal object.
- **Moment:** An event of nil duration.
- **Mutability:** Substitutability of one object by another (Chapter V, Compositions of Relationships).
- **Name:** Name and its subtypes, Synonym, Homonym, Alias, and Concept ID—Chapter II.
- **Number:** Number is an expression of Quantitative Value and therefore a subtype of both Expression and Quantitative Value. **Format** is a kind of expression of Value in symbolic form. This makes Format a subtype with two parents, **Value** and **Symbol.**
- **Object Class (a Subtype of an Aggregate Object):** Object Class does not convey any information on multiplicity of occurrence of the same object instance. A **list** is a subtype of an aggregate object that conveys more information than a class. It distinguishes between occurrences of the same object instance.
- **Observation, Inquiry, and Reporting:** Processes that are polymorphisms of a generic "inquiry" process, which changes the state of the object queried/observed to "queried/observed," and may or may not change it in other ways.
- **Object Instance:** An individual object that is a member of a class of object instances and has the information that distinguishes its identity from every other member of the class.
- **Object Partition:** Object Partition is a criterion for dividing an object class into mutually exclusive subtypes. A partition may be exhaustive (the subtypes in the partition collectively cover all possible members of the partitioned class) or inexhaustive (the subtypes do not cover all possible members of the partitioned class).
- **Object Property:** Attributes, relationships, effects of events, and constraints associated with the object.
- **Pattern:** This is the root of the Metamodel of Knowledge. All its components are polymorphisms of Pattern; an object instance is also a kind of pattern—a meaningful pattern of information.

- **Perspective:** A classification scheme. It is expressed in a network of objects and relationships. It is also a **Composition**. Compositions are also subtypes of relationships. A Composition is a synonym for Expression. Perspective is the same as Composition, which is a subtype of Relationship.
- **Pick:** A polymorphism of *Process* and the *Instance of* relationship. Pick, the polymorphism, may also have subordinate polymorphisms. For instance, one polymorphism may pick a single item out of a collection or assembly of items, whereas another might pick a class of similar items out of that collection of parts, and yet another polymorphism could pick a batch of similar or dissimilar parts out of the collection.
- **Polymorphism:** Synonym for subtype.
- **Precision: Precision** is a synonym for Accuracy, and Exhaustiveness is a synonym for Completeness. Note that less precise and less complete patterns convey less information than their more precise or more complete counterparts. Therefore, the more precise or more complete pattern is a subtype of its less precise or less complete counterpart.
- **Process:** A subtype of two parents—event and relationship. Processes use resources to produce products. Process inherits the features of Relationship, combined with temporal information from Event, such as cycle time. Combined with temporal information from Event, the features inherited from Relationship acquire new characteristics like temporal succession, productivity, reversibility, temporal mutability—the time dependence of mutability between objects; temporal order (how far back into history does a process reach to articulate rules about a change of state at present; temporal degree), repeatability and concurrency; for idempotent relationships: the number of times a process loops back to the same product or reuses the same resource. A Reporting Process changes the state of an object from Unknown to a known value. An Inquiry changes the state of an object from Unknown to Observed. It may or may not change other features that constitute the overall state of the object.
- **Process Owner (Various Kinds):** Responsible for execution of a process; R: Responsible for the process; A: Has the authority to govern the process.
- **Product:** An object produced by a process.
- **Proximity Metric:** Measures of similarity. May also be a measure of distance (Chapter IV, Measure of Similarity).
- **Purpose or Goal:** An objective. It is a polymorphism of information.
- **Ranges:** A range is a region in state space. In a unidimensional-sequenced space, a lower bound may be distinguished from an upper bound.
- **Recursive Relationship:** A relationship between objects that belong to the same object class.
- **Relationship: Relationship** is an interaction. It is a polymorphism of a List, which in turn is a polymorphism of Aggregate Object.
- **Representation:** A polymorphism of expression.
- **Resource:** An object that may be used by a process.
- **Resource Consumption** is a polymorphism of Resource Life, in which the capacity of a resource to engage is diminished over time by a known process. If a process changes the state of a resource, it is considered consumed, and the changed resource is a Product (it could be a work product, a waste product, or a byproduct).
- **Resource Life:** A temporal polymorphism of Capacity; when time is added to the meaning of capacity, the capacity to engage with objects will change over time. When the capacity decreases, we might conceive of an "unknown" process that has engaged the capacity of an object. The "un-

known" process starts "consuming" it or diminishing its capacity for engagement. If the decline is precipitous at a particular point time after the resource is created, that interval may be considered the life of the object.

- **Reversibility and Reversion (of Processes):** Reversion is a process that is the inverse of another process—it restores the original states of all involved objects, that is, undoes the effects of the reversed process.
- **Rule Constraint:** A rule that constrains a nominal, ordinal, or ratio scaled Value by tying them together into an irreducible fact; a kind of Constraint.
- **Saga:** A process with no definite end, which is also a supertype of a process with a definite end. An endless saga is a polymorphism of Saga, in which it is definitely known that the process will not end.
- **Size:** A polymorphism of Capacity.
- **State, State Space, Trajectory in State Space, and Set of Possible Trajectories in State Space:** All are subtypes of Aggregate Object. The last two are also Compositions. A composition is a subtype of aggregate object. Trajectory in State Space and Set of Possible Trajectories in State Space are actually subtypes of Composition and therefore a subtype of Aggregate Object, once removed.
- **Subtype and Supertype:** Subtypes of Object Class. A subtype is created from a supertype by the subtyping relationship.
- **Subtyping Relationship:** A kind of relationship that incorporates and extends a meaning by adding information.
- **Supply Chains:** Polymorphisms of Process, wherein extended enterprises create and deliver products and services to consumers of these services.
- **Symbols:** Objects like text, pictures, sound, odor, and other items that may be sensed by an actor.
- **Symmetry:** The lack of sequencing information. Note that processes cannot be symmetric; they incorporate information on the flow of time, which is asymmetrical.
- **Temporal Succession:** Sequence in time; a supertype of Process and subtype of relative location (a succession enables a predecessor to locate its successor in time and vice versa). Causality is a polymorphism of succession, and Process is a polymorphism of causality.
- **The Expression of a Rule:** A meaning may have many expressions. Each expression is a perspective of that meaning. Therefore, Expression and Perspective are identical. Expression is the result of Express (Expression of and Express are synonyms; their inverse is Expressed By[1]). Express is a polymorphism of the subtyping relationship (as is "**instance of**").
- **Tracking Process:** A process obtained by infusing temporal information into the proximity metric. It is a polymorphism of the proximity metric and Event **Unit of Measure:** A map from a quantitative domain to the domain of numbers.
- **Transformation, Input, and Output Processes (Subtypes of Process):** Transformation processes use resources to create products. Input processes convey resources to transformation processes and output processes convey products from transformation processes. They are all polymorphisms of Process, and every business process consists of all three, input, transformation, and output process, assembled in tandem.
- **Transitive Relationship:** When a set of relationships implies another, the implied relationship is transitive with respect to the others. In a transitive triad of relationships, any two relationships in the triad imply the third. Transitive relationships and the property of transitivity encapsulate the meaning of implication, which is distinct from causality.

- **Truncation:** Slices a pattern into a part. Truncate relates an object to its truncation. A truncated pattern conveys less information than the pattern that was truncated. It is therefore a supertype of the original pattern, and the inverse of Truncate is a polymorphism of the subtyping relationship.
- **Universal Perspective:** A subtype of Perspective.
- **Use:** The defining relationship between a process and its resources. The input process is a polymorphism of "Use."
- **Value: Value** encapsulates the concept of existence and measurability. It may convey distinctness, an ordered sequence, a magnitude, the absence of magnitude (the Nil Value), Infinite magnitude, the absence of meaning (the Null Value), the concept of "All," "Any," and "Unknown."
- **Value Constraints:** A kind (subtype) of Rule Constraint in which specific values are permitted or excluded.
- **Value Sets:** A collection of values at a point in time.
- **View:** A conduit to the information conveyed by an object. A view consists of mechanisms such as displays, formatting, and sequencing rules, inclusion and exclusion criteria.

Moreover, *Agile Systems with Reusable Patterns of Business Knowledge*, a book by the same authors published by Artech House Publishers, extends the meanings above into shared business concepts at lower levels of the ontology (see Figure 1.2).

We have summarized RDF and OWL as follows to enable our readers to compare and contrast them with our approach. One key extension that the model in this book and its companions add to OWL and RDF concepts is the semantics of pattern and measurability. This enables the model in the series to integrate the model of ontology with business rules and business processes. Several OWL and RDF concepts such as value constraints, conjunction, disjunction, properties, and others may thus be naturally inferred and articulated by the integrated model of knowledge in this series of books.

The Dublin Core Metadata Initiative (DCMI) is a related initiative that has enriched the RDF vocabulary (as described later in this appendix). Many of these extensions are articulated in the concept of "audit attributes" of objects that flow from the metamodel of knowledge in this series. These "audit attributes" would support traceability and authentication needs mandated by recent regulations such as HIPAA and SOX (Sarbanes-Oxley regulations). Thus, the model in this series can enrich and extend the standards already recommended by OMG and the W3C consortium:

## RDF

RDF is an acronym for Resource Description Framework. It is a model of objects ("resources") and relationships. RDF provides simple semantics, and the model can be expressed in XML. It is a W3C standard for describing Web metadata such as resources, and for Web pages, the title, author, modification date, content, copyright information, and so forth.

RDF Schema describes properties and classes of RDF resources and has the semantics to generalize these concepts. However, RDF is not easy to comprehend. It is meant for computers.

## Examples

- Metadata for items in inventory, such as price and items on hand
- Metadata for schedules for such as timings of events

## RDF Rules

- Resources are identified by Web identifiers (URIs)
- Resources have properties and property values.

1. A **Resource** is anything that can have a URI, such as "http://www.GalaxySI.com"
2. A **Property** is a Resource that has a name, such as "author" or "home page"
3. A **Property value** is the value of a Property, such as "Amit Mitra" or "http://www.GalaxySI.com"
4. Note that a property value can be another resource

## RDF Metadata

### RDF Classes

| Element | Class of | Subclass of |
|---|---|---|
| Class | All classes | |
| Datatype | All Data types | Class |
| Resource | All resources | Class |
| Container (set of objects) | All Containers | Resource |
| Collection (set membership is restricted by some criteria) | All Collections | Resource |
| Literal | Values of text and numbers | Resource |
| List | All Lists | Resource |
| Property | All Properties | Resource |
| Statement | All RDF Statements | Resource |
| Alt | Containers of alternatives | Container |
| Bag | Unordered containers | Container |
| Seq | Ordered containers | Container |
| ContainerMembershipProperty | All Container membership properties | Property |
| XMLLiteral | XML literal values | Literal |

### RDF Attributes

| Attribute | Description |
|---|---|
| about | Resource definition |
| Description | Resource description |
| resource | The property being defined by a resource |
| ID | Element identifier |
| datatype | Data type of an element |
| li | List identifier |
| *n* | Node |
| nodeID | Elementary node identifier |
| parseType | Defines the parsing of an element |

| | |
|---|---|
| RDF | Root of an RDF document |
| base | XML base |
| lang | Language in which the content (of an element) is rendered |

## RDF Properties

| Property | Operates on | Produces | Description |
|---|---|---|---|
| domain | Property | Class | The domain of the resource. The domain defines what a property may apply to (operate on). |
| range | Property | Class | The range of the resource. It defines what the property may map to (produce). |
| subPropertyOf | Property | Property | The property of a property |
| subClassOf | Class | Class | Subtyping property |
| comment | Resource | Literal | User friendly resource description |
| label | Resource | Literal | User friendly resource name |
| isDefinedBy | Resource | Resource | Resource definition |
| seeAlso | Resource | Resource | Additional information about a resource |
| member | Resource | Resource | The property of being an instance of a kind of resource |
| first | List | Resource | The property of being the first member of a list |
| rest | List | List | The second and subsequent members of a list |
| subject | Statement | Resource | The subject of an assertion, i.e., the subject of a resource in an RDF statement |
| predicate | Statement | Resource | Similar to "subject": The predicate of an assertion |
| object | Statement | Resource | The object of the resource (in an RDF) Statement |
| value | Resource | Resource | The value of a property |
| type | Resource | Class | An instance of a class |

The Dublin Core Metadata Initiative (DCMI) has added to RDF by adding the following standard properties for RDF documents:

| DCMI Property | Definition |
|---|---|
| Title | A name given to the resource |
| Description | An account of the content |
| Identifier | An unambiguous reference to the resource |
| Contributor | An entity responsible for contributing to the content of a resource |
| Creator | An entity with the primary responsibility for creating the content |
| Coverage | The scope of the content |
| Format | The physical or digital rendering of a resource |
| Date | A date of an event in the life cycle of a resource |
| Language | The language the content is rendered in |
| Publisher | An entity responsible for making the resource available |

| DCMI Property | Definition |
|---|---|
| Relation | A reference to a related resource |
| Rights | Information about rights held in and over the resource |
| Source | A reference to a resource from which the present resource is derived |
| Subject | The topic of the content of the resource |
| Type | The nature or kind of content |

## OWL

OWL is an acronym for Web Ontology Language. It is a W3C standard language for ***processing*** and integrating Web information (as opposed to ***displaying***) in a standard way. OWL adds more functions and features to RDF, and like RDF, it is a part of the initiative to create the Semantic Web.

The Semantic Web is a vision of the Web in which information on the Web has explicit meanings, which machines automatically integrate and process. Therefore, OWL is meant to be used when information must be processed by automation, as opposed to (being displayed for) human operators. OWL can represent the meanings of terms and the relationships between meanings.

- OWL is written in XML and is based on the experience of DAML+OIL, which were standards that preceded it.
- Like RDF, OWL is meant for automation and is not user friendly
- OWL has a larger vocabulary than RDF and supports more automation of functional requirements
  - With OWL, automation can reason; therefore the language goes beyond the basic semantics of RDF
  - For example, OWL adds constructs such as disjointness, cardinality, equality, symmetry, and enumerated classes (a class may be described by exhaustively enumerating its instances)

There are three flavors of OWL:

- OWL Full (Has the full OWL syntax, however, sometimes axioms may not be fully decidable)
- OWL DL (A subset of OWL Full that guarantees computability and decidability). The subset of OWL constructs in OWL DL ensures that all conclusions are computable and can finish in finite time (i.e., all computations are decidable). OWL DL constrains OWL constructs; for example, while a class may be a subclass with multiple parents, it cannot be an instance of another class. OWL DL constrains OWL Full as follows:
  - Separates the following by making them disjoint: classes, individuals (thus classes may not be individuals), datatypes, datatype properties, object properties, annotation properties, ontology properties, data values, and the built-in vocabulary
  - In OWL DL, object properties are disjoint from datatype properties. Therefore, the following cannot be datatype properties:
    - inverse of,

- inverse functional,
- symmetric, and
- transitive
- OWL DL requires that no cardinality constraints be placed on transitive properties or their inverses or any properties they are subtypes of
- Annotations are restricted to certain conditions
- Axioms cannot have missing or extra components and must form a tree-like hierarchy
- Assertions of sameness or differences between individuals must be about named individuals (OWL adds equality and difference properties to RDF, that assert the sameness or distinctness of things)

- OWL Lite (A simpler subset of OWL DL), primarily supports those who only need classification hierarchies and simple constraints. It is meant to be a stepping stone in migrating towards applying the Semantic Web. For example, OWL Lite only permits cardinality values of 0 or 1. OWL Lite also forbids the following set operations (these are not an exhaustive set of OWL Lite restrictions):
    - oneOf
    - unionOf
    - complementOf
    - hasValue
    - disjointWith
    - DataRange

## OWL Classes

| Class | Description |
|---|---|
| AllDifferent | All listed individuals are mutually different |
| allValuesFrom | All values of a property of class X are drawn from class Y (or Y is a description of X) |
| AnnotationProperty | Describes an annotation. OWL has predefined the following kinds of annotations, and users may add more:<br>• Versioninfo<br>• Label<br>• Comment<br>• Seealso<br>• Isdefinedby<br>OWL DL limits the object of an annotation to data literals, URIs, or individuals (not an exhaustive set of restrictions) |
| backwardCompatibleWith | The ontology is a prior version of a containing ontology and is backward compatible with it. All identifiers from the previous version have the same interpretations in the new version. |
| cardinality | Describes a class that has exactly N semantically distinct values of a property (N is the value of the cardinality constraint) |
| Class | Asserts the existence of a class |
| complementOf | Analogous to the Boolean "not" operator. Asserts the existence of a class that consists of individuals that are NOT members of the class it is operating on |
| DataRange | Describes a data type by exhaustively enumerating its instances (this construct is not found in RDF or OWL Lite) |

| Class | Description |
|---|---|
| DatatypeProperty | Asserts the existence of a property |
| DeprecatedClass | Indicates that the class has been preserved to ensure backward compatibility and may be phased out in the future. It should not be used in new documents, but has been preserved to make it easier for old data and applications to migrate to the new version |
| DeprecatedProperty | Similar to depreciated class |
| differentFrom | Asserts that two individuals are not the same |
| disjointWith | Asserts that the disjoint classes have no common members |
| distinctMembers | Members are all different from each other |
| equivalentClass | The classes have exactly the same set of members. This is subtly different from class equality, which asserts that two or more classes have the same meaning (asserted by the "sameAs" construct). Class equivalence is a constraint that forces members of one class to also belong to another and vice versa. |
| equivalentProperty | Similar to equivalent class: i.e., different properties must have the same values, even if their meanings are different (for instance, the length of a square must equal its width) |
| FunctionalProperty | A property that can have only one, unique value. For example, a property that restricts the height to be nonzero is not a functional property because it maps to an infinite number of values for height |
| hasValue | Links a class to a value, which could be an individual fact or identity, or a data value (see RDF data types) |
| imports | References another OWL ontology. Meanings in the imported ontology become a part of the importing ontology. Each importing reference has a URI that locates the imported ontology. If ontologies import each other, they become identical, and imports are transitive. |
| incompatibleWith | The opposite of backward compatibility. Documents must be changed to comply with the new ontology. |
| intersectionOf | Similar to set intersection. Members are common to all intersecting classes. |
| InverseFunctionalProperty | Inverses must map back to a unique value. Inverse Functional properties cannot be many-to-one or many-to-many mappings. |
| inverseOf | The inverse relationship (mapping) of a property from the target (result) to the source (argument) |
| maxCardinality | An upper bound on cardinality (may be "many," i.e., any finite value) |
| minCardinality | A lower bound on cardinality |
| Nothing | The empty set |

| Class | Description |
|---|---|
| ObjectProperty | Instances of properties are not single elements but may be subject-object pairs of property statements, and properties may be subtyped (extended). ObjectProperty asserts the existence and characteristics of properties:<br>• RDF Schema constructs: rdfs:subPropertyOf, rdfs:domain and rdfs: range<br>• relations to other properties: owl:equivalentProperty and owl: inverseOf<br>• global cardinality constraints: owl:FunctionalProperty and owl: InverseFunctionalProperty<br>• logical property characteristics: owl:SymmetricProperty and owl: TransitiveProperty |
| oneOf | The only individuals, no more and no less, that are the instances of the class |
| onProperty | Asserts a restriction on a property |
| Ontology | An ontology is a resource, so it may be described using OWL and non-OWL ontologies |
| OntologyProperty | A property of the ontolology in question. See imports. |
| priorVersion | Refers to a prior version of an ontology |
| Restriction | Restricts or constrains a property. May lead to property equivalence, polymorphisms, value constraints, set operations, etc. |
| sameAs | Asserts that individuals have the same identity. Naming differences are merely synonyms. |
| someValuesFrom | Asserts that there exists at least one item that satisfies a criterion. Mathematically, it asserts that at least one individual in the domain of the "SomeValuesFrom" operator that maps to the range of that operator. |
| SymmetricProperty | When a property and its inverse mean the same thing (e.g., if Jane is a relative of John, then John is also a relative of Jane) |
| Thing | The set of all individuals |
| TransitiveProperty | If A is related to B via property P1 and B is related to C via property P2, then A is also related to C via property P1. For example, if a person lives in a house, and the house is located in a town, it may be inferred that the person lives in the town because "Lives in" is transitive with "Located in." |
| unionOf | Set union. A member may belong to any of the sets in the union to be a member of the resulting set |
| versionInfo | Provides information about the version |

## OWL Properties

| Property | Operates on (Domain) | Produces (Range) |
|---|---|---|
| allValuesFrom | Restriction | rdfs:Class |
| backwardCompatibleWith | Ontology | Ontology |
| cardinality | Restriction | xsd:nonNegativeInteger |
| complementOf | Class | Class |
| differentFrom | Thing | Thing |
| disjointWith | Class | Class |
| distinctMembers | AllDifferent | rdf:List |
| equivalentClass | Class | Class |
| equivalentProperty | Property | rdf:Property |
| hasValue | Restriction | value |
| imports | Ontology | Ontology |
| incompatibleWith | Ontology | Ontology |
| intersectionOf | Class | rdf:List |
| inverseOf | ObjectProperty | ObjectProperty |
| maxCardinality | Restriction | xsd:nonNegativeInteger |
| minCardinality | Restriction | xsd:nonNegativeInteger |
| oneOf | Class | rdf:List |
| onProperty | Restriction | rdf:Property |
| priorVersion | Ontology | Ontology |
| sameAs | Thing | Thing |
| someValuesFrom | Restriction | rdfs:Class |
| unionOf | Class | rdf:List |

## ENDNOTE

1 *Expression*, an object, is identical to *Expressed By*, its defining relationship; the information conveyed (and hence meaning) is identical. See Appendix II on functional programming. [337] in Appendix III (Chapter IV, section 2) is also recommended for further reading.

# About the Contributors

**Amar Gupta** is the Tom Brown Endowed chair of management and technology, professor of entrepreneurship, MIS, management of organizations, computer science, and Latin American studies at the University of Arizona. Earlier, he was with the MIT Sloan School of Management (1979-2004); for half of this 25-year period, he served as the founding co-director of the Productivity from Information Technology (PROFIT) initiative. Subsequent to his move to Arizona in 2004, he continued to maintain ties with MIT as a visiting professor in college of engineering. He has published over 100 papers and serves as associate editor of *ACM Transactions on Internet Technology*. At the University of Arizona, Professor Gupta is the chief architect of new multidegree graduate programs that involve concurrent study of management, entrepreneurship, and one specific technical or scientific domain. He has nurtured the development of several key technologies that are in widespread use today and is currently focusing on the area of the 24-hour knowledge factory.

**Amit Mitra** is a senior practice manager in TCS North American Global Consulting Practice and a former senior vice president of process improvement and enterprise architecture at Galaxe Solutions, where he established the practice. He is also the president and principal consultant at Sprybiz LLC. He is a alumnus of KPMG and the former chief methodologist of the American International Group. He is a seasoned practitioner in transforming the business of IT, facilitating business agility and enabling the Service Oriented Enterprise.

# Index